UMI ANNUAL COMMENTARY

# PRECEPTS FOR LIVING®

## MISSION STATEMENT

*W*e are called
of God to create, produce, and distribute
quality Christian education products;
to deliver exemplary customer service;
and to provide quality Christian
educational services, which will empower
God's people, especially within the Black
community, to evangelize, disciple,
and equip people for serving Christ,
His kingdom, and church.

Urban Ministries, Inc.
The African American Christian Publishing
& Communications Co.

# UMI ANNUAL SUNDAY SCHOOL LESSON COMMENTARY
## *PRECEPTS FOR LIVING® 2014–2015*
## INTERNATIONAL SUNDAY SCHOOL LESSONS
## VOLUME 17
## UMI (URBAN MINISTRIES, INC.)

Melvin Banks Sr., Litt.D., Founder and Chairman

C. Jeffrey Wright, J.D., CEO

All art: Copyright © 2014 by UMI.

Bible art: Fred Carter

# Get the *Precepts for Living*® eBook!

Do you enjoy the ease and freedom of reading books using a Kindle, iPad, NOOK, or other electronic reader? If so, there's good news for you! UMI (Urban Ministries, Inc.) is at the forefront of the latest technology and now publishes its annual Sunday School commentary, *Precepts For Living*®, in the leading eBook formats: Kindle (Amazon), NOOK (Barnes & Noble), and iBooks (Apple).

To purchase an eBook copy of *Precepts For Living*®, visit our website at www.PreceptsForLiving.com to find download links and step-by-step instructions.

If you've purchased *Precepts For Living*® for your eReader, be sure to leave a rating and a review at the iTunes, Barnes & Noble, or Amazon store sites to tell others what you think. Also, spread the word on your favorite social networking sites! Follow *Precepts For Living*® on Facebook and Twitter (with the handle @precepts4living).

PRECEPTS FOR LIVING®

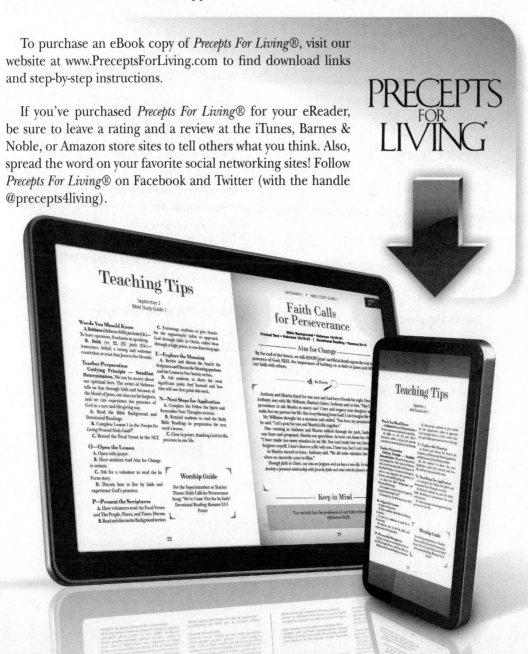

# CONTRIBUTORS

**Editor**
A. Okechukwu Ogbonnaya Ph.D.

**Associate Director of Adult
Content Development**
John C. Richards Jr., M. Div.

**Developmental Editor**
Ramon Mayo, M.A.

**Copy Editors**
Beth Potterveld, M.A.
Benton Sartore

**Layout Design**
Trinidad D. Zavala, B.A.

**Cover Design**
Kofi Bansa, B.A.

**Bible Illustrations**
Fred Carter

**Contributing Writers**
Essays/In Focus Stories
Melvin E. Banks Sr., Litt.D.
Jennifer King, M.A.
Judith St. Clair Hull Ph.D.
Rev. Samuel Green Jr.
Ramon Mayo, M.A.
Beverly Moore, M.S.
Kimberly Gillespie, M.Div.
Victoria Saunders-Johnson

**Bible Study Guide Writers**
Jean V. Garrison M.A.
Kimberly Gillespie M.Div.
Wayne Hopkins M.Div.
Odell Horne M.A.
Rev. Karl R. Hrebik M.Div.
Jennifer King M.A.
Angela Lampkin M.S.
Ramon Mayo M.A.
Beverly Moore M.A.
CaReese Rials M.Div.
Amy Rognlie
Elizabeth Simmington
Wan Smith M.A.
LaTonya Summers
Jeremy Wade M.Div.
Charlesetta Watson-Holmes M.Div.
Justin West M.Div.

**More Light on the Text**
J. Ayodeji Adewuya Ph.D.
Moussa Coulibaly Ph.D.
Richard Gray Ph.D.
Rukeia Draw-Hood Ph.D.
Kevin Hrebik D.Min
Judith St. Clair Hull, Ph.D.
Harvey Kwiyani Ph.D.
Kelly Whitcomb Ph.D.

Dear Precepts Customer,

It is our privilege to present the 2014–2015 *Precepts For Living*®. As you encounter God's Word through these lessons, we anticipate that you will find this resource to be indispensable.

*Precepts For Living*® comes to you in three versions: the Personal Study Guide (the workbook), the online version, and a large print edition. You will also notice that the biblical text for each lesson includes the New Living Translation in addition to the King James Version. This contemporary translation will enhance your textual understanding when you compare it side by side to the classic English translation. It is very helpful in illuminating your understanding of the text.

*Precepts For Living*® is designed to be a witness through our learning and sharing more of the Bible. Our intent is to facilitate innovative ways for pursuing a deeper understanding and practice of God's Word. One of the ways we strive to do this is by highlighting the larger narrative of God's work in salvation as a key part of understanding each biblical passage. We believe it is important to help you understand not only the particulars of the text but also the broad extent of God's revelation to us as well. This panoramic approach enhances our ability to witness to others about the saving power of Jesus Christ.

This year we explore the themes of hope, worship, God: the Holy Spirit, and justice. Each year of Bible study offers great potential for a more intimate and transformative walk with God.

We want to continually refine *Precepts For Living*® as we endeavor to meet our customers' needs. We are always looking for ways to enhance your study of the Bible, and your comments and feedback are vital in helping us. If you have questions or suggestions, we encourage you to please e-mail us at precepts@urbanministries.com or mail your comments to UMI, *Precepts For Living*®, PO Box 436987, Chicago, IL 60643-6987.

May God draw you closer to the fullness of life with Him through this book.

God's blessings to you,

*A. Okechukwu Ogbonnaya, Ph.D.*

A. Okechukwu Ogbonnaya, Ph.D.
Editor

# Uncovering the Benefits of Precepts

It is a great privilege to participate in Christian education and play a significant role in the spiritual formation of fellow Christians in our churches. *Precepts for Living*® is a resource that is designed to help you lead others toward greater knowledge and practice of following Jesus Christ. To that end, please take full advantage of the substantive offerings provided to you in this year's commentary. From the standpoint of your vocation as a teacher, it is very important to be aware of the great responsibility that goes along with your position. James 3:1 reminds us that we have such a great opportunity in front of us that we run the risk of greater judgment if we are derelict in our duties. This is a strong word that helps us understand the great influence we have when we help our students learn about God's Word. Being a teacher means participating in one of the church's greatest tasks, one that the ancient church called "catechesis." While this word is often associated with particular denominations and with a form of teaching that relies upon a systematic question-and-answer format, the central meaning of the word is teaching. It carries with it the idea of imparting the entirety of the faith to Christians. While many Sunday School teachers might not be familiar with this word, the truth is that every time we help others learn about God's Word and ways, we are participating in this great task of the church that has been with us from the beginning. Our participation in catechesis is central to the life of the church. Unfortunately, though, this gets lost amid other concerns. As a teacher, you have an opportunity to energize or revitalize this aspect of your church's ministry. Reflect on how you have prepared for the challenge.

What is the goal when you use *Precepts for Living*® to open up the riches of the Bible to your students? It is beyond the mere acquisition of "spiritual data." Certainly we want our students to grow in knowledge, but the knowledge we seek to pass on does not solely comprise Bible facts but includes a larger sense of comprehension where the information and doctrine conveyed is oriented toward a faithful life of discipleship. The People, Places, and Times; Background; In Depth; and More Light on the Text sections are there to help you provide insight and understanding of the text. But the sections include more than a simple compilation of information. In each lesson, you will also see In Focus stories and Lesson in Our Society and Make It Happen sections serving as catalysts for applying the biblical text to life situations. It is very important that we as teachers pass on knowledge that will enable our students to deepen their devotion to God in an upward focus and encourage them to better embody that devotion in a way that makes their lives a living witness to the world. Our hope from every lesson should be to inspire students to become the best living examples of the Scriptures with the understanding that their lives may be the only Bible some people ever read.

To best take advantage of this commentary, utilize the essays highlighting notable African Americans to emphasize quarterly themes and enhance the classroom experience.

We believe this commentary is a great tool to help form fully devoted followers of Christ, and we invite you to wholeheartedly partake in all of the resources provided here. May God be glorified as you play your part in this great task of the church!

# Creative Teaching

• **Energizing the Class.** If the class does not seem as enthusiastic or energy is low, after you open with prayer, have everyone stretch to the sky or outward. Then tell the class to shake off the low energy, and open up their hands to receive the love of God that is right there. You can always have a 30-second meet-and-greet time. This usually helps to wake people up so you can begin class on a higher energy level.

• **Two Teachers in One Class—Bring Out the Best in Both.** Taking turns works in some classes, but in others it creates tension and favorites. Encourage teachers to study together, and then divide the segments of the lesson. Perhaps one will teach the introduction while the other teaches a section of the text. Encourage them to also become a true team with each contributing throughout the lesson.

• **Remember.** Everyone cannot read or write on the same level. Use different teaching techniques and styles when teaching. How you learn affects how you teach, so be open and willing to learn and teach through various media.

• **Avoid Study in Isolation.** People often "get it" when they are involved with more than talking about the lesson. Why not allow the class to see the connections themselves? Try using a chart to have adult students work in pairs or groups to compare and contrast Bible persons such as David and Solomon or Ruth and Orpah, Naomi's daughters-in-law. To help the students get started, suggest specific categories for comparisons such as lifestyles, families, or public ministry. As class members search the Scriptures, they will learn and remember much more than if you told them about either person.

• **Group Studies.** Have the class form groups, and have each group read the Scripture lesson and a section of the Background for the text. Have each group create a two-minute skit about the Scripture to share with the class. Encourage the groups to use their imaginations and energy. You may want to have at least one "leader" in a group if you have more than two or three reserved people in your class.

• **Volunteers.** Many classes begin with reading the lesson. When class members have studied, this activity is more "bringing minds" together than about the actual lesson. Still some classes can benefit from dramatic and creative reading of Bible passages at any point in the lesson. When the passage under study lends itself, assign parts to volunteers. This need not be formal—standing up isn't even critical. This strategy works best in passages that have a story such as the conversation between Moses and his father-in-law, Jethro, or Paul confronting the merchants in Thessalonica. Assign one person to each speaking character in the Bible text. Feel free to be creative with giving the class roles as "the crowd." Make sure to assign a narrator who will read the nonspeaking parts. It is fun, it is fast, and it makes for memorable Bible reading.

• **Alternatives.** Select one or two persons from the class to read the Scripture lesson with enthusiasm and drama. Ask a few persons to develop a newspaper or magazine headline with a brief story that explains the headlines. Have another group write the headlines and a story that will be used in a cell phone video. (Let the class know that they should bring their cell phones—with video recording—so that most people can share in this activity.)

• **Materials.** You may want to have large sheets of paper, markers, glue or tape, newspapers, and magazines available on a weekly basis for the various activities.

• **Additional Methods.** Write the theme on a large poster board or sheet of paper, and ask each person to write a word or draw a picture that best describes the theme. Read the themes aloud, and discuss any of the pictures before you begin your class discussion or activities. If you have a very large class or time is limited, only select a few words and/or pictures for discussion. You can either lead the discussion or invite members of the class to do so.

• **Web sites.** Connect with us by logging on to urbanministries.com. E-mail us at precepts @urbanministries.com, and send us some of your favorite Teaching Tips for ages 18 and older that you want to share with others. If yours is selected, we will post them under our Teaching Tips sections for Precepts. If you have icebreaker activities, please submit them as well. Your submissions should be no longer than 125 words.

• **Closing.** At the end of the lesson, give your class the assignment of looking for scenes from films or television, advertisements, or parts of songs that either demonstrate the coming week's In Focus story, Lesson in Our Society section, or Make It Happen section. Encourage them to be creative and to come up with an explanation of how their contribution helps make the truth of the lesson come to life.

• **Prayer.** Have a Prayer Request Board for people to write their prayer requests on each Sunday. You may want to make this a weekly activity. Have someone read the prayer request and let the class decide which prayer requests they will pray for during the week. One Sunday School teacher has his class write their prayer requests on sheets of paper and place them in the middle of the floor once a year. He then shares with the class that he will write them all down in a prayer journal that he keeps and prays over them at least once a week. Be creative and create your own prayer journal or prayer tradition(s) within your class.

**Questions Related to the Heritage Profiles:**

1. Why are some people chosen over others to be recognized for their achievements?

2. When reading the Heritage Profiles, what contemporary person comes to mind? A family member or friend can be a part of your decision.

3. Have you ever been recognized for a special achievement? How did you feel, and who have you lifted up to receive a special award in your church, community, or family? Why?

4. List three things you believe are important that someone else knows.

5. What similarities do you see between the historical figure and your life? If there are none, share ways the person's life may have made an impact on your life and on future generations.

6. List three characteristics that stand out about the Heritage Profiles that you think are either positive or negative. List three characteristics about your life that you believe are either positive or negative. Compare the lists and write a short paragraph about the similarities and differences.

Remember that creative teaching can maximize your students' learning experience.

# TABLE OF CONTENTS

ix

# 2012–2016 Scope and Sequence—Cycle Spread

|  | FALL | WINTER | SPRING | SUMMER |
|---|---|---|---|---|
| **YEAR ONE 2012–13** | FAITH<br><br>**A Living Faith**<br>Psalm 46<br>1 Corinthians 13:1–13<br>Hebrews<br>Acts | GOD: JESUS CHRIST<br><br>**Jesus Is Lord**<br>Ephesians<br>Philippians<br>Colossians | HOPE<br><br>**Beyond the Present Time**<br>Daniel<br>Luke<br>Acts<br>1, 2 Peter<br>1, 2 Thessalonians | WORSHIP<br><br>**God's People Worship**<br>Isaiah<br>Ezra<br>Nehemiah |
| **YEAR TWO 2013–14** | CREATION<br><br>**First Things**<br>Genesis<br>Exodus<br>Psalm 104 | JUSTICE<br><br>**Jesus and the Just Reign of God**<br>Luke<br>James | TRADITION<br><br>**Jesus' Fulfillment of Scripture**<br>Zachariah<br>Malachi<br>Deuteronomy<br>Matthew | COMMUNITY<br><br>**The People of God Set Priorities**<br>Haggai<br>1, 2 Corinthians |
| **YEAR THREE 2014–15** | HOPE<br><br>**Sustaining Hope**<br>Jeremiah<br>Habakkuk<br>Ezekiel<br>Isaiah | WORSHIP<br><br>**Acts of Worship**<br>Psalm 95:1–7<br>Daniel<br>Matthew<br>Mark<br>Luke<br>John<br>Ephesians<br>Hebrews<br>James | GOD: THE HOLY SPIRIT<br><br>**The Spirit Comes**<br>Mark<br>John<br>Acts<br>1 Corinthians 12–14<br>1, 2, 3 John | JUSTICE<br><br>**God's Prophets Demand Justice**<br>Amos<br>Micah<br>Isaiah<br>Jeremiah<br>Ezekiel<br>Psalms<br>Zechariah<br>Malachi |
| **YEAR FOUR 2015–16** | COMMUNITY<br><br>**The Christian Community Comes Alive**<br>Matthew<br>John<br>1 John | TRADITION<br><br>**Sacred Gifts and Holy Gatherings**<br>Leviticus<br>Numbers<br>Deuteronomy | FAITH<br><br>**The Gift of Faith**<br>Mark<br>Luke | CREATION<br><br>**Toward a New Creation**<br>Genesis<br>Psalms<br>Zephaniah<br>Romans |

# He Reigns Over All

by Ramon Mayo

For most of my life I've lived near the Pacific Ocean and have visited it numerous times. When I was young I would walk out from the shore and watch, as the water would come up to my neck and then allow it to pull me back to the shore. Many times looking out over the vast expanse of the ocean the greatness of God confronted me. Escaping was not an option. Here, I was compelled to think about God. He was Creator of all things; seen and unseen; above and below the water; beyond the great horizon.

Today the ocean still pulls me in like a steel rod to a magnet. The waters of the oceans and seas have always been a mystery to man. Even now explorers and oceanographers plumb their depths and find new discoveries. More and more scientists are finding new creatures at the bottom of the ocean floor. About 75% of the world is covered by water. It is no wonder we have spent centuries in awe of it. The vast expanse of water that surrounds our planet is enough to make us realize how vast and great God is.

The sea not only represents chaos and mystery, but the awesome power of God. This can be seen in the pages of Scripture as the first couple of lines in Genesis state, "the earth was without form and void and darkness was upon the face of the deep and the spirit of God moved upon the face of the waters" (Genesis 1:2, KJV). In the midst of chaos and the mystery of the waters, the Spirit hovers poised to break into the chaos, at the ready to display God's power. One of the greatest miracles recorded in the Bible is Israel's crossing of the Red Sea. It is another testimony to the awesome power of God as He takes control of something that men fear—the raging sea. He does what He wants with the sea, showing that He is sovereign over all creation. He is not like the gods of the Egyptians and Canaanites. He is not restricted to land, but can do whatever He pleases even with the waters of the sea.

Even in our baptism as believers in Christ we face the terror of water in a symbolic way. We are buried with Christ, as the waters overtake us, and we rise again to new life. The hands and arms that hold us are more than just those of the pastor or minister. They represent the power of God as He is in control of our life and decides to give us a new one. Going down into the water self-sufficient and coming up with the help of Another is a powerful lesson. We realize He is the only one who can do it. Because He is sovereign over all, we are forced to let go and trust Him.

Nowhere is this seen more clearly than when Jesus walks on water. The disciples' minds are blown after seeing Jesus hovering over the sea of Galilee. It is here we find the disciples bowing down and worshiping Him as the Son of God (Matthew 14:22–33). They are dumbfounded when they see the One who created and set the boundaries for the seas walk over those same seas. It is a case of the artist entering into his own masterpiece, still able to shape and paint it as He wills. Peter is invited to walk toward Jesus and succeeds in his attempt. Suddenly he sinks, as he focuses on the water and not Jesus. It is this reality that unravels their perception of Him. They know that they are not dealing with the ordinary.

In the story of Jesus and the calming of the seas, the Lord and the disciples are heading to the other side of the sea of Galilee. In the midst of their nautical journey, a storm arises. The boat reels back and forth as the wind kicks up waves. Water laps over the sides of the boat. The disciples are panicked and terrified. They think that this will be the end for them. On the other hand, Jesus is asleep. He is asleep because the storm does not faze Him. He created it: wind, water, and all. In Colossians 1, Scripture says that He created the world and in Him all things hold together (see Colossians 1:16–17). The disciples were unaware that the One who holds all things together was not going to come apart because of a mere storm. Jesus gets up and rebukes the disciples. They have no faith. The reason they have no faith is that they don't know who is in the boat with them. With an authoritative word He orders the storm to cease and the waves and winds to be still. And they do. This is the power of God at work. The disciples bow down and worship Him. Their exact words: "What manner of man is this, that even the winds and the sea obey him!" (Matthew 8:27, KJV). Exactly. He was no mere man.

As believers, many times we do not see God in all of His awesome power. The trivial pursuits of the day run our lives and permeate our thoughts more than the greatness of Jesus. Suddenly we are hit with a crisis and our world is thrown into chaos, much like the disciples. We imitate Peter as we panic and take our eyes off Jesus. We imitate the disciples as we panic and become terrified at our circumstances. It is such a shame that, like them, we look at the terrible things around us and not the amazing God who is over us. The Creator and Sustainer of the universe. Our response of panic is begging to be transformed into a response of praise. We know that the God who created the storm has the power to cause it to cease. Only this will enable us to sit back and enjoy the ride. We know that the God who created the waters can take strides over it because it is under His command. This God who created the sea and the storm is with us on the sea and in the storm. If He created it, He has power over it. The One who said "let there be light" can speak the same word again when darkness covers our situation. The one who divided the waters and the seas from the dry land can also stop them from overwhelming us when they threaten our lives. Our task is to keep our eyes on Him. The water is not sovereign, God is.

Realizing that He is sovereign should cause us to worship Him with our every breath. The fiber of our being needs to be marshaled into praising and extolling God not just for what He has done but also for who He is. His greatness is unmatched. We can no longer go through life down and out about our situation because we have faith in a God who is faithful, loving, all-knowing, and all-powerful. This is the kind of God we serve. The winds and the waves obey Him. He is able to defy gravity and the natural laws He put into existence. This provokes us to worship and obey Him. The disciples saw what He did when He calmed the sea and realized that Jesus was no ordinary man. They had moved beyond ordinary. They were in the presence of the One who reigns over all.

# Sustaining Hope

The study of this quarter is an examination of prophetic literature, as well as material from the wisdom book of Job, on the subject of hope. It highlights the prophecies concerning restoration and return of the people of Israel from exile and the declarations of Job as examples of sustaining hope through communal and individual hardship and suffering.

## UNIT 1 • THE DAYS ARE SURELY COMING

The four lessons in this unit focus on the hope Israel experienced as seen through the eyes of the prophet Jeremiah as told to him by the Lord.

### Lesson 1: September 7, 2014
### A Vision of the Future
### Jeremiah 30:1–3, 18–22

People often find themselves in situations when they feel lost and alone. Jeremiah told of God's promise to restore the fortunes of the people, Israel and Judah, and to reestablish the covenant with them.

### Lesson 2: September 14, 2014
### Restoration
### Jeremiah 31:31–37

Frequently agreements and relationships must be revised and renewed. Jeremiah assured the people that God will make a new covenant with His people that will nurture and equip them for the present and future.

### Lesson 3: September 21, 2014
### A New Future
### Jeremiah 32:2–9, 14–15

Even in dire circumstances, some people take hopeful actions. While Jerusalem was under siege, God instructed the prophet Jeremiah to purchase property as a sign that there was a future for the people and their land beyond defeat and exile.

### Lesson 4: September 28, 2014
### Improbable Possibilities
### Jeremiah 33:2–11

So many times when they have done wrong things, people reach a point at which they stop and wonder which way to turn. Jeremiah said God is willing to forgive and bring recovery, healing, and restoration.

## UNIT 2 • DARK NIGHTS OF THE SOUL

The four lessons in this unit look at the messages of Habakkuk and Job as they each experienced hope and God's help during times when trouble turned sunny days into darkness.

### Lesson 5: October 5, 2014
### Rejoice Anyway
### Habakkuk 2:1–5, 3:17–19

Some people experience so many difficulties in life that they lose all hope for the future. Job and Habakkuk both affirmed that—no matter what calamities might come their way—they would trust God, rejoice in His presence in their lives, and praise Him for strength to carry on.

**Lesson 6: October 12, 2014**
**Even So, My Redeemer Lives**
**Job 19:1–7, 23–29**

Even when people admit their shortcomings, they are often ostracized by others and receive no justice. Job proclaimed that—no matter what happens—God, the Redeemer, lives and constantly sends forth steadfast love to all people.

**Lesson 7: October 19, 2014**
**Hope Complains**
**Job 24:1, 9–12, 19–25**

There are times when it seems as though the wicked people in the world get all the breaks and cannot be stopped from doing terrible things. Job complained that God supported the evil ones, though only for a while. At the same time he affirmed that God saves the needy and gives the poor hope in their struggles.

**Lesson 8: October 26, 2014**
**Hope Satisfies**
**Job 42:1–10**

People often wonder who or what controls the final outcomes in life's many challenges. Job declared that God can do all things and will ultimately prevail over all obstacles, restoring the fortunes of those who are faithful.

**UNIT 3 • VISIONS OF GRANDEUR**

The five lessons in this study focus on visions of God's glory as seen through the eyes of Ezekiel (and others) as God spoke through them to the people.

**Lesson 9: November 2, 2014**
**God's Divine Glory Returns**
**Ezekiel 43:1–12**

People look for a place in which they can experience some sense of release and orderliness, away from the chaos that sometimes surrounds them. Ezekiel's vision, given to him by God, revealed to the Israelites that God's calming presence and merciful glory could be felt in sacred places where He is truly worshiped.

**Lesson 10: November 9, 2014**
**The Altar, A Sign of Hope**
**Ezekiel 43:13–21**

Often people seek space in which they can find direction for making the most of life. Where can such space be found? The Israelites could hope for release from their iniquities by making sin sacrifices in the sacred space of the altar that stood before the temple.

**Lesson 11: November 16, 2014**
**A Transforming Stream**
**Ezekiel 47:1, 3–12**

Occasionally people feel as if they are stranded on a high cliff, forced to leap into dangerous and unknown waters. Where can they find what they need to make the plunge? The life-giving water in Ezekiel's vision is a symbol of God's presence and blessings, which flow from His sanctuary and are now available to the earth and its people.

**Lesson 12: November 23, 2014**
**Transformation Continued**
**Ezekiel 47:13–23**

Sometimes life leaves people needing a new beginning. Ezekiel told the people that God restored the Israelites and the aliens among them with an inheritance of new land, signifying a new start.

**Lesson 13: November 30, 2014**
**Let Zion Rejoice**
**Isaiah 52:1–2, 7–12**

All people need to hear words of hope. Isaiah told God's people that He who reigns above is their help, shield, and salvation, and that they can put their hope in Him and rejoice.

# A Recipe for Hope

One thing we can count on is that sometime in our lives we will go through hard times. As a part of a community or as an individual, you do not need a prophet to predict that you will experience trouble in this journey of life. This is one of humanity's lowest common denominators, and many do not know how to sustain hope during the seasons of hardship and suffering that we all experience. When it comes to sustaining hope, the most basic principle is to place your hope in someone or something that is worthy of hope. Many place their hope in the next political candidate, only to have their hopes dashed when the candidate's promises fail. Others place their hope in relationships, only to see their trust and love abused or taken for granted. Often people place their hope in money, and the economy shows them how unstable riches and wealth can be. The surest way to sustain hope is to place it in God. Even when we do this, our hope can diminish and we can falter along the way. Sustaining hope is about persevering for the long haul. There is a recipe for sustaining hope during the hard times and it consists of four ingredients: promises, people, prayer, and presence.

## We Need Promises (Romans 15:4)

Paul explains to the church in Rome that we can persevere and continue in our walk with Christ because of the promises of Scripture. He says that the ultimate goal of the things that were written is that we would have encouragement and hope. These Scriptures written in the past sustain us in the present as we wait for their fulfillment in the future. We can only gain more hope as we learn and think on the fulfillment of what God has promised. What has He promised? He has promised us a kingdom where we live with Him forever (see Matthew 19:29). He has promised that we would have resurrected bodies and overflowing joy (see Psalm 16:9-11). Meditating on promises like these can only serve to steer us toward hope in God.

## We Need People (1 Thessalonians 4:13–18)

In 1 Thessalonians 4:13–18, Paul lets the believers know that they do not have to grieve as those who have no hope. He then goes on to explain the hope of the resurrection and the second coming of Jesus. He describes how the Lord will come and that all who believe, whether living or dead, will rise to be with Him forever. Then He says to encourage each other with these words. The way that we can sustain hope is by being surrounded by others who have the same hope. The people we have around us can either discourage us so that we throw that hope away, or encourage us so that we keep that hope in our hearts alive. This does not mean that we should avoid at all costs people who have no hope, for Jesus calls us to love and care for those in need. Instead, we must continue to remind each other of the hope in Jesus so that we can make it through the difficulties that we and others face.

**We Need Prayer (Psalm 65:5)**

The psalmist declares that God faithfully answers the prayers of His people. Then he further adds that the Lord is the hope of everyone on the face of the earth. Prayer, especially answered prayer, increases our hope. When we have seen God do amazing things in our lives, our hope is more steadfast and resilient. We know what God has done and this enables us to trust Him more for future acts. As we lean into prayer, we recall a big God who does big things and our small hope is enlarged to handle the storms of life.

**We Need Presence (Romans 5:5, 15:13)**

Paul explains in Romans 5 that we have a hope that doesn't disappoint us. Why? Because the love of God is overflowing in our hearts. We experience God's love. We experience that we are His and He will never leave us or forsake us. How does this happen? Through the presence of his Holy Spirit in our hearts, we know that God loves us. Later, in Romans 15:13, Paul prays that God would give the church in Rome joy and peace and that they would overflow with confident hope through the power of the Holy Spirit. Through the presence of God filling us with joy and peace, we have confident hope as we face the many trials of life.

That is the recipe for hope. When disaster strikes and crisis invades our lives, we can sustain hope through God's promises, people, prayer, and presence. Many things may trouble us and douse the fire of our hope. Every day we read of terrorist attacks, unstable economies, and unspeakable crimes, but we have a hope that will outlast the present age. With this kind of hope we can say like Jeremiah in Lamentations 3:21–23: "This I recall to my mind, therefore have I hope. It is of the LORD's mercies that we are not consumed, because his compassions fail not. They are new every morning: great is thy faithfulness."

# Learning Hope
### by Judith St. Clair Hull, Ph.D.

**I. Hope as an Attitude of the Personality**

My mother's father was an alcoholic, her mother addicted to gambling. My mom entered the hospital at seven years old, contracted three contagious diseases, went into a coma, but when she came back to consciousness, her eardrums were burst, creating a hearing disability for the rest of her life. And yet, my mom was a cheerful, optimistic person. Educators call this emotional intelligence.

Educator Howard Gardner described seven different intelligences or areas of learning giftedness. Some of us learn better in the area of verbal skills, others in mathematical or scientific thinking, some have musical talent, some have spatial intelligence in areas such as art or architecture, some have body intelligence and are great dancers or athletes, and others have interpersonal or intrapersonal skills. One intelligence not on Gardner's radar was emotional intelligence, which has been suggested by author Daniel Goleman. Emotional intelligence can be separated into two areas—one is emotional intelligence as an ability, the other as a trait. This latter distinction is the personality of my mother and all those who go through tough times and can always see the good side. They are the ones who see the glass as half full, while others see it as half empty.

**II. Hope That Can Only Be Found in God**

As educators we often see children who are going through more suffering than any child should have to. Some children who have suffered greatly reach adulthood triumphing over their difficulties, while others end up with their lives in ruins. What is the difference and how can we as Christian educators help our students—whether children, teens, or adults—develop hope in spite of their troubles?

Biblical hope is more than an optimistic view of what is happening now and will happen in the future. Hope in God happens because God has made the down payment for our future. God's promises are assured to us because of the death of Jesus on the cross and His subsequent resurrection. This is more than just a good mood or fanciful imagination. The hope of the believer is rooted in a historical event.

As we look through the Scriptures for this quarter, we see lots of examples of those who hoped in God even while dealing with terrible circumstances. And many of them do not seem to have optimistic personalities like my mother. One biblical character who stands out is Jeremiah, who has been called the weeping prophet. The Lord gave him a very sad job: to tell the people of Judah that their kingdom was coming to an end and even the beautiful temple of the Lord would be destroyed. Along with this sad message, Jeremiah was told that the people would not listen to him—no wonder Jeremiah wept and lamented! God also gave him a message that looked beyond the upcoming exile. We read in Jeremiah 31:33–34 that the day will come when God will put His words into the hearts of His people. He will be their God and they will be His people. No one will be ignorant of the Lord, because they will all know Him within their hearts. Although Jeremiah has been called the prophet of doom and gloom, he also was a prophet of hope. He did not speak of a wispy, airy Pollyanna hope. No! He dealt with the inevitable reality of his people's situation, but he also trusted in the God who loves with an everlasting love. Ultimately, Jeremiah placed his hope in what the Lord promised for the future.

### III. Building Hope in Our Students

So how do we build a hopeful attitude in our students? The Bible gives us an objective picture of hope that is based upon our trust in God to bring about the things that He has promised. He can accomplish this even with less than sanguine personalities. Hope can be discovered first of all through the many narratives of the Bible that describe how God is working to bring about the fulfillment of His Word in people's lives. Then students can be encouraged to memorize the promises of the Bible.

Students can also learn of how God works as they listen to the stories of witness in the lives of their contemporaries—in the church, in their community, and even from the lips of their Bible teachers. Yes, we have an obligation to tell how God has done great things for us and for others.

Hope in God as a feeling can be learned. However, attitude changes are much more difficult to affect than behavioral changes or changes of the intellect. One way to reach the heart is through music that involves the entire being. A gospel song that is planted deep within will come to mind amid troubles, and the attitude of a hopeful teacher and peers can be contagious. But the only truly effective way to reach that attitude is through the Holy Spirit. God Himself can transform the skepticism of our hearts into the wonderful comfort of resting in His promises.

Sources:
Dominy, Bert. "Hope" from *Holman Illustrated Bible Dictionary*, Brand, Chad, et. al., eds. Nashville, TN: Holman Bible Publishers, 2003.
Gardner, Howard. *Frames of Mind: The Theory of Multiple Intelligences*. New York: Basic Books, 1983.
Goleman, Daniel. *Emotional Intelligence*. New York: Bantam Books, 1995.
Simundson, Daniel J. "Hope" from *The Oxford Companion to the Bible*, Metzger, Bruce M. and Michael D Coogan, eds. New York: Oxford University Press, 1993.

# Sustained Hope in the African American Community

by Jennifer D. King

Hope. It's a word we use often, and one that most of us take for granted. When we say we "hope" in or for something, we are expressing a longing or desire for something. Job seekers hope that they will get the position they interviewed for. Newlyweds hope that they will have a long and enduring marriage. Parents hope that their children will grow up to become productive members of the community. The common denominator for those who hope is that there will be a positive change, an improvement of a situation, or the betterment of an existing condition.

There is, perhaps, no better example of hope than that of the African American community—a community that generation after generation has lived with an abiding hope that the condition of their lives would both change and improve. The totality of the African American experience in the United States has been marked by terror, tenacity, and triumph. Their transition from slavery to freedom has been rife with violence, instability, and inequality. Yet, in the period of 373 years, African Americans have incredibly moved from enslaved chattel to men and women occupying the highest seats of the same government that once bought and sold them and denied their humanity.

One has to marvel at the survival mechanisms that enabled such an incredible movement. Certainly, the retention of a sense of value and self-worth in the face of unparalleled hostility, cruelty, and oppression was critical to Black upward mobility. African spirituality, songs, dances, and folk tales were not only retained by the slaves but also passed on to their progeny. In this way, the slaves resisted the subhuman role their slave owners attempted to force upon them. Despite the trauma they endured, the enslaved Africans maintained their hope by drawing upon and retaining their African traditions that not only built their self-esteem, but which they could express in the areas of their life that were relatively free from the domination of their White slave owners.

Similarly, the sustained hope of the African slaves was carried forward through the emotional and psychological resilience demonstrated through their extraordinarily strong kinship bonds. While the institution of slavery actively discouraged family ties, both maternal and paternal, the slaves clung to the strongest of their African traditions: family. Maintaining the family unit was a formidable task for African slaves. Separation of couples and families through forcible sales was a hallmark of slavery. Even if his wife or children were not sold away from him, African men were powerless to defend their wives and daughters against rape, and their sons against whippings and other forms of brutality. In the face of such obstacles, African parents continued to not only raise their natural children, but also to assume responsibility for the children around them orphaned through the death or sale of their parents. To the best of their ability, slave parents taught their children the skills necessary to endure their bondage, but also taught them African values that empowered them to rely on the love of their families, the reverence of their elders, and other values. All these virtues not only expressed their belief in their own humanity, but that differed greatly from those of their masters that frequently promoted degradation, devaluation, and self-hatred.

Through Christianity, the sustained hope of the African slaves becomes an enduring communal and collective experience. Given the oppressive obstacles and barriers faced by the enslaved Blacks, it is remarkable that it is the slave experience that is directly responsible for reshaping the American Christian experience. The slave trade had kidnapped and transported millions of Africans to the American South to provide the manual labor needed to sustain the lucrative cotton and tobacco crops. These captured slaves brought with them a myriad of religious beliefs including, for some, the belief in a single and benevolent Provider who was responsible for the creation of the entire universe. On the plantations and under the watchful eyes of their owners, slaves were introduced to the rudiments of Christianity in various ways. Some slave masters allowed their slaves to observe their worship from segregated areas of the church. White ministers who preached directly to the slaves frequently used these opportunities to stress the need for the slaves to remain subservient and to "obey" their masters. In this way, Christianity was perverted. Rather than a means for salvation, Christianity was used as an enabling tool to maintain the institution of slavery.

During the latter part of the 1700s, Black men were licensed under the Methodist denomination to preach to the slaves. These ministers very quickly recognized the similarity between their position as slaves and that of the Children of Israel held in bondage in the Old Testament. Clearly, the same hope of liberation yearned for by God's "chosen people" was echoed in the lives of the slaves. Through preaching and teachings from both the Old and New Testaments, the slaves encountered and embraced a God who was willing to intervene on behalf of the oppressed. If God could provide an Exodus for Israel, He could and would, they believed, liberate the African slaves. Equally important was their belief that worship was primarily a communal, rather than private, experience. Rather than seeking a private devotional time with God, the Africanisms retained by the slaves dictated that worship included an encounter both with God and with the community of believers. Thus, the very genesis of the Black church experience was one of collective hope.

In the South, independent Black churches grew out of the efforts of denominational missionary societies. For Blacks living in the North, through the assistance of benevolent organizations called African Societies, independent Black churches gradually began to flourish. Consequently, by 1810, there are records of numerous independent Black churches from various denominations throughout the country.

The Christianity practiced by the enslaved Africans and over the centuries by the emancipated Blacks was quite different from what had been introduced to them from white Christians. Euro-centric Christianity was blended with African practices, cultural wisdom, and music, and Christian worship among Blacks was gradually transformed away from a hate-filled and controlling mechanism to a meaningful and centralizing force within the African American community. At the heart of its robust and very often animated worship, Black Christians fully embraced Jesus' message of justice and hope.

It was through the church that the sustained hope of African Americans would henceforth be centralized and mobilized, and from the pulpits of the Black church the needs and the desires of the majority of African Americans would be articulated. Following the mass migration of almost half a million Blacks from southern states between 1914 and 1920—the largest migration of people in American history—the members of the northern Black churches assisted their brothers and sisters with their settlement into urban cities by giving them housing and employment leads. Black churches also nurtured education by sending monies to support Christian Black colleges. Through the churches, many Blacks were introduced to social organizations, many of which focused on the upward mobility of African Americans. Lodges, fraternal organizations, and Black social and political organizations such as the National Association for the Advancement of Colored People (NAACP) introduced Black churchgoers to new and radical ideas such as racial uplift and social activism. From the pulpit and pews of the Black church came a call for the end of segregation and discrimination, and an insistence on full access by Blacks to equal education, employment, and housing. Through their collective voices, formerly marginalized African Americans forced America to listen to and acknowledge them.

Hope has sustained the African American community through many difficulties and in recent years this hope has been sorely tested. African Americans have witnessed the gradual decay of many fine urban cities into slums, the infiltration and ravages of drugs, the deterioration of public school education, and the proliferation of Black-on-Black crime and violence. Gone are the thousands of small Black-owned businesses that dotted the urban landscape of the '60s and '70s. Within far too many Black communities, single, female-headed households have become commonplace. Historically Black colleges are now competing with white schools to attract the brightest Black students. Perhaps most sad is the growing decline in attendance at Black churches. In the face of all of this, hope still prevails within the African American community. Nowhere was that more clearly seen than in the election and subsequent re-election of America's first African American president.

In November of 2008, the collective hopes of millions of African Americans were recognized with the election of Barack Hussein Obama as the forty-fourth president of the United States. In 2008, Blacks voted in record numbers—2 million more than ever before. For the first time in American history, the gap between White and Black voters was almost erased. So we see that despite the continuing hardships faced by the African American community, it did not give up; rather it maintained its long and enduring legacy of hope.

*Jennifer King holds a B.A. with honors in English and has served as a Superintendent of Sunday School for Bay Area Christian Connection.*

# PAUL CUFFE

## (1759?–September 9, 1817)

### (Businessman, Sea Captain, Abolitionist)

The seed of Pan Africanism can be clearly seen in the life of Paul Cuffe. Cuffe was born free on Cuttyhunk Island, Massachusetts. No exact date of birth can be given but it was approximately 1759. One of many enslaved Blacks who could trace their ancestry to the Ashanti empire in West Africa, Cuffe's father Kofi was a skilled tradesman who earned his freedom. He married Paul's mother, Ruth Moses, a Native American. Kofi died when Paul was a teenager. Paul refused the last name of Slocum given by his father's owner and chose to use his father's first name. In choosing the name of his African heritage, Paul Cuffe was already showing small signs of his destiny to make a name for himself and empower African Americans.

During his teenage years Paul taught himself navigation, mathematics, and other nautical skills. His first journey as a member of a whaling vessel was at sixteen. From the time of the Revolutionary War until several years after, Paul began to buy shares in different ships and build his shipping enterprise. Eventually he owned shares in ten ships. Cuffe and his brother David also built their own boat and smuggled supplies through British blockades during the war. Cuffe's success as a whaling ship captain eventually translated into being a ship owner. This late 18th century position would be similar to owning a commercial airline today. Cuffe owned several sailing vessels that sailed from ports along the coast of Massachusetts. In 1793, he married Alice Pequit and they later had six children: Paul, Mary, Alice, William, Ruth, and Rhoda. During the same year of his marriage, the Fugitive Slave Act gave slave owners the right to retrieve and capture an escaped slave in another state. This new law put Cuffe and his crew in constant danger as they made shipping expeditions up and down the Atlantic coast.

Cuffe became a political activist when he was in his twenties. In 1778, he and his brother John refused to pay taxes, claiming that if they were not allowed to vote, then they suffered from "taxation without representation." He organized a petition to sway the Massachusetts government to allow African and Native Americans the right to vote or free them from taxation. The petition did not influence the Massachusetts General Court to allow them the right to vote, but it did influence the creators of the Massachusetts Constitution to give freedom to all Massachusetts citizens.

Cuffe was a Quaker, and his religious beliefs could be clearly seen in his activities as a philanthropist. He donated to many causes and organizations that helped to uplift African Americans. One of these causes was the building of a school in his hometown of Westport, Massachusetts. This school was established on his own property and was open to children of all races. Cuffe was also an abolitionist who used his connections with free Blacks and other Quakers to rally against slavery and the slave trade. During this time, he advocated for organizations that helped African Americans to participate in the leadership and planning of these organizations.

Cuffe earned a reputation as the wealthiest African American and the largest employer of free African Americans. Although he gained enormous wealth and business success, he became frustrated and discouraged by the status of African Americans in the United States. This led him to believe the best course to take was to establish an independent African nation with returnees from America. In this way, two objectives would be accomplished: gain freedom for African Americans and modernize Africa.

After British abolitionists paved the way in creating the colony of Sierra Leone, Cuffe decided to follow the same path. In January of 1811, he sailed for the West African coast to Freetown. With an entirely African American crew, the expedition safely arrived at their destination. Shortly thereafter Cuffe organized the "Friendly Society of Sierra Leone," which would serve as a trading organization for those Blacks who had returned to Africa. The long-term goal of this organization was to generate enough business to foster a large-scale emigration of African Americans to Sierra Leone.

Cuffe hoped that once there African Americans would spread the Gospel, start new businesses, and abolish slavery and the slave trade.

In 1815, Cuffe led a second expedition to Sierra Leone. The returnees numbered thirty-eight. Once there, they settled into new homes among the former English residents and refugees from Nova Scotia. After this initial success, Cuffe hoped to bring even more returnees and organize larger groups of African Americans who wanted to live a new life of freedom and equality. This plan would soon be overtaken by the American Colonization Society, which was much larger and well funded. The Society created the colony of Liberia and began a similar emigration program. In the uproar of many White and Black Americans debating the validity of the program, Cuffe's plans were overshadowed and eclipsed. Cuffe died on September 9, 1817.

Sources:
Becker, Chrisanne. *100 African Americans Who Shaped American History.* San Francisco: Bluewood Books, 1995.
"Cuffe, Paul, Sr. (1759-1817)." http://blackpast.org/?q=aah/cuffe-paul-sr-1759-1817. Accessed August 23, 2013.
Julye, Vanessa. "Paul Cuffe (1759-1817)." http://www.fgcquaker.org/sites/www.fgcquaker.org/files/attachments/Paul%20Cuffe.pdf. Accessed August 23, 2013.

# Teaching Tips

## Words You Should Know

**A. Heap** (Jeremiah 30:18) *tel* (Heb.)—A mound on which a city had previously stood.

**B. Engaged** (v. 21) *'arav* (Heb.)— To stand with certainty alongside someone as a lender stands with a debtor assured that the debt will be repaid.

## Teacher Preparation

**Unifying Principle—A Promise Assured.** People often find themselves in situations when they feel lost and alone. How do they regain a sense of belonging? Jeremiah tells of God's promise to restore the fortunes of the people, Israel and Judah, and to reestablish the covenant with them.

**A.** Read the Bible Background.

**B.** Read the Devotional Readings.

**C.** Reread the Focal Verses in a modern translation.

## O—Open the Lesson

**A.** Open with prayer.

**B.** Have students read the Aim for Change in unison.

**C.** Ask for a volunteer to read the In Focus story.

**D.** Ask for two or three volunteers to share a personal experience where they felt completely alone and hopeless.

## P—Present the Scriptures

**A.** Ask for volunteers to read the Focal Verses.

**B.** Read and discuss The People, Places, and Times.

**C.** Read and discuss the Background section.

**D.** Encourage students to remember that God never leaves them.

## E—Explore the Meaning

**A.** Review and discuss the Search the Scriptures and Discuss the Meaning questions.

**B.** Ask students to share the most significant point they learned and how to use that point this week.

## N—Next Steps for Application

**A.** Complete the Follow the Spirit and Remember Your Thoughts sections.

**B.** Remind students to read the Daily Bible Readings in preparation for next week's lesson.

**C.** Close in prayer, thanking God for His presence in our life.

## Worship Guide

For the Superintendent or Teacher
Theme: A Vision of the Future
Song: "Great Is Thy Faithfulness"
Devotional Reading: Jeremiah
29:10–14

# A Vision of the Future

**Bible Background • JEREMIAH 30**
**Printed Text • JEREMIAH 30:1–3, 18–22**
**Devotional Reading • JEREMIAH 29:10–14**

## Aim for Change

By the end of the lesson, we will: REVIEW God's written promise to restore the people and the land of Israel and Judah as of old; IMAGINE and EXPRESS the feelings of safety in a community that has great promise for the future; and PLAN a way to invite people who are not part of the covenant community to become members of the church and Sunday School.

## In Focus

Shirley cried softly as she packed the last of the kitchen items. Four months ago Fred, her husband of three years, had told her that he had fallen in love with one of his co-workers and wanted a divorce. After Fred moved out, Shirley had struggled emotionally and financially. Now, she could not afford to pay the rent with her part-time salary. Shirley had repeatedly called Fred and tried to get him to go to marriage counseling, but he refused. He told her, "It's over. You need to accept that and move on with your life." When she and Fred had married, he had accepted a position with a firm that required them to move more than six hundred miles from her friends and family. She was too embarrassed to call her sister and tell her that Fred had left her. As she closed the last box of dishes, she wondered what was going to happen to her and how she would manage without her husband. In the midst of her suffering Shirley realized she was not alone. God was present and had a plan for her life.

*Jesus Christ has promised never to leave us alone. In spite of the darkness around, He is ever present. In today's lesson, we will see that although Israel and Judah had been punished for their sins, God had every intention of redeeming and restoring them.*

## Keep in Mind

"For, lo, the days come, saith the LORD, that I will bring again the captivity of my people Israel and Judah, saith the LORD: and I will cause them to return to the land that I gave to their fathers, and they shall possess it" (Jeremiah 30:3).

"For, lo, the days come, saith the LORD, that I will bring again the captivity of my people Israel and Judah, saith the LORD: and I will cause them to return to the land that I gave to their fathers, and they shall possess it" (Jeremiah 30:3).

## Focal Verses

**KJV** **Jeremiah 30:1** The word that came to Jeremiah from the LORD, saying,

**2** Thus speaketh the LORD God of Israel, saying, Write thee all the words that I have spoken unto thee in a book.

**3** For, lo, the days come, saith the LORD, that I will bring again the captivity of my people Israel and Judah, saith the LORD: and I will cause them to return to the land that I gave to their fathers, and they shall possess it.

**18** Thus saith the LORD; Behold, I will bring again the captivity of Jacob's tents, and have mercy on his dwellingplaces; and the city shall be builded upon her own heap, and the palace shall remain after the manner thereof.

**19** And out of them shall proceed thanksgiving and the voice of them that make merry: and I will multiply them, and they shall not be few; I will also glorify them, and they shall not be small.

**20** Their children also shall be as aforetime, and their congregation shall be established before me, and I will punish all that oppress them.

**21** And their nobles shall be of themselves, and their governor shall proceed from the midst of them; and I will cause him to draw near, and he shall approach unto me: for who is this that engaged his heart to approach unto me? saith the LORD.

**22** And ye shall be my people, and I will be your God.

**NLT** **Jeremiah 30:1** The LORD gave another message to Jeremiah. He said,

**2** "This is what the LORD, the God of Israel, says: Write down for the record everything I have said to you, Jeremiah.

**3** For the time is coming when I will restore the fortunes of my people of Israel and Judah. I will bring them home to this land that I gave to their ancestors, and they will possess it again. I, the LORD, have spoken!"

**18** This is what the LORD says: "When I bring Israel home again from captivity and restore their fortunes, Jerusalem will be rebuilt on its ruins, and the palace reconstructed as before.

**19** There will be joy and songs of thanksgiving, and I will multiply my people, not diminish them; I will honor them, not dispise them.

**20** Their children will prosper as they did long ago. I will establish them as a nation before me, and I will punish anyone who hurts them.

**21** They will have their own ruler again, and he will come from their own people. I will invite him to approach me," says the LORD, "for who would dare to come unless invited?

**22** You will be my people, and I will be your God."

---

### The People, Places, and Times

**Judah.** Located between the Mediterranean Sea and Dead Sea, Judah lies in southern Palestine. Following the death of King Solomon, the united kingdom of Israel split into two. Two tribes, Judah and Benjamin, remained loyal to King Rehoboam and became the Southern Kingdom of Judah. The other ten tribes followed King Jeroboam and are generally referred to as the Northern Kingdom of Israel. Judah's capital city and central place of worship was the city of Jerusalem. Prior to its destruction by the Babylonians in 587 B.C., Judah was ruled by a succession of nineteen kings, all from the line of David.

**Jeremiah.** Jeremiah is known as the weeping prophet, so much so that there is an entire book of the Bible dedicated to his sorrow: the book of Lamentations. Most of the anguish he experienced was due to the sinful nature of the Israelites and their rejection of God. Subsequently, this also led to their captivity. But, Jeremiah also experienced grief because both he and his message were rejected by the people.

Jeremiah's ministry stretched from 626 B.C. to some time after the destruction of Jerusalem in 587 B.C., which places him after Zephaniah and a contemporary with Ezekiel, and Habakkuk in history. A very popular and often quoted Scripture is derived from God calling Jeremiah to be God's prophet: "Before I formed you in the womb I knew you" (from Jeremiah 1:5, NIV).

## Background

In the book that bears his name, Jeremiah was clearly operating as a prophet. Throughout the book, Jeremiah declared the sins of the people (including idolatry) and God's judgment against them. One cannot fail to see the prophet's sadness and sympathy as he denounced Judah's ungodly behavior and the impending doom it would bring about. Present-day Christians should be just as sad when we see unchecked sin abound. While Jeremiah frequently issued harsh denunciations, the prophet's love for the people was evident. His prophecies, however, fell on deaf ears. The people of Judah were using the temple as a good luck charm. They mis-

takenly believed that no real harm could befall the city that housed the magnificent temple of Jerusalem. They ignored the fact that Shiloh, which was Israel's central place of worship before David elevated Jerusalem, had fallen to the Philistines as punishment for the wickedness of Israel. This was proof that God recognized the difference between hypocritical ritual and true religion. The nation of Judah failed to heed the words of Jeremiah and would not repent or turn away from its wickedness.

## At-A-Glance

1. The Prophet Called to Write the Vision (Jeremiah 30:1–2)
2. A Future of Restoration (v. 3)
3. A Future with a Kingdom (v. 18)
4. A Future with Joy and a Renewed Covenant (vv. 19–22)

## In Depth

### 1. The Prophet Called to Write the Vision (Jeremiah 30:1–2)

Prior to the destruction of Jerusalem, Jeremiah, who continues to speak out against false priests and prophets, is imprisoned for treason. It is important to note that God no longer has the prophet speaking directly with the people. His people still have access to His Word even though they will no longer have access to His messenger. God tells Jeremiah to write all the words that He had given him in a book. Here we see a loving God making a way for a people who have been continually unfaithful to Him.

Often referred to as the "Book of Consolation," it is believed that this portion of Jeremiah's prophecy comes to him shortly after the sacking of Jerusalem by the Babylonians. Jeremiah's ministry covered a period of about forty years. He is the last prophet to Judah, and, more importantly, he is a first-hand witness to the moral decay of the nation. He had warned that God's judgment was imminent. Jeremiah saw for himself how the nation made alliances with the idol-worshiping nations around them and even began to adopt pagan worship and religious practices. For these sins and the injustice that resulted from them, God would soon judge the nation of Judah.

## 2. A Future of Restoration (v. 3)

Just as God said, and just as Jeremiah prophesied, Jerusalem fell to the Babylonians in 587 B.C. The city was utterly destroyed and many of the people were deported. Jeremiah emphasizes that God had not forgotten nor forsaken His people—a people who had failed to heed the Word of God, refused to repent, and were now suffering the consequences of their sin. God's love for His people was enduring. Even in captivity, His thoughts were turned toward them. Yes, they were being punished, but God intended that the people of Judah would be restored to Him and returned to their land.

In this verse, we see Jeremiah delivering a more specific message of hope to the people of Judah. His message is not simply one that contains words of comfort and consolation to a suffering people. It is, actually, a vision for their future! Even though it is their fault that they have come into captivity, we will see that God still loves His people and that He cares deeply for them. We must be careful to remember that it is only a trick of the enemy to make us believe that our sins separate us from the loving care and concern of God. Through the blood of His Son Jesus Christ, we are always in the thoughts of God, and there is nothing that can separate us from His love.

## 3. A Future with a Kingdom (v. 18)

In this verse we see that God's vision for His people's future includes their liberation and restoration. This vision is divinely comprehensive and includes all of God's people. Jeremiah's referral to "Jacob" informs us that God is addressing Israel as a united nation and not just the Southern Kingdom of Judah. Just as God had been present with the patriarchs Abraham, Isaac, and Jacob, so too would He be present with their captive children. The prophet references "tents" and "dwellingplaces" as a reminder to the people of both Israel and Judah that they have now become wanderers and sojourners in foreign and alien lands, but this is coming to an end.

Jeremiah continues to show that even more acts of mercy for the people of God are forthcoming. God will once again rebuild Jerusalem, and He will do it on the "heap" or ruins of their former capital. Although Jerusalem had been destroyed, remnants of its foundations and portions of the walls surrounding the city remained. God would use these painful physical reminders to restore the city. The mention of a "palace" implies that the restoration would not only include the rebuilding of the city but a restoration of the kingdom itself.

## 4. A Future with Joy and a Renewed Covenant (vv. 19–22)

Jeremiah prophesies that following their restoration the people of Israel would finally give the appropriate response to the God of their salvation—thanksgiving. Recognizing, at last, the source of their joy, the people would now worship God honestly and joyfully. Then the worship of the people would not only be true but also marked by joyfulness. Jeremiah goes on to prophesy that God would increase their numbers. This would be a sign to the pagan nations around them that the blessing of God rested once again on the nation He had called out of nothingness.

Here, we are now given even further glimpses of God's vision for His people. No longer would foreign and ungodly rulers govern the people of God. Instead, their ruling class would rise from among them. The God-appointed "nobles" would be men who both knew and understood their prior suffering and afflictions. More importantly, we are now presented with a clear pre-figuration of Christ as both our Mediator and Righteous Judge. Like the governors, Jeremiah predicts in this verse, Christ knew the full suffering of mankind. As Mediator, it is the role of Christ to "draw near" or to go to the Father, not for Himself, but for the express purpose of intervening on behalf of man. Christ's role as a High Priest is also seen here. In the same way Moses drew near to God to plead for the Children of Israel who had sinned in the desert wilderness, so too did Jesus draw near to His Father to plead for us. It was only Jesus who could and did bridge the gap between the Creator and the creation.

## Search the Scriptures

1. How did God instruct Jeremiah to communicate with the people (Jeremiah 30:2)?

2. Where did God tell Jeremiah the city of Jerusalem would be rebuilt (v. 18)?

3. What were some of the signs of restoration that would accompany God's people (vv. 18–20)?

## Discuss the Meaning

1. When we accept Jesus Christ as our Lord and Savior, what are some of the promises God has given us about our future?

2. How do you imagine the captives reading these promises felt about their future? How much do you think it prompted them to reflect on their past sins?

## Lesson in Our Society

We need only walk down the streets of any major urban city to see ruin and decay. Once-prosperous cities and towns are full of abandoned and boarded-up buildings. There are no signs of thriving businesses, and entire neighborhoods are blighted and empty. The people who remain in these areas sometimes look as forlorn as the property surrounding them. These are all signs of hopelessness. Through Jesus Christ, there is hope for the restoration and renewal of the communities and the people who live in them. We must be as diligent as Jeremiah in sharing the Word that God not only loves but also cares for His people and that He has a plan for their future.

## Make It Happen

Consider ministries that are helping to rebuild and restore communities that have been devastated by crime, poverty, or natural disaster. Pray and ask God to show you where there is time in your busy schedule to demonstrate His love through you. Next, ask Him to give you a tender and understanding heart.

## Follow the Spirit

What God wants me to do:

_____

_____

_____

_____

## Remember Your Thoughts

Special insights I have learned:

_____

_____

_____

_____

## More Light on the Text

Jeremiah 30:1–3, 18–22

**1 The word that came to Jeremiah from the LORD, saying, 2 Thus speaketh the LORD God of Israel, saying, Write thee all the words that I have spoken unto thee in a book.**

For most of the preceding chapters of his book, Jeremiah has been instructed by God to speak words of condemnation to the nation of Israel for their behavior. Beginning with this chapter, however, Jeremiah receives "word" (Heb. *davar*, **dah-VAHR**, message or edict) from the Lord to "write" (Heb. *katav*, **kah-TAHV**, to register or record in writing) his message to the nation of Israel. God wants Jeremiah to write down the prophecy instead of speaking it because His message is to be preserved for future generations to read and understand. God knew that Jeremiah would not be taken into captivity with the rest of the Jewish nation, and by having him write the prophecy instead of speaking it, those Jews in captivity to the Babylonians could have a source of hope that even their bondage was in accord with God's divine plan for them. Later, while a captive of the Babylonian empire, Daniel would read and take heed of Jeremiah's prophecy, responding with a repentant heart (cf. Daniel 9:2–4).

**3 For, lo, the days come, saith the LORD, that I will bring again the captivity of my people Israel and Judah, saith the LORD: and I will cause them to return to the land that I gave to their fathers, and they shall possess it.**

Through Jeremiah, God wants His chosen people to understand that their "captivity" (Heb. *shevut*, **sheh-VOOT**, exile or ill fortune) to the Babylonians will come to an end. The nations of Israel and Judah are to be consoled with this promise. For that reason, many scholars assert that this chapter of Jeremiah begins a Book of Consolation to the Jewish nations held in captivity. God has promised that He "will bring again the captivity" (Heb. *shuv*, **SHOOV**, turn back or ever turn away), the exile of His chosen people. Jeremiah is to write the prophecy so that there will be no misunderstanding by future generations of God's sure hand on their situation. Jeremiah is to write the prophecy so that when the captivity has ended and the nations of Israel and Judah are restored to their former land in Palestine, there will be no doubt how the restoration came about and who was the source of that restoration. Through Jeremiah, God pledges to the Jewish nations that the promise He made to "their fathers" (Heb. *'av*, **AHV**, father or ancestor), that they would "possess" (Heb. *yarash*, **yah-RASH**, to seize, inherit, or occupy) the land of Palestine, would one day be a reality.

**18 Thus saith the LORD; Behold, I will bring again the captivity of Jacob's tents, and have mercy on his dwellingplaces; and the city shall be builded upon her own heap, and the palace shall remain after the manner thereof.**

Through Jeremiah, the Lord continues His promise to the Jewish nations now in bondage. The nations are to understand and believe that they will not always feel like nomads or wanderers living in "tents" (Heb.

19

'ohel, **OH-hel**, nomadic dwelling thus symbolic of wilderness life) like their forefathers Abraham, Isaac, and Jacob had to do. Tents will one day give way to permanent dwelling places in the land that God has promised to them. God also promises to "have mercy" (Heb. *racham*, **rah-KHAM**, to have pity or compassion) on those dwellings, a promise of divine protection. Further, the city will be rebuilt upon her own "heap" (Heb. *tel*, **TEL**, former ruins). In ancient times, sites for cities were often chosen for their strategic importance, whether commercial or military, and for that reason, when a city was destroyed, a new city would often be erected on the exact same spot. Finally, God promises that the "palace" (Heb. *'armon*, **ar-MONE**, royal citadels or temple) will once again be "after the manner thereof" (Heb. *mishpat*, **meesh-PAHT**, what is proper and right). It will once more be a place of righteousness and judgment. Even the palace is to be rebuilt to its former glory and in its former spot and will once more be the host of sacred feasts with offerings of sacrifice to the Most High God.

**19 And out of them shall proceed thanksgiving and the voice of them that make merry: and I will multiply them, and they shall not be few; I will also glorify them, and they shall not be small. 20 Their children also shall be as aforetime, and their congregation shall be established before me, and I will punish all that oppress them.**

All of these promises (permanent dwellings, divine protection, increase of children, the restoration of the cities and temple in their original places) were to result in the people offering "thanksgiving" (Heb. *todah*, **toe-DAH**, hymn of praise) to the Lord God. This thanksgiving would be accompanied by voices expressing great joy and happiness. God would have demonstrated His faithfulness and love for His chosen people. In their present state of bondage, such an occurrence would have been hard to imagine, but the nations were to have faith in God. Their sufferings were to be mixed with hope for their future. As in many African societies, children in Israelite culture were a valuable possession and a sign of prosperity. Thus the the size and fortunes of the various tribes of Israel would be restored and increased and children would be "as aforetime" (Heb. *qedem*, **KEH-dem**, from of old)—bountiful, playing in the streets of their cities, and inheriting their parents' estates. Further, God will sit and watch over their "congregation" (Heb. *'edah*, **eh-DAH**, assembly) to protect their worship practices and will "punish" (Heb. *pakad*, **pah-KAHD**, to impose a penalty on) any who would seek to "oppress" (Heb. *lakhats*, **lah-KHATS**, to force themselves upon or afflict) His chosen nation.

**21 And their nobles shall be of themselves, and their governor shall proceed from the midst of them; and I will cause him to draw near, and he shall approach unto me: for who is this that engaged his heart to approach unto me? saith the LORD.**

It must have pleased Jeremiah to be writing a prophecy that was intended to assure the Children of Israel that at the end of their captivity to the Babylonians, their leadership structure would once again be in place. This is because the leaders were primarily responsible for the nation's exile. Their "nobles" (Heb. *'addir*, **ad-DEER**, leading men or rulers) would be selected from their own tribes. Moreover, their "governor" (Heb. *mashal*, **mah-SHAL**, king or one who exercises authority over) will come from one of their tribes and the Lord God will cause him to "draw near" (Heb. *karav*, **kah-RAHV**, to approach or be brought close) to Him. Scholars agree that this is a foreshadowing of the Messiah who is to come and who will be able to offer Himself to God on behalf of the people. God, who sees and judges on the basis of the "heart" (Heb. *lev*, **LEV**, the seat of the affections, intellect, and memory), is mindful of any who would seek to approach Him. Only Christ the Messiah would be found worthy for such a task. Only Christ, acting as the High Priest of the people, could have so "engaged" (Heb. *'arav*, **ah-RAV**, pledged as security) His heart.

**22 And ye shall be my people, and I will be your God.**

God will accept the sacrifice of this King and Ruler, thus ensuring the continuing relationship between Himself and the Jewish nations. Christ as High Priest and King will be the Mediator between God and the people. As the people accept Christ, God will accept the people.

Sources:

Alexander, David, et al. *Eerdman's Handbook to the Bible.* Grand Rapids, MI: Wm. B. Eerdmans Publishing Company, 1994. 398–405.

Dunn, James D. G. and John W. Rogerson. *Commentary on the Bible.* Grand Rapids, MI: Wm. B. Eerdmans Publishing Company, 2003.

Elwell, Walter A. *Baker Theological Dictionary of the Bible.* Grand Rapids, MI: Baker Book House Company, 1996. 389–390.

English, E. Schuyler and Marian Bishop Bower, eds. *The Holy Bible: Pilgrim Edition.* New York: Oxford University Press, 1952.

Howley, G.C.D., F.F. Bruce, and H. L. Ellison. *The New Layman's Bible Commentary.* Grand Rapids, MI: Zondervan, 1979.

Keener, Craig S. *The IVP Bible Background Commentary: New Testament.* Downers Grove, IL: InterVarsity Press, 1993.

## Say It Correctly

Aforetime. a-**FOR**-time.
Jeroboam. je-ruh-**BO**-um.

## Daily Bible Readings

**MONDAY**
Act with Justice and Righteousness
(Jeremiah 22:1–9)

**TUESDAY**
Hear the Words of This Covenant
(Jeremiah 11:1–10)

**WEDNESDAY**
Only the Lord Will Be Exalted
(Isaiah 2:10–19)

**THURSDAY**
Turn from Your Evil Way
(Jeremiah 18:1–10)

**FRIDAY**
A Future with Hope
(Jeremiah 29:10–14)

**SATURDAY**
Hope for Israel's Neighbors
(Jeremiah 12:14–17)

**SUNDAY**
The Days Are Surely Coming
(Jeremiah 30:1–3, 18–22)

# Teaching Tips

## Words You Should Know

**A. Covenant** (Jeremiah 31:31) *berit* (Heb.)—A political or financial agreement with signs and pledges by both parties.

**B. Hearts** (v. 33) *lev* (Heb.)—The seat of the affections, intellect, and memory.

**C. Hosts** (v. 35) *tsaba'* (Heb.)—An organized army for service or battle.

## Teacher Preparation

**Unifying Principle—Hope for Tomorrow.** Sometimes agreements and relationships must be revised and renewed. How can the faithful make sure all aspects of their lives encourage wholeness and spiritual growth in present circumstances? Jeremiah assures the people that God will make a new covenant with His people that will nurture and equip them for the present and the future.

**A.** Read the Bible Background and Devotional Readings.

**B.** Read the Focal Verses in a modern translation.

**C.** Read the companion lesson in *Precepts For Living Personal Study Guide*®.

## O—Open the Lesson

**A.** Ask a student to begin the class with a prayer.

**B.** Ask a volunteer to read the In Focus story. Discuss.

**C.** Read the Aim for Change and talk about how God's new covenant gives us hope for the future.

## P—Present the Scriptures

**A.** Ask for volunteers to read The People, Places, and Times.

**B.** Read the Focal Verses in the NLT Translation.

## E—Explore the Meaning

**A.** Review and discuss the Discuss the Meaning questions and the Lesson in Our Society section.

**B.** Ask volunteers to share the most significant point they learned and to give examples of how they can use those points in this week.

## N—Next Steps for Application

**A.** Allow time for students to complete the Follow the Spirit and Remember Your Thoughts sections.

**B.** Remind students to read the Daily Bible Readings in preparation for next week's lesson.

## Worship Guide

For the Superintendent or Teacher
Theme: Restoration
Song: "God Will Take Care of You"
Devotional Reading: Hebrews
8:1–7, 13

# Restoration

**Bible Background • JEREMIAH 31**
**Printed Text • JEREMIAH 31:31–37**
**Devotional Reading • HEBREWS 8:1–7, 13**

## Aim for Change

By the end of the lesson, we will: KNOW God's new covenant to reveal Himself to all the people, forgive their sins, and hold them accountable; SENSE the relief and joy that come from starting over in agreement with someone; and MAKE plans for renewing our personal covenant with God.

## In Focus

Lauren and Bill were standing at the altar. Seated in the pews behind them were their grown children and grandchildren. Although they had been married for years, they had decided to renew their marriage vows. As he stood at the altar and looked at his bride, Bill also remembered how the first twenty years of their marriage had been a nightmare for his wife and children. Bill had struggled with his alcoholism, insisting that he "didn't have a problem" even though he had been fired from several jobs. Lauren had worked a full-time and a part-time job to pay the rent and other bills. She had to take care of the children alone. Five years ago, Lauren had finally insisted that Bill join a substance abuse program. Lauren had also talked Bill into attending church with her. A year later, Bill accepted Christ as his personal Savior. As he stood at the altar, he thanked God for giving him Lauren and for giving him an opportunity to renew his covenant of marriage with such a wonderful woman. God's love is forever. Even when we sin and turn away from God, He wants us to return to Him and His care and protection.

*In this lesson, we will see that even though Israel had repeatedly sinned against Him, God wanted to renew His covenant with them.*

## Keep in Mind

"Behold, the days come, saith the LORD, that I will make a new covenant with the house of Israel, and with the house of Judah" (Jeremiah 31:31).

"Behold, the days come, saith the LORD, that I will make a new covenant with the house of Israel, and with the house of Judah" (Jeremiah 31:31).

## Focal Verses

**KJV** Jeremiah **31:31** Behold, the days come, saith the LORD, that I will make a new covenant with the house of Israel, and with the house of Judah:

**32** Not according to the covenant that I made with their fathers in the day that I took them by the hand to bring them out of the land of Egypt; which my covenant they brake, although I was an husband unto them, saith the LORD:

**33** But this shall be the covenant that I will make with the house of Israel; After those days, saith the LORD, I will put my law in their inward parts, and write it in their hearts; and will be their God, and they shall be my people.

**34** And they shall teach no more every man his neighbour, and every man his brother, saying, Know the LORD: for they shall all know me, from the least of them unto the greatest of them, saith the LORD: for I will forgive their iniquity, and I will remember their sin no more.

**35** Thus saith the LORD, which giveth the sun for a light by day, and the ordinances of the moon and of the stars for a light by night, which divideth the sea when the waves thereof roar; The LORD of hosts is his name:

**36** If those ordinances depart from before me, saith the LORD, then the seed of Israel also shall cease from being a nation before me for ever.

**37** Thus saith the LORD; If heaven above can be measured, and the foundations of the earth searched out beneath, I will also cast off all the seed of Israel for all that they have done, saith the LORD.

**NLT** Jeremiah **31:31** "The day is coming," says the LORD, "when I will make a new covenant with the people of Israel and Judah.

**32** This covenant will not be like the one I made with their ancestors when I took them by the hand and brought them out of the land of Egypt. They broke that covenant, though I loved them as a husband loves his wife," says the LORD.

**33** "But this is the new covenant I will make with the people of Israel on that day," says the LORD. "I will put my instructions deep within them, and I will write them on their hearts. I will be their God, and they will be my people.

**34** And they will not need to teach their neighbors, nor will they need to teach their relatives, saying, 'You should know the LORD.' For everyone, from the least to the greatest, will know me already," says the LORD. "And I will forgive their wickedness, and I will never again remember their sins."

**35** It is the LORD who provides the sun to light the day and the moon and stars to light the night, and who stirs the sea into roaring waves. His name is the LORD of Heaven's Armies, and this is what he says:

**36** "I am as likely to reject my people Israel as I am to abolish the laws of nature!"

**37** This is what the LORD says: "Just as the heavens cannot be measured and the foundations of the earth cannot be explored, so I will not consider casting them away for the evil they have done. I, the LORD, have spoken!"

## The People, Places, and Times

**Covenants.** A covenant is not simply an agreement between two parties. Covenants are not arbitrary; they are binding. Covenants are special relationships by which the parties enter into a binding commitment with one another. This committed relationship makes a demand on each party. In the Bible, we see all types of covenants. There are the covenants that are made between groups and nations, as is the case in Joshua 9 when the people of Gibeon covenant with the Children of Israel (Joshua 9:6, 15). Still another type of covenant is demonstrated in the relationship between David and Saul's son Jonathan. This relationship is not a trivial friendship. The Scriptures tell us "that the soul of Jonathan was knit with the soul of David, and Jonathan loved him as his own soul" (1 Samuel 18:1). Throughout the Old Testament, the covenant between God and the Children of Israel provides that God offers His love and protection, and in return His people pledge to worship and serve Him alone.

**Babylonian Captivity.** This is the period in biblical history when the people of Judah were defeated and taken away by the powerful nation of Babylonia. Following a year-long siege, the capital city of Jerusalem and the temple were destroyed in 587 B.C. Deportation or removal of defeated foes was a common military practice of the Babylonians and other nations. The actual deportation of the people of Judah took place in three waves. The first was in 606 B.C. when Daniel and his friends were taken along with other prospects to work in the Babylonian government. The second happened in 588 B.C., when King Zedekiah and more leaders were removed from Judah. The third occurred in 582 B.C. when Nebuchadnezzar took 4,600 heads of families along with their wives and children. The Babylonians probably only took the people who would be useful to them in Babylon. This would include the priests, craftsmen, business owners, and the wealthy. The Bible implies that the captives were resettled in a single area which allowed them to continue to practice their religion and culture. Theoretically, the nation of Judah ceased to exist after 587 B.C., and the former inhabitants of Judah no longer had a homeland. The people who were left behind in Judah, the "Am Ha'aretz," or people of the land, primarily the poor and elderly, are described as suffering from widespread famine in the book of Lamentations.

## Background

Jeremiah, the final prophet to the Southern Kingdom of Judah, was from Anathoth, a priestly community belonging to the tribe of Benjamin. Under the instruction of the Lord, Jeremiah wrote to people of Judah who had been captured and taken into captivity by the powerful nation of Babylonia. Despite admonitions and warnings delivered by the godly prophets like Jeremiah, the people of Judah had shown themselves unwilling to change and unrepentant. Here we see that Judah knowingly and willfully breached their covenant with God. Although they continued to go through the motions of worship, it was only a ritualized affair that greatly displeased God. Their religious pomp was not backed by faithfulness to God. Adding to this were religious leaders who preached superstition and predicted that the temple in Jerusalem could never fall into the hands of the Babylonians.

Jeremiah continued to prophesy to the people of Judah. He let them know that God would restore their relationship with Him through a new covenant. This new covenant would bind them to the Lord in a unique and different way. It would also give them the abili-

26

ty to obey the stipulations of the covenant and to experience the Lord in their midst.

## In Depth

### 1. God Offers a New Covenant (Jeremiah 31:31–32)

We must keep in mind that Judah's continued unfaithfulness and failure to return to God was a national breach of their covenant with Him. This initial covenant was made on Mount Sinai after the Exodus of the Children of Israel from Egypt. Now, Jeremiah declares that God is instituting a new covenant. There is to be a change in the relationship between God and His chosen people. Jeremiah clearly names the nations or "houses" of Israel and Judah as parties and ultimate recipients of this new covenant.

Jeremiah points out that this new covenant will be quite different from the previous Mosaic covenant. We will recall that while Moses was talking to God, the Children of Israel had grown impatient and subsequently constructed a golden calf to worship (Exodus 32). Thus the initial covenant was broken before Moses could even come down from Mount Sinai.

Moreover, the phrase "I took them by the hand" shows us the parental approach God used toward Israel. It is very interesting to note that the imagery Jeremiah uses to denote God's faithfulness toward Israel is that of a "husband." While a husband-wife rela-

tionship certainly makes the point of faithfulness, it is a bit odd that such an analogy would be used to describe the relationship between the Creator and His obviously inferior creation. Here we see the loving quality of God's character exemplified. As the Children of Israel wandered through the hostile desert, God, like a loving husband, had protected them and provided for Israel. This imagery also foreshadows Christ's fulfillment in the New Testament as a loving husband of His bride, the church (cf. Ephesians 5:23).

### 2. A Covenant of Love (vv. 33–34)

Jeremiah goes on to point out a major difference between the Mosaic and the new covenant: its character. The previous covenant had been written on stone tablets. It had been a legalistic mechanism whereby the people would follow the laws and statutes of God. This new covenant would be intrinsic in nature, and so it would be inscribed in their hearts. Here we see that God wants His people to recognize the corrupting effects of their sin: that it actually destroys them both externally and internally. Our faithfulness to God is predicated on a relationship with Him that is intensely personal and intimate. His laws must be seared into our hearts so that we may serve Him because our very wills have been changed.

More importantly, God declares that "I will be their God, and they will be my people" (from v. 33, NLT). This clearly describes God's great promise—one that will be asserted in each successive covenant with man—that does not need to ever be expanded. Jeremiah knows that the earlier Mosaic covenant relied heavily on legalism. Thus the laws, the temple, and the sacrificial offerings would stand as proof of the absolute forgiveness of the people's sins. All of these objects stimulated fear and uncertainty in the people. Instead, the new covenant would rely on love rather than fear as the principal motivation for obedience and faithfulness to God.

### 3. A Covenant of Everlasting Intimacy (vv. 35–37)

In these verses, Jeremiah offers even greater hope to the captives to whom he is writing. It is God, the prophet posits, who can control the uncontrollable. The intricate cycles of day and night and the motion and movement of seas are under the sovereign control of God. God alone orders and controls nature. Jeremiah now presents a powerful image for his reader. In order for Israel not to belong to God, God would have to discard His control of nature itself—something that clearly cannot happen since God alone is sovereign.

Only God is all knowing, or "omniscient." Since there is no one who can know these marvelous secrets of nature, then the captives could rest in their assurance that Israel would again be a nation of God's chosen people. God and God alone, the prophet declares, is able to restore His people and only He can hold any power against them. Jeremiah is clear that the blessings of God's new covenant will be experienced by a fully restored nation. More importantly, present-day believers have the assurance through Christ Jesus that the blessings of God's new covenant have been extended to us.

### Search the Scriptures

1. With whom is God making the new covenant (Jeremiah 31:31)?

2. Rather than a law on tablets, where will the new covenant be written (v. 33)?

3. What assurances does God offer the people about their former transgressions and sins (v. 34)?

### Discuss the Meaning

1. This portion of Scripture is widely believed to have been written while the people were still in captivity. Why do you think God wanted them to hear this before they were released?

2. When we accept Christ, He responds, "Henceforth, I call you not servants ... I have called you friends" (from John 15:15). What should be our response to Christ as believers? Does your relationship with Christ reveal that He is your friend?

### Lesson in Our Society

In today's world, agreements are constantly made and broken. It seems that no one's word can be trusted. Corporations make agreements with their customers that they readily break. Governments make agreements with their citizens and with other nations, only to break those as well. God gives us more than just a flimsy human agreement. His new covenant is backed by Jesus' death on the Cross. This was His demonstration and pledge of His love for us. Our response ought to be one of gratitude and sharing this love with others.

### Make It Happen

The Lord told His people that "I will remember [your] sin no more" (from Jeremiah 31:34). Again and again we see that God continues to forgive and love His people despite their sins. As recipients of this amazing love, we do not want to take it for granted. We need to pray and examine our lives. If there is any old anger, hurt, betrayal, or heartbreak, it only means that God is presenting us with an opportunity to forgive and be forgiven. Only then can we renew our relationship with Him.

## Follow the Spirit

What God wants me to do:

_____

_____

_____

_____

## Remember Your Thoughts

Special insights I have learned:

_____

_____

_____

_____

## More Light on the Text

Jeremiah 31:31–37

**31 Behold, the days come, saith the LORD, that I will make a new covenant with the house of Israel, and with the house of Judah: 32 Not according to the covenant that I made with their fathers in the day that I took them by the hand to bring them out of the land of Egypt; which my covenant they brake, although I was an husband unto them, saith the LORD.**

God knew that Jeremiah would not be taken into captivity with the rest of the Israelite nation and so had him write his prophecy so future generations would be able to read of God's plans for them and have a sense of hope (cf. Jeremiah 30:2–3). Beginning with this passage, the "LORD" (Heb. *Yehovah*, **yeh-ho-VAW**, the self-existing One) would continue His message of hope to the nations of Israel and Judah. God's promise includes the making of a "new covenant" with the nations of Israel and Judah (cf. Hebrews 8:8–9). Previously God had covenanted with the people at Mount Sinai. Moses was given God's laws for the nations to observe. These laws required effort on the part of the Israelites and could be understood in a more material sense. The new covenant that God will make in "days" (Heb. *yom*, **YOME**, sometime later or the future) to "come" (Heb. *bo'*, **BOE**) looks forward to the time of Christ and the grace of God that will be available only through Him. Even though God took the Children of Israel by the hand, led them out of Egypt, and walked with them in the wilderness the way a husband would guide his wife, they would be unfaithful to Him and break their covenant. This Mosaic covenant the Israelites were able to "brake" (Heb. *parar*, **pah-RAR**, to make void, or to annul) because it demanded a particular behavior. However, the new covenant that God was promising through Jeremiah to make with the nations, would be grounded in the work of Christ and require only acceptance of Christ to trigger God's grace. In this way, the new covenant was to be a much better covenant between God and His people.

**33 But this shall be the covenant that I will make with the house of Israel; After those days, saith the LORD, I will put my law in their inward parts, and write it in their hearts; and will be their God, and they shall be my people.**

Because God's new "covenant" (Heb. *berit*, **be-REET**) would be located in the "inward parts" (Heb. *kerev*, **KEH-rev**) of each person and written on the hearts, it differentiates itself from the old covenant that was written on stone. The old covenant was written by the finger of God on stone tablets, and through Moses, was laid before the people for them to accept or reject. Under the old covenant, if God's laws were accepted, then they would be followed and could be received into their hearts. However, the possibility remained that they could reject God's law. Embedded within the old covenant were the kernels of righteousness that would be the fruit of obedient adherence to the commands of the law, but those kernels were presented externally to the people. The new covenant was to be internal and righteousness would come on the basis of belief in the Messiah, Jesus Christ. Because of Christ, God's blessings would be bestowed spiritually on the basis of grace, not commanded but freely given. Through union with Christ, those who believed, whether Jew or Gentile, would be God's people and God would be their God. The promise of a new covenant should be understood as a completion of the old covenant where God pledged this special relationship between Himself and His people (cf. Exodus 29:45 and Leviticus 26:12).

**34 And they shall teach no more every man his neighbor, and every man his brother, saying, Know the LORD: for they shall all know me, from the least of them unto the greatest of them, saith the LORD: for I will forgive their iniquity, and I will remember their sin no more.**

The light and knowledge of God will be freely available to all who believe. Under the new covenant, it will no longer be necessary for anyone to receive individual instruction and have others "teach" (Heb. *lamad*, **lah-MAHD**, to instruct) the ways of God, because everyone will personally have access to God and His wisdom. Nothing of God will be hidden from His people because His laws and precepts will be written internally upon each individual heart, and all will know for themselves what pleases or displeases God. In the event that errors in judgment are made,

God will forgive their "iniquity" (Heb. *'avon*, **ah-VONE**, wrongdoing or transgressions) and in forgiving will remember the offense no more. This is a glorious promise to future Israel and to all who come to God through Christ because of them.

**35 Thus saith the LORD, which giveth the sun for a light by day, and the ordinances of the moon and of the stars for a light by night, which divideth the sea when the waves thereof roar; The LORD of hosts is his name: 36 If those ordinances depart from before me, saith the LORD, then the seed of Israel also shall cease from being a nation before me for ever.**

These verses proceed to show why God by His intrinsic nature cannot fail in the fulfillment of the covenant He has made with Israel. God created, God controls, and God sustains. God put the sun in place and established its purpose to give light and heat to the earth. He then put the moon in place and the stars with it. According to His "ordinances" (Heb. *khukkah*, **khook-KAH**, limits, enactments or something prescribed), they have their regular duties and functions. God "divideth" (Heb. *raga'*, **rah-GAH**, to cause to rest) the bounds for the sea, and when the waves threaten to overrun its bounds, He quiets those waves with a word. These things must be so because they all exist to serve Him (cf. Psalm 119:90–91). God's people and His church need only look around and observe nature to understand that as it is subject to His ordinances and relies on His faithfulness for its continuance, so too His holy people and His church, "the seed of Israel," will not cease or come to an end without His sanction.

**37 Thus saith the LORD; If heaven above can be measured, and the foundations of the earth searched out beneath, I will also cast**

off all the seed of Israel for all that they have done, saith the LORD.

It is nearly impossible for man to measure the heavens or to determine the foundations of the earth. God's Word established the heavens and the earth, and that same Word declares that they are hung upon nothing (cf. Job 26:7). Believing this to be true, God's people and His church can be assured that He has the power and the goodness to be faithful to the promises He has made. Iniquities will be pardoned and forgotten, nations will be rebuilt, future generations will be enlarged and protected, and God will be their God through all eternity. This is the gift of grace to all "the seed" (Heb. *zera'*, **ZEH-rah**, meaning descendants, offspring, or posterity) of Israel who embrace Christ as Lord and Savior.

Sources:
Alexander, David, et al. *Eerdman's Handbook to the Bible.* Grand Rapids, MI: Wm. B. Eerdmans Publishing Company, 1994. 398–405.
Dunn, James D. G. and John W. Rogerson. *Commentary on the Bible.* Grand Rapids, MI: Wm. B. Eerdmans Publishing Company, 2003.
Elwell, Walter A. *Baker Theological Dictionary of the Bible.* Grand Rapids, MI: Baker Book House Company, 1996. 389–390.
English, E. Schuyler and Marian Bishop Bower, eds. *The Holy Bible: Pilgrim Edition.* New York: Oxford University Press, 1952.
Howley, G.C.D., F.F. Bruce, and H. L. Ellison. *The New Layman's Bible Commentary.* Grand Rapids, MI: Zondervan, 1979.
Keener, Craig S. *The IVP Bible Background Commentary: New Testament.* Downers Grove, IL: InterVarsity Press, 1993.

## Say It Correctly

Iniquity. in-**IH**-qui-tee.
Ordinance. **OR**-din-ans.

## Daily Bible Readings

**MONDAY**
A Better Covenant
(Hebrews 8:1–7, 13)

**TUESDAY**
Mediator of a New Covenant
(Hebrews 9:11–15)

**WEDNESDAY**
Ministers of a New Covenant
(2 Corinthians 3:4–11)

**THURSDAY**
I Will Gather Them
(Jeremiah 31:7–11)

**FRIDAY**
Hope for Your Future
(Jeremiah 31:12–17)

**SATURDAY**
Set Up Road Markers
(Jeremiah 31:18–25)

**SUNDAY**
I Will Make a New Covenant
(Jeremiah 31:31–37)

# Teaching Tips

## Words You Should Know

**A. Beseiged** (Jeremiah 32:2) *tsur* (Heb.)— Encircle and enclose a fortified area as an aggressive military strategy.

**B. Redemption** (v. 7) *ge'ullah* (Heb.)— Reclamation of inheritance or family members from servitude or difficulties.

## Teacher Preparation

**Unifying Principle—Property for Sale**. Even in dire circumstances, some people take hopeful actions. What gives them the confidence to do so? While Jerusalem was under siege, God instructed the prophet Jeremiah to purchase property as a sign that there was a future for the people and their land beyond defeat and exile.

**A.** Pray for the participants and clarity.

**B.** Read both translations of the text.

## O—Open the Lesson

**A.** Ask the class to think about their future.

**B.** Instruct everyone to meditate on how much better their future can be than whatever they imagined before they put God in the equation.

**C.** Pray and introduce the lesson title and Aim.

**D.** Ask a volunteer to read the Keep in Mind verse to the class.

## P—Present the Scriptures

**A.** Instruct participants to read the In Focus story silently to themselves.

**B.** Request volunteers to read the Focal Verses.

**C.** Use The People, Places, and Times; Background; Search the Scriptures; At-A-Glance; and In Depth to clarify the verses.

## E—Explore the Meaning

**A.** Depending on the size of the class, divide the group and have participants discuss the Lesson in Our Society questions.

**B.** Come back together as a class. Instruct students to read Search the Scriptures and think about their answers individually. Ask for volunteers who feel comfortable sharing their responses.

**C.** Examine Discuss the Meaning as a group.

**D.** Give the class time to complete the Make it Happen activity silently.

## N—Next Steps for Application

**A.** Summarize the lesson.

B. Close with prayer.

## Worship Guide

For the Superintendent or Teacher
Theme: A New Future
Song: "It's a New Season"
Devotional Reading: Isaiah 12

# A New Future

**Bible Background • JEREMIAH 32**
**Printed Text • JEREMIAH 32:2–9, 14–15 | Devotional Reading • ISAIAH 12**

## ———————— Aim for Change ————————

By the end of this lesson, we will: RETELL the hopefulness of Jeremiah's purchase of a field while he awaits the invasion and siege of Jerusalem; APPRECIATE hope and hopeful actions in the face of deep hardship; and REVIEW our personal times of hardship in the past that held, and hold, hope for the future.

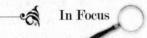

## ———————— In Focus ————————

Rico was a young man whose family had instilled in him the importance of owning property ever since he was a little boy. At the age of twenty-six, he had just saved up enough money for the down payment on his first home when the economy crashed in 2008. All around him companies were laying off, downsizing, and going out of business. So many of his friends had lost jobs and were moving back in with their parents. His older colleagues complained about the depreciated value of their homes.

At this point Rico was torn. The news reports said banks and Wall Street were to blame, and the housing and automotive industries were suffering the worst effects. His gut feeling told him this was a bad time to make such a large purchase, but he remembered the things he was taught about ownership. Rico decided the best thing he could do was seek the advice of a financial planner. The planner informed Rico that it was a great time to purchase. He informed him that real estate was at an all-time low. He told Rico not to worry; despite how things appeared, the market would recover and, at some point, the future would be bright again.

*Today's lesson will show us that even in dire circumstances, we can take hopeful actions.*

## ———————— Keep in Mind ————————

"Thus says the LORD of hosts, the God of Israel: Houses and fields and vineyards shall again be bought in this land" (Jeremiah 32:15).

"Thus says the LORD of hosts, the God of Israel: Houses and fields and vineyards shall again be bought in this land" (Jeremiah 32:15).

# Focal Verses

**KJV** **Jeremiah 32:2** For then the king of Babylon's army besieged Jerusalem: and Jeremiah the prophet was shut up in the court of the prison, which was in the king of Judah's house.

**3** For Zedekiah king of Judah had shut him up, saying, Wherefore dost thou prophesy, and say, Thus saith the LORD, Behold, I will give this city into the hand of the king of Babylon, and he shall take it;

**4** And Zedekiah king of Judah shall not escape out of the hand of the Chaldeans, but shall surely be delivered into the hand of the king of Babylon, and shall speak with him mouth to mouth, and his eyes shall behold his eyes;

**5** And he shall lead Zedekiah to Babylon, and there shall he be until I visit him, saith the LORD: though ye fight with the Chaldeans, ye shall not prosper.

**6** And Jeremiah said, The word of the LORD came unto me, saying,

**7** Behold, Hanameel the son of Shallum thine uncle shall come unto thee saying, Buy thee my field that is in Anathoth: for the right of redemption is thine to buy it.

**8** So Hanameel mine uncle's son came to me in the court of the prison according to the word of the LORD, and said unto me, Buy my field, I pray thee, that is in Anathoth, which is in the country of Benjamin: for the right of inheritance is thine, and the redemption is thine; buy it for thyself. Then I knew that this was the word of the LORD.

**9** And I bought the field of Hanameel my uncle's son, that was in Anathoth, and weighed him the money, even seventeen shekels of silver.

**14** Thus saith the LORD of hosts, the God of Israel; Take these evidences, this evidence of the purchase, both which is sealed, and

**NLT** **Jeremiah 32:2** Jerusalem was then under siege from the Babylonian army, and Jeremiah was imprisoned in the courtyard of the guard in the royal palace.

**3** King Zedekiah had put him there, asking why he kept giving this prophecy: "This is what the LORD says: 'I am about to hand this city over to the king of Babylon, and he will take it.

**4** King Zedekiah will be captured by the Babylonians and taken to meet the king of Babylon face to face.

**5** He will take Zedekiah to Babylon, and I will deal with him there,' says the LORD. 'If you fight against the Babylonians, you will never succeed.'"

**6** At that time the LORD sent me a message. He said,

**7** "Your cousin Hanamel son of Shallum will come and say to you, 'Buy my field at Anathoth. By law you have the right to buy it before it is offered to anyone else.'"

**8** Then, just as the LORD had said he would, my cousin Hanamel came and visited me in the prison. He said, "Please buy my field at Anathoth in the land of Benjamin. By law you have the right to buy it before it is offered to anyone else, so buy it for yourself." Then I knew that the message I had heard was from the LORD.

**9** So I bought the field at Anathoth, paying Hanamel seventeen pieces of silver for it.

**14** "This is what the LORD of Heaven's Armies, the God of Israel, says: 'Take both this sealed deed and the unsealed copy, and put them into a pottery jar to preserve them for a long time.'

**15** For this is what the LORD of Heaven's Armies, the God of Israel, says: 'Someday people will again own property here in this

this evidence which is open; and put them in an earthen vessel, that they may continue many days.

**15** For thus saith the LORD of hosts, the God of Israel; Houses and fields and vineyards shall be possessed again in this land.

land and will buy and sell houses and vineyards and fields.'"

## The People, Places, and Times

**Zedekiah.** Zedekiah was the last king of Judah and son of King Josiah. His birth name was actually Mattanyahu, but it was changed by Nebuchadnezzar when he appointed Zedekiah king of Judah. Zedekiah attempted a revolt against Babylon, which prompted the military turmoil that is present in our text. Ultimately, Zedekiah was captured in a very gruesome manner; he was forced to watch the killing of his children and spent the remainder of his life as a prisoner in Babylon. These events mark the beginning of the Babylonian exile. The Judeans were deported to Babylonia and the temple was destroyed (2 Kings 24–25; 2 Chronicles 36).

**Babylonia.** This tremendously wealthy and powerful nation was located between the Tigris and Euphrates Rivers in southern Mesopotamia. Babylonia is one of the world's most ancient kingdoms and its people, religion, and culture are mentioned throughout the Old Testament. It reached the height of militaristic power during the period known of Old Babylonia. Babylonia eventually fell to Assyrian reign. Later, under the rule of King Nebuchadnezzar, Babylonia completely devastated the Southern Kingdom of Judah. King Solomon's temple was looted and destroyed, and the people, including the prophets Daniel and Ezekiel, were carried off into captivity for seventy years. The Babylonian empire eventually fell to the Persians and never regained its former prominence as a world power.

## Background

Jeremiah is the longest book in the Bible (by word count) and is a part of the biblical category known as the "prophets." This genre can be divided in two sub-categories: major and minor. The major prophets are Isaiah, Jeremiah, Ezekiel, and Daniel, and then the minor prophets comprise the last twelve books of the Old Testament. The distinguishing factor between major and minor is based solely on the length of the books. It has nothing to do with importance or status.

A prophet is one who serves as a medium of communication between the human and divine worlds. Prophets helped to shape Judaism and Christianity. Over the course of time, they became a mainstay as much-needed divine messengers for the nation as well as for individuals. Not all prophets have biblical books of the same name. The Bible is actually full of prophets; the only difference is that some wrote while others didn't. Various types of prophets existed in both the Old and New Testaments, and their delivery and characters were uniquely different. Biblical prophets were concerned with things of the past, present, and future. Not only did some have the gift of foresight (prediction), but they also had the "forth-sight" to discern present times and admonish wrongdoing. Prophets did not have superstar appeal; most were not eloquent or charismatic and their messages were contrary to what popular culture wanted to hear.

## At-A-Glance

1. The Plot (Jeremiah 32:2–5)
2. The Prophecy (vv. 6–9)
3. The Purpose (vv. 14–15)

## In Depth

### 1. The Plot (Jeremiah 32:2–5)

Jeremiah was going to Anathoth to take care of the land deal when he was accused of desertion and thus imprisoned in the palace of the king. Based on the information provided, at the time of the text the year is between 588–587 B.C. and Nebuchadnezzar is the king of Babylon. Judah is still free but has been surrounded by the Babylonian army for eighteen months. Now that King Zedekiah has Jeremiah in his custody, the king asks a question, or rather interrogates him. The question is in fact a quote previously spoken by Jeremiah that has evidentially ravished the emotional well-being of the king. The king has either heard the prophecy on more than a few occasions or understands the weight of the words because he quotes them verbatim. Basically the message is that Zedekiah will not succeed and Jerusalem will be occupied by the Babylonians. The Lord makes it clear that although the Babylonians will hold Zedekiah captive, God will administer the punishment. Even more discouraging is the warning that fighting will prove futile because there is no chance for Judah to win. The king is shaken by the prophecy and wants an explanation for why Jeremiah spoke the dispiriting words.

### 2. The Prophecy (vv. 6–9)

The previous section was centered on the king asking Jeremiah about his prophecy. Oddly Jeremiah provides an extensive response, but never answers Zedekiah's ques-

tion. Instead Jeremiah goes into what the reader assumes is an explanation of a revelation God has given him. God told Jeremiah about a proposition that his cousin would present to him concerning a portion of land in their hometown. When the event transpired just as the Lord said it would, Jeremiah was very diligent concerning the transaction. This particular manifestation of God's words was confirmation that the revelations he received really were from God.

As a side note, when Hanameel says, "By law you have the right to buy it" (v. 7), he is speaking of the law of redemption, which can be explained as a "keep it in the family" clause. If an owner was not able to care for the family land or didn't want it for whatever reason, the closest relative had the first right to purchase the property. One may attribute Jeremiah's diligence to wanting to ensure there was no disputing the authenticity of the transaction. His prophecy was for all of Judah, so he ensured that all the men who were in the courtyard could bear witness and hear as he spoke the words of the Lord. Undoubtedly they would go spread the word that Jeremiah had shared and tell of all the subsequent events that took place.

### 3. The Purpose (vv. 14–15)

God's purpose is revealed here. This is not just a foolish transfer of land from one family member to another during a time of military occupation, but a sign of hope. Jeremiah took care in preserving the deeds as a sign that the day would come when the land would once again be of value. It is very likely that during this time everyone wanted to sell and no one wanted to buy because all of the land could any day become the property of Babylon. This is yet another message given to the prophet from God. This time the message is of hope and comes in the form of action, not just words. It was so during ancient times and still holds true today: when a country is in despair, the housing and real estate market is a gauge used to measure recovery and stability. People buy when they are planning to stay and settle. The actions of Jeremiah signify something far greater than words; like the old saying goes . . . put your money where your mouth is.

## Search the Scriptures

1. What was the purpose of putting the sealed deeds in a pottery jar (Jeremiah 32:14)?

2. How was the king of Babylon going to be able to capture Jerusalem (v. 3)?

## Discuss the Meaning

When we envision our future, do we plan based on the future God has given us, or do we look at things only as they appear right before us?

## Lesson in Our Society

Jeremiah speaks regarding the faith and future of a nation. The same way God sent prophets to the nation of Israel, He sends messages and messengers to the nations of today. What are some of the things that we do as a nation that God may be displeased with? Now think about it on a smaller level. What are some of the things your local community may do that are displeasing to God? When the appointed messenger, your pastor, speaks doom and hope, does it affect the actions of the community?

## Make It Happen

Think about a past experience in your life that was filled with despair. Even though you may not have been hopeful at the time, try to remember if there were any signs of hope that everything would work out in the end.

## Follow the Spirit

What God wants me to do:

_____

_____

_____

_____

## Remember Your Thoughts

Special insights I have learned:

_____

_____

_____

_____

## More Light On the Text

Jeremiah 32:2–9, 14–15

**2 For then the king of Babylon's army besieged Jerusalem: and Jeremiah the prophet was shut up in the court of the prison, which was in the king of Judah's house.**

The siege by Babylon's army had begun a year earlier (cf. 2 Kings 25:8) and would last for an additional six months. Jeremiah had predicted that King Nebuchadnezzar of Babylonia would be successful in his efforts to capture Israel and Judah and take its inhabitants captive back to Babylonia. Now even in the midst of being "besieged" (Heb. *tsur*, **TSOOR**, to shut up or enclose) by the foreign invaders, King Zedekiah hardened his heart against Jeremiah and imprisoned God's prophet in the court of his palace. This court was probably the courtyard of the palace guards and located within the palace grounds. Jeremiah was not bound and had the freedom to have visitors and to walk the courtyard, but he was "shut up" (Heb. *kala'*, **kah-LAH**, to restrain or restrict or forbid) in the court and would have been unable to have an audience for any more of his prophecies. King Zedekiah imprisoned Jeremiah even though it was obvious that he was a prophet of God.

**3 For Zedekiah king of Judah had shut him up, saying, Wherefore dost thou prophesy, and say, Thus saith the LORD, Behold, I will give this city into the hand of the king of Babylon, and he shall take it; 4 And Zedekiah king of Judah shall not escape out of the hand of the Chaldeans, but shall surely be delivered into the hand of the king of Babylon, and shall speak with him mouth to mouth, and his eyes shall behold his eyes.**

Zedekiah was incensed that Jeremiah would "prophesy" (Heb. *nava'*, **nah-VAH**, to be under the influence of divine spirit) as he did. The phrase "wherefore dost thou prophesy" is better understood as "how dare you prophesy" such a disaster upon Jerusalem and its king. Jeremiah prophesied that Nebuchadnezzar would capture Jerusalem as an agent of God's displeasure with His chosen nation and its leadership. Even though Jerusalem was at that moment under siege by the Babylonians, Zedekiah would not humble himself before God or His prophet (cf. 2 Chronicles 36:12). Further, Jeremiah indicated that even though King Zedekiah would try to "escape" (Heb. *malat,* **mah-LOT,** to slip away or flee), he would not be able to do so. Instead, he would be delivered into the hands of the Babylonians, where he would stand before their king, look into his eyes, and hear from his mouth the punishment to be exacted upon him. In some older African cultures the phrase "mouth to mouth and eye to eye" is used as a reference to wrestling or a swordfight. It carries the nuance of the fear

and terror exuding from another warrior in close proximity. No wonder Zedekiah was furious. Jeremiah speaking in the name of Yahweh had implied that the King will be coward groveling with fear when he meets the King of Babylon.

**5 And he shall lead Zedekiah to Babylon, and there shall he be until I visit him, saith the LORD: though ye fight with the Chaldeans, ye shall not prosper.**

Once captured by the Babylonians, King Zedekiah would be led in chains to Babylon. He would be forcibly removed from his throne and dragged along by horses. This is a picture of complete and utter humiliation. There in Babylon he would remain a prisoner until God "visit[ed] him" (Heb. *pakad,* **pah-KAHD,** to punish) with death. Some scholars assert that Zedekiah found a degree of favor with Nebuchadnezzar in Babylon because he was not put to death but rather died of natural causes, even receiving some honor at his funeral (cf. Jeremiah 34:4–5). This suggest that Zedekiah repented of his sin sometime before his death.

**6 And Jeremiah said, The word of the LORD came unto me, saying, 7 Behold, Hanameel the son of Shallum thine uncle shall come unto thee saying, Buy thee my field that is in Anathoth: for the right of redemption is thine to buy it. 8 So Hanameel mine uncle's son came to me in the court of the prison according to the word of the LORD, and said unto me, Buy my field, I pray thee, that is in Anathoth, which is in the country of Benjamin: for the right of inheritance is thine, and the redemption is thine; buy it for thyself. Then I knew that this was the word of the LORD.**

God instructed Jeremiah to be prepared for a visit from his cousin Hanameel, who would approach Jeremiah to purchase his property located in Anathoth. The right of redemption was spelled out in Leviticus 25:24–34 and illustrated in Ruth 4:3–4 and would have been known to most Israelites of the time. It is probable that Hanameel's father Shallum was dead and the property had passed to his son. It is also probable that the siege by the Assyrians had made money a scarce possession throughout the region and Hanameel needed money. Jeremiah was not married (cf. Jeremiah 16:2) and had already been told by God that the Babylonians would be victorious over Israel and Judah and take possession of all the lands of those nations. For that reason, there was not much value in purchasing land within Israel or Judah at that time. Because Jeremiah did not have a wife or children, he would only be able to use the property while he lived and then could leave it only to a relative until the time of Jubilee, when the land would revert back to the original owner. Still, he knew that when Hanameel visited him in prison and requested that he purchase the land, he had been sent by God.

**9 And I bought the field of Hanameel my uncle's son, that was in Anathoth, and weighed him the money, even seventeen shekels of silver.**

Scholars estimate a shekel of silver to be worth about five dollars in U.S. dollars today and seventeen shekels would be equivalent to about seven ounces of silver. Jeremiah, as a priest, would not have had a lot of money, but by being frugal, he could have had sufficient funds to purchase the field from his cousin. The prophet knew that God had sent Hanameel to him and therefore did not haggle over the price. Rather, in front of the appropriate witnesses (cf. v. 12), Jeremiah counted out the seventeen shekels of silver

and purchased the field in accord with God's further purpose.

**14 Thus saith the LORD of hosts, the God of Israel; Take these evidences, this evidence of the purchase, both which is sealed, and this evidence which is open; and put them in an earthen vessel, that they may continue many days.**

The land purchase agreement between Jeremiah and Hanameel, witnessed by those present, would have been written down on two documents. These documents or "evidences" (Heb. *sefer*, **SEH-fer**, missive or writing) of the purchase were to be placed in a clay pot to be retrieved at some future date. One document was to be sealed (this was probably the original document which contained the terms and conditions of the agreement), while the second document that summarized the agreement was to remain "open" (Heb. *galah*, **gah-LAH**, uncovered or exposed) so that it could be housed in a public register for any person to have access to.

**15 For thus saith the LORD of hosts, the God of Israel; Houses and fields and vineyards shall be possessed again in this land.**

God then reveals the reason that Jeremiah was to purchase the field from his cousin. Jeremiah had already been told that the Babylonians would be successful in their siege of Jerusalem and would lay the land to waste. During the seventy years that the Children of Israel would be in bondage in Babylonia, the land that made up the nations of Israel and Judah would be desolate and in ruin. Houses and fields and vineyards would all be destroyed. In purchasing Hanameel's field, God was communicating to future generations through Jeremiah that His chosen people will once again possess the land promised to them.

40

Sources:

Brueggmann, Walter. *To Build, To Plant: Jeremiah 26–52*. Grand Rapids, MI: Wm. B. Eerdsmans Publishing Company, 1991.

Dunn, James D. G. and John W. Rogerson. *Commentary on the Bible*. Grand Rapids, MI: Wm. B. Eerdmans Publishing Company, 2003. English, E. Schuyler and Marian Bishop Bower, eds. *The Holy Bible: Pilgrim Edition*. New York: Oxford University Press, 1952.

Howley, G.C.D., F.F. Bruce, and H. L. Ellison. *The New Layman's Bible Commentary*. Grand Rapids, MI: Zondervan, 1979.

Keener, Craig S. *The IVP Bible Background Commentary: New Testament*. Downers Grove, IL: InterVarsity Press, 1993.

Keown, Gerald L., Pamela J. Scalise, and Thomas G. Smothers. *Word Biblical Commentary, Volume 27: Jeremiah 26–52*. Dallas, TX: Word Books Publisher, 1995. 169.

## Say It Correctly

Chaldean. chal-**DEE**-en.
Zedekiah. ze-de-**KAY**-ah.
Hanameel. ha-na-**MEEL**.
Anathoth. a-na-**THOTH**.

## Daily Bible Readings

**MONDAY**
The Steadfast Love of God
(Jeremiah 32:16–23)

**TUESDAY**
Provoking God
(Jeremiah 32:26–35)

**WEDNESDAY**
Very Soon My Anger Will End
(Isaiah 10:20–25)

**THURSDAY**
I Will Surely Gather Them
(Jeremiah 32:36–44)

**FRIDAY**
The Wolf and Lamb Live Together
(Isaiah 11:1–12)

**SATURDAY**
Surely God Is My Salvation
(Isaiah 12)

**SUNDAY**
Hope for a Distant Future
(Jeremiah 32:2–9, 14–15)

# Notes

# Teaching Tips

## Words You Should Know

**A. Iniquity** (Jeremiah 33:8) *'avon* (Heb.)— Sin or wickedness, often with a focus on the guilt or liability incurred and the punishment to follow.

**B. Prosperity** (v. 9) *shalom* (Heb.)—Peace, safety, well-being, wholeness.

## Teacher Preparation

**Unifying Principle—Laughter Will Return.** So many times when they have done wrong things, people reach a point at which they stop and wonder which way to turn. How can people seek renewal and accept help to turn their lives around? Jeremiah says God is willing to forgive and bring recovery, healing, and restoration.

**A.** Pray as you prepare and read over the lesson.

**B.** Read both translations of the text.

**C.** Complete companion lesson in *Precepts For Living Personal Study Guide®*.

## O—Open the Lesson

**A.** Pray and introduce the lesson title.

**B.** Ask for a volunteer to read the Aim for Change.

**C.** Read the Keep in Mind verse to the class.

## P—Present the Scriptures

**A.** Instruct participants to read the In Focus story silently.

**B.** Request volunteers to read Focal Verses.

**C.** Use The People, Places, and Times; Background; Search the Scriptures; At-A-Glance; and In Depth to clarify the verses.

## E—Explore the Meaning

**A.** Depending on the size of the class, divide the group and have participants discuss Lesson in Our Society.

**B.** Come back together as a class. Instruct students to read Search the Scriptures and think about their answers individually. Ask for volunteers who feel comfortable sharing their responses.

**C.** Examine Discuss the Meaning as a class.

## N—Next Steps for Application

**A.** Allow participants time to complete the Make It Happen and Aim for Change individually.

**B.** Summarize the lesson.

**C.** Close with prayer and allow students to thank God for His hope, healing, and forgiveness in their lives.

## Worship Guide

For the Superintendent or Teacher
Theme: Improbable Possibilities
Song: "God Specializes"
Devotional Reading: Jeremiah 9:17–24

# Improbable Possibilities

**Bible Background • JEREMIAH 33**
**Printed Text • JEREMIAH 33:2–11**
**Devotional Reading • JEREMIAH 9:17–24**

## Aim for Change

By the end of this lesson, we will: REALIZE that God's promise to follow punishment with forgiveness and restoration is still a valid promise; AFFIRM that with God, punishment, forgiveness, and healing come as a package; and DESIGN a thank offering for hope, healing, and forgiveness we receive from God.

## In Focus

Carolyn played Division I tennis for a powerhouse team. She was the first person in her family to go to college, and everyone was very proud of her. Her family was relatively poor, so she would not have been able to attend school if not for her scholarship. One day an alum approached Carolyn after tennis practice. The woman expressed her love for tennis, the school, and Carolyn's unique skill set. As the woman was leaving, she gave her a bag and said, "I thought you could use a new racket."

Inside the bag was a large amount of money. Carolyn knew that this was no mistake. She knew it was against the rules, but her family needed the money. It was a month later when Carolyn's coach and athletic director approached her before practice. They somehow found out about the money she had taken and were forced to release her from both the team and school. Carolyn was devastated. She knew that she had disappointed God and her family. She had no idea where to turn, so she prayed and asked God to forgive her and help her turn her life around.

*In today's lesson, we learn that God is willing to forgive and bring recovery, healing, and restoration.*

## Keep in Mind

"Call unto me, and I will answer thee, and show thee great and mighty things, which thou knowest not" (Jeremiah 33:3).

"Call unto me, and I will answer thee, and show thee great and mighty things, which thou knowest not" (Jeremiah 33:3).

## Focal Verses

**KJV** **Jeremiah 33:2** Thus saith the LORD the maker thereof, the LORD that formed it, to establish it; the LORD is his name;

**3** Call unto me, and I will answer thee, and show thee great and mighty things, which thou knowest not.

**4** For thus saith the LORD, the God of Israel, concerning the houses of this city, and concerning the houses of the kings of Judah, which are thrown down by the mounts, and by the sword;

**5** They come to fight with the Chaldeans, but it is to fill them with the dead bodies of men, whom I have slain in mine anger and in my fury, and for all whose wickedness I have hid my face from this city.

**6** Behold, I will bring it health and cure, and I will cure them, and will reveal unto them the abundance of peace and truth.

**7** And I will cause the captivity of Judah and the captivity of Israel to return, and will build them, as at the first.

**8** And I will cleanse them from all their iniquity, whereby they have sinned against me; and I will pardon all their iniquities, whereby they have sinned, and whereby they have transgressed against me.

**9** And it shall be to me a name of joy, a praise and an honour before all the nations of the earth, which shall hear all the good that I do unto them: and they shall fear and tremble for all the goodness and for all the prosperity that I procure unto it.

**10** Thus saith the LORD; Again there shall be heard in this place, which ye say shall be desolate without man and without beast, even in the cities of Judah, and in the streets of Jerusalem, that are desolate, without man, and without inhabitant, and without beast,

**NLT** **Jeremiah 33:2** "This is what the LORD says—the LORD who made the earth, who formed and established it, whose name is the LORD:

**3** Ask me and I will tell you remarkable secrets you do not know about things to come.

**4** For this is what the LORD, the God of Israel, says: You have torn down the houses of this city and even the king's palace to get materials to strengthen the walls against the siege ramps and swords of the enemy.

**5** You expect to fight the Babylonians, but the men of this city are already as good as dead, for I have determined to destroy them in my terrible anger. I have abandoned them because of all their wickedness.

**6** Nevertheless, the time will come when I will heal Jerusalem's wounds and give it prosperity and true peace.

**7** I will restore the fortunes of Judah and Israel and rebuild their towns.

**8** I will cleanse them of their sins against me and forgive all their sins of rebellion.

**9** Then this city will bring me joy, glory, and honor before all the nations of the earth! The people of the world will see all the good I do for my people, and they will tremble with awe at the peace and prosperity I provide for them.

**10** This is what the LORD says: You have said, 'This is a desolate land where people and animals have all disappeared.' Yet in the empty streets of Jerusalem and Judah's other towns, there will be heard once more

**11** the sounds of joy and laughter. The joyful voices of bridegrooms and brides will be heard again, along with the joyous songs of people bringing thanksgiving offerings to the LORD. They will sing, 'Give thanks to the LORD of Heaven's Armies, for the LORD is good. His faithful love endures forever!' For

11 The voice of joy, and the voice of gladness, the voice of the bridegroom, and the voice of the bride, the voice of them that shall say, Praise the LORD of hosts: for the LORD is good; for his mercy endureth for ever: and of them that shall bring the sacrifice of praise into the house of the LORD. For I will cause to return the captivity of the land, as at the first, saith the LORD.

I will restore the prosperity of this land to what it was in the past, says the LORD."

## The People, Places, and Times

**Chaldea.** Nebuchadnezzar's father, who was a Chaldean, seized Babylon around 626 B.C., and at some point in ancient history Chaldean and Babylonian became synonymous. More correct, however, is the term Neo-Babylonian, which marks the period Chaldeans ruled Babylon. Babylon was located in the lower regions of the Tigris and the Euphrates Rivers, which is present-day Iraq. The larger area to which Chaldea belonged is Mesopotamia. Aside from the aforementioned Iraq, parts of present-day Iran, Syria, and Turkey comprise Mesopotamia. The region is known for its desert terrain.

## Background

The word "LORD" in this text is translated from the Hebrew word Yahweh. Whenever the Bible uses the name of Yahweh, there's a prevailing promise for God's people. The name Yahweh is used for God whenever His personal relationship with His people is highlighted.

Throughout the Bible, God reminds the Children of Israel several times: "I am Yahweh your God, who brought you out of the land of Egypt, out of the house of bondage. You shall have no other gods before me" (Deuteronomy 5:6–7, World English Bible). This consistent declaration reminded the

Children of Israel, and us today, of an offer of partnership, provision, and a potent prescription for power!

Yahweh is the God of covenant. Just as seen in today's lesson, God will take care of His people. Yahweh made the Earth (Genesis 2:4), Yahweh spoke to Moses on Mt. Sinai (Exodus 19:1–6), Yahweh is my shepherd, I shall not want (Psalm 23:1). This is the Lord we know.

In Jeremiah, the Judeans are on the brink of captivity, but this would not be the first time the Israelites experienced oppression. They were enslaved in Egypt, and Yahweh provided them a passage to freedom. Yahweh is willing to make the same provisions for us today!

## At-A-Glance

1. A Point of Clarity (Jeremiah 33:2–6)
2. Laughter Shall Return (vv. 7–11)

## In Depth

### 1. A Point of Clarity (Jeremiah 33:2–6)

Chapter 33 serves as a reassurance that the covenant God had with Israel was still binding despite what was going on currently and about to happen. This text begins with a point of clarity. God is saying, if you want to know something, be sure you call on the right God. One of Judah's transgressions was that they were faithless and had gone astray by entertaining other deities. God wanted to ensure there was no confusing the author of the message. In essence, God's message is "I alone, the One who created the Earth, am capable of revealing things beyond your knowledge." God goes on to cite a specific example: attempting to fight the Chaldeans would be futile because God has already decided to give them victory as a form of punishment against Judah.

The text is clear that Judah's effort will be in vain and their defeat will be great. The entire nation will suffer destruction; every dwelling from the smallest cottage to the grandest palace of the king will be affected. The loss will extend beyond possessions and wealth; there will even be death. God will turn aside while the Chaldeans wreak havoc on them and the consequences of their wickedness unfold. God reiterates the terms of their punishment prior to confirming the promise.

### 2. Laughter Shall Return (vv. 7–11)

God's actions are similar to a parent. If a child does something wrong, the parent reprimands the child. The purpose of the reprimand is to correct because the parent realizes the behavior is detrimental to the child's well-being. God makes it clear that once Judah has been corrected, He will come and restore the relationship. Once a child has been disciplined, the parent then reassures the child of the love at the foundation of the discipline. The reassurance in this case is restoration. The restoration will come in many forms: land revitalization, healing, peace, truth, liberation, forgiveness, and unity again with God. God will bring Judah back not only from physical but emotional discipline, and things of the heart such as joy, singing, and laughter shall return.

God's message seems like an improbable possibility to the Children of Israel. The nation is on the brink of captivity, and as such, the inhabitants can't imagine the sun shining again after the storm. God asserts that a new day will dawn and all will be well. He avows that not only will they be freed from captivity and reclaim what is rightfully theirs, but they will experience abundant peace. God seeks and is able to restore His children to their rightful place even when we fall short. God's love is just and all encompassing. It is inclusive of everything we need to take our rightful place in God's kingdom.

### Search the Scriptures

1. What did God say happened because of Judah's wickedness (Jeremiah 33:5)?

2. "The joyful voices of _____ and _____ will be heard again, along with the joyous songs of people bringing thanksgiving offerings to the LORD" (v. 11, NLT).

### Discuss the Meaning

We often read biblical accounts or hear the testimony after the test and wonder why people took God's Word for granted. If we are honest, we too are guilty of having doubts. In light of today's lesson, do you need to make any adjustments?

### Lesson in Our Society

Although incarceration rates are high, more and more we are becoming a society that does not fear punishment. God's punishment, healing, and forgiveness are all a part of His love for us. No one should expect to commit a crime and not have to suffer the repercussions. On a more personal level, when we take our relationships for granted,

47

mistreat someone, or don't own up to our responsibilities, there is a consequence.

## Make It Happen

Think about an instance when you did something wrong. What were the ways in which God extended hope, healing, and forgiveness to you afterward? Use these thoughts to assist you in completing the last section of the Aim for Change.

## Follow the Spirit

What God wants me to do:

_____

_____

_____

_____

## Remember Your Thoughts

Special insights I have learned:

_____

_____

_____

_____

## More Light on the Text

Jeremiah 33:2–11

**2 Thus saith the LORD the maker thereof, the LORD that formed it, to establish it; the LORD is his name; 3 Call unto me, and I will answer thee, and show thee great and mighty things, which thou knowest not.**

A second time God visits Jeremiah while he is imprisoned and speaks to him. God's purpose in speaking to the nations of Israel and Judah through the prophet is to assure them that He is able to accomplish what He desires, so He affirms for the nations exactly who is speaking to them. The "LORD" (Heb. *Yehovah*, **yeh-ho-VAH**, the self-existing One) God who is addressing this prophecy through Jeremiah is the same one who was the "maker" (Heb. *'asah*, **ah-SAH**, to produce, fashion or make to come to pass) of the earth. He formed it so that He could establish it. The message from God is simple: if He was able to make, "form" (Heb. *yatsar*, **yah-TSAR**, to shape clay or metal), and "establish" (Heb. *kun*, **KOON**, to make secure) the earth and all that is in it, He is able to accomplish any request Israel and Judah might make to Him. They need only to "call" (Heb. *kara'*, **kah-RAH**, to cry out for help) upon Him and He has promised to "answer" (Heb. *'anah*, **ah-NAH**) them. God even offers to extend what they might pray for by showing (Heb. *nagad*, **nah-GOD**, to announce) them great and mighty things of which they "knowest" not (Heb. *yada'*, **yah-DAH**, to understand).

**4 For thus saith the LORD, the God of Israel, concerning the houses of this city, and concerning the houses of the kings of Judah, which are thrown down by the mounts, and by the sword.**

The Lord affirms for Israel that He is their God and has been watching their plight. He wants them to know that He is aware that the attack by the Babylonians has destroyed their homes and left the palace in a heap of rubble. The Chaldean army was famous for its use of the battering ram, and other instruments of war had been used to siege the city of Jerusalem for over a year. In order to patch the holes in the wall that fortified the city, the inhabitants of Jerusalem were using the rubble from the homes and royal dwellings that had been destroyed in the fighting. It is probable that the forces of Nebuchadnezzar directed their most violent assaults at the dwellings of the nobility and leadership in an effort to dishearten the inhabitants of the city. Some commentators suggest that "mounts" (Heb. *solelah*, **so-leh-LAH**, siege ramps) refers to the ramparts that the soldiers within the city built in order to fight the Babylonians.

**5 They come to fight with the Chaldeans, but it is to fill them with the dead bodies of men, whom I have slain in mine anger and in my fury, and for all whose wickedness I have hid my face from this city.**

The normal practice of taking the dead bodies of the slain and placing them on a heap outside of the city gate was not possible during the siege by the Babylonians. The bodies could not be left in the homes or on the street, so they were piled up and left by the walls where the battle was raging. Seeing all the dead and rotting bodies would have been visible evidence to the Israelites within the city of God's great displeasure with them. Jeremiah is telling the people that God in his "anger" (Heb. *'af*, **AHF**, meaning to be enraged) also has permitted the slaying of His chosen people because of their sin. His righteousness has caused Him to hide his face from the city, or turn His back on it and its plight (cf. Micah 3:4).

**6 Behold, I will bring it health and cure, and I will cure them, and will reveal unto them the abundance of peace and truth.**

The Lord will initially heal Judah with the cure of bringing the exiles back from Babylon and rebuilding the city and temple. Through Jeremiah, God continues to speak to future generations of the Children of Israel (also to us who are heirs to the promises), stating that He will bring both health and the cure for the disease of sin that has caused Him to turn His back on His chosen people. Christ is the source of this cure (cf. John 1:17) that He

accomplished by offering Himself up on the Cross. In accepting Christ as their Messiah, God is promising that He will "reveal" (Heb. *galah*, **gah-LAH**, to uncover) to them just how deep and full His "peace" (Heb. *shalom*, **shah-LOME**, welfare, health, prosperity) and "truth" (Heb. *'emet*, **EH-met**, faithfulness, reliableness) are.

**7 And I will cause the captivity of Judah and the captivity of Israel to return, and will build them, as at the first.**

What joy it must have been for Jeremiah to write this promise of God to bring the captives of the nations of Israel and Judah back to their Promised Land and to restore them to a status and situation that equaled their state before their bondage to the Babylonians. And what faith it must have prompted in the prophet to believe God's promise while he himself was being held prisoner in Zedekiah's courtyard.

**8 And I will cleanse them from all their iniquity, whereby they have sinned against me; and I will pardon all their iniquities, whereby they have sinned, and whereby they have transgressed against me.**

God's promise to His chosen people and to His church is that though they at present are reprehensible to Him because of sin, He will cleanse them from that sin. But not that sin only; He will cleanse them from all their "iniquities" (Heb. *'avon*, **aw-VONE**, violations or offenses). Further, God will "pardon" (Heb. *salakh*, **sah-LAKH**, to release or forgive) all of the wrong and evil done against His holy person. Only then would His people be fit to reoccupy the land that had been promised.

**9 And it shall be to me a name of joy, a praise and an honour before all the nations of the earth, which shall hear all the good**

that I do unto them: and they shall fear and tremble for all the goodness and for all the prosperity that I procure unto it.

The suffering that the Israelite nations would undergo and all the pain and misery of God's chosen people would cause the other nations of the earth to take note. Then, once the Children of Israel had repented, been forgiven, and been restored to their own land and the land repopulated, their homes rebuilt, and their worship of God renewed, all the nations would hear of the good that God had done for His chosen people. In response, those nations would "fear" (Heb. *pakhad*, **pah-KHAD**, to be in dread) and "tremble" (Heb. *ragaz*, **rah-GAZ**, to shake with fear) before the God of the Israelites, and He would receive honor from this. Additionally, the Jews thus being restored and noting the reactions of the other nations would glorify God by being obedient to His will. The "prosperity" Jeremiah mentions in this verse is the same word in the original text as "peace" in verse 6. It is the fullness of God's goodness that would cause them to tremble and fear. Experiencing God's goodness and the resulting "prosperity" in this fashion, His chosen people would fear to offend Him and forfeit His favor once more. God would also glorify Himself by taking a people that had been reprehensible to Him and making their name a joy, praise, and honor before all the other nations of the earth.

**10 Thus saith the LORD; Again there shall be heard in this place, which ye say shall be desolate without man and without beast, even in the cities of Judah, and in the streets of Jerusalem, that are desolate, without man, and without inhabitant, and without beast, 11 The voice of joy, and the voice of gladness, the voice of the bridegroom, and the voice of the bride, the voice of them that shall say, Praise the LORD of hosts: for the LORD is good; for his mercy endureth for ever: and of them that shall bring the sacrifice of praise into the house of the LORD. For I will cause to return the captivity of the land, as at the first, saith the LORD.**

As the Babylonians besieged Jerusalem and the surrounding nations of Judah and Israel and were about to completely overrun its fortifications, all one could see was "desolate" ruins. Jeremiah had prophesied that the people of the land would be carried off as captives of war and that the land would appear to be without a single "inhabitant" (Heb. *yashav*, **yah-SHAV**, people who live in a certain area). No men roaming about the cities, streets deserted and empty, and no animals to be seen. Such a scene could only evoke an overwhelming sense of sadness. But God here promises that voices of sadness will one day be turned to voices of joy and gladness. God promises that the voice of the bridegroom and the voice of the bride will ring out in praises to the Lord of hosts. In His "mercy" (Heb. *khesed*, **KHEH-sed**, favor, faithfulness, or loyal love), God will return the inhabitants of the land and restore them to a condition that will equal their state when they first occupied the Promised Land. Then their weeping will be turned to joy, and they will bring their "sacrifice of praise" to the house of the Lord. This wondrous promise is intended to give hope and encouragement to the Children of Israel and, by extension, to all who will share in God's favor because of them.

Sources:

Achtemeier, Paul J., Roger S. Boraas, Michael Fishburne, et al. eds. *Harper Collins Bible Dictionary*. New York: HarperCollins Publishers, 1996. 154, 550.

Brueggmann, Walter. *To Build, To Plant: Jeremiah 26–52*. Grand Rapids, MI: Wm. B. Eerdsmans Publishing Company, 1991.

Dunn, James D. G. and John W. Rogerson. *Commentary on the Bible*. Grand Rapids, MI: Wm. B. Eerdmans Publishing Company, 2003.

English, E. Schuyler and Marian Bishop Bower, eds. *The Holy Bible: Pilgrim Edition*. New York: Oxford University Press, 1952.

Howley, G.C.D., F.F. Bruce, and H. L. Ellison. *The New Layman's Bible Commentary*. Grand Rapids, MI: Zondervan, 1979.

Keener, Craig S. *The IVP Bible Background Commentary: New Testament*. Downers Grove, IL: InterVarsity Press, 1993.

Strong, James. *Strong's Exhaustive Concordance*. Grand Rapids, MI: Zondervan, 2001.

## Say It Correctly

Procure. **PRO**-kyur.
Desolate. de-**SO**-let.

## Daily Bible Readings

**MONDAY**
In Returning You Shall Be Saved
(Isaiah 30:9–17)

**TUESDAY**
Where Are Your Gods?
(Jeremiah 2:26–32)

**WEDNESDAY**
I Will Bring You to Zion
(Jeremiah 3:11–15)

**THURSDAY**
I Will Heal Your Faithlessness
(Jeremiah 3:19–23)

**FRIDAY**
The Hope of Israel
(Jeremiah 17:12–17)

**SATURDAY**
The Lord Acts with Steadfast Love
(Jeremiah 9:17–24)

**SUNDAY**
Voices of Mirth and Gladness
(Jeremiah 33:2–11)

## Notes

_____

_____

_____

_____

# Teaching Tips

## Words You Should Know

**A. Vision** (Habakkuk 2:3) *khazon* (Heb.)—Oracle, prophecy, divine communication.

**B. Faith** (v. 4) *'emunah* (Heb.)—Firmness, fidelity, steadfastness, steadiness.

## Teacher Preparation

**Unifying Principle—The Rewards of Patience.** Some people experience so many difficulties in life that they lose all hope for the future. Where can they turn for direction when things get really bad? Habakkuk affirms that—no matter what calamities might come their way—they will trust God, rejoice in His presence in their lives, and praise Him for strength to carry on.

**A.** Pray for your students and that God will bring clarity to this lesson.

**B.** Study and meditate on the entire text.

**C.** Prepare to present examples of the benefits of being patient.

**D.** Complete the companion lesson in the *Precepts for Living Personal Study Guide®*.

## O—Open the Lesson

**A.** Open with prayer, including the Aim for Change.

**B.** Introduce today's subject, Aim for Change, and Keep in Mind verses. Discuss.

**C.** Share your presentation.

**D.** Ask, "Are there rewards for being patient?"

**E.** Share testimonies.

**F.** Have a volunteer summarize the In Focus story. Discuss.

## P—Present the Scriptures

**A.** Have volunteers read the Focal Verses.

**B.** Use The People, Places, and Times; Background; Search the Scriptures; At-A-Glance outline; In Depth; and More Light on the Text to clarify the verses.

## E—Explore the Meaning

**A.** To interact with the Discuss the Meaning, Lesson in Our Society, and Make It Happen sections, divide the class into groups. Assign one or two sections to each group depending on the class size.

**B.** Have them select a representative to report their responses to the rest of the class.

## N—Next Steps for Application

**A.** Summarize the lesson.

**B.** Close with prayer and praise God for giving us relationships.

## Worship Guide

For the Superintendent or Teacher
Theme: Rejoice Anyway
Song: "Hallelujah Anyhow!"
Devotional Reading: Psalm 56:8–13

# Rejoice Anyway

**Bible Background • JOB 1; PSALM 56; HABAKKUK 1–3**
**Printed Text • HABAKKUK 2:1–5, 3:17–19**
**Devotional Reading • PSALM 56:8–13**

## Aim for Change

By the end of the lesson, we will: HEAR God's message of patience for the people and assurance that God will act with justice; EXPERIENCE the feeling of joy when we have patiently awaited God's promises; and PRACTICE responding to difficulties by trusting in God's presence and by praising God for strength to endure.

 In Focus

He could hear the clock ticking on the wall. Michael waited in silence for the phone to ring. His foot kept tapping and he knew it was his nerves. When he stopped tapping his foot, he began to tap the pen on the table. *How come they haven't called already?* he thought to himself. For Michael, any longer was too much longer. He had just been in an interview after months of getting no responses from any companies he applied to. The bills were piling up, and he began to wake up at night wondering how he was going to care for his wife and kids. He wondered if God even cared about his family. There was nothing left for Michael to do. He felt like he could not go on any longer without an answer from God. Michael thought for a moment about their situation. He knew that God was in control of it all. He also knew that God deserved to be praised before he even got a job. So Michael began to shout "Hallelujah!" and "Thank You, Jesus" as an act of faith in God's care. While he was shouting and praising God, the phone rang.

*While waiting for God, hold on to every promise from His Word. Praise God for what He has done. Praise God for what He is doing. Praise God for what He will do.*

## Keep in Mind

"Although the fig tree shall not blossom, neither shall fruit be in the vines; the labour of the olive shall fail, and the fields shall yield no meat; the flock shall be cut off from the fold, and there shall be no herd in the stalls: Yet I will rejoice in the LORD, I will joy in the God of my salvation" (Habakkuk 3:17–18).

"Although the fig tree shall not blossom, neither shall fruit be in the vines; the labour of the olive shall fail, and the fields shall yield no meat; the flock shall be cut off from the fold, and there shall be no herd in the stalls: Yet I will rejoice in the LORD, I will joy in the God of my salvation" (Habakkuk 3:17–18).

## Focal Verses

**KJV** **Habakkuk 2:1** I will stand upon my watch, and set me upon the tower, and will watch to see what he will say unto me, and what I shall answer when I am reproved.

**2** And the LORD answered me, and said, Write the vision, and make it plain upon tables, that he may run that readeth it.

**3** For the vision is yet for an appointed time, but at the end it shall speak, and not lie: though it tarry, wait for it; because it will surely come, it will not tarry.

**4** Behold, his soul which is lifted up is not upright in him: but the just shall live by his faith.

**5** Yea also, because he transgresseth by wine, he is a proud man, neither keepeth at home, who enlargeth his desire as hell, and is as death, and cannot be satisfied, but gathereth unto him all nations, and heapeth unto him all people.

**3:17** Although the fig tree shall not blossom, neither shall fruit be in the vines; the labour of the olive shall fail, and the fields shall yield no meat; the flock shall be cut off from the fold, and there shall be no herd in the stalls:

**18** Yet I will rejoice in the LORD, I will joy in the God of my salvation.

**19** The LORD God is my strength, and he will make my feet like hinds' feet, and he will make me to walk upon mine high places. To the chief singer on my stringed instruments.

**NLT** **Habakkuk 2:1** I will climb up to my watchtower and stand at my guardpost. There I will wait to see what the LORD says and how he will answer my complaint.

**2** Then the LORD said to me, "Write my answer plainly on tablets, so that a runner can carry the correct message to others.

**3** This vision is for a future time. It describes the end, and it will be fulfilled. If it seems slow in coming, wait patiently, for it will surely take place. It will not be delayed.

**4** Look at the proud! They trust in themselves, and their lives are crooked. But the righteous will live by their faithfulness to God.

**5** Wealth is treacherous, and the arrogant are never at rest. They open their mouths as wide as the grave, and like death, they are never satisfied. In their greed they have gathered up many nations and swallowed many peoples."

**3:17** Even though the fig trees have no blossoms, and there are no grapes on the vines; even though the olive crop fails, and the fields lie empty and barren; even though the flocks die in the fields, and the cattle barns are empty,

**18** yet I will rejoice in the LORD! I will be joyful in the God of my salvation!

**19** The Sovereign LORD is my strength! He makes me as surefooted as a deer, able to tread upon the heights. (For the choir director: This prayer is to be accompanied by stringed instruments.)

## The People, Places, and Times

**Habakkuk.** A prophet of the late seventh century. His name in Hebrew means "embrace" or "ardent embrace." As the chosen human instrument for God, he spoke the Word of God to the people. Not much is known about Habakkuk the person other than he may have been a Levite who was familiar with the temple singers. This is due to the musical notation that is found at the conclusion of the book that bears his name.

**Prophet.** One called to receive and declare a word from God after being prompted by the Holy Spirit. Prophets were usually called to speak a word concerning the present and the future. Their words could be addressed to nations as well as individuals. God used prophets to speak of injustice and wickedness in the nation of Israel. This was accomplished not only through verbal means; sometimes prophets were called to demonstrate their message through physical acts. Habakkuk was a prophet. Other known prophets are Moses, Samuel, Elijah, and Elisha.

## Background

As with many righteous religious leaders, Habakkuk faced a lot of wickedness and injustice during his time. This was a time when, after a period of reform under King Josiah, many in Israel had fallen back into godlessness and idolatry. Instead of speaking out against national sin and addressing the perpetrators of wickedness, Habakkuk addressed himself to God. He could not stand to see the wicked get away with their crimes and sinful actions. He complained to God and asked, "How long, O LORD...?" (from 1:2). Habakkuk's personal plea was a radical departure from the usual activity of the prophets who pronounced judgement and encouraged the people to repent of their ways. This time he questioned the justice of God.

God answered by explaining His plans to judge the wicked and to assure Habakkuk to not worry. God reminded Habakkuk He is indeed righteous and will judge the wicked. The form in which this judgment would come left Habakkuk amazed and astounded: It would be through the Chaldeans. The Lord would assign a wicked nation to discipline His people. This was something that Habakkuk could not comprehend. Why would the Lord allow a nation who was more wicked than Judah to conquer them? Why would He send a pagan nation to conquer His chosen people? The Lord addressed this question and gave Habakkuk reason to rejoice and trust in Him.

## At-A-Glance

1. Habakkuk Trusts God for an Answer (Habakkuk 2:1–3)
2. Habakkuk Must Continue to Trust (vv. 4–5)
3. Habukkuk Trusts God Enough to Rejoice (vv. 3:17–19)

## In Depth

**1. Habakkuk Trusts God for an Answer (Habakkuk 2:1–3)**

Habakkuk has asked questions of God and now stands like a watchman waiting for an answer. This attitude and posture shows that Habakkuk had faith and trust in God. His questions were not questions based on doubt, but a rock-solid faith in God. He embraced the hard questions and is willing to receive the answer that God would give.

This is the second time Habakkuk receives a response from God: "Then the LORD said to me" (v. 2, NLT). God instructs Habakkuk to write down the vision as he receives it. The written vision gives Habakkuk credibility be-

56

fore speaking it to the people. The written vision also serves as a guarantee God will act and does act.

The Lord also assures Habakkuk of the vision's timing. The vision would come to pass in a future time. God says that the vision will be delayed, but it will come to pass. It will not be delayed indefinitely. It will be delayed but not denied! Habakkuk is given assurance that the vision will come to pass in God's timing. Then the Lord encourages him to wait for the vision to be fulfilled. The assurance that what God has spoken will come to fruition will enable Habakkuk to wait and endure the injustice of the present.

### 2. Habakkuk Must Continue to Trust (vv. 4–5)

In the vision, God assures Habakkuk to remain committed to God in the midst of the injustice and violence taking place around him. "Look at the proud! They trust in themselves, and their lives are crooked. But the righteous will live by their faithfulness to God" (v. 4, NLT). God gives Habakkuk the right way to respond to the wickedness around him: trust. Trust will separate the righteous from the wicked. Trust in the Lord distinguishes God's people from those who trust in themselves. God lets Habakkuk know that he is supposed to live by faith. Faith should permeate all aspects of his life. His whole way of being should be characterized by trusting in God, not himself.

The Lord then describes the character of the wicked. They drink excessively and are full of pride. They have an insatiable greed and attempt to bring everything under their ownership. This is also a picture of the Babylonian ruler who will come to conquer Judah. It is a picture of someone who is not in a relationship with God but is against God and His people. This is the type of person who

symbolizes the opposite of God's mandate to live by faith. It is the perfect example of someone who trusts in nothing but himself. These people are self-centered and only seek their own gratification. This is not the way the righteous live. The righteous are called to live by faith in a God who takes care of them and will remedy every injustice.

### 3. Habakkuk Trusts God Enough to Rejoice (vv. 3:17–19)

Habakkuk describes utter disaster for an agricultural way of life (v. 17). Nothing that is planted grows and the animals fail to reproduce. It is a sad picture that spoke to the mostly agricultural society in those times. The first hearers would have seen this as the worst thing that could happen to someone. It is a scene where there is no sign of life or growth. There is no provision that the land can give. It is barren. This is a picture of poverty and devastation.

After painting this scene, the next words are surprising. "Yet I will rejoice in the LORD, I will joy in the God of my salvation" (v. 18). Habakkuk says that in the midst of utter devastation and loss, he will rejoice. The key thing to realize is what he is rejoicing in. Habakkuk does not say he will rejoice in this situation, but that He will rejoice in the Lord. His joy will come from the God of his salvation. It is not the circumstances that give him a reason to rejoice; Habakkuk rejoices because the Lord is his strength and will support him and make him firm and stable as a deer on a high mountain.

### Search the Scriptures

1. What is the significance of Habakkuk standing on a tower to hear God answer (Habakkuk 2:1)?

2. What does it mean for the just to live by faith (v. 4)?

## Discuss the Meaning

Society's moral barometer is shifting to acceptance of immoral behavior as the norm; injustices for some and justice for others. Has the body of Christ lost its hope?

## Lesson in Our Society

There are two types of people in this world: those who trust in themselves and those who trust in God. When life comes crashing down, those who trust in themselves have no reason to rejoice. They cannot sustain joy in times of disappointment. Belief, hope, and trust in God are prerequisites for enduring the daily challenges of life. When disappointment and suffering appear, our trust in God is the primary factor that can sustain our joy. In this world full of crime, economic crisis, and terrorism, we can rejoice in knowing God, who is sovereign over all.

## Make It Happen

The problems and trials of life can bring us down. Sometimes our patience can wear thin and our joy can decrease. Think of one thing that you have been waiting God to act on. It could be a job opportunity or a loved one coming to know Jesus. It has to be something that hasn't happened yet. Praise and thank God as an act of faith that He will bring it to pass. Let God be your joy in the absence of the thing that you have been waiting for.

## Follow the Spirit

What God wants me to do:

_____

_____

_____

_____

## Remember Your Thoughts

Special insights I have learned:

_____

_____

_____

_____

## More Light on the Text

**Habakkuk 2:1–5; 3:17–19**

**1 I will stand upon my watch, and set me upon the tower, and will watch to see what he will say unto me, and what I shall answer when I am reproved.**

Do you ever look around and think the world is an unjust place? Do you ever wonder why God allows certain things to happen? If not, you are probably not being honest with yourself. God has placed the book of Habakkuk in the Bible for us to know that He is ready for our questions. First Habakkuk looks around and saw all sorts of wickedness among his own people. He sees them perpetrating violence and destruction on one another. He asks God to show him why He is allowing these things to go on. God's answer is even more shocking: He will punish His people, the Israelites, by allowing the Babylonians (Chaldeans, KJV) to conquer them. This amazes Habakkuk. It seems to him that the sins of Israel were light in comparison with the extreme violence and destruction of the Babylonians. We can see some parallels among some African American communities. Black-on-Black crime seems to be abundant, and yet, when the police force, etc. of the mainstream move in, we may see things are even worse for our people.

Habakkuk, whose name in Hebrew is *Khabakkuk* (**kha-bak-KOOK**) and means "to embrace," fully embraces his people and his faith in Yahweh, the God of Israel, and yet he has questions. He figuratively stands at the "towers," a watchtower or siege enclosure (*matsor*, **MAH-tsor**), and waits to see what God will do in answer to his doubts. "When I am reproved" may not be the best translation. The Hebrew for "reproved" is *tokhekhat* (**toe-kheh-KHAHT**) and does mean to be corrected, but whether this refers to a rebuke of Habakkuk or by him is not clear. But it is certain that Habakkuk is patiently waiting for God's answer to his complaint.

**2 And the LORD answered me, and said, Write the vision, and make it plain upon tables, that he may run that readeth it.**

Israel lay at the crossroads for many cultures; thus they learned to write on papyrus scrolls, inscribe on soft clay tablets, and chisel on stone tablets. The picture here is probably writing on a large, wooden tablet with large, clear letters that could be easily read, so legible that even a hurried passersby could read the message and pass it on. Picture the billboard on an interstate expressway, and you will get the idea. Not only is the message clear, but the message is meant to be shared.

**3 For the vision is yet for an appointed time, but at the end it shall speak, and not lie: though it tarry, wait for it; because it will surely come, it will not tarry. 4 Behold, his soul which is lifted up is not upright in him: but the just shall live by his faith.**

Habakkuk lives between the times of the promise and the fulfillment. Although God is using the Babylonians to punish His own people, in the end the Babylonians will be judged for their excessive cruelty to the Israelites. Habakkuk wants God to bring judgment on the Babylonians right away, but he has to wait. In verse 3 God assures Habakkuk that the prophecy will come to pass. He says it will "tarry" (Heb. *mahah*, **mah-HAH**)

or linger but it will not "tarry" (Heb. *'achar*, **ah-KHAR**) or remain behind. This word is often used in conjunction with the word for appointed time and has the connotation of being late. Habakkuk was instructed to wait because the vision would come to pass at the appointed time and not be late. This is not unlike our own lives, as we learn to wait patiently for the Lord to act. But what should Habakkuk do in the meantime? He is to continue living a life of faith.

The Hebrew word used for faith in verse 4 is *'emunah* (**eh-moo-NAH**). The synonym for this is literally firmness and can be translated as faith, faithfulness, or moral fidelity. This reminds us that very few words can be translated exactly into another language. The Hebrew word for faith here encompasses both faith and faithfulness.

"The just shall live by faith" was the standard upon which the Protestant Reformation was started—the phrase that helped Martin Luther see that buying indulgences, performing good deeds, or living a moral life could not give us salvation. Salvation only comes by grace through faith in Jesus Christ. This is how the New Testament writers interpreted this verse. Paul quotes this phrase in Romans 1:17 and in Galatians 3:11. Hebrews 10:37–38 quotes verses 3–4 in this way: "For yet a little while, and he that shall come will come, and will not tarry. Now the just shall live by faith: but if any man draw back, my soul shall have no pleasure in him." The New Testament writers clearly saw this as referring to the second coming of our Savior. Habakkuk 2:3 refers to "it," but the writer of Hebrews makes clear that "it" is not a thing but a "He"—Jesus Christ, the promised Messiah. Biblical prophecy is often that way; there is a partial fulfillment soon after the prophecy—the Babylonians were already poised to conquer Israel, but they would be totally out of the picture in seventy years, when the people of Judah had the opportunity of returning to their land. Then there is a grander fulfillment of biblical prophecy, often referring to the first or second coming of Jesus. The life of the believer or just (whether in the Old Testament or the New) is to be a life of faith, putting our full trust in our Lord.

The fourth verse begins with the phrase "Behold, his soul which is lifted up is not upright in him." This refers to the Babylonian king or the Babylonian people who would soon conquer Judah. In so many words, this description calls them arrogant, which contrasts with Habakkuk and God's chosen people who are to humbly trust and wait for God.

**5 Yea also, because he transgresseth by wine, he is a proud man, neither keepeth at home, who enlargeth his desire as hell, and is as death, and cannot be satisfied, but gathereth unto him all nations, and heapeth unto him all people.**

The Babylonians and other imperial powers were well-known for their over-indulgence in alcoholic beverages and drunkenness. For example, Babylonia was overthrown while their leaders were in the midst of a drunken feast (Daniel 5). The Bible warns in several places of the dangers of drinking, especially drinking to excess (Proverbs 23:31–32). Secondly, the Babylonians are called "proud" (Heb. *yahir*, **yah-HERE**), which also means arrogant or haughty, just as the accusation in verse 4. And thirdly, the Babylonians are portrayed as rapacious, seeking to devour all the surrounding nations, just as death and hell seek to swallow everyone.

**3:17 Although the fig tree shall not blossom, neither shall fruit be in the vines; the labour of the olive shall fail, and the fields shall yield no meat; the flock shall be cut off from the fold, and there shall be no herd in** the stalls: **18 Yet I will rejoice in the LORD, I will joy in the God of my salvation.**

Habakkuk is not an unrealistic optimist. He knows that God is going to bring awful judgment upon His people through the Babylonians. This ruthless army will not only take all the food that God's people are growing, but they will destroy the trees and vines so that for years to come, no olives, grapes, or figs will grow. In addition they will take all the herds—the sheep, the goats, and other animals. But in the midst of all this, Habakkuk gives a ringing testimony that he will trust in the Lord, no matter what the situation. So in spite of everything, Habakkuk will rejoice.

The third and last chapter of Habakkuk is a prayer in the form of a psalm. After all the questions, Habakkuk sings of the power and justice of God that bring him to the triumph of faith. We tend to think that the beauty of psalms lies in their ability to express the feelings that are in our own hearts, and they certainly do that. But our singing can be a spiritual discipline in which the very character and feelings of God's people become impressed within us. As we take within ourselves the words of Habakkuk, the inspired words of God are being planted in our hearts. Imagine composing a tune to go with verses 17 and 18—what increasing faith will grow in our hearts, even in the midst of difficult circumstances!

**19 The LORD God is my strength, and he will make my feet like hinds' feet, and he will make me to walk upon mine high places. To the chief singer on my stringed instruments.**

The reason for Habakkuk's confidence in the midst of the expectations of great horrors for the Israelites is his trust in the Lord God. The Hebrew for "LORD" is Yahweh, which is the personal name by which God identifies Himself to His chosen people. Vowels were not written in ancient Hebrew and so the translators of the KJV Bible surmised that the pronunciation for "LORD" was Jehovah. Today we say **YAH-way**, but it is impossible to know how it was pronunounced in ancient Israel. This epithet came to be pronounced 'Adonai (**ah-doe-NIGH**), meaning "my Lord" and is a common title for God.

The hind can be a variety of animals that are swift and sure-footed, such as deer or gazelles. These animals can confidently climb up the mountains with their nimble feet and strong legs. Habakkuk is imagining himself climbing upon spiritual mountaintops because God is giving him the strength and confidence so that even when troubles come he can trust in the Lord.

Evidently this chapter was written for the levitical choir, accompanied by stringed instruments.

Habakkuk himself may have been a Levite, one of the official temple workers, but not descended directly from the Aaronic priestly line. Two of the stringed instruments mentioned in the Old Testament are the lyre and the harp. The lyre was shaped like a rectangle or a trapezoid and had a varied number of strings. It was used to accompany singing, either sacred or secular. The harp had its origins in Egypt and was used primarily in temple music. So you can imagine whatever your favorite string instruments—guitar, violin, or harp—being used to accompany these beautiful verses.

Sources:
Brand, Chad, Charles Draper, and Archie England, eds. *Holman Illustrated Bible Dictionary*. Nashville, TN: Holman Bible Publishers, 2003.
Guthrie, Steven R. "Love the Lord with All Your Voice." *Christianity Today*. June 2013.
Keck, Leander, gen. ed. *The New Interpreter's Bible*. Vol. 3. Nashville, TN: Abingdon Press, 1999.
Meyers, Allen C., ed. *The Eerdmans Bible Dictionary*. Grand Rapids, MI: Wm. B. Eerdmans Publishing Company, 1996.
Morgan, G. Campbell. *The Minor Prophets: The Men and Their Messages*. Old Tappan, NJ: Fleming H. Revell, 1960.
Pfeifer, Charles F. and Everett F. Harrison, eds. *The Wycliffe Bible Commentary*. Chicago, IL: Moody Press, 1962.
Rachmacher, Earl D., Th.D., gen. ed. *The Nelson Study Bible New King James Version*. Nashville, TN: Thomas Nelson Publishers, 1997.
Smith, Ralph L. *Micah–Malachi. Word Biblical Commentary*. Vol. 32. Dallas, TX: Word Books Publisher, 1984.
*Today's Parallel Bible*. Grand Rapids, MI: Zondervan, 2000.
Walvoord, John F. and Roy B. Zuck, eds. *The Bible Knowledge Commentary: Old Testament*. Wheaton, IL: Victor Books, 1985.

## Say It Correctly

Babylonian. bab-y-**LO**-ni-an.
Chaldean. kal-**DE**-an.
Habakkuk. ha-**BA**-kuk.

## Daily Bible Readings

**MONDAY**
How Long Shall I Cry Out?
(Habakkuk 1:1–5)

**TUESDAY**
Why Are You Silent?
(Habakkuk 1:12–17)

**WEDNESDAY**
The Lord Has Turned Against Me
(Ruth 1:12–21)

**THURSDAY**
Blessed Be the Name
(Job 1:13–21)

**FRIDAY**
Be Gracious to Me, O God
(Psalm 56:1–7)

**SATURDAY**
In God I Trust
(Psalm 56:8–13)

**SUNDAY**
Yet I Will Rejoice
(Habakkuk 2:1–5, 3:17–19)

# Teaching Tips

## Words You Should Know

**A. Reproach** (Job 19:3, 5) *kherpah* (Heb.)—To insult, shame, humiliate, be ashamed.

**B. Latter Day** (v. 25) *'akharon* (Heb.)—Following, subsequent, last of time.

## Teacher Preparation

**Unifying Principle—Confident of Redemption.** Even when people admit their shortcomings, they are often ostracized by others and receive no justice. Where can they get strength and reassurance? Job proclaims that no matter what happens God, the Redeemer, lives and constantly sends forth steadfast love to all people.

**A.** Pray for your students and that God will bring clarity to this lesson.

**B.** Study and meditate on the entire text.

**C.** Prepare to present current examples of redemption.

**D.** Complete the companion lesson in the *Precepts for Living Personal Study Guide®*.

## O—Open the Lesson

**A.** Open with prayer, including the Aim for Change.

**B.** Introduce today's subject, Aim for Change, and Keep in Mind verse. Discuss.

**C.** Share your presentation.

**D.** Ask, "Do you feel redeemed by your circle of family and friends?"

**E.** Share testimonies.

**F.** Have a volunteer summarize the In Focus story. Discuss.

## P—Present the Scriptures

**A.** Have volunteers read the Focal Verses.

**B.** Use The People, Places, and Times; Background; Search the Scriptures; At-A-Glance outline; In Depth; and More Light on the Text to clarify the verses.

## E—Explore the Meaning

**A.** To interact with the Discuss the Meaning, Lesson in Our Society, and Make It Happen sections, divide the class into groups. Assign one or two sections to each group.

**B.** Have them select a representative to report their responses to the rest of the class.

## N—Next Steps for Application

**A.** Summarize the lesson.

**B.** Close with prayer and praise God for redeeming us.

## Worship Guide

For the Superintendent or Teacher
Theme: Even So, My Redeemer Lives
Song: "My Redeemer Lives"
Devotional Reading: 1 Chronicles
16:28–34

# Even So, My Redeemer Lives

**Bible Background • JOB 19; PSALM 57**
**Printed Text • JOB 19:1–7, 23–29**
**Devotional Reading • 1 CHRONICLES 16:28–34**

## Aim for Change

By the end of the lesson, we will: UNDERSTAND that Job had unwavering belief in God's redemption even as he was made to suffer; AFFIRM that, though we suffer much, God loves us and offers us redemption; and ACKNOWLEDGE ways we are loved and blessed during times of trouble.

## In Focus

Angela had been battling cancer for over six months. After so many sessions of chemotherapy, she was a shell of her former self. Her husband, Tim, could barely hold himself together as he watched his wife suffer. He often looked at her and wondered how she continued to be optimistic and keep her faith in God. She still prayed and thanked God every day. Since she was diagnosed with cancer, they had not missed one Sunday morning church service. Tim endured it although the hope and optimism that he experienced from Angela and the people at church grated on him. *How could God do this to my wife?* he asked himself.

One day while driving home, Angela began quietly humming a praise and worship song they had heard in church. Tim couldn't take it anymore. Frustrated, he asked her, "How can you sing a song like that in a time like this?" Angela was shocked by his question but then calmly collected herself. "Songs like that were made for times like this," she responded. "I don't know if the Lord will take away this cancer, but I know for certain that I will see Him. That gives me hope."

*Even in suffering, God gives us hope and the ability to look toward His redemption.*

## Keep in Mind

"For I know that my redeemer liveth, and that he shall stand at the latter day upon the earth" (Job 19:25).

"For I know that my redeemer liveth, and that he shall stand at the latter day upon the earth" (Job 19:25).

# Focal Verses

**KJV** Job 19:1 Then Job answered and said,

2 How long will ye vex my soul, and break me in pieces with words?

3 These ten times have ye reproached me: ye are not ashamed that ye make yourselves strange to me.

4 And be it indeed that I have erred, mine error remaineth with myself.

5 If indeed ye will magnify yourselves against me, and plead against me my reproach:

6 Know now that God hath overthrown me, and hath compassed me with his net.

7 Behold, I cry out of wrong, but I am not heard: I cry aloud, but there is no judgment.

23 Oh that my words were now written! oh that they were printed in a book!

24 That they were graven with an iron pen and lead in the rock for ever!

25 For I know that my redeemer liveth, and that he shall stand at the latter day upon the earth:

26 And though after my skin worms destroy this body, yet in my flesh shall I see God:

27 Whom I shall see for myself, and mine eyes shall behold, and not another; though my reins be consumed within me.

28 But ye should say, Why persecute we him, seeing the root of the matter is found in me?

29 Be ye afraid of the sword: for wrath bringeth the punishments of the sword, that ye may know there is a judgment.

**NLT** Job 19:1 Then Job spoke again:

2 "How long will you torture me? How long will you try to crush me with your words?

3 You have already insulted me ten times. You should be ashamed of treating me so badly.

4 Even if I have sinned, that is my concern, not yours.

5 You think you're better than I am, using my humiliation as evidence of my sin.

6 But it is God who has wronged me, capturing me in his net.

7 I cry out, 'Help!' but no one answers me. I protest, but there is no justice.

23 "Oh, that my words could be recorded. Oh, that they could be inscribed on a monument,

24 carved with an iron chisel and filled with lead, engraved forever in the rock.

25 But as for me, I know that my Redeemer lives, and he will stand upon the earth at last.

26 And after my body has decayed, yet in my body I will see God!

27 I will see him for myself. Yes, I will see him with my own eyes. I am overwhelmed at the thought!

28 How dare you go on persecuting me, saying, 'It's his own fault'?

29 You should fear punishment yourselves, for your attitude deserves punishment. Then you will know that there is indeed a judgment."

## The People, Places, and Times

**Job.** Job is a man from the land of Uz (ancient Edom). Although not an Israelite, we do know that Job has a relationship with God. He is wealthy and is blessed with many children. Job experienced great prosperity until he is tested by God and loses everything. In the midst of his suffering and doubt, Job remains faithful to God.

**Redeemer.** In the ancient Near East, the redeemer or kinsman-redeemer was a person's nearest living blood relation. This person was called upon to continue the family line, in case there was no male descendant left, through marrying the widow of the next of kin. This person was also called upon to redeem the inheritance of those who found themselves impoverished and also those who had sold themselves into slavery. Jesus is often spoken of as humanity's kinsman-redeemer as He is near us in His humanity and has redeemed us from our slavery to sin.

### Background

Job had experienced the destruction of his wealth, his children, and his health. His wife had told him to curse God but he refuses. Job accepted that everything he has experienced has come from the hand of God. Soon his friends came to his side and sat with him. As they sat, they began to try to explain Job's situation. In trying to explain his current calamities, they began to blame Job and say that he is responsible for everything that has happened to him. The rest of the book (chapters 3–37) is a back and forth between Job and his friends which culminates in the final verdict given by God in chapters 38–42. Job is restored and given double what he had before.

In chapter 19, Job was responding to the argument from Bildad. Bildad argued that the trials Job experiences were punishments set aside for those who were wicked. The implication was that Job was wicked. Job then vented his frustration at the accusations being placed on him. He also stated his innocence in their sight and how it was God who was responsible for the trials that he was experiencing. In spite of it all, Job expected God to change his situation and vindicate

Him. He expressed his hope in God as his Redeemer and the opportunity to be in His presence.

## At-A-Glance

1. Job Speaks to His Friends' Verbal Attack (Job 19:1–7)
2. Job's Response to His Situation (vv. 23–29)

### In Depth

**1. Job Speaks to His Friends' Verbal Attack (Job 19:1–7)**

Job speaks to his friends' verbal attacks. "How long will you torture me? How long will you try to crush me with your words? You have already insulted me ten times. You should be ashamed of treating me so badly" (vv. 2–3, NLT). He is frustrated with the way his friends have talked to him. They have accused him of wrongdoing and it has been insulting. Their words have been crushing to him. This shows us the power of our words, especially when people are dealing with tragedy and hardship in their life.

Job states that if he has done wrong, then that is his concern and not theirs. It is not for them to show him his sin, because his sin is for him alone to deal with. Job clarifies to his friends they are unable to humiliate him because God already has. He says God is like a hunter who has trapped him in a net. He doesn't need them to do the same.

**2. Job's Response to His Situation (vv. 23–29)**

Job desires for his words to be written down. Why? So his testimony of innocence could be recorded for future generations. By saying this, Job is stating his innocence not only to his friends but for those to come and ultimately to God. He states that he wants his words to be engraved with an iron pen. This way the message could last forever and not changed. Job was confident of his innocence and wanted everyone to know, even those who had not existed yet.

Job reaffirms his unconditional faith and trust in God in all situations. "For I know that my redeemer liveth, and that he shall stand at the latter day upon the earth: and though after my skin worms destroy this body, yet in my flesh shall I see God" (vv. 25–26). Job knows God will remove him from his circumstance even if it happens after his death. He uses the term "redeemer" in reference to God. He knows that only God can redeem him from death and take up the cause of his innocence. Job sees beyond his present situation and look to the time when he will be able to stand in the presence of God.

## Search the Scriptures

1. How did Job defend himself against the accusations of his friends (Job 19:4–6)?

2. Why did Job refer to God as his Redeemer (v. 25)?

## Discuss the Meaning

1. Whom do you turn to in times of suffering?

2. How can we know that God is with us in our suffering and pain?

## Lesson in Our Society

There is so much suffering in the world we live in. During these times, many people turn to many things to medicate the pain. Some turn to drugs, alcohol, and sex. Others turn to milder things like shopping and food. Those who believe in Christ look to Him as their redemption and hope. In our suffering we can be assured that God is for us and not against us. Whether or not we are freed from our suffering, we will be able to see our Redeemer and be in His presence forever.

## Make It Happen

Think about the times that you have experienced God's blessing even amid suffering. Maybe it was during a time of illness or the loss of income. Make a list of the ways that God showed you His love and care in times of suffering. It could have been through the words of a friend or a sermon. It could have been through unexpected provision or a small comfort. As you make the list, thank God that He does not leave us alone in our suffering.

## Follow the Spirit

What God wants me to do:

_____

_____

_____

_____

## Remember Your Thoughts

Special insights I have learned:

_____

_____

_____

_____

## More Light on the Text

Job 19:1–7, 23–29

1 Then Job answered and said, 2 How long will ye vex my soul, and break me in

**pieces with words? 3 These ten times have ye reproached me: ye are not ashamed that ye make yourselves strange to me.**

What is Job's mood at this point? His three friends are unable to see that suffering might not be caused by the sin of the sufferer, and Job is trying to tell them that he is sure from his personal experience that this is not so. Do you think someone remains sick because they lack faith? This is just the same situation—we need to be careful not to judge the heart of another or how God is working in their lives. God does not always heal and He often allows suffering to come into our lives to strengthen us. The Apostle Paul had some sort of physical disability or sickness. He asked God three times to heal him, but God refused and said that His power was made perfect through Paul's weakness (2 Corinthians 12:7–9). In other words, because Paul had this disability, people were more apt to give glory to God for Paul's ministry than to credit Paul himself.

Job is often credited with patience, but this is not the case. Job perseveres in spite of it all, but he is not feeling very patient! "How long?" he asks. The Hebrew is *'ad* (**AD**), which is almost as if asking if it will last forever. Job seems to be feeling angry here—do you blame him? All three of his friends are ganging up against him. They are trying to vex him and break him in pieces with their words. "Break" in Hebrew is *daka'* (**dah-KAH**), which literally means to crush into powder. This is not used here in the literal, physical sense, but a psychological sense of to humiliate or oppress.

Job says that his so-called friends have tried ten times to accuse him. He is not literally counting the number of times with his ten fingers, but this is a Hebrew idiom meaning many times and completely, and Job is saying that it is too many times to accuse a friend. And so he basically asks, "Are

you not ashamed to abuse me?" They are not succeeding in making Job feel ashamed, but they should feel ashamed for treating him this way.

**4 And be it indeed that I have erred, mine error remaineth with myself.**

Scholars have interpreted this verse in a variety of ways. "With myself" (Heb. *'itti*, **ee-TEE**) is an emphatic expression; in other words, it is as if Job had underlined it. So the most logical interpretation is that Job says he alone is responsible to God for his own sin. This is something that his friends could neither see nor understand. No one else can see what transpires between Job and the Lord. If Job has sinned, his sin is not hurting his friends; it only hurts Job, so he thinks they should stop bothering him about it. And by using the word "erred" (Heb. *shagah*, **shah-GAH**), Job is intimating a smaller sin, probably done in ignorance, not the huge sin that would be expected to bring on the great suffering that Job is enduring.

**5 If indeed ye will magnify yourselves against me, and plead against me my reproach.**

Job's accusers are acting as if they are his moral superiors—they are magnifying themselves. They think that they are pure, because obviously God is not punishing them. A "reproach" (Heb. *kherpah*, **kher-PAH**) is a condition of disgrace in which Job feels he is being treated like a terrible sinner.

**6 Know now that God hath overthrown me, and hath compassed me with his net.**

Job feels that it is God who has unjustly caused his suffering, which makes Job's friends view him as a great sinner, and he finds that humiliating. The word "overthrown" (Heb. *'avat*, **ah-VAHT**) means to bend or pervert the cause of someone or something. Job thinks that God has ruined his reputation as an upright man. He says that God has compassed or surrounded him with a net like a hunter catching his prey.

**7 Behold, I cry out of wrong, but I am not heard: I cry aloud, but there is no judgment.**

The picture here is like the person being assaulted in broad daylight, but no one listens to his or her cries for help. In this case, Job is crying out for God's help, but seemingly God has His ears shut. Job is not accusing God of being unjust. He is just complaining that he has not received a fair and equitable response from God; God is not answering.

**23 Oh that my words were now written! oh that they were printed in a book! 24 That they were graven with an iron pen and lead in the rock for ever!**

Job desires vindication and it certainly does not seem to be happening. He wishes that the facts of his life could be written down for the future—so it could be seen that he is not guilty of horrendous sins. First he thinks of the facts being written down in a scroll, the book format of his day. Then he thinks he really desired a permanent record, inscribed in stone with the letters filled in with lead so in the future, it could be seen that he is innocent. Job's desire is answered by God in far greater ways than Job could ever imagine. The story of his suffering and his godly life is recorded in the book of Job, and many more are reading it than were even alive on earth in his days. You and I know of his innocence and even more important, God was watching the pain of every boil on his body, the holes in his heart for every one of his dead children, and the hurtful words of his closest friends. God saw his suffering as well as his righteousness. And yes, a permanent written record was made

of his suffering, and it is the book of Job in our Bibles!

**25 For I know that my redeemer liveth, and that he shall stand at the latter day upon the earth: 26 And though after my skin worms destroy this body, yet in my flesh shall I see God: 27 Whom I shall see for myself, and mine eyes shall behold, and not another; though my reins be consumed within me.**

Have you heard the "Messiah" sung recently and been thrilled to hear the words, "I know that my Redeemer liveth"? Old Testament believers did not fully understand the idea that we will go to live in heaven with the Lord after we die. Elsewhere in the book of Job, we don't see that Job firmly believed that he would go to heaven when he died. But in these verses, Job is speaking under the inspiration of the Holy Spirit of the wonderful truth that he would someday see his living Redeemer. Old Testament prophets often spoke of things that they didn't fully understand, especially in the references to Jesus, our Messiah. But with this statement we seem to see a turning in the attitude of Job—yes, in the end God will vindicate him.

A redeemer (Heb. *ga'al*, **gah-ALL**) in Israelite society was the next of kin and had certain responsibilities and privileges, such as buying back family property which had been lost as a result of indebtedness, marrying a widow, avenging, delivering, purchasing, ransoming, and redeeming. David spoke of God being his Redeemer (Psalm 19:14) and so did Isaiah (44:6), and it is certainly in this sense that Job speaks of his Redeemer. Only God could vindicate him of his sins. And since Job expects to die soon, he saw the only hope of God declaring him innocent as happening after he died. So if God vindicated Job after he died, would that really help him? Job expresses in these verses the belief that even though his physical body would be eaten by worms as it lay in the grave, his physical body would also be resurrected and he would be face to face with his Redeemer.

We read the word "reins" in the KJV and wonder what this is referring to. This is how the KJV translates the Hebrew word *kilyah* (**keel-YAH**), which actually refers to the kidneys, which were viewed as the seat of the emotions. The NIV translation renders this as: "How my heart yearns within me!" Particularly as we get older or as we experience terminal diseases, the thought that excites us is that we will soon see Jesus.

**28 But ye should say, Why persecute we him, seeing the root of the matter is found in me? 29 Be ye afraid of the sword: for wrath bringeth the punishments of the sword, that ye may know there is a judgment.**

Now Job returns to his complaints concerning his so-called friends. We think of the ninth commandment: "Thou shalt not bear false witness against thy neighbour" (Exodus 20:16). Job knows in his heart that he is not guilty of the gross sins his friends are accusing him of. We, too, should remember that whether in a court of law or a whisper of gossip, we should not accuse someone of doing anything wrong unless we have seen it for ourselves, or we will suffer punishment from God. When we get to the end of the book of Job, we will see that God judges the three for their accusations against Job. They had repeatedly harassed an innocent victim. The root of the matter was not found in Job.

Sources:
Andersen, Francis I. *Job: Introduction and Commentary*. Tyndale Old Testament Commentaries. Downers Grove, IL: InterVarsity Press, 1976.
Brand, Chad, Charles Draper, and Archie England, eds. *Holman Illustrated Bible Dictionary*. Nashville, TN: Holman Bible Publishers, 2003.
Clines, David J.A. *Job 1–20*. Word Biblical Commentary, Vol. 17. Dallas, TX: Word Books Publisher, 1989.
Gray, John. *The Book of Job*. Sheffield, England: Sheffield Phoenix Press, 2010.
Keck, Leander, gen. ed. *The New Interpreter's Bible*. Vol. 3. Nashville, TN: Abingdon Press, 1999.
Meyers, Allen C., ed. *The Eerdmans Bible Dictionary*. Grand Rapids, MI: Wm. B. Eerdmans Publishing Company, 1996.
Rachmacher, Earl D., Th.D., gen. ed. *The Nelson Study Bible New King James Version*. Nashville, TN: Thomas Nelson Publishers, 1997.
*Today's Parallel Bible*. Grand Rapids, MI: Zondervan, 2000.
Walvoord, John F. and Roy B. Zuck, eds. *The Bible Knowledge Commentary: Old Testament*. Wheaton, IL: Victor Books, 1985.

## Say It Correctly

Uz. **OOTZ**.
Intimation. in-ti-**MAY**-shun.

## Daily Bible Readings

**MONDAY**
Forsaken by Family and Friends
(Job 19:13–21)

**TUESDAY**
Why Do You Stand Far Off?
(Psalm 10:1–11)

**WEDNESDAY**
Do Not Fear
(Isaiah 44:1–8)

**THURSDAY**
God's Purpose for Me
(Psalm 57:1–6)

**FRIDAY**
My Heart Is Steadfast
(Psalm 57:7–11)

**SATURDAY**
Loves That Endures Forever
(1 Chronicles 16:28–34)

**SUNDAY**
My Redeemer Lives!
(Job 19:1–7, 23–29)

# Teaching Tips

## Words You Should Know

**A. Almighty** (Job 24:1) *Shadday* or *(El) Shadday* (Heb.)—Powerful.

**B. Grave** (v. 19) *She'ol* (Heb.)—Realm of the dead.

**C. Job** *'Iyob* (Heb.)—Hated or persecuted one.

## Teacher Preparation

**Unifying Principle—Defiant Faithfulness.** Sometimes it seems as though wicked people get all the breaks and cannot be stopped from doing terrible things. How can this picture be changed? Job complains that God supports the evil ones, but only for a while; however, he affirms that, even so, God saves the needy and gives the poor hope in the battles they are waging.

**A.** Pray for your students and for lesson clarity.

**B.** Read through Job 24 several times.

## O—Open the Lesson

**A.** Open with prayer, including the Aim for Change.

**B.** Introduce today's lesson title.

**C.** Have your students read the Aim for Change and Keep in Mind verse together. Discuss.

**D.** Tell the class to read the In Focus story silently, then discuss it.

## P—Present the Scriptures

**A.** Have volunteers read the Focal Verses.

**B.** Use the People, Places, and Times; Background; Search the Scriptures; At-A-Glance outline; In Depth; and More Light on the Text to clarify the verses.

## E—Explore the Meaning

**A.** Divide the class into groups to discuss the Discuss the Meaning, Lesson in Our Society, and Make It Happen sections. Tell the students to select a representative to report their responses.

**B.** Connect these sections to the Aim for Change and the Keep in Mind verse.

## N—Next Steps for Application

**A.** Summarize the lesson.

**B.** Close with prayer.

## Worship Guide

For the Superintendent or Teacher
Theme: Hope Complains
Song: "I Will Trust in the Lord"
Devotional Reading: Jeremiah 14:14–22

# Hope Complains

**Bible Background • JOB 5, 24; PSALM 55:12–23**
**Printed Text • JOB 24:1, 9–12, 19–25**
**Devotional Reading • JEREMIAH 14:14–22**

## Aim for Change

By the end of this lesson, we will: EXPLORE Job's complaint about the appearance that God does nothing to call wicked people to account; APPRECIATE that, although the timing of God's justice is often unknown to us, it is certain; and DETERMINE ways to help God bring justice to the poor and weak.

### In Focus

A young man named Craig had finally been released from jail. Happy to get out, Craig was also fearful and anxious about returning to society. How would he take care of himself? How would he be able to get hired with a felony on his record? The odds were stacked against him. On top of that, he felt anger and frustration at the events which led him to this particular moment in his life. Craig had not done anything wrong except be in the wrong place at the wrong time. While he and his friends were hanging out in front of their apartment building, police officers came by and proceeded to frisk them for drugs. One of the officers planted drugs in Craig's jacket. He had no record or any history of being affiliated with drugs or dealers, but he had no voice in the courtroom. He ended up spending years in prison for a crime he did not commit. As Craig walked past his old church, he began to cry out to God. He didn't know that Pastor Johnson, his old pastor, saw him from his study. The pastor came out and embraced Craig. In the weeks that followed, Pastor Johnson helped Craig land a job and a place to stay. Craig also began to go back to school to be a lawyer and be an advocate for those who needed a voice against injustice.

*In today's lesson, we will look at Job's analysis of the wicked and his demand that God bring justice for the oppressed.*

## Keep in Mind

"Why, seeing times are not hidden from the Almighty, do they that know him not see his days?" (Job 24:1).

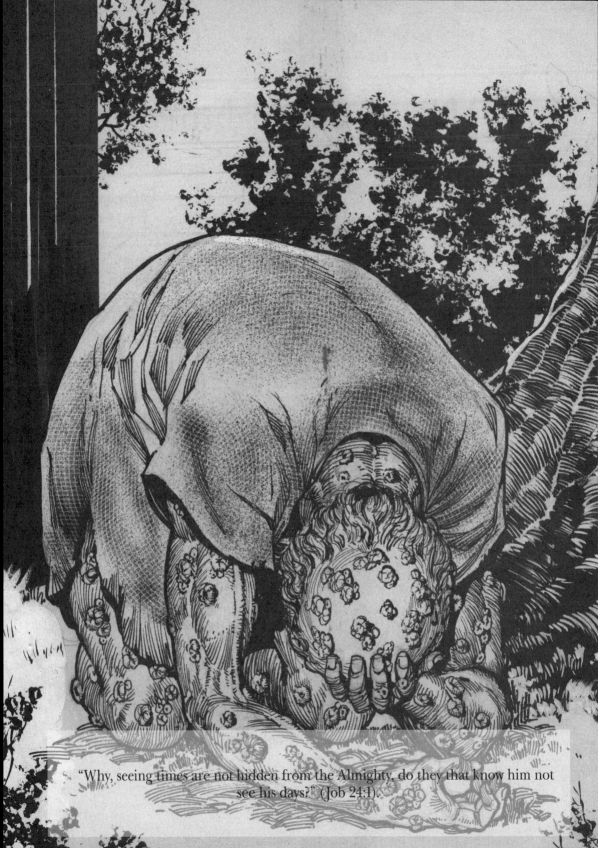

"Why, seeing times are not hidden from the Almighty, do they that know him not see his days?" (Job 24:1).

## Focal Verses

**KJV** **Job 24:1** Why, seeing times are not hidden from the Almighty, do they that know him not see his days?

**9** They pluck the fatherless from the breast, and take a pledge of the poor.

**10** They cause him to go naked without clothing, and they take away the sheaf from the hungry;

**11** Which make oil within their walls, and tread their winepresses, and suffer thirst.

**12** Men groan from out of the city, and the soul of the wounded crieth out: yet God layeth not folly to them.

**19** Drought and heat consume the snow waters: so doth the grave those which have sinned.

**20** The womb shall forget him; the worm shall feed sweetly on him; he shall be no more remembered; and wickedness shall be broken as a tree.

**21** He evil entreateth the barren that beareth not: and doeth not good to the widow.

**22** He draweth also the mighty with his power: he riseth up, and no man is sure of life.

**23** Though it be given him to be in safety, whereon he resteth; yet his eyes are upon their ways.

**24** They are exalted for a little while, but are gone and brought low; they are taken out of the way as all other, and cut off as the tops of the ears of corn.

**25** And if it be not so now, who will make me a liar, and make my speech nothing worth?

**NLT** **Job 24:1** "Why doesn't the Almighty bring the wicked to judgment? Why must the godly wait for him in vain?

**9** The wicked snatch a widow's child from her breast, taking the baby as security for a loan.

**10** The poor must go about naked, without any clothing. They harvest food for others while they themselves are starving.

**11** They press out olive oil without being allowed to taste it, and they tread in the winepress as they suffer from thirst.

**12** The groans of the dying rise from the city, and the wounded cry for help, yet God ignores their moaning.

**19** The grave consumes sinners just as drought and heat consume snow.

**20** Their own mothers will forget them. Maggots will find them sweet to eat. No one will remember them. Wicked people are broken like a tree in the storm.

**21** They cheat the woman who has no son to help her. They refuse to help the needy widow.

**22** God, in his power, drags away the rich. They may rise high, but they have no assurance of life.

**23** They may be allowed to live in security, but God is always watching them.

**24** And though they are great now, in a moment they will be gone like all others, cut off like heads of grain.

**25** Can anyone claim otherwise? Who can prove me wrong?"

## The People, Places, and Times

**Pledge.** A pledge is a security given for future payment. Pledges were often oppressive to the poor. Many times wicked men would take pledges from the poor of things they could hardly do without. Legislation can be found in the Bible regarding the proper taking of pledges. A man's clothing could not be taken (Amos 2:8; Job 24:10) although his outer garment could be taken for the day and returned at night (Exodus 22:26; Deuteronomy 24:12–13). A widow's clothing could not be taken as a pledge (Deuteronomy 24:17). Additionally, a mill for breadmaking could not be taken for a pledge (Deuteronomy 24:6). Those who took pledges were not allowed to enter into the debtor's house to take the pledge (Deuteronomy 24:10).

**Uz.** Uz is the poetic name for Edom (the southernmost part of Transjordan) according to Jewish tradition. According to the description of Job's friends, it seemed to be inhabited or bordered by Temanites, Namathites, and Buzites. Due to lack of archaeological evidence, Uz is sometimes thought of as part of Edom, but the Bible is not explicit about the location of Uz, and a more general location of east of Palestine would make it accessible to the Sabateans and Chaldeans (Job 1:15–17).

### Background

Date and authorship of the book of Job is uncertain. Some Jewish scholars believe that the book was written by Moses, some Christian scholars believe that Solomon is the author, while others believe Job is an autobiography written during the time of the prophets Isaiah or Zechariah, or that it was written by an anonymous author during the period of the exile or post-exile. Job was a wealthy and righteous man who, through a series of events, lost his possessions, his children, and his health. As a result, Job began to question God about suffering. Job's friends (Eliphaz, Bildad, and Zophar) mourned with him over his great loss. After the time of mourning had ended, Job's friends wrongly assumed that all suffering is the result of sin and began to persuade Job to repent of his sins. Job,

however, was not suffering because of sin. God was orchestrating the circumstances in Job's life to prove Satan wrong. While this might seem like a diabolical chess match between God and Satan, the nature of God was revealed to Job as he wrestled with his faith. Job began to plead for justice amid his seemingly unjust situation. As he complained to God, he listed the oppression and injustice that he saw before his very eyes.

## At-A-Glance

1. Job's Questions (Job 24:1)
2. The Plight of the Oppressed (vv. 9–12)
3. Change in Perspective (vv. 19–25)

### In Depth
#### 1. Job's Questions (Job 24:1)

Almighty, Powerful, Mighty One are all names for God that can be used in this verse. It is fitting that Job uses the term Almighty in reference to God. Injustice has been committed, and Job looks to the ultimate power and authority in the universe to right the wrongs on earth. Yet, the wicked seemed to be in control and the godly had no defender from these evil men. In anguish, Job cries out to the Almighty, but God's silence only compounds his suffering. Job asks the question "Why?" He believes God is the Almighty One, and he also believes that God is righteous and just. If this is the case, then why are the wicked allowed to oppress the poor and innocent? Job asks the age-old question of humanity: "If God is all-powerful and always good, how can He allow evil to flourish?" Bewilderment is beginning to set in. Justice has not been served.

## 2. The Plight of the Oppressed (vv. 9–12)

Job is concerned about injustice in this diatribe to the Almighty. He is crying out in anguish at the cruelty of this world. Job lists many issues that continue to plague humanity to this day. He looks around and sees slavery, unfair wages, and debt entanglement. The widow's child is taken from her and the poor go about naked. Although the poor work to produce food and wine, they are hungry and thirsty. He complains that justice does not prevail in the world because the wicked are prosperous and successful. God is allowing this wickedness to thrive. Job takes it a step further and says that God is ignoring the cries of the dying and the wounded. No one is brought to justice for this wrong. There is no relief. Job is in anguish because of this great wrong.

## 3. Change in Perspective (vv. 19–25)

Finally, Job begins to argue that the wicked will not get away with their sin. He realizes that the wicked are punished in death. This is a fact of life as much as "drought and heat consume snow" (v. 19). The wicked will soon be forgotten by family members and friends. Though they were once rich, secure and great, God will strip them of their riches and they will die like everyone else. Job likens their demise to a tree being destroyed in a storm. From the outside they look like they will stand strong, but they are not what they appear to be. In death, they will be broken by the power and judgment of God. Job is convinced that judgment for the wicked is certain and harsh, and that there will be no relief for them. The downfall of the wicked will be swift and brutal. God will answer the cries of the oppressed and deliver them from evil. Job has renewed hope in God the Deliverer.

## Search the Scriptures

1. How does God seem to respond to injustice at times (Job 24:12)?

2. What is the cost of wickedness (vv. 22–24)?

## Discuss the Meaning

1. What do you believe about God, the wicked, and injustice?

2. How can we handle situations where justice does not come swiftly?

## Lesson in Our Society

The Civil Rights Act of 1964 outlaws discrimination based on race, color, religion, sex, or national origin in specific settings. Additional civil rights acts have expanded the specific settings of the Civil Rights Act of 1964 to general settings across a wide variety of American life and have expanded the categories of protection to cover age and disability. These laws were passed to protect vulnerable people from injustice.

The laws in Uz to protect people from oppression were not enforced in this passage of Job. However, Job's final conclusion was that God will judge those who oppress other people. The oppressors will lose their riches, status, and even their own lives.

## Make It Happen

Are there widows and poor people in the neighborhood to whom your church can minister? Are there lawyers in your church who can help the oppressed fight against discrimination based on the Civil Rights Act of 1964? Is your group praying for God to bring justice on the wicked? Pray and act in the fight against oppression of the widows and the poor in your community.

## Follow the Spirit

What God wants me to do:

_____

_____

_____

_____

## Remember Your Thoughts

Special insights I have learned:

_____

_____

_____

_____

## More Light on the Text

Job 24:1, 9–12, 19–25

**1 Why, seeing times are not hidden from the Almighty, do they that know him not see his days?**

Job is wondering why God doesn't make some sort of judicial calendar so people could clearly understand His plan for justice. This is the way we humans think; we want justice to be done right away. But God's justice is different from ours (cf. Isaiah 55:8–9). There is a time of final justice—judgment day—but no one knows when that will be. God does not deal with us as parents deal with toddlers. We may not be punished for wrong immediately or rewarded for good right away. That would make us just God's toddler-puppets, but He desires for us to do what is good, no matter what the consequences may be. Just as Job was a very godly man, God is able to trust His strongest followers to keep close to Him even when times are tough.

Job is speaking of justice for those who know God. The Hebrew for "know" is *yada'* (**yaw-DAH**), and it means more than just an intellectual understanding that there is a God; it means to respond to Him, to recognize His rights as God Almighty, and to esteem Him as God. Job thought that especially those who worship God and obey Him deserve to have Him answer them in regard to punishment and reward for the things they do. "Why?" (Heb. *maddua'*, **mad-DOO-ah**) asks Job, not seeking the answer, but expressing sorrow that he does not know the answer.

**9 They pluck the fatherless from the breast, and take a pledge of the poor. 10 They cause him to go naked without clothing, and they take away the sheaf from the hungry; 11 Which make oil within their walls, and tread their winepresses, and suffer thirst. 12 Men groan from out of the city, and the soul of the wounded crieth out: yet God layeth not folly to them.**

Job begins to look at the suffering of others who seem innocent and powerless also (vv. 2–8). He wonders why they, too, suffer unjustly. This leads to asking the question of why an omnipotent God, a God of love and justice, allows suffering in this world, particularly when bad things happen to good people. The entire book of Job wrestles with this problem which theologians have termed theodicy. Christians have come up with several answers. One is that God allows pain because it refines and purifies us, so that the end result outweighs the suffering endured. Second, if good were the only choice open to us human beings, we would not have a genuine choice. So our evil choices cause much of the suffering in this world. Although these reasons do not fully explain all the problems in this world, God calls upon us as His followers to trust in His sovereign design and His love for us, even when things seem upside down to us.

Job is beginning to grow and look beyond his own problems to see that others are in similar situations. This is one area where we definitely should be growing spiritually when we ourselves are suffering—it should make us more sensitive to the plight of others. The first example Job mentions is the cruel person plucking (Heb. *gazal*, **GAH-zal**) or snatching an infant to pay for a debt. This word properly used means to strip off skin from flesh. This highlights the severity of the injustice. We can imagine the pain of the widow whose sons were going to be taken from her to work as slaves to pay off the debt of her dead husband (2 Kings 4:1–7). The example is exaggerated in verse 9, a hyperbole; it would not make sense to take an infant as a slave. A baby would have to be fed and cared for until old enough to do any worthwhile work, but Job is making the point of the cruelty that would cause a person to snatch a child from his or her mother. The next example is likely an exaggeration also. While those in poverty may not be running around naked, they are destitute and dressed in rags.

And the next three examples show extreme worker exploitation. Farm workers carry the sheaves (Heb. *'omer*, **OH-mer**) or bundles of grain but do not have enough to eat. Others crush olive oil, but it is implied that they receive no oil for their work. They work in the winepress (Heb. *yekhev*, **yeh-KHEHV**) where grapes were squeezed and bruised to make wine but they don't even have water to drink. Job sees that people are wounded and dying; they are crying out for help, but God doesn't seem to be doing anything about it. In each of these examples, we see suffering that is not caused by God, but is caused by the wealthy owners of the agricultural businesses. But Job says that injustice is not confined to agriculture; there are cries from those in the city as well. Before we blame God for this type of suffering, we must remember that He is not the cause of it; human beings should set these injustices to right. Not only does God want us to trust Him to bring about justice in the end, but He also wants us to help others in their distress as we are able.

**19 Drought and heat consume the snow waters: so doth the grave those which have sinned. 20 The womb shall forget him; the worm shall feed sweetly on him; he shall be no more remembered; and wickedness shall be broken as a tree.**

Job's side of the debate so far has been that God ignores the wicked and they are not punished for their sins, while the innocent face suffering as God turns His face away. But Job seems to be changing his ideas, since we read in 19:25–27 that he is expecting to meet his Redeemer face to face in the afterlife. Although he does not have a clear idea of hell for the wicked, he realizes that the faithful can expect a glorious future after death, and there will be punishment for evildoers in the end. Job acknowledges that just as snow is melted away by heat and drought (Heb. *tsiyah*, **TSEE-yah**) or dryness, so the wicked will come to the end of their lives and be remembered no more (vv. 19–20). Even if they have a well-attended funeral, they will soon be forgotten.

**21 He evil entreateth the barren that beareth not: and doeth not good to the widow. 22 He draweth also the mighty with his power: he riseth up, and no man is sure of life. 23 Though it be given him to be in safety, whereon he resteth; yet his eyes are upon their ways. 24 They are exalted for a little**

**while, but are gone and brought low; they are taken out of the way as all other, and cut off as the tops of the ears of corn.**

Again Job returns to the idea that the wicked "evil entreateth" (Heb. *ra'ah*, **ra-AH**) or do evil to the poor and helpless. This time it is not to the widowed mother but to the woman who faces great problems alone—maybe she has no children, a disgrace in that era, or maybe she is a widow without anyone to help her. In most societies, lone women are at a disadvantage. We all know elderly women and single moms who are in poverty, but in the ancient patriarchal society, things were even worse for women. People think they can get away with taking advantage of women who are alone because they have no one to stand up for them. But in spite of the ancient context, God commended women who spoke up for themselves. Read Numbers 36 to see how God defended the rights of the daughters of Zelophehad.

Job says he feels like doing the right thing is not worth it, because in spite of the good things he did, he is suffering. Then God gives him spiritual insight and he understands the final end of the wicked. Instead of Job standing on slippery ground, the wicked will be feeling the ground pulled out from under them. And then to continue this picture, God is holding Job by his hand, as a father takes the hand of his child as they walk along a dangerous road. God is helping him and guiding him. Even if his physical health and strength may fail, God is his strength forever. Yes, and the unfaithful will finally be destroyed. Job has not reached the end of his wrestling match with his friends and with God, but he will get there!

**25 And if it be not so now, who will make me a liar, and make my speech nothing worth?**

Job is very sure of himself here—he says that no one can prove wrong what he has just said. How could his friends insist that the wicked are always immediately punished and the good never suffer? Job gives examples from real life that prove otherwise. And yet he is not saying things are just backward of what they say. Yes, evildoers are punished, we just don't know when—it could be upon their death. Yes, God will reward those who follow Him, but again, we don't know when, and the greatest rewards will surely come after we die.

Sources:

Adeyemo, Tokunboh, ed., et al. *Africa Bible Commentary: A One-Volume Commentary Written by 70 African Scholars*. Nairobi, Kenya: Word Alive Publishers, 2006.

Andersen, Francis I. *Job: An Introduction and Commentary*. Tyndale Old Testament Commentaries. Downers Grove, IL: InterVarsity Press, 1976.

*Archaeological Study Bible, New International Version*. Grand Rapids, MI: Zondervan, 2005. 732–734.

Ferguson, Sinclair B., ed., et al. "Theodicy." *New Dictionary of Theology*. Downers Grove, IL: InterVarsity Press, 1988.

*Jewish Study Bible, Tanakh Translation*. New York: Oxford University Press, 2004. 1499–1505, 1535–1536.

*Key Word Study Bible, New International Version*. Chattanooga, TN: AMG International, 1996. 584, 608–609.

*Life Application Study Bible, New International Version*. Wheaton, IL: Tyndale House Publishers, 1997. 764–765.

*Quest Study Bible, New International Version*. Grand Rapids, MI: Zondervan, 2003. 733–734.

## Say It Correctly

Theodicy. thee-**AH**-di-see.
Hyperbole. hi-**PER**-bo-lee.

## Daily Bible Readings

**MONDAY**
Set a Time to Remember Me
(Job 14:7–13)

**TUESDAY**
You Destroy the Hope of Mortals
(Job 14:14–22)

**WEDNESDAY**
Why is My Pain Unending?
(Jeremiah 15:10–18)

**THURSDAY**
Our Hope is in God
(Jeremiah 14:14–22)

**FRIDAY**
Shelter from the Storm
(Psalm 55:1–8)

**SATURDAY**
I Call Upon God
(Psalm 55:12–23)

**SUNDAY**
The Poor and the Mighty
(Job 24:1, 9–12, 19–25)

# Notes

_____

_____

_____

_____

# Teaching Tips

## Words You Should Know

**A. Abhor** (Job 42:6) *ma'as* (Heb.)—To reject, despise, refuse.

**B. Burnt offering** (v. 8) *'olah* (Heb.)—Sacrifice that is entirely burned.

## Teacher Preparation

**Unifying Principle—Who's in Control?** People often wonder who or what controls the final outcome in life's many challenges. Where can people find answers to life's ultimate questions? Job declares that God can do all things and will ultimately prevail over all obstacles, restoring the fortunes of those who are faithful.

**A.** Pray for your students and for lesson clarity.

**B.** Research Job 42 several times.

**C.** Complete the companion lesson in the *Precepts For Living Personal Study Guide®*.

## O—Open the Lesson

**A.** Open with a prayer, including the Aim for Change.

**B.** Introduce today's lesson title.

**C.** Have your students read the Aim for Change and Keep in Mind verse together. Discuss.

**D.** Tell the class to read the In Focus story silently, then discuss it.

## P—Present the Scriptures

**A.** Have volunteers read the Focal Verses.

**B.** Use the People, Places, and Times; Background; At-A-Glance outline; In Depth; and More Light on the Text to clarify the verses.

## E—Explore the Meaning

**A.** Discuss the Search the Scriptures section.

**B.** Divide the class, and have them answer the questions in the Discuss the Meaning and Lesson in Our Society sections, then report their responses. Connect these sections to the Aim for Change and Keep in Mind verse.

## N—Next Steps for Application

**A.** Ask students to read the Make it Happen section and give ideas for how to respond to family members and friends who are going through something outside of their control.

**B.** Summarize the lesson.

**C.** Close with prayer allowing students to thank God for sustaining them in their trials and rewarding their hope in Him.

## Worship Guide

For the Superintendent or Teacher
Theme: Hope Satisfies
Song: "Trouble Don't Last Always"
Devotional Reading: Galatians 1:11–19

81

# Hope Satisfies

**Bible Background • JOB 42; PSALM 86**
**Printed Text • JOB 42:1–10**
**Devotional Reading • GALATIANS 1:11–19**

## Aim for Change

By the end of this lesson, we will: EXPLORE the conclusion of Job and God's conversation; AFFIRM that God will answer our questions in ways best for us; and BECOME involved in an active and hopeful prayer life.

## In Focus

Deborah remembered when she and her husband bought a home in 1980. This was the dream home that they had prayed for. They had saved enough for a down payment and knew that the time was right. They saw their children grow up there and planned to be there for life. This all changed after her husband experienced a stroke, and they refinanced their home. The mounting medical bills worried her husband, who did not want Deborah to be left to pay his medical expenses upon his untimely demise. After his death, she learned that the refinanced mortgage loan was not a fixed rate mortgage, but an adjustable rate mortgage.

Soon Deborah's mortgage payments went from $1000 a month to $1700 a month. Deborah, who lived on a fixed income, was in danger of losing her home. She sought the help of legal aid. They soon discovered that she had been a victim of a now bankrupt company's tactic of offering subprime loans to minorities. Deborah didn't know how it was going to turn out, but hoped in God's goodness. Sometime later a mortgage assistance program reduced her mortgage and gave her financial assistance as well.

*In today's lesson, we will look at how Job's hope in the Lord was rewarded.*

## Keep in Mind

"And the LORD turned the captivity of Job, when he prayed for his friends: also the LORD gave Job twice as much as he had before" (Job 42:10).

"And the LORD turned the captivity of Job, when he prayed for his friends: also the LORD gave Job twice as much as he had before" (Job 42:10).

## Focal Verses

**KJV** **Job 42:1** Then Job answered the LORD, and said,

**2** I know that thou canst do every thing and that no thought can be withholden from thee.

**3** Who is he that hidest counsel without knowledge? therefore have I uttered that I understood not; things too wonderful for me, which I knew not.

**4** Hear, I beseech thee, and I will speak: I will demand of thee, and declare thou unto me.

**5** I have heard of thee by the hearing of the ear: but now mine eye seeth thee.

**6** Wherefore I abhor myself, and repent in dust and ashes.

**7** And it was so, that after the LORD had spoken these words unto Job, the LORD said to Eliphaz the Temanite, My wrath is kindled against thee, and against thy two friends: for ye have not spoken of me the thing that is right, as my servant Job hath.

**8** Therefore take unto you now seven bullocks and seven rams, and go to my servant Job, and offer up for yourselves a burnt offering; and my servant Job shall pray for you: for him will I accept: lest I deal with you after your folly, in that ye have not spoken of me the thing which is right, like my servant Job.

**9** So Eliphaz the Temanite and Bildad the Shuhite and Zophar the Naamathite went, and did according as the LORD commanded them: the LORD also accepted Job.

**10** And the LORD turned the captivity of Job, when he prayed for his friends: also the LORD gave Job twice as much as he had before.

**NLT** **Job 42:1** Then Job replied to the LORD:

**2** "I know that you can do anything, and no one can stop you.

**3** You asked, 'Who is this that questions my wisdom with such ignorance?' It is I— and I was talking about things I knew nothing about, things far too wonderful for me.

**4** You said, 'Listen and I will speak! I have some questions for you, and you must answer them.'

**5** I had only heard about you before, but now I have seen you with my own eyes.

**6** I take back everything I said, and I sit in dust and ashes to show my repentance."

**7** After the LORD had finished speaking to Job, he said to Eliphaz the Temanite: "I am angry with you and your two friends, for you have not spoken accurately about me, as my servant Job has.

**8** So take seven bulls and seven rams and go to my servant Job and offer a burnt offering for yourselves. My servant Job will pray for you, and I will accept his prayer on your behalf. I will not treat you as you deserve, for you have not spoken accurately about me, as my servant Job has."

**9** So Eliphaz the Temanite, Bildad the Shuhite, and Zophar the Naamathite did as the LORD commanded them, and the LORD accepted Job's prayer.

**10** When Job prayed for his friends, the LORD restored his fortunes. In fact, the LORD gave him twice as much as before!

## The People, Places, and Times

**Dust and Ashes.** To sit or to lie in dust and ashes was often a sign of repentance and humiliation in the ancient Near East. Dust represented man's frailty, and to lie in dust was to recognize the frailty of one's humanity in committing a wrong or experiencing grief due to the loss of a loved one, famine, or other calamity. Ashes symbolized worthlessness; to throw ashes on one's head was to humble oneself and acknowledge one's worthlessness in the sight of God. These gestures were not mandated by God but originated in the culture of the time.

**Eliphaz, Bildad, and Zophar.** Job's friends mourned with him for seven days after he suffered great loss. They then encouraged Job to confess his sin of pride, as they believed that it was the reason for his suffering. Eliphaz appealed to personal experience, Bildad pointed to universal wisdom, and Zophar declared what he felt was common sense. They all agreed that Job's problems were his own doing and that questioning God simply made matters worse.

## Background

After Eliphaz, Bildad, and Zophar finished speaking to Job concerning his suffering, a young man named Elihu spoke. Elihu rebuked the three friends for being unable to give Job a reasonable answer for why he was suffering. However, Elihu was only able to give a partial answer to Job's question by saying that people cannot understand all that God allows but must trust Him. This was the best answer that a human could give, yet it was incomplete because Elihu did not have all of the facts.

Finally, the Lord spoke! Instead of answering Job's question directly, God asked Job a series of questions that no human could possibly answer. God showed that He is eternal, holy, and incomprehensible!

## At-A-Glance

1. Job's Response to the Lord (Job 42:1–6)
2. The Lord Responds to Job's Friends (vv. 7–9)
3. The Lord Reverses Job's Situation (v. 10)

## In Depth

### 1. Job's Response to the Lord (Job 42:1–6)

Job understands his humanity in a new way. He has an encounter with God that causes him to re-evaluate his perspective. Job repents of complaining, as he now knows that God is sovereign. His spiritual eyes have been opened, and he humbles himself in dust and ashes.

Job is now conscious of the fact that he did not speak in the right way concerning God. His speech only served to hide God's true purposes rather than reveal them. He sought to understand God and his ways but fell short. His repentance is an acknowledgment that God is in control and that He alone knows what is best for His creation.

### 2. The Lord Responds to Job's Friends (vv. 7–9)

The Lord is angry with Job's friends. They are deserving of His wrath. He demands a sacrifice from Job's friends as a payment for defaming the name of the Almighty. Seven bulls and seven rams, which represent a sin offering, must be taken to Job, who will pray for his friends. Only then will the Lord forgive Job's friends and not treat them as their sins deserve.

The Lord calls Job's friends to account for their bad advice and counsel. They spoke for God when they too did not understand God. In fact, God says they did not speak about Him correctly. They accused Job and did not have the right to do so. As a result, their sins must be atoned for and they must rely on the prayers of the one whom they sought to accuse.

### 3. The Lord Reverses Job's Situation (v. 10)

Job prays for his friends, and the Lord accepts His prayer. Job is accepted because he has already repented of his arrogance and pride. God reverses Job's situation and brings him out of "captivity." It is also recorded that the Lord gives Job twice as much as he had before. This is all detailed in the rest of the chapter (vv. 11–17). All this happened as a result of Job's prayer for his friends.

Throughout the story of Job, we see him questioning God and His goodness. Now we see God giving Job even more than what he had before. The Lord knew the whole story while Job only knew a piece of it. Amid the wrestling, Job comes to have his spiritual eyes opened—not after he is blessed, but during the time of his trial. When Job first experienced his troubles, he had no idea that the Lord would restore him. When he began to pray for his friends, he had no idea that God was about to bless him with twice as much as he had before.

### Search the Scriptures

1. How was Job able to see God when God did not make a physical appearance (Job 42:5)?

2. Why was the Lord's wrath kindled against Eliphaz, Bildad, and Zophar (v. 7)?

### Discuss the Meaning

1. In what ways do we speak for God without truly understanding Him?

2. How can we maintain our hope even when we do not see God's purpose in our trials?

### Lesson in Our Society

There are many people in our society who are experiencing the trials of life. Because of this, their hope grows thin and they resort to relieving the pain they feel through addictive and destructive behaviors. Even as believers, we often question God's ways and whether He is good to us. This lesson shows us that the Lord can sustain us in our hope when we maintain intimate communication with Him. When our hope fades, He can strengthen us until His purpose is finally revealed.

### Make It Happen

Evaluate the circumstances in your life and pray that the Lord would open your spiritual eyes to see what He is doing. But do not stop there! Pray that the Lord would show you how to respond to your family and friends who are going through circumstances that are beyond their control. Offer wisdom, prayer, and silence. We as humans cannot know what God is doing in someone's life unless we seek God for our friend in need. Only speak when your friend is in danger or when the Lord shows you, then remain silent and let the Lord reveal an answer.

### Follow the Spirit

What God wants me to do:

_____

_____

_____

_____

## Remember Your Thoughts

Special insights I have learned:

_____

_____

_____

_____

## More Light on the Text

Job 42:1–10

**1 Then Job answered the LORD, and said, 2 I know that thou canst do every thing, and that no thought can be withholden from thee. 3 Who is he that hideth counsel without knowledge? therefore have I uttered that I understood not; things too wonderful for me, which I knew not.**

Now we come to the end of the book. When Job says "I know" (Heb. *yada'*, **yaw-DAH**), he is acknowledging the omnipotence of God. God knows everything and He is all powerful. Job has had the amazing experience of God Himself speaking to him. God did not say the things that Job was hoping for or expecting. Instead of speaking about justice issues, God spoke of His mighty creation. Job and his friends had thought of God as the great moral accountant, chalking up our rights and wrongs, and dishing out appropriate punishments and rewards.

In verse 3, Job quotes what God said earlier, intensifying the action with the verb "hideth" which is more complete than "darkeneth" (Heb. *khashak*, **khah-SHAHK**). There God said that Job was speaking out of ignorance when he brought his complaints before Him (38:2). "Hideth" in verse 3 is *'alam* (Heb. **ah-LAM**), which is speaking of God's grand designs for the universe that are concealed from us human beings. These are things that Job cannot speak of, because they are hid-den from him and from us. God is the great I AM—He exists in the past, the present, and the future, all simultaneously. His plans take all of these things into account. What if we pray that it will not rain on our Sunday School picnic, while the farmer is praying for much-needed rain on his crops? How can God take all of these things into account? We don't know—He just does.

So what did Job say after hearing what God had to say about Himself? First of all, he discovered that God is much more than some superior human being. We miss by a long shot when we try to make God in our own image or imagine Him as the being who will meet our specific needs. When we pray, we often think we know just what God should do to answer our prayers, when in reality, God has the whole picture and we do not.

**4 Hear, I beseech thee, and I will speak: I will demand of thee, and declare thou unto me. 5 I have heard of thee by the hearing of the ear: but now mine eye seeth thee. 6 Wherefore I abhor myself, and repent in dust and ashes.**

Job begins verse 4 by quoting God as He had spoken to him (38:3). God says that He wants to question Job, and Job must answer Him. This is a rhetorical question—one that Job answers in his mind, not aloud. But in verse 5, Job is ready with his answer, or non-answer in this case. When Job brought all his questions to God, he only asked from the point of view of a man who had a rather superficial knowledge of God—things that he had heard from others. But now that God Himself has talked with Job, Job's view of God has greatly expanded. Now Job knows God's voice, and he sees God with his very eyes and takes Him to heart. This is now a personal relationship with the God of the universe. His view of God is far bigger and yet more intimate.

To see our holy God as He really is always causes us to realize how sinful we are in comparison. We think of Isaiah in the temple as God in His holiness appeared to him. Isaiah said, "Woe is me! for I am undone; because I am a man of unclean lips, and I dwell in the midst of a people of unclean lips: for mine eyes have seen the King, the LORD of hosts" (from Isaiah 6:5). We find Job saying a similar thing in verse 6. "I abhor myself" can have several different meanings. The verb in Hebrew is *ma'as* (**mah-AHS**) and can also mean to melt or submit. Job does not utterly hate himself. Although his three friends had accused him of doing terrible things, Job is not agreeing to their accusations. He still maintains that he has done nothing so awful that he deserves the troubles he has experienced. He is aware of his arrogance before the Lord. When coming face to face with God, all these things must have been going through Job's mind. The last words that we hear from Job show his desire to "repent in dust and ashes." The Hebrew word for "repent" is *nakham* (**nah-KHAHM**), in which we see him sighing, breathing strongly with a sense of sorrow, and regretting his ignorant and hasty words before God.

**7 And it was so, that after the LORD had spoken these words unto Job, the LORD said to Eliphaz the Temanite, My wrath is kindled against thee, and against thy two friends: for ye have not spoken of me the thing that is right, as my servant Job hath. 8 Therefore take unto you now seven bullocks and seven rams, and go to my servant Job, and offer up for yourselves a burnt offering; and my servant Job shall pray for you: for him will I accept: lest I deal with you after your folly, in that ye have not spoken of me the thing which is right, like my servant Job. 9 So Eliphaz the Teman-**

**ite and Bildad the Shuhite and Zophar the Naamathite went, and did according as the LORD commanded them: the LORD also accepted Job.**

Now we switch from poetry to prose as we come almost to the end of the book. God defends Job by speaking to his friends. Evidently Eliphaz was the oldest of the three men, and so he is chosen by God as the representative. The three friends have the very narrow view of God mentioned earlier—that God is the great moral police officer, a God of immediate retribution, quickly meting out punishment when people sin and quickly bestowing material riches on the righteous. Sometimes this is true, but often it is not. Some greedy people use all their wiles to pile up stuff for themselves. Other very good people generously give away much of their goods to help others. When we accuse people of wrongdoing, just because they are suffering, we are imputing to God a very limited character. We read in Hebrews 12:6 that the one "the Lord loveth he chasteneth, and scourgeth every son whom he receiveth." Yes, those who suffer are more likely to be God's favorite children. This is similar to the way good parents treat their children. They do not ignore them and let them do whatever they want. This is really not the loving way to parent. Good parents do not give their children everything they want. This would just make them lazy. And that is somewhat the way that God treats us. He allows hardship into our lives for a variety of reasons, but one is to strengthen us spiritually, to teach us to stay on our knees before Him.

When we look at people who seem successful even though they are very immoral, we may be forgetting God's grace and mercy to sinners as He waits for them to repent. Often people die without ever turning to God and then they are punished, because they have ignored the great grace of God. The book of Job should open our eyes to see more of the sovereign greatness of God. He alone does what He wants, because He alone sees the whole picture. The first chapter of Job let us as readers in on a conversation between God and Satan, so we could see why God allowed Job to suffer. But so far as we can see, God never shared this information with Job; Job had to trust God that He was working in the best interests of all those who love Him. Hopefully, this study has helped us to catch a greater vision of the greatness of our God.

Job was certainly not perfect, but he passionately desired to communicate honestly with God. His friends, on the other hand, just mouthed platitudes that they had heard. But even worse, they arrogantly thought they knew why Job was suffering, even though they had no real evidence for sin on his part. So God commanded them to make a sacrifice of seven bulls and seven rams which probably signified complete atonement. Eliphaz, Bildad, and Zophar must have felt humiliated. They had thought they were the righteous ones, but God accuses them of sin and validates Job's righteousness. To make things even worse, they need Job's prayers of intercession for their own sakes. And the Lord accepts Job's prayer for them.

**10 And the LORD turned the captivity of Job, when he prayed for his friends: also the LORD gave Job twice as much as he had before.**

Here God has asked Job to take a step of faith. He first has to intercede for his so-called friends, and then the Lord gives him twice as much as he had before. Job had no idea that this would be the result, and he surely had to wait many years for this to happen. He lived 140 years more and in this time he had seven sons and three daughters, the same number as he had lost. Although children cannot be replaced with other children, nevertheless, these were amazing children. We look at the names of the daughters—Jemima, which means dove; Kezia, which means cinnamon; and Kerenhappuch, which means a container of expensive eye makeup. These are fitting names as they were the most beautiful women in all the land. Job lived to see his children grow up and have his grandchildren, and his grandchildren grow up and have his great-grandchildren. His herds grew from nothing to double the number of sheep, camels, oxen, and donkeys than he had before. Not only did Job's material blessings increase, but because of his experiences he gained the privilege of knowing God in a unique and powerful way.

Sources:

Adeyemo, Tokunboh, ed., et al. *Africa Bible Commentary: A One-Volume Commentary Written by 70 African Scholars*. Nairobi, Kenya: Word Alive Publishers, 2006.

Andersen, Francis I. *Job: An Introduction and Commentary*. Tyndale Old Testament Commentaries. Downers Grove, IL: InterVarsity Press, 1976.

*Archaeological Study Bible, New International Version*. Grand Rapids, MI: Zondervan, 2005. 732–734.

Clines, David J. A. *Word Biblical Commentary: Job 38–42*. Vol. 18B. Nashville, TN: Thomas Nelson, 2011.

*Jewish Study Bible, Tanakh Translation*. New York: Oxford University Press, 2004. 1499–1505, 1561–1562.

*Key Word Study Bible, New International Version*. Chattanooga, TN: AMG International, 1996. 584, 627.

*Life Application Study Bible, New International Version*. Wheaton, IL: Tyndale House Publishers, 1997. 764–765, 779, 805, 813, 820.

*Quest Study Bible, New International Version*. Grand Rapids, MI: Zondervan, 2003. 755–756.

## Say It Correctly

Eliphaz. el-ee-**FAHZ**.
Bildad. bill-**DAD**.
Zophar. zoh-**FAR**.
Jemima. dzeh-mee-**MAH**.
Kezia. keh-zee-**AH**.
Kerenhappuch. **KEHR**-ehn-**HAP**-ouk.

## Daily Bible Readings

**MONDAY**
I Wait for You, O Lord
(Psalm 38:9–15)

**TUESDAY**
You Alone Are God
(Psalm 86:1–10)

**WEDNESDAY**
Give Strength to Your Servant
(Psalm 86:11–17)

**THURSDAY**
God Has Called You to Hope
(Ephesians 1:11–19)

**FRIDAY**
My Hope is from God
(Psalm 62:1–8)

**SATURDAY**
You Are the Hope of All
(Psalm 65:1–5)

**SUNDAY**
Wonderful Things I Did Not Know
(Job 42:1–10)

# Notes

# Teaching Tips

## Words You Should Know

**A. Glory** (Ezekiel 43:5) *kavod* (Heb.)— Abundance, splendor, riches, reputation.

**B. Abominations** (v. 8) *to'evah* (Heb.)— Disgusting things in a ritual or ethical sense.

## Teacher Preparation

**Unifying Principle—Seeking a Place of Peace.** People look for a place where they can experience some sense of release and orderliness, away from the chaos that sometimes surrounds them. Where can such a place be found? Ezekiel's vision, given to him by God, reveals to the Israelites that God's calming presence and merciful glory can be felt in sacred places where He is truly worshiped.

**A.** Read the Bible Background and Devotional Readings.

**B.** Complete Lesson 9 in the *Precepts For Living Personal Study Guide*®.

**C.** Reread the Focal Verses in a modern translation.

## O—Open the Lesson

**A.** Open with prayer.

**B.** Have students read Aim for Change in unison.

**C.** Ask for a volunteer to read the In Focus story.

**D.** Discuss how God's presence makes the church gathering sacred.

## P—Present the Scriptures

**A.** Ask for volunteers to read the Focal Verses and The People, Places, and Times. Discuss.

**B.** Read and discuss the Background section.

**C.** Encourage students to give thanks for God's holy and merciful presence.

## E—Explore the Meaning

**A.** Review and discuss Search the Scriptures, the Discuss the Meaning questions, and the Lesson in Our Society section.

**B.** Ask students to share the most significant point they learned and how to use that point this week.

## N—Next Steps for Application

**A.** Complete the Follow the Spirit and Remember Your Thoughts sections.

**B.** Remind students to read the Daily Bible Readings in preparation for next week's lesson.

**C.** Close in prayer, thanking God for His presence in our life.

## Worship Guide

For the Superintendent or Teacher
Theme: God's Divine Glory Returns
Song: "Oh The Glory of Your Presence"
Devotional Reading: Psalm 138

# God's Divine Glory Returns

**Bible Background • EZEKIEL 40:1–43:12**
**Printed Text • EZEKIEL 43:1–12**
**Devotional Reading • PSALM 138**

## ——————— Aim for Change ———————

By the end of the lesson, we will: COMPREHEND the vision of God's holy and merciful glory in the temple; ASSOCIATE a sense of holiness of place with the presence and mercy of God; and GROW in respect for the sacredness of worship settings.

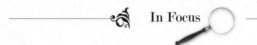

## In Focus

Roger had not been to church in a long time. When he bumped into his childhood friend Pam at the grocery store, he was convicted. She talked about the new pastor and the way that certain people were growing in God. He was even jealous that some of the young people whom he had seen in diapers were now actively serving in the church and passionate for the Lord. In spite of all his career accomplishments and financial wealth, he knew that something was desperately missing in his life. He decided to get back to faithfully attending church starting this Sunday.

He had come to Sunday worship a little early, and no one was around. He saw the empty pews that reminded him of what it was like to be in the service worshiping with the people of God. Roger felt overwhelmed just being there in the silence. As he walked down the center aisle, a surge of emotions came over him as he remembered the days when he was passionately following Jesus. Tears began to well up in his eyes. He knew that this was what he was missing.

*Although God is everywhere, certain places remind us of His presence and encourage us to live holy lives before Him.*

## ——————— Keep in Mind ———————

"So the spirit took me up, and brought me into the inner court; and, behold, the glory of the LORD filled the house" (Ezekiel 43:5).

"So the spirit took me up, and brought me into the inner court; and, behold, the glory of the LORD filled the house" (Ezekiel 43:5).

# Focal Verses

**KJV** **Ezekiel 43:1** Afterward he brought me to the gate, even the gate that looketh toward the east:

**2** And, behold, the glory of the God of Israel came from the way of the east: and his voice was like a noise of many waters: and the earth shined with his glory.

**3** And it was according to the appearance of the vision which I saw, even according to the vision that I saw when I came to destroy the city: and the visions were like the vision that I saw by the river Chebar; and I fell upon my face.

**4** And the glory of the LORD came into the house by the way of the gate whose prospect is toward the east.

**5** So the spirit took me up, and brought me into the inner court; and, behold, the glory of the LORD filled the house.

**6** And I heard him speaking unto me out of the house; and the man stood by me.

**7** And he said unto me, Son of man, the place of my throne, and the place of the soles of my feet, where I will dwell in the midst of the children of Israel for ever, and my holy name, shall the house of Israel no more defile, neither they, nor their kings, by their whoredom, nor by the carcases of their kings in their high places.

**8** In their setting of their threshold by my thresholds, and their post by my posts, and the wall between me and them, they have even defiled my holy name by their abominations that they have committed: wherefore I have consumed them in mine anger.

**9** Now let them put away their whoredom, and the carcases of their kings, far from me, and I will dwell in the midst of them for ever.

**10** Thou son of man, shew the house to the house of Israel, that they may be ashamed

**NLT** **Ezekiel 43:1** After this, the man brought me back around to the east gateway.

**2** Suddenly, the glory of the God of Israel appeared from the east. The sound of his coming was like the roar of rushing waters, and the whole landscape shone with his glory.

**3** This vision was just like the others I had seen, first by the Kebar River and then when he came to destroy Jerusalem. I fell face down on the ground.

**4** And the glory of the LORD came into the Temple through the east gateway.

**5** Then the Spirit took me up and brought me into the inner courtyard, and the glory of the LORD filled the Temple.

**6** And I heard someone speaking to me from within the Temple, while the man who had been measuring stood beside me.

**7** The LORD said to me, "Son of man, this is the place of my throne and the place where I will rest my feet. I will live here forever among the people of Israel. They and their kings will not defile my holy name any longer by their adulterous worship of other gods or by honoring the relics of their kings who have died.

**8** They put their idol altars right next to mine with only a wall between them and me. They defiled my holy name by such detestable sin, so I consumed them in my anger.

**9** Now let them stop worshiping other gods and honoring the relics of their kings, and I will live among them forever.

**10** Son of man, describe to the people of Israel the Temple I have shown you, so they will be ashamed of all their sins. Let them study its plan,

**11** and they will be ashamed of what they have done. Describe to them all the specifica-

of their iniquities: and let them measure the pattern.

**11** And if they be ashamed of all that they have done, shew them the form of the house, and the fashion thereof, and the goings out thereof, and the comings in thereof, and all the forms thereof, and all the ordinances thereof, and all the forms thereof, and all the laws thereof: and write it in their sight, that they may keep the whole form thereof, and all the ordinances thereof, and do them.

**12** This is the law of the house; Upon the top of the mountain the whole limit thereof round about shall be most holy. Behold, this is the law of the house.

tions of the Temple—including its entrances and exits—and everything else about it. Tell them about its decrees and laws. Write down all these specifications and decrees as they watch so they will be sure to remember and follow them.

**12** And this is the basic law of the Temple: absolute holiness! The entire top of the mountain where the Temple is built is holy. Yes, this is the basic law of the Temple.

## The People, Places, and Times

**Inner Court.** The inner court was a separate area in the temple reserved only for the priests. This separate area contained ten golden lampstands. It also contained a table for the shewbread, which was constantly on display and replaced every Sabbath. An altar of incense stood in the inner court before the entrance into the Holy of Holies, where the glory of the Lord was manifested. As a member of the priesthood, Ezekiel was qualified to have access to this area of the temple (1:2).

**The River Chebar.** The Chebar was a river that ran through the land of the Chaldeans. Many of the captive Jews settled here. Many believe that the Chebar was the royal canal of Nebuchadnezzar that joined the Tigris and Euphrates. Ezekiel sat here among the captives and received many of his visions and prophetic words at this location (1:1–3).

## Background

During the final section of the book of Ezekiel, there is a special focus on the coming restored temple. These visionary narratives provide a glimpse of God's plans for His land and His people. Here we can see Ezekiel's priestly concerns and knowledge come into play. The temple was described in architectural terms in the previous chapters and as such it is empty and lifeless. Now the glory of God came to the temple. As a result, the temple was full of life. Ezekiel then begins to talk of what that means for those who serve and worship in the temple. Since the glory of God is now present in the temple, its worshipers must be holy. It must not continue to be business as usual. As a priest, Ezekiel stressed the holiness that is required by God and the putting away of all things that would defile the temple.

## At-A-Glance

1. The Return of the Glory (Ezekiel 43:1–5)
2. Return to the Glory (vv. 6–9)
3. The Requirements for the Glory (vv. 10–12)

## In Depth

### 1. The Return of the Glory (Ezekiel 43:1–5)

After describing the measurements and the physical description of the temple, Ezekiel is brought to the gate of the east. There he has a vision of the glory of the Lord with both an aural component (the "noise of many waters") and a visual component ("the earth shined with his glory"). He notices that this vision is similar to the ones in previous chapters where the Lord called him to destroy the city (Ezekiel 9:5–11) and the one that he received at the river Chebar (Ezekiel 1–3). The Spirit takes Ezekiel up into the inner court of the temple, and he observes that the glory of the Lord fills the house.

This is the return of God's glory to the temple. It is important to note that without the glory of God, the temple is just another building. The glory of God animates it and gives it life. Ezekiel recognizes this and falls on his face. The proper response to experiencing the glory of God is authentic worship. Notice that Ezekiel didn't sing a song or begin to preach. He fell on his face because it was God who was there and took center attention.

### 2. Return to the Glory (vv. 6–9)

Next, as Ezekiel is face down in submission to God and His glory, God speaks to him. He lets Ezekiel know that the temple must not be defiled by Israel anymore. He refers to Israel's past actions and the abominations that they committed in the temple. They must treat the glory of God with reverence. It is not enough that God's glory has returned to them; they also must return to Him. They must put away their whoredom and the carcasses or memorials of their kings. This word is not just for the common people of Israel but also her kings and leaders. What

God is saying in these verses is that He will not share His glory with anyone else. He will not be worshiped alongside other man-made gods, whether they are statues or men.

God's glory would return to the temple, but Israel needed to return to Him. Without His glory, they would be just like the temple in the absence of His glory—a lifeless shell. God promises them that if they would return to Him by putting away these abominations, then He would dwell with them forever. This is God's desire and plan, and this is the true reason the temple is to be rebuilt. God wants to be with His people in a life-giving and sustaining way!

### 3. The Requirements for the Glory (vv. 10–12)

Ezekiel is now commanded to show the temple or "house" to the "house of Israel," so that they would be ashamed of their sins and the things that they have done to defile God's name. Ezekiel is instructed to show them the pattern of the house. The Lord says that if they see the pattern and are ashamed of their sins, then he is to show them all the measurements and architectural design of the temple. He is to show them the decorations and the ritual acts that are to be performed in the temple. This is what they are to do in order to maintain the presence of God's glory in the temple.

God also says that there is one major requirement or law from which all other requirements are derived: the law of holiness. The Lord lets Ezekiel know that the temple and the mountain that it sits on are to be holy. This means that the people are to be holy in their behavior and actions. Both the place where the Lord's glory rests and the people who are blessed to have His presence among them are to be holy. Holiness is required to experience the glory of God.

## Search the Scriptures

1. What was Ezekiel's reaction to seeing the glory of the Lord (Ezekiel 43:3)?

2. What did the Lord ask the children of Israel to remove and put away (v. 9)?

## Discuss the Meaning

1. In what ways can we as God's people defile His name in the 21st century?

2. How can we experience the glory of the Lord today?

## Lesson in Our Society

Our society has lost the sense of the sacred. Most people live as if everything is banal and trivial. This type of attitude has even spread to the church. Our worship of God sometimes can be dull and lifeless and treated as something that is man-made and common. God's presence is always near when His people gather. His glory is meant to be experienced in these settings. The attitude of sacredness and sensitivity to the presence of God ought to permeate our gatherings and continue with us once we go our separate ways. God is a holy God and deserves to be treated as such.

## Make It Happen

How can you grow in respect for the sacredness of worship settings? One of the ways you can do this is to begin to pray when you step through the doors of your church. Say a prayer to calm your heart and focus your mind on God. In this way you can remind yourself of the reason you are there and go in with a desire to experience the glory of God and to worship Him.

## Follow the Spirit

What God wants me to do:

_____

_____

_____

_____

_____

## Remember Your Thoughts

Special insights I have learned:

_____

_____

_____

_____

_____

## More Light on the Text

**Ezekiel 43:1–12**

Just as God showed the Apostle John a revelation of the future in a vision, which included the New Jerusalem (Revelation 21:2), so he permitted Ezekiel a similar partial vision of the new temple (begun in Ezekiel 40). The whole purpose of the restored temple would be to receive God's glory, which would arrive from the east. This coming glorious event would perfectly reverse Ezekiel's prior vision of the glory departing toward the east (10:1–22; 11:22–25).

**1 Afterward he brought me to the gate, even the gate that looketh toward the east: 2 And, behold, the glory of the God of Israel came from the way of the east: and his voice was like a noise of many waters: and the earth shined with his glory.**

God's actions and symbols are never accidental, and the emphasis here on the east is significant for several reasons in addition to the prophetic context. This is the direction to which God's presence departed in Ezekiel 11:23. The sun rises in the east, so God's glory followed the path of the rising sun as it cast its light on the temple. Entering the east gate led directly to the main entrance to the temple, which was a direct path to the Holy of Holies. Directly to the east of the temple mount is the Mount of Olives and the Garden of Gethsemane, both of which have momentous biblical significance, including both Jesus' agony (Matthew 26:36–39) and His parting ascension (Acts 1:9–12). This gate is also the one into which Jesus rode on a donkey on Palm Sunday (Mark 11:1–11)—another example of God's incarnate glory entering the temple from the east. The word for east in Hebrew (*kadim,* **kah-DEEM**) also means first or at the beginning, indicating that God's glory has existed since the beginning and is primal (first and fundamental).

**3 And it was according to the appearance of the vision which I saw, even according to the vision that I saw when I came to destroy the city: and the visions were like the vision that I saw by the river Chebar; and I fell upon my face. 4 And the glory of the LORD came into the house by the way of the gate whose prospect is toward the east. 5 So the spirit took me up, and brought me into the inner court; and, behold, the glory of the LORD filled the house.**

Ezekiel had two prior experiences with God's glory: 1) he saw in a vision the destruction of Jerusalem when the glory left, moving toward the east (10:1–22; 11:22–25), and 2) he saw a vision of the glory when he was called to the ministry of prophecy by the river Chebar (Kebar River, NLT), where the glory had come from the north (1:25–3:15). Nothing could be more natural

than to fall prostrate before such brilliant radiance (cf. 1:28).

Since Ezekiel witnessed the glory departing, it was altogether fitting that he is given a preview of its return. For Old Testament believers, the glory of the Lord was a tangible reality that wasn't witnessed often, but whenever it appeared, it was unforgettable and beyond description. Numerous Scriptures attempt to capture it, e.g., Psalm 24:9–10, which seems appropriate for Ezekiel's vision: "Lift up your heads, O ye gates; even lift them up, ye everlasting doors; and the King of glory shall come in. Who is this King of glory? The LORD of hosts, he is the King of glory."

For New Testament believers, God's glory is usually an intangible concept but we are not without examples of New Testament references to His tangible glory, e.g., "who [is] the brightness of his glory, and the express image of his person" (Hebrews 1:3), among others from the beginning to the end of the New Testament (cf. Matthew 1:23; Revelation 21:23). One would be correct to say that in the Christian era, Jesus' veil of humanity was removed momentarily during His transfiguration, revealing the glory of God (Matthew 17:2).

**6 And I heard him speaking unto me out of the house; and the man stood by me. 7 And he said unto me, Son of man, the place of my throne, and the place of the soles of my feet, where I will dwell in the midst of the children of Israel for ever, and my holy name, shall the house of Israel no more defile, neither they, nor their kings, by their whoredom, nor by the carcases of their kings in their high places.**

Even in a vision, Ezekiel does not behold God directly, but rather he hears Him from within the Holy of Holies; His glory makes it beyond man's ability to perceive Him directly. Although God dwells in heaven and earth cannot contain Him, still He chooses to dwell on earth. Isaiah 66:1 captures the balance, "Thus saith the LORD, The heaven is my throne, and the earth is my footstool: where is the house that ye build unto me? and where is the place of my rest?" (cf. "throne" in Jeremiah 3:17, 17:12, with "footstool" in Psalm 99:5, 132:7). In this speech, God dedicates the restored temple Himself, essentially saying that the soles of His feet are on the same ground as the soles of mankind. The difference is that wherever God chooses to make His earthly habitation must be holy and sacred.

The word "dwell" in Hebrew is *shakhan* (**shah-KHAN**), which means "reside," "inhabit," or "rest" and is the root of the word "Shekinah" (which does not appear in Scripture), referring to the glory of God that appeared in a cloud to guide the Israelites (Exodus 16:10). This cloud also appeared to Moses on Mount Sinai (Exodus 24:16–17, 33:22) and filled the tabernacle in the wilderness when it was finished (Exodus 40:34–38). It also filled Solomon's temple on the day of its dedication (1 Kings 8:10–11). Interestingly, the Hebrew for tabernacle, *mishkan* (**mish-KAHN**), also comes from the same root. Some theologians connect this dwelling or settling of the divine presence with the New Testament use of the Greek *parousia* (**par-oo-SEE-ah**), which means "presence" or "coming" (cf. 2 Thessalonians 2:8; 2 Peter 1:16).

The Lord's speech reassures the Ezekiel declaring that His return is permanent, which provides hope not only for Ezekiel but for the captives in Babylon. From the beginning, God's presence marked and accompanied every move of the nation of Israel, and by itself distinguished Israel from all other nations, and her God from all other gods. Israel was not complete without God's presence, and now it not only will return, but this time it will be home "forever."

**8 In their setting of their threshold by my thresholds, and their post by my posts, and the wall between me and them, they have even defiled my holy name by their abominations that they have committed: wherefore I have consumed them in mine anger.**

God reminds Ezekiel why His presence had departed from the people: because of their cumulative and collective sins, represented by their spiritual "whoredom" (v. 7), which is another word for idolatry. This is illustrated by the temple example. The corruption of the temple was a sign of the overall moral corruption of the nation. Apparently, the temple authorities had permitted either actual burials of deceased kings on the temple mound or had erected memorials to them, neither of which glorified the living God, the King of glory, in what was supposed to be His sacred temple. Instead they had defiled (Heb. *tame'*, **tah-MAY**) or profaned God's name and treated it with disrespect. The notion that only the thickness of a wall or the threshold (Heb. *saf*, **SAHF**) or timber that lies under a door separated such profane things from God's exalted sacred place was an abomination against God's holiness. It was complete and total disobedience to do this on the sacred temple grounds. Ezekiel points out the Lord's consuming of the nation due to these grave sins.

**9 Now let them put away their whoredom, and the carcases of their kings, far from me, and I will dwell in the midst of them for ever. 10 Thou son of man, shew the house to the house of Israel, that they may be ashamed of their iniquities: and let them measure the pattern.**

The prophet's message is continued even beyond the time of the prophets and even into our current day and age. The message of the prophets has taken similar forms throughout the history of faith, but the theme barely varies—turn from the death of evil and turn to the life of God; put sin out of your heart and purify your temple so God may dwell within you—culminating in today's ultra-succinct Gospel in a nutshell, "repent and be saved."

The temple is God's symbolic dwelling. It is His earthly residence, which is not to be defiled in any way. It is the ultimate paradox that the infinite, uncontainable God chooses to be present among mortal, finite humanity—a paradox perfectly embodied in the life of Jesus Christ: "who is the image of the invisible God" (from Colossians 1:15). This same paradox creates the ultimate tension in humanity—at any given time, how much is the profane rejected and the glory of the sacred presence welcome in our hearts? God wants to be King over all and will share His glory with no one else.

The use of the word "ashamed" as the purpose of the vision stands in stark contrast to modern thinking that tends to avoid the subject at all costs. Yet shame, like guilt or fear, can be a valuable emotion if it leads one to transformation—much like the sensation of burning helpfully teaches one to withdraw from or avoid things that burn. Only from within the healthy experience of shame in confessing one's sins can one truly repent and thus fully experience God's mercy and grace.

**11 And if they be ashamed of all that they have done, shew them the form of the house, and the fashion thereof, and the goings out thereof, and the comings in thereof, and all the forms thereof, and all the ordinances thereof, and all the forms thereof, and all the laws thereof: and write it in their sight, that they may keep the whole form thereof, and all the ordinances thereof, and do them. 12 This is the law of the house; Upon the top of the mountain the whole limit thereof round about shall be most holy. Behold, this is the law of the house.**

The ultimate disaster for Israel was the Lord's departure. Even captivity by her enemies did not compare to His absence. Conversely, the ultimate blessing for Israel would be His permanent return. The element on which both departure and return hinged was Israel's faithlessness or her faithfulness. As a result, it is not enough that the people be aware of God's return. They must know everything involved with the temple, including its design (both exits and entrances) and the laws and teachings associated it, which refer to the instructions originally laid out through Moses. Just as Jesus came not to destroy the law and the prophets but to fulfill them (Matthew 5:17), so Ezekiel promises that God will restore the blessings associated with Him originally through Moses (both His presence and worship of Him). Ezekiel was exhorted to deliver the message of hope both orally and in hard copy. One can only imagine the depth of meaning and significance that his vision would have brought for the languishing exiles. Many today are in self-imposed exile, imprisoned by their own bondages, and held in bondage by their addictions and profane habits. Not so different from the people of Ezekiel's time, they are in desperate need of the hope of God's glory entering their temple and evicting their darkness and sin. By receiving Him, they experience the sacred place of God's glorious presence within their hearts.

## Summary

Ezekiel's vision of hope for exiled Israel could also be compared to Martin Luther King Jr.'s vision for a racially torn America, which he cast for a downtrodden people who desperately needed to be infused with hope for the future. Just as Ezekiel's vision superseded his people and his time, so King's "I Have a Dream" speech also was a timeless message and vision for all humanity, for any who could see with new eyes the difference that a holy God could make in an evil world. Perhaps King had Solomon's words in mind that "where there is no vision, the people perish" (Proverbs 29:18).

Sources:
Allen, Leslie C., ed. *Word Biblical Commentary: Ezekiel 20–48.* Dallas, TX: Word Book Publishers, 1990.
Barlow, Rev. George. *The Preacher's Homiletic Commentary: Lamentations and Ezekiel.* Grand Rapids, MI: Baker Books, reprint 1996.
Blenkinsopp, Joseph. *Ezekiel. Interpretation: A Bible Commentary for Teaching and Preaching.* Louisville: John Knox Press, 1990. 210–216.
Bryant, T. Alton, ed. *The New Compact Bible Dictionary.* Grand Rapids, MI: Zondervan, 1967.
Cooper, Lamar Eugene, Sr. *Ezekiel.* The New American Commentary, vol. 17. Nashville, TN: Broadman and Holman Publishers, 1994. 374–390.
Craigie, Peter C. *Ezekiel.* Louisville, KY: Westminster John Knox Press, 1983. 286–293.
Duguid, Iain M. *Ezekiel. The NIV Application Commentary.* Grand Rapids, MI: Zondervan, 1999. 487–497.
Jensen, Robert W. *Ezekiel.* Brazos Theological Commentary on the Bible. Grand Rapids, MI: Brazos Press, 2009. 305–312.
Strong, James. *The New Strong's Exhaustive Concordance of the Bible.* Nashville, TN: Thomas Nelson Publishers, 1990.
Wright, Christopher J. H. *The Message of Ezekiel: A New Heart and a New Spirit.* Downers Grove, IL: InterVarsity Press, 2001. 333–348.

## Say It Correctly

Chebar. keh-**VAR**.
Shekinah. sheh-kee-**NAW**.

## Daily Bible Readings

**MONDAY**
God's Glory and Greatness
(Deuteronomy 5:23–29)

**TUESDAY**
God's Exalted Name
(Psalm 138)

**WEDNESDAY**
Standing on Holy Ground
(Exodus 3:1–6)

**THURSDAY**
God's Holy Place
(Psalm 24)

**FRIDAY**
Worshiping in Awe
(Psalm 5)

**SATURDAY**
God Examines Humankind
(Psalm 11)

**SUNDAY**
God's Glory Returns to the Temple
(Ezekiel 43:1–12)

# Teaching Tips

## Words You Should Know
**A. Horns** (Ezekiel 43:15, 20) *keren* (Heb.)—Projections from the altar.

**B. Bullock** (vv. 19, 21) *par* (Heb.)—A young bull or steer.

## Teacher Preparation
**Unifying Principle—Relishing Special Places.** Sometimes people seek space in which they can find direction for making the most of life. Where can such space be found? The Israelites can hope for release from their iniquities by making sin sacrifices in the sacred space of the altar that stood before the temple.

**A.** Read the Bible Background and Devotional Readings.

**B.** Complete Lesson 10 in the *Precepts For Living Personal Study Guide®*.

**C.** Reread the Focal Verses in a modern translation.

## O—Open the Lesson
**A.** Open with prayer.

**B.** Have students read Aim for Change in unison.

**C.** Ask for a volunteer to read the In Focus story.

**D.** Discuss what it means to have a sacred space.

## P—Present the Scriptures
**A.** Ask for volunteers to read the Focal Verses and The People, Places, and Times. Discuss.

**B.** Read and discuss the Background section.

**C.** Encourage students to give thanks for the sacred space God has given us in Jesus Christ.

## E—Explore the Meaning
**A.** Review and discuss Search the Scriptures, the Discuss the Meaning questions, and the Lesson in Our Society section.

**B.** Ask students to share the most significant point they learned and how to use that point this week.

## N—Next Steps for Application
**A.** Complete the Follow the Spirit and Remember Your Thoughts sections.

**B.** Remind students to read the Daily Bible Readings in preparation for next week's lesson.

**C.** Close in prayer, thanking God for His atonement and renewal of our lives.

## Worship Guide

For the Superintendent or Teacher
Theme: The Altar, A Sign of Hope
Song: "Is Your All on the Altar?"
Devotional Reading: Psalm
130:1–131:3

# The Altar, A Sign of Hope

**Bible Background • EZEKIEL 43:10–46:24**
**Printed Text • EZEKIEL 43:13–21**
**Devotional Reading • PSALM 130:1–131:3**

## Aim for Change

By the end of this lesson, we will: REVIEW the instructions Ezekiel received for building a new altar and making offerings; REFLECT on the value of finding personal sacred spaces for atonement and renewal; and IDENTIFY and USE personal sacred spaces for atonement and renewal.

 In Focus

The retreat was almost over and RaShaunda was a little anxious. Everyone seemed to be having these amazing experiences during the nightly gatherings. It seemed as if God had a special message for each person—except her. She was becoming a little frustrated.

People were talking about the new direction that God had given them and how their issues were being resolved, and she felt left out. Some had even said they were going to give their lives to the ministry or to serving overseas in missions. RaShaunda heard the words of the speakers, but she felt like something was missing. It all sounded the same to her. She longed for God to speak directly into her life. She had spent $200 to be here for a whole week without her comfy mattress and other luxuries. As the last speaker was talking, he began to share how we needed to create space and time for God to speak to us and how He is not silent, but we often are not listening. RaShaunda felt convicted and walked out of the room to a quiet place surrounded by trees next to the main meeting hall. There she knelt in prayer and confession. This had now become holy ground.

*We often need to find personal space for reflecting on and renewing our relationship with God.*

## Keep in Mind

"And when these days are expired, it shall be, that upon the eighth day, and so forward, the priests shall make your burnt offerings upon the altar, and your peace offerings; and I will accept you, saith the Lord GOD" (Ezekiel 43:27).

"And when these days are expired, it shall be, that upon the eighth day, and so forward, the priests shall make your burnt offerings upon the altar, and your peace offerings; and I will accept you, saith the Lord GOD" (Ezekiel 43:27).

117

## Focal Verses

**KJV** **Ezekiel 43:13** And these are the measures of the altar after the cubits: The cubit is a cubit and an hand breadth; even the bottom shall be a cubit, and the breadth a cubit, and the border thereof by the edge thereof round about shall be a span: and this shall be the higher place of the altar.

**14** And from the bottom upon the ground even to the lower settle shall be two cubits, and the breadth one cubit; and from the lesser settle even to the greater settle shall be four cubits, and the breadth one cubit.

**15** So the altar shall be four cubits; and from the altar and upward shall be four horns.

**16** And the altar shall be twelve cubits long, twelve broad, square in the four squares thereof.

**17** And the settle shall be fourteen cubits long and fourteen broad in the four squares thereof; and the border about it shall be half a cubit; and the bottom thereof shall be a cubit about; and his stairs shall look toward the east.

**18** And he said unto me, Son of man, thus saith the Lord GOD; These are the ordinances of the altar in the day when they shall make it, to offer burnt offerings thereon, and to sprinkle blood thereon.

**19** And thou shalt give to the priests the Levites that be of the seed of Zadok, which approach unto me, to minister unto me, saith the Lord GOD, a young bullock for a sin offering.

**20** And thou shalt take of the blood thereof, and put it on the four horns of it, and on the four corners of the settle, and upon the border round about: thus shalt thou cleanse and purge it.

**NLT** **Ezekiel 43:13** "These are the measurements of the altar: There is a gutter all around the altar 21 inches deep and 21 inches wide, with a curb 9 inches wide around its edge. And this is the height of the altar:

**14** From the gutter the altar rises 3 1/2 feet to a lower ledge that surrounds the altar and is 21 inches wide. From the lower ledge the altar rises 7 feet to the upper ledge that is also 21 inches wide.

**15** The top of the altar, the hearth, rises another 7 feet higher, with a horn rising up from each of the four corners.

**16** The top of the altar is square, measuring 21 feet by 21 feet.

**17** The upper ledge also forms a square, measuring 24 1/2 feet by 24 1/2 feet, with a 21-inch gutter and a 10 1/2-inch curb all around the edge. There are steps going up the east side of the altar."

**18** Then he said to me, "Son of man, this is what the Sovereign LORD says: These will be the regulations for the burning of offerings and the sprinkling of blood when the altar is built.

**19** At that time, the Levitical priests of the family of Zadok, who minister before me, are to be given a young bull for a sin offering, says the Sovereign LORD.

**20** You will take some of its blood and smear it on the four horns of the altar, the four corners of the upper ledge, and the curb that runs around that ledge. This will cleanse and make atonement for the altar.

**21** Then take the young bull for the sin offering and burn it at the appointed place outside the Temple area.

**21** Thou shalt take the bullock also of the sin offering, and he shall burn it in the appointed place of the house, without the sanctuary.

---

## The People, Places, and Times

**Altar.** An altar is a place where sacrifices can be made. It was an object that assisted in worship in ancient Near Eastern culture. Two types of altars can be found in the Bible. One type of altar was made of earth or unhewn stones piled up into a heap. This type of altar was mostly used by God's people during pre-Mosaic times and was readily available for the average worshiper. The second kind of altar was one made of metal or hewn stone and had horns attached to it. This type of altar could be found in the temple and only the Levitical priests could make sacrifices on these.

**Sin Offering.** A sin offering was an expiatory sacrifice to cleanse from sin. Various animals were used depending on the status of the worshiper. The priest or the whole community used a young bullock (Leviticus 4:3–12). A male goat was used for an Israelite ruler (4:22–26). The common person would use a lamb or female goat, while a poorer person would use two turtledoves (4:27–5:13). The animal was killed, and the blood was sprinkled over the altar. Sin offerings were made for unintentional sins that if done consciously or willingly would have caused someone to be executed.

**Cubits, Handbreadths, Spans.** A cubit was the length from the elbow to the tip of the middle finger. A span was a measurement of half a cubit or the distance between a thumb and the little finger on an outstretched hand. A handbreadth was the distance between the index finger and the little finger. All of these measurements are approximate.

## Background

Ezekiel's vision of a future temple is described beginning in Ezekiel 40. This future temple would be the ideal place for the worship of God. Ezekiel described the general architectural design and measurements of the temple. Once he described this, he was approached by a heavenly messenger who took him toward the East Gate. Here Ezekiel witnessed the return of the glory of the Lord. As he saw the shining presence of God, he immediately fell down prostrate in worship and submission. Then the heavenly messenger spoke to him regarding the holiness of the temple. Based on this, Israel was called on to repent of their sins and remove anything that would defile the temple. Finally, the basic law of the temple is given: holiness.

## At-A-Glance

1. The Details of the Altar Offer Hope
(Ezekiel 43:13–18)
2. The Priests of the Altar Offer Hope
(vv. 18–19)
3. The Sacrifice on the Altar Offers
Hope (vv. 20–21)

## In Depth

**1. The Details of the Altar Offer Hope (Ezekiel 43:13–18)**

Ezekiel communicates the precise measurements of the altar. The altar is specifically designed for the sacrificial offerings and also for symbolic teaching on the nature and ways of God. Ezekiel gives the measurements of the altar. Three things can be observed concerning the construction and measurements of the altar for the future temple. The first thing that we notice is the "bottom" or gutter, which was a sump for catching the sacrificial blood (v. 17, Leviticus 4:7). The third thing is that the priest who performs the sacrifices approaches it on stairs that faced east (v. 17).

Both of these things symbolize the holiness of God and the holiness that God requires of His people. The sump was put there to cleanse the court of blood. The inner court was to be holy and free from all defilement. This sump would remove the leftover sacrificial blood which was considered holy. Due to its sacredness this blood was to be used for no other purpose and would defile any common person or thing it came into contact with. It was definitely a reminder that this was sacred space. The stairs facing east would ensure that the priest approached the Lord facing the Holy of Holies and not toward the sun. Facing the sun was a prominent feature of worship in many idolatrous cultures of the time. These small details let Israel know that the worship of God is a holy thing and something not to be taken lightly.

## 2. The Priests of the Altar Offer Hope (vv. 18–19)

Ezekiel's vision then describes the type of priests who will minister at the altar. The priests will come from the line of Zadok. Zadok was the joint high priest during David's reign and the high priest during the reign of Solomon. When Abiathar the high priest conspired against Solomon, he was put into retirement and Zadok was made sole high priest because of his loyalty to the king. Choosing priests from the line of Zadok points to the desire for a righteous high priest. In fact, in Hebrew, Zadok's name is from the same root as the word for righteousness (*tsedeq*, **TSEH-dehk**). As believers we have a righteous High Priest who is sin-

less: Jesus Christ. He has access and authority with God the Father because of His righteousness. Just like the priests in Ezekiel's vision, He can approach God and minister to Him on our behalf (v. 19, cf. Hebrews 5:1–2).

## 3. The Sacrifice on the Altar Offers Hope (vv. 20–21)

The priests were charged with presenting a sin offering to God for the people. This sin offering was to be a young bullock or male steer. As a sin offering it would be offered to God for the unwilling and unconscious sins of the people. It would be the first step in dedicating the altar and making it holy to God. The blood of the sacrifice would be sprinkled on corners of the altar and on the horns of the altar. The rest of the animal would be taken outside of the sanctuary and burned.

We can see in these verses that the altar is a symbol of hope for the Children of Israel and for us. Dedicating the altar to the service of God represents renewed closeness to God for His people. The altar, the sacrifice, and as stated earlier, the high priest are symbols of Christ. The altar symbolizes Christ because, in order to get to the Holy of Holies where God dwells, one must pass by the altar. The only way to get to God is through Jesus Christ. The sacrifice is also a symbol of Christ as He is our sin offering and cleanses us from sin that we consciously or unconsciously commit. The high priest symbolizes Christ because He is righteous and represents the people before God. Christ is our High Priest who represents us before the Father. In this way, the altar symbolizes our hope in Christ.

## Search the Scriptures

1. What was the reason the altar's stairs were designed to face east (Ezekiel 43:17)?

2. What was the purpose of the sin offering (v. 20)?

## Discuss the Meaning

1. In what ways can we create sacred space to honor God?

2. How does Christ as our sin offering give us hope?

## Lesson in Our Society

Many in our society long for a place where they can go to find peace and refreshment. Our 24/7 busy world is yearning for a sacred space to keep out the noise and pollution of life. Constant attention to technology, overwhelming workloads, and endless recreational distractions make it hard to carve out space for God. As believers, we can always go to Christ in prayer and worship. He is our sacred space and an altar that brings us near to God.

## Make It Happen

Many times in our lives we experience a need for atonement and renewal. There are many ways that we can go about setting apart space and time for this. Try taking a personal retreat for a day. We can also make special appointments with God to praise and thank Him, even if only for a moment. We can use our time before work or going to bed for prayer, praise, and confession.

## Follow the Spirit

What God wants me to do:

## Remember Your Thoughts

Special insights I have learned:

## More Light on the Text

### Ezekiel 43:13–21

Sinful humanity needs a mediator to commune with a holy God and a place for that mediation to take place. In Old Testament times, that place was a physical altar of sacrifice; in New Testament times, that place was a symbolic altar of sacrifice within one's heart, made possible by Jesus' ultimate sacrifice. The altar of Ezekiel's visionary temple points toward the altar set up outside Jerusalem, the cross. This vision from the ancient prophet spans the two testaments and reaches into the future to offer a view of things to come, and also fulfills things begun in the past. In the immediate context, exiles soon would be returning home to rebuild the temple and reinstate the sacrificial system. In the future, prophetic context, the passage is the shadow of the substance and reality of Jesus. This theme continues to the church age, where God's dwelling place and temple became the body of Christ, and look toward the time when God dwells in His new creation.

The subject of altars is rich with symbolism, ritual, and meaning for believers throughout history. In God's house, the altar was the hearth, a place of fire—which is a symbol for His presence in various capacities. Altars are also connected with and symbolic of places where the ritual of purification meets God's mercy and grace. Altars are places that connect the profane with the sacred, and they are places where sacrifices are considered to be gifts and prayers. This is a place, whether physical or spiritual, to seek God and to be found by Him.

**13 And these are the measures of the altar after the cubits: The cubit is a cubit and an hand breadth; even the bottom shall be a cubit, and the breadth a cubit, and the border thereof by the edge thereof round about shall be a span: and this shall be the higher place of the altar. 14 And from the bottom upon the ground even to the lower settle shall be two cubits, and the breadth one cubit; and from the lesser settle even to the greater settle shall be four cubits, and the breadth one cubit. 15 So the altar shall be four cubits; and from the altar and upward shall be four horns. 16 And the altar shall be twelve cubits long, twelve broad, square in the four squares thereof. 17 And the settle shall be fourteen cubits long and fourteen broad in the four squares thereof; and the border about it shall be half a cubit; and the bottom thereof shall be a cubit about; and his stairs shall look toward the east.**

Many have interpreted the modern equivalent of an ancient "long" cubit (cf. 40:5) to translate the physical description of the altar shown to Ezekiel—ranging 24–32 square feet at the base, and ranging 10–16 feet in height. According to some, a cubit is the distance from the elbow to the fingertips plus a hand-breadth, and the handspan—inexact at best. Scholars collectively agree, however, that it is a large altar, four times larger than the one in the wilderness tabernacle (Exodus 27:1–8), and on par with the bronze al-

tar in Solomon's temple (2 Chronicles 4:1). Ezekiel includes instructions on the "settle" (Heb. *'azarah*, **ah-ZAH-rah**), the place where the priests would stand and assist the high priest as he made the various sacrifices. Also, the simple construction—four layers of progressively smaller squares with a stairway facing east and horns at each of the four corners at the top—belies the divine intent and symbolism.

Throughout Israel's history, even proper sacrifices were meaningless without a proper attitude and lifestyle that was congruent with the ritual. Various prophets address this core truth: Amos forever and poetically captures the concept (Amos 5:21–24, especially v. 24); Isaiah writes about offerings made in vain (Isaiah 1:12–17); Micah makes a memorable statement similar to the classic passage in Amos (Micah 6:6–8, especially v. 8); and David also writes many memorable and often-quoted words on the subject (e.g., Psalm 51:16–17). In the New Testament, Paul continues the unabated theme of offering one's body, i.e. life, as a spiritual worship (Romans 12:1); and Peter echoes a similar thought to offer spiritual sacrifices that are acceptable to God (1 Peter 2:5).

**18 And he said unto me, Son of man, thus saith the Lord GOD; These are the ordinances of the altar in the day when they shall make it, to offer burnt offerings thereon, and to sprinkle blood thereon. 19 And thou shalt give to the priests the Levites that be of the seed of Zadok, which approach unto me, to minister unto me, saith the Lord GOD, a young bullock for a sin offering.**

The priests, as well as the altar, were to be consecrated and pure. The purity of the priests was even evident in their bloodline, as they were to be Levites from the seed of Zadok. The seed of Zadok had been loyal to King David and King Solomon, and thus their line continued on to be priests. They were seen as not only loyal to these particular kings but also loyal to God. The priests were also to be set apart through the offering of a young bullock. A sin offering was given for sins that were committed unconsciously. The purity of the priests who would minister at the altar would not be taken for granted. Every measure would be taken to ensure that they remained pure and their sins were atoned for.

**20 And thou shalt take of the blood thereof, and put it on the four horns of it, and on the four corners of the settle, and upon the border round about: thus shalt thou cleanse and purge it. 21 Thou shalt take the bullock also of the sin offering, and he shall burn it in the appointed place of the house, without the sanctuary.**

When speaking of the Hebrew sacrificial system, to "purge" is translated "make atonement" in most versions (Heb. *kafar*, **kah-FAR**) and also means "expiate," "forgive," or "reconcile." Once the sacrificial lifeblood had been used for atonement, the animal had to be burned in another area (cf. Leviticus 8:17)—just as Jesus was put to death outside of the temple (Hebrews 13:11–13). Today, our acceptance into God's presence comes because of Jesus' atoning blood on the Cross, which each of us symbolically sprinkles on the altar of our heart. We, like Ezekiel's people, then are cleansed and forgiven, and God accepts us. In this way, the practice continues as a metaphor for all those who believe in Jesus Christ.

Even in Jesus' day, Jews continued to practice the rituals prescribed by Moses and reinstated by Ezekiel. In fact, Jesus Himself only addresses those who take advantage of observers of the sacrificial laws (Matthew 21:12–

13), and not those who practice these laws. It was not until the temple was destroyed again in A.D. 70 that Jews abandoned the sacrificial system completely. Hebrews states clearly that it was the blood of Jesus, not the blood of animals, that sealed the new covenant (Hebrews 10:1–8; cf. Matthew 26:28), and Ezekiel's vision does not contradict this eternal truth. These systems of worship were created to communicate spiritual truth. All the passages about a kingdom of priests in both the Old and New Testaments finally will have converged, and all the Old Testament typology will have found ultimate fulfillment.

## Summary

The seven days of purification that began just after this portion of the vision (43:25) might seem excessive to today's impatient worshipers, who might complain if a service runs over by seven minutes. Indeed, our drive-through world of convenience stands in sharp contrast to the many biblical exhortations to wait on God (Psalm 25:5; Hosea 12:6), to seek Him diligently (Deuteronomy 4:29), and to worship Him with all of one's heart, soul, mind, and strength (Matthew 22:37). Impatience has no place in God's kingdom, and impatient Christians are the antonym of a humble penitent seeking God's favor, blessing, and presence at the altar of sacrifice. It is this kind of attitude that God accepts.

Sources:
Allen, Leslie C., ed. *Word Biblical Commentary: Ezekiel 20–48.* Dallas, TX: Word Books, 1990.
Barlow, Rev. George. *The Preacher's Homiletic Commentary: Lamentations and Ezekiel.* Grand Rapids, MI: Baker Books, reprint 1996.
Blenkinsopp, Joseph. *Ezekiel. Interpretation: A Bible Commentary for Teaching and Preaching.* Louisville, KY: John Knox Press, 1990. 210–216.
Bryant, T. Alton. *The New Compact Bible Dictionary.* Grand Rapids, MI: Zondervan, 1967.
Cooper, Lamar Eugene, Sr. *Ezekiel.* The New American Commentary, vol. 17. Nashville, TN: Broadman and Holman Publishers, 1994. 374–390.

Duguid, Iain M. *Ezekiel.* The NIV Application Commentary. Grand Rapids, MI: Zondervan, 1999. 487–497.

Strong, James. *The New Strong's Exhaustive Concordance of the Bible.* Nashville, TN: Thomas Nelson Publishers, 1990.

Wright, Christopher J. H. *The Message of Ezekiel: A New Heart and a New Spirit.* Downers Grove, IL: InterVarsity Press, 2001. 333–348.

## Say It Correctly

Zadok. tsaw-**DOKE**.
Abiathar. ab-yaw-**THAR**.

## Daily Bible Readings

**MONDAY**
Quest for a True Altar
(Joshua 22:21–34)

**TUESDAY**
Pulling Down False Altars
(Judges 6:24–32)

**WEDNESDAY**
A Costly Altar and Sacrifice
(2 Samuel 24:17–25)

**THURSDAY**
You, O Lord, Are My Hope
(Psalm 71:1–8)

**FRIDAY**
Hope in the Lord Forevermore
(Psalm 130–131)

**SATURDAY**
I Will Accept You
(Ezekiel 43:22–27)

**SUNDAY**
The Ordinances for the Altar
(Ezekiel 43:13–21)

# Notes

_____

_____

_____

_____

# Teaching Tips

## Words You Should Know

**A. House** (Ezekiel 47:1) *bayit* (Heb.)—Dwelling, temple.

**B. Cubits** (v. 3) *'ammah* (Heb.)—A measure of distance (the forearm), roughly 18 inches.

## Teacher Preparation

**Unifying Principle—Life Needs Water.** Sometimes people feel as if they are stranded on a high cliff and forced to leap into dangerous and unknown waters. Where can they find what they need to make the plunge? The life-giving water in Ezekiel's vision is a symbol of God's presence and blessings, which flow from God's sanctuary and are available to the earth and its people.

**A.** Read the Bible Background and Devotional Readings.

**B.** Complete Lesson 11 in the *Precepts For Living Personal Study Guide®*.

**C.** Reread the Focal Verses in the NLT.

## O—Open the Lesson

**A.** Open with prayer, thanking God for His refreshing and healing grace.

**B.** Have students read Aim for Change.

**C.** Ask for a volunteer to read the In Focus story.

**D.** Discuss how to live by faith and experience God's presence.

## P—Present the Scriptures

**A.** Ask for volunteers to read the Focal Verses and The People, Places, and Times. Discuss.

**B.** Read and discuss the Background section to help the students understand the context of today's lesson.

**C.** Encourage students to ask questions.

## E—Explore the Meaning

**A.** Review and discuss Search the Scriptures, the Discuss the Meaning questions, and the Lesson in Our Society section.

**B.** Ask students to share the most significant point they learned and how to use that point this week.

## N—Next Steps for Application

**A.** Complete the Follow the Spirit and Remember Your Thoughts sections.

**B.** Remind students to read the Daily Bible Readings in preparation for next week.

**C.** Ask if there are any prayer needs, then close in prayer.

## Worship Guide

For the Superintendent or Teacher
Theme: A Transforming Stream
Song: "There's a River of Life
(Flowing Out of Me)"
Devotional Reading: Psalm 1

112

# A Transforming Stream

**Bible Background • EZEKIEL 47:1, 3–12**
**Printed Text • EZEKIEL 47:1, 3–12**
**Devotional Reading • PSALM 1**

──────────────── **Aim for Change** ────────────────

By the end of the lesson, we will: KNOW about Ezekiel's vision of life-giving water; APPRECIATE our covenant with God as an ever-deepening river of blessings; and COMMIT to communing with God daily.

──────── 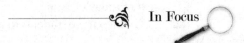 **In Focus** ────────

Sharla awoke abruptly, her heart pounding. She lay still, willing herself to calm down. She was experiencing these anxiety attacks more and more recently, and she knew why. On top of the fact that she and Chris were struggling with their marriage, the bills for Chris's medical issues were piling up. It seemed like every time they thought they were going to get ahead in life, Chris had another medical crisis.

Just yesterday, his boss had warned him that if he missed any more work, he would be out of a job. Sharla thought about how hard it was already to make ends meet, and her heart started to pound again. What would happen to them? Would they lose their home? Would they have to declare bankruptcy?

Finally, she dragged herself out of bed and onto her knees. "God," she prayed, "I don't know what to do. I'm so afraid, and I need Your help." Not knowing what else to pray, she stayed quiet, still kneeling. After a few moments of silence, Sharla began to feel a sense of peace overwhelm her heart. God would provide.

Through God, we can experience peace and provision even in the midst of trouble. *In today's lesson, we learn that God is the source of everything we need.*

──────────────── **Keep in Mind** ────────────────

"And it shall come to pass, that every thing that liveth, which moveth, whithersoever the rivers shall come, shall live: and there shall be a very great multitude of fish, because these waters shall come thither: for they shall be healed; and every thing shall live whither the river cometh" (Ezekiel 47:9).

"And it shall come to pass, that every thing that liveth, which moveth, whithersoever the rivers shall come, shall live: and there shall be a very great multitude of fish, because these waters shall come thither: for they shall be healed; and every thing shall live whither the river cometh" (Ezekiel 47:9).

# Focal Verses

**KJV** **Ezekiel 47:1** Afterward he brought me again unto the door of the house; and, behold, waters issued out from under the threshold of the house eastward: for the forefront of the house stood toward the east, and the waters came down from under from the right side of the house, at the south side of the altar.

**3** And when the man that had the line in his hand went forth eastward, he measured a thousand cubits, and he brought me through the waters; the waters were to the ankles.

**4** Again he measured a thousand, and brought me through the waters; the waters were to the knees. Again he measured a thousand, and brought me through; the waters were to the loins.

**5** Afterward he measured a thousand; and it was a river that I could not pass over: for the waters were risen, waters to swim in, a river that could not be passed over.

**6** And he said unto me, Son of man, hast thou seen this? Then he brought me, and caused me to return to the brink of the river.

**7** Now when I had returned, behold, at the bank of the river were very many trees on the one side and on the other.

**8** Then said he unto me, These waters issue out toward the east country, and go down into the desert, and go into the sea: which being brought forth into the sea, the waters shall be healed.

**9** And it shall come to pass, that every thing that liveth, which moveth, whithersoever the rivers shall come, shall live: and there shall be a very great multitude of fish, because these waters shall come thither: for they shall be healed; and every thing shall live whither the river cometh.

**10** And it shall come to pass, that the fishers shall stand upon it from Engedi even

**NLT** **Ezekiel 47:1** In my vision, the man brought me back to the entrance of the Temple. There I saw a stream flowing east from beneath the door of the Temple and passing to the right of the altar on its south side.

**3** Measuring as he went, he took me along the stream for 1,750 feet and then led me across. The water was up to my ankles.

**4** He measured off another 1,750 feet and led me across again. This time the water was up to my knees. After another 1,750 feet, it was up to my waist.

**5** Then he measured another 1,750 feet, and the river was too deep to walk across. It was deep enough to swim in, but too deep to walk through.

**6** He asked me, "Have you been watching, son of man?" Then he led me back along the riverbank.

**7** When I returned, I was surprised by the sight of many trees growing on both sides of the river.

**8** Then he said to me, "This river flows east through the desert into the valley of the Dead Sea. The waters of this stream will make the salty waters of the Dead Sea fresh and pure.

**9** There will be swarms of living things wherever the water of this river flows. Fish will abound in the Dead Sea, for its waters will become fresh. Life will flourish wherever this water flows.

**10** Fishermen will stand along the shores of the Dead Sea. All the way from En-gedi to En-eglaim, the shores will be covered with nets drying in the sun. Fish of every kind will fill the Dead Sea, just as they fill the Mediterranean.

**11** But the marshes and swamps will not be purified; they will still be salty.

unto Eneglaim; they shall be a place to spread forth nets; their fish shall be according to their kinds, as the fish of the great sea, exceeding many.

11 But the miry places thereof and the marishes thereof shall not be healed; they shall be given to salt.

12 And by the river upon the bank thereof, on this side and on that side, shall grow all trees for meat, whose leaf shall not fade, neither shall the fruit thereof be consumed: it shall bring forth new fruit according to his months, because their waters they issued out of the sanctuary: and the fruit thereof shall be for meat, and the leaf thereof for medicine.

12 Fruit trees of all kinds will grow along both sides of the river. The leaves of these trees will never turn brown and fall, and there will always be fruit on their branches. There will be a new crop every month, for they are watered by the river flowing from the Temple. The fruit will be for food and the leaves for healing."

## The People, Places, and Times

**Ezekiel.** Ezekiel was a prophet of God while the Israelites were in Babylon and was active for twenty-two years. He was born to a priestly family during a time of political upheaval both nationally and within the surrounding kingdoms. Among the Israelites exiled to Babylon, the destruction of the temple in Jerusalem in 587 B.C. occurred during his lifetime.

**Ezekiel's Visions.** Ezekiel's vision of the river is the third major vision in the book of Ezekiel. Visions are, in essence, waking dreams. They were seen by numerous Bible characters including Abraham, Peter, and Paul (Genesis 15; Acts 10; 2 Corinthians 12). Visions contain messages from God concerning the individual experiencing the vision or for the larger community of His people. Most of the time visions contain things that are beyond the scope of what could happen in real life. They are rich with symbolism and usually have to be interpreted in much the same way as dreams. The Lord seemed to communicate to Ezekiel major portions of his prophecy through visions.

## Background

The first three chapters of Ezekiel detail the calling and commissioning of Ezekiel as a prophet of God. The rest of the book of Ezekiel can be divided into three main sections. The first section, chapters 4–24, is prophetic messages of judgment upon Israel and Jerusalem, ending with the prediction of the fall of Jerusalem in chapter 24. The second section, chapters 25–32, is prophetic messages of God's judgment of foreign nations. The third section, chapters 33–48, is predictions of Israel's restoration and redemption, and include details concerning the temple, the sacrificial system, and the rebuilding of Jerusalem. These last chapters also point toward the re-establishment and exaltation of the kingdom of God.

Chapters 1–24 reveal God in the fall of Jerusalem and the ensuing national destruction. Chapters 25–32 teach God's revelation of Himself through His judgments upon the nations, and chapters 33–48 emphasize God's character through the restoration and renewal of Israel—both literally and spiritually.

It is in the context of this last section that Ezekiel receives a multi-part vision of the new temple of God that is to come during the future thousand-year reign of Christ on earth. In today's lesson, we will examine the last part of Ezekiel's "temple tour" where Ezekiel is standing just inside the gate of the temple and sees the river flowing from under the temple.

## At-A-Glance

1. The Rise of the River
(Ezekiel 47:1, 3–6)
2. The Result of the River
(vv. 7–12)

## In Depth

### 1. The Rise of the River (Ezekiel 47:1, 3–6)

Ezekiel's third vision begins as he is standing in the inner court of the new temple in Jerusalem. He sees water coming out from under the temple, flowing from the side of the altar. In Revelation 22:1, we also see "the river of the water of life, as clear as crystal, flowing from the throne of God and of the Lamb" (NIV). It is significant that this river proceeds from where God dwells. God's presence has been associated with water elsewhere in Ezekiel (1:24, 43:2). Likewise, the flow of God's Spirit, through Jesus, brings energizing life and healing to those who will accept Him.

As the river flowed from the temple and over the mountains, instead of eventually waning to a trickle, it gained in depth and strength. Ezekiel, in his vision, waded into the river. It was ankle-deep (v. 3). A little farther downstream, the river was knee-deep, then waist-deep (v. 4). One final check re-vealed that the river was so deep that "no one could cross" (v. 5, NIV).

And so it is with our spiritual life. When we first begin our relationship with God, we wade out ankle-deep. We learn the first things about God. As we begin to mature, we search out the deeper things of God that require some "knee-deep" wading into the river. And then there are some things that we will never fully understand, and we must be content to say with the Apostle Paul, "Oh, the depth of the riches of the wisdom and knowledge of God! How unsearchable his judgments, and his paths beyond tracing out!" (Romans 11:33, NIV). When we are in covenant with God, His river in our lives grows ever deeper as we spend time communing with Him and getting to know Him better.

### 2. The Result of the River (vv. 7–12)

The waters that proceed from God have a healing, restorative effect. Even the lowest, saltiest body of water in the world, the Dead Sea, will be made fresh by the healing river of God (v. 8). In place of this "dead" water where no life can be sustained, there will be "swarms of living creatures" (v. 9, NIV). This signifies great provision for humankind—fishermen will stand along the shore from one end of the country to the other to fill their nets with the abundance of fish (v. 10). Fruit trees of all kinds will bear bountiful crops—a different kind of fruit every month, because "the water from the sanctuary flows to them. Their fruit will serve for food and their leaves for healing" (v. 12, NIV).

How we wish the water of the sanctuary would flow over us—that healing, reviving presence of God in our lives. How we need His grace, His healing, His forgiveness to wash away the stagnant, dead waters of our lives. Only when we bask in His presence and soak up the living water of His words will we become bountifully fruitful servants of God.

Our fruitfulness is not just for us. The fruit we bear is to serve as food to those who are hungry for the Gospel. Our green leaves of revival and purity will be for the healing of others who are sick or wounded. Wash us in Your living water, O God!

## Search the Scriptures

1. Where did Ezekiel's vision of the river begin (Ezekiel 47:1)?

2. Who is guiding Ezekiel through this vision (vv. 1, 3–8)?

3. What was growing on both sides of the river (v. 12)?

## Discuss the Meaning

1. Why is it significant that the wellspring of the river was at the temple? How can we apply this image of the river to our lives?

2. What happened when the river flowed into the Dead Sea? What happens when God's Spirit is allowed to flow unhindered in our lives?

3. Describe the trees that grew along the banks of God's river. What kind of spiritual principle can we learn from these trees?

## Lesson in Our Society

According to scientists, 97 percent of all water on Earth is salty. Another 2 percent of Earth's water is ice, leaving about 1 percent of all water on Earth for human use. Water conservation and pollution are major concerns in our world today, yet this is approximately the same quantity of water that has cycled continuously for centuries. God has blessed all of mankind—both saved and sinner—with the life-giving gift of water.

We've all seen the pleas for help from poverty-stricken countries where people are dying for lack of pure water. God's people

should not be hardened to the plight of these nations, but we should do what we can to help. God calls believers to hold out a cup of cold water to those who are thirsty—both literally and spiritually (cf. Matthew 25:35).

God's living water is available to quench the thirsty souls of those around us. God's well will never run dry; His river will never be dammed up. But it is up to us to lead the lost and dying to the water's Source.

## Make It Happen

What is happening in your life spiritually? Is your stream growing stronger and deeper over time, or is it drying up and becoming stagnant? This week, examine your life. Compare your life today to where you were spiritually a year ago. Are you in ankle-deep? Knee-deep? Ask God for a desire to go deeper into His river and commit to commune with Him daily.

## Follow the Spirit

What God wants me to do:

_____

_____

_____

_____

## Remember Your Thoughts

Special insights I have learned:

_____

_____

_____

_____

_____

## More Light on the Text
### Ezekiel 47:1, 3–12

Ezekiel is a book of visions. This passage is a fitting climax to the book and to Ezekiel's entire experience. Whereas the vision of the dry bones had announced the removal of the curse of death (37:1–14), the vision in this passage proclaimed the renewal of all aspects of life. This visionary experience depicts the temple as a source of blessing for the land. Ezekiel sees the river that would heal the land issuing out of the temple—an emblem of the power of God's grace under the Gospel. The temple has been measured; then the glory of God returned through the east gate, which is permanently closed since God will remain with His people. It is important to note that Ezekiel's vision of a life-giving, healing river comes immediately before his account of the boundaries and divisions of the land. Before it could be inhabited again, the land must be healed and cleansed of all defilement. There are several elements of the Christian life seen in these eleven verses.

**1 Afterward he brought me again unto the door of the house; and, behold, waters issued out from under the threshold of the house eastward: for the forefront of the house stood toward the east, and the waters came down from under from the right side of the house, at the south side of the altar.**

After Ezekiel's guided tour of the temple (Heb. *bayit*, **BAH-yit**), he is brought back to the entrance of the temple building to the inside of the inner court. Upon reaching the gate of the temple, he sees waters that has their spring under the threshold of that gate. These waters, which look toward the east and pass to the south of the altar of burnt offerings on the right of the temple, run from the west to the east. The most important fact about the river is its Source. The river

issues directly from the presence of God Himself. This is the reason it is able to give life and sustenance, for they are both gifts of the living God. The river has its spring out of sight—the fountainhead is invisible—but it proceeds out of the sanctuary of God. We need to remember that all renewal in the church and the world flows by God's wonderful grace from His presence and is not something that can be generated or controlled by humans.

**3 And when the man that had the line in his hand went forth eastward, he measured a thousand cubits, and he brought me through the waters; the waters were to the ankles. 4 Again he measured a thousand, and brought me through the waters; the waters were to the knees. Again he measured a thousand, and brought me through; the waters were to the loins. 5 Afterward he measured a thousand; and it was a river that I could not pass over: for the waters were risen, waters to swim in, a river that could not be passed over.**

The divine messenger takes Ezekiel to explore the extent of this stream. A measuring line is used to mark off four one-thousand-cubit intervals, approximately one-third of a mile each. At each interval, Ezekiel is taken out into the stream to examine its depth. The waters increase so that they become a river in which one could swim. What an amazing transformation that a river so tiny at its source could become a mighty river in just over a mile! The depth increases at each interval from the ankles to the knees to the loins or waist and finally to a depth in which one must swim. At the four-thousand-cubit mark, the stream has become a river of such magnitude that it cannot be crossed. The river appears so torrential or so wide that it is not possible to swim across it. A miracle is no doubt at work, something like the unspent jar of meal and unfailing cruse of oil in 1 Kings 17:12–16 or like the growth of the kingdom of God from mustard seed to a spreading tree (Mark 4:31–32).

We all have plenty of room for improvement! With each step of obedience, Ezekiel finds himself going deeper into dependence on the grace of God. With each venture of forward progress, more of Ezekiel is submerged in the river with less of him being visible. The Christian life is progressive in nature, showing growth that is both measurable and discernible. God does not make us grow. We must choose to walk on into greater maturity.

Ezekiel has gone so far from the shore that he can no longer walk back. Wherever the river flows, that is where he is going. The current is so strong and the volume of water is so great that Ezekiel is in over his head. Still God is carrying him and there is no danger of the prophet drowning. God is still in control of the water and the life of the prophet.

**6 And he said unto me, Son of man, hast thou seen this? Then he brought me, and caused me to return to the brink of the river. 7 Now when I had returned, behold, at the bank of the river were very many trees on the one side and on the other.**

Ezekiel must have been left in such utter amazement that he continues to stare at the scene. He is brought right back to the brink—back to the starting point. But there is more to see. Ezekiel is a new sight that he had not noticed before. Both sides of the river are lined with trees. The purpose of the river is becoming clearer. Its basic purpose is to bring life. Many trees line its sides. Every kind of fruit tree grow on both sides. There is an oasis of trees growing in the wilderness of Judah, between Jerusalem and the Dead Sea. What a sight, and what a miracle!

**8 Then said he unto me, These waters issue out toward the east country, and go down into the desert, and go into the sea: which being brought forth into the sea, the waters shall be healed.**

The guide does not leave the prophet in doubt concerning the interpretation of what he has just seen. Ezekiel learns that the river, which he has just seen, eventually flows into the sea. "The sea" here is referring to the Dead Sea since contextually it was located in the "east country" and its waters needed healing. Through the waters of the temple the waters of the Dead Sea are miraculously healed. The word "healed" (Heb. *rafa'*, **rah-FAH**) normally refers to the healing of a diseased body. However in this case, the miracle involves the neutralizing of the corrupting chemicals in the water so it becomes fresh and life is no longer suppressed.

**9 And it shall come to pass, that every thing that liveth, which moveth, whithersoever the rivers shall come, shall live: and there shall be a very great multitude of fish, because these waters shall come thither: for they shall be healed; and every thing shall live whither the river cometh.**

The thoroughness of the healing is evident in the phrase "whithersoever the rivers shall come." Everywhere else, the river brought its life-giving power. Every living thing will abound in the "healed" waters. The absence of living creatures in the Dead Sea has been remarked by ancient and modern writers. In the same way, the living water that Jesus gives brings life to those dead in trespasses and sins (cf. John 4:14). Ezekiel's river is similar to the rivers in the Garden of Eden and the eternal state (cf. Revelation 22:2–3).

**10 And it shall come to pass, that the fishers shall stand upon it from Engedi even unto Eneglaim; they shall be a place to spread forth nets; their fish shall be according to their kinds, as the fish of the great sea, exceeding many.**

Ordinarily, the salt and minerals of the Dead Sea permit no life in it of any kind, but in the ideal (coming) age, it will miraculously teem with life. The entire Dead Sea and Arabah plain, where the Dead Sea is located, are healed by these waters, causing the Dead Sea to swarm with marine life to the extent that fishermen fish its entire length from Engedi (a town on the sea's western shore) to Eneglaim, an uncertain location believed to be a place on the southwestern shore of the Dead Sea.

**11 But the miry places thereof and the marishes thereof shall not be healed; they shall be given to salt.**

The guide informs Ezekiel that there will be exceptions to the remarkable picture of life that he has just seen. The Arabah blooms (cf. Isaiah 35:1–2, 6–7; Joel 3:18); only the miry places or swamps along with the marshes or small pools of water are not healed. They are left to provide salt for the people. These are places to which the living water does not reach and indicate that life and health are solely due to the stream, which proceeds from beneath the throne of God.

**12 And by the river upon the bank thereof, on this side and on that side, shall grow all trees for meat, whose leaf shall not fade, neither shall the fruit thereof be consumed: it shall bring forth new fruit according to his months, because their waters they issued out of the sanctuary: and the fruit thereof shall be for meat, and the leaf thereof for medicine.**

The vision comes to a conclusion with a focus on the abundance of the growth of the trees and their benefits for human use. Both banks are filled with "all" (Heb. *kol*, **KOLE**), literally "every" tree, to suggest profusion and variety. Their fruit provides meat (Heb. *ma'akal*, **MAH-ah-khahl**) or food, and their leaves provide healing. The source of the land's redemption and healing comes from the temple or sanctuary. This is the dwelling place of God and His throne. He will heal the land in the time of the consummation of the kingdom. Ultimately, the river of life in Ezekiel, as in Revelation, anticipates the new creation. In this new creation, God will have lifted the curse from the earth forever and will dwell in life-giving abundance with His redeemed people gathered from all nations.

Source:
Buttrick, George Arthur, ed. *The Interpreter's Bible.* Vol. 6. Nashville, TN: Abingdon Press, 1956. 327.
Cooper, Lamar Eugene Sr. *Ezekiel.* The New American Commentary, Vol. 17. Nashville, TN: Broadman and Holman Publishers, 1994. 39.
Henry, Matthew. *Matthew Henry's Complete Commentary on the Bible.* http://www.biblestudytools.com/commentaries/matthew-henry-complete/ezekiel/47.html. Accessed August 22, 2013.
Keil, C. F., and F. Delitzsch. *Ezekiel and Daniel.* Commentary on the Old Testament, Vol. 9. Peabody, MA: Hendrickson Publishers, 1996. 7.
*NIV Study Bible, 10th Anniversary Edition.* Grand Rapids, MI: Zondervan, 1995. 1219, 1285.

## Say It Correctly

Engedi. en-ge-**DEE**.
Eneglaim. en-eg-**LA**-im.

## Daily Bible Readings

**MONDAY**
Forsaking the Living Water
(Jeremiah 2:5–13)

**TUESDAY**
Living Water Shall Flow from Jerusalem
(Zechariah 14:1–8)

**WEDNESDAY**
Let the Thirsty Come to Me
(John 7:37–44)

**THURSDAY**
Guided to the Water of Life
(Revelation 7:13–17)

**FRIDAY**
Give Me This Water
(John 4:7–15)

**SATURDAY**
Planted by Streams of Water
(Psalm 1)

**SUNDAY**
Water Flowing from the Sanctuary
(Ezekiel 47:1, 3–12)

# Notes

# Teaching Tips

## Words You Should Know

**A. Inheritance** (Ezekiel 47:13–14, 22–23) *nachalah* (Heb.)—Possession, property, heritage, portion, share.

**B. Sojourn** (v. 22) *gur* (Heb.)—To abide, travel in, inhabit, be a stranger.

## Teacher Preparation

**Unifying Principle—A New Beginning.** Sometimes life leaves people needing a new beginning. What is available to everyone to make that happen? Ezekiel tells the people that God restored the Israelites and the aliens among them with an inheritance of new land, signifying a new start.

**A.** Read the Bible Background and Devotional Readings.

**B.** Complete Lesson 12 in the *Precepts For Living Personal Study Guide®*.

**C.** Reread the Focal Verses in a modern translation.

## O—Open the Lesson

**A.** Open with prayer.

**B.** Have students read Aim for Change in unison.

**C.** Ask for a volunteer to read the In Focus story.

**D.** Encourage students to think about a time when they made a new beginning. Ask for volunteers to share with the class.

## P—Present the Scriptures

**A.** Ask for volunteers to read the Focal Verses; The People, Places, and Times; and Background. Discuss.

**B.** Read the Acts passage from the Bible Background section. Discuss the connection between the passage in Acts and the passage in Ezekiel. What is the main idea we can gain from both passages?

## E—Explore the Meaning

**A.** Review and discuss Search the Scriptures, Discuss the Meaning, and the Lesson in Our Society sections.

**B.** Ask students to share the most significant point they learned and how to use that point this week.

## N—Next Steps for Application

**A.** Complete the Follow the Spirit and Remember Your Thoughts sections.

**B.** Remind students to read the Daily Bible Readings in preparation for next week's lesson.

**C.** Close in prayer, asking God to provide ways for us to show His love to others.

## Worship Guide

For the Superintendent or Teacher
Theme: Transformation Continued
Song: "The Family of God"
Devotional Reading: Psalm 51:1–13

# Transformation Continued

**Bible Background • EZEKIEL 47:13–23; ACTS 2:37–47**
**Printed Text • EZEKIEL 47:13–23**
**Devotional Reading • PSALM 51:1–13**

## Aim for Change

By the end of the lesson, we will: KNOW what God's Word says about sharing our inheritance with all those who live among us; FEEL the importance of affirming and appreciating one another as children of God who have made, or can make, new beginnings together; and EMBRACE new beginnings as gifts from God to be enjoyed with others.

### In Focus

Andrea wearily brushed her hair from her eyes, then unbuckled her son from his car seat. "Let's go, big guy," she whispered. Taking a deep breath, she headed toward the church doors. It had been three years since she last went through those doors. But life had not turned out how she thought it would, and now her heart was broken. For weeks, she had argued with herself about going back to church. At one time she had been very involved—how would people respond to her now? Would they judge her for what she had done and what had been done to her? And what of the baby, Isaac? She hugged him tight to her chest. She had to take the chance. She had nowhere else to go, and she desperately needed someone to help her face life as a now-single parent. Andrea held her breath as she opened the door and slipped into the familiar building.

"Andrea!" She turned to find herself in the embrace of an old friend, and tears sprang to her eyes. She was going to be OK.

*God wants His church to be a loving community where people can find support to make a new beginning. In today's lesson, we learn that God offers new beginnings to everyone who will accept Him.*

## Keep in Mind

"So shall ye divide this land ... unto you, and to the strangers that sojourn among you" (from Ezekiel 47:21–22).

"So shall ye divide this land ... unto you, and to the strangers that sojourn among you" (from Ezekiel 47:21–22).

# Focal Verses

**KJV** **Ezekiel 47:13** Thus saith the Lord GOD; This shall be the border, whereby ye shall inherit the land according to the twelve tribes of Israel: Joseph shall have two portions.

**14** And ye shall inherit it, one as well as another: concerning the which I lifted up mine hand to give it unto your fathers: and this land shall fall unto you for inheritance.

**15** And this shall be the border of the land toward the north side, from the great sea, the way of Hethlon, as men go to Zedad;

**16** Hamath, Berothah, Sibraim, which is between the border of Damascus and the border of Hamath; Hazarhatticon, which is by the coast of Hauran.

**17** And the border from the sea shall be Hazarenan, the border of Damascus, and the north northward, and the border of Hamath. And this is the north side.

**18** And the east side ye shall measure from Hauran, and from Damascus, and from Gilead, and from the land of Israel by Jordan, from the border unto the east sea. And this is the east side.

**19** And the south side southward, from Tamar even to the waters of strife in Kadesh, the river to the great sea. And this is the south side southward.

**20** The west side also shall be the great sea from the border, till a man come over against Hamath. This is the west side.

**21** So shall ye divide this land unto you according to the tribes of Israel.

**22** And it shall come to pass, that ye shall divide it by lot for an inheritance unto you, and to the strangers that sojourn among you, which shall beget children among you: and they shall be unto you as born in the country among the children of Israel; they shall

**NLT** **Ezekiel 47:13** This is what the Sovereign LORD says: "Divide the land in this way for the twelve tribes of Israel: The descendants of Joseph will be given two shares of land.

**14** Otherwise each tribe will receive an equal share. I took a solemn oath and swore that I would give this land to your ancestors, and it will now come to you as your possession.

**15** These are the boundaries of the land: The northern border will run from the Mediterranean toward Hethlon, then on through Lebo-hamath to Zedad;

**16** then it will run to Berothah and Sibraim, which are on the border between Damascus and Hamath, and finally to Hazer-hatticon, on the border of Hauran.

**17** So the northern border will run from the Mediterranean to Hazar-enan, on the border between Hamath to the north and Damascus to the south.

**18** The eastern border starts at a point between Hauran and Damascus and runs south along the Jordan River between Israel and Gilead, past the Dead Sea and as far south as Tamar. This will be the eastern border.

**19** The southern border will go west from Tamar to the waters of Meribah at Kadesh and then follow the course of the Brook of Egypt to the Mediterranean. This will be the southern border.

**20** On the west side, the Mediterranean itself will be your border from the southern border to the point where the northern border begins, opposite Lebo-hamath.

**21** Divide the land within these boundaries among the tribes of Israel.

**22** Distribute the land as an allotment for yourselves and for the foreigners who have joined you and are raising their families

have inheritance with you among the tribes of Israel.

**23** And it shall come to pass, that in what tribe the stranger sojourneth, there shall ye give him his inheritance, saith the Lord GOD.

among you. They will be like native-born Israelites to you and will receive an allotment among the tribes.

**23** These foreigners are to be given land within the territory of the tribe with whom they now live. I, the Sovereign LORD, have spoken!"

## The People, Places, and Times

**Boundaries of Israel.** The land of Israel's borders have changed over the years and have differed from the Bible's description. In Ezekiel's vision, the western boundary of the Mediterranean Sea has been the most stable permanent boundary. The eastern boundary is in Syria. The northern boundary is Lebanon. The southwest border goes along Syria and the Jordan River to the western bank of the Dead Sea. It later follows the desert of Kadesh Barnea and then goes along the Brook of Egypt to the Mediterranean.

## Background

Ezekiel received numerous visions from God regarding the future restoration of Israel. In chapter 47, he received a vision of a river of life flowing from the temple. This river would produce an abundance of fish and trees, which possessed leaves of healing. This river symbolized the Holy Spirit and its life-giving vitality to God's people.

After Ezekiel received this vision, he received another regarding the boundaries of the nation of Israel. The boundaries would be the same general boundaries that were given when the Israelites approached the Promised Land. The big difference when it came to this inheritance is that it would be available to strangers as well. The Gentiles would have a share in the inheritance of Israel along with the native-born Israelites. This

points toward the fellowship and mutual sharing within the life of the church.

## At-A-Glance

1. Instructions for the Inheritance
(Ezekiel 47:13–14)
2. Illustrating the Inheritance
(vv. 15–20)
3. Included in the Inheritance
(vv. 21–23)

## In Depth

**1. Instructions for the Inheritance (Ezekiel 47:13–14)**

Ezekiel receives instructions from God on dividing the inheritance of the land among the twelve tribes. First, God lets them know that He is the one who gives the border or boundaries of the inheritance. It is not determined by man or by chance. Israel's inheritance comes from God and God alone. Next, he is given instruction that Joseph will inherit two portions of the land. These two portions would be given to the tribes of Ephraim and Manasseh, tribes descended from the two sons of Joseph. Joseph was the older son of Jacob's favorite wife, Rachel. The double portion is because his two sons were adopted by Jacob, so they became two tribes of Israel and therefore each get a portion in the inheritance (Genesis 48). The Lord reminds Ezekiel of the equal participation of all the tribes in the inheritance. No one would be left out. They all would be included in what God gave to Israel.

The Lord also reminds them that they are receiving the inheritance based on His promise "concerning the which I lifted up mine hand to give it unto your fathers." This means that His giving of the land of Israel was sealed with a binding oath. It was a sure thing and would not be taken away. The inheritance was a promise from God, and He is faithful to do what He promised.

### 2. Illustrating the Inheritance (vv. 15–20)

Ezekiel then receives details concerning the borders of the land of Israel. This is in anticipation of the next chapter, where he will receive the boundaries of the tribes. First, the borders of the entire nation are given because God promised the whole land to a whole Israel. They were promised this land not as isolated tribes but as a community. This was their portion together as a people.

The Lord then goes on to give Ezekiel the northern border, which reached the border of Damascus and Lebo-Hamath. Damascus was an ancient trading city and the capital of Syria. Lebo-Hamath was a city situated on the Orontes river in Syria. Then the Lord gives the eastern border, which runs along Syria then follows the Jordan River and the Dead Sea. The land to the east of the Jordan is not mentioned, probably because it is regarded as unclean (Joshua 22:19, 25, 27). Next, the border south travels southwest to the desert of Kadesh Barnea. This has been the most southerly border in Israel's biblical history. The land then spreads out toward the river of Egypt, which has been the most common border with Egypt (Joshua 15:4; 1 Kings 8:65) The western border of the nation of Israel is the Mediterranean Sea.

This border was actually never realized in Old Testament history. All of these borders indicate that the inheritance was a real tangible thing and that it coincided with the original boundaries for the land (Numbers 33:50–34:15).

### 3. Included in the Inheritance (vv. 21–23)

Next, God reiterates the goal of dividing the land among the twelve tribes. Then we see further instructions regarding those who were not Israelites by birth. The Lord says that they are to receive a share in the inheritance. This is unprecedented. Earlier Old Testament passages regarding foreigners and strangers talk about fair treatment and showing hospitality. This takes it a step further and includes them in the citizenship of Israel. This foreshadows the Gentiles being included in the family of God and receiving the blessings of citizenship in the kingdom of God. This can be seen in Acts 2:42–47, where those who are part of the church all share and have everything in common.

### Search the Scriptures

1. How many shares of land would be given to the descendants of Joseph (Ezekiel 47:13)?

2. What was the qualification for Gentiles to receive a share of the land (v. 22)?

### Discuss the Meaning

1. What is our inheritance today as believers?

2. How can believers today create community with other believers?

### Lesson in Our Society

Life is full of new beginnings. Some new beginnings are planned, joyful occasions: a wedding, a birth, a new home, a new career opportunity. But sometimes people need new beginnings for reasons that are anything but planned or joyful: the loss of a spouse or child, the loss of a job or relationship, or the onset of a devastating health issue. The church is a place that should be a haven for people seeking a new beginning. Just as Christ provides redemption and salvation for all, His church should provide acceptance, support, and fellowship to those who need a new start in life.

## Make It Happen

The members of the early church shared everything with each other—food, possessions, prayer, work, and fellowship. From this example and God's instruction in Ezekiel for even the "outsiders" to be included in the inheritance, we see that God values His people supporting one another through life's ups and downs. As believers, we need to make sure that we share our "inheritance" with one another as well as with those who are outside the body of Christ. Ask God to show you how you can share with those both inside and outside your church. Donate food and clothing to a local food bank or homeless shelter. Volunteer to cook meals for those who are sick or mothers who have just given birth. God has given you a new beginning; make sure you are available to help others who are in desperate need of the new beginning that only Christ can offer.

## Follow the Spirit

What God wants me to do:

_____

_____

_____

_____

## Remember Your Thoughts

Special insights I have learned:

_____

_____

_____

_____

## More Light on the Text
### Ezekiel 47:13–23

In this part of Ezekiel's vision, Israel finally and forever will be repaired to essentially the same as the original designations given by Moses (Numbers 34; Joshua 13–19). In Ezekiel's "new" Promised Land, the distribution is no longer for a divided or scattered kingdom; rather, now the twelve tribes are reunited as a single entity, under a single "prince" (Ezekiel 48:21).

Part of what makes this vision radical is that in Ezekiel's time, the tribes of the nation of Judah are in exile, with the northern tribes having been scattered long before, leaving even the term "twelve tribes of Israel" largely theological rather than actual. Even when the exiles returned, it wasn't to reclaim all of their land, but instead the territory they occupied was a small unimpressive province around Jerusalem and Judea. While our passage focuses on 47:13–23, the whole context of land boundaries extends to 48:29.

**13 Thus saith the Lord GOD; This shall be the border, whereby ye shall inherit the land according to the twelve tribes of Israel: Joseph shall have two portions. 14 And ye shall inherit it, one as well as another: concerning the which I lifted up mine hand to give it unto your fathers: and this land shall fall unto you for inheritance.**

It is noteworthy that the land allotment begins and ends with "Thus saith the Lord GOD," making it clear that this isn't Ezekiel's interpretation or a later editor's compilation. Rather, this is a prophetic word from God. God made a "unilateral promise" to Israel's forefathers, and now that promise inexplicably is inserted into Ezekiel's vision (339). There is no explanation provided of how the northern tribes will reassemble, or why whole tribes are uprooted and arbitrarily planted elsewhere. Moreover, the straight east-west lines pay no attention to the natural topography of the land. It is not the wisdom of men or circumstance that determines the boundaries but the promise of God.

Because the Levites have no portion, having provision within the "holy" areas (45:4, 48:13), Joseph is a name for the consolidated tribes of Joseph's two sons, Ephraim and Manasseh (48:4–5). This retains the original number of twelve tribes who would own land. Even in Ezekiel's utopian vision, the number of tribes must be twelve, just as other numbers of twelve were critical in other parts of biblical history, e.g., the apostles replacing Judas rather than being content with eleven (Acts 1:26). There is also the significance of the number twelve, particularly throughout the book of Revelation, e.g., chapter 21.

The stress is on the principle of equality for "one as well as another" (Heb. *'akh*, **AKH**, brother or kindred), which is preserved with the allotment for the priests even though they aren't numbered among the twelve tribes. In this renewed Israel, any inequities would be a distant memory. It wasn't that Israel deserved this grace, but it was about God fulfilling His promise to Abraham (Genesis 12:7, 15:7, 17:8).

15 And this shall be the border of the land toward the north side, from the great sea, the way of Hethlon, as men go to Zedad; 16 Hamath, Berothah, Sibraim, which is between the border of Damascus and the border of Hamath; Hazarhatticon, which is by the coast of Hauran. 17 And the border from the sea shall be Hazarenan, the border of Damascus, and the north northward, and the border of Hamath. And this is the north side. 18 And the east side ye shall measure from Hauran, and from Damascus, and from Gilead, and from the land of Israel by Jordan, from the border unto the east sea. And this is the east side. 19 And the south side southward, from Tamar even to the waters of strife in Kadesh, the river to the great sea. And this is the south side southward. 20 The west side also shall be the great sea from the border, till a man come over against Hamath. This is the west side.

The borders are listed in clockwise order, starting with the north (the parallel passage in Numbers 34 starts in the south), basically from the Mediterranean (the "great sea") heading east to somewhere between Damascus to the south and Hamath (modern Hama) to the north, following a somewhat unclear line of several cities that long ago disappeared into history. It is impossible to identify them with certainty. The eastern border is clearer, from the Jordan River to the Dead Sea. The southern border starts in northern Sinai at the oasis of Kadesh Barnea, also called the "waters of strife" (Numbers 27:14) where Moses struck the rock in anger to give the Children of Israel water. Next the boundary line winds westward to the river (also known as the "brook of Egypt") to the Great Sea or Mediterranean, which of course is the western border.

**21 So shall ye divide this land unto you according to the tribes of Israel.**

As noted, the division of land in Ezekiel's vision is neither practical according to Israel's geography, nor does it fit with the actual history of the nation and its tribes. As some scholars have noted, the boundaries in Ezekiel are more concerned with theology than with a well-functioning map. This theological statement includes sweeping provisions for long-awaited and much-needed equality and security. The designation of boundaries was intended to furnish every household with what they needed to flourish economically. This is a picture of economic equality for all the people of God. Ezekiel's vision was the description of a new beginning, the essence of a new start, the picture of a new lease on life.

**22 And it shall come to pass, that ye shall divide it by lot for an inheritance unto you, and to the strangers that sojourn among you, which shall beget children among you: and they shall be unto you as born in the country among the children of Israel; they shall have inheritance with you among the tribes of Israel. 23 And it shall come to pass, that in what tribe the stranger sojourneth, there shall ye give him his inheritance, saith the Lord GOD.**

The "strangers" (Heb. *gar*, **GAR**, a foreigner), translated "sojourners" or "aliens" in other versions, were foreigners and immigrants who lived in Israel. They were a familiar presence in Israel's history and, according to Hebrew laws, they were a people who always needed special protection as they were vulnerable to exploitation and oppression. Israel held unforgettable memories of having been "strangers" who had been enslaved and exploited in Egypt, which would be expected of any people with such a history. Indeed, God Himself reminds them often of how He delivered them from bondage while they were foreigners (e.g., Deuteronomy 6:12; Judges 6:8; 1 Samuel 10:18)—and that memory was the basis for Israel's laws regarding the just treatment of strangers or aliens who sojourned among them (e.g., Leviticus 19:33–34, the last verse of which includes another reminder of why they are to obey this law). Those resident aliens who had adopted the Hebrew laws and religion became proselytes, which entitles them to the rights and privileges of native Israelites (Isaiah 56:3–8). This reference includes the portion of Isaiah that describes God's house as a "house of prayer for all people" (v. 7). The land would be divided by lot or a portion would be allocated to Israelites and foreigners living in the land of Israel.

### Summary

Ezekiel's vision included not only a new temple but also new land. The new allotments leave no room for discrimination and are a model for economic justice. If any theme dominates the Old Testament, it is justice and righteousness (e.g., Psalm 99:4; Isaiah 9:7; Amos 5:24). If any phrase describes God's character, it is just and righteous (cf. Exodus 34:6–7; Numbers 14:18; Psalm 145:17; 2 Thessalonians 1:6), and by extension this also should describe each of God's people. In the end, after every human form of government ultimately has failed to secure an equitable and righteous common good, in God's kingdom described by Ezekiel, there will be God's new creation full of justice and mutual love.

Sources:

Blenkinsopp, Joseph. *Ezekiel. Interpretation: A Bible Commentary for Teaching and Preaching.* Louisville, KY: John Knox Press, 1990. 232–237.

Cooper, Lamar Eugene, Sr. *Ezekiel.* The New American Commentary, vol. 17. Nashville, TN: Broadman and Holman Publishers, 1994. 415–417.

Duguid, Iain M. *Ezekiel.* The NIV Application Commentary. Grand Rapids, MI: Zondervan, 1999. 538–551.

Jensen, Robert W. *Ezekiel.* Brazos Theological Commentary on the Bible. Grand Rapids, MI: Brazos Press, 2009. 338–342.

Strong, James. *The New Strong's Exhaustive Concordance of the Bible.* Nashville, TN: Thomas Nelson Publishers, 1990.

Taylor, John B. *Ezekiel: An Introduction and Commentary.* Tyndale Old Testament Commentaries. Vol. 22. Downers Grove, IL: IVP Academic, 1969. 272–273.

Wright, Christopher J. H. *The Message of Ezekiel: A New Heart and a New Spirit.* Downers Grove, IL: InterVarsity Press, 2001. 359–362.

## Daily Bible Readings

**MONDAY**
God Declares New Things
(Isaiah 42:5–9)

**TUESDAY**
A New Song, a New Way
(Isaiah 42:10–16)

**WEDNESDAY**
A New and Right Spirit
(Psalm 51:1–13)

**THURSDAY**
New Mercies Every Morning
(Lamentations 3:19–26)

**FRIDAY**
A New Birth, a Living Hope
(1 Peter 1:1–7)

**SATURDAY**
All Who Believed Were Together
(Acts 2:37–47)

**SUNDAY**
Inheritance for You and the Immigrants
(Ezekiel 47:13–23)

## Say It Correctly

Hethlon. kheth-**LONE**.
Zedad. tseh-**DAWD**.
Hamath. khah-**MAWTH**.
Berothah. be-ro-**THAW**.
Sibraim. siv-**RAH**-yim.
Hazarhatticon. kha-**TSER** hat-tee-**KONE**.
Hauran. khav-**RAWN**.
Hazarenan. khah-**TSAR** ey-**NONE**.
Kadesh. kaw-**DESH**.

## Notes

_____

_____

_____

_____

# Teaching Tips

## Words You Should Know

**A. Uncircumcised** (Isaiah 52:1) *'arel* (Heb.)—Man whose foreskin is not removed.

**B. Unclean** (v. 1) *tame'* (Heb.)—Bodily or religiously polluted or defiled.

**C. Watchman** (v. 8) *tsafah* (Heb.)—A person who kept guard over a town or building and watched for oncoming threats.

## Teacher Preparation

**Unifying Principle—Seeking Words of Hope.** All people need to hear words of hope. Where will they find hopeful words? The psalmist and Isaiah tell God's people that God who reigns above is their help, shield, and salvation, and that they can put their hope in God and rejoice.

**A.** Review the Aim for Change and pray for the ability to teach the class in a way that the students will meet its objectives.

**B.** Read Isaiah 52 several times.

**C.** Complete the companion lesson in the *Precepts For Living Personal Study Guide®*.

## O—Open the Lesson

**A.** Open today's lesson by including the Aim for Change in your prayer.

**B.** Read the Aim for Change and Keep In Mind verse.

**C.** Give students a few minutes to read the In Focus story, and discuss.

## P—Present the Scriptures

**A.** Allow a few minutes for the students to read through the Focal Verses.

**B.** Get volunteers to read The People, Places, and Times; Background; Search the Scriptures; At-A-Glance; In Depth; and More Light on the Text sections.

## E—Explore the Meaning

**A.** Assign the following sections to groups of students to explore: Discuss the Meaning; Lesson in Our Society; and Make It Happen. Choose a representative from each group to share their assignment and responses.

**B.** Encourage students to review the Aim for Change and memorize the Keep In Mind verse to make sure they've gotten the most out of the lesson.

## N—Next Steps for Application

**A.** Have students identify ways they can encourage others. Some suggestions include inviting others to church or using social media to evangelize.

**B.** End your class in prayer, thanking God for bringing you and your students out of darkness and into His marvelous light.

## Worship Guide

For the Superintendent or Teacher
Theme: Let Zion Rejoice
Song: "Our God Reigns"
Devotional Reading: Psalm 42:5–11

# Let Zion Rejoice

**Bible Background • ISAIAH 52:1–2, 7–12; PSALM 33**
**Printed Text • ISAIAH 52:1–2, 7–12**
**Devotional Reading • PSALM 42:5–11**

## Aim for Change

By the end of the lesson, we will: KNOW Isaiah's words of hope, good news, and rejoicing; EXPRESS great joy through heartfelt worship for the Lord's salvation; and RESPOND to God's blessings with exuberant worship.

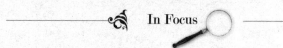

## In Focus

Chaunel knew that if her son Hakim did not change his behaviors, he was going to end up in jail. For four years, she prayed, fasted, and stood in proxy for him in many altar calls, but recently he was in the wrong place at the wrong time with the wrong people. Hakim said he did not do what he was accused of, and Chaunel believed him. She, out of all people, knew her son—and she knew when he was lying. This time, he was not. But, her biggest dilemma was to decide whether to leave him in jail or to come up with the money required to get him out. There was nothing more that she wanted but to get to her only child and bring him home. Soon she received a letter from Hakim. In the letter he wrote that he had been going to chapel services in jail and decided to give his life to the Lord. He let her know that although he was physically imprisoned, he was truly free because he was spiritually free. Chaunel put the letter down and began to run around the house. She couldn't help it. She had to rejoice at the good news of Hakim's salvation.

*In today's lesson, we learn that the people of God have good cause for rejoicing. They have received His Good News of salvation.*

## Keep in Mind

"How beautiful upon the mountains are the feet of him that bringeth good tidings, that publisheth peace; that bringeth good tidings of good, that publisheth salvation; that saith unto Zion, Thy God reigneth!" (Isaiah 52:7).

"How beautiful upon the mountains are the feet of him that bringeth good tidings, that publisheth peace; that bringeth good tidings of good, that publisheth salvation; that saith unto Zion, Thy God reigneth!" (Isaiah 52:7).

# Focal Verses

**KJV** Isaiah 52:1 Awake, awake; put on thy strength, O Zion; put on thy beautiful garments, O Jerusalem, the holy city: for henceforth there shall no more come into thee the uncircumcised and the unclean.

2 Shake thyself from the dust; arise, and sit down, O Jerusalem: loose thyself from the bands of thy neck, O captive daughter of Zion.

7 How beautiful upon the mountains are the feet of him that bringeth good tidings, that publisheth peace; that bringeth good tidings of good, that publisheth salvation; that saith unto Zion, Thy God reigneth!

8 Thy watchmen shall lift up the voice; with the voice together shall they sing: for they shall see eye to eye, when the LORD shall bring again Zion.

9 Break forth into joy, sing together, ye waste places of Jerusalem: for the LORD hath comforted his people, he hath redeemed Jerusalem.

10 The LORD hath made bare his holy arm in the eyes of all the nations; and all the ends of the earth shall see the salvation of our God.

11 Depart ye, depart ye, go ye out from thence, touch no unclean thing; go ye out of the midst of her; be ye clean, that bear the vessels of the LORD.

12 For ye shall not go out with haste, nor go by flight: for the LORD will go before you; and the God of Israel will be your reward.

**NLT** Isaiah 52:1 Wake up, wake up, O Zion! Clothe yourself with strength. Put on your beautiful clothes, O holy city of Jerusalem, for unclean and godless people will enter your gates no longer.

2 Rise from the dust, O Jerusalem. Sit in a place of honor. Remove the chains of slavery from your neck, O captive daughter of Zion.

7 How beautiful on the mountains are the feet of the messenger who brings good news, the good news of peace and salvation, the news that the God of Israel reigns!

8 The watchmen shout and sing with joy, for before their very eyes they see the LORD returning to Jerusalem.

9 Let the ruins of Jerusalem break into joyful song, for the LORD has comforted his people. He has redeemed Jerusalem.

10 The LORD has demonstrated his holy power before the eyes of all the nations. All the ends of the earth will see the victory of our God.

11 Get out! Get out and leave your captivity, where everything you touch is unclean. Get out of there and purify yourselves, you who carry home the sacred objects of the LORD.

12 You will not leave in a hurry, running for your lives. For the LORD will go ahead of you; yes, the God of Israel will protect you from behind.

## The People, Places, and Times

**Zion.** Synonymous with Jerusalem, but most commonly referred to a specific mountain near Jerusalem, Mount Zion. It is also regarded as a synonym for the people of God. It later became a term that denoted the church (Hebrews 12:22–23) as well as the heavenly city (Revelation 14:1).

**Jerusalem.** Name means the Foundation of Peace. It is located in the Judean mountains and was the ancient capital of Israel (and specifically Judah during the divided monarchy). Its elevation is remarkable, and there were two main approaches to the city (from the Jordan Valley by Jericho and the Mount of Olives). It is full of pools and fountains, including the Well of Job, the Pool of Hezekiah, and the Pool of Bethesda. There are many gates and gardens there; most famous is the Garden of Gethsemane. During its long history, it is said to have been destroyed twice, besieged 23 times, attacked 52 times, and captured and recaptured 44 times.

### Background

Isaiah can be divided into two main sections. The first deals with judgment and the second deals with hope. Isaiah 52 deals with hope. It is not just any hope but a hope sourced in the compassion and sovereignty of God. The amazing thing about this hope is it is written about Jerusalem's captivity before it even happens! Then, it offers encouragement because it tells of her future deliverance.

Jerusalem was taken captive as a consequence of disobedience (and idolatry). There were three deportations of Israelites to Babylon, probably 597 B.C., 587 B.C., and 582 B.C. God allowed them to be held by the Babylonians for seventy years! Most of the captives were treated as colonists. The Babylonian captivity was brought to a close after the fall of Babylon to Cyrus the Great. Cyrus issued a decree at approximately 536 B.C. for the Jews to return and rebuild Jerusalem (Ezra 1:2).

## At-A-Glance

1. Get on Your Mark (Isaiah 52:1–2)
2. Get Set (vv. 7–10)
3. Go (vv. 11–12)

### In Depth

#### 1. Get on Your Mark (Isaiah 52:1–2)

Seventy years is a long time to be in a bad situation. By then, hope would be long gone and replaced by the slumber of complacency, apathy, and resentment. Forecasting the depression, heaviness, and lack of energy to do nothing more than sleep, Isaiah 52:1 commands the exiles taken to Babylonia to wake up. With freedom arriving seven decades later, the sleeping captives might have mistaken it for a dream and missed out on the opportunity to return home. So, the first order of business is to arouse the captive. Loosely translating the verse, it might read, "Wake up! Stretch! Get out of your pajamas and put on some clothes. The captor will not bother you anymore!" Isaiah further declares that "there shall no more come into thee the uncircumcised and the unclean." This means that Jerusalem would not have foreigners ruling over her.

He further instructs them in verse 2, in case they cannot believe their ears. He tells them to shake off the dust that has settled on them from sitting so long. They are so used to sitting that he has to tell them to get up. "Arise!" he commands, and tells them to take their place as the children of the Most High God. Instead of sitting down in the dirt, they are to take a position more suitable to their status as children of the King of the universe. They are to release themselves from the yoke that held them captive. As believers, we are also called to arise and take our rightful position as children of God. We are to no longer live in bondage and under the yoke of spiritual slavery.

### 2. Get Set (vv. 7–10)

The captives do not have to go out to find word of God's salvation; He sends the news to them! In our text, the prophet assures that a messenger will come to bring the good tidings. The watchmen proclaims salvation, and the sound will be so beautiful that the captives will break forth in song. Isaiah makes reference to the feet of the messenger and says they are beautiful because of the message that he is running to give to the captives. It is a message of peace, salvation, and good news.

The watchmen will see the messenger coming and begin to sing for joy. Isaiah states that they would see eye to eye. They would see the same thing. This may have been a reference to the prophets as Ezekiel called them "watchmen" in a later prophecy (Ezekiel 3:17, 33:1–11). The prophets and leaders will have the same good news and be in unity. They will relay their joy to the people, and the people will break forth in song.

The content of the messenger's message has to do with redeeming Jerusalem. After a seventy-year captivity, Isaiah states, the waste or ruined places of Jerusalem will begin to sing. This is because Jerusalem will be rebuilt and restored and will be the Lord's possession, not under foreign rule. After seventy years of captivity, this will be a comfort to God's people. This is definitely good news to make them sing and shout for joy!

Isaiah further describes the redemption of Jerusalem. He states that the "LORD hath made bare his holy arm in the eyes of all the nations." This will not be a private event. It will be known among all the nations. They will see that the Lord is still looking out for His people. They will see His power and His salvation. The Lord does not want to keep the salvation of His people a secret. Why? He wants other nations to worship and serve Him as well.

### 3. Go (vv. 11–12)

The Israelites are instructed to depart from Babylon. During their departure, they are to touch nothing that is unclean. They are in a foreign land, surrounded by a culture of idolatry and wickedness. The Lord instructs them to stay holy even though they have been exposed to the wickedness of a foreign people. They are to return to Him as worshipers bearing the holy vessels of the temple. They are to remain holy and get rid of anything that would defile them.

Although they may have been brought into captivity in haste and uncertainty, it will not be the way they will leave. They are instructed to depart in peace, in confidence, and not as one being pursued. It seems contradictory—to be told to leave a place of bondage but not so fast. Imagine being trapped in an elevator for hours and being told to walk out slowly when the door finally opens. Why are they told to exit slowly? This instruction is similar to customary evacuation procedures—to stay calm and exit carefully. They are to depart in peace knowing that the Heavenly Father has delivered them, gone before them, and that this is a place where they will never have to be again.

## Search the Scriptures

1. What makes the messenger's feet beautiful (Isaiah 52:7)?

2. What will the watchmen do when they see the messenger (v. 8)?

3. How are the people of God told to depart (v. 11)?

## Discuss the Meaning

1. What happened that caused Jerusalem to fall asleep, become weak, and settled with dust?

2. Why were they told to leave, but not in a hurry?

## Lesson in Our Society

Our society is bombarded with bad news. The newspaper and television are filled with stories of terrorist attacks and collapsing economies. We are constantly seeing the embarrassing sins of celebrities and high-profile preachers. This bad news saturation ought to make us hungry and thirsty for good news that brings hope. As believers, we have the good news that brings hope: the Gospel. There is enough hope in the Good News of the Gospel to drown out all of the bad news that the world throws at us. This kind of hope is enough to make us go all out in praising God and rejoicing.

## Make It Happen

Think of a situation you can't wait to get out of—your job, single parenthood, financial hardship, or a relationship. Now, consider today's lesson and apply what you've learned. This might include: warding off complacency, rejoicing with deliverance in mind, and leaving confidently knowing that God's deliverance is sure.

## Follow the Spirit

What God wants me to do:

_____

_____

_____

_____

## Remember Your Thoughts

Special insights I have learned:

_____

_____

_____

_____

## More Light on the Text
### Isaiah 52:1–2, 7–12

This portion of the great prophet includes passages that are much beloved today, which have been described by some as poetic and literary beauty. These verses fall between the third and fourth of what are known as Isaiah's four "Servant Songs." The verse immediately after our portion begins the famous "Fourth Servant Song," which many Christian commentators agree is a series of prophecies about the Christ, and frequently is titled "Suffering Servant." The first song, 40:1–4, introduces the servant. In the second, 49:1–6, the servant identifies himself to the world, and in the third, 50:4–11, the servant declares his confidence in the divine. In this passage, Isaiah's message is one of divine comfort and hope, which is explicit in 51:12: "I, even I, am he that comforteth you."

**1 Awake, awake; put on thy strength, O Zion; put on thy beautiful garments, O Jerusalem, the holy city: for henceforth there shall no more come into thee the uncircumcised and the unclean. 2 Shake thyself from the dust; arise, and sit down, O Jerusalem: loose thyself from the bands of thy neck, O captive daughter of Zion.**

Isaiah uses the same dual or double imperative in 51:9 (also "Awake, awake") and v. 17 (also translated "Rouse yourself"), which in Hebrew is 'ur (**OOR**), and means to wake, rise, or stir up. Zion variously refers to God's people, Jerusalem or Israel. From Hanson, both Zion and Jerusalem "depict the Holy City as a mother of the children of Israel" (147). In this case, it clearly refers to Jerusalem, and her strength refers to the power of her God. For such a great occasion, it is time for her to dress her best. In Hebrew, strength is *'oz* (**OZE**), and means might or power, while beauty is *tiph'arah* (**tif-ah-RAH**), which means comeliness or glory, as in fine garments (cf. Psalm 96:6).

As sovereign, God is the one who determines the future, and God has heard the cry of His people from bondage—now it is time to wake up, for freedom has arrived. In times past, Israel has drunk from the cup of God's wrath, but now that time has passed and the time of comfort has come. Now is the time to stand up and prepare for a time of celebration. This time, Israel's enemies will not be permitted entrance, as all unholiness will be prohibited—the holy city will be kept holy.

A biblical parallel can be seen in Matthew 10:14, referencing the disciples shaking the dust off their feet from places where they were not welcome. There is a clear sense of the people of God being set free or liberated and leaving behind the chains of bondage. Also evident is the fact that God's love reaches out to people in their bondage (cf. Romans 5:8).

**7 How beautiful upon the mountains are the feet of him that bringeth good tidings, that publisheth peace; that bringeth good tidings of good, that publisheth salvation; that saith unto Zion, Thy God reigneth! 8 Thy watchmen shall lift up the voice; with the voice together shall they sing: for they shall see eye to eye, when the LORD shall bring again Zion.**

To describe the feet of the good news runner or messenger, Isaiah selects the Hebrew word *na'ah* (**nah-AH**), also meaning to be pleasant or comely, which is only used twice elsewhere in the Old Testament (cf. Psalm 93:5 referring to the beauty of God's house, and Song of Solomon 1:10 referring to adorned cheeks). This verse is a direct parallel to Nahum 1:15, "Behold upon the mountains the feet of him that bringeth good tidings, that publisheth peace!"

As Isaiah has inspired many modern songs from his poetic prowess, this portion is well known. Many believe that he wrote in lyrical mode with the intent for the verses to be sung, much like the Psalms. Because of God's trustworthiness and reliability, just the news of the coming event is as good as the event. Using "prophetic" perfect tense, Israel's release has come to pass—as-good-as-done. It is a historical reality which is ready to take place. Such "future is here" language dovetails with 2 Corinthians 5:17, "all things have become new" (NKJV).

These are the feet that bring words that thrill the heart longing for just this announcement, "Your God reigns!" Even Jesus was not handsome, but rather plain in appearance (Isaiah 53:2) and certainly on the Cross He was a repulsive sight—yet how beautiful those pierced, bleeding feet that carried the message from His day to today: our God reigns.

News is not always good, but in this case the adjective makes all the difference. This is "good tidings," a phrase almost synonymous today with the Gospel. The remaining descriptors in the verse further reinforce that this isn't an ordinary victory by any means.

**9 Break forth into joy, sing together, ye waste places of Jerusalem: for the LORD hath comforted his people, he hath redeemed Jerusalem. 10 The LORD hath**

made bare his holy arm in the eyes of all the nations; and all the ends of the earth shall see the salvation of our God.

At first, it is the voice of a lone arriving messenger, and then those on the watchtower join in, and now the city will raise its voice in song as a choir. The people of the "waste places" are the suffering and disoriented remnant of the nation. Now all that has changed, as God has returned and "made bare his holy arm." This means God will comfort His people with His strong arm of deliverance and salvation (cf. 40:10, 51:9) in the eyes of all the nations. This is an anthropomorphism indicating both strength and preparation for action. Surely such reassurances spell divine comfort for all of God's people (cf. 40:1–2), starting in Jerusalem and including the whole world (cf. 42:1–12).

They hear first and then see, just as Israel first heard about the coming Messiah, and then finally saw Him with their eyes (e.g., Simeon, Luke 2:25–32). Similarly, today, most everyone has heard about Christ's second coming, and one day every eye will see Him (Revelation 1:7). Isaiah's prophecy about God's triumphant return to Zion runs parallel to Ezekiel's account of God's glory returning to the temple from a recent lesson exploring Ezekiel 43:1–12. Another parallel today is the body of Christ waiting expectantly for Jesus to return triumphantly to the Mount of Olives from which He ascended, which is due east of the temple mound from which direction Ezekiel saw the glory of God returning to His temple.

**11 Depart ye, depart ye, go ye out from thence, touch no unclean thing; go ye out of the midst of her; be ye clean, that bear the vessels of the LORD. 12 For ye shall not go out with haste, nor go by flight: for the LORD will go before you; and the God of Israel will be your reward.**

Now comes the climax of Isaiah's message with another dual imperative. His intention is to show how the march from Babylon displays not only God's power and sovereignty but His holiness. This is a religious, not a military march, which was to be void of anything that could hurt the purity of God's people. There will be no more defiling or staining of Zion; the sins that brought judgment will be left behind.

The "vessels" are speculated to be either: 1) the actual vessels that had been stolen from the temple by King Nebuchadnezzar (see 2 Chronicles 36:7, 10, 18; Ezra 1:7–11; Jeremiah 27:16–22), or 2) symbolic of the total worship experience that had been stopped since the Babylonian exile.

As stated, the actual victory is declared in prophetic perfect tense, and the outcome is certain even though the battle is still ongoing. This reminds us of a common expression of the hope of the ages, "We're on the winning team." For believers, this is not pie-in-the-sky wishful thinking but present inspiration from tomorrow's, future perfect, as-good-as-done, coming reality. In a real sense, Isaiah—even before Christ's time—captured the Christian's irrepressible hope that stands strong regardless of circumstances and the direness of one's present reality.

The passage evokes an unmistakable comparison to the Exodus, but Isaiah reverses it. The "new Exodus" will be a journey of peace and safety. Flight implies seeking safety, but here safety is guaranteed. Here, God both leads and protects; there is no Pharaoh chasing them, and the former anxiety and fear are left in the dust. God will go before them and He will also be their "reward" (Heb. *asaf*, **ah-SAHF**) or rearguard. This is similar to the pillar of cloud that protected them from the Egyptian army prior to crossing the Red Sea (Exodus 14:19-20). All is well—the King has returned in victory to His people—all is well (cf. 51:16).

### Summary

While in the ancient world, the literal existence of bondage and exile was common, most today do not experience such ugly realities. The sad truth, however, is that these practices are not entirely relegated to the history books, and in the modern world slavery still exists, e.g., human trafficking. The notion of freedom from bondage, whether literal or metaphorical, is simultaneously powerful and profound. In Isaiah 52:3–6, not covered in the lesson, Israel's oppressors and those who spoke with contempt about her God met their just ends, a principle which can be extended because it speaks to our sovereign God's character of justice and righteousness. With passages such as these, God ensures that for those who trust in Him, all of their persecutors will be prosecuted, and all of their fellow prisoners will be liberated.

We are often anxious about what tomorrow will bring, but when our faith burns brightly, our fear subsides and our hope is restored because we know in our hearts that our future is secure. To help us through troubled times, it is important to maintain a remembrance of God's presence in our lives, both past and present, in times of deliverance from bondage and in times of victory and restoration. We must not permit ourselves to forget our God, like Israel often forgot (Isaiah 51:13). We must not forget His grace, our salvation, or our great future. We must remember that our God reigns!

Sources:
Goldingay, John. *The Message of Isaiah 40–55: A Literary-Theological Commentary.* New York: T&T Clark International, 2005. 417–460.

Grogan, Geoffrey W. *Isaiah—Ezekiel.* The Expositor's Bible Commentary, vol. 6. Grand Rapids, MI: Zondervan, 1986. 296–297.
Hanson, Paul D. *Isaiah 40–66. Interpretation: A Bible Commentary for Teaching and Preaching.* Louisville, KY: John Knox Press, 1995. 142–153.
*Smith's Bible Dictionary.* Peabody, MA: Hendrickson Publishers, 2000. 292–303.
Strong, James. *The New Strong's Exhaustive Concordance of the Bible.* Nashville, TN: Thomas Nelson Publishers, 1990.
Westermann, Claus. *Isaiah 40–66: A Commentary.* The Old Testament Library. Philadelphia, PA: The Westminster Press, 1969. 246–258.

## Say It Correctly

Zion. **ZEYE**-on.
Bethesda. beh-**THEZ**-duh.

## Daily Bible Readings

**MONDAY**
Hope in God!
(Psalm 42:5–11)

**TUESDAY**
Fear, Awe, and Praise
(Psalm 33:1–9)

**WEDNESDAY**
O Lord, We Hope in You
(Psalm 33:10–22)

**THURSDAY**
Hope Set on the Living God
(1 Timothy 4:4–11)

**FRIDAY**
The God of Our Salvation
(Psalm 85:1–7)

**SATURDAY**
God is Our Shield
(Genesis 15:1–6)

**SUNDAY**
God Before Us, God Behind Us
(Isaiah 52:1–2, 7–12)

# Acts of Worship

The study of this quarter is primarily from the New Testament. Its three units follow the theme of worship as it pertains to a human response to God.

## UNIT 1 • IN AWE OF GOD

The four lessons in this unit explore the amazing power of God in Hebrews, Matthew, and Luke. In Lesson 3, Luke's account of the Christmas story recalls the praise and adulation expressed to God by both the angels and shepherds.

**Lesson 1: December 7, 2014**
**Worship Christ's Majesty**
**Hebrews 1:1–9**
Some people do seemingly miraculous things with their gifts and talents. For the true miracle of Jesus Christ, the gift of salvation, God's people respond with worship.

**Lesson 2: December 14, 2014**
**Make a Joyful Noise**
**Psalm 95:1–7a**
Many realize that a power beyond them gives meaning to their lives. The psalmist declared that God is the rock of their salvation and is worthy of praise and worship.

**Lesson 3: December 21, 2014**
**Glory to God in the Highest**
**Luke 2:8–20**
Sometimes an event in people's lives causes spontaneous celebration. Angels announced the birth of the Savior and a multitude of the heavenly host praised God.

**Lesson 4: December 28, 2014**
**In Awe of Christ's Power**
**Matthew 14:22–36**
Many things inspire awe in people. Matthew wrote about the times when Jesus miraculously healed the sick and walked on water to meet His disciples in a boat, which led them to worship Him as truly the Son of God.

## UNIT 2 • LEARNING TO PRAY

The four lessons in this unit look at prayer as found in Luke, John, Hebrews, and James.

**Lesson 5: January 4, 2015**
**A Model for Prayer**
**Luke 11:1–13**
People build intimate, trusting relationships by having open communication with one another. Jesus teaches that nurturing a relationship with God requires persistent prayer.

**Lesson 6: January 11, 2015**
**Jesus Prays for His Disciples**
**John 17:6–21**

Small, intimate groups exist in the midst of a larger community. Jesus prayed that the disciples would be united and protected as they brought new people into their community in an unsafe world.

**Lesson 7: January 18, 2015**
**Jesus Intercedes for Us**
**Hebrews 4:14–5:10**

People often have someone who makes special efforts on their behalf. The writer of Hebrews informed us that God appointed Jesus, the High Priest, as an intercessor on behalf of His people.

**Lesson 8: January 25, 2015**
**We Pray for One Another**
**James 5:13–18**

Illness is part of being human. James taught that the prayer of faith brings healing and offered Elijah's prayer as an example of prayer's effectiveness.

**UNIT 3 • STEWARDSHIP FOR LIFE**

The four lessons in this study examine various aspects of stewardship from Matthew, Luke, and Ephesians.

**Lesson 9: February 1, 2015**
**Feasting and Fasting**
**Daniel 1:5, 8–17; Matthew 6:16–18**

People often restrict their diet for both physical and spiritual reasons. The Scripture teaches that fasting is good stewardship that gives physical and spiritual benefits.

**Lesson 10: February 8, 2015**
**Serving Neighbors, Serving God**
**Luke 10:25–34**

People of goodwill take care of and serve their neighbors. The parable of the Good Samaritan teaches that when the faithful serve their neighbor, they serve God.

**Lesson 11: February 15, 2015**
**Serving the Least**
**Matthew 25:31–46**

Opportunities for serving others are all around us, although believers do not always recognize or respond to them. Matthew says that believers should serve others as if they were the Lord, and God will judge the believers accordingly.

**Lesson 12: February 22, 2015**
**Clothed and Ready**
**Ephesians 6:10–20**

Only proper preparation can give assurance that certain things are accomplished. Putting on the whole armor of God teaches that in order to best serve God, Christians need to fortify themselves with truth, righteousness, peace, faith, salvation, the Word of God, and prayer.

# The Rightful Object of Our Worship

Everyone worships someone or something. The essential question in life is not whether I will worship something, but who or what do I worship? Many would like to believe that they do not worship anything. They would rather exist in a secular universe devoid of God and talk of worship. The fact is even those who would like to dismiss worship as something primitive often worship themselves or their ideas. There is an innate desire in us as human beings for someone or something to be our ultimate allegiance and the primary motivating factor of our lives. When you look around at the daily lives of those around you, we can easily observe what holds their ultimate allegiance. You can tell by the way they treat their possessions or relationships. You can tell by the way they relate to their jobs and their recreational activities. We are all worshiping something. These objects of worship are never worth our time and attention. We worship them and receive nothing in return. We experience their fragility and futility. There is an emptiness that comes with worshiping things that are not worthy of our worship. It is the inevitable result of idolatry. Idolatry is worshiping anything that is not God Himself. It is placing our proper desire for worship onto an object that is not worthy of worship. As Christ-followers, we have the Son of God Himself as an object of worship.

He is the rightful object of worship because of His person, purpose, and position.

**His Person**

Jesus is the sinless Son of God. He is the second Person of the Trinity. All of the attributes of God the Father can be attributed to Jesus. He is faithful. He is loving. He is holy. He is sovereign. In fact Jesus said Himself that if you have seen Him, you have seen the Father. He is the image of the invisible God. Many people want to see God. They desire to know exactly what God is like. What pleases Him and what displeases Him? In Jesus we get our answer to that question. Jesus is also a man. He is the Word made flesh that came down to dwell among us. In Jesus we see the perfect man. The life of Jesus shows us the life that we were created for. When we examine the Gospels, we are struck by the way Jesus handled different situations. Through it all, His humanity and His deity shine through. One of the reasons Jesus is our rightful object of worship is who He is.

**His Purpose**

The Apostle John stated that "the Son of God came to destroy the works of the devil" (1 John 3:8, NLT). Jesus came to earth with a grand purpose. It was planned before the foundation of the world that Jesus would atone for the sins of humanity. Jesus came to model the life we are to live as humans, but that wasn't all. He also came to remove the barrier to living that life: sin. As the sinless Son of God, Jesus came to be a sacrifice for the world. Instead of coming to rule as a king, He died as a criminal for a greater purpose. This purpose and plan was to give His blood for the forgiveness of our sins so that nothing could stand in the way of our having a relationship with God the Father. Sin made us distant enemies, but Jesus' work on the Cross made us sons and daughters. He is the rightful object of worship because He gave us a right relationship with the Father.

### His Position

Jesus died, but that was not the end of the story. Three days later, He rose again. With a new resurrected body, Jesus had conquered death and was given all authority in heaven and in earth. For forty days He stayed with the disciples, teaching them about the kingdom of God, and then He ascended into heaven to be with His Father. Now He sits at the right hand of God as our advocate. Paul says that "he is far above any ruler or authority or power or leader or anything else—not only in this world but also in the world to come. God has put all things under the authority of Christ and has made him head over all things for the benefit of the church" (Ephesians 1:21–22, NLT). Christ is the ruler of the universe. There is nothing that exists that is not under His authority. He is the King of kings and the Lord of lords. He has no rivals or competitions. There is no one that He can be compared to. This is why He is the rightful object of worship.

As we look at our lives, let us examine whether we are worshiping the idols of this world or the rightful object of worship: Jesus Christ. Let's take a close look at our financial budgets and the way we spend our time. Let's reflect on what makes us angry, happy, or sad. Sometimes there is a clue hidden in our emotions on what truly holds our allegiance. The Westminster Confession states that "the chief end of man is to glorify God and enjoy him forever." Is this your main goal in life? We were created to worship, and it is not a matter of whether we worship or not, but who will be our object of worship. This world gives worship to things that are not worthy of worship. The followers of Christ have Jesus Christ as our object of worship. Because of His person, purpose, and position, we can give Him all of our money, time, and effort. It is through Him that we can fulfill the first and greatest commandment to love God with all our heart, soul, and mind. This is the rightful response toward the rightful object of our worship.

# Surrender: The Best Teacher of Worship

by Beverly Moore, M.A.

Acts of worship such as praise, thanksgiving, and giving are valuable and required expressions of our love and appreciation for God. However, at the heart of worship is our ability to be vulnerable by placing our complete trust in our God whom we cannot see. As Christian educators, we are instruments of God used in the spiritual formation of His people. We are charged with helping others cultivate an intimate relationship with God through the transforming study and application of His Word. Worship is a lifestyle, one that must be taught with repetition and modeling. To use worship as a teaching tool requires the ability to be transparent with your students. Students are able to relate to teachers who are able to be real about their struggles yet show them how they are able to overcome them through surrendering to God. This is ultimately an act of worship.

I am reminded of Moses, whom God used as His instrument to deliver His people out of bondage in Egypt after years of captivity. Throughout the Pentateuch, we see Moses in his humanity relate to God and the people he was called to serve. God uses Moses to lead His people because of the intimate relationship he developed with God through his surrendered life. The relationship Moses had with God could only be cultivated through continual dependence, fidelity, and surrender to God's will. Moses could not teach the Children of Israel how to worship God without having seen God proved in his own life. Indeed Moses had plenty of object lessons in knowing not just God's acts, but also His ways (Psalm 103:7). And so it is with us in today's context as Christian educators: pastors, ministers, and teachers alike, our lives often become object lessons where we too are called upon to surrender all to Jesus. It is in these experiences that we obtain the best lessons to pass on to others.

In the book of Deuteronomy, Moses prepares the Children of Israel to take possession of the Promised Land. That generation survived the wilderness through God's sustaining power and goodness. Moses was tasked as God's mouthpiece with reiterating God's laws, commandments, and ordinances, and instilling in them specific directions for how to worship. God was very clear: He did not want the people, whom He had chosen and called out from among the other nations of the world as His treasured possession, to copy the pagan worship practices (Deuteronomy 12:1–5, 29–32). God through Moses established acceptable worship to Him and shared with them the blessings of obedience to His commands. Most notably, God instructed the Children of Israel "You shall love the LORD your God with all your heart, and with all your soul, and with all your might. Keep the words that I am commanding you today in your heart" (Deuteronomy 6:5–6). This passage of Scripture is included in what is known in the Jewish culture as the *Shema*, which in Hebrew is the first word of the commandment and means to "listen" or "hear." Faithful Jews still recite the *Shema* as an expression of their devotion to God today, and it is a good practice for us as Christians to call to mind and live out the *Shema*. Loving God with all our heart, soul, and might is to surrender to God in every area of our lives.

To use worship as a teaching tool is to usher people into the presence of God by aiding their understanding of what it means to live in unbroken fellowship with the Lord. Living in unbroken fellowship with God in response to His goodness and redemptive work through Jesus Christ means that we live our lives as modeled by our Lord, who showed us how to be one with the Father (John 17:21–23). As mentioned above, worship is a lifestyle; therefore we should see every aspect of our lives as worship to the Lord. We can be accustomed to compartmentalizing our lives—church lives versus the rest of our social lives—but true worship recognizes God in everything that we do. As the theologican and statesman Abraham Kuyper has said, "There is not a square inch in the whole domain of our human existence over which Christ, who is Sovereign over all, does not cry: 'Mine!'" In these words is a challenge for us to surrender on a daily basis.

We can also use worship as a means of showing people how to deal with life's adverse situations. In these times worship is not automatic, and a conscious decision to believe God over circumstances is needed. Through worship, we are able to draw strength from the presence and power of God and His Word. As Christian educators, we are directly responsible for equipping the saints in how to count it as joy when they experience hardships (James 1:2). Martin Luther said the very highest worship of God is that we trust Him: "God cannot be worshiped unless you ascribe to Him the glory of truthfulness and all goodness which is due to Him." We are central as influencers for God to instruct and facilitate students in learning how to redirect negative circumstances, especially those thoughts born through spiritual attacks. By living a life surrendered to God, our reasonable act of worship (Romans 12:1), we entrust our lives to the One who is sovereign. In other words, we teach our students through the Word of God how to respond differently when they are hit with life's blows, sure in knowing that God is good and trustworthy when circumstances are not.

Finally, our worship teaches students who God is, to know His character, and to be personally affirmed because of His acceptance. Jesus, our Master teacher, shows us through His life and ministry how we are to reflect the knowledge of God's character. Jesus said, "Those who speak on their own seek their own glory; but the one who seeks the glory of Him who sent is true and there is nothing false in Him" (John 7:18, NRSV). Jesus was affirmed by His relationship with His Father and did not seek the glory of man (John 5:30, 41). When He met the woman at the well, He noted that "true worshipers will worship the Father in spirit and in truth for the Father seeks such as these to worship Him" (from John 4:23, NRSV). At the heart of God's character is the knowledge that His intentions and motives are always pure, good, and in our best interest. We are affirmed in our place in Him by knowing that we are accepted as one of His beloved, chosen in Him before the foundation of the world (Ephesians 1:4–6). With that said, we wear the brand of Jesus by receiving our identity in Him. We know who we are and whose we are, and because we place our trust in His goodness and faithfulness, total surrender is not burdensome. Our lives are hidden in Christ in God (Colossians 3:3). We are able to teach students how to base their identity on who they are in Christ, not the labels of the world, nor the past, nor the present whether good or bad. Bruce Wilkerson said in his book *The Seven Laws of the Learner*: "Application must ultimately lead the students from studying the Bible to obeying the Lord...Christianity is not a set of facts but relationship with a living Person Jesus Christ" (160). As teachers, our function in the body of Christ is to cultivate true worship of God, which is more than just a mere performance of religious ritual, but a surrender of our hearts and lives to the King of the Universe, Jesus Christ.

*Beverly Moore is a Bible Teacher and Independent Church Marketing Communications Consultant.*

Sources:
Luther, Martin. "On the Freedom of a Christian," *Luther's Works*, vol. 31. Philadelphia: Fortress Press, 1957. 350, 353.
Wilkerson, Bruce. *The Seven Laws of the Learner: How to Teach Almost Anything to Practically Anyone!*, Sisters, OR: Multnomah Publishers, 1992. 160.

# Worship from an African Perspective

by Dr. Moussa Coulibaly

It is an early Sunday morning in a small village. The livestock are released. One can hear the noise of metal. Some farmers are getting ready to go to the fields, but those who are Christians are preparing themselves for church. Though a poor community in a rural area, they have been touched by the love of Jesus Christ. To refuse to farm on Sunday seemed foolishness to other villagers. For these Christians, it is not only an act of obedience to their Lord, but also an act of sacrifice and thanksgiving for all that He has done. At about 9:00 a.m., the service starts. After the whole church prays together, the songs begin. Loud voices are heard from afar as these melodious songs in the vernacular language praise the Lord for His power, love, and grace. Everyone is singing, and no one is a spectator. The drummers expertly lead the congregational singing with a rhythmic beat that induces the desire to dance. Some cannot hold in their feelings or stand in one place. Their desire is to move up and down or go up front to make a circle and dance. Young and old, women and men, all are involved in this joyful celebration of the Lord. The mood felt in the awesome presence of God dismisses fears and anxieties. This is a typical way of worship that can be witnessed all over churches in the sub-Saharan Africa.

Worship is the rendering of the Greek word *proskunein* (**pros–KOO-nayn**), which means to fall prostrate. Bromiley states that the usage of the word demonstrates that those who fall voluntarily or consciously declare by their attitude the subject of their worship. Best states that worship is a "simultaneous expression of dependency and worth" and an indication of the insufficiency of the worshiper before the subject of his worship. Worship therefore includes a deep knowledge of the Lord and a precise self-knowledge of the worshiper in his relation to whom he worships. As African Christians, we have been alienated previously from our culture and we had to struggle to capture the real figure of Christ that was presented to us clothed in white.

We cherish dearly whatever object we value. Most often, some of our attitude toward things or people we value or put in high esteem stems from the perceived worth of the subject in relation to our own. Peter, for instance, during the miraculous catch of fish in Luke 5:8, said to Jesus: "Depart from me; for I am a sinful man, O Lord" (KJV). Isaiah also expresses awe and reverence for God when he saw His majesty and his own sinfulness; he therefore cried out: "It's all over! I am doomed, for I am a sinful man. I have filthy lips, and I live among a people with filthy lips. Yet I have seen the King, the LORD of Heaven's Armies." (Isaiah 6:5, NLT). It means that genuine worship comes from the recognition of our true selves and the revelation of God to us.

African worship is imbedded in culture. However, as Africans, we have struggled since the introduction of Christianity by missionaries to capture a real sense of worship. Alienation from African culture and the wrong perception of Christ as displayed to us by early missionaries led many Africans to lose their real sense of worship. It was forbidden at a certain period to use African musical instruments for worship. Instruments such as djembe (drum), balafon (xylophone), and the like could stir emotions in Africans to express their deepest feeling of appreciation of the majesty, holiness, and love of God more than the organ or guitar. African worship is full of exuberance with shout of praises, clamor, clappings, and dance. Spontaneous inspired songs with a repetitive chorus for the church to sing in unison usually generate a feeling of participation by all the members of the congregation. Not every congregation does as stated above. Urban churches conduct worship in a variety of ways, many of which are modern and foreign to the general African culture.

Emotions are part and parcel of the African style of worship. Jesus told the Samaritan woman that the true worshiper will worship in spirit and truth (John 4:23–24). Wiersbe explains this phrase to imply objective and subjective aspects of worship that we should strive to balance. While the objective aspect is concerned with reasoning, the subjective calls upon the feelings and emotions. Objectivity alone in worship can bring dryness in a service, while subjectivity alone would also lead to mere emotionalism without a real grasp on reality. We Africans

from our cultural practice most often identify with the subjective worship, freely expressing our innermost feeling by crying, clapping, jumping, and dancing. Although not all the churches in Africa worship this way, the majority do.

Whatever joy or delight we can find in that type of worship, it cannot benefit us unless we discover who Jesus really is. "Who do people say I am?" This was Jesus' question to the disciples in Luke 9:18. It is in an encounter with Jesus that His real identity is discovered. It could be a challenging or crisis situation like in Matthew 14:33. When the disciples saw Jesus walking on water and calming the wind when He entered the boat, they could not do anything but exclaim, "You are really the Son of God!" (NLT). In the case of the Roman centurion in Matthew 27:54, a miraculous event was witnessed. The centurion experienced the earthquake and exclaimed, "This man truly was the Son of God!" (NLT). This discovery of Jesus' identity triggered a sense of awe to all those who witnessed it. In Africa today, there is an ongoing search in many Christians' minds for who Jesus really is. Their struggle to appropriate the Christ in a relevant African context is due to the alienation of Africans from themselves in the early part of European evangelism in Africa. This leads us to forcefully reiterate the equally important objective aspect of worship. As Africans, we also need a major understanding of God's self-revelation to the world through the life and ministry of Jesus Christ. Philip rightly asked Jesus to show the Father and that will be enough (John 14:8).

Worship also involves attitude and action. We should exhibit reverence when we approach the Lord of Hosts. It reminds me of a scene I witnessed in a church, where a ministry leader fell flat on the floor with her face on the ground during church service to express humility for playing the role of God in a drama that just ended. Indeed, some may think she was too spiritual or she exaggerated, but it should be reiterated that our God deserves an attitude of total fear, surrender, submission, and humility from us. The frenzied excitement of worship is important, but the reverence should not be out of place. Is He not the "fearsome God" (Genesis 31:53) of Jacob's father Isaac? People in rural churches in Africa will openly testify to God's kindness in their lives or answered prayer, and then will celebrate it with spontaneous rhythmic songs to the glory of our Lord and Savior. These answered prayers could range from healing, to protection from a fatal accident, to success in an exam, business, or harvest.

Worship has a cultural function in that the one who worships should know his or her own identity. In the past, African culture has been ignored in the worship service with undeniable consequences in the appraisal of true worship by Africans. There is, however, today a danger of attempting to lead African Christians to adopt one type of worship that may appear to best suit a changing society made up of major diversities. Best again emphasizes that musicians should adjust their musical choice according to the cultural sensibilities of the congregation. This will ensure that the congregation will connect with the worship by being their true selves and at the same time connect with the objective reality of God. In this way, congregations can worship Him in spirit and in truth, for the Father seeks such to worship Him (John 4:23).

*Moussa Coulibaly holds a Ph.D. from Trinity Evangelical Divinity School. He currently serves in his home country of Burkina Faso, founding five elementary schools and one secondary school with almost 2,000 students; planting over 20 churches; and founding Elim Bible Institute which teaches in two different languages.*

# GWENDOLYN BROOKS
## (1917–2000)
### Poet

Poetry is often regarded as something for the rich in high society. In fact, it is one of the most accessible literary art forms. It is art for the people. No one proves this more than Gwendolyn Brooks. Writing prolifically since she was a child, Gwendolyn Brooks earned a reputation as a poet for the people. She was born in Topeka, Kansas, in 1917. Before long, the Great Migration took her family from Topeka to Chicago, and she was a lifelong Chicagoan, residing in the South Side until her death. During her early years, Gwendolyn's family experienced hardship and financial struggles.

Brooks began writing poetry as a child and published her first poem in a children's magazine when she was thirteen. She attended four different high schools throughout the city. An all White, an all Black, and an integrated school gave her a unique perspective on race that influenced her work. By the age of sixteen, Brooks had become prolific, publishing seventy-five poems. These poems, which included sonnets, ballads, and free verse, were being published in the *Chicago Defender*, a primarily African American newspaper. Gwendolyn's work at this time contained a robust description and celebration of inner-city life.

During this time, she is quoted as saying, "I felt that I had to write. Even if I had never been published, I knew that I would go on writing, enjoying it, and experiencing the challenge."

In 1936, she graduated from Wilson Junior College. Later, in 1939, she married Henry Blakely and they had two children. During this time, Brooks met with James Weldon Johnson and Langston Hughes. Both literary greats urged her to read more modern poetry and to write more. During her early years, she was also Director of Publicity for the NAACP. By 1943, she had earned an award from the Midwest Writers Conference. A few years later, in 1945, Brooks' first published book, *A Street in Bronzeville*, earned her a Guggenheim Fellowship and several other awards. She later published *Annie Allen*, which was so well received that it made her the first African American to win a Pulitzer Prize in literature.

She first began teaching with a poetry workshop at Columbia College in 1963. After this she taught creative writing at a number of universities including Northeastern Illinois University, Elmhurst College, Columbia University, Clay College of New York, and the University of Wisconsin.

Brooks received many awards from the government. She was invited to the White

House by John F. Kennedy to participate in the Library of Congress public readings. In 1968, she became the poet laureate of Illinois. In this role, she created workshops and public readings to make poetry more accessible to everyday people. In 1985, she became the appointed poetry consultant to the Library of Congress. Later, in 1994, she was selected by the National Endowment of Humanities to be a Jefferson Lecturer, the highest award the federal government can give to a poet.

Gwendolyn Brooks was a prolific author. She authored over twenty books of poetry and a number of non-fiction works. In 1953, Brooks published her only long fiction work, *Maud Martha*. At a conference held at Fisk University, Gwendolyn decided to become more involved in the Black arts movement. Although nothing about her poetry had changed, she became one of the premiere spokespeople for "the Black aesthetic." She championed art that spoke of Black life as human. Gwendolyn Brooks will be especially remembered as a poet who visited schools, colleges, universities, prisons, hospitals, and drug rehabilitation centers all over the nation. While attending to her duties as poet laureate for the state of Illinois, Brooks hosted annual literary awards ceremonies, where she gave out prizes from her own meager funds. She was truly a poet for the people.

# Teaching Tips

## Words You Should Know

**A. Majesty** (Hebrews 1:3) *megalosune* (Gk.)—Greatness; another name for God.

**B. Angel** (v. 4) *angelos* (Gk.)—Messenger, one who is sent.

## Teacher Preparation

**Unifying Principle—Better Than Angels.** Some people do seemingly miraculous things with their gifts and talents. How do Christians respond? For the true miracle of Jesus Christ, the gift of salvation, God's people respond with worship.

**A.** Read through the Focal Verses at least two times, then spend quiet time meditating on them.

**B.** Read through the lesson and make notes on important points to highlight, keeping in mind the Aim for Change and Keep in Mind verse.

**C.** Review your notes and reread the Focal Verses once more, adding any additional points to your notes.

## Open the Lesson

**A.** Begin with prayer.

**B.** Share the topic, the Unifying Principle, and the Aim for Change objectives.

**C.** Ask a volunteer to read the In Focus illustration aloud.

## Presenting the Scripture

**A.** Solicit an individual to read the Focal Verses aloud.

**B.** Have another volunteer read the passage again and tell the class to mark any words or sentences that stick out or evoke a question.

**C.** Ask the class to share any words or sentences they marked.

**D.** Read the Keep in Mind Verse.

## Explore the Meaning

**A.** Read and discuss the Background and The People, Places, and Times portions of the lesson.

**B.** Offer any clarification on the lesson.

**C.** Split the class in two groups. Have each group answer the questions in Search the Scripture and read the Discuss the Meaning section.

## Next Steps for Application

**A.** Explore the Lesson in Our Society.

**B.** Review the key point of Make It Happen.

**C.** Have anyone share concluding thoughts or ways they will commit to applying the passage to their lives.

## Worship Guide

For the Superintendent or Teacher
Theme: Worship Christ's Majesty
Song: "Before the Throne of
God Above"
Devotional Reading: 1 Timothy
1:12–17

# Worship Christ's Majesty

**Bible Background • HEBREWS 1:1–9**
**Printed Text • HEBREWS 1:1–9**
**Devotional Reading • 1 TIMOTHY 1:12–17**

## Aim for Change

By the end of this lesson we will: CONSIDER why Jesus is worthy of adoration and worship; AFFIRM that Jesus' superiority and God's anointing of Him "with the oil of gladness" leads to our response of worship; and GUIDE adults into the practice of meaningful worship.

 In Focus

Maya Angelou's written works have touched many lives across our nation and the world. Through her poetry and autobiographical books, she has inspired, encouraged, and challenged individuals and communities to lead better lives. Indeed, Dr. Angelou has been regarded by many as one of the greatest poets of the nation in the twentieth century. Perhaps nothing suggests this more than when President Clinton bestowed upon her the title Poet Laureate (or a poet who speaks for one's country). This honor is considered the highest honor that a poet can receive. It is an honor that comes with a special authority; it is an honor that signals to an audience, "Listen up, I'm speaking! I have something important to say."

*While humans ascribe honor to each other based on accomplishments, in today's lesson the author of Hebrews calls our attention to the honor and majesty of Jesus. The author offers specific reasons that Jesus is worthy of the highest honor and majesty, and that we as Christians should worship Him. Jesus is God, and when He speaks and acts, He is displaying the will of God. Because of this, He is worthy of the highest honor and most deserving of worship!*

## Keep in Mind

"[Jesus] being the brightness of his glory, and the express image of his person, and upholding all things by the word of his power, when he had by himself purged our sins, sat down on the right hand of the Majesty on high" (Hebrews 1:3).

"[Jesus] being the brightness of his glory, and the express image of his person, and upholding all things by the word of his power, when he had by himself purged our sins, sat down on the right hand of the Majesty on high" (Hebrews 1:3).

## Focal Verses

**KJV** **Hebrews 1:1** God, who at sundry times and in divers manners spake in time past unto the fathers by the prophets,

**2** Hath in these last days spoken unto us by his Son, whom he hath appointed heir of all things, by whom also he made the worlds;

**3** Who being the brightness of his glory, and the express image of his person, and upholding all things by the word of his power, when he had by himself purged our sins, sat down on the right hand of the Majesty on high:

**4** Being made so much better than the angels, as he hath by inheritance obtained a more excellent name than they.

**5** For unto which of the angels said he at any time, Thou art my Son, this day have I begotten thee? And again, I will be to him a Father, and he shall be to me a Son?

**6** And again, when he bringeth in the firstbegotten into the world, he saith, And let all the angels of God worship him.

**7** And of the angels he saith, Who maketh his angels spirits, and his ministers a flame of fire.

**8** But unto the Son he saith, Thy throne, O God, is for ever and ever: a sceptre of righteousness is the sceptre of thy kingdom.

**9** Thou hast loved righteousness, and hated iniquity; therefore God, even thy God, hath anointed thee with the oil of gladness above thy fellows.

**NLT** **Hebrews 1:1** Long ago God spoke many times and in many ways to our ancestors through the prophets.

**2** And now in these final days, he has spoken to us through his Son. God promised everything to the Son as an inheritance, and through the Son he created the universe.

**3** The Son radiates God's own glory and expresses the very character of God, and he sustains everything by the mighty power of his command. When he had cleansed us from our sins, he sat down in the place of honor at the right hand of the majestic God in heaven.

**4** This shows that the Son is far greater than the angels, just as the name God gave him is greater than their names.

**5** For God never said to any angel what he said to Jesus: "You are my Son. Today I have become your Father." God also said, "I will be his Father, and he will be my Son."

**6** And when he brought his supreme Son into the world, God said, "Let all of God's angels worship him."

**7** Regarding the angels, he says, "He sends his angels like the winds, his servants like flames of fire."

**8** But to the Son he says, "Your throne, O God, endures forever and ever. You rule with a scepter of justice.

**9** You love justice and hate evil. Therefore, O God, your God has anointed you, pouring out the oil of joy on you more than on anyone else."

### The People, Places, and Times

**Sin.** Sin is defined as breaking the law of God. The concept of sin was very common among the Jewish people before and during the life of Jesus. Most good Jews would have learned at a early age the laws regarding sin from the Pentateuch (the first five books of the Jewish Bible and the Old Testament). Sin forms a separation between a holy God and His people. Leviticus details the required responses of the people to rectify their sin against God. In Leviticus 4:1–5:19, for example, we learn that a primary duty of the priests of Israel was to sacrifice an animal regularly to God for the forgiveness of the people's sins.

**Purification Rituals.** Purification rituals were a set of sacrifices and actions designed to make an individual or a group of people holy before God. Because the book of Hebrews was written to a predominantly Jewish-Christian audience, the proclamation that Jesus "cleansed us from our sins" would have had profound meaning for them (v. 3, NLT). It would have served as a powerful reminder that no longer must they spill the blood of an animal to be in God's presence. Rather, Jesus' sacrifice, once and for all, allows them to have access to a holy God (Hebrews 9:11–14). No longer must a priest serve on their behalf to enact purification rituals, either. As the author of Hebrews explains, Jesus not only replaces the animal sacrifice, but the high priest as well (chapters 7–8). No longer are the old rituals necessary. Jesus' sacrifice for their sins is lasting and completely effectual. The key point is that with the sacrifice of Jesus, a new type of purification of sins has been established.

## Background

The early Christians were composed of Jews and Gentiles. The letter of Hebrews, however, appears to be intended for a primarily Jewish-Christian audience. Over and over, the letter refers to ideas and concepts that have historical importance for Jews. For example, the author talks about "purification for sins," a "high priest," and Israel's time in the wilderness. In addition, the author refers to key figures in Israel's history, such as the prophets, Moses, Joshua, and the priest Melchizedek.

Many of the references to Jewish history are to instruct these new Christians. By drawing on language and themes that would have had significance for the audience, the author is instructing and encouraging these fledgling Christians to press forward in their new faith. The author contrasts their Jewishness to their Christian identity and explains how being a follower of Christ is similar to and different from Judaism. The author is careful to point out that because Christ is superior to figures in their Jewish history, including highly esteemed angels, He is worthy of their faith and worship.

## At-A-Glance

1. The Son of God (Hebrews 1:1–3)
2. Superior to the Angels (vv. 4–9)

## In Depth

### 1. The Son of God (Hebrews 1:1–3)

You will notice that in verses 1–3 the name Jesus is not mentioned; neither is the title Christ (Messiah). Almost startlingly, "Jesus" is not invoked until Hebrews 2:9. Not mentioning Jesus in this section seems most likely to do with the focus of the author. By not mentioning His name until later, the author wishes to draw the attention of the readers to who Jesus is. And for this author, discussion of Jesus' identity begins not with His name but with the fact that He is God's Son, and thus God Himself. Jesus' divinity is highlighted.

If the readers forget that Jesus is God, then they will forget the importance of His message and His life, and they will not offer Him the worship He deserves. If Jesus was just a man, then His message was just a good word spoken by a human being. If Jesus' actions were just human actions, then He was just a good human being. But this is not so, says the author in these opening verses. Jesus' message is connected to the very mind of God. Jesus' actions are connected to the very will of God. Jesus is God.

### 2. Superior to the Angels (vv. 4–9)

In this set of verses, the author continues to build upon the description of Jesus. Let me sketch you a picture, the author seems to say. Imagine the angels. They're pretty important, aren't they? Pretty powerful. Pretty amazing creatures. Well, where do you think Jesus stands in comparison? Higher, the author contends! Jesus is more important, more powerful, and more amazing.

But the most important point to realize here is the same as in the previous verses. Jesus is superior to the angels because His identity is connected directly and inseparably to God. "The name he has inherited is superior to theirs" (v. 4). Next the author asks, "For to which of the angels did God ever say, 'You are my Son; today I have become your Father'? Or again, 'I will be his Father, and he will be my Son'?" (v. 5, NIV). The answer to these rhetorical questions is "none." But the author doesn't stop there. He continues to hammer the point of Jesus' divinity home for the audience. As if he hasn't been clear, "And again, when God brings his firstborn into the world, he says, 'Let all God's angels worship him'" (v. 6, NIV). In verses 7–9, the author elaborates even more on the deity (divinity) of Jesus, God's Son.

The author reiterates Jesus' divinity to caution his readers to heed His message and live lives faithful to God. As the letter unfolds, the author continues discussing who Jesus is as a reason to worship Him through obedience.

### Search the Scriptures

1. Who has appointed Jesus the heir of all things (Hebrews 1: 2)?

2. How does Jesus sustain all things (v. 3)?

### Discuss the Meaning

The passage informs us that God has spoken through His Son. Why is it important to remember that God speaks through Jesus? Can you recall what God has spoken through Jesus?

### Lesson in Our Society

People in society often esteem other people. Presidents, kings, queens, athletes, and celebrities receive praise for their status and achievements. When President Obama was elected, for example, many thought he would take the "presidential throne" as a type of savior.

Today's passage draws our attention to the one who is most deserving of all our praise and worship: Jesus, God's Son. How often do we find ourselves worshiping Him instead of finding ourselves at the feet of a person in society?

### Make It Happen

Sometimes when we read the Bible, it is tempting to view Jesus as a man. Even Christians can forget the significance of Jesus being God. How can you shape your worship of Jesus to start with the fact that He is God instead of what He's done for you?

### Follow the Spirit

What God wants me to do:

_____

_____

_____

_____

## Remember Your Thoughts

Special insights I have learned:

_____

_____

_____

_____

## More Light on the Text

**Hebrews 1:1–9**

This passage underscores the uniqueness and superiority of Jesus and the finality of God's revelation in Him.

**1 God, who at sundry times and in divers manners spake in time past unto the fathers by the prophets, 2 Hath in these last days spoken unto us by his Son, whom he hath appointed heir of all things, by whom also he made the worlds;**

The first four verses of Hebrews are only a single sentence in the Greek text. Unlike modern translations that have three or four sentences, the King James Version retains the sense of the original Greek text in one rich and complete sentence.

In this epistle, the writer begins with God. God is the initiator of revelation; therefore, the focus is on Him, not man. The first and second verses contrast the methods of communication God used in the past with the method He used then. The phrase "at sundry times and in divers manners spake" refers to the fact that God chose the times and methods to communicate. The Old Testament records the clouds, dreams, visions, etc. that God used to communicate with His people. God also used the prophets to reveal His Word. The reference to "prophets" here is not limited to the traditional prophets but includes men of God like Moses, David, and Solomon, to mention a few.

The phrase "in these last days" refers to both the present and end times. There is a clear sense that God has reached the climax of His self-revelation. He has saved the best for last. There is a definite intention to show that this last revelation of God is superior to what He has done in the past. The fact that God has already "spoken unto us by his Son" suggests that, at the time of writing this epistle, the revelation had been completed.

Even though most English translations say "his son" or "the Son," the Greek has no definite article. It simply says "son." The writer assumes that the readers know whom he is talking about. The lack of the definite article "the" makes this statement stronger. Instead of identifying whom God spoke through, it emphasizes the nature of the one whom God spoke through. Unlike the prophets, the Son is more than a messenger. His divine nature makes Him the right and only capable bearer of God's complete revelation. The rest of Hebrews elaborates on this truth about the identity and the superiority of the revelation of God though Jesus Christ.

The phrase "appointed heir of all things, by whom also he made the worlds" indicates that Christ embodies a dual motif of sonship and creation. When speaking of Jesus as God's heir, Psalm 2:7–8 says, "Thou art my Son; this day have I begotten thee. Ask of me, and I shall give thee the heathen for thine inheritance, and the uttermost parts of the earth for thy possession." Everything God has belongs to Jesus. The Bible also reveals that Jesus is co-creator with God (Colossians 1:16–17). This shows the superiority of the Son and also His pre-existence. He is eternal and therefore superior to any other revelation of God. The word translated as "worlds" (Hebrews 1:2, KJV) or "universe" (NIV) is *aion* (Gk. **eye-OWN**). It literally means ages or times. The preferred interpretation is "ages," which suggests that Jesus not only created the world but also controls the events of history.

**3 Who being the brightness of his glory, and the express image of his person, and upholding all things by the word of his power, when he had by himself purged our sins, sat down on the right hand of the Majesty on high;**

In verse 3, we get a complete Christology. The first part of the verse talks about the Son's relationship with God, the second part deals with the work of the Son, and the third part refers to His exaltation—the pre-existence, incarnation, and exaltation of Christ. The phrase "brightness of his glory" could mean that Jesus is either the reflection or the radiance of the glory of God. The Bible tells us that God is inapproachable, but that Jesus makes it possible to know Him truly and intimately. What a blessing! The "express image of his person" means "the imprint or seal of God's nature," and the word translated as "person" connotes "the reality or actuality of His being." Thus, Jesus fully represents God (cf. Colossians 2:9), and upholds all things by the word of His power. This is not a passive holding up but an active sustaining. Jesus is not only Creator of the universe, but He is also sustaining it by His word. The exaltation of Christ is an allusion to Psalm 110:1. Jesus used this verse in silencing the Pharisees concerning his position of Messiah (Matthew 22:41–46). The Son of David who is also the pre-incarnate God would come down to earth to "purge" (Gk. *katharismos*, **ka-tha-rees-MOSE**) or to cleanse and wash away our sins. The word "purge" is usually used in the context of the ritual washings and purifications mentioned in Leviticus. The writer of Hebrews uses this term to describe the ritual holiness given to us through Christ's sacrifice. It was through His death and resurrected triumph over all of God's enemies die and then be raised to heaven in triumph over all of God's enemies including death. This gave Him the right to be seated on the right hand of the "The Majesty on high," which is a title for God. It is a sign of kingship and royal authority.

**4 Being made so much better than the angels, as he hath by inheritance obtained a more excellent name than they.**

The phrase "better than" or "superior to" is used thirteen times in the Christology presented in Hebrews. Christ is the revelation that is superior to all others. He is the One we are to serve and worship. His revelation holds more sway in our lives than any other. In the Old Testament, a name (Gk. *onoma*, **OH-no-mah**) is associated with reputation, and Christ's name and reputation is superior to the angels.

Verse 4 introduces the major subjects of the discussion that is to follow: Christ and the angels. To counter the worship of angels, the writer shows the real position of the angels in contrast to Christ. Christ is directly related to the Father and the angels are not. Christ inherited the universe and the angels are under His dominion. Christ has a more excellent name due to His pre-existence, incarnation, and exaltation to the right hand of God.

**5 For unto which of the angels said he at any time, Thou art my Son, this day have I begotten thee? And again, I will be to him a Father, and he shall be to me a Son?**

Hebrews 1:5–14 continues the explanation of who Jesus Christ is, and Hebrews 2:1–4 challenges the reader to respond appropriately. The author follows this pattern throughout the epistle. He always gives the explanation of who Jesus is and then the challenge to respond appropriately. Beginning with verse 5, we find frequent references to, or quotations from, the Old Testament (thirty or more), especially the Psalms. Verse 5 is a combination of two Old Testament quotations: Psalm 2:7 and 2 Samuel 7:14. The truth from Psalm 2:7 ("Thou art my Son; this day have I begotten thee") concerning Jesus' relationship to God was very significant for the early church's understanding of Christ. This truth was announced from heaven at Jesus' baptism (Mark 1:10–11) and preached by Paul (Acts 13:33–34). The reference to 2 Samuel 7:14 is taken from the promise to David that he will always have a son to reign on the throne. This passage carries messianic expectation that the Messiah would be a son of David. The verse in particular shows that not only would the Messiah be a son of David but also a son of God. None of the kings of Israel could claim both of these titles in reality. The only true fulfillment of this was through Christ the son of David and the Son of God.

**6 And again, when he bringeth in the first -begotten into the world, he saith, And let all the angels of God worship him. 7 And of the angels he saith, Who maketh his angels spirits, and his ministers a flame of fire.**

The term "first begotten" is translated from the Greek word *prototokos* (**pro-TOE-toe-kose**). It does not mean the first to be created. Rather, it indicates privilege, authority, and inheritance. Its meaning centers on the firstborn son's rights and position. Christ has the highest authority. The phrase "all the angels of God worship him" emphasizes His exalted state as God because only God can be worshiped. Since the angels worship Him, do not worship the angels. Worship Christ. This seals the exaltation of Christ over the angels.

Even the angels know that He is superior, and therefore they bow down and worship Him. This is not an exaltation of His human nature but the recognition of who He truly is as the Son of God.

Verse 7 contains an Old Testament quotation from Psalm 104:4. It further shows the superiority of Christ over angels. They not only worship Him, but serve Him. Psalm 104:4 is taken from a passage about creation. While Christ created the world, the angels were just instruments in the overall act of creation. They are ministers or servants and agents of God in creating the world. The angels are subordinate to Christ. They are spirits and flames of fire. This suggests their temporality and transient nature. This is placed in contrast to the eternality of the Son.

**8 But unto the Son he saith, Thy throne, O God, is for ever and ever: a sceptre of righteousness is the sceptre of thy kingdom. 9 Thou hast loved righteousness, and hated iniquity; therefore God, even thy God, hath anointed thee with the oil of gladness above thy fellows.**

These verses are a quotation of Psalm 45:6–7. Psalm 45 is a marriage psalm calling a princess to heed the king's call and "forget also thine own people and thy father's house" (v. 10) in order to enter the king's palace, where there is great joy. This king loves righteousness and hates sin. This psalm has many messianic applications. Hebrews 1:8–9 refers to the Son as God and says that His throne is exalted forever. Christ is superior to the angels—"anointed with the oil of gladness above thy fellows."

Sources:

Hamilton, Victor P. *Handbook on the Pentateuch: Genesis, Exodus, Leviticus, Numbers, Deuteronomy.* Grand Rapids, MI: Baker Academic, 2005.

Keener, Craig S. *The IVP Bible Background Commentary.* Downers Grove, IL: Intervarsity Press, 1993

## Say It Correctly

Superior. soo-**PEE**-ri-or.
Subordinate. su-**BOR**-din-it.
Allusion. uh-**LOO**-shin.

## Daily Bible Readings

**MONDAY**
Great and Awesome God
(Daniel 9:3–10)

**TUESDAY**
O Lord, Hear and Forgive
(Daniel 9:11–19)

**WEDNESDAY**
God the Almighty Reigns
(Revelation 19:1–8)

**THURSDAY**
First and Last, Beginning and End
(Revelation 22:8–14)

**FRIDAY**
My Son, the Beloved
(Matthew 3:13–17)

**SATURDAY**
Honor and Glory Forever
(1 Timothy 1:12–17)

**SUNDAY**
The Son Reflects God's Glory
(Hebrews 1:1–9)

# Notes

# Teaching Tips

## Words You Should Know

**A. Psalms** (Psalm 95:2) *zemir* (Heb.)—an instrumental song; a song with words accompanied by musical instruments. The beauty of musical instruments as a part of worship was greatly developed by King David.

**B. Thanksgiving** (v. 2) *todah* (Heb.)—adoration, praise. Appears approximately 30 times in the Old Testament, a dozen of these in the Psalms.

## Teacher Preparation

**Unifying Principle—Sing a Song of Praise.** Many people realize that a power beyond them gives meaning to their lives. How do they respond to this knowledge? The psalmist declares that God is the rock of their salvation and is worthy of praise and worship.

**A.** Set aside time to pray that you will teach in a way that students will meet the lesson aim.

**B.** Study Psalm 95 in its entirety, using a commentary and concordance.

**C.** Encourage students to become willing to shed inhibitions in worship and praise God exuberantly.

## O—Open the Lesson

**A.** Begin today's lesson with prayer, including the Aim for Change.

**B.** Read the Aim for Change and Keep In Mind verse.

**C.** Have students read the In Focus story, and discuss.

## P—Present the Scriptures

**A.** Have volunteers take turns reading through the Focal Verses.

**B.** To clarify the verses, use The People, Places, and Times; Background; Search the Scriptures; In Depth; and More Light on the Text.

## E—Explore the Meaning

**A.** Assign three groups one of each of the following sections: Discuss the Meaning, Lesson in Our Society, and Make It Happen. Tell each group to select a representative to share their assignment and responses.

**B.** Relate the Aim for Change and the Keep In Mind verse to the application sections.

## N—Next Steps for Application

**A.** Invite students to tell why various worship styles are most meaningful to them and the ways these lead to God.

**B.** Have students summarize today's lesson.

**C.** Close with prayer, thanking God for this example of praise and worship.

## Worship Guide

For the Superintendent or Teacher
Theme: Make a Joyful Noise
Song: "Total Praise"
Devotional Reading: 1 Kings 8:54–62

# Make a Joyful Noise

**Bible Background • PSALM 95:1–7a**
**Printed Text • PSALM 95:1–7a**
**Devotional Reading • 1 Kings 8:54–62**

## Aim for Change

By the end of the lesson, we will: DISCERN that God is the Creator of the earth and the maker of humankind, and God is truly worthy of praise; EXPERIENCE the enthusiasm, power, and excitement that comes when believers praise God as their divine King; and SHED inhibitions in worship and praise God exuberantly.

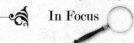

## In Focus

After months of indecision and trying to convince himself otherwise, David finally resigned from the praise and worship team. Sure, the new job promotion had him busier than before, but not to the point where he wouldn't use his singing gift for God. But, that's the excuse he gave to his pastor. He hoped one day he could be bold enough to be honest about his resignation.

Six months ago, a new minister of music was hired, and the church seemed livelier. Compliments poured in about the song choices and compositions. People no longer had to be told to get up and praise God because they were now doing it on their own. Everybody seemed pleased, except David. He desperately wanted to express himself like everyone else, but he felt a little jealous of the new music minister. He knew that he could not praise God the way he wanted to because of the condition of his heart. He knew he had to deal with that before he made any attempts at worshiping God during the service.

*God is worthy of our praise and worship. How do we ensure that we worship Him in spirit and in truth?*

## Keep in Mind

"O come, let us sing unto the LORD: let us make a joyful noise to the rock of our salvation" (Psalm 95:1).

"O come, let us sing unto the LORD: let us make a joyful noise to the rock of our salvation" (Psalm 95:1).

## Focal Verses

**KJV** **Psalm 95:1** O come, let us sing unto the LORD: let us make a joyful noise to the rock of our salvation.

**2** Let us come before his presence with thanksgiving, and make a joyful noise unto him with psalms.

**3** For the LORD is a great God, and a great King above all gods.

**4** In his hand are the deep places of the earth: the strength of the hills is his also.

**5** The sea is his, and he made it: and his hands formed the dry land.

**6** O come, let us worship and bow down: let us kneel before the LORD our maker.

**7a** For he is our God; and we are the people of his pasture, and the sheep of his hand.

**NLT** **Psalm 95:1** Come, let us sing to the LORD! Let us shout joyfully to the Rock of our salvation.

**2** Let us come to him with thanksgiving. Let us sing psalms of praise to him.

**3** For the LORD is a great God, a great King above all gods.

**4** He holds in his hands the depths of the earth and the mightiest mountains.

**5** The sea belongs to him, for he made it. His hands formed the dry land, too.

**6** Come, let us worship and bow down. Let us kneel before the LORD our maker,

**7a** for he is our God. We are the people he watches over, the flock under his care.

### The People, Places, and Times

**Gods.** These were idols worshiped by other nations and sometimes the Israelite people. In the ancient Near East, different nations worshiped a variety of gods. The Israelite worship of Yahweh was unique in that the people were commanded to worship only one God as opposed to the surrounding nations, who worshiped a roster of different deities dedicated to different aspects of life. Although the Israelites did not worship these deities, they often declared their one God to be supreme over the many other gods of the nations.

**Rock of Our Salvation.** Many times the Bible refers to God as a Rock or the Rock of our salvation. This may have been because during their trek in the wilderness God gave Israel water from a rock (Numbers 20:1–13). It also could have been due to the benefits of a rock as a shade during the heat (Isaiah 32:2) and the safety of

a rock when hiding from or fighting an enemy (Psalm 31:2, 3; 104:18).

**Pasture.** Shepherds would keep their sheep in a pen during the night and let them out into the pasture during the day. These were areas where they could find grass and vegetation to eat freely. In ancient Palestine, pasture was not necessarily an abundant field of greenery but the rocky bare hills. The shepherd led the sheep to eat just what they needed for that day. The best pasture was usually on the plateaus east of the Jordan and the mountains of Palestine and Syria.

### Background

Psalm 95 is an invitation to worship. Perhaps the crowd or congregation had grown weary. It seemed that they'd stopped believing, and were no longing expecting God to fulfill His promises. The author who tired of their passivity essentially said, "Don't just stand there; do something!"

Through the psalm, the psalmist exhorted the people to serve God.

One cannot worship God with a hardened heart, as this psalm warns. In verse 8 of the same psalm, the psalmist used the testing at Meribah (also known as Massah) as an example. At Meribah, the Israelites sinned against God (Exodus 17:1–7). "Is the Lord among us or not?" they complained. Not trusting God in the wilderness kept them out of the Promised Land. In our text, the psalmist admonished the congregation to not let the same happen to them. "Come, let us sing to the one who'll save us," he urged. The same testing is referenced in Hebrews 3:7 and 4:7 as a warning to believers.

## At-A-Glance

1. Praise Him (Psalm 95:1–2)
2. Adore Him (vv. 3–5)
3. Worship Him (vv. 6–7)

## In Depth

### 1. Praise Him (Psalm 95:1–2)

Praising God was as natural to the psalmist as breathing. Psalms is full of praises, adoration, and worship to God. Even when things were bad, the psalmist poured out his heart to the Rock of his salvation. The "Rock" is a recurrent metaphor for God in Psalms, used over 20 times.

The psalmist sees the worship of God as something to be done corporately. He exhorts the congregation with the words "Come, let us sing together." It is an invitation to praise the Rock of our salvation, but at the same time the psalmist is also leading the way by including himself in the invitation. He says "us" so that the call is personal as well as corporate.

The psalmist says, "Let's shout joyfully." Praising God should be joyful and exuberant, not a solemn and sad occasion. Our deepest joy is to be found in God, and this joy must have full expression. Shouting joyfully was a way of celebrating God and all that He had done for His people.

The tools that the psalmist prescribes to be used in worship are thanksgiving and psalms of praise. Our worship of God is to be permeated by thanksgiving. We have received nothing outside of what God has given us. This is enough motivation for thanks. Psalms of praise were songs written for the express purpose of praising and adoring God in small and large settings.

### 2. Adore Him (vv. 3–5)

As if the people had asked why they should praise the Lord, the psalmist answered. "Because He is great." Then, he gave evidence of God's greatness by recalling that He held the deep places of the earth in His hand. Essentially he challenged, "If things that are out of sight and out of reach are in His hands, how much more so are your problems?"

Scripture often used Creation as evidence of God's power. The Lord made the sea and dry land, and both are under His control. No matter how much an angry sea rages, it can go no farther than the boundary the Lord sets. It's as if the psalmist set a challenge: "If the Lord set an end to something seemingly uncontrollable, would He not have an end to this?"

### 3. Worship Him (vv. 6–7)

The psalmist recognized pride can hinder our relationship with God. The antidote to pridefulness is worship. By showing God how much He is worth to us, we realize our true worth in relationship to Him. This is a surefire cure for pride: "Bow down and worship the

Lord who made us." Psalm 100:3 also points to God as our Creator, saying, "... it is he that hath made us, and not we ourselves."

Who tells the maker what to do? Isaiah 45:9 echoes, "Does the clay say to the potter, 'What are you making?'" (NIV). Further, in verse 7, the psalmist challenged the reader to know that He is their God, not the other way around. We are His sheep, in His pasture, and cannot be plucked out of His hand.

Jesus further illustrated the sheep-shepherd relationship when He proclaimed Himself the Good Shepherd (John 10). There, Jesus confronted the Pharisees who had set themselves up as shepherds of the people.

## Search the Scriptures

1. How should we come into His presence (Isaiah 53:2)?

2. What is the posture for worship (v. 6)?

## Discuss the Meaning

1. Why did the psalmist refer to God as a Rock?

2. How does Scripture point to Creation as evidence of God's power?

## Lesson in Our Society

Our society promotes pridefulness, often concealing it as self-confidence. Bestseller lists tout titles that reveal seven or ten steps to self-promotion. The Bible shows us that promotion comes from the Lord (Psalm 75:6). Our text reminds us that one must come before the Lord humbly and with thanksgiving—certainly not positions of pride, especially while on bended knee.

## Make It Happen

This week, practice joyfulness. No matter how challenging your days get, sing songs of praise to God. Remember that you belong to God, not the other way around. Instead of standing, complaining, and prolonging your pain, get on your knees and worship. Bow down and thank Him for the things that are good and right.

## Follow the Spirit

What God wants me to do:

_____

_____

_____

_____

## Remember Your Thoughts

Special insights I have learned:

_____

_____

_____

_____

## More Light on the Text
### Psalm 95:1–7a

This passage is filled with commands and exhortations about praise and worship. In ancient Israel, many of the psalms were part of the worship services, especially psalms of praise such as this one. Imperative forms are used twice inviting the people to worship (vv. 1, 6). These commands to come to worship are followed by numerous exhortations for the people to rejoice, exult, come into God's presence, and shout with songs (vv. 1–2), as well as to bow down in worship and kneel before God (v. 6). The quantity of verbs calling the people to worship must have overwhelmed the worshipers. Accompanied by these exhortations are repeated reminders of who they are called to worship—the Lord (v. 1), the Rock of our salvation (v. 1), the great God (v. 3), the great King over all divine things (v. 3), and our God (v. 7a). Again and again the psalm impresses on the people how, why, and who they should worship. We all need reminders from time to time of the many ways God shows His power in our lives so we can worship with awe and joy, and this psalm serves to do just that.

Because a call to worship appears twice (vv. 1–2 and v. 6), it is possible that the psalm was originally part of a processional that concluded with the prophetic exhortation of vv. 7b–11. There is no explicit historical evidence for the original setting, but the psalm was a part of Jewish Sabbath worship during the Roman period, and as a result it became a call to worship in Christian services as well. Since antiquity, its words have charged the faithful to glorify God.

**1 O come, let us sing unto the LORD: let us make a joyful noise to the rock of our salvation. 2 Let us come before his presence with thanksgiving, and make a joyful noise unto him with psalms.**

The psalm begins the call to worship with an imperative (come), followed by four verbs exhorting the people to sing and rejoice in God's presence. It is more than an invitation to worship the Lord, the Rock our salvation; it is a powerful summons to "make a joyful noise" or to worship God with a joy that compels His people to shout. The psalmist is filled with such jubilation at God's power that words are not enough. Music is necessary to express such wonderment.

The people are urged to enter God's presence. In the Old Testament, God's presence is described as His very face. God is not just a transcendent Creator and Ruler who is not involved personally with His creation. God interacts face to face with

those who worship Him, and since their worship brings them face to face with their Creator, they must sing!

**3 For the LORD is a great God, and a great King above all gods.**

The psalm begins the explanation of the reasons for worshiping God. Not only is the Lord a great God, but He is also greater than all other gods. In antiquity, the Israelites always had neighbors who worshiped other gods, and the Old Testament narrates many times when the Israelites were tempted to, and sometimes did, worship those false deities. Here the psalm contains a metaphor the people would comprehend because they were ruled by kings and understood the authority and power that a king had. Just as David, Solomon, and the other Israelite kings had authority and power over the people, so the Lord has authority and power over all gods. For anyone tempted to worship other gods, this psalm reminds them that their God is the one with power over everything.

**4 In his hand are the deep places of the earth: the strength of the hills is his also. 5 The sea is his, and he made it: and his hands formed the dry land.**

God is the Creator of all things. The deep places and the hills represent creation from top to bottom. Similarly, v. 5 mentions water and dry land. These opposite pictures of the depths and the hills, as well as water and dry land, form an all-encompassing picture of God's creation. In addition, the reference to the sea and the dry land echoes the Exodus, reminding the people of the miraculous ways in which God saves those of faith. Bookending these verses with God's hands also creates an image of His hands encompassing all of creation. God created everything and cares for everything.

In the Old Testament, God's hand represents not only the things He touches and tends to, but also His power and strength. Literally, God's hand touches all parts of the earth, including the heights of the mountains. Metaphorically, God's power and strength as Creator are reflected in the very foundations and heights of creation. God's hand is both powerful and caring, and tends to all of His creation.

**6 O come, let us worship and bow down: let us kneel before the LORD our maker.**

Parallel to verse 1 in structure, this verse once again commands the people to worship God, adding new forms of worship to the noisy singing and rejoicing of vv. 1–2. Although the first exhortative verb, *shakhah* (Heb. **shah-KHAH**), is translated "worship," it also means to bow down because it carries the connotation of submitting to someone in authority. As a result, all three verbs describing worship in this verse indicate physical bowing before God the Creator. The final verb for kneeling, *barak* (Heb. **bah-RAHK**), can also indicate blessing in other contexts where God blesses the faithful, establishing a relationship between God as the one who blesses and the people as worshipers. In addition, the epithet for God as our Maker reminds the people that God has created not only the earth and the sea but also the people, and they should worship Him by surrendering to Him.

**7a For he is our God; and we are the people of his pasture, and the sheep of his hand.**

Similar to v. 3, 7a explains why the people should worship with submission. Quite simply, the Lord is our God. The metaphor shifts from God as Creator to God as Shepherd. Now God's hand of care and power is involved in tending to His flock. The remainder of the psalm carries out this metaphor by reminding the people that their ancestors did not always follow God, even though they knew about His works. Amid a psalm of praise and worship, the final verses serve as a reminder of the need for such psalms. Even God's faithful can forget how to worship God, so the psalm calls the people to keep worshiping God with song and submission lest they too forget His power and mighty deeds.

Sources:
Bellinger, W. H. *Psalms: Reading and Studying the Book of Praises.* Peabody, MA: Hendrickson Publishers, 1990.
Mays, James Luther. *Psalms. Interpretation: A Bible Commentary for Teaching and Preaching.* Edited by James Luther Mays, Patrick D. Miller, Jr. and Paul J. Achtemeier. Louisville, KY: Westminster John Knox Press, 1994.
McCann, J. Clinton, Jr. "The Book of Psalms." Vol. IV of The New Interpreter's Bible. 12 vols. Edited by Leander E. Keck, et al. Nashville, TN: Abingdon Press, 1996. 641–1280.
*The Word in Life Study Bible.* Nashville, TN: Thomas Nelson, 1993. 149.
*The New Spirit Filled Life Bible.* Nashville, TN: Thomas Nelson, 2002. 687–688, 760.

## Say It Correctly

Exhortation. eks-or-**TAY**-shun.
Transcendent. tran-**SEN**-dent.

## Daily Bible Readings

**MONDAY**
Hold Fast to God
(Deuteronomy 13:1–8)

**TUESDAY**
Devote Yourselves to the Lord
(1 Kings 8:54–62)

**WEDNESDAY**
Worship with Reverence and Awe
(Hebrews 12:22–29)

**THURSDAY**
Sing Praises to God
(1 Chronicles 16:7–15)

**FRIDAY**
Ascribe Greatness to Our God
(Deuteronomy 32:1–7)

**SATURDAY**
A Sacrifice of Praise to God
(Hebrews 13:6–15)

**SUNDAY**
Let Us Worship and Bow Down
(Psalm 95:1–7a)

# Notes

_____

_____

_____

_____

# Teaching Tips

## Words you should know

**A. Joy** (Luke 2:10) *chara* (Gk.)—Gladness, happiness; or the cause or object of such.

**B. Messiah** (v. 11) *Christos* (Gk.)—Christ, the Anointed One.

## Teacher Preparation

**Unifying Principle—Spontaneous Joy!** Sometimes an event in people's lives causes spontaneous celebration. What might cause people to be wild with joy? Angels announced the birth of the Savior and a multitude of the heavenly host praised God.

**A.** Read through the Focal Verses at least two times, then spend quiet time meditating on them.

**B.** Read through the lesson, noting important points to highlight, and keeping in mind the Aim for Change and Keep in Mind verse.

**C.** Review your notes and reread the focal verses once more, adding any additional points to your notes.

## Open the Lesson

**A.** Begin with prayer.

**B.** Share the topic of the lesson, the Unifying Principle, and the Aim for Change objectives.

**C.** Ask a volunteer to read the In Focus illustration aloud.

## Presenting the Scripture

**A.** Solicit an individual to read the Focal Verses aloud.

**B.** Have a volunteer read the passage again and tell the class to mark any words or sentences that stick out or evoke a question.

**C.** Ask the class to share any words or sentences they marked.

**D.** Read the Keep in Mind verse.

## Explore the Meaning

**A.** Read and discuss the Background and The People, Places, and Times portion of the lesson.

**B.** Offer any clarification on the lesson.

**C.** Split the class in two groups. Have each group answer the questions in Search the Scripture and read Discuss the Meaning.

## Next Steps for Application

**A.** Explore the Lesson in Our Society.

**B.** Review the key point of Make It Happen.

**C.** Have anyone share concluding thoughts or ways they're committing to applying the passage.

## Worship Guide

For the Superintendent or Teacher
Theme: Glory to God in the Highest
Song: "Joy to the World"
Devotional Reading: Psalm 19

174

# Glory to God in the Highest

**Bible Background • LUKE 2**
**Printed Text • LUKE 2:8–20**
**Devotional Reading • PSALM 19**

## —— Aim for Change ——

By the end of this lesson we will: EXPLORE the events that led to the angels' spontaneous joy and the shepherds' pilgrimage to see Jesus; FEEL the unrestrained joy that comes with the good news of the Savior's birth; and PARTICIPATE in worship events of Advent and Christmas.

## In Focus

After a grueling day at work, Gina was excited to be home. Going through her usual after-work ritual, she parked her car in the driveway and shuffled over to the mailbox. Once she was in the house, she sat in her favorite chair in the living room and began glancing over the mail. In the stack of mail were advertisements, bills, and a community newsletter. But towards the bottom of the stack, a turquoise envelope stuck out. *Hmm*, Gina thought to herself, *what could this be?* Quickly Gina set aside all the other mail and went straight for the mysterious letter.

Teasing it open, to her great surprise, inside was a picture of a lady who looked vaguely familiar. It took a moment for Gina to realize who it was, but after a few seconds Gina exclaimed, "Oh, Jenelle! Jenelle!" It was one of her best friends from college whom Gina hadn't seen in years. Jenelle was having a baby, and had written Gina to invite her to the baby shower next month. Gina, completely overjoyed and full of delighted surprise, jumped up from her chair and repeated, "Oh, Jenelle! That's so exciting!" She wasn't going to miss this celebration.

*The shepherds were astounded by the angels' announcement. Today's lesson reminds us of the good news Jesus brings to the world, and invites us in again to revel in its joy and to praise God because of it.*

## —— Keep in Mind ——

"And the shepherds returned, glorifying and praising God for all the things that they had heard and seen, as it was told unto them" (Luke 2:20).

"And the shepherds returned, glorifying and praising God for all the things that they had heard and seen, as it was told unto them" (Luke 2:20).

## Focal Verses

**KJV** **Luke 2:8** And there were in the same country shepherds abiding in the field, keeping watch over their flock by night.

**9** And, lo, the angel of the Lord came upon them, and the glory of the Lord shone round about them: and they were sore afraid.

**10** And the angel said unto them, Fear not: for, behold, I bring you good tidings of great joy, which shall be to all people.

**11** For unto you is born this day in the city of David a Saviour, which is Christ the Lord.

**12** And this shall be a sign unto you; Ye shall find the babe wrapped in swaddling clothes, lying in a manger.

**13** And suddenly there was with the angel a multitude of the heavenly host praising God, and saying,

**14** Glory to God in the highest, and on earth peace, good will toward men.

**15** And it came to pass, as the angels were gone away from them into heaven, the shepherds said one to another, Let us now go even unto Bethlehem, and see this thing which is come to pass, which the Lord hath made known unto us.

**16** And they came with haste, and found Mary, and Joseph, and the babe lying in a manger.

**17** And when they had seen it, they made known abroad the saying which was told them concerning this child.

**18** And all they that heard it wondered at those things which were told them by the shepherds.

**19** But Mary kept all these things, and pondered them in her heart.

**20** And the shepherds returned, glorifying and praising God for all the things that they had heard and seen, as it was told unto them.

**NLT** **Luke 2:8** That night there were shepherds staying in the fields nearby, guarding their flocks of sheep.

**9** Suddenly, an angel of the Lord appeared among them, and the radiance of the Lord's glory surrounded them. They were terrified,

**10** but the angel reassured them. "Don't be afraid!" he said. "I bring you good news that will bring great joy to all people.

**11** The Savior—yes, the Messiah, the Lord—has been born today in Bethlehem, the city of David!

**12** And you will recognize him by this sign: You will find a baby wrapped snugly in strips of cloth, lying in a manger."

**13** Suddenly, the angel was joined by a vast host of others—the armies of heaven—praising God and saying,

**14** "Glory to God in highest heaven,

and peace on earth to those with whom God is pleased."

**15** When the angels had returned to heaven, the shepherds said to each other, "Let's go to Bethlehem! Let's see this thing that has happened, which the Lord has told us about."

**16** They hurried to the village and found Mary and Joseph. And there was the baby, lying in the manger.

**17** After seeing him, the shepherds told everyone what had happened and what the angel had said to them about this child.

**18** All who heard the shepherds' story were astonished,

**19** but Mary kept all these things in her heart and thought about them often.

**20** The shepherds went back to their flocks, glorifying and praising God for all they had heard and seen. It was just as the angel had told them.

## The People, Places, and Times

**Shepherds.** These were men who looked after sheep. Throughout the Bible, there are a number of references to shepherds. Scholars agree that a reason for the common reference to shepherds is most likely because, where the Israelites lived, the pastoral way of living was widespread. But shepherding was not a glamorous form of work; rather, it was a humble job. Understanding the lowliness of shepherds makes our passage for today that much more meaningful when we consider that God decided that they should be among the first to receive the news that the Messiah and Savior had been born.

**Bethlehem.** In the story of Jesus' birth, Bethlehem is the key town. Historically, Bethlehem was known as the city of David, referring to the famous King David who ruled the people of Israel hundreds of years before Jesus' birth. Bethlehem was not a large town, so when the shepherds arrived, they probably had little difficulty finding Joseph, Mary, and Jesus. Also there is evidence that Joseph had a significant connection to Bethlehem, perhaps being an owner of a piece of land, which is the reason he and Mary journeyed there for the census. It was also known as the city that was prophesied to be the birthplace of the Messiah (Micah 5:2, Matthew 2:5-6)

## Background

By the time we arrive at the story of the angel of the Lord bringing news of Jesus' birth to the shepherds, several events have already occurred. The angel Gabriel had been sent by God to inform Mary that God was giving her a son named Jesus, who would be "the Son of the Highest" and would rule a kingdom that would be established forever (Luke 1:26-38). Pregnant Mary and her fiancé Joseph had traveled at least 70 miles (from Nazareth to Bethlehem) to register under a census by Quirinius, governor of Syria. After no suitable room could be found for her to deliver the child, Mary delivered Jesus into a manager where animals stayed nearby (Luke 2:1–7).

## At-A-Glance

1. The Angel of the Lord Delivers a Message (Luke 2:8–14)
2. The Shepherds Spread the Message (vv. 15–18)
3. Mary and the Shepherds Respond (vv. 19–20)

## In Depth

**1. The Angel of the Lord Delivers a Message (vv. 8–14)**

In these six verses, the angel of the Lord appeared. The angel of the Lord is commonly referenced as a heavenly being who is a special messenger or servant of God. Typically, the angel comes to accomplish the explicit will of the Lord. Beside the stories of Jesus' birth, the angel of the Lord also appears in the Old Testament, for example, to Moses at the burning bush (Exodus 3). The angel of the Lord came to (or stood before) the shepherds who were tending to their flock at night. The nighttime setting gives an interesting contrast when the glory of the Lord appears with the angel of the Lord. The glory is said to have "shone round about them," suggesting an image of radiating light. No wonder the shepherds became afraid. Imagine walking at night and a comet suddenly appearing before you. Fear would seem like the natural response.

But the angel of the Lord quickly reassured these fearful shepherds by announcing good news of "great joy." The angel told the shepherds that he brought a message that should evoke the opposite feelings. Whereas the shepherds were afraid after having been startled by the angel, the angel said the message of Jesus' birth should turn their fear into joy!

## 2. The Shepherds Spread the Message (vv. 15–18)

After receiving the news of Jesus' birth from the angel of the Lord and witnessing the multitude of angels praising God, the shepherds did two things: they believed the message was from God, and they went to see this child. Their excitement is obvious! "Let us now go even unto Bethlehem, and see this thing which is come to pass, which the Lord hath made known to us" (from v. 15). Then instead of delaying, the shepherds acted "with haste" (v. 16). The shepherds' belief in the angel's message and their prompt journey to Bethlehem are remarkable. When the shepherds saw Jesus and realized that things were as the angel of the Lord had announced (v. 17), they could not contain what they heard; they shared it with those present, who reacted with wonder. It is not clear what they were most surprised by: perhaps by their receiving this message, or the message itself—that is, perhaps they wondered how this baby in the manger would be the Savior and the Messiah they anticipated from the Lord.

## 3. Mary and the Shepherds Respond (vv. 19–20)

Mary's response to the shepherds' statements was different from the others'. Whereas they wondered at the shepherds' words, Mary pondered them "in her heart." The language here might suggest that unlike the others, Mary's reaction was internal and private, while the others outwardly responded. Following Mary's reaction is the shepherds' response to the unfolding events. Like the angels who had appeared before them, the shepherds now glorify and praise God to others. Like the angels, they experience the same joy and thankfulness to God, and they respond with worship.

## Search the Scriptures

1. How did the angels say the shepherds would find the baby (Luke 2:12)?
2. Where did the angels go after they appeared before the shepherds (v. 15)?

## Discuss the Meaning

The shepherds couldn't keep the angel's message to themselves; they had to share it. Why do you think they did this? What do you think the appropriate reaction should have been to the shepherds' message?

## Lesson in Our Society

"News is like the new reality show," it has been said. Our culture has become so obsessed with news that you can find it anywhere and at anytime you want. News has almost become entertainment. You can get rapid news updates on your smartphone, Facebook, and Twitter. The unfortunate thing is that we often pay too much attention to stories that don't matter; and the stories that do matter hardly affect us because we've become so numb to hearing them all the time. In our news society, how are we hearing the "good news" of Jesus' birth that the angel of the Lord announced to the shepherds?

## Make It Happen

How can you read the story of Jesus afresh and with joy? Take time during this season to read through the story in different ways, each time concentrating on what Jesus' coming into the world truly means. Try reading it aloud. Another time, try doing a slow reading (concentrating on each word). Read it at home with your family. Read it outside in an open field or area. Read it in a public place, focusing on what the "good news" might mean to the people around you. And finally, remember what it means in your life, and allow yourself to be drawn to worship and praise God.

## Follow the Spirit

What God wants me to do:

_____

_____

_____

_____

## Remember Your Thoughts

Special insights I have learned:

_____

_____

_____

_____

## More Light On the Text
### Luke 2:8–20

Luke introduces us to the chronological historical events leading to the birth of Jesus—the long-expected Messiah (Luke 2:1–3). It was during the reign of Caesar Augustus, the emperor of Rome. According to this account, the emperor had issued a decree that all the inhabitants of the empire should be taxed, each in his or her province. The intent of this historicity probably is to give the reason Mary and Joseph had to go to Bethlehem. The account of Christ's birth is told in a simple and straightforward manner.

**8 And there were in the same country shepherds abiding in the field, keeping watch over their flock by night. 9 And, lo, the angel of the Lord came upon them, and the glory of the Lord shone round about them: and they were sore afraid.**

In the following few verses, Luke details the strange events that happened after the birth of Christ—the angelic announcement of the birth. He informs his readers about shepherds living in the same country (or region), who were keeping their flock at night. The fact that the shepherds were out grazing their herd by night contradicts the assumption that Christ was born in December. Shepherds never kept flocks outside during the winter months because of the cold. It was customary to send flocks out after the Passover until the first rain in October or November. The actual month and year of Christ's birth are impossible to prove. Throughout the centuries, different Christian sects have given hundreds of suggestions for the date of His birth, to no avail. However, we do not need to speculate. One thing is certain: He was born of a virgin in Bethlehem of Judea according to Scriptures. That suffices.

As the shepherds watched their flock that night, the angel suddenly appeared to them. The glory of the Lord shone around them. The "glory" *doxa* (Gk. **DOKE-sah**) is the manifestation of God's greatness and is used here as in the Old Testament. It often symbolizes the presence of God (Exodus 24:16; 1 Kings 8:11; Isaiah 6:1–6). It describes the radiating splendor and majesty of God's presence. The glory of God, or God's presence, is seen or felt in different forms. To the Israelites in the wilderness, it was seen as a pillar of cloud and fire (Exodus 13:21). To Moses, it was seen as a burning bush (Exodus 3:1–2). To the worshipers in the temple, it was felt as the radiance of His glory (1 Kings

8:10–11). This same radiance appeared to Peter, James, and John on the Mount of Transfiguration (Matthew 17:1–2). This phenomenon was often associated with the appearance of an angel. There is a luminous aspect of glory, as described by the phrase "shone round about them." The reaction of the shepherds was consistent with Zacharias' and Mary's reactions when Gabriel visited them (1:12, 29). Moses, too, was terrified when he encountered the burning bush (Exodus 3). The shepherds were all overwhelmed by fear and wonder because of the strange supernatural happening. "They were sore afraid" underlies this fact.

**10 And the angel said unto them, Fear not: for, behold, I bring you good tidings of great joy, which shall be to all people. 11 For unto you is born this day in the city of David a Saviour, which is Christ the Lord.**

Here the reassuring words of the angel, "Fear not" (cf. 1:13, 30), were echoed. The angel told them not to fear and gave them the reason not to. He was bearing "good tidings (news) of great joy, which shall be to all people." "Bring good tidings," *euaggelizo*, (Gk. **ew-an-ghel-EED-zo**), is a verb which means to announce or declare good news. The English verb "evangelize" is a transliteration of the Greek and can mean to preach, especially the Gospel. Hence, evangelism is the act of preaching, and evangelists are those who preach or proclaim the Good News of the Gospel. *Euaggelizo* referred to any type of happy news in the Greek translation of the Old Testament, but in the New Testament it is used for the Gospel of salvation, which is through Christ's redemptive sacrifice. The angel qualified the Good News that he announced to the shepherds. It was "good tidings of great joy (Gk. *megas*, **MEH-gahs,** great; *chara*, **kha-RAH,** joy) ...

to all people." The great news was not only for all people, but also it will bring joy to all people. The words "all people" (Gk. *pas to laos*, **PAHS toe la-OSE**) have the idea of all people groups everywhere. Therefore, this Gospel is for people (all nationalities) and is intended by God to bring joy to all people universally. What is the good news? The angel announced that the long-expected Messiah, the hope of Israel, the Savior, was born "this day in the city of David." Notice how the angel described this newborn Babe that was born.

First, He is a "Saviour," *soter* (Gk., **so-TARE**), which means a deliverer, a preserver. It was a name given by the ancients to deities, princes, kings, and men who had brought deliverance to their country. It is used repeatedly for both God and His Christ, the medium of God's salvation to men.

Secondly, He is Christ. The word "Christ" is a direct transliteration of the Greek, *Christos* (**khrees-TOSE**), which means anointed (the anointed one). The equivalent in Hebrew is Messiah, which is another epithet of Jesus. In Jewish thought, there were a number of different forms the Messiah might take. For some the Messiah would be the king of the Jews, a political leader who would defeat their enemies and bring in a golden era of peace and prosperity. In Christian thought, the term Messiah refers to Jesus' role as a spiritual deliverer, setting His people free from sin and death.

In Old Testament times, anointing with oil was part of the ritual of commissioning a person for a special task. Thus, the phrase "anointed one" was applied to the person in various cases. Messiah is used more than 30 times to describe kings (1 Samuel 2:35, 26:9), priests (Leviticus 4:3, 5, 16), and the patriarchs (Psalm 105:15). The Persian king Cyrus was referred as an anointed one or messiah as well (Isaiah 45:1). The word is also used concerning King David, who became the model of the messianic king who would come at the end of the age (2 Samuel 22:51; Psalm 2:2). During the time of Daniel, the 6th century B.C., the word Messiah was used as an actual title of the future king (Daniel 9:25–26). Even later, as the Jewish people struggled against their political enemies, the Messiah came to be thought of as a political, military ruler. Because Jesus' humble birth did not coincide with most understandings of Messiah, the majority of modern Jews still do not accept Jesus as the Messiah and are still waiting for one. However, the angel announced to the shepherds that the cause of the strange event they observed is the birth of the Christ—the long-anticipated Messiah of Israel. The Gospels show how many were eagerly hoping and watching out for the Messiah. Andrew met Jesus and told Simon Peter his brother, "We have found the Messias, which is, being interpreted, the Christ" (John 1:41). The woman at the well said to Jesus, "I know that Messias cometh, which is called Christ: when he is come, he will tell us all things" (John 4:25).

Thirdly, He is the "Lord." The word is a translation of the Greek, *kurios* (**KOO-ree-ose**), meaning master. It signifies ownership, one with supreme authority over a person or a group. It is a title of honor expressive of servants' respect and reverence to their masters. It was used in reference to princes, chiefs, and the Roman emperor. In the African context, servants, students, or apprentices call their owners, teachers, or instructors "master" as sign of respect, never their names. The Igbo call their master *Nna anyi ukwu* ("our big father" or "dad") or *Oga*. To them the owner, teacher, or instructor has the same responsibility and care over them as their real father during the time they are

under them. As such they have the obligation to respect them as they respect their birth father. "Lord" is often used in the New Testament for God and the Messiah—the Christ. It was the usual way of referring to Yahweh in Greek. Because God's name was considered too holy to pronounce, Jews instead said Adonai ("my Lord"), which is *kurios* in Greek. Here the angel's designation of the newborn babe as the Lord identified Him as the possessor and supreme owner of all creation. Later in the Bible, the Apostle Peter declared that God made Jesus "both Lord and Christ" (Acts 2:36). While "Messiah," or Christ (the Anointed One), refers to Jesus' humanity, *Kurios*, "Lord," refers to His deity as the Supreme Being.

Who were the shepherds? Why did the angel announce the news first to the shepherds? What are the implications of announcing the birth of the Christ to the shepherds first? The Bible is silent about who the shepherds were. However, they probably were pious Jews who, like many others, had been praying and waiting for the promised Messiah and Deliverer.

There seems to be a number of reasons and theological implications for the role of the shepherds in the events of that night. The main reason is probably for the purpose of identification. Shepherding in the Jewish tradition was a lowly occupation and treated with contempt. Due to occasions of dishonesty among those in this profession, shepherds were not allowed to testify in court. Therefore, the announcement was to identify Christ's humility with the shepherds (cf. Philippians 2:7–8). The announcement also identified His mission—caring and protecting. In both the Old and New Testaments, shepherds can symbolize those who care for God's people. Christ later identifies Himself in John's Gospel as the "Good Shepherd" (John 10:2, 11, 12, 14, 16). David writes, "The Lord is my shepherd" (Psalm 23:1). A number of passages in both Testaments use imagery to identify the Lord as the Shepherd of His people (Isaiah 40:11; Jeremiah 23:1–4; Hebrews 13:20; 1 Peter 2:25; 5:2).

Shepherds at the time of Jesus were not only poor, but also considered outsiders. Their work, like that of the tax collectors, made them ceremonially unclean. Therefore, the implication is that the Gospel came first to the social outcasts of Jesus' day. This accounts for the recurring emphasis in Luke of Jesus' identification with both the poor and the societal outcasts of His day. He ate with "sinners" (Luke 7:37–39; 19:7). He said that He did not have a place to lay His head (Luke 9:58; cf., Matthew 8:20). He declared that He was commissioned to preach and care for the poor, the sick, and the less privileged in the society (Luke 4:18–19). Even at death He was buried in a borrowed grave (Matthew 27:57–60).

**12 And this shall be a sign unto you; Ye shall find the babe wrapped in swaddling clothes, lying in a manger. 13 And suddenly there was with the angel a multitude of the heavenly host praising God, and saying, 14 Glory to God in the highest, and on earth peace, good will toward men.**

After the announcement, the angel did not instruct the shepherds to go and see the Child. He assumed they would. However, he did inform them how they would recognize Him. They would find Him, rather than being surrounded by grandeur and glory, wrapped in swaddling clothes and lying in a manger. This information was necessary because there are probably other children born in Bethlehem on this same day, but no others would be lying in a manger. As the

angel announced the news to the shepherds, he was suddenly joined by "a multitude of the heavenly host praising God." The word "host" (Gk. *stratia*, **strah-tee-AH**) means an army. "Multitude," *plethos* (Gk. **PLAY-thohs**), quantifies the number of these angels that appear before the shepherds as a great or large number, probably too many to count. The host is described as "heavenly," which means they are celestial beings or angels. The heavenly host filled the air with praises to God singing, "Glory to God in the highest, and on earth peace, good will toward men." What does this host of angels mean by the song? What message do they convey through this chorus?

By the phrase "glory to God in the highest," the angels seem to declare the purpose of the birth of the newborn Child. His birth brings the highest degree of glory to God. Here the angels foresaw the ultimate purpose of Christ on earth, i.e., to glorify God through His death and resurrection. Creation glorifies God, but not so much as redemption. The heavenly hosts not only praise God but they also bless those on earth with peace. The NLT more clearly captures the sense of the Greek here than KJV: "and peace on earth to those with whom God is pleased." The Greek translated as "good will" (KJV) or "pleased" (NLT) is *eudokia* (**ew-doh-KEE-ah**), which means good will or favor. The grammar is difficult, so that it could refer to people who show good will toward one another or people who have God's good graces. However, there is no need to quibble over the grammar because Mosaic Torah commands us to love one another, so to show good will toward others is favorable to God (see Deuteronomy 6:5; Matthew 22:37–39; Mark 12:30–31; Luke 10:27). Jesus' birth brings a blessing of peace to such people. Isaiah said centuries before that He shall be called "the Prince of Peace"

(Isaiah 9:6). Thirdly, the birth of Christ reveals God's "good will" for humankind. Right from Creation, God has never willed otherwise. His desires for humanity have always been for our good or well-being, and He seeks to convince us of that desire. We can see this through the creation narrative (Genesis 1:28–31). The psalmist said, "The LORD God is a sun and shield ... no good thing will he withhold from them that walk uprightly" (Psalm 84:11). The Lord through Jeremiah assured Israel of His desire for them, "For I know the thoughts that I think toward you, saith the LORD, thoughts of peace, and not of evil, to give you an expected end" (Jeremiah 29:11). God's wish for mankind is to "have all men to be saved" (1 Timothy 2:4). Peter wrote, "The Lord is not ... willing that any should perish, but that all should come to repentance" (2 Peter 3:9). Here the angels proclaim the wish of God for all for us.

**15 And it came to pass, as the angels were gone away from them into heaven, the shepherds said one to another, Let us now go even unto Bethlehem, and see this thing which is come to pass, which the Lord hath made known unto us. 16 And they came with haste, and found Mary, and Joseph, and the babe lying in a manger.**

After these spectacular and supernatural happenings, the shepherds decided to go to Bethlehem to see for themselves what the angels had told them. They never questioned or doubted the story, but went rather to see this strange event which the Lord had revealed to them through the angels. The clause "which the Lord hath made known unto us" confirms the fact that they accepted the message of the angels as truth from God. Hence, they hurried with excitement into Bethlehem to visit the newborn child. They find not only what the angel has told them concerning the child (v. 12), but they also saw Mary and Joseph with the baby in the manger. What happened to their flocks, whether the shepherds left them by themselves under the protection of God or under the care of some other people, the Bible does not tell us. How they found the right manger, the Bible does not say. However, the verb used here, "found" (Gk. *aneurisko*, **an-ew-RIS-ko**), seems to show that they searched before they found the child.

**17 And when they had seen it, they made known abroad the saying which was told them concerning this child. 18 And all they that heard it wondered at those things which were told them by the shepherds. 19 But Mary kept all these things, and pondered them in her heart.**

The shepherds were the first to hear the Good News of the birth of the Savior; they were also the first to proclaim it to others. Their message was simple; they declared what the angels told them concerning the child, and what they had seen. Their message left the listeners with wonder and marvel. However, "Mary kept all these things, and pondered them in her heart." "All these things" includes the story the shepherds told—the appearance of the angel and the heavenly host. This story adds to the chain of miraculous events regarding the Christ, which began with the initial visit of Gabriel announcing to Mary that she would be the mother of the Messiah. The word "kept" is the Greek *suntereo* (**soon-teh-REH-oh**), and means to preserve, to conserve something of great importance. Hence, it is translated as "treasured" by New American Standard Bible and New International Version. Mary preserved the words of the shepherds in her heart with all the strange things that had been taking place, and she meditated upon them as future events unfolded.

**20 And the shepherds returned, glorifying and praising God for all the things that they had heard and seen, as it was told unto them.**

After visiting the newborn, and finding the child as the angels had told them, the shepherds returned, glorifying and praising God. The object of their joyful praise is obvious—the long-expected Messiah is born and they have been witnesses. The birth of a Redeemer brings joy and peace to those who accept Him. Here the shepherds accepted the good tidings. Therefore, they praised and worshiped the Lord, and proclaimed to others the wonders of God's dealing with mankind. Like the shepherds, we are called to declare the birth of the Savior and His purpose to the world. Christ was born to bring peace and redemption. This event occurred over two thousand years ago, but it is still as relevant today as it was then. He came that we might have peace, He suffered that we might be healed, and He died that we might live. That is the message of Christmas.

Sources:
Alexander, David and Pat Alexander. *Eerdmans Handbook to the Bible.* Grand Rapids, MI: Wm.B. Erdmans Publishing Co., 1992.
Green, Joel B and Scot McKnight. *Dictionary of Jesus and the New Testament.* Downers Grove, IL: InterVarsity Press, 1992.

## Say It Correctly

Historicity. hi-sto-**RI**-ci-tee.
Caesar. **CEE**-zer.
Augustus. au-**GU**-stus.

## Daily Bible Readings

**MONDAY**
Give Thanks to God's Holy Name
(1 Chronicles 16:35–41)

**TUESDAY**
Praising and Thanking God Together
(2 Chronicles 5:2–14)

**WEDNESDAY**
The Heavens Proclaim God's
Handiwork
(Psalm 19)

**THURSDAY**
God's Glory Over All the Earth
(Psalm 108:1–6)

**FRIDAY**
Our Hope of Sharing God's Glory
(Romans 5:1–5)

**SATURDAY**
Expecting a Child
(Luke 2:1–7)

**SUNDAY**
A Savior Born This Day
(Luke 2:8–20)

# Teaching Tips

## Words You Should Know

**A. Gennesaret** (Matthew 14:27) *Gennesaret* (Gk.)—A lovely and fertile region near the sea of Galilee.

**B. Of little faith** (v. 31) *oligopistos* (Gk.)—Puny, small trust, short burst of belief, uncertain of belief.

## Teacher Preparation

**Unifying Principle—Believing in Miracles.** Many things inspire awe in people. How do Christians know what is truly worth their reverence? Matthew tells about the times when Jesus miraculously walked on water to meet His disciples in a boat, which led them to worship Him as truly the Son of God, and when Jesus healed the sick.

**A.** Pray for God to make you aware of your weaknesses and strengthen your faith.

**B.** Intercede for your students as they study this week's lesson that the Lord would touch them in a special way.

**C.** Study the Scriptures to obtain full insight of the context. Meditate and record your own personal application.

**D.** Read the Focal Verses in several translations for clarity.

## O—Open the Lesson

**A.** Open the class, taking prayer requests specifically for where students need to see God move in their lives.

**B.** Review the Aim for Change and ask students what they hope to learn today.

**C.** Briefly discuss the In Focus story and ask if students have encountered such a situation.

**D.** Tie the discussion into today's Keep in Mind verse to help them believe the Lord.

## P—Present the Scriptures

**A.** Review the Background and The People, Places, and Times to make sure students understand the backdrop for today's lesson.

**B.** Have volunteers read the Focal Verses.

**C.** Find parallels between the biblical culture and today's context when it comes to what we believe during stormy situations.

## E—Explore the Meaning

**A.** Ask students to share where they are in their faith walk. Where are they having trouble believing for the Lord to act on their behalf?

**B.** Break students into partners or small groups to review Search the Scriptures and Discuss the Meaning.

## N—Next Steps for Application

**A.** Ask students how they plan to apply this week's lesson to their lives and encourage them to write down their plan.

## Worship Guide

For the Superintendent or Teacher
Theme: In Awe of Christ's Power
Song: "Break Every Chain"
Devotional Reading: Mark 9:15–24

# In Awe of Christ's Power

**Bible Background • MATTHEW 14:22–36**
**Printed Text • MATTHEW 14:22–36**
**Devotional Reading • MARK 9:15–24**

## —————————— Aim for Change ——————————

By the end of the lesson, we will: REVIEW the disciples' response to Jesus' miracles; BE inspired by the miracles of Jesus and yearn to become faithful worshipers; and BELIEVE in Jesus' miracles and commit to being prayerful encouragers of others.

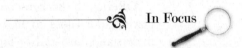

## —————————— In Focus ——————————

Warren had been between jobs for over two years. To stay afloat, he took a job that called for a considerable pay cut. He and his wife Angela had to downsize their lifestyle, which included significant cuts in giving. They visited a church where the preacher brought a powerful word that encouraged them to trust God for their provision. Warren became more and more frustrated and angry with God. He cried out to the Lord and asked for a miracle. He knew that this current job was not paying the bills, but he decided to work as hard as he could, expecting God to provide for his family's needs. While at work, he gave excellent service to a frazzled customer. It turned out that the customer was the head of human resources at a company that was expanding. He loved Warren's personality and pursuit of excellence and gave Warren his card. Within two weeks, Warren had a job that paid more than his previous job. As he walked into his new workplace, he heard in his spirit, "Why did you doubt My ability to bless you?"

*How many times do we doubt the Lord's ability to do the impossible in our lives? In today's lesson, we take a look at one of Jesus' greatest miracles that science still cannot explain.*

## —————————— Keep in Mind ——————————

"And when they were come into the ship, the wind ceased. Then they that were in the ship came and worshipped him, saying, Of a truth thou art the Son of God" (Matthew 14:32–33).

"And when they were come into the ship, the wind ceased. Then they that were in the ship came and worshipped him, saying, Of a truth thou art the Son of God" (Matthew 14:32–33).

# Focal Verses

**KJV** **Matthew 14:22** And straightway Jesus constrained his disciples to get into a ship, and to go before him unto the other side, while he sent the multitudes away.

**23** And when he had sent the multitudes away, he went up into a mountain apart to pray: and when the evening was come, he was there alone.

**24** But the ship was now in the midst of the sea, tossed with waves: for the wind was contrary.

**25** And in the fourth watch of the night Jesus went unto them, walking on the sea.

**26** And when the disciples saw him walking on the sea, they were troubled, saying, It is a spirit; and they cried out for fear.

**27** But straightway Jesus spake unto them, saying, Be of good cheer; it is I; be not afraid.

**28** And Peter answered him and said, Lord, if it be thou, bid me come unto thee on the water.

**29** And he said, Come. And when Peter was come down out of the ship, he walked on the water, to go to Jesus.

**30** But when he saw the wind boisterous, he was afraid; and beginning to sink, he cried, saying, Lord, save me.

**31** And immediately Jesus stretched forth his hand, and caught him, and said unto him, O thou of little faith, wherefore didst thou doubt?

**32** And when they were come into the ship, the wind ceased.

**33** Then they that were in the ship came and worshipped him, saying, Of a truth thou art the Son of God.

**34** And when they were gone over, they came into the land of Gennesaret.

**35** And when the men of that place had knowledge of him, they sent out into all that

**NLT** **Matthew 14:22** Immediately after this, Jesus insisted that his disciples get back into the boat and cross to the other side of the lake, while he sent the people home.

**23** After sending them home, he went up into the hills by himself to pray. Night fell while he was there alone.

**24** Meanwhile, the disciples were in trouble far away from land, for a strong wind had risen, and they were fighting heavy waves.

**25** About three o'clock in the morning Jesus came toward them, walking on the water.

**26** When the disciples saw him walking on the water, they were terrified. In their fear, they cried out, "It's a ghost!"

**27** But Jesus spoke to them at once. "Don't be afraid," he said. "Take courage. I am here!

**28** Then Peter called to him, "Lord, if it's really you, tell me to come to you, walking on the water."

**29** "Yes, come," Jesus said.

So Peter went over the side of the boat and walked on the water toward Jesus.

**30** But when he saw the strong wind and the waves, he was terrified and began to sink. "Save me, Lord!" he shouted.

**31** Jesus immediately reached out and grabbed him. "You have so little faith," Jesus said. "Why did you doubt me?"

**32** When they climbed back into the boat, the wind stopped.

**33** Then the disciples worshiped him. "You really are the Son of God!" they exclaimed.

**34** After they had crossed the lake, they landed at Gennesaret.

**35** When the people recognized Jesus, the news of his arrival spread quickly throughout the whole area, and soon people were bringing all their sick to be healed.

country round about, and brought unto him all that were diseased;

**36** And besought him that they might only touch the hem of his garment: and as many as touched were made perfectly whole.

**36** They begged him to let the sick touch at least the fringe of his robe, and all who touched him were healed.

## The People, Places, and Times

**Sea of Galilee.** Although not explicit in Matthew's account, it is more clear on Mark's Gospel (6:45–53) that Jesus walked on the Sea of Galilee, located north of Jerusalem. Scholars estimate that Jesus did many of His most notable miracles, at least eighteen, in and around the communities bordering this body of water.

**The Apostle Peter.** Peter and his brother Andrew were the first disciples called by Jesus (Mark 1:16–17). He was known for his impulsive nature and forceful personality, as well as his special relationship with Jesus. Jesus Himself changed his name from Simon to Peter (or Cephas), which means "rock."

Peter was the first of the disciples to recognize Jesus as the Messiah. And though Peter denied Jesus three times before Jesus' crucifixion, after receiving the gift of the Holy Spirit on the day of Pentecost, Peter was the first to preach to the crowds. He ultimately became one of the Gospel's most passionate and tireless ambassadors, suffering persecution, beatings, and imprisonment until he was martyred around A.D. 67.

## Background

In the preceding verses, Jesus dealt with the devastating news of the imprisonment and execution of His cousin John the Baptist at the hands of Herod the tetrarch (Matthew 14:1–13). He sought to get away from the crowd and retreated by Himself to a remote place to rest. However, crowds of people from surrounding towns began to seek af-

ter Jesus. As the evening set in, the disciples sought to send the people on their way to fend for themselves for dinner, but Jesus objected. He ordered His disciples to give the people something to eat. The disciples were perplexed at Jesus' command, but it was all a setup for a display of His unquestionable power and convincing proof of His ability to defy natural law. With five loaves and two fishes, Jesus blessed His Father and turned little into overflow, feeding five thousand men, not including women and children (Matthew 14:13–21). After this, Jesus sent the disciples away by boat to the other side of the Sea of Galilee while He recharged in prayer.

## At-A-Glance

1. Jesus Replenishes His Power
(Matthew 14:22–23)
2. Jesus Defies the Laws of Nature
(vv. 24–27)
3. Jesus Calls Peter to Step Out
(vv. 28–29)
4. Jesus' Power Declared
(vv. 30–36)

## In Depth

**1. Jesus Replenishes His Power (Matthew 14:22–23)**

Jesus, after His exhausting time of ministry and meeting the spiritual and natural needs of the people, again seeks to commune alone with His Father in prayer. Jesus sends the disciples ahead of Him by boat while dismissing the crowds that gathered to see Him. He sought to be alone with His Father to recharge and regroup. In this scene, we see the humanity of Jesus and the dependency that He had on the Father and the Holy Spirit in His daily life and ministry. Through Jesus, we have a model for how we should carve out time away from the busyness of life to steal away with the Father. In His presence we are refreshed, renewed, and empowered to continue on with His purpose. It sets the perfect stage for the next scene, in which we see the perfect exhibition of the divinity of Jesus Christ.

### 2. Jesus Defies the Laws of Nature (vv. 24–27)

Matthew shifts the scene. While on the boat, the disciples encounter torrential winds and waves in their travel, which is very unsettling even for the trade fishermen to navigate. In this brewing storm, between 3 and 6 o'clock in the morning, the disciples see a figure walking toward them and become terrified. Out of fear, their imaginations take them to the worst possible scenario, and they conclude that it was a threatening figure. They begin to scream out with terror, "It's a ghost!" not realizing that it was Jesus (v. 26, NLT). Upon their reaction, Jesus immediately calls on His disciples to calm down and "take courage" (v. 27, NLT) because He has arrived on the scene among the waves and wind. Jesus' appearance on the water is not an everyday occurrence, and it is not something that has been repeated. He defies all natural laws by walking on the water. Scholars are still trying to rationalize how this could have happened, and if it really occurred as recorded. However, as Christians, we accept it as truth because the One who created the seas has the power to walk on them and is sovereign over all the earth.

### 3. Jesus Calls Peter to Step Out (vv. 28–29)

Peter, being often the spokesman of the group and bold enough to ask the tough questions, puts Jesus to the test after hearing His voice. Peter responds, "Lord, if it's really you, tell me to come to you, walking on the water" (v. 28, NLT). It was Peter's personality to take Jesus at His word and take risks of faith which would prove to be invaluable for his future role in the church. No one since has successfully walked on water, but in the Spirit, as we receive a word from the Lord to do something, we have the ability to defy the odds through the power of the Holy Spirit. Jesus said: "I tell you the truth, anyone who believes in me will do the same works I have done, and even greater works, because I am going to be with the Father. You can ask for anything in my name, and I will do it, so that the Son can bring glory to the Father" (John 14:12–13, NLT).

### 4. Jesus' Power Declared (vv. 30–36)

We can only imagine what the other disciples were thinking as Peter launched out into the deep. As he continued, he began to notice within his natural senses what was happening around him and became afraid. The wind got stronger, and as it pressed his body, he began to get nervous, which caused him to take his eyes off Jesus. As Peter became frightened, he began to sink and cry out to Jesus to save him because he thought he was going to drown. Matthew notes again that Jesus immediately reacts and stretches out His hand to pull Peter from the water and get him to safety. Jesus then asks him, "Why did you doubt me?" (v. 31, NLT). Once Jesus and Peter got into the boat, the winds and waves ceased and everything was still and peaceful. They worshiped, acknowledging that Jesus "truly is the Son of God" (v. 33). Again, how often do we take our eyes off Jesus when things don't look like what we expect, even though we have been given a word from the Lord to go forward in faith?

After this, Jesus landed on the opposite shore in Gennesaret. The people immediately heard that Jesus was there and sought out His healing and miracles. Jesus' power is evident in the fact that people desired to touch the fringes of His robe in order to be healed. These fringes are actually the tassels spoken of in Numbers 15:37–41. For the Jews, they were a reminder to obey God's Word and also a symbol of authority. The passage records that those who touched the fringes were healed. This is a small window into the awesome power of Jesus.

## Search the Scriptures

1. What was Peter's response to the sight of Jesus walking on water (Matthew 14:28)?

2. How did Jesus react to the disciples and Peter's trouble on the water (vv. 27, 31)?

## Discuss the Meaning

1. What are the implications for this lesson in today's context? Drawing on the example of Scripture, what things can we do corporately and individually to step out on faith?

2. Jesus' response to Peter's cry for help was immediate. What does that mean for when you cry out for help? What keeps us in fear?

## Lesson in Our Society

God is still performing signs and wonders today as we call on the name of His Son Jesus. We should seek the Lord's will for our lives to receive vision and be empowered by the Holy Spirit to get in alignment to make the miraculous happen in our age. The same power that raised Jesus from the dead lives within us. Just as the apostles turned the world upside down at the word of the Lord to establish the church, we live on as His fruit on the earth.

## Make It Happen

We are encouraged to fix our eyes on Jesus, the Author and Finisher of our faith, who for the sake of the joy set before Him endured the Cross and is seated at the right hand of the throne of God (Hebrews 12:2). If we truly believe that Jesus ever lives to make intercession for us, we must trust that we are safe in His arms and follow His lead.

## Follow the Spirit

What God wants me to do:

_____

_____

_____

_____

## Remember Your Thoughts

Special insights I have learned:

_____

_____

_____

_____

## More Light on the Text

### Matthew 14:22–36

**22 And straightway Jesus constrained his disciples to get into a ship, and to go before him unto the other side, while he sent the multitudes away.**

Jesus multiplied bread for five thousand people in a desert place (vv. 13–21) where He had retreated with His disciples. His withdrawal was motivated by a report of Herod's beheading of His cousin John the Baptist and by the king's comments about Him and the miracles He was performing (vv. 1–2, 13). After feeding the people with the bread, they were overwhelmed and wanted to appoint Him king (John 6:15). Jesus rejected this as a potential threat to His mission on earth. Jesus' purpose on earth was to serve, not to be served (Matthew 20:28; Mark 10:45, NLT).

This situation led Jesus to constrain His disciples to leave the scene immediately while He dismissed the crowd. The Greek word for constrained is *anagkazo* (**ah-nahng-KAHD-zo**), which means to physically or mentally compel or force somebody to do something. It is derived from *anagke* (Gk. **ah-NAHNG-kay**), which means necessity or need. There was an imperative motive for Jesus to send His disciples ahead. Carson states that Jesus wanted to "tame a messianic uproar" (Matthew, 343).

The disciples had to go to "the other side," which according to scholars refers to the western side of the Sea of Galilee. However, the synoptic parallel in Mark adds "to Bethsaida" (6:45), where Luke 9:10 also locates the feeding of the five thousand. Some scholars suggest that the desert place where the feeding took place was closer but separated from Bethsaida by a bay. Jesus intended the disciples to wait for Him at Bethsaida, but the contrary wind took them to Gennesaret. A similar situation happened in Acts 27:15, where the boat driving Paul and the other crew members was carried away from its initial course by a strong wind.

**23 And when he had sent the multitudes away, he went up into a mountain apart to pray: and when the evening was come, he was there alone.**

After He has sent them away, He climbed the mountain to communicate with the Father. At some critical periods of Jesus' earthly ministry, He isolated Himself from the crowd and even His disciples to pray. Luke

5:16 explains that Jesus was withdrawing in the wilderness for prayer in periods of great popularity. In Matthew 6:6, Jesus entreats us to withdraw in our closet to pray to God. It is therefore important for us Christians today to emulate our Lord and retreat ourselves from noise and busyness at times to pray.

He was alone at evening. We should not be confused about the use of "evening" twice in this chapter in the narrative sequence. The Jews divided the day into three periods: morning, noon, and evening (cf. Psalm 55:17). The evening was in turn subdivided into two parts: the first evening began at sunset (twilight) and the second began when the sun was fully set (dusk) (cf. Exodus 12:6 literally "between the evenings"). The Greek word for evening was *opsios* (**OP-see-ose**) which could refer either to the period before sunset or right after sundown, but was sometimes used for the two. In context, however, it is logical to ascribe the first mention of evening (14:15) to the first evening and the current one after sunset. Jesus was left praying alone when it was night.

**24 But the ship was now in the midst of the sea, tossed with waves: for the wind was contrary.**

While Jesus was on the mountain praying, the disciples were on the sea tossed with waves. They encountered a contrary wind that would eventually lead them to Gennesaret. Mark 6:48 tells us that Jesus saw that the disciples were battling with the contrary wind. We cannot be certain if Jesus saw them physically or supernaturally. The current event is taking place after they had left the desert place for quite a long time. Still, John states that it was already night when they encountered the wind. It would have been difficult for Jesus to see from such a long distance. Some suggest that it was the full moon and Jesus could see from the mountain. In any case, if Jesus in the beginning of His ministry could see Nathanael (John 1:50) from afar, it is not unlikely that He could see the disciples by the divine endowments of the Holy Spirit.

**25 And in the fourth watch of the night Jesus went unto them, walking on the sea.**

The Jews divided the night into three watches and the Romans divided it into four between 6 p.m. and 6 a.m. Jesus therefore came to the disciples between three and six o'clock in the morning.

Around this time, Jesus appeared to them in an unprecedented fashion by walking on the sea. Great figures of Old Testament history such as Moses, Joshua, Elijah, and Elisha did miracles involving parting of water bodies, but never has it been recorded that anyone walked on water (Exodus 14:21, 22; Joshua 3:15–17; 2 Kings 2:8, 14). This action of Jesus clearly portrays His divine nature. There was probably no boat left for Him to join the disciples.

**26 And when the disciples saw him walking on the sea, they were troubled, saying, It is a spirit; and they cried out for fear.**

The disciples saw someone walking on water at night and with a contrary wind. The disciples could not fathom this scene, assuming the being they saw was a spirit. The Greek word for spirit here is *phantasma* (**FAHN-tahs-mah**), meaning phantom or "a ghost" (NLT). Our perception of reality always shapes our responses and reactions. They expressed their inner feelings of fear outwardly by a strident noise. Their fear could have been due to prevailing cultural beliefs of the time. In the ancient Near East, the sea was thought to be the realm of powerful, chaotic beings (cf. Job 41; Revelation 13:1). They undoubtedly thought Jesus was a "ghost" that would do them harm. Their deduction that it was a ghost led them to fear,

*phobos* (**FOE-bose**), which means fear, dread, terror—that which is caused by intimidation or adversaries. Hagner compares the "fear of the disciples" to that of "all who are threatened by insecurity in the face of the unknown" (425).

**27 But straightway Jesus spake unto them, saying, be of good cheer; it is I; be not afraid.**

The Lord is always prompt in coming to rescue us. "Be of good cheer" or "do not be afraid" (NLT) are phrases of encouragement and comfort. It resonates when we have a challenging task ahead; it will re-echo if we are in peril or in the face of danger, such as the current case facing the disciples.

The Lord wants us to "be of good cheer" and not be afraid because of His presence. "It is I" is the translation of *ego eimi* (Gk. **eg-O ay-MEE**), which echoes the "I am" God's self-revelation to Moses in Exodus 3:14 and other similar passages like Isaiah 43:12. We have this promise of Jesus in Matthew 28:20: "I am with you always, even to the end of the age" (NLT). We should therefore not be afraid even in our darkest circumstances or the most violent storm of our lives.

**28 And Peter answered him and said, Lord, if it be thou, bid me come unto thee on the water.**

Peter's request was not portraying a doubt about the identity of the one walking on water. Carson suggests the phrase "since it is you" is an acceptable rendering of "if it be thou." Peter is an extrovert as far as personality is concerned. His request might have been guided by the delegation of power Jesus granted them in Mark 6:12, 13, 30 over sicknesses and demons. Since it was the Lord, He can grant Peter with this authority over physical laws also.

**29 And he said, Come. And when Peter was come down out of the ship, he walked on the water, to go to Jesus.**

Jesus granted Peter's request by the word "come." It should not be perceived here as a mere invitation but rather as a delegation of power or a transfer of authority. Peter therefore took the first step and came out of the ship. Once he was out of the boat and on the sea, he could walk just as Jesus was doing. John 14:12 says that "anyone who believes in me will do the same works I have done..." (NLT).

**30 But when he saw the wind boisterous, he was afraid; and beginning to sink, he cried, saying, Lord, save me.**

We can perform greater works by faith as long as we keep on looking at the Lord who instructs us. Anytime we shift our focus from the Lord to the challenge, we will start to experience failure. Here Peter fails to look at the Lord, who instructed him to come, but rather focused on the wind.

When Peter realized he was sinking, he cried to Jesus, saying, "Lord save me." Our faith may fail us at times, but ultimately Jesus is our last recourse in peril or danger. Instinctively, Peter cried out of fear and despair for the rescue of the Lord.

**31 And immediately Jesus stretched forth his hand, and caught him, and said unto him, O thou of little faith, wherefore didst thou doubt?**

Jesus did not tarry in rescuing Peter. Without any delay, He stretched His hand to seize the drowning Peter. Peter walked quite a distance since Jesus could just stretch His hand to get hold of Him.

Jesus rebuked him after He got hold of him. The Greek word for "little faith" is *oligopistos* (**oh-lee-GO-pees-tose**), and it is used only by the Lord to gently rebuke His disci-

ples for their anxiety. Our cry of desperation will always be heard, and God will swiftly deliver us from our trouble, but we must expect a gentle rebuke from our loving Lord. This word suggests a quantification of faith just as Jesus explained the amount of faith required to move mountains in Matthew 17:20.

**32 And when they were come into the ship, the wind ceased.**

This verse indicates that Peter walked back with Jesus into the boat. When they (Jesus and Peter) entered the ship, the wind ceased.

**33 Then they that were in the ship came and worshipped him, saying, of a truth thou art the Son of God.**

When the wind ceased, the disciples realized the true personality of Jesus. This man could multiply five loaves of bread for five thousand people, walk on water, and still the wind. Who could that person be except the promised Son of God? The Roman officer and the soldiers made the same confession when they witnessed the events at Jesus' death and were filled with awe (Matthew 27:50–54).

The term used for worship is *proskuneo* (**pros-koo-NEH-oh**), which signifies to fall prostrate in front of the one being worshiped. The same word is used when Cornelius welcomed Peter into his house. Peter's objection that he was also a man points to the fact that the term is used only for divine being (Acts 10:25–26).

**34 And when they were gone over, they came into the land of Gennesaret.**

After crossing, they landed at Gennesaret, described as a triangular coastal land on the western side of the Sea of Galilee.

**35 And when the men of that place had knowledge of him, they sent out into all that country round about, and brought unto him all that were diseased;**

Jesus was already very famous and He could not move unnoticed. John even records that the people who were fed the previous day went after Jesus to the other side of the lake (John 6:24–25). The people of that area spread the news about Jesus' arrival in their territory, and they brought sick people to Jesus for healing. The term used to describe the sick people could mean physical or mental illness (Gk. *kakos*, **kah-KOSE**).

**36 And besought him that they might only touch the hem of his garment: and as many as touched were made perfectly whole.**

"The hem of his garments" probably refers to the fringes or tassels at the corner of the mantle, which was a Jewish religious requirement prescribed in Numbers 15:37–39 and Deuteronomy 22:12. The request to only touch the fringe of the garments might be due to the crowds at the place. Anyone who was able to touch Him was made perfectly whole, meaning a complete restoration, similar to the woman with the blood issue (Luke 8:44, 48).

Sources:
Attridge, Harold et. al. *The Harper Collins Study Bible New Revised Standard Version.* New York: Harper One, 2006. 1693, 1694, 1736.
Bromiley, G. W. *Theological Dictionary of the New Testament.* 7th Edition. Grand Rapids, MI: Eerdmans, 1978.
Carson, D. A. *The Expositor's Bible Commentary with the New International Version.* Grand Rapids, MI: Zondervan Publishing House, 1995.
Fullam, E. L. *Living the Lord's Prayer.* Lincoln, VA: Chosen Books, 1980.
Green, J. B. *The New International Commentary on the New Tesstament: The Gospel of Luke.* Grand Rapids, MI: Eerdmans, 1997.
Hagner, D. A. *Word Biblical Commentary: Matthew 14-28* Vol. 33. Dallas, TX: Word Books Publisher, 1995.
Hendriksen, W. *New Testament Commentary: Luke.* Carlisle, PA: The Banner of Truth Trust, 1978.
Howard, F. D. *The Gospel of Matthew: A Study Manual.* Grand Rapids, MI: Baker Book House, 1961.
Howard, M. J. *The New International Greek Testament Commentary: The Gospel of Luke.* Grand Rapids, MI: Eerdmans, 1978.
Keener, C. S. *The IVP Bible Background Commentary: New Testament.* Downers Grove, IL: Inter Varsity Press, 1993.
Morris, L. *Tyndale New Testament Commentary: Luke.* Grand Rapids, MI: Eerdmans, 1984.
Nolland, J. *Word Biblical Commentary: Luke 9:21–18:34.* Vol. 35B. Dallas, Texas: Word Books, 1993.
Ryrie, C. C. *The Ryrie Study Bible: New Testament, King James Version.* Chicago, IL: The Moody Bible Institute, 1976.
Tasker, R. V. *Tyndale New Testament Commentaries: Matthew.* Grand Rapids, MI: Wm. Eerdmans Publishing Company, 1961.
Unger, Merrill. *Unger's Bible Dictionary.* Chicago, IL: Moody Press, 1981. 387, 388, 847, 848.
Vine, W. E. *An Expository Dictionary of the New Testament Words.* 7th Edition. Old Tappan, NJ: Fleming H. Revell, 1966.
Wilson, N. S., and L. K. Taylor. *Tyndale Handbook of Bible Charts and Maps.* Wheaton, IL: Tyndale House Publisher, 2001.
Zodhiates, Spiros, Baker, Warren. eds. *Hebrew Greek Key Word Study Bible King James Version.* 2nd ed. Chattanooga, TN: AMG Publishers, 1991. 1749, 1766, 51.

## Say It Correctly

Gennesaret. juh-**NES**-uh-ret.
Galilee. **GAL**-uh-lee.
Bethsaida. beth-**SAY**-uh-duh.

## Daily Bible Readings

**MONDAY**
By Faith We Please God
(Hebrews 11:1–6)

**TUESDAY**
Where is Your Faith?
(Luke 8:19–25)

**WEDNESDAY**
I Believe; Help My Unbelief
(Mark 9:15–24)

**THURSDAY**
The Light Overpowers Darkness
(John 1:1–9)

**FRIDAY**
A Mustard-Seed-Sized Faith
(Matthew 17:14–20)

**SATURDAY**
Great is Your Faith
(Matthew 15:21–31)

**SUNDAY**
Oh, You of Little Faith
(Matthew 14:22–36)

# Notes

---

---

---

---

# Teaching Tips

## Words You Should Know

**A. Hallowed be** (Luke 11:2) *hagiazo* (Gk.)—To be sanctified, to be made holy and pure, to be venerated.

**B. Heaven** (v. 2) *ouranos* (Gk.)—The abode of God, God's dwelling or resting place, also the air or sky.

## Teacher Preparation

**Unifying Principle—Finding the Right Words.** People built intimate, trust-filled relationships by having open communication with one another. How do people maintain open communication? Jesus teaches that nurturing a relationship with God requires persistent prayer.

**A.** Pray that God will use you to help your students grow in His grace and knowledge.

**B.** Read the Scripture lesson in different translations and take note of what God specifically reveals for you and your students.

**C.** Review and complete the companion lesson in *Precepts for Living Personal Study Guide®*.

## O—Open the Lesson

**A.** Start off the class with prayer and ask students for prayer requests, what are they trusting God for: for themselves, family, friends, community, etc.

**B.** Ask students to share insights from last week's lesson and how they applied them during the week.

**C.** Probe students to tie together last week's and this week's lesson (Christ's power and His spiritual practice of prayer).

**D.** Read the Aim for Change and have students reflect on their own prayer lives.

## P—Present the Scriptures

**A.** Ask students about their understanding of the Lord's Prayer.

**B.** Also ask students to share their perception of God as Father.

**C.** Review the Scripture text and pull out key points from the In Depth section along with your own insight.

## E—Explore the Meaning

**A.** Engage students in conversation concerning their relationship with God as expressed through prayer.

**B.** Break up into groups and have each group explore Discuss the Meaning, Lesson in Our Society, and Make It Happen.

## N—Next Steps for Application

**A.** Have students set realistic goals for application to communicate and believe God for what He wants to do in their lives.

**B.** Close in prayer by inviting students to silently reflect and write out what God has spoken during the teaching time.

## Worship Guide

For the Superintendent or Teacher
Theme: A Model for Prayer
Song: "Give Us This Day"
Devotional Reading: Psalm 103:1–13

# A Model for Prayer

**Bible Background • LUKE 11**
**Printed Text • LUKE 11:1–13**
**Devotional Reading • PSALM 103:1–13**

## —————————— Aim for Change ——————————

By the end of the lesson, we will: UNDERSTAND the Lord's Prayer as a model for praying various kinds of prayers; ACCEPT the need for constant prayer; and DEVELOP a more disciplined prayer life as a means of growing a relationship with God.

## ———————— In Focus ————————

"Mommy, if God knows everything, why do we have to pray for Granddaddy?" Stella struggled to answer this question for her daughter Imani amid her own pain. Her father has been in intensive care for several weeks, and doctors didn't give her much hope for his recovery. She mustered up the strength to reply to little Imani.

"Because, sweetheart, although God knows everything, He wants to hear what is on our heart," Stella answered. Stella's father Raymond had taught her as a young child how to go to God in prayer, even after her mother died at the age of 13. As Stella stood by her father's bedside, memories of those precious moments flooded her mind, and she prayed that she and her husband Alan set a similar example for their children. Imani still questioned why we pray, but as she looked at her mother's calmness, she recognized her mother's faith in God to take care of her Granddaddy.

*In today's lesson, Jesus teaches His disciples a very valuable lesson about how our relationship with God is cultivated through prayer.*

## ———————— Keep in Mind ————————

"And he said unto them, When ye pray, say, Our Father which art in heaven, Hallowed be thy name. Thy kingdom come. Thy will be done, as in heaven, so in earth" (Luke 11:2).

"And he said unto them, When ye pray, say, Our Father which art in heaven, Hallowed be thy name. Thy kingdom come. Thy will be done, as in heaven, so in earth" (Luke 11:2).

## Focal Verses

**KJV** **Luke 11:1** And it came to pass, that, as he was praying in a certain place, when he ceased, one of his disciples said unto him, Lord, teach us to pray, as John also taught his disciples.

**2** And he said unto them, When ye pray, say, Our Father which art in heaven, Hallowed be thy name. Thy kingdom come. Thy will be done, as in heaven, so in earth.

**3** Give us day by day our daily bread.

**4** And forgive us our sins; for we also forgive every one that is indebted to us. And lead us not into temptation; but deliver us from evil.

**5** And he said unto them, Which of you shall have a friend, and shall go unto him at midnight, and say unto him, Friend, lend me three loaves;

**6** For a friend of mine in his journey is come to me, and I have nothing to set before him?

**7** And he from within shall answer and say, Trouble me not: the door is now shut, and my children are with me in bed; I cannot rise and give thee.

**8** I say unto you, Though he will not rise and give him, because he is his friend, yet because of his importunity he will rise and give him as many as he needeth.

**9** And I say unto you, Ask, and it shall be given you; seek, and ye shall find; knock, and it shall be opened unto you.

**10** For every one that asketh receiveth; and he that seeketh findeth; and to him that knocketh it shall be opened.

**11** If a son shall ask bread of any of you that is a father, will he give him a stone? or if he ask a fish, will he for a fish give him a serpent?

**12** Or if he shall ask an egg, will he offer him a scorpion?

**NLT** **Luke 11:1** Once Jesus was in a certain place praying. As he finished, one of his disciples came to him and said, "Lord, teach us to pray, just as John taught his disciples."

**2** Jesus said, "This is how you should pray: "Father, may your name be kept holy. May your Kingdom come soon.

**3** Give us each day the food we need,

**4** and forgive us our sins, as we forgive those who sin against us. And don't let us yield to temptation.'

**5** Then, teaching them more about prayer, he used this story: "Suppose you went to a friend's house at midnight, wanting to borrow three loaves of bread. You say to him,

**6** 'A friend of mine has just arrived for a visit, and I have nothing for him to eat.'

**7** And suppose he calls out from his bedroom, 'Don't bother me. The door is locked for the night, and my family and I are all in bed. I can't help you.'

**8** But I tell you this—though he won't do it for friendship's sake, if you keep knocking long enough, he will get up and give you whatever you need because of your shameless persistence.

**9** "And so I tell you, keep on asking, and you will receive what you ask for. Keep on seeking, and you will find. Keep on knocking, and the door will be opened to you.

**10** For everyone who asks, receives. Everyone who seeks, finds. And to everyone who knocks, the door will be opened.

**11** "You fathers—if your children ask for a fish, do you give them a snake instead?

**12** Or if they ask for an egg, do you give them a scorpion? Of course not!

**13** So if you sinful people know how to give good gifts to your children, how much

**13** If ye then, being evil, know how to give good gifts unto your children: how much more shall your heavenly Father give the Holy Spirit to them that ask him?

more will your heavenly Father give the Holy Spirit to those who ask him."

---

## The People, Places, and Times

**Disciples.** Disciples are followers or apprentices. Whether a rabbi or philosopher, many in the culture of biblical times who were thought to have expertise had followers sitting under their teaching. A disciple followed a rabbi in the hopes of becoming just like the rabbi themselves. Jesus had many disciples, but there were twelve apostles who were sent to establish the church, which continues to stand from their witness today.

**Kingdom.** In this passage Jesus speaks of the kingdom of heaven. The kingdom of God is God's manifested rule on earth as it is in heaven, bringing forth His way of doing and being in the earth. The theocracy was God's original intent at creation (Genesis 1:26–31). The kingdom also refers to the reign of God, which through prayer brings humanity in partnership with God to bring forth His divine rulership in every realm. In Mark and Luke's Gospel, it is mentioned 46 times and is synonymous with the term "kingdom of heaven" in the Gospel of Matthew.

## Background

Prayer is a major theme of Luke's Gospel. Scholars note that Luke records at least eleven instances of Jesus praying and two times where He teaches His disciples how to pray (Luke 11:1–13, 18:1–14). The placement of this discourse on the Lord's Prayer is interesting to note because in the last verses of the previous chapter, Luke shares Jesus' sending out the seventy (Luke 10:1–12), where He calls on them to "pray for the Lord of the harvest" to increase the harvest for more laborers in the kingdom. As well, he tells of

Jesus by the Holy Spirit rejoicing in the Lord upon the return of the seventy for revealing Himself as His Father and how no one can know this relationship except they be chosen (Luke 10:21–22). The chapter closes with Jesus visiting Mary and Martha's house; while Martha is busy serving, Mary chooses to listen to the Master teach, which was unheard of in this culture. Martha calls attention to Mary's behavior, but rather than rebuke her as expected, Jesus commends Mary for doing what was necessary at the moment: fellowship with Him (Luke 10:38–42). In summary, what we learn leading up to today's lesson is the power of communion, how prayer and being still enough to listen enable us to tap into God's power.

## At-A-Glance

1. The Structure of Prayer
(Luke 11:1–4)
2. Persistent in Prayer
(vv. 5–8)
3. Pursuing Through Prayer
(vv. 9–13)

## In Depth

### 1. The Structure of Prayer (Luke 11:1–4)

This particular text is traditionally noted as a passage taught to be recited, rather than a model for prayer, hence the words "when you pray say." However "The Lord's Prayer" is actually "the disciple's prayer." Many of the men who followed Jesus were first followers of John the Baptist, so they were familiar with the forerunner's practices of spiritual retreats in the wilderness (fasting, prayer, repentance). After walking with Jesus they sensed that there was something different about His posture of prayer, and just as John taught his disciples, they too wanted to be taught by their leader. Jesus outlines the structure or pattern of prayer for His disciples placing emphasis on five key points: adoration (honoring the Father, coming in humble reverence), submission (His will/kingdom first, His way of doing and being), supplication (asking for His daily provision), repentance (forgiveness of sins, ours and others), and protection (from the evil one and awareness of our own selfishness).

### 2. Persistent in Prayer (vv. 5–8)

What Jesus taught His disciples about prayer was a significant departure from Jewish and other surrounding ancient religious cultures because He reveals God in a personable way. By sharing an example they can relate to, how friends and neighbors treat each other in the time of need, Jesus lets His disciples (and ultimately us) know that God is good, merciful, compassionate, and would not turn us away if we pursue Him for what we need. Jesus also taught in Luke 18:1–8, that as we cry out to God for help and are persistent in looking to Him to meet our needs, He will answer. We do not need to be persistent because God cannot hear, He is toying with us, or He is in need of the attention; the purpose of prayerful persistence is for us to get our minds in accord with His. Hence within Matthew's account following of the Lord's Prayer, we also find Jesus teaching to take no thought for our lives but to seek first the Kingdom and everything else will be added (Matthew 6:25–33).

### 3. Pursuing Through Prayer (vv. 9–13)

Jesus teaches us how to ask, seek, and knock for the things of God. To ask God for something is to come to Him knowing that He is able to supply. The writer of Hebrews teaches us that we have to come to God with faith believing that He is God and a rewarder of those who diligently seek Him (Hebrews 11:6). Jesus teaches that we must come to God knowing He is able to grant or supply our need, and (if we are asking in alignment with His Word) that He will do it for His glory (John 14:12–14). If we seek after God, His way of doing and being, we will find Him. Searching for Him is intentional and requires focus. In another parable, Jesus likens seeking after the kingdom to one who is in pursuit of something valuable and precious (Matthew 13:44–45). To seek after God is to esteem Him above all, and Jesus reiterates what Jeremiah prophesied: that God is willing to be found by one in honest pursuit (Jeremiah 29:13). Finally, to knock is to approach expecting a welcomed entry. Again Jesus emphasizes the character of His Father as one who is willing to open the door for His children to receive from Him all the good things He has in store for them. It is the Father's nature to lovingly provide the Holy Spirit, who is the gateway to communion with the Father and the Son. The Triune God is able and willing to abide with us. All we have to do is ask.

### Search the Scriptures

1. What was Jesus doing before His disciples asked Him to teach them how to pray (Luke 11:1)?

2. What example does Jesus give to reveal how God the Father responds to our prayers (vv. 11–13)?

### Discuss the Meaning

1. What kind of model does Jesus give us on how to make our prayer life more

personal? What practices help make alone time with God more intimate?

2. Why do you think Jesus placed such emphasis on being persistent in prayer?

## Lesson in Our Society

Our Lord encourages us in the prayer of faith as the key to a vibrant relationship with His Father. The Holy Spirit is available to us to guide into truth and reveal the nature and character of God; all we have to do is ask, seek, and knock. What would happen in our communities if we really took God at His word, and through the power of prayer we received the strategy to go into the streets to stop the violence through the power of love?

## Make It Happen

Jesus says if we "being evil know how to give good gifts to our children how much more will the heavenly Father give the Holy Spirit to those who ask Him!" (Luke 11:13 paraphrase). As the old saying goes, "much prayer, much power; little prayer, little power; no prayer, no power." We must not be slack in the posture of prayer. As the Lord has taught His disciples, take this lesson and examine your prayer pattern and times of intimacy with the Lord. See where there is room for improvement in your relationship with God.

## Follow the Spirit

What God wants me to do:

_____

_____

_____

_____

## Remember Your Thoughts

Special insights I have learned:

_____

_____

_____

_____

## More Light on the Text
### Luke 11:1–13

The prayer in this passage is paralleled in Matthew 6:9–13, and is commonly called the Lord's Prayer. Some scholars believe that the prayer has been taught twice. The current one is believed to be the latter version. It, therefore, suggests that the disciple asking the question was not there when it was first taught in the Sermon on the Mount. This explains some variations on the text. The prayer has been used for liturgy in the church throughout the ages, but many scholars now believe it was meant to be a pattern of prayer.

**1 And it came to pass, that, as he was praying in a certain place, when he ceased, one of his disciples said unto him, Lord, teach us to pray, as John also taught his disciples.**

The impression Jesus' prayer life created has motivated a disciple to request a teaching on the subject. The identity of the particular disciple is not given in the text and the geographical location of the scene is not stated either. As it would have appeared discourteous and irreverent for the disciple to interrupt Jesus, he therefore waited for Him to finish. The disciple added "as John also taught his disciples," showing that religious leaders taught their followers how to pray. The scenario echoes the centrality of prayer in Jesus' life and presents the disciple's willingness to learn (Green, 438, 440). This suggests that they wanted to grow in the likeness of their Master (Luke 6:40).

**2 And he said unto them, when ye pray, say, Our Father which art in heaven, Hallowed be thy name. Thy kingdom comes. Thy will be done, as in heaven, so in earth.**

Morris suggests that Jesus' introductory phrase for this prayer in Matthew 6:9, to pray "after this manner," indicates the prayer was rather a pattern. Here however, Jesus is more exact, saying, "When ye pray, say." This means that we should conceive it as both words for prayer and a pattern of prayer to emulate. The prayer is comprised of two sets of petitions. The first set is interested in God and His rule in the universe, while the second sets has three petitions dealing with the needs of the disciples. Howard therefore rightly states that the prayer begins with "a theocentric attitude" (457).

Jesus introduced the prayer with the phrase "Our Father in heaven." The Greek word is *Pater* (**pah-TARE**) with the corresponding Aramaic term *abba* (**AH-bah**). The use of the first person plural "our" suggests that the prayer should be conducted in community with others and it also means that there is a personal relationship between the one praying and God. Christians have a personal God, not an impersonal one.

After the address comes a clause with utmost importance: "hallowed be thy name." Hallowed means "made holy, reverenced." The name is not only a label but also communicates something essential or substantive about the nature of its bearer. The sanctification of the name of God implies two responsibilities. God should sanctify His name, which He never fails to do. It also calls on the one praying to sanctify the name of God by their life (Isaiah 29:23). "Thy

kingdom come" is a petition for God's reign to be manifested in the world. This has an immediate dimension in everyday life and a future eschatological dimension when God will establish His kingdom at the restoration of all things. In this verse the KJV includes the phrases "which art in heaven" and "Thy will be done, as in heaven, so in earth" but NLT does not. This is because some ancient manuscripts of Luke include these phrases, while others do not. Most scholars think that the manuscripts that add these phrases did so because they are included in Matthew's version (6:9–10), so the scribes wanted to harmonize the two passages. In addition, many more manuscripts of Luke have been found since the translation of the KJV, some of which are several centuries older than the ones available to the KJV translators. These older manuscripts tend to be more reliable because over time scribes often revised the Gospels to make them agree with each other. However, it is not necessary for the Gospels to always agree word for word in their accounts of Jesus' ministry, and the fact that Matthew and Luke agree so closely despite the disciples passing on his teaching primarily through oral tradition for quite some time before writing His story is a remarkable testimony to the truth of Jesus' ministry.

**3 Give us this day our daily bread.**

The bread could be anything necessary for the sustenance of physical life, or the provision for human need. The Greek word *epiousios* (**eh-pee-OO-see-ose**), translated as "daily," is however difficult to convey because the word has no other known usage. Its only usage in the New Testament is found in Matthew 6:11 and Luke 11:3. Basically it could have two meanings. The traditional one related to time is translated as "daily" meaning everyday. In this case it portrays a total dependence on God for our everyday needs. The example of the rich fool fits the situation where we are no longer dependent on God but ourselves; he said: "you have enough stored away for years to come. Now take it easy! Eat, drink, and be merry!" (from Luke 12:19, NLT). The word also recalls Jesus' warning to let "tomorrow worry about itself" (Matthew 6:34, NLT). Others, however, conceived *epiousios* in terms of measure or quantity and therefore assume that it speaks of the appropriate amount for the individual, like in the case of the manna. Both conceptions are important because even in the case of the manna, God wanted to teach the people of Israel to depend on Him. The leftovers from the day before went rotten apart from the reserve for the Sabbath (Exodus 16:15–24).

**4 And forgive us our sins; for we also forgive every one that is indebted to us. And lead us not into temptation; but deliver us from evil.**

The word for forgive here is *aphiemi* (Gk. **ah-FEE-eh-mee**), and it is composed of two words: *apo* (**ah-POE**), meaning from, and *hiemi* (**HEE-eh-mee**), meaning to send. It therefore means to send forth or send away. When used for debts, it means a complete cancellation, and when used for sins, it means the remission of punishment due to sinful conduct. The clause on forgiveness in the context of this prayer does not suggest that God's forgiveness depends on human activity as we may suppose. We should be mindful as Christians that our salvation is not dependent on our good deeds. However, for our prayers to be answered, we need to be cleansed from our sins, because they might be a barrier to God hearing our prayer (Isaiah 59:1–2). The context probably suggests therefore that we forgive our offenders

so that God will not hold our sins against us and generate a barrier to the answer.

The Greek word for temptation is *peirasmos* (**pay-rahs-MOSE**). It also means trial or test. The petition "lead us not into temptation" is not a suggestion that God tempts His people into sin, for James clearly defeats this conception: "God is never tempted to do wrong and he never tempts anyone else either" (from 1:14, NLT). The source of our temptation is our own desires (v. 14). Marshall suggests that "to enter into temptation" does not mean "to be tempted" but rather "to succumb to temptation" (461–462). Keener also, on the basis of other ancient Jewish prayers, suggests a similar reading: "let us not sin when we are tested." This fits with 1 Corinthians 10:13, which states that when we are tempted, God in His faithfulness will show us a way out (NLT).

**5 And he said unto them, Which of you shall have a friend, and shall go unto him at midnight, and say unto him, Friend, lend me three loaves; 6 For a friend of mine in his journey is come to me, and I have nothing to set before him? 7 And he from within shall answer and say, Trouble me not: the door is now shut, and my children are with me in bed; I cannot rise and give thee.**

It is suggested that these three verses all constitute one question. The beginning of the question can be rephrased, "Can you imagine..." In other words, Jesus is asking which of them would do what the character portrayed in the example does or wanted to do.

The scenario pictures a single-room peasant home. The father shares the same bed or sleeping mat with the children. For the father to get up and satisfy his friend's request, he must disturb the whole family. The friend who came to ask is short of bread and has a visitor in the middle of the night. It is suggested that three loaves is the appropriate number for an evening meal. The basis for the request is friendship. It is evident from the scenario that none of the hearers will do as the character portrayed. The story suggests that in extreme challenge, when we appeal to friends, they will naturally assist us. It also implies that prayer is an issue of relationship. Indeed, Jesus is our friend (John 15:15), and will never let us down when we call on Him. In our need we will find God yet more reliable than any friend, which prepares us for the challenge to trust Him.

**8 I say unto you, Though he will not rise and give him, because he is his friend, yet because of his importunity he will rise and give him as many as he needeth.**

Friendship should be a sufficient reason for the friend to give a hand of assistance. In case the friend does not value the friendship that much, he will act to avoid the embarrassment to the one seeking or for his importunity or "shameless persistence" (NLT). In Nolland's view, God's reliability in comparison to a friend "prepares the challenge to venture with God" (632).

**9 And I say unto you, Ask, and it shall be given you; seek, and ye shall find; knock, and it shall be opened unto you. 10 For every one that asketh receiveth; and he that seeketh findeth; and to him that knocketh it shall be opened.**

From this example, Jesus entreats the disciples to ask, seek, and knock. To ask is to make a request for something that we do not possess, and it may not require an effort from us to receive it when granted. To seek is to look for something that is lost; it might require effort from us to get it. To knock implies a persistent effort to see a closed door opened. It happens when we want to get access to something which is locked.

These three may suggest variants or levels of prayers. Green explains that the instruction to ask, seek, and knock is universal. It is an encouragement "to recognize God's fidelity and expansiveness of his goodness to respond" (*The Gospel of Luke*, 449).

**11 If a son shall ask bread of any of you that is a father, will he give him a stone? Or if he asks a fish, will he for a fish give him a serpent? 12 Or if he shall ask an egg, will he offer him a scorpion?**

After the example with friendship and the encouragement to ask, seek, and knock, Jesus uses the illustration of a father-son relationship. This means that prayer is above all about relationship. Here Jesus demonstrates a human father's willingness to answer his child's request in spite of his innate wickedness. Human beings are evil by nature; however, they demonstrate kindness to their children. It is very hard to conceive of a father who will do such evil to his child by giving him something that would harm him instead of what he asked for.

**13 If ye then, being evil, know how to give good gifts unto your children: how much more shall your heavenly Father give the Holy Spirit to them that ask him?**

Jesus then draws the conclusion and proves, as Nolland puts it, that "the fatherhood of God is more dependable than the flawed human fatherhood" (632). God will bestow the Holy Spirit to whomever asks Him. Morris believes this gift of the Spirit refers to the work of the Spirit in Christian life as generally found in Romans 8 (196). In this case, it may imply an issue of relationship because Romans 8:9 states "...those who do not have the Spirit of Christ living in them do not belong to him at all" (NLT). Finally, 1 Corinthians 2:12 states that we have received God's Spirit to "know the wonderful things God has freely given us" (NLT). The suggestion is that we should first seek the Spirit, who will lead us to discover all that God has in store for us.

Sources:

Abraham, Kenneth A. *The Matthew Henry Study Bible, King James Version.* Dallas, TX: World Bible Publishers, 1994. 1990.

Attridge, Harold et al. *The Harper Collins Study Bible New Revised Standard Version.* New York: Harper One, 2006. 1770, 1785–1786.

Cabal, Ted et al. *The Apologetics Study Bible, Holman Christian Standard.* Nashville, TN: Holman Bible Publishers, 2007. 1509, 1536.

Fullam, E. L. *Living the Lord's Prayer.* Lincoln, VA: Chosen Books, 1980.

Green, J. B. *The New International Commentary on the New Testament: The Gospel of Luke.* Grand Rapids, MI: Eerdmans, 1997.

Hendriksen, W. *New Testament Commentary: Luke.* Carlisle, PA: The Banner of Truth Trust, 1978.

Keener, C. S. *The IVP Bible Background Commentary: New Testament.* Downers Grove, IL: Inter Varsity Press, 1993.

Marshall, I. H. *The New International Greek Testament Commentary: The Gospel of Luke.* Grand Rapids, MI: Eerdmans, 1978.

Morris, L. *Tyndale New Testament Commentary: Luke.* Grand Rapids, MI: Eerdmans, 1984.

Nolland, J. *Word Biblical Commentary: Luke 9:21–18:34.* Vol. 35B. Dallas, Texas: Word Books, 1993.

Vine, W. E. *An Expository Dictionary of the New Testament Words.* 7th Edition. Old Tappan, NJ: Fleming H. Revell, 1966.

Unger, Merrill. *Unger's Bible Dictionary.* Chicago, IL: Moody Press, 1981. 632.

Zodhiates, Spiros, Baker, Warren. eds. *Hebrew Greek Key Word Study Bible, King James Version.* 2nd ed. Chattanooga, TN: AMG Publishers, 1991. 1681, 1743.

## Say It Correctly

Persistence. per-**SIS**-tenz.

## Daily Bible Readings

**MONDAY**
Whenever You Pray
(Matthew 6:1–8)

**TUESDAY**
You Shall Not Profane My Name
(Leviticus 22:26–33)

**WEDNESDAY**
Bless God's Holy Name
(Psalm 103:1–13)

**THURSDAY**
God's Kingdom Has Come Near
(Luke 10:1–11)

**FRIDAY**
Do Not Worry about Your Life
(Matthew 6:25–34)

**SATURDAY**
The Lord Will Not Abandon You
(Psalm 37:27–34)

**SUNDAY**
Lord, Teach Us to Pray
(Luke 11:1–13)

# Notes

_____

_____

_____

_____

# Teaching Tips

## Words You Should Know

**A. Pray** (John 17:9) *erotao* (Gk.)—To ask for something; to beseech, desire, entreat, or request.

**B. Glorified** (v. 10) *doxazo* (Gk.)—To honor, praise, to recognize, to bring honor and to make glorious, to give importance; the manifestation of all that Jesus has and is.

## Teacher Preparation

**Unifying Principle—A Friend in High Places**. Small, intimate groups exist within a larger community. How can a small group impact the larger community? Jesus prayed that the disciples would be united and protected by God as they brought new people into their community in an unsafe world.

**A.** Pray that students will be one with God and other believers.

**B.** Read the focal verses in multiple translations.

## O—Open the Lesson

**A.** Review the Aim for Change and In Focus story to set up the discussion.

**B.** Collectively pray for the study of today's lesson, that it will create a sense of unity for the class (small group).

## P—Present the Scriptures

**A.** Read the Focal Verses; The People, Places, and Times; and Background to set up context.

**B.** Ask students to think through the difference(s) between what we have historically called the Lord's Prayer and why this text by scholars is known as the real "Lord's Prayer."

## E—Explore the Meaning

**A.** Review and discuss Search the Scriptures, Discuss the Meaning, and Lesson in Our Society.

**B.** Discuss the implication of Jesus' prayer for believers to be unified with Him and His Father. How far are we from this reality?

## N—Next Steps for Application

**A.** Invite students to implement ideas from the Make It Happen section.

**B.** Close in prayer and ask students to be diligent in praying for unity in the body of Christ.

## Worship Guide

For the Superintendent or Teacher
Theme: Jesus Prays for His Disciples
Song: "Somebody Prayed for Me"
Devotional Reading: John 15:1–11

# Jesus Prays For His Disciples

**Bible Background • JOHN 17**
**Printed Text • JOHN 17:6–21**
**Devotional Reading • JOHN 15:1–11**

## Aim for Change

By the end of the lesson, we will: REVIEW Jesus' prayer for the unity of all who believe in Him; EXPERIENCE intimacy with Jesus and God the Father through prayer; and UNITE in prayer for one another and for unity in Jesus Christ.

## In Focus

Ashley and Morgan were best friends through thick and thin. Having grown up together in their tough neighborhood, they learned how to rely on each other. Both girls had aspirations to do something big with their lives, and as they graduated from high school and later college, they remained close, although they moved to different cities. Over the years, they were able to stay connected through their weekly calls. At the end of their calls, they made it a point to cover each other in prayer, and in times of crises, they each knew the other was never far away. Now as adults, they have stayed connected through those weekly calls. Ashley says, "It is nice to know that I am covered in prayer, and I have someone who knows me and cares about my life." Morgan feels the same way. "She keeps me grounded and I know when times get tough who I can count on and trust. I don't know what I would do if I didn't have my sister, my friend Ashley."

*The prayers of our loved ones are wonderful, but it's even more assuring to know that even before going to the Cross, Jesus prayed not only for His disciples but those who would believe based on their witness.*

## Keep in Mind

"That they all may be one; as thou, Father, art in me, and I in thee, that they also may be one in us: that the world may believe that thou hast sent me" (John 17:21).

"That they all may be one; as thou, Father, art in me, and I in thee, that they also may be one in us: that the world may believe that thou hast sent me" (John 17:21).

211

## Focal Verses

**KJV** **John 17:6** I have manifested thy name unto the men which thou gavest me out of the world: thine they were, and thou gavest them me; and they have kept thy word.

**7** Now they have known that all things whatsoever thou hast given me are of thee.

**8** For I have given unto them the words which thou gavest me; and they have received them, and have known surely that I came out from thee, and they have believed that thou didst send me.

**9** I pray for them: I pray not for the world, but for them which thou hast given me; for they are thine.

**10** And all mine are thine, and thine are mine; and I am glorified in them.

**11** And now I am no more in the world, but these are in the world, and I come to thee. Holy Father, keep through thine own name those whom thou hast given me, that they may be one, as we are.

**12** While I was with them in the world, I kept them in thy name: those that thou gavest me I have kept, and none of them is lost, but the son of perdition; that the scripture might be fulfilled.

**13** And now come I to thee; and these things I speak in the world, that they might have my joy fulfilled in themselves.

**14** I have given them thy word; and the world hath hated them, because they are not of the world, even as I am not of the world.

**15** I pray not that thou shouldest take them out of the world, but that thou shouldest keep them from the evil.

**16** They are not of the world, even as I am not of the world.

**17** Sanctify them through thy truth: thy word is truth.

**NLT** **John 17:6** "I have revealed you to the ones you gave me from this world. They were always yours. You gave them to me, and they have kept your word.

**7** Now they know that everything I have is a gift from you,

**8** for I have passed on to them the message you gave me. They accepted it and know that I came from you, and they believe you sent me.

**9** "My prayer is not for the world, but for those you have given me, because they belong to you.

**10** All who are mine belong to you, and you have given them to me, so they bring me glory.

**11** Now I am departing from the world; they are staying in this world, but I am coming to you. Holy Father, you have given me your name; now protect them by the power of your name so that they will be united just as we are.

**12** During my time here, I protected them by the power of the name you gave me. I guarded them so that not one was lost, except the one headed for destruction, as the Scriptures foretold.

**13** "Now I am coming to you. I told them many things while I was with them in this world so they would be filled with my joy.

**14** I have given them your word. And the world hates them because they do not belong to the world, just as I do not belong to the world.

**15** I'm not asking you to take them out of the world, but to keep them safe from the evil one.

**16** They do not belong to this world any more than I do.

**17** Make them holy by your truth; teach them your word, which is truth.

**18** As thou hast sent me into the world, even so have I also sent them into the world.

**19** And for their sakes I sanctify myself, that they also might be sanctified through the truth.

**20** Neither pray I for these alone, but for them also which shall believe on me through their word;

**21** That they all may be one; as thou, Father, art in me, and I in thee, that they also may be one in us: that the world may believe that thou hast sent me.

**18** Just as you sent me into the world, I am sending them into the world.

**19** And I give myself as a holy sacrifice for them so they can be made holy by your truth.

**20** "I am praying not only for these disciples but also for all who will ever believe in me through their message.

**21** I pray that they will all be one, just as you and I are one—as you are in me, Father, and I am in you. And may they be in us so that the world will believe you sent me.

## The People, Places, and Times

**John.** One of the sons of Zebedee, this apostle and his brother James were among the first hand-picked by Jesus to walk alongside Him and carry on His earthly ministry, as well as establish the church. He is the disciple who is noted in his own Gospel as "the one whom Jesus loved" (John 13:23, 19:26), but his weaknesses were also portrayed in the Gospels, such as seeking to call down fire on those who did not receive Jesus (Luke 9:53–54). Nonetheless, he was a part of Jesus' inner circle, as he was with Jesus at the Transfiguration (Matthew 17:1–9), witnessed His raising Jairus' daughter from the dead (Mark 5:37), and was given charge to take care of Mary (John 19:26–27). He is believed to be the only apostle not to die a martyr's death. He was exiled to the island of Patmos, but his demise was not as brutal as the others. John the apostle, in addition to his Gospel account, also penned three epistles, and his most profound biblical contribution, the book of Revelation.

slant is focused on highlighting Jesus' deity (God incarnate) and His humanity (the Word made flesh who dwelt among humanity). John's Gospel was the last one written, and he does not repeat many of the accounts noted in the other synoptic Gospels (i.e., Matthew, Mark, and Luke). He does still provide convincing proofs of Jesus' messianic authority as "the Christ," Son of the Living God, Savior and Lord. Throughout John's account, Jesus is portrayed as one who stays in complete oneness with His Father and is singularly focused on accomplishing the Father's will. In the chapters leading up to this time of prayer before the Crucifixion, Jesus is careful to prepare His disciples for what is to come: both sorrow and triumphant joy. Most notably, He informs the disciples of the coming Holy Spirit who will be their Helper, Comforter, and Advocate (John 14:16–17, 26, 15:26, 16:7–8), and through this unbroken fellowship He will continue to reveal Himself and remain in contact henceforth.

## Background

John's Gospel provides a more intimate account of both the public and private ministry of Jesus Christ. The apostle's editorial

## At-A-Glance

1. Prayer for Unity (John 17:6–10)
2. Prayer for Protection (vv. 11–19)
3. Prayer for Future Believers
(vv. 20–21)

## In Depth

### 1. Prayer for Unity (John 17:6–10)

Jesus acts in His role as High Priest by praying on behalf of His disciples. In the preceding verses, He opens His intimate conversation with His Father by calling attention to the fact that He has accomplished the Father's will on earth, having brought glory to His name as the only true God by using His authority (John 17:1–5). The time has come for Him to return to His Father in heaven, but before the end of His earthly ministry, He intercedes on behalf of His chosen disciples who would go on to carry out His ministry. Jesus emphasizes how He has manifested the name of the Lord, how He has given His chosen the Word, and that they know everything He has given them (vv. 6–7). Jesus prays for them to be kept as they go out into the world to accomplish the greater things He has already told them they would do (John 14:12–13). Jesus prays for their deliverance, and He prays for them to be one with Him as He is one with His Father. He prays that through them, His name would continue to be made great. In the power of this unity with God the Father and the Son, the church was born at Pentecost.

### 2. Prayer for Protection (vv. 11–19)

Continuing to make this request of His Father on their behalf, Jesus then moves on to pray for the protection of His chosen. Many of them expected Jesus to establish His earthly kingdom delivering them from Roman rule, but He had warned them of coming betrayal, Crucifixion, and Resurrection (John 12:27–33, 13:18–19, 21–29). He was departing soon and expressed His love for those who have walked with Him in His earthly ministry by calling them to be set apart for the Father's use. Though they will be in the world, their allegiance and citizenship has changed to the kingdom of heaven. Jesus was there to guard and protect His disciples from the world and the evil one. Now Jesus intercedes on their behalf that they would be protected, recognizing that all but one would be covered. That one was Judas Iscariot, whom He calls the "son of perdition" or destruction, that the Scripture would be fulfilled. He knows just as He has suffered hatred and rejection, believers would also experience enemy attacks and rejection because of His name, but He has us covered. Jesus also asks that followers past, present, and future be made holy in His truth. For their sakes, He has consecrated Himself as a living sacrifice and stood in the gap on our behalf.

### 3. Prayer for Future Believers (vv. 20–21)

Jesus also prays for those who would believe in Him based on their witness. This prayer can be summed up as a desire for a unity that would mimic the unity that Jesus has with the Father. It is a mutual connection where Jesus is one with the Father, and the Father is one with Jesus. Jesus is "in" the Father, and the Father is "in" Jesus. Jesus prays that they would be as close as He and the Father are. This is a huge, all-encompassing prayer that borders on asking for a miracle. Jesus prays that we as believers would be together and close, just as the first and second Persons of the Trinity. That is beyond our comprehension. Secondly, Jesus asks that the unity of believers would show the world that Jesus was sent by the Father. The unity of the believers would authenticate whether Jesus was sent from God and would cause the world to believe in Him as Savior.

## Search the Scriptures

1. What makes Jesus' disciples set apart and holy (John 17:6)?

2. Who is Jesus referring to when He says: "Neither pray I for these alone, but for them also which shall believe on me through their word" (v. 20)?

## Discuss the Meaning

1. Jesus prays for believers to be one with each other. How is this made possible, and how do we maintain unity as the church?

2. As a Christian, do you expect to be hated and rejected by the world? How does it make you feel to know that Jesus already prayed for you?

## Lesson in Our Society

The text from today's lesson is considered by biblical scholars to be the real Lord's Prayer as we see the passion of the Christ in prayer for all of us. As we look at our world today we see division and strife. This is the opposite of what Jesus prayed for His disciples. Many in the same church are at odds with each other over trivial matters and do not exhibit the oneness that Christ desired as He prayed this prayer to the Father. We as believers have a mandate from God to strive for unity and to seek the unity of our neighborhoods and communities as well.

## Make It Happen

God has shown us His love through the sending of His Son to die for us. As the church, we must reflect this love by maintaining our relationship with Him and extending this great love out to others. Christ laid the sure foundation for us to be one with

the Father by faith, and this oneness is to be manifested in our relationships with other believers. It has been said that the most segregated hour of the week is on Sunday during church. Show our oneness as believers by inviting other believers who are of a different culture or background into your home for a meal and a time of fellowship and prayer.

## Follow the Spirit

What God wants me to do:

_____

_____

_____

_____

## Remember Your Thoughts

Special insights I have learned:

_____

_____

_____

_____

## More Light on the Text
### John 17:6–21

Consider the story of a village chief in Malawi, Africa. As a civil leader—which, in that context, also made him a spiritual leader of his community—he believed that his success as a leader would depend on his people's sense of being united. When there were fights among the villagers, he was usually discouraged, feeling he had failed at his task of leading the community. To restore unity whenever fights erupted in the village, he reminded the striving villagers that life is much bigger than what they were fighting about, and that their community was even larger than the five hundred people that actually lived in the village. In his understanding, the community included the spiritual reality of God's presence in the village, and that of the ancestors, the strangers, all humanity regardless of distance from his village, and even future generations of people connected to the village. As such, leadership, for him, was a spiritual exercise and the unity that he considered the measure of his success was a spiritual phenomenon. He believed that the unity he desired for his community was only possible with God's help. Consequently, he prayed for this unity every time he said a prayer: every time, and everywhere. He prayed for unity when he prayed over a meal, or for a sick person, even when he buried the dead. In praying for unity for His disciples, Jesus set the example for him and for all of us today in John 17.

**6 "I have manifested Your name to the men whom You have given Me out of the world. They were Yours, You gave them to Me, and they have kept Your word. 7 Now they have known that all things which You have given Me are from You. 8 For I have given to them the words which You have given Me; and they have received them, and have known surely that I came forth from You; and they have believed that You sent Me.**

Jesus makes a transition here from praying for Himself (vv. 1–5) to praying for His disciples. He begins with a rehearsal of His ministry to them. In His three and half years with the disciples, He had given them the words that God had given to Him. He had revealed to them the glory of God—the glory about which John says, "We beheld [Jesus'] glory, the glory as of the only begotten of the

Father" (from 1:14). And He manifested—revealed—to the disciples the name of the Father. This language of "the name of the Father" appears three more times in this chapter (vv. 11–12, and 26) in addition to three other times in the Fourth Gospel (5:43, 10:25, and 12:28). The word used here for "name" is *onoma* (Gk. **OH-no-mah**), which means more than just a person's name, but functions more like a title to encompass the person's entire identity and character. Such usage of someone's name is still common in most Middle Eastern and African cultures. In John's language, the name of the Father is the Father Himself, and includes all His attributes (Brown 754–756). In the Old Testament, we find "the name of the Lord" occasionally used in place of "the Lord" (Isaiah 30:27–28, 55:13; Psalm 20:1, 7). Therefore, in revealing the name of the Father to the disciples, Jesus was really revealing the essential nature of who God is and what God does. Indeed, He had told Philip earlier that night, "He that hath seen me hath seen the Father" (John 14:9). Jesus came to make God known.

In His prayer, Jesus reveals further that the disciples were given to Him by the Father. Thus, the disciples were God's gift to Jesus—and a means through which Jesus would be glorified (17:10). Carson observes that, "Christians often think of Jesus as God's gift to us; we rarely think of ourselves as God's gift to Jesus" (184). Some scholars have argued that this giving of disciples to Jesus is about the doctrine of predestination. However, while that may be true, Jesus might also have meant that God gave Him (or entrusted to Him) these men and women for their discipleship and ministry training for the salvation of the world—a future phenomenon at the time of Jesus' prayer—dependent on the witness of these disciples whom the Father has given him "out of the same world" (vv. 21, 23). That they were given to Him by the Father might seem strange since the Gospels tell of Jesus choosing His disciples (Matthew 4:18–22; Mark 1:16–20, 2:13–14; Luke 5:1–11; John 1:35–51). However, even for our leaders today, disciples—a title that is closer to students or followers than to members—are given by the Father. They are a solemn endowment and must be taken seriously. As the best rabbi there ever was, Jesus taught them the words of the Father. He modeled for them how to live a life surrendered to the Father's will. Since they were good disciples, they received Jesus' words and believed He was sent from the Father.

The disciples had received the Father's words, and they had kept them. This is a presumptive statement though, since the disciples evidently did not understand Jesus' mission until much later. However, Jesus was confident that the powerful Word that He had shared with them in the previous months had taken roots. Carson adds, "They may not yet enjoy massive comprehension and profound faith; but at least Jesus can say that the disciples have come to know 'with certainty that I [Jesus] came from you [the Father], and they believed that you sent me" (184). In receiving and keeping Christ's words, the disciples recognized everything Jesus gave them was indeed from God. These words are spirit and life (6:63) and are also the word of eternal life (6:68).

**9 "I pray for them. I do not pray for the world but for those whom You have given Me, for they are Yours. 10 And all Mine are Yours, and Yours are Mine, and I am glorified in them. 11 Now I am no longer in the world, but these are in the world, and I come to You. Holy Father, keep through Your name those whom You have given Me, that they may be one as We are. 12 While I was with them in the world, I kept them in Your name. Those whom You gave Me I have kept; and none of them is lost except the son of perdition, that the Scripture might be fulfilled.**

When He offered this prayer, Jesus had come to the very last few hours of His earthly ministry. He had taught His disciples everything He needed to teach them, and now, in the mood of a farewell conversation—one that started in John 13—He needed now to pray for them. This prayer takes the form of intercession, *erotao* (**eh-roe-TAH-oh**), a Greek word that is translated "to ask, request, or beseech, sometimes on behalf of someone else." Jesus' intercession in this chapter covers not only the 11 disciples who were there with Him, but also many who had believed in Him in the course of His ministry, and many more who would believe in Him in the years to follow (17:20). These were the disciples that were given to Him by the Father and He has kept or protected them except for Judas Iscariot who is the "son of perdition." It should encourage the believers of our day that both Christ and the Spirit have continued to intercede for us (Romans 8:26–27, 34; Hebrews 7:25). In addition, God expects us to intercede for one another (Isaiah 59:16). In interceding for His disciples, Jesus sets a good example of spiritual leadership. Leonard Ravenhill, in *Why Revival Tarries*, said, "A pastor who is not praying is playing." Leading God's people ought to be first achieved in prayer. Leaders must pray for their followers.

Jesus prayed for the protection of His disciples from disunity and from the evil one. He prays that they would be one or united in the same way as He and the Father. Jesus had been present among them as their leader, but He was soon to leave them as lambs in a world filled with wolves (Luke 10:3). There was a real danger of the sheep scattering after the shepherd was taken away. Jesus wants them to stay together, and here, He goes beyond the new commandment—love one another (John 13:34)—to loving them in a specific way by praying for them. Jesus is showing us here that there are issues in life that teaching and counseling will not resolve without the help of prayer. Even though all disciples belong to Christ and to the Father (v. 10) and are therefore covered and protected in this never-changing relationship with God, praying for them was still very necessary. In this belonging to God, they would make Christ glorified (Gk. *doxazo*, **doke-SAHD-zo**, to lift up, bring honor to, and make glorious). The lives of the disciples would be a testimony to God's goodness to the world, and through this testimony, Jesus would be glorified, drawing many people to Himself (John 12:32).

**13 But now I come to You, and these things I speak in the world, that they may have My joy fulfilled in themselves. 14 I have given them Your word; and the world has hated them because they are not of the world, just as I am not of the world. 15 I do not pray that You should take them out of the world, but that You should keep them from the evil one. 16 They are not of the world, just as I am not of the world.**

The theme of joy was critical in the tough circumstances around this chapter. However, Jesus prayed in the hearing of the disciples to strengthen their assurance of their relationship with God, and that in being so assured, the joy which Jesus finds in the Father's love may be fully reproduced in the disciples' hearts (Bruce 333). This joy, which is their strength (Nehemiah 8:10; Hebrews 12:2), would come through the Word that Jesus had given them and from the memory that He prayed for them on the night He was betrayed. Living in a world that would hate

them as it had hated their master, they would need the joy to remain wholehearted in their obedience to His commands (Morris 674). This obedience should not imply that the disciples were robotic followers of Christ. Prior to this prayer, Jesus had called them friends (15:15).

This small community of believers would be persecuted in the world, but Jesus does not wish them to be spared from the hostility that was sourced in the "evil one" which is another name for Satan. He only asks the Father to protect them from the evil one through the power of the Father's name, just as He had taught them to pray, "deliver us from the evil one" (Matthew 6:13). Of course, in the Jewish thought, the name of the Lord is a strong, protective tower (Proverbs 18:10). Sometimes, in the face of persecution and martyrdoms, it seems that they were not protected at all. However, their protection is guaranteed, they are the apple of the Lord's eye, and whatever persecution they encounter, God was always in control. Since they do not belong to this world, God will not leave them alone. Jesus had told them, "Blessed are you when they revile and persecute you, and say all kinds of evil against you falsely for my sake. Rejoice and be exceedingly glad, for great is your reward in heaven, for so they persecuted the prophets who were before you" (Matthew 5:11–12).

**17 Sanctify them by Your truth. Your word is truth. 18 As You sent Me into the world, I also have sent them into the world. 19 And for their sakes I sanctify Myself, that they also may be sanctified by the truth.**

To be sanctified is to be set aside for God's purposes. This sanctification involves their consecration for the task entrusted to them; it involves their further inward purity and endowment with all the spiritual resources for carrying out the task (Bruce 334). This work is done by the Holy Spirit through the Word of truth—in John, Jesus is both the Word and Truth—and is directed toward their mission. Jesus was sent by the Father into the world, and now He sends His disciples into the same world. The disciples need to be consecrated to serve as apostles—the "sent ones." The Greek word here is *apostello* (**ah-poe-STEL-lo**), which means "to order to go to an appointed place" or "to send away." The entire Christian community is, thus, to be sanctified, as it is an apostolic community sent by Christ to be His witnesses in the world.

As Christ was sent by the Father, He also sent the disciples into the world. The mission of the Christ informs and shapes the mission of the disciples. The Father has sanctified or set apart and sent Christ into the world (10:36), and here we see Jesus praying for the sanctification of the disciples whom He then sends into the world. But the Father had sent Christ in the power of the Holy Spirit. His ministry was inaugurated by His own encounter with the Spirit during His baptism. The disciples' going into all the world would wait as well for the coming of the Spirit upon them (Acts 2). Jesus commanded them not to depart from Jerusalem—not to go anywhere—until they had been endowed with the Spirit's power. Alhough the Holy Spirit is not mentioned in John 17, the whole prayer can be interpreted in light of His role in the life of the believer. Indeed, both the sanctification and the sending of the disciples is a work of the Spirit, for without the Spirit, there is no mission.

Jesus also sanctifies Himself for the same purpose of God's mission in the world. This is not sanctification for the remittance of sin or personal holiness, for Christ is the spotless Lamb of God. "His sanctification does not make him any holier, but rather establishes the basis for the disciples' sanctification" (Carson, 192). Jesus meant, "For them, I sanctify myself." With the impending Cross on His mind and the disciples hearing Him pray, Jesus sets a basis for the disciples' obedience later by resolving afresh to do the Father's will—which in His case meant death on the Cross. Jesus sets Himself apart to perform the redemptive work on the Cross so that the beneficiaries of that work might set themselves apart for the work of mission (Carson 193). He shows the disciples that the Father's will reigns supreme, and the disciples' best response to God's will is surrender. In this sense, Christ's sanctification resembles the sacrificial lamb being prepared for the offering (Brown 766–767). Christ Himself would later say, "Not my will, but yours be done" (Luke 22:42, NIV; see also Matthew 26:42, John 18:11).

**20 "I do not pray for these alone, but also for those who will believe in Me through their word; 21 that they all may be one, as You, Father, are in Me, and I in You; that they also may be one in Us, that the world may believe that You sent Me.**

Jesus continues to pray even for the future disciples who would believe in Him through the ministry of the apostles. He especially prays for their unity, that they may all be one just like He and the Father are one. He had already taught them that by their love toward one another, the world would know that they are His disciples (John 13:35). In this love, they would form a nucleus of a new apostolic community that would live its life through the Holy Spirit while preaching the Good News of salvation to others. Their manifest oneness would give public confirmation both of their relationship with Jesus and that of Jesus with the Father (Bruce 335). This expanding unity would generate a multiplying witness throughout the world, and that is how the church grows (Carson 199). While debates about what this unity looks like continue (see Brown 775), it is helpful to realize that such love is possible through God's power and not only human effort.

Sources:

Abraham, Kenneth A. *The Matthew Henry Study Bible, King James Version*. Dallas, TX: World Bible Publishers, 1994. 2155–2158.

Brown, Raymond Edward. *The Gospel According to John Xiii–Xxi: A New Introduction and Commentary*. Garden City, NY: Doubleday, 1966.

Bruce, F. F. *The Gospel of John: Introduction, Exposition and Notes*. Grand Rapids, MI: Wm. B. Eerdmans, 1983.

Carson, D. A. *The Farewell Discourse and Final Prayer of Jesus: An Exposition of John 14–17*. Grand Rapids, MI: Baker Book House, 1980. 173–207.

Meyer, F. B. *Gospel of John: The Life and Light of Man, Love to the Uttermost*. Fort Washington, PA: Christian Literature Crusade, 1988.

Morris, Leon. *The Gospel According to John: The English Text with Introduction, Exposition and Notes*. Grand Rapids, MI: Eerdmans, 1971. 716-738.

Unger, Merrill. *Unger's Bible Dictionary*. Chicago, IL: Moody Press, 1981. 596.

Zodhiates, Spiros, Baker, Warren. eds. *Hebrew Greek Key Word Study Bible, King James Version*. 2nd ed. Chattanooga, TN: AMG Publishers, 1991. 1709, 1717.

## Say It Correctly

Consecration. kon-se-**KREY**-shun.
Crucifixion. kroo-si-**FIK**-shun.
Intercession. in-ter-**SE**-shun.
Gethsemane. geth-**SE**-ma-nee.
Sanctification. sank-ti-fi-**KA**-shun.

## Daily Bible Readings

**MONDAY**
Revealing the Words of the Lord
(Exodus 4:27–31)

**TUESDAY**
Treasuring God's Word in Your Heart
(Psalm 119:9–16)

**WEDNESDAY**
Obey the Words of the Lord
(Jeremiah 35:12–17)

**THURSDAY**
Abide in My Love
(John 15:1–11)

**FRIDAY**
This is Eternal Life
(John 17:1–5)

**SATURDAY**
Making Known the Lord's Name
(John 17:22–26)

**SUNDAY**
Sanctified in the Truth
(John 17:6–21)

# Notes

# Teaching Tips

## Words You Should Know

**A. High Priest** (Hebrews 4:14) *archiereus* (Gk.)—Head or chief clergy, who offered sacrifices to God and appeared in the presence of God to make intercession for the people.

**B. Order** (Hebrews 5:6, 10) *taxis* (Gk.)—Arrangement, regularity, sequence.

## Teacher Preparation

**Unifying Principle—Someone's On My Side.** People often have someone who makes special efforts on their behalf. What qualifies and motivates a person to make that special effort? The writer of Hebrews informs us that God appointed Jesus, the High Priest, as an intercessor on behalf of His people.

**A.** Pray, interceding for your students for God to speak to your students during their study time to place you all on one accord.

**B.** Read The People, Places, and Times; Background; and More Light on the Text.

**C.** Complete the companion lesson in the *Precepts for Living Personal Study Guide®*.

## O—Open the Lesson

**A.** Open with prayer, asking students to make prayer requests on behalf of others' needs before their own.

**B.** Review the Aim for Change, asking students to keep in mind what they are to "do" in your time together.

**C.** Read and discuss the In Focus story and have students comment on what they heard.

**D.** Ask students to recall a time and discuss when they needed someone to represent their interest personally.

## P—Present the Scriptures

**A.** Read through the Focal Verses and have students discuss what "jumped out" for them as they read the text.

**B.** Highlight the salient points from the In Depth section along with what the Lord revealed to you during your own study. Have students also share.

## E—Explore the Meaning

**A.** Have students break into groups to discuss Search the Scriptures and Discuss the Meaning.

**B.** Have students report their consensus and share points of difference.

## N—Next Steps for Application

**A.** Ask students to partner up and take prayer requests spoken at the start of class to pray for next week.

**B.** End class with prayer and praise to God for the mercy and grace we receive through Jesus Christ our High Priest.

## Worship Guide

For the Superintendent or Teacher
Theme: Jesus Intercedes for Us
Song: "Every Prayer"
Devotional Reading: Psalm 107:1–15

# Jesus Intercedes for Us

**Bible Background • HEBREWS 4**
**Printed Text • HEBREWS 4:14–5:10**
**Devotional Reading • PSALM 107:1–15**

## Aim for Change

By the end of the lesson, we will: REVIEW how Jesus fulfills the role of intercessor with God for His people; APPRECIATE that Christians do not stand alone before God with their sins; and PRAY with thanksgiving for our intercessor with God and tell others about Him.

### In Focus

Aiesha loved her big brother Jay. They were eight years apart and their parents divorced when she was young, so when her dad left home, she held tightly to Jay. Aiesha could always count on Jay to look out for her. While their mom was at work, he made sure she did her homework and her chores, but he also took her out to do fun things too like movies and ball games. Even when Jay started dating and eventually married, he still looked out for his little sister. When Aiesha was a senior in high school, she wanted to stay out with her friends past her curfew. It was Jay who intervened and convinced Mom to trust Aiesha to make good decisions and allow her to stay out later. Jay was proven right. Even when she had the opportunity to make bad choices, she remembered Jay's defense of her to their mom, and rather than cave to peer pressure, she called her brother to come get her.

*Jesus is our Elder Brother and our High Priest who is seated at the right hand of God with all power and majesty. We will explore how He makes intercession for us every day.*

## Keep in Mind

"For we have not an high priest which cannot be touched with the feeling of our infirmities; but was in all points tempted like as we are, yet without sin" (Hebrews 4:15).

"For we have not an high priest which cannot be touched with the feeling of our infirmities; but was in all points tempted like as we are, yet without sin" (Hebrews 4:15).

## Focal Verses

**KJV** **Hebrews 4:14** Seeing then that we have a great high priest, that is passed into the heavens, Jesus the Son of God, let us hold fast our profession.

**15** For we have not an high priest which cannot be touched with the feeling of our infirmities; but was in all points tempted like as we are, yet without sin.

**16** Let us therefore come boldly unto the throne of grace, that we may obtain mercy, and find grace to help in time of need.

**5:1** For every high priest taken from among men is ordained for men in things pertaining to God, that he may offer both gifts and sacrifices for sins:

**2** Who can have compassion on the ignorant, and on them that are out of the way; for that he himself also is compassed with infirmity.

**3** And by reason hereof he ought, as for the people, so also for himself, to offer for sins.

**4** And no man taketh this honour unto himself, but he that is called of God, as was Aaron.

**5** So also Christ glorified not himself to be made an high priest; but he that said unto him, Thou art my Son, to day have I begotten thee.

**6** As he saith also in another place, Thou art a priest for ever after the order of Melchisedec.

**7** Who in the days of his flesh, when he had offered up prayers and supplications with strong crying and tears unto him that was able to save him from death, and was heard in that he feared;

**8** Though he were a Son, yet learned he obedience by the things which he suffered;

**9** And being made perfect, he became the author of eternal salvation unto all them that obey him;

**NLT** **Hebrews 4:14** So then, since we have a great High Priest who has entered heaven, Jesus the Son of God, let us hold firmly to what we believe.

**15** This High Priest of ours understands our weaknesses, for he faced all of the same testings we do, yet he did not sin.

**16** So let us come boldly to the throne of our gracious God. There we will receive his mercy, and we will find grace to help us when we need it most.

**5:1** Every high priest is a man chosen to represent other people in their dealings with God. He presents their gifts to God and offers sacrifices for their sins.

**2** And he is able to deal gently with ignorant and wayward people because he himself is subject to the same weaknesses.

**3** That is why he must offer sacrifices for his own sins as well as theirs.

**4** And no one can become a high priest simply because he wants such an honor. He must be called by God for this work, just as Aaron was.

**5** That is why Christ did not honor himself by assuming he could become High Priest. No, he was chosen by God, who said to him, "You are my Son. Today I have become your Father."

**6** And in another passage God said to him, "You are a priest forever in the order of Melchizedek."

**7** While Jesus was here on earth, he offered prayers and pleadings, with a loud cry and tears, to the one who could rescue him from death. And God heard his prayers because of his deep reverence for God.

**8** Even though Jesus was God's Son, he learned obedience from the things he suffered.

**10** Called of God an high priest after the order of Melchisedec.

**9** In this way, God qualified him as a perfect High Priest, and he became the source of eternal salvation for all those who obey him.

**10** And God designated him to be a High Priest in the order of Melchizedek.

## The People, Places, and Times

**Melchizedek or Melchisedec.** A mysterious biblical character, he is first referenced in the book of Genesis as the king of Salem and "priest of the Most High God" (Genesis 14:17–20). Even though there is no biblical record of Melchizidek's ancestry, he is obviously a real person. Since he lived in the area occupied by descendants of Ham (Canaan), it is quite possible his ancestry is Hamitic from which Africans descended. His encounter with Abram (who would later be renamed Abraham) was after the defeat of Chedorlaomer and the kings allied with him, including the king of Sodom. Abraham's victory was not a single-handed success but was given by the hand of the Lord, who moved on his behalf. King Melchizedek, whose name means "My king is righteousness," brought out bread and wine to celebrate Abram and spoke a blessing over him. In response to God's goodness and honor, Abram gave King Melchizedek, the high priest of the Most High God, one-tenth of the spoils of his victory. This is the first biblicial instance of the tithe.

## Background

The book of Hebrews, known as one of the general epistles, was tailored and penned to reach a primarily Jewish audience and is rich with displays that compare and contrast the Torah and the new covenant. Its purpose is to exhort a second-generation church that had experienced persecution not to lose their faith. They were in danger of reverting back to Judaism and so the book of Hebrews often points out the preeminence of Christ over all held dear within the Jewish culture and nation. Scholars' opinion vary on the authorship of Hebrews. Many believe Paul wrote it, even though he did not sign it like his other letters. Nonetheless, it was counted as an inspired source and included in the Bible. A major theme of the book of Hebrews is showing Jesus as the Christ, the Son of God, in His position in the lives of believers as Savior, Priest, and King through His deity and humanity. It should also be noted that this audience of believers was the second generation of the church, who were enduring persecution for their faith. Hebrews sought to provide sound doctrine for them to follow, to further root them in the faith by teaching Christ's superiority over angels and prophets, including Moses, and His position as the great High Priest.

## At-A-Glance

1. Jesus the Great High Priest (Hebrews 4:14–16)
2. Jesus and Earthly High Priests (vv. 5:1–5)
3. Jesus and Melchizedek High Priest Forever (vv. 6–10)

## In Depth

### 1. Jesus the Great High Priest (Hebrews 4:14–16)

Jesus in His role as our High Priest puts an end to the need to petition anyone else for the forgiveness of sins. The writer reiterates to his audience that Jesus as the Son of God is the profession of the faith, and that because of Him we are able to approach the throne of God. Through this passage, Christians are invited to stand strong in this belief in the face of those who argue differently. Throughout the opening of Hebrews, the writer makes the point that Jesus is the expressed image of God, just as in the world a child is the very reflection of his father in DNA, behavior, and character (Hebrews 1:3). Because of what Jesus accomplished through His death and resurrection, He is seated at the right hand of the Father with all power and majesty. This makes Him more than qualified to represent God to the people and the people to God. We are therefore reminded that we do not have a High Priest who cannot empathize with our struggles, but He was at all points tempted or tried as we are, but He did not sin (v. 15). As we stand in His righteousness, we are implored to come boldly to the throne of grace and receive what we need from God in the name of Jesus, just as He promised we could (John 14:13, 16:26–27).

### 2. Jesus and Earthly High Priests (vv. 5:1–5)

The writer goes on to draw comparisons to the office of high priest to show how Jesus perfects the custom. Under the Mosaic Law, God set apart the high priest to represent Himself to the people and the people to Him. God specifically established the priesthood to hail from the lineage of Aaron; he wore special clothing while functioning as priest. While before the people, he wore a uniform of great grandeur, and each piece represented a facet of his office on behalf of the people; however, when he went before the Lord in the Holy of Holies, he was stripped of that grandeur to represent the people. The high priest once a year entered the Holy of Holies to make atonement of sins for himself and the people. The point the writer makes is that God the Father established His Son as the high priest when we called Him out in His humanity to represent the people by bearing our sins and glorifying His name (v. 5, John 12:28).

### 3. Jesus and Melchizedek High Priest Forever (vv. 6–10)

The writer closes this phase of his argument by introducing the order of Melchizedek and makes the link that Jesus is the High Priest forever. He draws this conclusion because in Old Testament Scripture, Melchizedek has no recorded father, his priesthood predates Aaron's, he is also a king, and he has no recorded end. Psalm 110:3–5 is a prophetic foreshadow of Christ saying: "The LORD has taken an oath and will not break his vow: You are a priest forever in the order of Melchizedek" (v. 4, NLT). Melchizedek is the shadow of Christ as he combined kingship and priesthood in his person; Jesus remains in the office of Priest and King forever, which is why we call Him Lord. Jesus in the days of His humanity remained faithful by staying in a posture of prayerful submission to God. Although He is the Son of God, He still suffered and knows the experience of what it takes to obey God, which again solidifies why He is the great High Priest who knows the feeling of our infirmities in this earthly body. Later the author of Hebrews writes that Christ entered into the heavenly Holy of Holies to apply His blood on the mercy seat on our behalf and now remains in the presence of God to make intercession for us (Hebrews 9:11–12).

## Search the Scriptures

1. Where can we go to receive mercy and the grace to help in times of need (Hebrews 4:14–16)?

2. How does Christ as High Priest compare among the priests of the Old Testament (vv. 5:1–5)?

## Discuss the Meaning

1. What does it mean to for us today that Jesus "in the days of His flesh offered up prayers of pleadings and though He were a Son he learned obedience by the things which He suffered" (Hebrews 5:7)?

2. How does knowing Jesus is our High Priest add value to your relationship with Him?

## Lesson in Our Society

If you ever have need for a lawyer, it is always good to have one who is able to best represent your interest. Isn't it great to know that in heaven we have the best representation that money cannot buy, but was purchased with the blood of Christ? Hebrews 7:25 says He lives forever to intercede with God on their behalf. Praise God, Jesus intercedes for us!

## Make It Happen

Today and throughout the week, reflect on the fact that Jesus ever lives to intercede on your behalf. Live intentionally with the thought that no matter what you experience, there is grace to help in your time of need, and share this grace with others.

## Follow the Spirit

What God wants me to do:

_____

_____

_____

_____

## Remember Your Thoughts

Special insights I have learned:

_____

_____

_____

_____

## More Light on the Text

**Hebrews 4:14–5:10**

**14 Seeing then that we have a great high priest, that is passed into the heavens, Jesus the Son of God, let us hold fast our profession. 15 For we have not an high priest which cannot be touched with the feeling of our infirmities; but was in all points tempted like as we are, yet without sin. 16 Let us therefore come boldly unto the throne of grace, that we may obtain mercy, and find grace to help in time of need.**

The author turns our attention to Jesus as the great High Priest. The adjective "great" (Gk. *megas*, **MEH-gahs**) places Him in a different category than any other high priest. He is the High Priest of all high priests. The phrase "passed into the heavens" is similar to what the high priest did on the Day of Atonement. He "passed through" the curtain of the temple and entered the Holy of Holies, where the Ark of the Covenant was placed. The Holy of Holies was where God resided. Jesus' passing into the heavens suggests that He has gone into the very presence of God.

This passage has two admonitions: to hold fast our profession and approach the throne of grace. Both are possible only through Jesus Christ, our great High Priest. Jesus was "touched with the feeling of our infirmities." This does not mean that He experienced every circumstance that we have experienced. It means He experienced and felt what we have felt in our own particular moments of weaknesses and suffering. He has experienced the same emotions and pain. As a man, Jesus has experienced what we are going through; thus, we know that when we approach God in prayer, we will receive sympathy and understanding. When we pray, we can also approach God with great hope and expectation because we know we will find forgiveness, mercy, and help to overcome our problems. The mention of the "throne of grace" alludes to the area of the Ark of the Covenant which was called "the mercy seat." This was where the high priest sprinkled the blood of the sacrifice to make atonement with God for the people. The author is saying that unlike those other high priests who went into the Holy of Holies trembling, we can come boldly to God because of the work of Jesus our great High Priest.

**5:1 For every high priest taken from among men is ordained for men in things pertaining to God, that he may offer both gifts and sacrifices for sins:**

This section does not discuss all the features of this office, but highlights those that correspond with what the author wants to say about Jesus as High Priest (vv. 1–4). A high priest must be one of the people in order to fulfill his role effectively. He is taken from among men to mediate between them and

God. These points are essential in understanding the priesthood of Jesus. One of the functions of a high priest is to "offer both gifts and sacrifices" or to make atonement for sin. The high priest must be holy in all that he is and does. The life of the high priest was governed by a particular set of rules regulating his behavior even down to his apparel when offering sacrifices for the people. The high priest was a representative for the people in "things pertaining to God." Jesus is also holy and pure and able to represent the people before God not because of what He wears or adhering to certain ritual regulations but because He is holy in His very nature.

**2 Who can have compassion on the ignorant, and on them that are out of the way; for that he himself also is compassed with infirmity.**

Another function of the priest is to empathize with the people. Even though this is not a specific function stated for Aaron, it is implied in his responsibility. The word translated "compassion" is *metriopatheo* (Gk. **meh-tree-oh-pah-THEH-oh**). It is used only here in the New Testament and means to act in moderation or to control one's emotion. A high priest is expected to have compassion toward those who are ignorant and "on them that are out of the way" ("going astray," NIV; see also Leviticus 4; Numbers 15:22–31). The high priest is to be compassionate toward those who have ignorantly sinned against the Lord. He should neither dismiss sin lightly nor severely condemn the sinner. He ought to act in moderation. Jesus is able to have compassion because He was a man, and although He was without sin, He could identify with human weakness.

**3 And by reason hereof he ought, as for the people, so also for himself, to offer for sins.**

The high priest in the Old Testament also had to offer sacrifices for himself (Leviticus 16:11) because, like the people, he had sinned. His task, therefore, was not to condemn sinners but to stand in solidarity with them. In doing this he could offer a sacrifice for them. By recognizing his own weakness, he could be deeply compassionate toward and patient with those who were not walking in the truth.

**4 And no man taketh this honour unto himself, but he that is called of God, as was Aaron.**

A high priest must be "called" (Gk. *kaloumenos*, **kah-LOO-men-ose**) or selected by God. One cannot just decide to enter into this high office and mediate between God and people. Since sinful humanity has violated God's righteous law, we cannot select the mediator. Only God can decide whom He wants as mediator. Aaron and his sons were appointed as priests by God Himself (Exodus 28). The connection between this office and Christ's role as High Priest is clearly stated in verse 5.

**5 So also Christ glorified not himself to be made an high priest; but he that said unto him, Thou art my Son, to day have I begotten thee. 6 As he saith also in another place, Thou art a priest for ever after the order of Melchisedec.**

Although Christ is compared to the high priest and they are both called by God, Christ is superior. In verse 4, the phrase "he that is called of God" indicates that the calling to the office of the high priest is an honor that God gives to whomever He chooses. However, a stronger word, *doxazo*

(**doke-SAHD-zo**), which means "to glorify, praise, or honor," is used to describe Jesus' becoming High Priest. Christ is glorified or exalted to this office. In verse 5, God's call is expressed in the words of Psalm 2:7 (which was also quoted in Hebrews 1:5).

Verse 6 is a quotation of Psalm 110 (which was also quoted in Hebrews 1:13). Unlike Aaron, Melchisedec was both king and priest. No king in Israel functioned as both a king and a priest. As priest and king, Melchizedek had no predecessor and no successor. Similarly, Christ is our High Priest forever. His perfect work of atonement is perpetual; thus, He cannot be succeeded. Jesus Christ is the Son of God, our High Priest and King.

**7 Who in the days of his flesh, when he had offered up prayers and supplications with strong crying and tears unto him that was able to save him from death, and was heard in that he feared;**

Verse 7 emphasizes the humanity of Jesus, which was previously mentioned in Hebrews 2:9–18. The phrase "in the days of his flesh" refers to His earthly ministry. The phrase "offered up prayers and supplications" is a reference to Jesus' "High Priestly" prayer in the Garden of Gethsemane (Matthew 26:36–46; Mark 14:32–42; Luke 22:40–46). The Gospel accounts clearly describe the fervency and intensity of this prayer. All this shows Jesus can completely empathize with our human condition of weakness.

Jesus prayed for deliverance from death, and He was heard. God's answer was not that He would escape death, but that He would be resurrected. His prayer was heard because He "feared" God (or because of His "reverent submission," NIV). This does not mean that Jesus was afraid of God. Rather, it means that He had the proper attitude of reverence in His duty.

**8 Though he were a Son, yet learned he obedience by the things which he suffered;**

Through His suffering, Jesus learned obedience. This does not mean that He was at any time disobedient. Rather, He learned how to submit in obedience, laying down His will and rights. The writer engages in word-play between the verb forms for "learning" (Gk. *emathen*, **EH-mah-thehn**) and "suffering" (Gk. *epathen*, **EH-pah-thehn**). In doing so, the writer suggests the falsity of the common understanding that obedience always results in peace and disobedience in suffering. Jesus' life and His death on the Cross prove that obedience can lead to suffering.

**9 And being made perfect, he became the author of eternal salvation unto all them that obey him;**

The phrase "being made perfect" (a single word in Greek; Gk. *teleiotheis*, **teh-lay-oh-THASE**) is not a reference to moral perfection but to the satisfactory completion of Christ's role as High Priest. The same word is used in the Greek translation of the Old Testament to mean "consecrated" or "ordained" (Leviticus 8:33; Numbers 3:3). Upon completion of this responsibility, Jesus became the "author" or source of eternal salvation for all who obey Him, just as He learned to obey God. The Greek word for "author" (*aitios*, **EYE-tee-ose**) could also be translated as "cause." The term "eternal salvation" is to be equated with eternal life, which Christ offers to those who believe in Him. Therefore, the reference to eternal salvation here is a description of Christ's work. His work of procuring salvation as our High Priest is eternally efficacious—a perpetual priesthood.

**10 Called of God an high priest after the order of Melchisedec.**

Verse 10 ends this discussion of Jesus as our High Priest the way it began: with God's calling. It also introduces the new thought "after the order of Melchisedec," which points to His role as both Priest and King. He is a High Priest, but a different kind of high priest. As the pre-incarnate Son of God, He is one with royal authority.

Sources:

Attridge, Harold, et al. *The Harper Collins Study Bible, New Revised Standard Version.* New York: Harper One, 2006. 23.

Cabal, Ted, et al. *The Apologetics Study Bible, Holman Christian Standard.* Nashville, TN: Holman Bible Publishers, 2007. 1821–1822.

Unger, Merrill. *Unger's Bible Dictionary.* Chicago, IL: Moody Press, 1981. 881-886.

Unger, Merrill. *Unger's Bible Handbook: The Essential Guide to Understanding the Bible.* Chicago, IL: Moody Press, 1967. 747, 756–757.

Zodhiates, Spiros, Baker, Warren, eds. *Hebrew Greek Key Word Study Bible, King James Version.* 2nd ed. Chattanooga, TN: AMG Publishers, 1991. 1695, 1761.

## Say It Correctly

Melchisidec. mel-ki-si-**DEK**.
Infirmity. in-fir-mi-**TEE**.

## Daily Bible Readings

**MONDAY**
The Grace of God Has Appeared
(Titus 2:11–15)

**TUESDAY**
An Advocate with God
(1 John 2:1–6)

**WEDNESDAY**
Our Faithful High Priest
(Hebrews 3:1–6)

**THURSDAY**
Jesus Prayed in Anguish
(Luke 22:39–46)

**FRIDAY**
Gratitude for God's Steadfast Love
(Psalm 107:1–15)

**SATURDAY**
Boldness and Confidence through Faith
(Ephesians 3:7–13)

**SUNDAY**
A Great High Priest
(Hebrews 4:14–5:10)

# Notes

# Teaching Tips

## Words You Should Know

**A. Sick** (James 5:14) *astheneo* (Gk.)—To be weak, feeble, without strength, powerless.

**B. Fervent** (v. 16) *energeo* (Gk.)—To be operative, to be at work, to put forth power.

## Teacher Preparation

**Unifying Principle—Help! I'm in Trouble.** Illness is part of being human. How can believers overcome illness? James teaches that the prayer of faith brings healing and offers Elijah's prayer as an example of prayer's effectiveness.

**A.** Pray for the students that will attend, and for God to give you clarity on the lesson and its application.

**B.** Study examples of the prayers offered in 1 Kings 18:25–40.

**C.** Bring index cards so that students can write down prayer requests anonymously. Allow students to pick a card and commit to praying for the needs of their fellow classmate.

## O—Open the Lesson

**A.** Open with prayer and the Aim for Change.

**B.** Ask students to think about a time in their lives when they were in need of prayer. What were the emotions they experienced during that time?

**C.** Tell the class to read the In Focus story silently, then discuss it.

## P—Present the Scriptures

**A.** Have volunteers read the Focal Verses.

**B.** Use The People, Places, and Times; Background; and Search the Scriptures to clarify verses.

## E—Explore the Meaning

**A.** Break the class into groups of 2 or 3. Have the students discuss hindrances to spending time in prayer.

**B.** Come up with a list of hindrances. Look for patterns and brainstorm practical solutions for spending more time with God and praying for others.

## N—Next Steps for Application

**A.** Summarize the lesson.

**B.** Close with prayer.

## Worship Guide

For the Superintendent or Teacher
Theme: We Pray for One Another
Song: "Somebody Prayed For Me"
Devotional Reading: Lamentations 3:52–58

# We Pray for One Another

**Bible Background • JAMES 5:13-18**
**Printed Text • JAMES 5:13-18**
**Devotional Reading • LAMENTATIONS 3:52-58**

## Aim for Change

By the end of the lesson, we will: EXPLORE James' admonitions for prayer and its power to heal; AFFIRM that prayer is powerful and yields good results; and PRAY for the sick.

## In Focus

Latonya had come to visit her friend Sandy in the hospital. She hesitated to say something, although she knew something needed to be said. Sandy had gotten pneumonia, and at her age, pneumonia is a very serious thing. Latonya wanted to pray for her friend, but she was scared of being embarrassed. She convinced herself that she could pray for her silently, but this didn't sit well with her. She couldn't escape the Holy Spirit nudging her to pray out loud for healing as a sign of faith. How could she do it? She wasn't super spiritual or a preacher. Then she remembered her grandmother, who wasn't a preacher but encouraged the whole family to go to God in prayer. She remembered how her grandmother would rise early and pray for all those she knew and for the nation. Latonya also remembered how her grandmother would grab the olive oil from the kitchen and anoint any of them if they were sick. She knew God had already called her to pray. All she had to do was earnestly call on God believing that He would answer. She reached out to Sandy and laid her hands on her hand and began to call on God for her healing.

*If we have a relationship with God, then His power to heal is available for all those who believe.*

## Keep in Mind

"Therefore, confess your sins to one another, and pray for one another so that you may be healed. The effective prayer of a righteous man can accomplish much" (James 5:16).

"Therefore, confess your sins to one another, and pray for one another so that you may be healed. The effective prayer of a righteous man can accomplish much" (James 5:16).

# Focal Verses

**KJV** **James 5:13** Is any among you afflicted? let him pray. Is any merry? let him sing psalms.

**14** Is any sick among you? let him call for the elders of the church; and let them pray over him, anointing him with oil in the name of the Lord:

**15** And the prayer of faith shall save the sick, and the Lord shall raise him up; and if he have committed sins, they shall be forgiven him.

**16** Confess your faults one to another, and pray one for another, that ye may be healed. The effectual fervent prayer of a righteous man availeth much.

**17** Elias was a man subject to like passions as we are, and he prayed earnestly that it might not rain: and it rained not on the earth by the space of three years and six months.

**18** And he prayed again, and the heaven gave rain, and the earth brought forth her fruit.

**NLT** **James 5:13** Are any of you suffering hardships? You should pray. Are any of you happy? You should sing praises.

**14** Are any of you sick? You should call for the elders of the church to come and pray over you, anointing you with oil in the name of the Lord.

**15** Such a prayer offered in faith will heal the sick, and the Lord will make you well. And if you have committed any sins, you will be forgiven.

**16** Confess your sins to each other and pray for each other so that you may be healed. The earnest prayer of a righteous person has great power and produces wonderful results.

**17** Elijah was as human as we are, and yet when he prayed earnestly that no rain would fall, none fell for three and a half years!

**18** Then, when he prayed again, the sky sent down rain and the earth began to yield its crops.

## The People, Places, and Times

**Elders**. These were Christians who presided over the gatherings. The term "elder" was taken from the Jewish synagogue. They were the rulers of synagogue life, and this is the function they had in the life of the church. Elders were not always the oldest in terms of age, but had Christian maturity. They were called on to perform certain functions in the church, such as pastoral care and church discipline. In the New Testament, the terms bishops, elders, and presbyters are used interchangeably. Historically, these became separate offices and roles in the church.

**Anointing**. This word means to smear or rub with oil. It was used to designate and bless those who had been chosen by God to carry out a particular task. In the Old Testament, priests and kings were anointed with oil when they were set apart for their office. Anointing was also done to prepare bodies for burial and to refresh the skin after washing. Because of its sacred and religious connotations, it became a symbol of God's presence and power. This is why anointing the sick became a customary Christian ritual, accompanied by prayer for healing.

**Elias**. Elias is the Greek spelling of Elijah. Elijah means "My God is Jehovah." He was a prophet during the reigns of Ahab and

Ahaziah. The Bible says that he came from the region of Thisbe (1 Kings 17:1) and challenged idolatry. Known for his bold challenging of the monarchy of Israel at the end of his ministry, Elijah was taken up into heaven to be with God. For this reason, the Jews expected Elijah to return soon in order to prepare the Israelites for the coming of the Messiah.

## Background

James has been called the Proverbs of the New Testament, because it is full of wisdom and practical teaching about the Christian life. This epistle was written prior to 70 A.D., but a more precise date is difficult. James 1:1 identifies the author as "James, a servant of God and of the Lord Jesus Christ" (KJV). If this was James the son of Zebedee, he died in the early 40s A.D. (before 44); if James the brother of Jesus, then he died in the 60s A.D. In James 1:5, Christians are admonished to ask God for wisdom if they lack it, because God gives wisdom freely and generously.

Some of the themes that are discussed in this epistle are spiritual growth, maturing in Christ, enduring temptation, and demonstrating the faith. James was calling the church to practice holy living. He was encouraging the church to allow their faith to be demonstrated in their lifestyles.

Historically, James 5:13–18 has been used to claim healing. While healing is addressed, the main idea of the passage is prayer. From Genesis to Revelation, countless examples are given of people entreating God in prayer. In the Old Testament, we read about prayers that moved God to act powerfully and miraculously. David offered prayers of confession for sin. Prophets like Moses and Elijah offered prayers on behalf of Israel for deliverance. In the New Testament, Jesus gives a model for prayer, and New Testament letters often ended with a focus on prayer.

James uses this portion of the letter to apply prayer to illness. James 5:13–20 deals with various issues involving prayer. James here deals with prayer of the individual (v. 13), the prayer of the elders (vv. 14–15), the prayer of friends and companions for one another (v. 16), and the prayer of the prophet Elijah (vv. 17–18). No matter what circumstances believers find themselves in, prayer is the recommended remedy.

## At-A-Glance

1. The Exhortation to Pray
(James 5:13–16)
2. The Example of Prayer (vv. 17–18)

## In Depth

**1. The Exhortation to Pray (James 5:13–16)**

An initial reading of James 5:13–18 would suggest that this passage is about healing. A deeper study reveals that the overall theme is prayer. Verse 13 specifically addresses prayers of the individual Christians who have been experiencing suffering. James asks, "Is any among you afflicted?" The Greek word *kakopatheo* (**kah-koe-pah-THEH-oh**) means "to suffer misfortune" and is not used for illness. During suffering or misfortune prayer is the conduit to our strength. As we navigate the trials of life, we may feel tempted to question the goodness of God and others. Prayer will help Christians to stay positive and keep our eyes on God even in our darkest hour. In contrast, the believer is also admonished to sing psalms when things are going good. No matter what the circumstance, the believer's focus is toward God.

Then attention is given to the Christian who experiences sickness. James instructs them to rely upon the leaders of the church. Traditionally oil was used to cleanse wounds. Christians may have used the oil to symbolically entrust the issue to God. Turning the issue over in faith shows trust that God is able to heal and enable the believer to endure present sufferings. James reminds the church that prayer offered in faith will bring results. God is faithful to heal the sick person and forgive sin.

Next James highlights the relationship between being sick spiritually versus physically. Confession of sin is needed to restore and heal not only the physical body but the spiritual relationship with God. Many do not realize that their illnesses can be due to unconfessed sin in their lives. We are then told that the effectual fervent prayers of a righteous person can accomplish a lot in prayer. Effective prayers are those that line up with God's will and produces results. Knowing and distinguishing God's will require spending consistent time with Him.

### 2. The Example of Prayer (vv. 17–18)

Elijah is mentioned as an example of someone who offered up prayers that received answers from God. He is said to be a "man of like passions." Here James lets us know that Elijah was not a superman, and he did not have any special right to have his prayers answered more than we do. Elijah is shown to be a human with the same types of fears and doubts as we have. This is an encouragement to step out in faith and pray. One of the heroes of the Old Testament is shown to be a normal person who prayed to God in faith.

James also states the kind of prayer that Elijah prayed. It was an effectual, fervent prayer; that is, it was a serious and earnest prayer that reached the heart of God. It was a prayer that was full of energy and life, not necessarily a lot of words or vain rambling.

The prayer Elijah prayed was a bold and convincing petition to the God who could do the impossible. This prayer opened and closed the heavens. Christians are encouraged to pray in a similar fashion and expect results. The Christian should expect God to heal and forgive sin.

### Search the Scriptures

1. What is the purpose of confession in the life of a believer who is sick (James 5:16)?

2. What does "the effective and fervent prayer of a righteous man availeth much" mean (v. 16)? —great prayer and produces results

### Discuss the Meaning

1. What does it mean when a believer's prayer is not answered?

2. What is the difference between sickness and affliction?

### Lesson in Our Society

We are living in a world with modern conveniences like iPads, smartphones, and GPS. These gadgets are meant to make life easier, but often wind up distracting us from practicing spiritual disciplines like prayer. Our lesson today reminds us to pray regardless of the situation. Praying for our brothers and sisters in Christ will keep us sensitive to one another. Through prayer, we can stay connected to our power source: God. He strengthens us to endure the intrusions that appear in life that we never imagined we would encounter.

### Make It Happen

This week, spend time praying for the needs of your fellow Bible study members. Please write your prayer request on an index card for distribution to fellow class members.

## Follow the Spirit

What God wants me to do:

_____

_____

_____

_____

## Remember Your Thoughts

Special insights I have learned:

_____

_____

_____

_____

## More Light on the Text

### James 5:13–18

**13 Is any among you afflicted? let him pray. Is any merry? let him sing psalms.**

James advises believers on how to respond to different life circumstances. The believers experienced times of joy and times of sorrow (vv. 13–18; 1:2–3). James urged them to turn constantly to communication with God in whatever circumstances life brought their way. This needs to happen during times of "affliction" (Gk. *kakopatheo*, **kah-koe-pah-THEH-oh**, to suffer misfortune) as well as when "merry" (Gk. *euthumeo*, **ew-thoo-MEH-oh**). In regards to affliction, it may not be removed, but it certainly can be transformed. Divine help and blessings are conveyed to the Christian in response either to his or her own prayers or the intercessions of other Christians on the individual's behalf. In all circumstances, it is a Christian's duty and privilege to pray. The Greek word

*psallo* (**PSAL-loh**) primarily meant "to play a stringed instrument" and later could also mean "to sing to the harp." It can refer to any sounding of God's praises, alone or in the company of others, vocally with or without musical instrument (cf. Romans 15:9; 1 Corinthians 14:15; Ephesians 5:19). Through singing, we can express our thanks to God. It is a natural response to the condition of good health, which is recognized as a gift from God.

**14 Is any sick among you? let him call for the elders of the church; and let them pray over him, anointing him with oil in the name of the Lord:**

In the case of being severely "sick" (Gk. *astheneo*, **ahs-theh-NEH-oh**), when the body may be tormented with pain and the mind considerably disturbed, it is not easy to turn one's concentration to prayer. The word here means to be without strength and feeble and can be applied to any number of sicknesses. In any case, the exhortation is to call the elders of the church to pray over the sick and anoint the afflicted person with oil in the name of the Lord (cf. Mark 6:13). The word "oil" (Gk. *elaion*, **EL-eye-on**) specifically means olive oil (from the root *elaia*, **el-EYE-ah**, "olive"). Oil is the symbol of the Holy Spirit, the divine presence (1 John 2:20, 27). In biblical times, it was used for medicinal purposes (Luke 10:34). The prayer for sickness is accompanied by the oil as a symbol of the divine presence in healing the body. The emphasis on "in the name of the Lord" reminds the reader that the Lord is the Healer, not the elders. It is neither the oil nor the elders that brings the healing. The Lord Himself is the Healer. The anointing of oil is done in His name.

**15 And the prayer of faith shall save the sick, and the Lord shall raise him up; and if he have committed sins, they shall be forgiven him.**

The expression "shall raise him up" means to restore to physical health. Physical healing is a form of redemption. Here James is offering God's prescription for healing and the forgiveness of sins. The Greek word used for "the sick" (*ton kamnonta*, **tone KAHM-non-tah**) is from a verb whose primary meaning is "to grow weary," in the sense of growing weary by reason of sickness. The verb *egeiro* (**eh-GAY-roh**) means to rise up, raise up, or awaken (see Matthew 1:24 from sleep; John 11:11–12 from death; 11:29 from sitting). The word is used many times for the resurrection of Christ and of believers. In this case it is used in the sense of being raised up from sickness, in contrast to being weak and without strength, with the implication of not being able to rise.

The clause "and if he have committed sins" does not mean that the sickness is necessarily due to sin. The conditional words "and if" (*kan*, **KAHN**) show that it may or may not be. The Bible does not teach that all sickness is due to sin committed by the person suffering, but it is a possibility (Mark 2:5–11; 1 Corinthians 11:28–30).

**16 Confess your faults one to another, and pray one for another, that ye may be healed. The effectual fervent prayer of a righteous man availeth much.**

Confess is the Greek word *exomologeo* (**ehk-so-mo-lo-GEH-o**), which means to speak out and make public or agree with. The believers are to agree with God and with one another concerning their "faults" (Gk. *paraptoma*, **pah-RAHP-toh-mah**), which means a "deviation from the right path" (see Matthew 5:23–24). There is great power in intercessory prayer. The Greek word *deesis* (**DEH-ay-sees**),

translated "prayer," has a more restricted meaning. It denotes a petition, a supplication (Luke 1:13; Romans 10:1). Sin is the enemy of personal and community life; it must be confessed before the throne of grace (Proverbs 28:13; 1 John 1:8–10; see Psalm 32:1). The word "healed" (Gk. *iaomai*, **ee-AH-oh-my**) has both a physical and spiritual meaning. It can mean "to be cured from a sickness" or "to be free from error or sin." It is possible considering the context that James has both in mind in this verse.

A righteous person is one who fears God and obeys His Word. His prayers differ from those of others by virtue of their earnestness and their helpfulness. The word *energeo* (Gk., **en-air-GEH-oh**) is translated "effectual fervent." It can also be rendered "active or operative" or "working." It describes the prayer that has the power to produce the desired effect. The grammar of the word suggests prayer is inwardly working on the righteous person, bringing them in line with the will of God. The Lord listens to the righteous because they fear God and are aligned with His will and purpose. Before prayer changes the situation, prayer changes the person. The prayer from this person produces the desired effect in much the same way as the prayers of Elijah did.

**17 Elias was a man subject to like passions as we are, and he prayed earnestly that it might not rain: and it rained not on the earth by the space of three years and six months.**

Here the reader's attention is drawn to one outstanding example of the efficacy of a righteous man's prayer, Elias [Elijah] (see 1 Kings 17–18). Being "a man subject to like passions (Gk. *homoiopathes*, **ho-moy-oh-pah-THASE**) as we are" means Elijah experienced the same things that all human beings experience. This word is the same used by Paul when explaining to the people of Lystra that he and Barnabas were not gods but men of "like passions" (Acts 14:15). In using this word, James says that Elijah was not a super human; he was a human being just as we are. Elijah "prayed earnestly" means literally, he "prayed in prayer." With this phrase, James points to the earnestness of Elijah's prayer by translating a certain Hebrew grammatical construction into Greek. The Hebrew infinitive absolute denotes intensity and sincerity. When found in the Old Testament, the English translation usually renders it as "certainly" or "surely" (Genesis 2:17 "surely die"; Luke 22:15 "with desire, I have desired"). It is similar to the African American church where someone describes a sermon or song by saying that person "really preached" or "really sang." In other words, James says Elijah "surely prayed" or "really prayed." James wants his readers to know that they too can pray this same type of prayer. All the true followers of the Lord can effectively pray with intensity and sincerity and see their prayers answered.

**18 And he prayed again, and the heaven gave rain, and the earth brought forth her fruit.**

Elijah's prayer for rain to return and water the dry land is an illustration of the sick returning to life after the prayer of faith. A time of being sick is like a period of dryness. But the prayers of people made righteous through the blood of Jesus are efficient to bring new life. The example of Elijah praying for rain is intended to show that nothing is impossible for believers who call on God in prayer. Elijah prayed with boldness and waited on God. We are called to pray with boldness and to wait on God in every situation (Hebrews 4:16).

Sources:

Davids, Peter H. *The Epistle of James, The New International Greek Testament Commentary.* Grand Rapids, MI: Eerdmans, 1982.

Vincent, Martin R. *Vincent's Word Studies in the New Testament: Matthew, Mark, Luke, Acts, James, 1 Peter, 2 Peter, Jude, King James Version.* Peabody, MA: Hendrickson Publishers, 1985.

## Say It Correctly

Anoint. a-**NOI**-nt.

## Daily Bible Readings

**MONDAY**
Let Us Seek God's Favor Together
(Zechariah 8:18–23)

**TUESDAY**
Pray to the Lord for Us
(Jeremiah 42:1–6)

**WEDNESDAY**
We Pray to God for You
(2 Thessalonians 1:5–12)

**THURSDAY**
You Heard My Plea
(Lamentations 3:52–58)

**FRIDAY**
Never Ceasing to Pray for You
(1 Samuel 12:19–25)

**SATURDAY**
The Prophets' Suffering and Patience
(James 5:1–12)

**SUNDAY**
The Prayer of Faith
(James 5:13–18)

# Teaching Tips

## Words You Should Know

**A. Defile** (Daniel 1:8) *ga'al* (Heb.)—To pollute, stain, desecrate.

**B. Countenance** (vv. 13, 15) *mar'eh* (Heb.)—Sight, appearance, vision.

## Teacher Preparation

**Unifying Principle—The Cuisine of Resistance.** People often restrict their diet for both physical and spiritual reasons as Daniel and his friends. What are some of the benefits of restricting a diet? The Scripture teaches that fasting is good stewardship that gives physical and spiritual benefits.

**A.** Read the Bible Background and Devotional Readings.

**B.** Complete Lesson 9 in the *Precepts For Living Personal Study Guide®*.

**C.** Reread the Focal Verses in a modern translation.

## O—Open the Lesson

**A.** Open with prayer.

**B.** Have students read the Aim for Change in unison.

**C.** Ask for a volunteer to read the In Focus story.

**D.** Discuss what it means to fast.

## P—Present the Scriptures

**A.** Ask for volunteers to read the Focal Verses and The People, Places, and Times. Discuss.

**B.** Read and discuss the Background section.

**C.** Encourage students to praise God for blessing them with His presence during times of fasting.

## E—Explore the Meaning

**A.** Review and discuss the Search the Scriptures and Discuss the Meaning questions and the Lesson in Our Society section.

**B.** Ask students to share the most significant point they learned and how to use that point this week.

## N—Next Steps for Application

**A.** Complete the Follow the Spirit and Remember Your Thoughts sections.

**B.** Remind students to read the Daily Bible Readings in preparation for next week's lesson.

**C.** Close in prayer, thanking God for his spiritual provision during fasting.

## Worship Guide

For the Superintendent or Teacher
Theme: Feasting and Fasting
Song: "Guide me, O Thou Great Jehovah"
Devotional Reading: 2 Chronicles 7:11–18

# Feasting and Fasting

**Bible Background • DANIEL 1:5, 8–17, MATTHEW 6:16–18, 9:14–17**
**Printed Text • DANIEL 1:5, 8–17, MATTHEW 6:16–18**
**Devotional Reading • 2 CHRONICLES 7:11–18**

## Aim for Change

By the end of this lesson, we will: KNOW and understand what Jesus said about fasting and those who fast; FEEL the value of being connected with God through fasting; and DECIDE to voluntarily fast and pray in order to draw near to God.

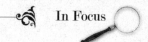

## In Focus

Debbie had grown up in the church and knew all the traditions that came along with it. She knew about fasting because the church mandated fasting twice a week. As she began to experience life as an adult, she realized that all of the rituals she followed were just that, an established pattern of repetitive behavior. She only did it because the church told her to do it and not through any understanding of why she was fasting. After realizing she was having some issues that neither she or the church could handle, she began to search her heart. Debbie remembered that she had heard repeatedly that "some things only come out through fasting and prayer" (Mark 9:29). She began to seek God and the Scriptures regarding fasting. She learned that fasting was not just a tradition but a vital discipline in seeking God. Soon Debbie understood the benefits of fasting and how her experience brought her closer to God. She started to understand that fasting was more than going without all food and drink for a period or refraining from certain foods as Daniel had done, but it was about by denying herself in order to have a closer relationship with God.

*In this week's lesson, we learn that fasting is not just the absence of food. It is hungering after the presence of God*

## Keep in Mind

"But thou, when thou fastest, anoint thine head, and wash thy face; That thou appear not unto men to fast, but unto thy Father which is in secret: and thy Father, which seeth in secret, shall reward thee openly" (Matthew 6:17–18).

"But thou, when thou fastest, anoint thine head, and wash thy face; That thou appear not unto men to fast, but unto thy Father which is in secret: and thy Father, which seeth in secret, shall reward thee openly" (Matthew 6:17–18).

# Focal Verses

**KJV** **Daniel 1:5** And the king appointed them a daily provision of the king's meat, and of the wine which he drank: so nourishing them three years, that at the end thereof they might stand before the king.

**1:8** But Daniel purposed in his heart that he would not defile himself with the portion of the king's meat, nor with the wine which he drank: therefore he requested of the prince of the eunuchs that he might not defile himself.

**9** Now God had brought Daniel into favour and tender love with the prince of the eunuchs.

**10** And the prince of the eunuchs said unto Daniel, I fear my lord the king, who hath appointed your meat and your drink: for why should he see your faces worse liking than the children which are of your sort? then shall ye make me endanger my head to the king.

**11** Then said Daniel to Melzar, whom the prince of the eunuchs had set over Daniel, Hananiah, Mishael, and Azariah,

**12** Prove thy servants, I beseech thee, ten days; and let them give us pulse to eat, and water to drink.

**13** Then let our countenances be looked upon before thee, and the countenance of the children that eat of the portion of the king's meat: and as thou seest, deal with thy servants.

**14** So he consented to them in this matter, and proved them ten days.

**15** And at the end of ten days their countenances appeared fairer and fatter in flesh than all the children which did eat the portion of the king's meat.

**NLT** **Daniel 1:5** The king assigned them a daily ration of food and wine from his own kitchens. They were to be trained for three years, and then they would enter the royal service.

**1:8** But Daniel was determined not to defile himself by eating the food and wine given to them by the king. He asked the chief of staff for permission not to eat these unacceptable foods.

**9** Now God had given the chief of staff both respect and affection for Daniel.

**10** But he responded, "I am afraid of my lord the king, who has ordered that you eat this food and wine. If you become pale and thin compared to the other youths your age, I am afraid the king will have me beheaded."

**11** Daniel spoke with the attendant who had been appointed by the chief of staff to look after Daniel, Hananiah, Mishael, and Azariah.

**12** "Please test us for ten days on a diet of vegetables and water," Daniel said.

**13** "At the end of the ten days, see how we look compared to the other young men who are eating the king's food. Then make your decision in light of what you see."

**14** The attendant agreed to Daniel's suggestion and tested them for ten days.

**15** At the end of the ten days, Daniel and his three friends looked healthier and better nourished than the young men who had been eating the food assigned by the king.

**16** So after that, the attendant fed them only vegetables instead of the food and wine provided for the others.

**17** God gave these four young men an unusual aptitude for understanding every aspect of literature and wisdom. And God gave Daniel the special ability to interpret the meanings of visions and dreams.

**16** Thus Melzar took away the portion of their meat, and the wine that they should drink; and gave them pulse.

**17** As for these four children, God gave them knowledge and skill in all learning and wisdom: and Daniel had understanding in all visions and dreams.

**Matthew 6:16** Moreover when ye fast, be not, as the hypocrites, of a sad countenance: for they disfigure their faces, that they may appear unto men to fast. Verily I say unto you, They have their reward.

**17** But thou, when thou fastest, anoint thine head, and wash thy face;

**18** That thou appear not unto men to fast, but unto thy Father which is in secret: and thy Father, which seeth in secret, shall reward thee openly.

**Matthew 6:16** "And when you fast, don't make it obvious, as the hypocrites do, for they try to look miserable and disheveled so people will admire them for their fasting. I tell you the truth, that is the only reward they will ever get.

**17** But when you fast, comb your hair and wash your face.

**18** Then no one will notice that you are fasting, except your Father, who knows what you do in private. And your Father, who sees everything, will reward you.

## The People, Places, and Times

**Pulse.** In Hebrew, this includes everything that is grown from sown seed. This means not only vegetables but also fruit, legumes, grains, and bread. It was very similar to a healthy vegetarian diet. This type of food was eaten in a partial fast as opposed to meat and dairy and other delicate foods. Eating pulse was not a condemnation of meat eating in general, but regarded by the participant as a way to humble themselves before God.

**Eunuch.** A eunuch was commonly one who was castrated. These men were guardians of the women of the court and were chosen because they could not harm them sexually. Eunuchs were also placed in charge of other court offices because of their proclivity to single-minded focus. This ability to focus was from their not having powerful sexual desires or family responsibilities. In the ancient world, they were considered remarkable for their faithfulness to their masters. Eunuchs were common in the royal courts

of the Jews, Persians, Babylonians, Romans, and Greeks. In the Law it was forbidden for eunuchs to be a part of public worship (Deuteronomy 23:1). Elsewhere, Jesus commends those who have figuratively made themselves eunuchs for the kingdom of God (Matthew 19:12).

## Background

During the conquest of Jerusalem, Nebuchadnezzar, the Babylonian king, took the royal youths to Babylon to be raised in his courts. This included eating at the king's table and receiving a Babylonian education. These royal captives would then be a part of the Babylonian culture and government. Daniel and his three friends Hananiah, Mishael, and Azariah were taken to Babylon to be a part of the court. They were to be trained in all the arts and sciences of Babylon and eat at the king's table. Despite being subjected to a foreign power the four friends resisted conforming to the aspects of Babylonian culture that jeopardized their faithfulness to God. At the same time they rose in prominence and authority and promoted the Hebrew God as the God of all the earth. They were in Babylon but not of Babylon. These four friends serve as an example to Christians who do not belong to this world although we live in it. The first test that Daniel and his friends would encounter had to do with their training. This would determine the trajectory for their lives as pilgrims in a strange land. Would they choose to become fully absorbed into the Babylonian ways, or would they choose to live distinctive lives even while they were in exile far away from home?

## At-A-Glance

1. The Appointment of the King
(Daniel 1:5)
2. The Abstinence of Daniel and His
Friends (vv. 8–14)
3. The Approval of God
(vv. 15–17; Matthew 6:16–18)

## In Depth

**1. The Appointment of the King (Daniel 1:5)**

Nebuchadnezzar had gathered together some of the best-looking and educated young men of Judah to be a part of his royal court. In order for them to be fully indoctrinated into the Babylonian culture, he started with something basic: food. For three years they were to be fed food and drink from the king's table. We do not know exactly what this food consisted of, but we do know that meat was the main dish. Wine was also served along with the food. By starting off with something as basic as food, Nebuchadnezzar was showing that he had complete control and they were dependent on him. This was central to the indoctrination process. The royal youths had to believe that their provision and sustenance came from Nebuchadnezzar and not from God.

**2. The Abstinence of Daniel and His Friends (vv. 8–14)**

Daniel understood the ways of God and had already decided that he would not defile himself with any of the king's meat or drink. This was the first step in resisting the king's attempts to conform him to the ways of Babylon. Next this decision in the heart became an outward action. Since Daniel had gained favor with the head eunuch, Melzar, he requested that he and his friends Hananiah, Mishael, and Azariah be given only water and pulse for ten days. He wanted to prove that their faces would be fairer and fatter than all the other children who ate the king's meat. By doing this, he was protesting the sovereignty of Nebuchadnezzar over their lives while at the same time promoting the king's interests. He knew the king would be interested more in the results and not the means by which the results came.

Their eating habits reflected their dependence on God's and not Nebuchadnezzar's provision. In this way, they resisted the attempts of Nebuchadnezzar to make them part of Babylon and turn them away from God. Daniel and his friends used the simple act of eating food as a way to defy the claims of Nebuchadnezzar and Babylon over their lives. By doing this, they showed that they were first and foremost loyal to God and not an earthly king. This also became a way for them to display the power of God to a people who did not believe in Him. For Daniel and his friends, this was a risk, but it was worth it to remain loyal to God and promote His name in a foreign land.

## 3. The Approval of God (vv. 15–17; Matthew 6:16–18)

After Daniel and his friends had completed the ten days with only the water and pulse, their countenances were fairer and fatter than the other young men in the court. Daniel and his friends had chosen to remain loyal to God, and it paid off. Melzar, their guardian, noticed the difference between their physical constitution and the other children. This caused him to take away the king's portion of food and give them a full diet of pulse and water for the next three years. These young Hebrew boys proved their appearance and countenance were looking better than the other young men who had been given the king's portion of meat and drink. The ten-day test had worked!

During their three years there, Daniel and his friends were not only stronger and more good looking, but they also grew stronger mentally. The text says that God gave them "knowledge and skill in all learning and wisdom." It also says that Daniel specifically could understand all kinds of dreams. This gives a hint at the future destiny of the young men. They would rise to become influencers in Babylonia, and use that influence in the court as worshipers of the one true God. Their first step in remaining loyal to God proved to be the foundation of the ministry and calling for their lives. This was all because they chose to eat the cuisine of resistance from the beginning of their time in Babylon.

Later on in the New Testament, Jesus shows His disciples how to receive approval from God in regards to fasting. He says not to be like the hypocrites who make themselves look miserable in order to display to the world what they are doing. Jesus says that fasting is to be done toward God. It is not to show people how super-spiritual you are, but it is a way to deny yourself in order to seek God and His kingdom. Similar to Daniel and his friends, God will see your secret fasting and reward you.

## Search the Scriptures

1. What did Daniel believe would happen to him if he ate the king's meat (Daniel 1:8)?

2. What was the purpose of Daniel asking the eunuch for ten days to eat pulse (v. 12)?

## Discuss the Meaning

1. What are some of the ways that we can resist the influence of the surrounding culture?

2. How is fasting connected to our relationship with God?

## Lesson in Our Society

In our society, many people eat all kinds of different diets. Some eat fast food and junk food on an everyday basis. Some are vegetarian or vegan. Others have allergies, while others abstain from carbohydrates. Whatever the diet, food is a constant topic of conversation. Whether it is about the health of food or the taste of food, the topic is always on our minds and in our talk on a daily basis. As Christians, we believe that all of life is under the sovereignty and Lordship of Christ. This can even be reflected in the food that we eat. For the believer, eating is not just a physical act, but also deeply spiritual. We can show this by fasting and abstaining from food altogether or from certain foods. This does not earn any merit or favor with God, but displays the closeness and intimacy that we already have with Him.

## Make It Happen

Fasting can be a challenging practice for those of us who have grown up in the junk and convenience food culture. Not only do we eat foods that are not good for us, but we also eat way more than is needed. Commit yourself to fasting at least once during this next week. It can be a partial fast like Daniel and his friends or a fast from all food altogether. We can also choose to fast from television or social media. Make sure to accompany this fast with prayer and take note of anything the Lord may say to you during this time.

## Follow the Spirit

What God wants me to do:

_____

_____

_____

_____

## Remember Your Thoughts

Special insights I have learned:

_____

_____

_____

_____

## More Light on the Text

### Daniel 1:5, 8–17

Daniel 1 establishes that Daniel and his Hebrew comrades are among the youths chosen to serve the king directly and eat and drink the king's portions. They are in exile and therefore at the mercy of a foreign ruler when they encounter a dilemma that is both political and religious. Consuming the king's food and drink would violate God's commandments, while refusing to consume

them would violate the king's command. Daniel and his friends stand firm, and as a result, God gives them wisdom and discernment. The rest of the book shows time and again God's grace, favor, and omnipotence with these Hebrew youths who remain faithful both in their hearts and in their practices, even when their lives are at risk in a foreign culture.

**5 And the king appointed them a daily provision of the king's meat, and of the wine which he drank: so nourishing them three years, that at the end thereof they might stand before the king.**

**8 But Daniel purposed in his heart that he would not defile himself with the portion of the king's meat, nor with the wine which he drank: therefore he requested of the prince of the eunuchs that he might not defile himself.**

The Law of Moses requires that Israelites refrain from eating certain kinds of foods that were not restricted in all other cultures. Only animals with split hooves that chewed cud were allowed, so meat from cattle and sheep was acceptable, but pork was not (Leviticus 11:3–8; Deuteronomy 14:6–8). Since the foreign rulers did not observe such restrictions, consuming the king's portions was problematic because the meat would not be kosher. Consuming wine was generally acceptable for Israelites, with the exceptions of the priests when they entered the tabernacle or temple (Leviticus 10:9) and those making a Nazarite vow for a certain period of time (Numbers 6:3). However, in the ancient world, both the meat and the wine could have been sacrificed to the king's gods, so if Daniel and his fellow Hebrews wanted to be sure they were not engaging in practices related to worship of other gods, it was necessary to refrain from consuming the king's foods.

**9 Now God had brought Daniel into favour and tender love with the prince of the eunuchs. 10 And the prince of the eunuchs said unto Daniel, I fear my lord the king, who hath appointed your meat and your drink: for why should he see your faces worse liking than the children which are of your sort? then shall ye make me endanger my head to the king. 11 Then said Daniel to Melzar, whom the prince of the eunuchs had set over Daniel, Hananiah, Mishael, and Azariah, 12 Prove thy servants, I beseech thee, ten days; and let them give us pulse to eat, and water to drink. 13 Then let our countenances be looked upon before thee, and the countenance of the children that eat of the portion of the king's meat: and as thou seest, deal with thy servants. 14 So he consented to them in this matter, and proved them ten days. 15 And at the end of ten days their countenances appeared fairer and fatter in flesh than all the children which did eat the portion of the king's meat. 16 Thus Melzar took away the portion of their meat, and the wine that they should drink; and gave them pulse.**

This was a miraculous event in the ancient world. In antiquity, as in two-thirds of the world today, meat was only available to the wealthiest people, so it was a great privilege to be offered the king's portions, even if they were leftovers from a religious sacrifice. To be thin was a sign of poverty or illness, so the fact that the Hebrew youths have gained weight was a sure sign that God is with them.

**17 As for these four children, God gave them knowledge and skill in all learning and wisdom: and Daniel had understanding in all visions and dreams.**

God not only strengthens Daniel and his friends physically but also gives them the wisdom and discernment necessary to survive in a foreign culture. The fact that God gives them precisely the skills the king requires indicates even more that God provides the faithful with what they need no matter where they are.

### Matthew 6:16–18

In this part of the Sermon on the Mount, Jesus explains the proper ways to observe God's commandments. Matthew 5:17–7:12 is a collection of instructions. Jesus does not abolish the laws established through Moses, but instead he addresses the distinctions between hypocritical and genuine observance (Matthew 5:17). Very little is dictated about fasting in Old Testament law, with only the fast of the Day of Atonement, Yom Kippur, explicitly ordained (Leviticus 16:29–34; 23:27–32). In fact, the Old Testament includes instances of fasting in ancient Israel for purposes such as repentance (Jonah 3:5), petition (2 Samuel 12:16) and mourning (1 Samuel 31:13). Fasting served numerous purposes, but in each case the individual or community humbled themselves before God by refraining from food and drink and often by putting on sackcloth instead of their everyday clothing. In Matthew 6, Jesus does not eliminate fasting as a religious ritual, but He establishes stipulations concerning the intention of the faster, especially in the case of voluntary fasts, which individuals could practice regularly on Mondays and Thursdays. Such fasts should not be about a public display of piety.

Fasting as addressed in Matthew 6 and a kosher diet as observed in Daniel 1 are distinct religious practices associated with eating and drinking. Fasting in antiquity typically involved refraining from all food and drink for a short period of time. Today fasting may involve complete abstention from eating and drinking, or it may involve avoiding certain foods, but in all cases the duration is short and for a specific purpose. In contrast, a kosher diet is to be observed regularly as a daily devotion to God, with occasional abstention from additional foods such as leavened bread during Passover (Exodus 3:15; Leviticus 23:5–6). In the Roman period and later, some faithful Christians and Jews further restricted their daily diets as a practice of faith, as with John the Baptist, who ate locusts and honey (Matthew 3:4). What is clear from the Bible is that dietary habits are associated with faith practices for Jews and Christians.

**16 Moreover when ye fast, be not, as the hypocrites, of a sad countenance: for they disfigure their faces, that they may appear unto men to fast. Verily I say unto you, They have their reward. 17 But thou, when thou fastest, anoint thine head, and wash thy face;**

In addition to refraining from eating and drinking, the Israelites would sometimes wear sackcloth, put ashes on their heads, and refrain from washing as a way of acknowledging their humble situation when they fasted. Whether they were mourning somebody's death, asking for forgiveness for sin, or pleading for help for a personal or community crisis, fasting was a way of acknowledging their situation of loss or need. This is not the type of fasting that Jesus addresses. Instead, He points out that at times people do not fast with these intentions, but with the purpose of calling attention to themselves as pious. The word "hypocrite" in Greek has the basic meaning of one who pretends that the situation is different from what it really is. To make yourself look mournful or needy when you are not serves the purpose of getting other people to look at you and either pity you for your situation or laud you for your piety. Instead, it is better to wash so that you do not stand out.

**18 That thou appear not unto men to fast, but unto thy Father which is in secret: and thy Father, which seeth in secret, shall reward thee openly.**

The word for secret here in Greek is *kruptos* (**kroop-TOSE**), and it refers specifically to hidden things, the types of things that only God can see. This is the crux of Jesus' statement about fasting. Fasting can serve a number of important religious purposes, but it should remain between the believer and God because it is not a performance for all to see. Voluntary fasts should be practiced not for public display but for true repentance, mourning, or plea for God's help. Everything we do should come from the heart, and God always knows what is in our hearts because God alone knows our secrets.

Sources:

Boring, M. Eugene. "Matthew." Vol. VIII. *New Interpreter's Bible Commentary.* 12 vols. Edited by Leander E. Keck, et al. Nashville: Abingdon Press, 1995. 87–506.

Gowan, Donald E. *Daniel: Abingdon Old Testament Commentaries.* Nashville: Abingdon Press, 2001.

Miller, Steven R. *The New American Commentary: Daniel.* Nashville, TN: Broadman and Holman, 1994.

Senior, Donald W. *Matthew: Abingdon New Testament Commentaries.* Nashville: Abingdon Press, 1998.

Smith-Christopher, Daniel L. "The Book of Daniel: Introduction, Commentary, and Reflections." Vol. VII. *New Interpreter's Bible Commentary.* 12 vols. Edited by Leander E. Keck, et al. Nashville: Abingdon Press, 1996. 17–152.

Towner, W. Sibley. *Daniel, Interpretation, a Biblical Commentary for Teaching and Preaching: New International Commentary on the New Testament.* Atlanta, GA: John Knox Press. 1984.

## Say It Correctly

Kosher. **KOH**-shur.
Hananiah. hah-nah-**NIGH**-ah.
Mishael. **MEE**-shah-el.
Azariah. ah-zar-**RIGH**-ah.
Yom Kippur. **YOME** kih-**POOR**.
Hypocrite. **HIH**-poh-criht.

## Daily Bible Readings

**MONDAY**
Draw Near to Me, O Lord
(Psalm 69:5–18)

**TUESDAY**
Help Me, O Lord My God
(Psalm 109:21–27)

**WEDNESDAY**
Humility Before God
(Luke 18:9–14)

**THURSDAY**
If My People Humble Themselves
(2 Chronicles 7:11–18)

**FRIDAY**
Humble Yourselves Before God
(2 Chronicles 34:24–33)

**SATURDAY**
An Appropriate Time for Fasting
(Matthew 9:9–17)

**SUNDAY**
To Honor God
(Daniel 1:5, 8–17; Matthew 6:16–18)

# Notes

# Teaching Tips

## Words You Should Know

**A. Neighbor** (Luke 10:27, 29, 36) *plesion* (Gk.)—One who is near, a fellow person or creature.

**B. Love** (v. 27) *agapao* (Gk.)—To express goodness and kindness to another as a choice of one's will, not dependent upon common interests or friendship; God's love towards man.

**C. Mercy** (v. 37) *eleos* (Gk.)—Compassion upon witnessing another's misery, typically caused by the commission of sins (by self and/or others).

## Teacher Preparation

**Unifying Principle—Do You Know Your Neighbor?** People of goodwill take care of and serve their neighbors. Why would they do this? The parable of the good Samaritan teaches that when the faithful serve their neighbor, they serve God.

**A.** Pray for clarity and application for you and students.

**B.** Review and complete the companion lesson in *Precepts for Living Personal Study Guide®*.

## O—Open the Lesson

**A.** Have students read the Keep in Mind verse and In Focus story.

## P—Present the Scriptures

**A.** Give students a few minutes to silently read The People, Places, and Times, and Background.

**B.** Have students read Focal Verses.

**C.** Use the In Depth content and Search the Scriptures to facilitate discussion on the Focal Verses.

## E—Explore the Meaning

**A.** Encourage students to view the lesson from the lawyer's viewpoint using Discuss the Meaning.

**B.** Read Lesson in Our Society and discuss commonalities between serving neighbors in the 1st century and 21st century.

## N—Next Steps for Application

**A.** Read Make it Happen and re-read the Aim for Change aloud.

**B.** Pray with students that God will bring two neighbors to mind whom they need to serve.

**C.** Have them write these names down and specific ways they sense they need to show mercy and love toward them.

**D.** Close in prayer.

## Worship Guide

For the Superintendent or Teacher
Theme: Serving Neighbors, Serving God
Song: "Come Thou Fount"
Devotional Reading:
Matthew 22:33–40

# Serving Neighbors, Serving God

**Bible Background • LUKE 10:25–34**
**Printed Text • LUKE 10:25–34**
**Devotional Reading • MATTHEW 22:33–40**

## Aim for Change

By the end of the lesson, we will: EXAMINE Jesus' teaching about compassion for our neighbors; REFLECT on the connection between serving our neighbors and serving God; and EXPAND our vision and application of service to neighbors and to God.

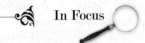 In Focus

She just could not understand him. Truthfully, she had no desire to. He was just too different. The old man did not think like her, look like her, or believe as she did. He had a reputation of being cold and sometimes rude. The neighborhood children were afraid of him, and her neighbors kept their distance. Why should she be the one to reach out now that he was ill? Where were his children? They probably avoided him for good reason. Where were his friends? Ha! He probably didn't have any. Yet, she felt drawn to him. So, Mary brought Mr. Martinez a meal. Three hours later, she realized how dreadfully wrong she had been. Mr. Martinez was a man filled with pain as a result of being wrongly accused of a crime. Having been betrayed by a "friend," he was slow to trust. He lost his family in the process and was overwhelmed by guilt and feelings of abandonment. His pride had prevented him from re-connecting with them upon being released. Now he suffered—alone. By serving him one meal, Mary became a true neighbor and gave him hope.

*We are exhorted to love God and our neighbors. This lesson reveals the connection between the two and encourages us to expand our definition of neighbor.*

## Keep in Mind

"Which now of these three, thinkest thou, was neighbour unto him that fell among the thieves? And he said, He that shewed mercy on him. Then said Jesus unto him, Go, and do thou likewise" (Luke 10:36–37).

"Which now of these three, thinkest thou, was neighbour unto him that fell among the thieves? And he said, He that shewed mercy on him. Then said Jesus unto him, Go, and do thou likewise" (Luke 10:36–37).

# Focal Verses

**KJV** **Luke 10:25** And, behold, a certain lawyer stood up, and tempted him, saying, Master, what shall I do to inherit eternal life?

**26** He said unto him, What is written in the law? how readest thou?

**27** And he answering said, Thou shalt love the Lord thy God with all thy heart, and with all thy soul, and with all thy strength, and with all thy mind; and thy neighbour as thyself.

**28** And he said unto him, Thou hast answered right: this do, and thou shalt live.

**29** But he, willing to justify himself, said unto Jesus, And who is my neighbour?

**30** And Jesus answering said, A certain man went down from Jerusalem to Jericho, and fell among thieves, which stripped him of his raiment, and wounded him, and departed, leaving him half dead.

**31** And by chance there came down a certain priest that way: and when he saw him, he passed by on the other side.

**32** And likewise a Levite, when he was at the place, came and looked on him, and passed by on the other side.

**33** But a certain Samaritan, as he journeyed, came where he was: and when he saw him, he had compassion on him,

**34** And went to him, and bound up his wounds, pouring in oil and wine, and set him on his own beast, and brought him to an inn, and took care of him.

**NLT** **Luke 10:25** One day an expert in religious law stood up to test Jesus by asking him this question: "Teacher, what should I do to inherit eternal life?"

**26** Jesus replied, "What does the law of Moses say? How do you read it?"

**27** The man answered, "'You must love the Lord your God with all your heart, all your soul, all your strength, and all your mind.' And, 'Love your neighbor as yourself.'"

**28** "Right!" Jesus told him. "Do this and you will live!"

**29** The man wanted to justify his actions, so he asked Jesus, "And who is my neighbor?"

**30** Jesus replied with a story: "A Jewish man was traveling from Jerusalem down to Jericho, and he was attacked by bandits. They stripped him of his clothes, beat him up, and left him half dead beside the road.

**31** "By chance a priest came along. But when he saw the man lying there, he crossed to the other side of the road and passed him by.

**32** A Temple assistant walked over and looked at him lying there, but he also passed by on the other side.

**33** "Then a despised Samaritan came along, and when he saw the man, he felt compassion for him.

**34** Going over to him, the Samaritan soothed his wounds with olive oil and wine and bandaged them. Then he put the man on his own donkey and took him to an inn, where he took care of him.

## The People, Places, and Times

**Lawyer.** Lawyers or experts in law (Gk. *nomikos*, **no-mee-KOHS**) are generally believed to be scribes who specialized in studying, teaching, and defending the Law of Moses. They may have been associated with the Pharisees who were well-versed in Mosaic Torah, and Luke groups them together several times (7:30; 11:53). Therefore, they were considered religious and moral authorities, and highly revered among common Jews. As proclaimed "protectors" of the Law, lawyers (scribes) are often found in Scripture questioning Jesus on religious matters. Luke uses the term frequently. They are often portrayed as arrogant, unbelieving, and hypocritical (see Matthew 23:23–28).

**Jerusalem to Jericho.** The journey from Jerusalem to Jericho was 17 miles long and on a steep decline of approximately 3,000 feet (thus the term "going down from Jerusalem"). The winding road was filled with rocky places and caves that served as hiding places for robbers. It was known to be a dangerous route, as robberies were common, especially for lone travelers.

**Samaritans.** In 721 B.C., the Northern Kingdom of Israel was defeated by Assyria, and its people were deported. The king of Assyria repopulated the area with foreigners, and those people intermarried with Jews. The result was Samaritans, a mixed race of people with some Jewish ancestry, and "impure" religion, being a combination of Jewish traditions and pagan/idol worship. Samaritans were, therefore, despised by Jews, and the relationship between the two people groups was a hostile one.

## Background

Jesus has just sent out His disciples to preach the kingdom of God and to heal the sick and cast out demons. He gave them instructions for the mission, and they faithfully followed them, and saw the power of God in tangible signs. They were amazed and came back rejoicing when giving Jesus the full report of their ministry. Jesus takes the time to let them know that although what they witnessed was amazing, it pales in comparison to the fact that their names are "written in heaven" (Luke 10:20). This causes Jesus to rejoice and thank God. Jesus thanks God that what He has told them has been kept from the wise and the proud of this world. In contrast, it has been given to those who are "babes" in understanding (v. 21).

This sets the stage for a teacher of the law to ask a question. Many times the teachers of the law, along with the scribes and Pharisees, questioned Jesus in order to test and trap Him. This was done to discredit Jesus' ministry. The questions were usually popular questions of the day or ones in which whatever answer was given would place you in a particular theological camp. Jesus was a master at not only giving the right answer but challenging the scribes and Pharisees to live a more God-pleasing life through the answers He gave.

## At-A-Glance

1. The Test (Luke 10:25–29)
2. The Parable (vv. 30–34)

## In Depth

### 1. The Test (Luke 10:25–29)

This conversation is considered a typical one between rabbis and their students. Questions about eternal life were common. Rabbis would often answer a question with a question ("How do you read it?") and affirm responses ("You have answered correctly"). However, the lawyer, coming from a mentality of authority, was not seeking to learn, but to test. As a learned, religious Jew, his response quoting Deuteronomy 6:5 and Leviticus 19:18 was the correct verbal response, but the motive behind his follow-up question (to justify himself) revealed the flaw in his heart. There was no intention to love his neighbor, only to maintain his reputation.

Jesus' response, "You have answered correctly," is not implying that eternal life is based on works. It is by faith in Christ alone. One who loves God with all His heart, soul, strength, and mind is one who has faith in Him, and desires to please Him through obedience. One cannot say that they love God, without obeying Him and loving others (John 15:9–14, 1 John 4:20–21).

### 2. The Parable (vv. 30–34)

As an illustration of neighborly love, Jesus tells this parable. During Jesus' time, Jewish religion and culture dictated that "good" Jews avoid impure things and people. Samaritans, as "mixed breeds," would fall into this category. Priests and Levites (along with Pharisees) were considered "holy" ones, striving to maintain the appearance of righteousness.

As such, a person would expect the priest or Levite to come to the aid of an injured fellow Jew. For many possible reasons, both of them selfishly and intentionally avoided the injured traveler. Unexpectedly, the Samaritan set aside cultural animosity to show compassion and serve another. He uses his time by going out of his way (takes him to an inn, and plans to return), his resources (his animal, oil, wine, money), and his energy (walks while allowing the man to ride). He is a picture of agape-love (love without commonalities or friendship) and mercy (compassion at seeing another's misery). It is undeniable that the Samaritan is the better person—the true neighbor. He illustrated that a neighbor is one who sees another who is in need, and using whatever resources he has, meets that need.

### Search the Scriptures

1. What does the lawyer say is the way to inherit eternal life? How consuming is the pursuit (Luke 10:27)?

2. What is implied to be one way for the lawyer to show love toward his neighbor (vv. 36–37)?

### Discuss the Meaning

Jesus' parable reveals that opportunities to be neighborly can come at any time. Our love for Him should compel us to show mercy. What are barriers to serving our neighbors? In what ways can we show mercy to others (e.g., the Samaritan gave money, etc.)?

### Lesson in Our Society

There are many examples of the lack of mercy and love in our society. There are executives who choose to lay off hard-working employees while accepting million-dollar bonuses. Some people take advantage of funds designated to help those in need. However, the opposite is true as well. There are tales of "heroes," people who rise up during tragedies to rescue, tend to, and provide for complete strangers. It is often said that this is the reflection of the good in humanity. In actuality, it is a reflection of God's love and mercy. Without Him, there would be no "good" in humanity.

### Make It Happen

We are often faced with unexpected opportunities to serve our neighbors. There are people with needs all around us, and we have specific resources to help. Whom is God impressing upon you to serve? What opportunities have you been presented with that you have chosen to ignore because it will cost you time, money, energy, or comfort? Ask God to reveal these to you. Pray that He would give you greater awareness of those around you and a boldness to serve in spite of difficulty.

## Follow the Spirit

What God wants me to do:

_____

_____

_____

_____

## Remember Your Thoughts

Special insights I have learned:

_____

_____

_____

_____

## More Light on the Text

Luke 10:25–34

Among the Bantu people of sub-Saharan Africa, the common life philosophy is called "ubuntu." It is, of course, known by different names in different Bantu languages, but its propositions are the same wherever one goes. Ubuntu is centered on the understanding that personhood is impossible in isolation. Thus, one cannot be a person without interacting with others; a person really exists only in relationships with other people—the community which makes him or her and which is also made by him or her. Thus, the community constitutes the individuals within it, but it also constituted by the same individual. They say, "I am because we are, and we are because I am." There is no personhood without community, but there is also no community without personhood. They find the Western maxim "I think therefore I am" too individualistic and misleading.

This sense of community usually works best when we encounter strangers, especially those strangers who are in need. This is when one's personhood—ubuntu—is stress-tested since the well-being of the other, or the stranger, is ubuntu's *telos* (Gk. **TEH-lohs**, end, goal, or purpose). In this sense then, ubuntu tells us that the answer to the lawyer's question, "Who is my neighbor?" is the entire world, especially those in need. But Jesus suggests further that love for the neighbor has to be predicated by love for God.

**25 And, behold, a certain lawyer stood up, and tempted him, saying, Master, what shall I do to inherit eternal life?**

Many readers bypass this initial story of the lawyer (Gk. *nomikos*, **no-mee-KOHS**; cf. Mark 12:28–34, the expert of the law "scribe," Gk. *grammateus*, **grah-mah-teh-OOS**)—who tested Jesus as they rush to the more popular story of the parable of the Good Samaritan. However, this dialogue between Jesus and the lawyer is not only a prelude to the parable, it has its own important place in Jesus' work with His disciples. In the Matthean and Marcan parallels, the scribe asks which is the greatest commandment (Matthew 22:34–40) or which is the first (Mark 12:28–34). In Mark's account, Jesus answers the question, and the scribe approves of Jesus' answer. Matthew's account is a shorter version and includes only the scribe's question and Jesus' answers. However, in Luke's writing here, the lawyer asks Jesus, "What shall I do to inherit eternal life?" Matthew and Luke say that the lawyer tested (Gk. *ekpeirazo*, **ek-pay-RAHD-zo**, to put to the test, try, tempt) Jesus. The lawyer was a recognized religious authority, and he tested Jesus, the unskilled Galilean lay and unofficial teacher, to see if He could give correct answers to tough theological questions. Thus, the lawyer tried to entrap

Jesus, wanting to discredit Him if He gave a wrong answer.

Luke's version does not seek to say which of the Torah commandments is the greatest, but rather inquires about the fundamental principle of all the commandments. "What shall I do to inherit eternal life?" One who knew the Mosaic law tested Jesus, not as in Matthew about individual laws, but about what he must do to inherit "eternal life," which is the goal of the entire law (Marshall 442). This question also appears in Luke 18:18, where Jesus had a conversation with the rich young ruler. It was a common theme in rabbinical debates of that time (Marshall 442). The word "inherit" (Gk. *kleronomeo*, **klay-ro-no-MEH-oh**, to receive an allotted share) is key to understanding that many Jews of the time thought that their eternal destiny was based on their Jewish descent plus their good deeds. They believed that their good deeds qualified them to receive a future blessing from God (Marshall 442).

**26 He said unto him, What is written in the law? how readest thou? 27 And he answering said, Thou shalt love the Lord thy God with all thy heart, and with all thy soul, and with all thy strength, and with all thy mind; and thy neighbour as thyself.**

Jesus answers the lawyer's question with two questions, taking him to the Old Testament whose authority the lawyer would not question, being an expert in the same. Marshall observes that some scholars believe that Jesus' question is actually, "How do you recite?" Thus the lawyer recalls the Shema from Deuteronomy 6, which he probably recited daily. However, Jesus is asking for more than just a recitation. He wants the lawyer to state his own interpretation of the Scriptures, thereby shifting the dialogue from Jesus' teaching to the lawyer's interpretation

of the law. Correctly, the lawyer recited two commandments: love God (Deuteronomy 6:5) and love your neighbor (Leviticus 19:18). Together these two commandments formed the heart of the Jewish religion (Marshall 443–444), but they also formed the core of Jesus' own teaching. Thus, Jesus and the lawyer end up at the same place in their conversation.

**28 And he said unto him, Thou hast answered right: this do, and thou shalt live. 29 But he, willing to justify himself, said unto Jesus, And who is my neighbour?**

Jesus observes that the lawyer is right in his interpretation, and tells him, "Do this, and you will live." However, having answered the question correctly, the lawyer asks for clarification, possibly to test Jesus further. Since loving your neighbor is a matter of life and death, the correct definition of a neighbor is of extreme importance. So, the lawyer asks, "Who is my neighbor?" In other words, he was saying, "Whom do I love?" Of course, he might have hoped that Jesus would understand—and justify—his bias against certain kinds of neighbors—neighbors who, in this case, did not belong to the Jewish family. Scholars agree that the general Jewish sense of the neighbor at the time was limited to members of the same people, religious communities, fellow Jews, or fellow members of the covenant (Marshall 444, 446). Marshall adds that there was a tendency among the Pharisees to exclude Samaritans, foreigners, and other ordinary people from the definition (444). Plummer observes that a Jew "except[ed] all Gentiles when he spoke of his neighbor" (285). Since the lawyer might have been a Pharisee, he could easily interpret the commandments in this exclusive manner. He agreed on loving neighbor, but he sought to define neighbor to include only

Jews. He wanted to define neighbor—which then defines for him who is not a neighbor.

In our contemporary context, this question may be used to justify our individualism while neglecting those neighbors that we do not like. Consequently, this question is of extreme relevance in our world where segregation tears the body of Christ apart just as much as it does any other community. Unity in diversity is a thorny subject even among Christians. Divisions take many forms and are prevalent in our communities. Black, White, Hispanic, Asian, Orthodox, Pentecostal, Roman Catholic, Lutheran, male, female, rich, poor, educated, and uneducated are just a few among the categories we use to classify our neighbors, usually to choose which neighbor to recognize or not recognize. Unfortunately, these discriminating definitions of neighbors affect the church's understanding of its mission in the world. God's mission is to invite all people into His kingdom without regard to our man-made qualifiers.

**30 And Jesus answering said, A certain man went down from Jerusalem to Jericho, and fell among thieves, which stripped him of his raiment, and wounded him, and departed, leaving him half dead. 31 And by chance there came down a certain priest that way: and when he saw him, he passed by on the other side. 32 And likewise a Levite, when he was at the place, came and looked on him, and passed by on the other side.**

The conversation takes a twist as Jesus brings in a parable to drive the lesson home.

In the parable, a man (supposedly a Jew) went down from Jerusalem to Jericho—a journey along a road that descends over 3,000 feet through treacherous desert and dangerous rocky country that could easily hide bandits. On his way, the man met robbers who vandalized him, stripped him, and

left him half-dead. While he lay half-conscious on the wayside, a priest and a Levite passed by, and upon seeing him, they went on the other side of the road. Both the priest and the Levite were well-known religious figures. The priests were descendants of Aaron and were responsible for everything to do with temple worship. Levites were a tribe of descendants of Levi but not of Aaron (who was also a descendant of Levi), and they assisted the priests in the temple. The Levite in this story seems overly inconsiderate as he "came and looked" at the wounded man and proceeded without offering help. Jesus' audience, however, might have expected that at the sight of a wounded fellow Jew, both the priest and the Levite would stop by to help him. There could be several reasons for their lack of action, among them: (1) their religious responsibilities may have prevented them from helping the wounded man since he might have appeared dead, as the law prohibited them from touching a corpse, (2) they might have been afraid of being attacked by the same robbers, and (3) they might have simply wanted nothing to do with the wounded person. It is possible that they were not indifferent to the wounded man, but their compassion might have been overcome by their commitment to religious purity.

**33 But a certain Samaritan, as he journeyed, came where he was: and when he saw him, he had compassion on him, 34 And went to him, and bound up his wounds, pouring in oil and wine, and set him on his own beast, and brought him to an inn, and took care of him.**

The plot of the story invites the audience to expect a Jewish layman to be the third traveler who responds to the wounded man, but Jesus brings a very unlikely person from a community hated by the Jews into the story—a certain Samaritan. The relationship between Jews and Samaritans was one of constant hostility. The Jews considered the Samaritans to be second-class citizens, the half-breed descendants of Jews who had intermarried with foreigners (see 2 Kings 17:24–40). In return, the Samaritans had occasionally troubled Israel. The ancient Jewish historian Josephus claims that in the years between 6 and 9 A.D., Samaritans defiled Passover by scattering bones in the temple. Consequently, the relations between Jews and Samaritans were especially difficult during Jesus' time. Still, we have here a Samaritan traveling in Jewish territory. His attending to the wounded Jew jeopardized his life, because he could have been easily blamed for the robbery. In addition, the Samaritans were bound by the same religious laws that bound the Jews, and therefore, the Samaritan risked defilement to take care of the possibly dead man—bandaging his wounds, pouring on oil and wine. Being a Samaritan, he could not expect any such kindness from the Jews. However, unlike the priest and the Levite, he fulfilled the law, showed compassion, and helped the wounded man.

He was moved by compassion—the same powerful emotion that moved Jesus to ministry, feeding the hungry and healing the sick, when He saw the multitudes weary and scattered like sheep without a shepherd (Matthew 9:36–38, 14:14; Mark 8:2). The word "compassion" here comes from the Greek word *splagchnizomai* (**splonk-NEED-zo-my**) which means "to be moved in one's gut, hence to be moved with compassion, have compassion" (the guts—inward parts, entrails—were thought to be the seat of love and pity). Love, empathy, and mercy are motivated by the need of another, while withholding mercy is essentially an act of

selfishness or self-protection. Jesus uses the story to contrast the lack of compassion shown by two members of the Jewish priesthood toward an unknown and unfortunate sufferer with the obedience to the law shown in practical compassion by the most unlikely of men, a Samaritan. Any Jew would be deeply humiliated for such an enemy of the Jews to show compassion to an injured Jew and pay expenses for his recuperation, while two Jewish religious officials did not. The story is not only to suggest that love can be found in unlikely places, but it paints a picture in the Samaritan that may—or must—be emulated. The mercy of the Samaritan made him give generously of his own supplies for the life of the wounded stranger: his oil and wine to cleanse and soothe the wounds, his bandage to bind them, and his own animal to carry the man. He also used his own money to pay for his care at the inn, promising to pay for any further expenses the man's care would require. In cultures like those of Africa, this Samaritan would be said to be a muntu—one who has ubuntu—and thus, is a person. The personhood of priest and the Levite would be diminished for not giving of themselves to help the needy. Love humanizes both the giver and the receiver—and that is what it takes to be a neighbor. Jesus finishes the conversation by telling the lawyer, "Go and do likewise." In other words, Jesus is saying, "Go and be a good neighbor; this is how you inherit eternal life."

Sources:
Cosby, Michael R. *Portraits of Jesus: An Inductive Approach to the Gospels.* 1st ed. Louisville, KY: Westminster John Knox Press, 1999. 86–87.
Dunn, James D. G., and J. W. Rogerson. *Eerdmans Commentary on the Bible.* Grand Rapids, MI: W.B. Eerdmans, 2003.
*Hebrew-Greek Key Word Study Bible, King James Version.* Chattanooga, TN: AMG Publishers, Inc., 1991.
Josephus. *The Antiquities of the Jews.* 18.2.2.
Keener, Craig S. *The IVP Bible Background Commentary: New Testament.* Downers Grove, IL: Intervarsity Press, 1993. 217–218.

Marshall, I. Howard. *The Gospel of Luke: A Commentary on the Greek Text.* Grand Rapids, MI: Eerdmans, 1978. 440–450.

Plummer, Alfred. *A Critical and Exegetical Commentary on the Gospel According to St. Luke.* 5th ed. Edinburgh: T. & T. Clark, 1975. 283–288.

Radmacher, Earl D., ed. *Nelson Study Bible, New King James Version.* Nashville, TN: Thomas Nelson Publishers, 1997. 1618–1619, 1714–1715.

Ryrie, Charles C. *Ryrie Study Bible, New International Version.* Chicago, IL: Moody Press, 1986. 1423.

Thompson, Richard P., and Thomas E. Phillips. *Literary Studies in Luke-Acts: Essays in Honor of Joseph B. Tyson.* Macon, GA: Mercer University Press, 1998.

Unger, Merrill F. *The New Unger's Bible Dictionary.* Chicago, IL: Moody Press, 1988. 762–765, 1116–1119.

Walvoord, John F., and Roy B. Zuck, eds. *The Bible Knowledge Commentary: New Testament.* Wheaton, IL: Victor Books, SP Publications, Inc., 1983. 233–234.

## Say It Correctly

Compassion. com-**PA**-shun.
Empathy. em-pa-**THEE**.
Samaritan. sa-**MARE**-ih-tin.
Levite. **LEE**-vite.
Ubuntu. u-boon-**TOO**.

## Daily Bible Readings

**MONDAY**
If You Wish To Be Perfect
(Matthew 19:16-22)

**TUESDAY**
Mercy Triumphs Over Judgment
(James 2:8-13)

**WEDNESDAY**
Keep the Instruction of Moses
(Matthew 23)

**THURSDAY**
Look to the Interests of Others
(Philippians 2:1-5)

**FRIDAY**
The First and Greatest Commandment
(Matthew 22:34-40)

**SATURDAY**
Live By The Spirit
(Galatians 5:10-17)

**SUNDAY**
Who is My Neighbor
(Luke 10:25-34)

# Notes

_____

_____

_____

_____

# Teaching Tips

February 15
Bible Study Guide 11

## Words You Should Know

**A. Separate** (Matthew 25:32) *aphorizo* (Gk.)—To set a boundary, divide.

**B. Cursed** (v. 41) *kataraomai* (Gk.)—Given over to destruction; to be judged and punished, rejected by God.

## Teacher Preparation

**Unifying Principle—Meeting Others' Needs.** Opportunities for serving others are all around us, even though believers do not always recognize or respond to them. What are the consequences of our action or inaction? Matthew says that believers should serve others as if they were the Lord, and God will judge the believers accordingly.

**A.** Pray for clarity and application, for you and your students.

**B.** Study the companion lesson thoroughly, in advance.

**C.** Prepare a personal story about a time someone came to your aid or find a short article that pertains to a stranger caring for another (e.g., accounts of adoptions, tragedies).

## O—Open the Lesson

**A.** Open by telling the story of a time you have been helped.

**B.** Introduce today's lesson title and Aim for Change. Pray for changed hearts.

**C.** Have students read the Keep in Mind verse and In Focus story.

## P—Present the Scriptures

**A.** Give students time to read The People, Places, and Times and Background.

**B.** Have students read the Focal Verses (aloud or silently), encouraging them to keep in mind the information presented in People, Places, and Times and Background.

**C.** Use the In Depth content and Search the Scriptures to facilitate discussion on the Focal Verses.

## E—Explore the Meaning

**A.** Explore Discuss the Meaning together, particularly Christ's connection of actions and eternal consequences.

## N—Next Steps for Application

**A.** Pray that God will reveal ways for us to serve the less fortunate.

**B.** Have students write any ways that immediately come to mind and begin creating a course of action.

**C.** Brainstorm, as a class, ways that they can serve individually and collectively.

## Worship Guide

For the Superintendent or Teacher
Theme: Serving the Least
Song: "Lord I'm Available to You"
Devotional Reading: Psalm 10:12–18

# Serving the Least

**Bible Background • MATTHEW 25:31–46**
**Printed Text • MATTHEW 25:31–46**
**Devotional Reading • PSALM 10:12–18**

## Aim for Change

By the end of the lesson, we will: UNDERSTAND Jesus' comments on our obligation to meet the needs of the less fortunate; EXPERIENCE how God's love for all inspires us to meet others' needs; and PARTICIPATE in serving the needs of others.

## In Focus

He walked past James everyday. Like clockwork, at 7 a.m., James arrived and stood on the corner and greeted people—a bit disheveled, but always friendly and upbeat. Marcus finally decided to ask his co-worker about James. "What is the story of the guy on the corner? He is punctual. He's there every day, seems like a pleasant personality. Why can't he just use those qualities to get a job? Dress him up a bit, he may be alright."

Sara smiled. "Oh, you're talking about James. He used to work here. He was so intent on making his mark in the business world that he neglected his family. After several failed interventions, his wife decided she'd had enough. She took their sons, eventually remarried, and moved out of state. He was shattered. But, he realized he needed to make a different mark in this world. He actually runs a shelter for homeless boys in the city. Fathering the fatherless. As for why he's outside, he stops here every morning to pray for those headed down the same path he was on. Helps him stay focused. As for getting a job—the one he had is yours."

*We are not called to serve ourselves, but instead to focus on serving the least of these as if they were the Lord Jesus Himself.*

## Keep in Mind

"And the King shall answer and say unto them, Verily I say unto you, Inasmuch as ye have done it unto one of the least of these my brethren, ye have done it unto me" (Matthew 25:40).

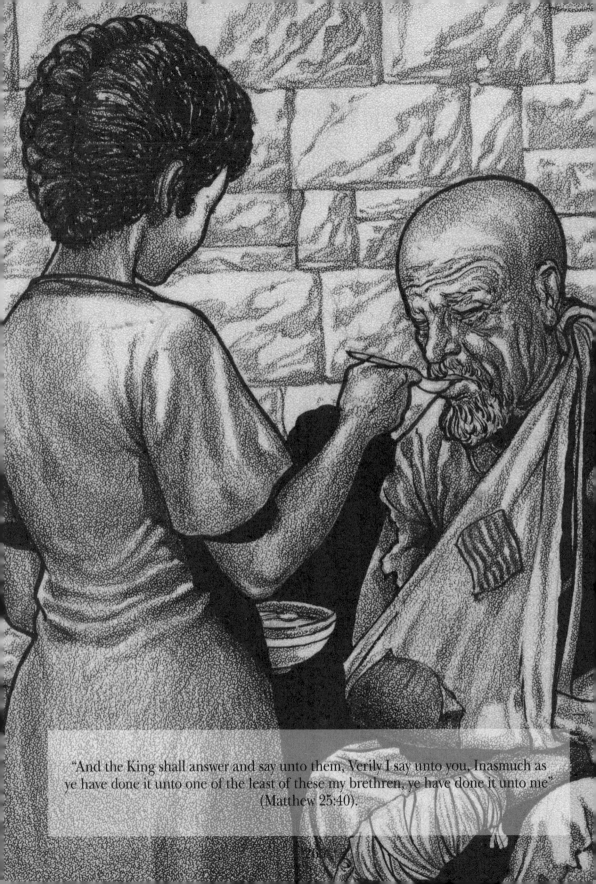

"And the King shall answer and say unto them, Verily I say unto you, Inasmuch as ye have done it unto one of the least of these my brethren, ye have done it unto me" (Matthew 25:40).

## Focal Verses

**KJV** **Matthew 25:31** When the Son of man shall come in his glory, and all the holy angels with him, then shall he sit upon the throne of his glory:

**32** And before him shall be gathered all nations: and he shall separate them one from another, as a shepherd divideth his sheep from the goats:

**33** And he shall set the sheep on his right hand, but the goats on the left.

**34** Then shall the King say unto them on his right hand, Come, ye blessed of my Father, inherit the kingdom prepared for you from the foundation of the world:

**35** For I was an hungred, and ye gave me meat: I was thirsty, and ye gave me drink: I was a stranger, and ye took me in:

**36** Naked, and ye clothed me: I was sick, and ye visited me: I was in prison, and ye came unto me.

**37** Then shall the righteous answer him, saying, Lord, when saw we thee an hungred, and fed thee? or thirsty, and gave thee drink?

**38** When saw we thee a stranger, and took thee in? or naked, and clothed thee?

**39** Or when saw we thee sick, or in prison, and came unto thee?

**40** And the King shall answer and say unto them, Verily I say unto you, Inasmuch as ye have done it unto one of the least of these my brethren, ye have done it unto me.

**41** Then shall he say also unto them on the left hand, Depart from me, ye cursed, into everlasting fire, prepared for the devil and his angels:

**42** For I was an hungred, and ye gave me no meat: I was thirsty, and ye gave me no drink:

**43** I was a stranger, and ye took me not in: naked, and ye clothed me not: sick, and in prison, and ye visited me not.

**NLT** **Matthew 25:31** "But when the Son of Man comes in his glory, and all the angels with him, then he will sit upon his glorious throne.

**32** All the nations will be gathered in his presence, and he will separate the people as a shepherd separates the sheep from the goats.

**33** He will place the sheep at his right hand and the goats at his left.

**34** Then the King will say to those on his right, 'Come, you who are blessed by my Father, inherit the Kingdom prepared for you from the creation of the world.

**35** For I was hungry, and you fed me. I was thirsty, and you gave me a drink. I was a stranger, and you invited me into your home.

**36** I was naked, and you gave me clothing. I was sick, and you cared for me. I was in prison, and you visited me.'

**37** Then these righteous ones will reply, 'Lord, when did we ever see you hungry and feed you? Or thirsty and give you something to drink?

**38** Or a stranger and show you hospitality? Or naked and give you clothing?

**39** When did we ever see you sick or in prison and visit you?'

**40** And the King will say, 'I tell you the truth, when you did it to one of the least of these my brothers and sisters, you were doing it to me!'

**41** Then the King will turn to those on the left and say, 'Away with you, you cursed ones, into the eternal fire prepared for the devil and his demons.

**42** For I was hungry, and you didn't feed me. I was thirsty, and you didn't give me a drink.

**43** I was a stranger, and you didn't invite me into your home. I was naked, and you

266

**44** Then shall they also answer him, saying, Lord, when saw we thee an hungred, or athirst, or a stranger, or naked, or sick, or in prison, and did not minister unto thee?

**45** Then shall he answer them, saying, Verily I say unto you, Inasmuch as ye did it not to one of the least of these, ye did it not to me.

**46** And these shall go away into everlasting punishment: but the righteous into life eternal.

didn't give me clothing. I was sick and in prison, and you didn't visit me.'

**44** Then they will reply, 'Lord, when did we ever see you hungry or thirsty or a stranger or naked or sick or in prison, and not help you?'

**45** And he will answer, 'I tell you the truth, when you refused to help the least of these my brothers and sisters, you were refusing to help me.'

**46** And they will go away into eternal punishment, but the righteous will go into eternal life."

## The People, Places, and Times

**Son of Man.** Christ refers to Himself as the Son of Man approximately 80 times throughout the Gospels. Although Matthew's main focus was to portray Christ as the King (vv. 34, 40), Son of Man is intended to show Christ's humanity—i.e., He has flesh, He suffers and dies. Whereas the name Son of David connects Him to Jews and Son of God connects Him to heaven, Son of Man qualifies Him to be the representative for all mankind as the perfect sacrifice and later, our advocate. He knows what it is to be rejected, hungry, thirsty, homeless, tempted, etc.

**Mount of Olives.** The Mount of Olives is a limestone ridge of hills that covers the eastern side of Jerusalem. There are several significant events associated with this mountain in the Old and New Testaments, among them this discussion, found in Matthew 24:1–25:46 and Luke 21:5–38.

## Background

After discussions with Jewish leaders, the disciples asked Christ two follow-up questions in 24:3: "When will this (the destruction of the temple) happen and what will be the sign of your coming and of the end of the age?" Matthew 24:4–25:46, known as the

Olivet Discourse, is His response. Christ describes end times for both Jews and Gentiles. He begins by prophesying the destruction of the temple in Jerusalem, lays out some of the signs of the end, informs them of His return, and shares parables to encourage preparation. He concludes with this passage on the actions and judgement of the righteous and unrighteous.

There is debate regarding this passage. One topic is whether the "brethren" in verse 40 are Jews, believers, or all people. It is unclear. However, what is apparent is the general principle that Christ expects His followers to care for others.

Another debate is based on the story's implication that our actions earn us eternal life or eternal punishment. It is written, "For God so loved the world ... that whosoever believeth in him should ... have eternal life" (John 3:16). Paul says, "For it is by grace you have been saved, through faith—and this not from yourselves, it is the gift of God—not by works, so that no one can boast" (Ephesians 2:8–9). Faith in Christ leads to eternal life. Showing mercy and serving the poor is a by-product of a life of faith. This passage is an illustration of James' writing "What good is it, dear brothers and sisters, if you say you have faith but don't show it by your actions?... So you see, faith by itself isn't enough. Unless it produces good deeds, it is dead and useless" (James 2:14, 17, NLT). Those who love Christ demonstrate it by their actions—by loving others.

## At-A-Glance

1. The Separation (Matthew 25:31–33)
2. The Blessed (vv. 34–40)
3. The Cursed (vv. 41–46)

## In Depth

### 1. The Separation (Matthew 25:31–33)

Jesus is describing His future return as the Son of Man "in his glory," accompanied by angels. This verse shows how He is both man and God. During that time, He will come as King, judging all people from all nations, based upon their righteousness. Christ uses the division of sheep and goats to illustrate His point. Jewish shepherds were in the habit of grazing their sheep and goats together during the day. However, the animals had different temperaments and needs, which would warrant separation at night. Even though together during the day, at night they were separated because sheep preferred open air, whereas goats needed to be kept warm. Sheep tend to flock together, while goats are more independent. However, sheep are generally more aloof even though they will stay inside fences more readily than goats. Both served important domestic and religious purposes in ancient Israel, so the eternal blessing of the sheep and condemnation of the goats is somewhat arbitrary here. If anything, it may be the characteristic of acting independently which could result in not caring for those in need that is the problem (however, see Ezekiel 34 where the rams and bucks are condemned for not leaving suitable grazing for the rest of the flocks and herds).

### 2. The Blessed (vv. 34–40)

Christ speaks well of those who are righteous, saying they are blessed heirs with rights to the kingdom. This blessing is connected to the outward expression of their faith: caring for strangers in need. His disciples would have understood this to be a basic expectation: Jews were commanded to care for those less fortunate—the hungry, thirsty, naked, imprisoned. Regardless of whether the "brothers" are Jews or Gentile Christians, Christ's point is that the recipients were regarded as representatives of Him. As they were served, He was served. Even more commendable, the righteous cared for "the least"—those without authority or power, without any previous relationship, as they are called strangers. This implies that no agenda existed beyond serving.

### 3. The Cursed (vv. 41–46)

In contrast to the blessed, those on the left are marked for destruction. Instead of being commended by the King, they are rejected. Their sin is one of inaction. Their failure to provide for the needs of others served as a reflection of their lack of faith in God, and love for Him and His people. They are assigned a place along with the devil, known for his selfish and evil ways. Their unrighteous acts (or lack of righteous acts) reflect a disregard for others (much like Satan). In the end, they will find themselves cast into eternal punishment.

## Search the Scriptures

1. What does Christ promise those who are at His right hand (Matthew 25:34)?
2. In contrast, what does He promise those on His left (v. 41)?

## Discuss the Meaning

Service is a reflection of the heart. Most people would not knowingly refuse the Lord if He was in need. However, hearts turned toward Him seek to serve all, regardless of their position in life. This follows Christ's example as "He made himself nothing" in order to serve us (Philippians 2:7). How do we know that those who are poor and less fortunate are important to God? In what way is it implied that we should not show favoritism as we seek to serve?

## Lesson in Our Society

Our society is keen on assigning places of honor based on certain criteria—looks, money, popularity, charisma, etc. As a result, those who are without these things often get overlooked. This is true even for believers. It is easier to serve those who we feel deserve our help—starving children in Africa or our friends, for example. However, we often ignore and make assumptions about the homeless man we see daily. It is important to note that Christ did not "fit in" with His community. He was not attractive (Isaiah 53:2), did not have money (Luke 8:1–3), and was homeless (Matthew 8:20). When we choose to serve "the least," we are often choosing to serve those who may be in similar situations as Christ when He walked the earth.

## Make It Happen

We are often faced with opportunities to serve those who are less fortunate than we are. Our care for those in need is a reflection of our heart and relationship with Christ. Christ is serious about this reality and teaches that there are places of eternal honor and eternal punishment reserved. Pray that God shows you ways to serve others. Be open to His challenging you to think out of the box and beyond your comfort zone. It could be serving the homeless in your community, traveling to serve people in a different country, fostering or adopting a child, or caring for a missionary. However He leads, remember His words that whatever you do to the least of these, you do to Him.

## Follow the Spirit

What God wants me to do:

_____

_____

_____

_____

## Remember Your Thoughts

Special insights I have learned:

_____

_____

_____

_____

## More Light on the Text

### Matthew 25:31–46

**31 When the Son of man shall come in his glory, and all the holy angels with him, then shall he sit upon the throne of his glory: 32 and before him shall be gathered all nations; and he shall separate them one from another, as a shepherd divideth his sheep from the goats: 33 and he shall set the sheep on his right hand, but the goats on the left.**

This passage of Scripture is not so much a parable as it is prophecy. It does, however, have some parabolic traits in that it details the shepherd, sheep, and goats. The point here is to describe the events of Jesus' second coming. When Christ returns, He will come back in His full glory, the same glory that clothed Him before He descended from heaven. His angels will accompany Him and will help gather all the people together at the same time. The Jews and Gentiles will not assemble in two different groups. Every nation will receive the same judgment before God.

Once more, Jesus teaches in a context with which the Jews were familiar. Sheep are usually milder and gentler while goats are more unruly and boisterous. Both animals grazed together during the daytime but were separated at night. In this passage, the sheep go one way and the goats go another. The right side symbolizes blessing, honor, and favor; the left side symbolizes worthlessness and condemnation.

**34 Then shall the King say unto them on his right hand, Come, ye blessed of my Father, inherit the kingdom prepared for you from the foundation of the world:**

Here, Jesus refers to Himself as "King" for the first and only time in Scripture. He called Himself by other titles, and in so doing used the first person, e.g., "I am the good shepherd." In this verse, He uses the third person. Although this is in the third person, we know that Jesus is referring to Himself since the King in this passage refers to God as "my Father."

Once the sheep completely separated, Jesus will address them, inviting them into God's kingdom. Matthew uses the Greek word *kleronomeo* (**klay-ro-no-MEH-oh**), meaning "to inherit or possess," signaling to the sheep to take possession of the kingdom. Jesus calls them blessed, not because of what they received (grace), but for what they did with what they received. He further says that this place has been prepared specifically for them since the beginning of the world.

**35 for I was an hungered, and ye gave me meat: I was thirsty, and ye gave me drink: I was a stranger, and ye took me in: 36 naked, and ye clothed me: I was sick, and ye visited me: I was in prison, and ye came unto me.**

Jesus lists some of the acts of compassion the sheep performed. The need for compassion still exists today, and many people feed the hungry, satisfy the thirsty, house the homeless, clothe the destitute, and visit the sick and imprisoned. In all of these actions Jesus said they encountered Him.

**37 Then shall the righteous answer him, saying, Lord, when saw we thee an hungered, and fed thee? or thirsty, and gave thee drink? 38 When saw we thee a stranger, and took thee in? or naked, and clothed thee? 39 Or when saw we thee sick, or in prison, and came unto thee?**

Few people have seen Jesus with unmistakable certainty. Though possible, it is a bit unlikely that anyone living today has had a face-to-face encounter with the Savior. Conversely, we may have seen Christ in others or recognized an opportunity to serve Him by ministering to others.

Here the righteous ask the King some questions. According to what they knew about Christ, He was never hungry, thirsty, a stranger, naked, sick, or imprisoned, and as a result they were confused. Evidently, they sacrificed themselves to attend to someone else, and their charity pleased God.

**40 And the King shall answer and say unto them, Verily I say unto you, Inasmuch as ye have done it unto one of the least of these my brethren, ye have done it unto me.**

Jesus calms the sheep by referring them to their merciful deeds born of God's love for them. The brethren of Christ were not only His siblings; they included all people who inhabited the land and shared a bond with Christ through His sufferings and afflictions. Jesus stresses the "least" of His brethren, highlighting the humility exercised by the righteous in serving those thought unworthy of service. He then identifies with those people, making their pain, sorrow, and tribulation His own.

**41 Then shall he say also unto them on the left hand, Depart from me, ye cursed, into everlasting fire, prepared for the devil and his angels: 42 for I was an hungered, and ye gave me no meat: I was thirsty, and ye gave me no drink: 43 I was a stranger, and ye took me not in: naked, and ye clothed me not: sick, and in prison, and ye visited me not.**

The Lord uses the same standards for both groups and parallels them to each other. Whereas Jesus invited those on the right to come, He commands those on the left to depart. Because the goats chose not to serve those in need, they were condemned to death. Just as God made the kingdom of heaven ready for the righteous, He made the everlasting fire ready for the unrighteous (Revelation 20:11–15).

Originally the everlasting fire was designated for Satan and his followers. But since the entrance of sin into the world and the introduction of death by sin, man was destined to join Satan in this inferno. God did not prepare this place for mankind because He is "not willing that any should perish" (2 Peter 3:9). But since God is just, man's disobedience demanded that he be punished unless he made proper atonement. Christ made that atonement, so man must live through the One who paid his debt. Otherwise, he must suffer God's judgment.

**44 Then shall they also answer him, saying, Lord, when saw we thee an hungered, or athirst, or a stranger, or naked, or sick, or in prison, and did not minister unto thee? 45 Then shall he answer them, saying, Verily I say unto you, Inasmuch as ye did it not to one of the least of these, ye did it not to me. 46 And these shall go away into everlasting punishment: but the righteous into life eternal.**

The goats' reply echoes the sheep's, but there may be a difference in the tone. While the sheep may have been pleasantly surprised by Jesus' report, the goats were desperately shocked by His convicting words. They pleaded hopelessly after hearing their sentence, but the King had rendered His ruling.

This contrast brings another issue to the surface. Neither the sheep nor the goats appear puzzled by their destination, but they seem bewildered by the reason for going there. None of them expected to live or die based on how they treated Jesus because no one believed they ever had the opportunity.

A similar circumstance exists today. Many people are not aware of the good they do through the Holy Spirit, and many don't recognize the chance to love as Christ loved and to serve Him by serving others.

Furthermore, some people believe they are sheep, when God sees them as goats. Jesus reiterates that the service done to others was also done to Him. Our service to our fellow man is not just leftover charity for those who are destitute but an act of service to Christ Himself.

Sources:

*Hebrew-Greek Key Word Study Bible, King James Version.* Chattanooga, TN: AMG Publishers, Inc., 1991.

Keener, Craig S. *The IVP Bible Background Commentary: New Testament.* Downers Grove, IL: Intervarsity Press, 1993. 118–119.

Radmacher, Earl D., ed. *Nelson Study Bible, New King James Version.* Nashville, TN: Thomas Nelson Publishers, 1997. 1620–1625.

Ryrie, Charles C. *Ryrie Study Bible, New International Version.* Chicago, IL: Moody Press, 1986. 1358.

Unger, Merrill F. *The New Unger's Bible Dictionary*. Chicago, IL: Moody Press, 1988. 72, 940–994, 1211.

Walvoord, John F., and Roy B. Zuck, eds. *The Bible Knowledge Commentary: New Testament*. Wheaton, IL: Victor Books, SP Publications, Inc., 1983. 80–81.

## Say It Correctly

Recipient. ri-**CIP**-ee-ent.

## Daily Bible Readings

**MONDAY**
You Must Be Ready
(Matthew 24:37–44)

**TUESDAY**
Compassion and Justice for the Poor
(Leviticus 19:9–15)

**WEDNESDAY**
Open Your Hand to the Poor
(Deuteronomy 15:7–11)

**THURSDAY**
Celebrate with Presents for the Poor
(Esther 9:19–23)

**FRIDAY**
Do Not Forget the Oppressed
(Psalm 10:12–18)

**SATURDAY**
Share Resources with the Poor
(Romans 15:22–28)

**SUNDAY**
Minister to the Least
(Matthew 25:31–46)

# Notes

_____

_____

_____

_____

# Teaching Tips

## Words You Should Know

**A. Wiles** (Ephesians 6:11) *methodeia* (Gk.)—Cunning arts, deceit, craft, trickery.

**B. Withstand** (v. 13) *anthistemi* (Gk.)—To set one's self against, to withstand, oppose.

## Teacher Preparation

**Unifying Principle—Always Be Prepared.** Only proper preparation can give assurance that certain things are accomplished. What does one do to be prepared? Putting on the whole armor of God teaches that in order to best serve Him, Christians need to fortify themselves with truth, righteousness, peace, faith, salvation, the Word of God, and prayer.

**A.** Read the Bible Background and Devotional Readings.

**B.** Complete Lesson 12 in the *Precepts For Living Personal Study Guide®*.

**C.** Reread the Focal Verses in a modern translation.

## O—Open the Lesson

**A.** Open with prayer.

**B.** Have students read the Aim for Change in unison.

**C.** Ask for a volunteer to read the In Focus story.

**D.** Discuss what it means to experience spiritual warfare.

## P—Present the Scriptures

**A.** Ask for volunteers to read the Focal Verses and The People, Places, and Times. Discuss.

**B.** Read and discuss the Background section.

**C.** Encourage students to praise God for giving them spiritual armor to withstand the assaults of the enemy.

## E—Explore the Meaning

**A.** Review and discuss the Search the Scriptures and Discuss the Meaning questions and the Lesson in Our Society section.

**B.** Ask students to share the most significant point they learned and how to use that point this week.

## N—Next Steps for Application

**A.** Complete the Follow the Spirit and Remember Your Thoughts sections.

**B.** Remind students to read the Daily Bible Readings in preparation for next week's lesson.

**C.** Close in prayer, thanking God for victory in spiritual warfare.

## Worship Guide

For the Superintendent or Teacher
Theme: Clothed and Ready
Song: "I'm a Soldier (in the Army of the Lord)"
Devotional Reading: Colossians 3:12–17

# Clothed and Ready

**Bible Background • EPHESIANS 6:10–20**
**Printed Text • EPHESIANS 6:10–20**
**Devotional Reading • COLOSSIANS 3:12–17**

## —————————— Aim for Change ——————————

By the end of the lesson, we will: EXAMINE the epistle's teaching to put on the whole armor of God; VALUE the feeling of being prepared to serve God; and ARM ourselves with those character traits needed to best serve God.

## In Focus

Clarence did not know how to respond. So many questions came his way. It took him a while to even think clearly about what just happened. His supervisor Dave had just singled him out and insulted him regarding his work. Everyone around the office knew that he was the most hard-working and accomplished employee at the company. How could this happen? Clarence understood why. He made it known that he was a Christian. His supervisor had grown up as an atheist and believed that religion was obsolete and ruining society. Once he found out Clarence was a Christian, he gave him a large workload and asked him to take on the most difficult projects. When he saw that this did not faze Clarence, he lashed out at him. Now all of his co-workers were curious about Clarence's peace and self-control. It seemed God had prepared him for this moment.

*In times of spiritual warfare, we can trust God to equip us with everything we need for the battles of life.*

## —————————— Keep in Mind ——————————

"Put on the whole armour of God, that ye may be able to stand against the wiles of the devil" (Ephesians 6:11).

"Put on the whole armour of God, that ye may be able to stand against the wiles of the devil" (Ephesians 6:11).

## Focal Verses

**KJV** **Ephesians 6:10** Finally, my brethren, be strong in the Lord, and in the power of his might.

**11** Put on the whole armour of God, that ye may be able to stand against the wiles of the devil.

**12** For we wrestle not against flesh and blood, but against principalities, against powers, against the rulers of the darkness of this world, against spiritual wickedness in high places.

**13** Wherefore take unto you the whole armour of God, that ye may be able to withstand in the evil day, and having done all, to stand.

**14** Stand therefore, having your loins girt about with truth, and having on the breastplate of righteousness;

**15** And your feet shod with the preparation of the gospel of peace;

**16** Above all, taking the shield of faith, wherewith ye shall be able to quench all the fiery darts of the wicked.

**17** And take the helmet of salvation, and the sword of the Spirit, which is the word of God:

**18** Praying always with all prayer and supplication in the Spirit, and watching thereunto with all perseverance and supplication for all saints;

**19** And for me, that utterance may be given unto me, that I may open my mouth boldly, to make known the mystery of the gospel,

**20** For which I am an ambassador in bonds: that therein I may speak boldly, as I ought to speak.

**NLT** **Ephesians 6:10** A final word: Be strong in the Lord and in his mighty power.

**11** Put on all of God's armor so that you will be able to stand firm against all strategies of the devil.

**12** For we are not fighting against flesh-and-blood enemies, but against evil rulers and authorities of the unseen world, against mighty powers in this dark world, and against evil spirits in the heavenly places.

**13** Therefore, put on every piece of God's armor so you will be able to resist the enemy in the time of evil. Then after the battle you will still be standing firm.

**14** Stand your ground, putting on the belt of truth and the body armor of God's righteousness.

**15** For shoes, put on the peace that comes from the Good News so that you will be fully prepared.

**16** In addition to all of these, hold up the shield of faith to stop the fiery arrows of the devil.

**17** Put on salvation as your helmet, and take the sword of the Spirit, which is the word of God.

**18** Pray in the Spirit at all times and on every occasion. Stay alert and be persistent in your prayers for all believers everywhere.

**19** And pray for me, too. Ask God to give me the right words so I can boldly explain God's mysterious plan that the Good News is for Jews and Gentiles alike.

**20** I am in chains now, still preaching this message as God's ambassador. So pray that I will keep on speaking boldly for him, as I should.

## The People, Places, and Times

**Principalities and Powers.** These are the evil and malicious spirits that oppose God and His people, both in the earthly realm and the heavenly realm (1:3, 20–21; 3:10). These powers were created by God and appear to be fallen angels that have rebelled against Him. Scripture declares that Jesus is the ultimate authority over them and that He disarmed them through His death on the Cross. Believers are called to resist and defeat these powers in our lives through the wisdom and power of God.

**Armor.** Armor has been used in battle since ancient times. The pieces of armor included resources for both offense and defense. The equipment of a Roman soldier was consistent for every soldier: a breastplate, a girdle or belt, a large door-like shield, a helmet, sword, spears, and sandals. In Paul's description of the Christian armor, it can be noted that there is no mention of a spear.

## Background

Ephesians is unique among the epistles, as it does not explicitly address a particular problem or concern in the church of Ephesus. It can best described as a model for what the church is supposed to be. In Ephesians, Paul has written a treatise defining what it means to be the church. He communicates to them that they are recipients of every spiritual blessing in Jesus Christ. They are saved by God's grace and mandated to practice good works and walk in a manner worthy of the calling they have received. Paul then proceeds to let them know how to live as the church. They are to exhibit morally pure lives and be filled with the Spirit. With this comes the ability to walk wisely and use their time for godly purposes. They are to mutually submit to one another, and this submission encompasses their home and work life.

Paul then concludes his letter with an exhortation to battle. The church is now described in a military perspective. Paul exhorts the Ephesian believers to be strong in the Lord and to put on the whole armor of God. He lets them know that they have a spiritual enemy who is out to destroy them. Then he proceeds to list the pieces of armor they will need in this battle.

## At-A-Glance

1. The Call to Arms (Ephesians 6:10–13)
2. The Soldier's Armor (vv. 14–17)
3. The Call to Prayer (vv. 18–20)

## In Depth

**1. The Call to Arms (Ephesians 6:10–13)**

Paul exhorts the Ephesian believers to be strong in the Lord and in His power. He gives them this exhortation for two reasons. The first is that with all the things he said they have been blessed with and all the duties they have been given, Satan will most definitely want to destroy them. Therefore, they need to be plugged into God's mighty power. The second reason is that they are not fighting a physical fight. Paul says that they do not wrestle against flesh and blood but against a hierarchy of evil spiritual forces.

Paul calls the believers to not only arm themselves with God's power, but further explains that believers ought to put on the full armor of God. This will enable followers of Jesus to resist the assaults of the enemy in the evil day. This evil day is the time of trial and testing that we all will experience in our walk with Jesus. Paul concludes his call to arms with an exhortation to stand. This is the final act of resistance. After preparing, Paul admonishes the believer to stand fully armed in the day of trouble.

## 2. The Soldier's Armor (vv. 14–17)

Next Paul describes the armor of God. This armor resembles the armor of a Roman soldier. It consists of a belt, breastplate sandals, shield, helmet, and sword. Paul describes these items as the virtues the Christian must put on in the fight against their spiritual adversaries. The equipment is listed in the exact order the Roman soldier would put them on. The first piece of armor is the belt of truth. The next piece of armor is the breastplate of righteousness. After the breastplate is the footgear, the readiness of the Gospel of peace.

Then Paul admonishes the Ephesian believers to take up the shield of faith. He also tells them to take the helmet of salvation. Next he calls them to take up the sword of the Spirit. He further explains that this is the Word of God. Being furnished with all these items, the Christian is completely armored and prepared for the battle.

## 3. The Call to Prayer (vv. 18–20)

The secret weapon of prayer is the last piece of the Christian's equipment for battle. Paul exhorts them to use all kinds of prayers in the battle against the spiritual forces of darkness. This praying and supplication is to be done "in the Spirit"; that is, these prayers should be motivated and directed by the Spirit of God, not selfish and man-centered ramblings. These prayers also are to be directed toward all the saints. We are called not only to look after ourselves but to stand with all of our brothers and sisters in Christ. We see here that our secret weapon consists of all kinds of prayers, being prayed in the Spirit, for all the saints.

Lastly, Paul makes a prayer request. He asks for them to pray for him. He is chained to a Roman guard and awaiting trial. His obvious prayer request would be that he would be released. Instead, Paul asks them to pray that he would preach the Gospel boldly. He wants the Lord to give Him not only courage but also the right words to say. His mind is on the Gospel being advanced. This is the true battle for the believer. It is not about managing our sin or maintaining our religious piety. It is a battle for the hearts and minds of those who do not know Jesus as Lord. This is the reason we need to make sure we are clothed and ready for battle.

## Search the Scriptures

1. Whom does Paul identify as the believers' opponent in battle (Ephesians 6:12)?

2. What is the purpose of taking up the shield of faith (v. 16)?

## Discuss the Meaning

1. What are situations where the Lord calls believers to put on the full armor of God and stand?

2. How can we be strong in the Lord and in the power of His might?

## Lesson in Our Society

The world is filled with fighting and hostility. Groups are often pitted against each other in opposition. Many lines are drawn in the sand, and we often resort to uncharitable words and even physical violence. The people of God are called to fight, but not against flesh and blood. We are engaged in a war against spiritual forces of darkness. Wherever we see opposition to God and His Gospel, we must know that it cannot be defeated by mere human methods. We must put on the full armor of God and rely on His power. It is our duty in these times to be clothed and ready.

## Make It Happen

The next time you are in a situation where your faith is being challenged or you are experiencing persecution, be sure to see the real enemy. Pray that the Lord would fill you with "the power of his might" and put on the whole armor of God. Create a checklist and examine whether you are clothed and ready with the full armor of God. If you are lacking a piece of equipment, pray that God would give it to you and share this with another Christian brother or sister who can mentor you in this area.

## Follow the Spirit

What God wants me to do:

_____

_____

_____

_____

## Remember Your Thoughts

Special insights I have learned:

_____

_____

_____

_____

## More Light on the Text

### Ephesians 6:10–20

Paul concludes this letter by dealing with a very serious topic: spiritual warfare, which unfortunately is usually overlooked or down-played by many churches. He charges the church to be aware of the type of conflict they are facing in the world, and summons them to prepare for battle. This battle, Paul reminds them, is not simply against humans, but against forces of evil that are not visible to the human eyes; they are not physical but spiritual. Therefore, the battle is spiritual, and as such, it must be fought and won with spiritual weaponry. Paul describes with precision, in the following passage, the church's weapons for this inescapable battle. He exhorts them to fully equip themselves with the divine armor in order to overcome.

**6:10 Finally, my brethren, be strong in the Lord, and in the power of his might. 11 Put on the whole armor of God, that ye may be able to stand against the wiles of the devil.**

Paul begins by addressing his readers as "my brethren," which emphasizes the bond and intimate relationship that exists between him and the Ephesian church. It also calls for their serious attention and intensifies the importance of the subject matter. He urges them to be strong (Gk. *endunamoo*, **en-doo-nah-MOH-oh**, to empower, to increase in strength) in the Lord and in the power (Gk. *kratos*, **KRAH-tose**, vigor or strength) of His might (Gk. *ischus*, **iss-KHOOS**, ability, power, or strength). Using these synonyms, Paul calls on the church to rely totally on the Lord for the strength and ability to face the onslaught of the enemy that surrounds them. He says in effect that only with a close and steadfast relationship with the Lord (the source of all power) will they be able to fight the battle that constantly awaits them in the world.

Jesus told His disciples that without Him, they could do nothing (John 15:1–5), but Paul writes, "I can do all things through Christ which strengtheneth me" (Philippians 4:13; cf. 2 Corinthians 12:9–10; 1 Timothy 1:12). We must totally rely on God's strength and power because He is all-powerful and

His might is infinite, as evidenced in creation and in history. By His power and strength, God not only created the heavens and the earth, but He caused the Red Sea and the Jordan River to be driven back, the moon to stand still, the mountains to tremble, and the rocks to melt. He raised Christ from the dead (Ephesians 1:20) and made alive those who were dead in trespasses and sins (2:1). In view of these and other deeds which reveal God's omnipotence in history, Paul exhorts believers to hold fast in the Lord, the one who "is able to do exceeding abundantly above all that we ask or think, according to the power that worketh in us" (3:20).

Although we rely totally on the strength and might of God, we must equip ourselves with the whole armor (Gk. *panoplia*, **pan-op-LEE-a**, full, total, or complete armor) of God, that ye may be able to stand against the wiles of the devil. We must recall at this point that Paul is writing from prison in Rome and probably guarded by a well-dressed and completely equipped soldier or soldiers. He has a complete picture and image of a soldier in military regalia and readiness for battle. He, therefore, writes to the brethren in Ephesus, and indeed Christians of all times, to be completely dressed and ready for battle. However, the Christian's armor is not like the Roman's, which is physical—it is God's armor, which is spiritual. It is this type of military regalia we use to withstand and overcome the wiles or craftiness of the devil.

There are a few things to learn here about the devil. First, it is a fact that demons, evil spirits, Satan, devils, or whatever name given them exist contrary to the belief of many today who say that evil spirits are a myth. However, we must be careful not to give the devil a place he does not deserve by attributing to him everything adverse that happens. We must not be afraid of him. This often leads to the worship of Satan and his agents. We must acknowledge their existence as Paul did, but we are not to be afraid of them or pay them homage.

Second, we must acknowledge that they possess some power, although their power is limited. God's power is unlimited and superior. Although evil spirits exist, we should not expend our energy daily thinking about and fighting them at the expense of other areas of ministry, as some churches do today. Instead, we must be ready for the enemy at all times by being equipped with God's own armor, which He has made available to us.

Third, we must acknowledge that Satan, the devil, is cunning and crafty, full of fury, and prowls around like a roaring lion looking for someone to devour (1 Peter 5:8, NIV). Having been cast out of heaven, he is full of fury and envy. His hatred is against God, His people, and all they stand for. He has a well-organized army and is out to destroy God's kingdom and to bring with him as many people as possible into hell. Satan's craftiness can be seen throughout Scripture. He mixes falsehood with some truth to make it plausible (Genesis 3:4, 5, 22); quotes Scripture out of context (Matthew 4:6); and masquerades as an angel of light (2 Corinthians 11:14). Therefore, we must be properly equipped to fight him, not with human armor but God's, Paul says. The call here is urgent.

**12 For we wrestle not against flesh and blood, but against principalities, against powers, against the rulers of the darkness of this world, against spiritual wickedness in high places. 13 Wherefore take unto you the whole armor of God, that ye may be able to withstand in the evil day, and having done all, to stand.**

After Paul establishes the fact of the devil's existence and power and urges his audience to be fully equipped with God's own armor, Paul now gives them the reason they should be so equipped: we are not fighting against "flesh and blood," i.e., against mere, frail humans (Galatians 1:16), with all their physical and mental weakness (Matthew 16:17; 1 Corinthians 15:50). Rather, we are fighting against all types of forces in all realms of life. However, the enemy knows how to use humans to do his work, so we are often deceived into thinking that the fight is against another human being.

Paul categorizes these forces as "principalities and powers" (Gk. Gk. *arche*, **ar-KHAY**, realm, principality; *exousia*, **ek-soo-SEE-ah,** authorities; cf. Ephesians 1:21), as the "rulers of the darkness of this world," which speaks of those who are in tyrannical control of the world of ignorance and sin. We are also fighting against spiritual forces of "wickedness in high places" (Gk. *epouranios*, **ep-oo-RAH-nee-ose**, heavenly places). Heavenly places here is the same word and therefore the same realm where Christ is enthroned at God's right hand and therefore has a special position and power above all others inhabiting this realm (1:20). It is also where the redeemed are seated with Him (2:6) as well as the home of the obedient angels (3:10).

Paul, in effect, says that since we are contending against an innumerable host of spiritual forces, we must be fully equipped and put on the full armor of God (v. 11). Paul repeats this call in verse 13. The repetition of this call intensifies its urgency. The word "wrestle" used in verse 12 can be misleading; since wrestling is viewed as a sport, it therefore can erroneously minimize the magnitude of the battle that is facing the Christian.

The explanation is probably that the battle is so intense and violent that it is like hand-to-hand combat. This battle is not like the phony wrestling on television, which is for entertainment and monetary gain;

the spiritual battle is serious and therefore requires a complete armament. It is only with such divine armament that we would "be able to withstand in the evil day," that is, in the day of severe trial and temptation and onslaught of the evil one (cf. Psalm 49:5). The implication here is that we must always be ready and on guard since we do not know when these crises will occur.

**14 Stand therefore, having your loins girt about with truth, and having on the breastplate of righteousness;**

To "stand," here and in verse 11, does not imply passivity, where a soldier is pictured standing like a brick wall waiting for Satan's attack. Rather, Paul paints a picture of a soldier equipped and drawn up in battle array, rushing into war making full use of God's weapons of war for attacks and defense. It is then that the soldier would be able to stand his ground and resist the evil one, and the devil will flee from him (James 4:7; cf. Matthew 10:22). The picture is that of a soldier who is alert, vigilant, one that is never asleep and never taken unaware by the devil, who cunningly likes to attack at odd times. This is the picture of the Christian Paul paints here, a strong and stable Christian who remains firm against the wiles of the devil (v. 11), even in a time of crisis or pressure.

In the next five verses, Paul details the six major pieces of the soldier's armor and gives the function of each one of them: the belt, the breastplate, the boots, the shield, the helmet, and the sword. They represent truth, righteousness, the Gospel of peace, faith, salvation, and the Word of God, respectively. All these pieces of spiritual armor equip us to battle against the evil powers.

The first piece of equipment which Paul lists is the belt of truth: "having your loins girt about with truth." The belt or the girdle, usually made of leather, is tied around the waist and used to brace the armor tight against the body. As the soldier buckles the belt, he feels a sense of hidden strength and confidence. One can see this watching people prepare to fight. One of the first things the fighters can do is take off their hair scarf or neck piece, tie it around their waist, and confidently beckon the other for a fight. As he or she waits for the other person to make a move, one could sense his or her feeling of confidence and inner strength. The belt is also used to hold daggers, swords, and other weapons to give the soldier freedom of movement when marching.

Paul says that the Christian's belt is truth. The two possible types of truth meant here are (1) the truth, as God's revelation in Christ and the Scripture, and (2) truth, as in honesty or integrity. Only the truth can dispel the devil's lies and set us free (John 8:31–36, 43–45). The psalmist says that God requires truth in the inward being (Psalm 51:6), and Paul says that we are to speak the truth in love (Ephesians 4:15). A common piece of advice is that if you speak the truth the first time, you will not worry to find another lie in future. Truth will always prevail, and lies and dishonesty will always be exposed. Honesty and integrity are marks of bravery, but lies are a sign of cowardice. The opposite of truth is lies, and the Bible says that Satan is the father of lies (John 8:44, NIV). Therefore we cannot beat him at his own game. Truth is the only thing that will dispel him, because he hates truth.

The second piece of the Christian's weaponry Paul mentions here is the breastplate (Gk. *thorax*, **THO-raks**) of righteousness. A breastplate is described as the armor that covers the body from neck to the thighs, the vital parts of the body. It consists of two parts, one for the back and the other for the front. Here, Paul says that the equipment for protection is righteousness (Gk. *dikaiosune*, **dee-keye-oh-SOO-nay**), which is often translated in Pauline epistles as "justification." This is theologically explained as the process whereby God through Christ puts the sinner in a right relationship with Himself. The most amazing gift for unjust sinners is to stand before the almighty, just God and not to be condemned, but accepted and clothed with God's righteousness through Christ as if they had not sinned. It is the believer's assurance that through Christ, all of our sins are forgiven and the barrier between God and us has been removed (Isaiah 59:1–2). This is the work of grace, which God wrought through the death of His Son Jesus on the Cross.

One of Satan's greatest weapons is slander, to accuse us through our conscience. Therefore, there is no greater defensive weapon for the Christian against the slanderous attack of the devil than the assurance of a right relationship with the Father through His Son (2 Corinthians 5:21). Paul assures the Roman believers of this fact: "There is therefore now no condemnation to them, which are in Christ Jesus, who walk not after the flesh, but after the Spirit ... Who shall lay any thing to the charge of God's elect? It is God that justifieth. Who is he that condemneth? It is Christ that died, yea rather, that is risen again, who is even at the right hand of God, who also maketh intercession for us" (Romans 8:1, 33–34). This relationship disarms the devil and offers protection for the Christian.

To successfully ward off the devil's unceasing slanderous attack, we must maintain that relationship with the Father by using the weapons of righteousness for the right hand and for the left (2 Corinthians 6:7). The righteousness referred to here, as well as in Ephesians 4:24 and 5:9, is a moral righteousness. Just as the Christian is to cultivate truth to overcome the deceptions of the devil, he also has to cultivate righteousness (i.e., moral integrity) in order to overcome the devil's slanderous attacks. Without integrity and a clear conscience, one cannot defend oneself against the accusations of the devil, who accuses the brethren night and day (Revelation 12:10).

**15 And your feet shod with the preparation of the gospel of peace;**

The next weapon in the apostle's list for warfare is the boot: the preparation of the Gospel of peace. The word translated "preparation" is the Greek word *hetoimasia* (**heh-toy-mah-SEE-ah**), which means "readiness, the act of preparedness." Paul says that the Christian should put on the Gospel of peace as his army boots. Boots protect soldiers from slipping, and from thorns or objects that can pierce through their feet and thereby hinder them from marching forward into battle. The Gospel (Good News) of peace is the protective mechanism by which we are shielded from the dangerous gimmicks the devil lays in our path to hinder our walk with the Lord. The more we are ready and prepared to testify about or confess Christ to others, the better we are protected from backsliding and falling into Satan's traps and temptation. This verse is also an allusion to the prophet Isaiah's proclamation, "How beautiful upon the mountains are the feet of him that bringeth good tidings, that publisheth peace" (from Isaiah 52:7, cf. Romans 10:15). The devil hates the Gospel (Good News) of Jesus Christ, because it is the power of God and salvation to everyone that believes (Romans 1:16).

Boots are a vital part of a soldier's armor, and with them securely strapped on, the soldier feels a certain amount of confidence and is ready for action. Without boots, the soldier will be ill-equipped and unprepared for battle.

**16 Above all, taking the shield of faith, wherewith ye shall be able to quench all the fiery darts of the wicked.**

The fourth weapon is the shield of faith, which we must take above all (Gk. *epi pasin*, **eh-PEE PA-sin**) in the sense that it is an indispensable part of the whole armor, rather than the most important part. The phrase can be rendered: "along with or besides all these, take also the shield of faith." The Greek word here, *thureos* (**thoo-reh-OHS**), was a large oblong, four-cornered shield, which covered the whole body, rather than the small round one that covered only a smaller part of the body. The *thureos* is specially designed to ward off all types of dangerous darts or missiles thrown, such as the arrows, javelins, spears, or stones that were used then.

The fiery darts also probably refer to the combustible arrowheads that set fire to the enemy's fortifications, boats, houses, or wooden shields. In order to quench the fiery darts, the shields are covered with metals. What are the fiery darts of the devil as they relate to the Christian warfare? They no doubt include the following: evil thoughts, lusts, false guilt, sinful passions, temptation of various kinds, doubts, disobedience, rebellion, malice, and fear (cf. 1 Corinthians 10:13–14; 2 Corinthians 10:4–6; James 1:13–15, etc.). The devil ceaselessly launches all these deadly, fire-tipped darts at us daily in different forms and combinations. There is one weapon to quench or extinguish them: the shield of faith. Proverbs 30:5 says that God is a shield to them that put their trust in Him. Faith here is reliance in and taking hold of the promises of God in the work Christ fulfilled on the Cross (1:20–22). In times of temptation, doubts, and depression, faith is claiming the power of God (Philippians 4:13). With faith, we can move mountains, Jesus told His disciples (Matthew 17:20; Luke 17:6).

**17 And take the helmet of salvation, and the sword of the Spirit, which is the word of God:**

Paul adds two more pieces of warfare equipment to the list: the helmet of salvation and the sword of the Spirit. We are to take these as weapons to fight the wicked one. Paul calls the helmet "the hope of salvation" in 1 Thessalonians 5:8, while here it is the "helmet of salvation." There seems to be no apparent difference in these passages, since salvation is both a present and a future reality. Hence, salvation is anchored in hope. This metaphor is used in the Old Testament, where the Lord wears the helmet of salvation on His head as He goes to vindicate His people, who had been oppressed (Isaiah 59:17). Therefore, just as soldiers receive a helmet from their army superiors in charge of supplies, Paul says we are to take (Gk. *dechomai*, **DE-kho-my**, to receive or accept) salvation through faith as a gift from God (2:8). The ancient helmets were cast from iron and brass (1 Samuel 17:5, 38) and they offered protection for the head like the breastplate provided for the heart. Salvation is also a protective (defensive) gear that assures the Christian in both the present and the future during times of crisis and persecutions. The assurance of God's salvation, which He has wrought through Christ in us, strengthens and carries the Christian to go on fighting without giving up, even in very difficult situations. It is the confidence that what God has begun in him, He will surely bring to completion (Philippians 1:6; cf. Psalm 138:8).

The final weapon that Paul urges the Christian to take is the sword of the Spirit.

While all the other five listed are primarily weapons for defense or protection, the sword is the only weapon which can clearly be used for both offense and defense. The word translated "sword" is the Greek word *machaira* (**MAH-kheye-rah**), which specifically refers to a small or short sword as opposed to a large or long one. Therefore, the combat envisaged here is in close quarters. The Christian's weapon of offense is the sword of the Spirit (or "spiritual sword"), which Paul identifies immediately as the Word (Gk. *rhema*, **RAY-ma**, the spoken word) of God. Jesus foreshadowed the importance of the Spirit's words when He promised His disciples that He would fill their lips with words through the Spirit when they are brought before magistrates (Matthew 10:17–20).

The Bible says that the Word of God is powerful and sharper than a double-edged sword (Hebrew 4:12), and so we ought to use it with confidence. The Word of God refers to both the written Word (the Scripture) inspired by the Holy Spirit (2 Timothy 3:16; 2 Peter 1:21) and the spoken word (*rhema*), the confession and testimony which will stand forever (Isaiah 40:8). Jesus applied the Word to fight Satan's temptations in the wilderness of Judea (Luke 4:1–13). John records the victory of the saints against Satan, saying, "And they overcame him by the blood of the Lamb, and by the word of their testimony" (from Revelation 12:11). The Word of God is the greatest weapon with which we can fight the devil and his gimmicks. It is amazing what victory we can have when we apply the Word of God. Through it, we dispel doubts, fears, and guilt; by it Satan is put to flight, and assurance of salvation is secured in our hearts.

The complete armor of God is made available to every Christian: truth as the girdle, righteousness as the breastplate, the Gospel as the boots, faith as the shield, salvation as the helmet, and the Word of God as the Spirit's sword (or the spiritual sword). Since the battle is not against humans, but spirits, we need all the specified weapons without leaving any out, so that we can withstand and stand firm against Satan's ceaseless onslaught against us. We must be fully equipped, always ready for battle.

**18 Praying always with all prayer and supplication in the Spirit, and watching thereunto with all perseverance and supplication for all saints; 19 And for me, that utterance may be given unto me, that I may open my mouth boldly, to make known the mystery of the gospel, 20 For which I am an ambassador in bonds: that therein I may speak boldly, as I ought to speak.**

After listing all the armor the Christian should put in use to fight against the wiles and wickedness of the devil, Paul explains how to use them by praying. Prayer and the Word are the two most important aspects of Christian living. Without either or both of them, the Christian's life is in jeopardy, and his life may even be at the mercy of Satan and his agents. No soldier of Christ can do anything on his or her own power without seeking strength and blessing from God, the all-powerful Father, even though he or she may have all their weapons. As a believer puts each piece of the armor on and makes use of it, he or she must rely on God through prayer. Hence, Paul says, put on the whole armor while praying and watching (vv. 18–20).

Prayer is not a one-time exercise, but should be done always (at all times), that is, constantly or habitually with all variety of prayers being "all prayer and supplication." The phrase "all prayer" (Gk. *pas,* **PAHS,** all; *proseuche,* **pro-sew-KHEE,** prayer) probably includes both public and private, church and family prayer. It will consist of supplication

(Gk. *deesis,* **DEH-ay-sees**), i.e., making a special request or seeking favor for some special necessity from God. It speaks of being specific instead of general in prayer. It should be done at all times, as we have already intimated, and it should be done through the Holy Spirit, who makes intercession for us even when we do not know how or what to pray (Romans 8:26–27, 34).

Paul calls on us to be alert (Gk. *agrupneo,* **ah-groop-NEH-oh,** to watch, be attentive) as we pray and with perseverance (Gk. *proskarteresis,* **pros-kar-TEH-ray-sees**) as we make supplication for the saints. This means we must be persistent and resolute in our prayer, not only for ourselves, but also for all members of the family of God in which we now belong. We shall not only be alert and watchful of Satan's strategies; we should be alert to know or be aware of the needs of others so that we can pray objectively, instead of rambling away without tangible things to pray for as we intercede for others.

Paul now, for the first time in the entire letter, makes a request for himself. He asks that when prayer is made on behalf of all the saints, they should remember him in a special way in their prayers. His two-fold request is clear, simple, and noble. First, he asks that God might give him the utterance (logos, i.e., the word) or the correct message when he opens his mouth to speak (Matthew 10:19); and second, that God might give him the courage at all times to deliver the message in a proper manner (Acts 4:13). The prayer request is important to him since it is for the sake of the Gospel, he says, "for which I am an ambassador in chains" (from v. 20, NKJV).

This echoes his request in Colossians 4:2–3, that he be endowed with power and boldness so that he could continue to make known the mystery of the Gospel. What is that mystery of the Gospel? That through Christ, there is full salvation for everyone who comes to Him in faith, both Jew and Gentile, and it is free. That through Christ the barrier of hostility which formerly existed between the Jews and Gentiles has now been removed and they are now one in God's new family (Ephesians 3:3–7, 9; cf. Romans 16:25; Colossians 1:26; 2:2). The Gospel is the mystery, which God through Christ made known, and Paul, though imprisoned at the time in a Roman jail, is an ambassador charged to proclaim this Good News.

Sources:
Lincoln, Andrew T. *Word Biblical Commentary Ephesians.* Dallas, TX: Word Books, 1990.
Martin, Ralph P. *Interpretation: Ephesians, Colossians, and Philemon.* Louisville, KY: John Knox Press, 1991.

## Say It Correctly

Principality. prin-ci-**PA**-li-tee.

## Daily Bible Readings

**MONDAY**
Ready with the Word
(Luke 4:1–12)

**TUESDAY**
The Battle Lines Drawn
(1 Samuel 17:19–30)

**WEDNESDAY**
Choosing the Right Equipment
(1 Samuel 17:31–39)

**THURSDAY**
The Battle is the Lord's
(1 Samuel 17:40–50)

**FRIDAY**
Put on the Lord Jesus Christ
(Romans 13:8–14)

**SATURDAY**
The Dress for God's Chosen Ones
(Colossians 3:12–17)

**SUNDAY**
The Whole Armor of God
(Ephesians 6:10–20)

# Notes

# The Spirit Comes

This quarter has three units tracing God's work through the Holy Spirit to empower disciples for the Christian faith.

## UNIT 1 • THE PLEDGE OF GOD'S PRESENCE

This is a five-lesson study of John's Gospel with a concluding lesson from Mark's Gospel. These studies focus on Jesus' teaching about and promise of the Holy Spirit.

### Lesson 1: March 1, 2015
### The Lamb of God
### John 1:29–34

In a world of competing religious and political values, people are not always clear how one system can be of any greater value than another. How can Christians know which set of beliefs carries more weight than all others do? John testifies that the baptism of the Holy Spirit surpasses water baptism and that the Spirit bears witness that Jesus is God's Son.

### Lesson 2: March 8, 2015
### Jesus Promises an Advocate
### John 14:15–26

Sometimes people know what is right, but struggle to follow through as they should. What motivates one to make the right choices? Jesus said that He would send the Holy Spirit to help His followers to love God and live according to God's commandments.

### Lesson 3: March 15, 2015
### The Spirit of Truth
### John 16:4b–15

It may be difficult to maintain a direction in life when a mentor is lost. How do people find the resources to carry on when the strength and vision of someone close to them is no longer available? Jesus promised His disciples that the Holy Spirit would be as real a presence to them as His physical presence was while He lived with them on earth.

### Lesson 4: March 22, 2015
### Receive the Holy Spirit
### John 20:19–23

A charismatic speaker can often lift and inspire an attentive audience. What is done and said to bring about such an effect? Jesus spoke peace to and empowered the disciples with the gift of the Holy Spirit.

### Lesson 5: March 29, 2015
### The One Who Comes
### Mark 11:1–11

People want to be in the presence of and pay homage to important people. Why are celebrity events important to us? The people celebrated Jesus' arrival in Jerusalem as the coming of God's kingdom.

## UNIT 2 • THE COMMUNITY OF THE BELOVED DISCIPLE

This is a five-lesson study for the Easter season. The Scriptures under consideration draw from 1 Corinthians as well as 1, 2, and 3 John. These letters provide a window into the work of the Holy Spirit in the community of faith.

### Lesson 6: April 5, 2015
### Resurrection Guaranteed
### 1 Corinthians 15:1–11, 20–22

People need to be reminded of important events that shape their identities and actions. What kind of event can make such an influence on their lives? Jesus' resurrection provided tangible evidence of the possibility of the same for those whose identity is formed by Christ Jesus.

## Lesson 7: April 12, 2015
### Love One Another
### 1 John 3:11–24

People wonder whether life is a random sequence of events or has an ordered purpose. How do believers measure meaning in life? John's letter indicates that the measure of people's lives is calculated by their faith in Christ and their love for one another.

## Lesson 8: April 19, 2015
### Believe God's Love
### 1 John 4:13–5:5

Community is built on unity and mutuality. What holds the members of a community together? The writer of 1 John says believers are made complete when as a community they abide in God's love and the Spirit of God's love abides in them.

## Lesson 9: April 26, 2015
### Watch Out for Deceivers!
### 2 John

People who spread lies and heresies are a threat to the faith community. How does the community deal with this threat? Having seen in the last lessons that those who remain faithful in their belief in Christ will have eternal life, the focus of 2 John shifts to a warning to beware of deceivers, lest they corrupt the community of believers.

## Lesson 10: May 3, 2015
### Coworkers with the Truth
### 3 John

Most people really appreciate the kindness and generosity they have experienced because of good hospitality. What is it about receiving hospitality that makes it so important? We see in 3 John that hospitality is one way Christians express their faith in Christ to others, making them faithful coworkers with the truth.

## UNIT 3 • ONE IN THE BOND OF LOVE

This is a four-lesson study of 1 Corinthians. This is a careful study of the final chapters of Paul's letter to the church in Corinth. These lessons move the learners to see the connection between loving one another and living as Christ's witness in the world.

## Lesson 11: May 10, 2015
### Gifts of the Spirit
### 1 Corinthians 12:1–11

Most humans seek opportunities to become loyal, contributing members of their societies. What motivates and empowers them to work together? Paul said that because one person does not possess all of the spiritual gifts, believers must work together for the church's common good.

## Lesson 12: May 17, 2015
### The Spirit Creates One Body
### 1 Corinthians 12:14–31

Organizations are composed of several interrelated, interdependent functional parts. Why is it important to value all the parts? In his letter, Paul told the Corinthian church that all spiritual gifts are necessary for the church's efficient operation.

## Lesson 13: May 24, 2015
### Gift of Languages
### Acts 2:1–7, 12; 1 Corinthians 14:13–19

Communication is important as groups implement programs that will affect the lives of others. What is needed to achieve the best communication possible? The need for finding a common understanding is necessary whether people are speaking in different native languages, as in Acts 2, or unknown spiritual languages, as in 1 Corinthians 14.

## Lesson 14: May 31, 2015
### The Greatest Gift is Love
### 1 Corinthians 13

Love is the primary requirement for societies attempting to make a positive influence on the world around them. What is it about love that is so indispensable? Paul told the Corinthians that love is needed to achieve fully the benefit of all spiritual gifts.

# Connecting to God the Holy Spirit

When we mention the Holy Spirit, many followers of Christ do one of two things: get excited about certain emotional experiences or cringe at the thought of the third person of the Trinity. But there is another way to think about and relate to the Holy Spirit. One of the issues in the Black church today is that we have mistakenly tied the Holy Spirit to emotionalism and not to what God's Word says about Him. Emotional and unusual experiences with the Holy Spirit are a good thing, but they are always secondary.

The Holy Spirit is God Himself. The implication for this is that we need to relate to Him in a way that goes beyond the search for goosebumps and wild experiences. It also means that we need not shy away from His activity even if it does bring about out-of-the-ordinary encounters with God. The apostles praying in the Upper Room did not shy away from the Holy Spirit, and neither did they go seeking a certain type of emotional experience. What they did seek and need was the presence and power of Jesus in their lives. Everything else was secondary.

As they prayed in the Upper Room, the Bible says that a mighty wind filled the house and tongues of fire hovered over each of their heads. After this, the Spirit enabled them to speak in foreign languages that they never studied or learned. This was the beginning of numerous experiences of the Holy Spirit for the church. They all were different externally, but the one thing that held them in common is that the Holy Spirit glorified Jesus and built up the church. The Holy Spirit wants more than just to give you goosebumps. The Holy Spirit's purpose from the very beginning is to bring glory to Jesus Christ. In John's Gospel, Jesus lets us know that the Holy Spirit would convict the world of sin, unrighteousness, and judgment. He also lets us know that the Spirit would bring His followers comfort and lead them into all truth. All of this activity of the Holy Spirit falls under the umbrella of glorifying Jesus.

Glorifying Jesus is a task that needs to be our highest priority. If that is the case, then the question must be asked: How can we connect to God the Holy Spirit in order for our lives to glorify Jesus? We must be intentional, available, and practical.

## Intentional

One of the things that makes it difficult for us to connect with the Holy Spirit is our avoidance of Him. Many people talk about God a lot. Even some unbelievers talk about God and believe in a "higher power." We also talk about Jesus. On the other hand, when it comes to the Holy Spirit, we are practically silent. It becomes an uncomfortable topic of conversation to bring up the Spirit of God. Maybe this is because in many circles the Holy Spirit is associated with unusual experiences and emotionalism. Maybe it's because Jesus and the Father can be kept at a distance. They are, after all, up in heaven. The Holy Spirit is the God who is with us and can disrupt our lives. Whatever the reason, keeping the Holy Spirit at a distance lends itself to not being intentional about seeking to be aware of His presence and leading in our lives.

In order to connect with the Holy Spirit, we have to be intentional about it. We must wake up with the desire to be led by Him. Our passion for Jesus to be glorified must consume us. Our need for the Holy Spirit needs to be our top priority. This means that we must be intentional in our prayers and cry out for Him to be with us and give us a fuller realization of His agenda in our lives.

## Available

Another thing that is needed to connect with the Holy Spirit is availability. The Bible speaks of being filled with the Spirit. If we are filled with other things, then we will not be able to be filled with the Spirit. Many times we can be filled with pride, anger, lust, and selfishness. We also can be filled with television shows, music, books, and other forms of media. We can be filled with busy schedules and to-do lists. We can even be filled with church activities devoid of the Holy Spirit. When we are filled with these other things, our availability will be reduced or nonexistent.

It is our responsibility to make ourselves available to the Holy Spirit. We are vessels to be filled and must empty ourselves of anything that is contrary to God's holiness (He is the *Holy* Spirit after all). We can exhale the wickedness and ungodliness and inhale the Spirit of God into our lives. The way we do

this is to repent of any wrong that we have committed and then ask forgiveness. Next we can commit ourselves to doing God's will and obeying Him. In this way we can become available to the Spirit and connect with Him and what He wants to do in our lives.

## Practical

The practical aspect of connecting to the Holy Spirit is to cultivate His presence through the spiritual disciplines. These are activities that we do, not to earn God's favor, but to make ourselves accessible to it. We do not work for or earn the Holy Spirit in any way, but we open ourselves up to His work by practicing the spiritual disciplines. Many people cringe at the word "discipline." It conjures up thoughts of army boot camp or school detention. Discipline is another way of saying training. We all need to be trained to recognize and yield to the Holy Spirit's work in our lives.

The spiritual disciplines are many and varied. They consist mainly of prayer, fasting, Bible study and meditation, solitude, silence, and service. There are many others, but these are some main tools that God uses to train us and make us able to connect to the Holy Spirit. Through the practice of these disciplines, we can cultivate the presence of the Spirit in our lives. They are essential as a means to foster dependence on God and connection to the Holy Spirit.

The church has an amazing task in bringing glory to Jesus Christ. This task was never meant to be accomplished on our own. This is why Jesus said, "I will not leave you comfortless: I will come to you" (John 14:18). He knew that we needed to connect with God the Holy Spirit in order to glorify Him. We can only do that as we become intentional, make ourselves available, and do what is practical. This is how we fulfill our call and connect with God the Holy Spirit.

# The Holy Spirit in the Classroom

by Victoria Saunders-Johnson

Mother Green, former teacher of the adult Sunday School class, waited until all the members filed out of the classroom. "Brother Alexander," she said, leaning her body hard on her cane with one hand as she grabbed his hand with the other. "Brother Alexander," she repeated. "Let me pray for you." The young teacher laid his briefcase down, appreciative that Mother Green had entrusted the class she had taught for over twenty years into his care. He was always grateful when she stopped to pray for him. "Lord," she shook his arm, "this here is a good godly man, good Christian, good teacher, good family man. You knew I was getting too old and sick to teach this class and You brought a bright, intelligent young man to take my place. I thank You, Lord. Now Lord, I can tell he studies Your Word. I know he spends long hours preparing to teach, I can tell. But Lord, teach him all about Your teacher, the Holy Spirit…" Mother Green continued to pray for his wife, his job, and his witness in the community, but Alexander got stuck on that one phrase about the Holy Spirit.

Throughout the eleven o'clock service, Alexander kept thinking, *What did she mean teach me all about Your teacher, the Holy Spirit? Aren't I depending on the Holy Spirit? Is Mother Green hearing something in my teaching that makes her question my reliance on Him?* He wanted to talk with her after service, but he knew her standard response from previous conversations: "Pray on it, son." Then she'd quote her favorite passage, "Trust in the LORD with all thine heart; and lean not unto thine own understanding. In all thy ways acknowledge him, and he shall direct thy paths" (Proverbs 3:5–6). In addition to his preparation for next week's class, Alexander took time to study a few passages in the book of John on the role of the Holy Spirit and His teaching.

**Holy Spirit's help.** In introducing the Spirit, Jesus says, "But the Comforter, which is the Holy Ghost, whom the Father will send in my name, he shall teach you all things" (from John 14:26). Jesus used the Greek word *parakletos* (**pa-RA-klay-toss**), meaning helper or comforter, a person summoned or called to one's aid, advisor, legal defender, mediator, or intercessor (1 John 2:1). The Holy Spirit is the third Person of the Trinity (not an it or thing but a Person). The Holy Spirit is willing to come alongside to minister and support all endeavors. As a teacher, He is not merely the assistant but the lead teacher. Leaning on Him for insight and instruction during preparation will keep one from inserting doubt into the teaching time. It also keeps instructors from bragging about their teaching skills. If lives are changed because of the class, it is the work of the Holy Spirit, not a gifted teacher. God's Spirit opens the teacher's mind to understand and be able to explain clearly to the class. One instructor Alexander knew always prays before teaching, "Lord, You stand up and I'll sit down. You teach, You know the hearts and minds of each person in the class and what's needed. You take my notes; edit out anything that should not be said." This kind of prayer indicates the instructor's humility and invitation for the Holy Spirit to take control and allow information to be shared that will build up and encourage the listeners. The Holy Spirit is God's way to partner with His children as they walk through this often difficult world. The enemy wages an all-out attack on the teachers of God's Word. He wants people to stay submerged in lies. The Holy Spirit will protect and fight on behalf of those in teaching ministry.

**Holy Spirit's promotion of Jesus.** The Holy Spirit will bring to mind the teachings and life of Christ. "The Holy Ghost...[brings] all things to your remembrance, whatsoever I have said unto you" (from John 14:26). "He shall testify of me" (from John 15:26). These verses apply specifically to the disciples and their being able to remember the teachings and sayings of Jesus. This is impossible without the Holy Spirit's help. In the same way, a teacher studies and reads several Scriptures, but it's impossible to bring to mind all that one has studied. The Holy Spirit is present, reminding the teacher of verses, principles, and anything else needed to lift Jesus up. It's important to keep in mind the entire Bible is all about Jesus! The Old Testament is the historical record of events before His coming, the four Gospels tell about His time on the earth, the New Testament letters talk about what happened when He left the earth, and Revelation teaches what will happen when He returns again. The Bible is filled with

so many different topics, it's easy to get distracted in a class filled with people all having their own opinions. The Holy Spirit is always there to help keep Jesus as the center.

For Bible teachers in the twenty-first century, it's essential to lift Jesus up. Unfortunately, many believe in universalism, thinking there are several ways to God. This is not true. Jesus said He is the only way to the Father (John 14:6). The Holy Spirit will bring Jesus' words and the Scriptures to the teacher's remembrance so he or she can teach Christ, His death, burial, and resurrection as the focal point. Christians need to be educated on different subjects, but their main concentration and understanding should first and foremost be Jesus Christ and God's Word. The teacher is the one who has to stay grounded, constantly leading the class back to how topics relate to Jesus Christ and the Word of God.

**Holy Spirit's presence and permanence.** Jesus promised that after He left the earth, the secure presence of the Holy Spirit would "abide with [us] for ever" (from John 14:16). Alexander remembered his seminary professor said, "This is my biggest comfort in teaching. I never have to stand at the podium alone; the Holy Spirit stands with me." Once people open their hearts to Christ, trusting Him for their salvation, the Holy Spirit takes up permanent residence in their hearts (2 Corinthians 1:22, 5:5; Ephesians 1:13–14). If the teacher walks into a class and he or she is the only Christian, God in the form of Holy Spirit will be present with him or her. The Holy Spirit is present, opening the hearts and minds of the students, impelling and urging them to embrace truth about Christ. When the Holy Spirit is in control, the teacher is being used by God to deliver His Word. The students, Christian and non-Christian, are receiving answers to their questions about life, healing from their past wounds, and gaining instructions for daily living. This experience cannot be taken for granted. When the Holy Spirit is at work, He ministers to the person in his or her individual area of need. The Holy Spirit is speaking to each person's special situation.

The Holy Spirit's presence also enables the teacher to respond effectively when answering questions. It's up to the teacher to remedy false opinions. The Holy Spirit helps the teacher to separate the mingling of worldviews from Christianity. Most students' thoughts are confused because of watching and listening to secular media and attending non-Christian institutions. In one Sunday School class, the students were always asked to discuss the Bible verses in small groups. After the group discussion, many of the students voiced opinions based upon their own feelings. Amazingly, the teacher said nothing to dispute the false notions. The Holy Spirit helps the teacher to maintain the purity of God's Word as well as demonstrate sensitivity toward those lacking knowledge or ask foolish questions to trick the class or cause confusion.

The following Sunday, Brother Alexander found himself praying differently about the class, asking the Lord for him to be more dependent on the Holy Spirit and less reliant on his own natural ability or personal study.

*Victoria Saunders-Johnson is a Bible teacher and freelance writer. She is the author of* Children and Sexual Abuse.

# The Holy Spirit and the Black Church

## by Rev. Samuel Green

The Holy Spirit is understood in the Christian tradition as a member of the Trinity. Christians believe that God manifests in the tri-fold persona of Father, Son, and Holy Spirit. While they are interpreted as being as one today, theologians and scholars in the early church argued over their rank and responsibilities. Nevertheless, through many controversies and battles in the development of the early church, what became orthodox or acceptable by the Christian faith was the belief in one God that is unified in three related persons and of equal substance. As the African theologian St. Augustine of Hippo writes in his book *On the Trinity*, Book 9, "Therefore, with respect to this issue, let us believe that the Father and Son and Holy Spirit are one God, creator and ruler of the entire creature, and that the Father is not the Son, nor the Holy Spirit the Father or the Son, but that there is a trinity of mutually related persons and a unity of equal substance."

For African American Christians, the development of the Black church as an institution can be attributed to the work of a strong faith in God and the power of the Holy Spirit. In light of the history of Blacks in the African Diaspora, there has been a consistent understanding of faith as a tool that helped Blacks overcome adversity. Blacks understood their faith to be rooted in a God of justice who stood on the side of the marginalized and victimized. This belief was helpful as Blacks relied on a hope of freedom despite the contradictory reality of bondage and evil.

However, the ways in which the Holy Spirit is defined and interpreted might vary. The Holy Spirit is believed to help persons manifest certain spiritual gifts and abilities that are given by God. According to Scripture, the Holy Spirit provides a number of gifts or benefits that enhance the Christian life. A spiritual gift has many forms and can be used by different people to do different things for God. One way to look at the lives of Black people and the intersection of the Holy Spirit is to examine their resilience in the face of oppression.

Along with faith, resilience has been a part of the lives of Blacks throughout the African Diaspora. Persons of African descent have triumphed through the evils of slavery and oppression because of a strong commitment to faith and a sense of determination that overcame adversity. Despite the attempts of White slave masters and oppressors who desired to dehumanize and destroy the lives of those whom they would enslave, Blacks were able to fight back through their faith and mobilization to believe that God would redeem them. One of the methods that Black Americans used to develop a Christian identity that was different from the faith preached by White slave masters was the use of resilience. According to historian Flora Wilson Bridges, due to the incorporation of a distinct spirituality, they were able to frame a future that was free from slavery. Black Americans rejected interpretations of biblical passages that supported slavery and inferiority to Whites. Instead Blacks used an understanding of freedom to guide them in interpreting the Bible, which led to their survival. A key aspect of this interpretation is a reading of Exodus and understanding of Jesus in Scripture that helped them develop a theology of God who cared about the poor and disinherited. In addition to a new way of interpreting Scripture, Blacks were able to form their own worship and rituals that reflected African traditional religions and a consciousness for who God was for them. As the Black church developed, the influence of worship as a form of resilience was instrumental in the struggles for equality and the freedom from racism. Resilience was liberating as the Spirit guided Blacks toward a new identity that was rooted in a present-day reality of a life of freedom with God.

As it pertains to worship in the Black church, the use of resilience to design different forms of liturgical and spiritual practices is also evident. Theologians Nicholas Cooper-Lewter and Henry Mitchell describe the charismatic indwelling of the Holy Spirit as the source in shouting or dancing in worship services. It is the presence of the Holy Spirit within the worshiper, which reflects the nature of God as being both spiritually and physically present. The connection of worship and resilience in the Black church can be found in the hymns and gospel songs that were written by Blacks. In these songs, the Holy Spirit led Blacks to see God as liberator and caregiver for all of creation in order to express trust, faith, hope and love. This is found in the Negro spiritual in the Black church, "I will trust in the Lord until I die." As a song that emphasized the resilience of Blacks, as the people of God, they were reminded to remain steadfast, dedicated, loving, vigilant and prayerful. For it was until death that the Holy Spirit led them to materialize their faith into practice in a world of despair.

Thus, resilience can be interpreted as a gift of the Holy Spirit. This ability of the Holy Spirit continues to shape the Black church as communities confront injustice. As a number of social issues continue to affect the Black community, it is essential for the Black church to utilize the gift of resilience in order to remain strong and viable. The Black community is gravely faced with the crises of a lack of employment, rising HIV/AIDS rates, increase in prison populations, violence, educational disparities, and other issues for which a prophetic witness must be given in order for the church to have a future. In our communities, the Holy Spirit still has power to guide, strengthen, and give hope despite turmoil. The Holy Spirit works within our communities to bring about transformation. It is the unity of the Black community, with the Black church as a foundation, that was demonstrated by the enslaved African ancestors that will encourage present-day Black Americans to overcome the evil and suffering in the world. As a form of action, resilience mobilizes communities to have faith and hope in God's redemption.

By the power of the Spirit, the continued resilience of Black Americans can be connected to the wider mission of the church and the will of God. It is God's Spirit that has sustained the Black church throughout many centuries and has led it to glimpses of justice.

Sources:

Augustine of Hippo. *On The Trinity.* 9.1.1.

Bridges, Flora Wilson. *Resurrection Song: African-American Spirituality.* Maryknoll, NY: Orbis Books, 2001. 166.

Cooper-Lewter, Nicholas, and Henry H. Mitchell. *Soul Theology: The Heart of American Black Culture.* Nashville: Abdingdon Press, 1986.

Harding, Vincent. *There Is a River: The Black Struggle for Freedom in America.* San Diego: Harvest Books, 1981.

Rusch, William G. *The Trinitarian Controversy.* Philadelphia: Fortress Press, 1980.

# BILL PICKETT

## December 5, 1870–April 2, 1932

### Cowboy and Actor

William "Texas Bill" Pickett was known as the "The Bull-Dogger" and "The Dusky Demon." Both of these monikers were given for his legendary prowess as a rodeo cowboy. Born on December 5, 1870, near the Travis County Line, about thirty miles north of Austin, Bill was a Texan through and through. He was of both African and Native American descent. As one of thirteen children by Thomas Jefferson and Mary Virginia Pickett, Bill became enamored with the life of a cowboy. After completing fifth grade education, he set off to work on a ranch.

While on the ranch, Pickett observed the herd dogs' technique of controlling steers. They bit the mouths of the steers and made them fall on their side. Soon Bill would perfect this technique for people and developed the art of bulldogging. He would grab the cow by the horns, twist the cow's neck, bite the cow's nose or upper lip, and produce the same results as the herd dogs. Pickett and his brothers went into business together and started their own horse breaking business. They named it Pickett Brothers Bronco Busters and Rough Riders. Their advertisements called attention to their specialty of training wild cattle.

In 1888 at a fair in Taylor, Texas, Bill entered his first rodeo contest. Pickett soon became a very popular rodeo performer. In 1904, one of his performances garnered huge attention at the Cheyenne Frontier Days event in Wyoming. This was the most popular national rodeo, and he became so popular that by 1905 he joined the rodeo company started by Buffalo Bill Cody: the Miller Brothers' 101 Ranch and Wild West show. Pickett became known for his trick roping, riding, and bulldogging skills.

Soon Pickett began to perform all over the United States and even traveled to Canada, Mexico, South America, and England. Although he gained notoriety as a rodeo cowboy, Pickett had to endure the racism of his time. In order to gain entry into different rodeo contests, he had to enter as a Native American rather than African American and was banned against competing against White cowboys. Due to overwhelming prejudice and racism, Pickett was even banned from performing in Madison Square Garden.

Despite the opposition against him, Pickett became the first Black cowboy movie star. As the star of *Crimson Skull* (1921) and the *Bull-Dogger* (1922), he was a cinematic trailblazer on top of being a rodeo star. Pickett was a close friend of Tom Mix, the biggest cowboy movie star of the time. Will Rogers also appeared in rodeos with Pickett from time to time and considered him to be a close friend. Pickett's image as a Black cowboy was nationally and internationally known.

Over the years, Pickett was awarded many honors for his rodeo skills. Pickett was the first Black man to be inducted into the Cowboy Hall of Fame in Oklahoma City. He also was inducted into the National Rodeo Hall of Fame in 1972. In 1989, he was inducted into the ProRodeo Hall of Fame and Museum of the American Cowboy in Colorado Springs, Colorado. The U.S. postage stamp issued with Pickett's image went on to be the most collected and famous stamp issued by the U.S. Postal Service.

# Teaching Tips

## Words You Should Know

**A. Baptize** (John 1:31, 33) *baptizo* (Gk.)— To dip repeatedly, to immerse, to submerge.

**B. Bear record** (vv. 32, 34) *martureo* (Gk.)— To affirm that one has seen or heard or experienced something, to testify.

## Teacher Preparation

**Unifying Principle—Reliable Testimony.** In a world of competing religious and political values, people are not always clear how one system can be of any greater value than another. How can Christians know which set of beliefs carries more weight than all others do? John testifies that the baptism of the Holy Spirit surpasses water baptism, and that the Spirit bears witness that Jesus is God's Son.

**A.** Read John 1, and research John 1:29–34 in a good commentary.

**B.** Pray for your students and for lesson clarity.

## O—Open the Lesson

**A.** Open with prayer and introduce today's lesson title.

**B.** Have your students read the Aim for Change and Keep in Mind verse. Discuss.

**C.** Instruct your students to read the In Focus story silently. Discuss.

**D.** Ask, "Whom would you trust to tell others about what kind of person you are?" Discuss.

## P—Present the Scriptures

**A.** Have volunteers read the Focal Verses.

**B.** Use The People, Places, and Times and Background to provide context. Ask the students to share how the information helps their understanding of the text.

**C.** Use the At-A-Glance outline and In Depth to clarify the verses.

**D.** Use Search the Scriptures to further clarify the text and discuss In Depth.

## E—Explore the Meaning

**A.** Divide students into groups of three. Each group will choose one person to be a judge. Instruct the other two students to pretend that each of them has been charged with a crime that they did not commit. Have the students take turns explaining to the judge why their partner is innocent.

**B.** Discuss how the students felt during their role play.

## N—Next Steps for Application

**A.** Summarize the lesson.

**B.** Use Make It Happen to provide practical steps that students can take.

**C.** Close with prayer.

## Worship Guide

For the Superintendent or Teacher
Theme: The Lamb of God
Song: "Lamb of God"
Devotional Reading: Joel 2:23–27

# The Lamb of God

**Bible Background • JOHN 1:29–34**
**Printed Text • JOHN 1:29–34**
**Devotional Reading • JOEL 2:23–27**

## Aim for Change

By the end of the lesson, we will: EXPLORE John's account of Jesus' baptism, RELIVE emotions felt while observing or participating in a baptism; and ASSESS how Christians live out their baptismal covenant.

## In Focus

Trey and Gwen were newlyweds. They met while volunteering with their church youth group. Trey had immediately noticed Gwen's outgoing personality and her sincere desire to seek God in her life. Trey was equally sincere in his desire to seek God, but still struggled sometimes as a new believer. Gwen admired his simple, easygoing nature and his willingness to work out his relationship with God. She knew that God was going to use him to minister to others.

Trey hadn't been baptized yet and decided that he wanted to take this next step. Gwen agreed that this was a great idea. On the day of the baptism ceremony, Gwen looked on proudly as Trey joined others at the front of the church. As she watched Trey being baptized by their pastor Glen couldn't help but clap wildly. Gwen noted that his face seemed brighter than ever. Trey's baptism was a turning point in his relationship with God. Afterward, Trey's confidence was strong. He was more bold. He began to readily share Christ with others and became a powerful blessing to other men in the church.

*In today's lesson, we'll discuss John the Baptist's ministry of water baptism and his announcement of Jesus' ministry of Spirit baptism.*

## Keep in Mind

"And I saw, and bare record that this is the Son of God" (John 1:34).

"And I saw, and bare record that this is the Son of God" (John 1:34)

## Focal Verses

**KJV** **John 1:29** The next day John seeth Jesus coming unto him, and saith, Behold the Lamb of God, which taketh away the sin of the world.

**30** This is he of whom I said, After me cometh a man which is preferred before me: for he was before me.

**31** And I knew him not: but that he should be made manifest to Israel, therefore am I come baptizing with water.

**32** And John bare record, saying, I saw the Spirit descending from heaven like a dove, and it abode upon him.

**33** And I knew him not: but he that sent me to baptize with water, the same said unto me, Upon whom thou shalt see the Spirit descending, and remaining on him, the same is he which baptizeth with the Holy Ghost.

**34** And I saw, and bare record that this is the Son of God.

**NLT** **John 1:29** The next day John saw Jesus coming toward him and said, "Look! The Lamb of God who takes away the sin of the world!

**30** He is the one I was talking about when I said, 'A man is coming after me who is far greater than I am, for he existed long before me.'

**31** I did not recognize him as the Messiah, but I have been baptizing with water so that he might be revealed to Israel."

**32** Then John testified, "I saw the Holy Spirit descending like a dove from heaven and resting upon him.

**33** I didn't know he was the one, but when God sent me to baptize with water, he told me, 'The one on whom you see the Spirit descend and rest is the one who will baptize with the Holy Spirit.'

**34** I saw this happen to Jesus, so I testify that he is the Chosen One of God."

### The People, Places, and Times

**Perea.** Perea was a large region located east of the Jordan River and to the northeast of Jerusalem. A large number of Jewish people lived in the Perean region. It was common for Jewish travelers living in Galilee to travel through Perea on their way to Jerusalem, rather than taking the more direct route through Samaria. Jesus spent considerable time preaching there toward the end of His earthly ministry. John the Baptist preached and baptized in the region as well. Herod Antipas ruled Perea and Galilee. He was later responsible for John the Baptist's imprisonment and execution.

**Baptism.** The act of baptism was a common Jewish practice. Ritual washing and immersion were used to symbolize purity and preparation for holy use or service. Priests were required to bathe themselves before entering the temple. For this reason, ritual baths were located nearby. Baptism was also used to indicate a change in status or membership and was used when Gentiles converted to the Jewish faith. John the Baptist used the ritual in conjunction with repentance of sin to prepare believers for the coming Messiah.

### Background

John the Baptist was a Nazarite, the son of Zacharias the priest and Elisabeth. His birth was foretold by the angel Gabriel. Gabriel told Zacharias and Elisabeth of John's birth and explained that he would be "great in the sight of the Lord" and would be "filled with the Holy Ghost" (from Luke 1:15). He was meant to lead many Israelites to the Lord and would prepare them for the coming of the Messiah. Gabriel also gave instructions that their son was never to drink wine or hard liquor, and that they should name him John. This news was surprising to Zacharias and Elisabeth, because they were very old and Elisabeth wasn't able to have children. Their baby was born, strong in the Spirit just as Gabriel had said. Prior to beginning his ministry in Israel, John lived in the Judean wilderness, between Jerusalem and the Dead Sea. Other accounts about John in the Gospels indicate that he wore camel hair and a leather belt, and ate locusts and honey (Mark 1:6). He lived in the wilderness until he began his ministry in Israel, around A.D. 26 or 27. John's ministry focused on calling for repentance, administering baptism, and prophesying about the coming Messiah. John's speaking style was bold and fearless. He urged people to confess their sins and repent. He was also critical of sin in the lives of local religious and political leaders. Shortly after bearing witness to Christ's arrival, John was imprisoned by Herod and beheaded. Jesus refers to John's witness and ministry in John 5:35, saying that "he was a burning and a shining light."

## At-A-Glance

1. John Announces Christ's Arrival
(John 1:29–31)
2. Jesus is the Son of God (vv. 32–34)

## In Depth

### 1. John Announces Christ's Arrival (John 1:29–31)

John presents Jesus as the "Lamb of God." The phrase alludes to the image of the sacrificial Passover lamb. More specifically, the phrase points to the redemptive nature of Christ's sacrifice. Animals were regularly used in Judaism as a sacrifice to cleanse sin. While the sacrifice of animals was an ongoing, repetitive process, John announces that Christ's atoning sacrifice would be a permanent solution. Furthermore, Christ's redemptive work is for everyone.

John had risen to popularity in the region. Crowds of people gathered to hear him speak and to be baptized (Mark 1:4–5; Luke 3:3, 7–17). His popularity had attracted the interest of the local religious leaders who sent a group of priests and Levites to determine John's identity (John 1:19–27). John had denied being the Christ or Elijah, and went on to explain that there would be a much greater man than himself who would be arriving soon after. A day after his explanation to the church leaders, John is now announcing that this is the man he had spoken of. Jesus is the greater one he had been waiting for.

### 2. Jesus is the Son of God (vv. 32–34)

Here John is reflecting on an event that is recorded in Matthew 3:13–17, Mark 1:9–11, and Luke 3:21–22. Jesus went to John to be baptized in the Jordan River. While John was baptizing Jesus, he witnessed the Holy Spirit rest on Jesus in the form of a dove. This event was significant, not only because of its spectacular nature, but because John had been told that this sign would mark the man who would baptize with the Holy Spirit. John clearly indicates God's direction in his baptism ministry and his testimony to Jesus' identity. God instructed him to baptize to prepare the people for Jesus' arrival.

John would certainly have known Jesus before baptizing Him; they were cousins. John's statement "I knew him not" probably refers to the fact that he didn't yet know Jesus' identity as the Lamb of God, the Son of God (vv. 31, 33). It was at the moment of Jesus' baptism that this was revealed to him. After his experience at Jesus' baptism, John was able to report definitively that Jesus is God's Son.

## Search the Scriptures

1. How do you think it felt for John to finally be able to declare Jesus' identity to everyone (John 1:29–30)?

2. John states that the Holy Spirit remained on Jesus. What is the significance of this distinction (v. 33)?

## Discuss the Meaning

1. When we look at the sin in our lives, it may be difficult to remember that Christ's sacrifice was a permanent solution for our sin. How do you think forgetting this fact might impact our relationship with God?

2. The Holy Spirit signaled that Jesus was the Son of God. How does the Holy Spirit support your belief in Jesus and His work in your life?

## Lesson in Our Society

People still "bear witness" today. Have you ever asked someone to provide you with a reference or letter of recommendation for a new job? Or maybe a former colleague has asked if you would share your experience of how they performed as a worker. These are modern-day examples of testifying to someone's identity or character. The Holy Spirit within each believer testifies to the fact that we are God's children (Romans 8:16). As His children, we have been charged with witnessing to the power and person of Christ. We are meant to be living recommendations of Christ's love.

## Make It Happen

John the Baptist provided witness testimony to the identity of Jesus as the Son of God and the redemptive sacrifice for the sins of humanity. Consider ways in which you could testify to the person of Christ this week. Ask God to reveal opportunities to share the love of Christ with your family, friends, and coworkers.

If you don't feel like you're a very reliable witness to the person and ministry of Christ, ask God what changes you can make in your life. Ask the Holy Spirit to give you strength to make those changes in your life.

## Follow the Spirit

What God wants me to do:

_____

_____

_____

_____

## Remember Your Thoughts

Special insights I have learned:

_____

_____

_____

_____

## More Light on the Text

### John 1:29–34

**29 The next day John seeth Jesus coming unto him, and saith, Behold the Lamb of God, which taketh away the sin of the world.**

As Jesus approaches John, John sees something, a sign, that affirms the identity of the one John is paving the way for. The Lamb of God, being divine, would take away the sin of the whole world. Jesus is the sacrificial Lamb who offered Himself without spot to God (Hebrews 9:24–28). The word for "taketh away" is *airo* (Gk., **EYE-row**), which means to take away, bear away, or carry off. It was language that would remind the listeners of Yom Kippur, the Day of Atonement, in which the scapegoat would be set loose into the wilderness to carry off the sin of the nation (Leviticus 16:20–22). The language here in John suggests that Jesus is not only the Passover Lamb, serving as a reminder of God's protection of His people in Egypt (Exodus 12), but that He is also an atoning sacrifice, accomplishing more than a normal Passover lamb ever could.

**30 This is he of whom I said, After me cometh a man which is preferred before me: for he was before me.**

John points out that Jesus is the one who he was referring to earlier (v. 27). He also adds that Jesus is "preferred before" (Gk. *emprosthen*, **EM-prohs-thehn**) John in rank, because He existed "before" (Gk. *protos*, **PRO-tohs**) John in time. John is speaking of Christ as the eternal Word who existed before creation. This is the basis of Christ's ranking above John. As the pre-incarnate Christ, Jesus will always be superior to every created thing because He is the Creator (John 1:1–3).

**31 And I knew him not: but that he should be made manifest to Israel, therefore am I come baptizing with water.**

John did not know the identity of the Christ, but that did not prevent him from carrying out his duty to baptize. He knew that through his ministry, the Christ would be "manifest" to Israel. The word "manifest" (Gk. *phaneroo*, **fah-nay-ROH-oh**) means more than just to appear. One may appear in a false identity, but to be made manifest is to appear as one truly is. This is significant because Jesus assumed the identity of an everyday Jewish man. Now His true identity would be revealed.

**32 And John bare record, saying, I saw the Spirit descending from heaven like a dove, and it abode upon him.**

This was the sign by which John was told he would know the identity of the Christ. We do not know whether it was an actual dove or if the emphasis is on the manner of the Spirit's descent. That is, it could be that John is describing the way in which the Spirit came down and hovered over Jesus. Doves were associated with God in various ways in Jewish tradition. A dove was used to let Noah know when the water had receded enough to reveal dry land (Genesis 8). As clean animals, doves were also used for sacrifices in the temple (Leviticus 5:7, 12:6).

**33 And I knew him not: but he that sent me to baptize with water, the same said unto me, Upon whom thou shalt see the Spirit descending, and remaining on him, the same is he which baptizeth with the Holy Ghost.**

John did not know who the Son of God would be. This does not mean that John did not know Jesus. John and Jesus were cousins, but John did not know that Jesus was the Christ, the one whom God would send after him. The Lord instructed John to baptize and look for the sign of the Spirit descending as the indicator of the Messiah's identity. John affirms that Jesus came to do more than baptize with water: He came to baptize with the Holy Spirit.

**34 And I saw, and bare record that this is the Son of God.**

In this concluding sentence of John the Baptist's testimony, John affirmed that he was an eyewitness to that which he had spoken. This language is from court language when testifying. All that John did not know before was made plain by the sign, and John knew that Jesus is the Son of God. This could only be known through revelation given by God.

Sources:

Alexander, David, and Pat Alexander. *Zondervan Handbook to the Bible*. Grand Rapids, MI: Zondervan, 1999. 240–41.

Barker, Kenneth L., and John R. Kohlenberger III, eds. *The Expositor's Bible Commentary*. Abridged Edition: New Testament. Grand Rapids, MI: Zondervan, 1994. 299–300.

Butler, Trent C., ed. "John the Baptist." *Holman Bible Dictionary*. Electronic Edition, Quickverse. Nashville, TN: Holman Bible Publishers, 1991.

——. "Passover." *Holman Bible Dictionary*. Electronic Edition, Quickverse. Nashville, TN: Holman Bible Publishers, 1991.

Easton, M. G. "John the Baptist." *Easton's Bible Dictionary*. 1st ed. Oklahoma City, OK: Ellis Enterprises, 1993.

Elwell, Walter A., and Robert W. Yarbrough. *Encountering the New Testament: A Historical and Theological Survey*. Grand Rapids, MI: Baker Books, 1998. 42–43.

McGrath, Allister E., and James I. Packer, eds. *Zondervan Handbook of Christian Beliefs*. Grand Rapids, MI: Zondervan, 2005. 240–41.

Thayer, Joseph. "Baptizo." *Thayer's Greek Definitions*. 3rd ed. Electronic Edition, Quickverse. El Cajon, CA: Institute for Creation Research, 1999.

——. "Martureo." *Thayer's Greek Definitions*. 3rd ed. Electronic Edition, Quickverse. El Cajon, CA: Institute for Creation Research, 1999.

Walvoord, John F., and Roy B. Zuck, eds. *The Bible Knowledge Commentary: An Exposition of the Scriptures*. Wheaton, IL: Victor Books, 1983. 274–75.

## Say It Correctly

Nazarite. **NA**-ze-rite.
Bethabara. beth-ah-**BA**-ra.
Esaias. eh-**SIGH**-as.

## Daily Bible Readings

**MONDAY**
The Spirit and Joseph
(Genesis 41:38–43)

**TUESDAY**
The Spirit and Bezalel
(Exodus 31:1–6)

**WEDNESDAY**
The Spirit and the Elders
(Numbers 11:11–25)

**THURSDAY**
Would that All Had the Spirit!
(Numbers 11:26–30)

**FRIDAY**
Make the Way Straight
(John 1:19–23)

**SATURDAY**
Why Are You Baptizing?
(John 1:24–28)

**SUNDAY**
I Saw the Spirit Descending
(John 1:29–34)

# Teaching Tips

## Words You Should Know

**A. Commandments** (John 14:15, 21) *entole* (Gk.)—Orders, commands, charges, precepts, injunctions.

**B. Comforter** (v. 16) *parakletos* (Gk.)—One who is called to one's side, especially called to one's aid; one who pleads another's cause before a judge.

## Teacher Preparation

**Unifying Principle—A Comforter and Much More.** Sometimes people know what is right, but struggle to follow through as they should. What motivates one to make the right choices? Jesus said that He would send the Holy Spirit to help His followers to love God and live according to God's commandments.

**A.** Read John 14, and research John 14:15–26.

**B.** Consider a moment in your life when you needed to make a decision but were unsure of the right thing to do.

**C.** Pray for your students and for lesson clarity.

## O—Open the Lesson

**A.** Open with prayer and introduce today's lesson title.

**B.** Have your students read the Aim for Change and Keep in Mind verse together.

**C.** Ask, "Can you recall a time when you had to make a tough decision but had no idea what to do?" Have students share their responses.

**D.** Read the In Focus story together. Discuss.

## P—Present the Scriptures

**A.** Have volunteers read the Focal Verses.

**B.** Use The People, Places, and Times and Background to provide context.

**C.** Use At-A-Glance and In Depth to clarify the verses. Be sure to acknowledge any themes that students have already noticed.

**D.** Use Search the Scriptures to further clarify the text and discuss In Depth.

## E—Explore the Meaning

**A.** Using masking tape, construct two mazes on the floor. Split students into teams. Instruct each team to select a member to attempt to walk the maze while blindfolded. After this, allow them to have someone whisper directions into the player's ear as they go through the maze again. Ask the students to reflect on their experience.

## N—Next Steps for Application

**A.** Summarize the lesson.

**B.** Use Make It Happen to provide practical steps that students can take.

**C.** Close with prayer.

## Worship Guide

For the Superintendent or Teacher
Theme: Jesus Promises an Advocate
Song: "Welcome Holy Spirit"
Devotional Reading: Psalm 23

# Jesus Promises an Advocate

**Bible Background • JOHN 14:15–26**
**Printed Text • JOHN 14:15–26**
**Devotional Reading • PSALM 23**

## Aim for Change

By the end of the lesson, we will: UNDERSTAND the significance of the Holy Spirit; RECOGNIZE the power available through the Holy Spirit; and PRAY for the guidance of the Holy Spirit in making decisions.

## In Focus

James and Trina had been experiencing tension in their marriage. Trina seemed less joyful lately. James asked if everything was OK. Trina insisted that she was fine. One night, James awoke to discover that Trina wasn't in bed. He noticed a light in the hallway. He listened closer and could hear muffled sobbing coming from their guest room. James' heart sank. He wanted to help fix it, but he didn't know how.

On his drive to work the next day, James prayed for Trina. James remembered a message that their pastor had preached about the Holy Spirit, so he prayed that the Holy Spirit would show him what to do. That afternoon, James remembered the deep feeling of love and appreciation he had for Trina on their wedding day. *I wonder if she knows that?* he thought. He knew what he needed to do. That night at dinner, James told Trina how much he still appreciated and loved her.

Trina's eyes filled with tears. "I didn't know you still felt that way." Trina explained she'd been sad because it seemed that James loved her less now. They talked about how they could show love toward each other more often.

*The Holy Spirit empowers us to live God-honoring lives and gives guidance. Today we will discuss the gift and ministry of the Holy Spirit.*

## Keep in Mind

"But the Comforter, which is the Holy Ghost, whom the Father will send in my name, he shall teach you all things, and bring all things to your remembrance, whatsoever I have said unto you" (John 14:26).

"But the Comforter, which is the Holy Ghost, whom the Father will send in my name, he shall teach you all things, and bring all things to your remembrance, whatsoever I have said unto you" (John 14:26).

## Focal Verses

**KJV** John 14:15 If ye love me, keep my commandments.

**16** And I will pray the Father, and he shall give you another Comforter, that he may abide with you for ever;

**17** Even the Spirit of truth; whom the world cannot receive, because it seeth him not, neither knoweth him: but ye know him; for he dwelleth with you, and shall be in you.

**18** I will not leave you comfortless: I will come to you.

**19** Yet a little while, and the world seeth me no more; but ye see me: because I live, ye shall live also.

**20** At that day ye shall know that I am in my Father, and ye in me, and I in you.

**21** He that hath my commandments, and keepeth them, he it is that loveth me: and he that loveth me shall be loved of my Father, and I will love him, and will manifest myself to him.

**22** Judas saith unto him, not Iscariot, Lord, how is it that thou wilt manifest thyself unto us, and not unto the world?

**23** Jesus answered and said unto him, If a man love me, he will keep my words: and my Father will love him, and we will come unto him, and make our abode with him.

**24** He that loveth me not keepeth not my sayings: and the word which ye hear is not mine, but the Father's which sent me.

**25** These things have I spoken unto you, being yet present with you.

**26** But the Comforter, which is the Holy Ghost, whom the Father will send in my name, he shall teach you all things, and bring all things to your remembrance, whatsoever I have said unto you.

**NLT** John 14:15 "If you love me, obey my commandments.

**16** And I will ask the Father, and he will give you another Advocate, who will never leave you.

**17** He is the Holy Spirit, who leads into all truth. The world cannot receive him, because it isn't looking for him and doesn't recognize him. But you know him, because he lives with you now and later will be in you.

**18** No, I will not abandon you as orphans—I will come to you.

**19** Soon the world will no longer see me, but you will see me. Since I live, you also will live.

**20** When I am raised to life again, you will know that I am in my Father, and you are in me, and I am in you.

**21** Those who accept my commandments and obey them are the ones who love me. And because they love me, my Father will love them. And I will love them and reveal myself to each of them."

**22** Judas (not Judas Iscariot, but the other disciple with that name) said to him, "Lord, why are you going to reveal yourself only to us and not to the world at large?"

**23** Jesus replied, "All who love me will do what I say. My Father will love them, and we will come and make our home with each of them.

**24** Anyone who doesn't love me will not obey me. And remember, my words are not my own. What I am telling you is from the Father who sent me.

**25** I am telling you these things now while I am still with you.

**26** But when the Father sends the Advocate as my representative—that is, the Holy Spirit—he will teach you everything and will remind you of everything I have told you.

## The People, Places, and Times

**Fatherless (Orphans).** Orphans were particularly vulnerable. In a patriarchal society where the family was reliant on the father, being orphaned was a difficult existence. Without a father, orphans had no one to provide for them and no representation in court. It was common for orphans to be mistreated and even murdered. Many relied on begging, or were sold into slavery. However, throughout Scripture, God instructs His people to be kind to orphans. He is sympathetic to their plight. In James' epistle, he describes pure and genuine religion as "caring for orphans and widows in their distress and refusing to let the world corrupt you" (from James 1:27, NLT).

## Background

Jesus and the disciples were preparing to celebrate the Passover festival. The Passover festival was celebrated in remembrance of the night that God spared the firstborn Israelites while under Egyptian rule. On the night that all firstborn Egyptians were killed, God passed over the homes of the Israelites. The Israelites had been instructed to wipe lamb's blood on their door posts as a sign, and God passed over their homes (Exodus 12:1–13).

It was just prior to the Passover festival, and Jesus was dining with the disciples in the Upper Room. Jesus knew that His time on earth was coming to a close. The announcement of His departure and pending arrival of the Holy Spirit followed several events that surprised and confused the disciples.

In John 13, Jesus took on the role of a servant and insisted on washing the disciples' feet. Peter was so disturbed by this that he initially resisted. Jesus' servant posture foreshadowed His sacrifice on the Cross. He was also setting an example of servanthood.

He was instilling a behavior for the disciples to adopt.

Even more shocking, Jesus then revealed to the disciples that one of them would betray Him (John 13:21). After the apostles questioned among themselves who it might be, Judas was revealed as the traitor and quickly departed. Jesus then began to explain that He must leave them. Again, Peter was so disturbed that he objected to what Jesus said. When Peter insisted that he would go with Jesus and even die for Him, Jesus explained that Peter would actually deny Jesus three times. Consider how disheartening these events would have been for the disciples. It was at this point that Jesus began explaining the ministry of the Holy Spirit.

## At-A-Glance

1. The Advocate is the Holy Spirit (John 14:15–17)
2. The Disciples are Not Abandoned (vv. 18–24)
3. The Holy Spirit is Jesus' Representative (vv. 25–26)

## In Depth

**1. The Advocate is the Holy Spirit (John 14:15–17)**

Jesus describes the relationship that exists between Himself and the disciples. The Greek verb translated as "keep" is *tereo* (Gk. **tay-REH-oh**), which has a sense of watching over or guarding. *Tereo* is in the future tense and can be translated "You will obey" (Mounce 420). Obeying Jesus' commandments is a natural result of their love for Him. This is a statement of relationship, rather than a command. The disciples' love for Jesus will result in their adherence to His teachings.

Jesus will ask the Father to send another Advocate who will remain with them forever. The Counselor-Advocate is the Holy Spirit. In Jesus' physical absence, the Spirit will guide them in the truth. Their relationship with the Holy Spirit is only possible because of their relationship with Jesus, because their love of Christ will allow them to recognize and receive the Spirit when He arrives. Here again, Jesus points to the future when the Holy Spirit will reside both *within* them and *beside* them.

### 2. The Disciples are Not Abandoned (vv. 18–24)

Jesus doesn't intend to leave them fatherless. He will reveal Himself to the disciples after His death, burial, and resurrection. Not only will He visit them physically, but He will send His Spirit. His resurrection ensures that they will have new life (vv. 19–20). Modern-day believers also have this new life in Christ because of His sacrificial death and resurrection.

When Christ lives again, the disciples will begin to understand the relationship between Jesus and the Father, and consequently, their new relationship with the Father. In verse 21, Jesus again speaks of the relationship between Himself and those who keep His commandments. People who love the Lord indicate as much by adhering to His teachings. Additionally, God loves those who love Jesus and keep His commandments. Loving Jesus and doing His commandments results in Jesus revealing Himself to the individual.

### 3. The Holy Spirit is Jesus' Representative (vv. 25–26)

The Father will send the Holy Spirit to represent Christ in the world in the same way that Christ was sent to the world to represent God. In Jesus' absence, the Holy Spirit will remind the disciples of His teachings. Additionally, the Spirit will help them to more fully understand all that Christ taught them during His ministry. This clearly indicates that the Holy Spirit was to be more than just a reminder to the disciples; the Holy Spirit would be an active teacher and guide to them.

### Search the Scriptures

1. What future event is Jesus referring to when He says that the Spirit will be in them (John 14:17)?

2. How do you think the disciples might have felt as they heard Jesus talk about leaving them (vv. 19, 25)?

### Discuss the Meaning

1. The Holy Spirit was sent to remind the disciples of Jesus' teachings and help their understanding of His commandments. Have you experienced this aspect of the Holy Spirit's ministry in your life?

2. Have you seen the Holy Spirit work in others? If so, what did you observe about their lives?

### Lesson in Our Society

Life is more enjoyable when we walk alongside others who are willing to encourage and support one another. Have you ever encountered a problem that seemed impossible to solve until you asked for help from someone? Remember how relieved you felt when you didn't have to figure it out on your own? This is similar to the Holy Spirit's ministry in believers' lives. He has been given to come alongside us and instruct us in how to live. We are not alone.

### Make It Happen

Ask God to reveal ways in which you can actively seek out the guidance of the Holy

Spirit in your life. This might be as simple as praying for the guidance of the Holy Spirit in a situation.

Or, you might find yourself relying solely on your own understanding when making decisions. Instead, prayerfully consider what the Holy Spirit is leading you to do.

## Follow the Spirit

What God wants me to do:

_____

_____

_____

_____

## Remember Your Thoughts

Special insights I have learned:

_____

_____

_____

_____

## More Light on the Text

### John 14:15–26

This section is a continuation of the discourse at the Passover table after the washing of the disciples' feet (John 13) and before their departure to the garden (14:31). In this chapter, Jesus gives them words of comfort and hope for the future. He reveals God's plan for them after He is gone to the Father. These revelations include the:

a) Promise of a place in and a way to heaven (vv. 1–7),

b) True face of God (vv. 8–11),

c) Promise of unlimited power in prayer for the disciples (vv. 12–14), and

d) Promise of the coming of another Comforter, the Holy Spirit, who will remain with them forever. This constitutes an important and fundamental doctrine in the Christian church—the gift, purpose, and work of the Holy Spirit.

**15 If ye love me, keep my commandments.**

Jesus begins this segment of the discourse with a conditional clause using the word "if" and ends with a a statement about the future ("keep my commandments"). The KJV and NLT translate this like a command, but it is a conditional with a simple future tense verb, not an imperative ("if you love me, you will keep"). The sense of the Greek is that the events of the conditional are not certain. As a result, Jesus is indicating that the disciples have a choice in the matter. They may choose to love Him, resulting in them keeping His commandments, or they may choose not to. It is not a lack of omniscience on Jesus' part that is of concern here but the free will of the disciples to love or not love Jesus. Jesus is saying that the proof of their love for Him is the keeping of His commandments. He would repeat this in various ways both in this chapter (vv. 21, 23) and in several other passages (e.g., 15:10). John also reiterates this in his first epistle (1 John 5:3).

In John 13:34, Christ defines His "new" commandment as loving one another, and all that He has been teaching them is summed up in this one commandment of love. Keeping all of His commandments can be done by keeping this single one: Love one another.

**16 And I will pray the Father, and he shall give you another Comforter, that he may abide with you for ever.**

The promise that follows seems to be directly linked with the preceding verse and the theme of loving obedience. It seems that His praying to the Father and the sending of the Comforter are conditional on the apostles' relationship with Him, evidenced by keeping His commandments. This relationship would motivate Him to pray (Gk. *erotao*, **eh-roh-TAH-oh**) to the Father on their behalf, and "he shall give you another Comforter." The word for prayer sheds light on Jesus' relationship with the Father. It means "to ask from another person of equal footing or familiarity." Jesus and the Father are both God, and this is the nature of their discourse.

Because of Jesus' prayer, "another Comforter" will come to the disciples. The word for "another" sheds light on the relationship of the Spirit to the Father and Son. It is not the word for "another of a different kind," *heteros* (Gk. **HEH-teh-rohs**), but for "another of the same kind," which is *allos* (Gk. **AH-lohs**). The word "Comforter" (Gk. *parakletos*, **pa-RAH-klay-tose**) has the idea of one called alongside to help. Hence, the New American Standard Bible translates it as "Helper." It has the idea of one who stands by another and exhorts or encourages. It is also translated "advocate" (NIV), meaning one called particularly in a law court to plead one's case (1 John 2:1), not as a professional pleader but as a friend.

This is the first of four times the function and activities of the Holy Spirit are mentioned in the discourse (see John 14:25–26, 15:26–27, 16:5–15). The idea here is that since Jesus is about to leave them, the Father will send the Holy Spirit, who will abide with them forever. The duration of the presence of the Comforter on earth with the disciples and believers is not temporary as Jesus' presence was, but permanent—forever.

We see here a picture of a discouraged group of people who are about to lose their Master through death, and their Master comes to encourage them. They are not going to be alone, He encourages them. He assures them that it is to their advantage that He depart so that the Holy Spirit would come and be with them permanently (16:7).

**17 Even the Spirit of truth; whom the world cannot receive, because it seeth him not, neither knoweth him: but ye know him; for he dwelleth with you, and shall be in you.**

This Comforter is called "the Spirit of truth." This defines one of the functions of the Holy Spirit. The word "Spirit" used here (Gk. *pneuma*, **puh-NEW-mah**, literally "wind" or "breath") is the same word Jesus used to describe to Nicodemus the function of the Spirit in conversion (3:8).

Truth is one of the characteristics of the Holy Spirit. This is not surprising, since truth is a recurrent theme in the Gospel of John (1:17). Jesus says earlier in this chapter that He is "the way, the truth, and the life" (from 14:6, cf. 8:32). From these and other passages, we learn that Christ is the embodiment of truth. Here the Spirit shares the same nature with Christ and communicates truth (15:26, 16:13), testifying about Christ.

Jesus says the "world" (Gk. *kosmos*, **KAHS-mose**), here meaning those who are unsaved, cannot receive this Spirit and gives two reasons for this lack. First, they do not see the Spirit because they are spiritually blind (see 2 Corinthians 4:4). Second, they do not know Him because they refuse to believe or understand Him (see 1 Corinthians 2:14).

Christ says the sinful nature of the world causes people to prefer darkness rather than light (John 3:19), and calls these people children of the devil, for they desire to do their father's will (8:44). Only those who believe in the Gospel of Christ are able to receive and know the Spirit of truth (1 John 4:6). In contrast to the world, the disciples know the Spirit or have experienced Him because He dwells in them, Jesus says. They have this privilege of knowing Him because of their belief and relationship with Christ.

The next point of interest in this verse is the use of the present and the future tenses, "for he dwelleth with you, and shall be in you." Some interpret this as a continuation of the presence or indwelling of the Holy Spirit in the believer. This agrees with the previous verse: "that he may abide with you for ever." Another interpretation is that while the Spirit dwells with them in a measure now, they would receive the Spirit in greater measure when He comes into their lives in His fullness at the baptism of the Holy Spirit (see John 3:34; cf. Matthew 3:11; Luke 11:13; John 1:31–33). It is believed that this was fulfilled on the day of Pentecost in Acts.

**18 I will not leave you comfortless: I will come to you.**

Jesus then assures His disciples of His continued presence. The word "comfortless" is the Greek *orphanos* (**or-fan-OSE**), from which we derive its English equivalent, "orphan." Other renderings of this word include "desolate" or "helpless." The next use of the word is found in James 1:27, where KJV renders it "fatherless."

It is common in African tradition, for example, to refer to an apprentice as the child of his master. The apprentice usually lives with and is generally regarded as part of the master's family. On many occasions, the master would include the apprentice in his inheritance upon his death.

There was probably a similar tradition among the Jews of Jesus' time. The disciples of a particular teacher were called his children, and if he died, they were considered orphans. In John 13:33, Jesus called His disciples children, and here He promises them that He will not leave them as orphans.

Jesus promises to them further, saying, "I will come to you." Is He referring to His immediate appearance after His resurrection, which happens approximately three days after this speech (John 20; Acts 1:3)? Or, is He talking about His coming in the Person of the Holy Spirit, therefore carrying forward the same trend of thought of verses 16 and 17? Alternatively, is He talking about His Second Coming, a thought He started with in this chapter (vv. 1–3)? All three are possible, and all three might be included in His thought.

**19 Yet a little while, and the world seeth me no more; but ye see me: because I live, ye shall live also.**

Jesus states that the world would not see Him because He would soon die and ascend into heaven. He further clarifies that the disciples will be able to see Him, because He would live again and give them access to eternal life through the power of the Holy Spirit.

**20 At that day ye shall know that I am in my Father, and ye in me, and I in you.**

Here Jesus describes the nature of the relationship He would have with the disciples and all who would subsequently follow Him. He says that they would know experientially that He is in the nature, soul, and thought of the Father; they would be in Him and He would be in them in the same manner. Although He would be away, the Spirit or Comforter would be in them and this would be their relational connection to Him.

**21 He that hath my commandments, and keepeth them, he it is that loveth me: and he that loveth me shall be loved of my Father, and I will love him, and will manifest myself to him.**

Jesus says that if the disciples not only have His commandments but obey them, it is proof that they love Him. This love for Him will be rewarded with love from both the Father and Son. Jesus says that He will manifest (Gk. *emphanizo*, **em-fah-NEED-zoh**) Himself to those who love Him. The word "manifest" means to exhibit for view, to show oneself. This would happen through the coming of the Comforter, the Holy Spirit.

**22 Judas saith unto him, not Iscariot, Lord, how is it that thou wilt manifest thyself unto us, and not unto the world?**

This Judas shares his name with the disciple who betrayed Jesus. He asks how Jesus can show Himself to the disciples and not to the world. Jesus gives His answer in the next verse.

**23 Jesus answered and said unto him, If a man love me, he will keep my words: and my Father will love him, and we will come unto him, and make our abode with him.**

Jesus says that if a person loves Him and obeys His words, then the Father will love them, and Jesus and the Father will come to and make their abode with that person. Here Jesus is speaking of the indwelling of the Holy Spirit in the life of the believer. This will be the method in which Jesus will manifest Himself to His disciples.

**24 He that loveth me not keepeth not my sayings: and the word which ye hear is not mine, but the Father's which sent me. 25 These things have I spoken unto you, being yet present with you.**

Jesus goes back to the love motif again. Stating it negatively (cf. v. 15), He reinforces the truth about loving Him and keeping His "sayings" (Gk. *logos*, **LOH-gohs**) or teachings. He says anyone who does not love Him would not keep His teachings. This is akin to verse 17, where we learned that the world cannot receive the Holy Spirit because they do not know Him.

In essence, he who rejects Christ will not even listen to His teachings, and in effect also rejects the Father since Jesus' teachings are the Father's (Luke 10:16; John 3:36, 13:20). Jesus refuses to take glory for Himself and says, "For all things that I have heard from my Father I have made known unto you" (from John 15:15). Again He gives the Father total credit for His teachings by saying, "For I have not spoken of myself; but the Father which sent me, he gave me a commandment, what I should say, and what I should speak" (12:49; compare vv. 47–48). The rejection of Christ and His teachings is, therefore, tantamount to rejection of God Himself.

"These things . . . spoken" (from 14:25) include all His teachings. It is not limited to His immediate sayings, but to all His teachings from the beginning of His ministry. This verse serves as a transition to the next, which deals more with the Holy Spirit and His work. It goes with the tone with which He started the discourse, and that is comforting and encouraging in view of His imminent departure from them.

**26 But the Comforter, which is the Holy Ghost, whom the Father will send in my name, he shall teach you all things, and bring all things to your remembrance, whatsoever I have said unto you.**

The conjunction "but" at the beginning of this verse clarifies the point of the previous verse. There Jesus seems to say, "Although I have been teaching you in person and will soon leave you, you are not losing anything, since you are about to receive the Comforter, the Holy Spirit, whose work includes bringing to your remembrance all My teachings." Here Christ mentions both the office and name of the Holy Spirit, both of which we have come across in the earlier verses of the chapter (vv. 16–18).

In verse 17, Jesus referred to the third Person of the Trinity as the Spirit of Truth, but here He calls Him the Holy Spirit, intentionally distinguishing Him from any other spirit. As we have already noted in verse 16, the Holy Spirit is from the Father. The new thing here is that Jesus is the medium through whom the Holy Spirit will be sent. This is the significance of the Father sending the Spirit "in [Jesus'] name."

The function of the Holy Spirit is to comfort, encourage, and communicate the truth. He also teaches (v. 26). He will both teach and remind us of Jesus' teachings. The work of the Holy Spirit is referenced here again in order to give the disciples confidence and encouragement to face Jesus' imminent departure. The Holy Spirit would have a dual function. He would both aid the disciples by recalling all that Jesus had taught them, and would also teach them Himself—even about future events (cf. 16:13).

Sources:

Barker, Kenneth L., and John R. Kohlenberger III, eds. *The Expositor's Bible Commentary*. Abridged Edition, New Testament. Grand Rapids, MI: Zondervan, 1994. 346, 349.

Barker, Kenneth L. *Zondervan Study Bible*. TNIV. Grand Rapids, MI: Zondervan, 2006. 1807–10.

Butler, Trent C., ed. "Fatherless." *Holman Bible Dictionary*. Electronic Edition, Quickverse. Nashville, TN: Holman Bible Publishers, 1991.

——. "Passover." *Holman Bible Dictionary*. Electronic Edition, Quickverse. Nashville, TN: Holman Bible Publishers, 1991.

Carson, D. A. *The Gospel According to John: Pillar New Testament Commentary*. Grand Rapids, MI: Wm. B. Eerdmans Publishing Company, 1991. 498–510.

Mounce, William D., and Robert H. Mounce, eds. *The Zondervan Greek and English Interlinear New Testament*. Grand Rapids, MI: Zondervan, 2008. 420.

Thayer, Joseph. "Entole." *Thayer's Greek Definitions*. 3rd ed. Electronic Edition, Quickverse. El Cajon, CA: Institute for Creation Research, 1999.

——. "Parakletos." *Thayer's Greek Definitions*. 3rd ed. Electronic Edition, Quickverse. El Cajon, CA: Institute for Creation Research, 1999.

Walvoord, John F., and Roy B. Zuck, eds. *The Bible Knowledge Commentary: An Exposition of the Scriptures*. Wheaton, IL: Victor Books, 1983. 323–324.

## Say It Correctly

Motif. mo-**TEEF**.
Iscariot. Is-**KAIR**-ee-ut.

## Daily Bible Readings

**MONDAY**
Is There No Balm in Gilead?
(Jeremiah 8:18–22)

**TUESDAY**
No One to Comfort Me
(Lamentations 1:17–21)

**WEDNESDAY**
Here is Your God!
(Isaiah 40:1–10)

**THURSDAY**
This is My Comfort
(Psalm 119:49–64)

**FRIDAY**
The Shepherd's Comfort
(Psalm 23)

**SATURDAY**
When the Advocate Comes
(John 15:18–26)

**SUNDAY**
An Advocate with You Forever
(John 14:15–26)

# Teaching Tips

## Words You Should Know

**A. Comforter** (John 16:7) *Parakletos* (Gk.)—One who encourages, helps, pleads the case for or represents another.

**B. Reprove** (v. 8) *elegcho* (Gk.)—To correct or criticize someone with the purpose of convincing him or her of sin or wrongdoing.

## Teacher Preparation

**Unifying Principle—Sorrow Turns to Joy.** It may be difficult to maintain a direction in life when a mentor is lost. How do people find the resources to carry on when the strength and vision of someone close to them is no longer available? Jesus promised His disciples that the Holy Spirit would be as real a presence to them as His physical presence was while He lived with them on earth.

**A.** Pray for clarity and application, for you and your students.

**B.** Study the companion lesson in the *Precepts for Living Personal Study Guide®*.

## O—Open the Lesson

**A.** Introduce today's lesson title and Aim for Change. Ask students to share their views on the Holy Spirit (Spirit of truth) and His role in their lives. Pray for clarity and for students to see the Spirit's activity in their lives.

**B.** Have students read the Keep in Mind verse and In Focus story.

**C.** In order to help them understand how the disciples were feeling, ask them to silently recall an experience of losing a loved one through death, moving, job change, etc.

## P—Present the Scriptures

**A.** Give students a few minutes to silently read The People, Places and Times, and Background.

**B.** Have students read Focal Verses (aloud or silently), encouraging them to keep in mind the information presented in The People, Places, and Times and Background.

**C.** Use In Depth content and Search the Scriptures to discuss the Focal Verses.

## E—Explore the Meaning

**A.** As a class, explore Discuss the Meaning to get a glimpse of a world without the activity of the Holy Spirit.

**B.** After reading Lesson in Our Society, have people share ways they have seen people function according to their "own truths," and how it has affected others.

## N—Next Steps for Application

**A.** Encourage students to write the names of any people who come to mind who have yet to choose Christ.

**B.** Encourage them to be prepared to share the Gospel.

## Worship Guide

For the Superintendent or Teacher
Theme: The Spirit of Truth
Song: "'Tis So Sweet to Trust in Jesus"
Devotional Reading: 1 Samuel 3:1–10

# The Spirit of Truth

**Bible Background • JOHN 16:4b–15**
**Printed Text • JOHN 16:4b–15**
**Devotional Reading • 1 SAMUEL 3:1–10**

## ———————— Aim for Change ————————

By the end of the lesson, we will: LEARN what Jesus says about how the Holy Spirit works on our behalf; EXPRESS our feelings about the loss of those close to us and the subsequent support we received; and FIND ways to tell others about how the Holy Spirit works on our behalf.

 In Focus

Ann was sixteen when her mother was diagnosed with terminal cancer. One day, she cried, sitting at her mother's feet, "I don't know how I'm going to live without you. You help me make all of my decisions. How will I know what to do?" Her mother, with tears in her eyes, said softly, "You will know. You'll be fine. Trust me. You'll do fine." At forty, Ann still remembers that conversation as if it were yesterday. There have been many decisions made over the last twenty-four years, some good, some not, but she is fine. Through college and graduate school, moving to another state, and marriage, she trusted in her mother's words. She made her decision on a college, then graduate school. She knew when it was time to make her first move to another state, and each move after that. And, when it came time to marry, she was certain Martin was the best man for her. Over time, God placed older women in her life to guide, love, encourage, and challenge her. Most importantly, He has done the same through the Holy Spirit. Ann has learned to seek God for wisdom and trust that He will provide. She still misses her mother, but she has learned that God provides.

*Today we will see how Christ encourages His disciples by promising to send a Helper.*

## ———————— Keep in Mind ————————

"Nevertheless I tell you the truth; It is expedient for you that I go away: for if I go not away, the Comforter will not come unto you; but if I depart, I will send him unto you" (John 16:7).

"Nevertheless I tell you the truth; It is expedient for you that I go away: for if I go not away, the Comforter will not come unto you; but if I depart, I will send him unto you" (John 16:7).

## Focal Verses

**KJV** **John 16:4b** And these things I said not unto you at the beginning, because I was with you.

**5** But now I go my way to him that sent me; and none of you asketh me, Whither goest thou?

**6** But because I have said these things unto you, sorrow hath filled your heart.

**7** Nevertheless I tell you the truth; It is expedient for you that I go away: for if I go not away, the Comforter will not come unto you; but if I depart, I will send him unto you.

**8** And when he is come, he will reprove the world of sin, and of righteousness, and of judgment:

**9** Of sin, because they believe not on me;

**10** Of righteousness, because I go to my Father, and ye see me no more;

**11** Of judgment, because the prince of this world is judged.

**12** I have yet many things to say unto you, but ye cannot bear them now.

**13** Howbeit when he, the Spirit of truth, is come, he will guide you into all truth: for he shall not speak of himself; but whatsoever he shall hear, that shall he speak: and he will shew you things to come.

**14** He shall glorify me: for he shall receive of mine, and shall shew it unto you.

**15** All things that the Father hath are mine: therefore said I, that he shall take of mine, and shall shew it unto you.

**NLT** **John 16:4b** "I didn't tell you earlier because I was going to be with you for a while longer.

**5** But now I am going away to the one who sent me, and not one of you is asking where I am going.

**6** Instead, you grieve because of what I've told you.

**7** But in fact, it is best for you that I go away, because if I don't, the Advocate won't come. If I do go away, then I will send him to you.

**8** And when he comes, he will convict the world of its sin, and of God's righteousness, and of the coming judgment.

**9** The world's sin is that it refuses to believe in me.

**10** Righteousness is available because I go to the Father, and you will see me no more.

**11** Judgment will come because the ruler of this world has already been judged.

**12** There is so much more I want to tell you, but you can't bear it now.

**13** When the Spirit of truth comes, he will guide you into all truth. He will not speak on his own but will tell you what he has heard. He will tell you about the future.

**14** He will bring me glory by telling you whatever he receives from me.

**15** All that belongs to the Father is mine; this is why I said, 'The Spirit will tell you whatever he receives from me.'"

## The People, Places, and Times

**The Passover.** Jesus and the disciples were in Jerusalem preparing for the Passover, one of the three annual Israelite festivals. During the Passover, an unblemished lamb was sacrificed and its blood sprinkled on the altar and in the temple. This sacrifice served as a memorial of Israel's preservation during the Exodus from Egypt, when the last plague of death "passed over" the Israelites' homes. It also pointed to sin and holy offerings required to be in right standing with God. It is no coincidence that these events, including the Crucifixion and Resurrection, occur during Passover season, when Christ became the sacrifice that protects God's people from death.

**Upper Room Discourse.** John 13–17 occurs after Jesus' triumphant entry into Jerusalem. By this time, the religious leaders (Pharisees and chief priests) have successfully begun turning the tide against Him. They have met with Judas, and agreed to pay him to identify Jesus and hand him over to be tried for His "sin"—claiming to be God. Jesus uses this time to prepare His disciples for what is to come in what is commonly known as the Upper Room Discourse. Several well-known passages are found in this portion of Scripture: John 14:1–7 (I am the way, truth, and life), John 14:15–21 (You are not orphans), John 15:1–17 (the true vine), John 17 (Christ's High Priestly prayer).

## Background

This Gospel is attributed to John, son of Zebedee and one of Christ's closest disciples. His purpose for writing the book is found in John 20:31: "But these are written so that you may continue to believe that Jesus is the Messiah, the Son of God, and that by believing in him you will have life by the power of his name" (NLT). John accomplished this by recording Christ's claims of being one with God, such as the "I AM" statements (e.g. 11:25, 14:6) and seven divine miracles (signs) that Christ performed. With such proof, John urged his readers to trust in Jesus for eternal life (3:16–21).

The antagonists throughout this Gospel are the Pharisees, Jewish religious leaders who claimed to have the truth as keepers of the Law, but who refused to believe the truth of Christ. Pride and legalism prevented them from seeing the truth, and even caused them to attribute God's action to Satan (cf. 9:13–34). As John wrote, "But though he had

done so many miracles before them, yet they believed not on him" (12:37).

In this particular passage, Christ told His disciples to expect the Holy Spirit, who will reveal more of the truth of who He is (His glory). The immediate recipients of His instructions were His apostles, but the principles also apply to His future followers.

## At-A-Glance

1. The Coming of the Holy Spirit
(John 16:4b–7)
2. Work of the Holy Spirit: Conviction
(vv. 8–11)
3. Work of the Holy Spirit: Guidance
(vv. 12–15)

## In Depth

### 1. The Coming of the Holy Spirit (John 16:4b–7)

Continuing His instructions, Jesus tells the disciples that after He leaves them, a Comforter or Advocate will arrive—the Holy Spirit. While they are understandably sad, He points out that they are so consumed with how His leaving affect them in the present, they are missing the future benefit—the Holy Spirit, who will abide with them forever (14:16). Jesus says that it would be expedient for Him to leave, because this would prepare the way for the Holy Spirit to come.

Until this point, Christ is the main target of the world's wrath. After His resurrection, the disciples would be. As such, they would need a Helper, an encourager and Advocate who does not have the physical limitations of a body and would indwell and equip all believers. After Jesus' departure, they would no longer be sad. The Holy Spirit would comfort them and bring them joy in the absence of Jesus' physical presence.

321

## 2. Work of the Holy Spirit: Conviction (vv. 8–11)

This Advocate would have a different role in believers' and unbelievers' lives. Ultimately He would function as a guide for both. The guidance of the Holy Spirit for unbelievers would be in the direction of initially submitting to the Lordship of Christ and turning away from sin. John refers to those who don't believe as "the world." This does not refer to the physical creation, but everyone who does not follow Jesus.

The Spirit would bring conviction to the world in three areas: sin, righteousness, and judgment. The Spirit reveals the things that people say, think, and do that offend God, working to convince them to turn away from sin and turn toward God. He is also the one who convinces the world that not only are they sinners, but that righteousness (or right standing) before God only comes from Christ's sacrifice—His death, resurrection, and return to heaven to reign with His Father. Finally, the Holy Spirit reveals that those who insist on rejecting God through unbelief stand condemned along with Satan, the prince of the world.

## 3. Work of the Holy Spirit: Guidance (vv. 12–15)

The Holy Spirit would come not only to convict the world, but also to guide believers as the Spirit of truth. The apostles are used to having Christ as their rabbi, teaching and guiding them. Now, they would have to rely on the Holy Spirit. Jesus comments that He has more to tell them but they could not bear it. When the Holy Spirit comes then He would lead them and guide them into all the truth that they could not handle at that moment.

During this time, the Pharisees lived by and enforced their version of truth, unable to grasp the real truth that was before them—Christ, as the Son of God. Christ tells His disciples that the Holy Spirit would come and "guide you into all truth." Not only would the Spirit come to help them understand and remember the things Christ taught (14:26), He would speak God's words to them, and tell them what is to come. They would go on to share these truths with the world, bringing glory to God. As a result, they helped to shape the New Testament Scriptures and led the church as it spread in the ancient Roman world.

## Search the Scriptures

1. What is the Holy Spirit's role to the world (John 16:8–11)?

2. What is one of the Holy Spirit's roles to the apostles and believers (vv. 12–15)?

## Discuss the Meaning

The Holy Spirit has often been relegated to being a mere "conscience" or the force behind emotional responses in church. This passage reveals that people's lives are affected for eternity by His ministry. What would happen if people were left to their own devices to determine what is offensive to God? How would the world have been impacted if the Holy Spirit had not guided the apostles in sharing their faith and writing what is now the New Testament?

## Lesson in Our Society

We live during a time when people mistakenly believe they can create their own truths depending upon how they feel, what they believe, and how much energy they put toward it. However, not believing something is true does not make it false. If a person does not believe the sky is blue, it does not change the reality that it is. The Holy Spirit is as living and active now as He was in John's day. He still points people to truth, using God's Word and other people. The Spirit of truth still convicts of sin, righteousness, and judgment. He still guides into all truth—just not those truths that make people comfortable.

## Make It Happen

The Holy Spirit still reveals sinners' need for Christ and works to convince them to believe in Him. If there are people in your life who do not believe in Christ, pray for them. Ask God for opportunities, grace, and wisdom through the Holy Spirit to share His truth with them.

## Follow the Spirit

What God wants me to do:

_____

_____

_____

_____

## Remember Your Thoughts

Special insights I have learned:

_____

_____

_____

_____

## More Light on the Text
### John 16:4b–15

This passage is a part of the Upper Room Discourse of John 13–17. The discourse includes Jesus' announcement of His betrayal and crucifixion. Jesus also lets the disciples know of the future. His intention is to warn them of the coming persecution and comfort them with the promise of His resurrection and the coming of the Holy Spirit.

In John 16, Jesus talks to the disciples concerning the work of the Holy Spirit in the world. This work would be important because of Jesus' physical absence from the earth. He lets them know that not only would the Holy Spirit show them the Father's love by making His home in them, but the Spirit would also work in the world. This work would consist of reproving or convicting. Jesus lets the disciples know that although He will not be with them, the Spirit would be there to guide them into all truth. He also speaks of how the Spirit's indwelling the disciples will glorify Jesus by declaring the Father's words.

**4b And these things I said not unto you at the beginning, because I was with you.**

Jesus had not needed to tell them about persecution and future troubles because He was present with them. From the very beginning, they had walked with Jesus and learned from Him. They had assisted Him in performing miracles and witnessed signs and wonders. They were His disciples. The Pharisees and the teachers of the law confronted Him and not His students. He was there to take the brunt of the attacks and be a shield to protect them. Soon He would leave, and they would be confronted as the ones who followed and learned from Him.

**5 But now I go my way to him that sent me; and none of you asketh me, Whither goest thou?**

In John 14:5, Thomas had asked, "Lord we don't know where you are going, so how can we know the way?" (NIV). He didn't ask Jesus where He was going but made a statement about how confused he was by Jesus' pronouncement of going away. Here, Jesus states that He was going "to him that sent me." This should have aroused curiosity within the disciples. If they followed Jesus for such a long time, they should have been hungry to know who sent Him. Jesus is speaking of His ascension to heaven to return to the Father. The confusion of the disciples indicates that they must have only thought of Jesus' departure on a purely physical level.

**6 But because I have said these things unto you, sorrow hath filled your heart.**

The disciples are sad because Jesus is leaving them. They don't understand that He is referring to His ascension and that He is going to the Father. They are merely thinking on an earthly level and do not realize that Jesus is the Son of God, sent to earth to die and rise again. At this point they are only thinking of Him as an earthly rabbi who would teach them things and perform some miracles. As a result, when Jesus talks about leaving, sorrow fills their hearts. They don't understand the broader spiritual implications.

**7 Nevertheless I tell you the truth; It is expedient for you that I go away: for if I go not away, the Comforter will not come unto you; but if I depart, I will send him unto you.**

In this section, Jesus tells them how important and necessary it is that He should leave them. Unless He departs, the Spirit will not come. He has already told them about the persecution they will encounter and the sorrow they will have at His leaving. Despite the fact that they are grieving His departure, He has a message of hope for them connected to His physical absence. There is a definite advantage for the disciples that He departs, because then the Spirit (Counselor) would come. "Expedient" (Gk. *sumphero*, **soom-FAIR-oh**) means profitable, beneficial, or for one's good. This word is used two other times in John (11:50, 18:14), and in both of these passages, the verb refers to Jesus' death and the fact that it will benefit everyone. It is profitable for them for

Jesus to leave, because at the moment He is localized. The only access to Him they could have is to be physically present with Him in Palestine. After Jesus ascends to heaven, the Spirit would then be with the disciples and those who came after Him, no matter where they found themselves. It is also expedient because as Jesus explains in the next verse, the Comforter would come with a definite agenda of convicting the world. This is something that could not happen until the ascension of Christ into heaven.

The use of the word "Comforter" adds another specific dimension in the activities of the Holy Spirit in view of the persecution that would come to them. The word in Greek is *parakletos* (**pah-RAH-klay-tose**), which can mean comforter, advocate or helper. In this passage, the Spirit takes on all of these roles in different ways as one who convicts the world and serves as God's messenger to believers and the world.

The phrase "I will send him unto you" and other passages indicate the manner in which the Holy Spirit is sent to us. He is the gift of God who emanates from the Father (14:16, 26) and is sent by the Son (15:26, 16:7; cf. Luke 24:49). Humans have no part in initiating the process. God takes the initiative. Furthermore, the coming of the Spirit, as we have noted, depends on the departure of Jesus (John 16:7, cf. 7:39). The role of the Spirit as Comforter is to be with the disciples to lead them and guide them in Jesus' absence. Up until this point, they had been following the incarnate Son. After Jesus leaves, they would be following the indwelling Spirit.

**8 And when he is come, he will reprove the world of sin, and of righteousness, and of judgment: 9 Of sin, because they believe not on me; 10 Of righteousness, because I go to my Father, and ye see me no more;**

**11 Of judgment, because the prince of this world is judged.**

These four verses constitute some of the fundamental beliefs in the Christian doctrine concerning the work of the Holy Spirit in the process of conversion. In them, Jesus reveals what hitherto has not been stressed, i.e., the Spirit's work to reprove or convict. The word "reprove" (Gk. *elegcho*, **el-ENG-kho**) means to convict, convince, or expose.

Jesus describes the threefold work of conviction by the Holy Spirit. First, He will convict the world of sin. The Holy Spirit will cause people to recognize their sinfulness in the sight of God. This includes the major sin of not believing in Christ. This rejection of the Gospel of Christ (and the rejection of His person) is the most serious offense because without Christ, all the other sins committed by a person cannot be forgiven.

Second, the Spirit convicts the world of righteousness. Here He will bring to their consciousness the standard of righteousness that God demands from all. That standard of righteousness is Christ, and without His presence in the world, we are at a loss for the true standard of what God requires for humanity. The "righteousness" here that God requires is communicated by the Greek word *dikaiosune* (**dee-keye-oh-SOO-nay**), which can also be translated "justification." It means being judicially right in the sight of God. Human justification is the gift of God through our belief in Christ. It is not earned; it is the work of faith. Jesus, however, lived a perfectly obedient life pleasing in God's sight. The Holy Spirit, therefore, will point toward Jesus' righteousness after Christ leaves and cannot show it Himself. His righteousness is the standard, and the role of the Holy Spirit is to illuminate that righteousness to the world. Therefore, the Spirit's work here is consistent with His function as a reminder of all the teachings of Christ (14:26).

The third work of the Spirit is to convict the world of judgment, "because the prince of this world is judged." The prince or ruler of this world refers to Satan (see 12:31, 14:30; 2 Corinthians 4:4; Ephesians 2:2; 1 John 4:4). Satan is the author and source of all evil and unbelief. The word "judged" (Gk. *krino*, **KREE-no**) is the language of a court of law and has the idea of being condemned. The noun form speaks of decision, passing a judgment, or verdict by a jury or a tribunal. The world, of course, is the world system ruled by the devil, whom Jesus referred to as their father (see John 8:44). Therefore, Jesus says that those who refuse to believe in the Gospel face the same fate of condemnation as their master the devil has already received (see Luke 10:18–20; John 3:36; Revelation 20:11–15, 21:8). The actual condemnation or defeat of the prince of this world was accomplished on the Cross. We see the work of the Holy Spirit is to reveal or expose not only the sin of unbelief, but also its result of judgment or condemnation, which awaits unbelievers. The Holy Spirit, on the one hand, brings people to the consciousness of their sins and leads them to repent and believe in the Gospel, while on the other hand, He also condemns those who refuse to repent, just like their master the devil.

**12 I have yet many things to say unto you, but ye cannot bear them now.**

The above sayings are no doubt hard to understand even to the disciples. They are perplexed and cannot make sense of what He is saying. Jesus recognizes their plight and says that He understands their situation. He realizes that they cannot comprehend all that He has been teaching—either the teachings are so highly spiritual that the disciples cannot fully understand them, or the disciples are so filled with emotion that they find it hard to bear the news of His imminent departure. Therefore, Jesus tells them that although He still has lots of things to tell them, He will not do so. The reason is they "cannot bear them now." "Bear" (Gk. *bastazo*, **bahs-TAD-zoh**) translates to carry, or bear something heavy or burdensome. In view of their emotional state, they could not carry the weight of what He wanted to say to them. It would be too much for them to take it all in. What are the things that would be too hard for them? They include "things to come" (from v. 13), both the immediate future and the end time events.

**13 Howbeit when he, the Spirit of truth, is come, he will guide you into all truth: for he shall not speak of himself; but whatsoever he shall hear, that shall he speak: and he will shew you things to come. 14 He shall glorify me: for he shall receive of mine, and shall shew it unto you. 15 All things that the Father hath are mine: therefore said I, that he shall take of mine, and shall shew it unto you.**

In this section, Jesus continues to explain to them the work of the Holy Spirit, whom He names the Spirit of truth (14:17, 15:26; cf. 1 John 4:6). His mission here is to guide the believer into all truth about Christ, not of Himself. He will be the medium of God's communication to mankind. Through the communication of the Holy Spirit, Christ will be glorified (cf. 15:26) because the Holy Spirit will not speak on His own authority, but whatever Christ reveals to Him (cf. 14:24). The word "glorify" (*doxazo*, **dok-SAHD-zo**) means to cause the dignity and worth of some person or thing to become manifest and acknowledged. Whatever can be known about Jesus, the Spirit will reveal to the disciples. Because Jesus is God incarnate, the Spirit will glorify Him by communicating for Him

and about Him to believers. What would the Spirit receive from Jesus? The truth about Jesus. He would communicate the truth about Jesus to the disciples and to the world. This would lead to Jesus being glorified.

In verse 15, Jesus equates Himself with the Father since the revelation is from both the Father and the Son through the Spirit. Here we see that God's Word—all truth—is a combined work of the Trinity.

Sources:

Grudem, Wayne. *Bible Doctrine*. Grand Rapids, MI: Zondervan, 1999. 104–10.

*Hebrew-Greek Key Word Study Bible*. King James Version. Chattanooga, TN: AMG Publishers, Inc., 1991.

Keener, Craig S. *The IVP Bible Background Commentary: New Testament*. Downers Grove, IL: InterVarsity Press, 1993. 260–63, 302–303.

Radmacher, Earl D., ed. *Nelson Study Bible*. New King James Version. Nashville, TN: Thomas Nelson Publishers, 1997. 1754–1755, 1792–1800.

Ryrie, Charles C. *Ryrie Study Bible*. New International Version. Chicago, IL: Moody Press. 1986. 1480–81.

Unger, Merrill F. *The New Unger's Bible Dictionary*. Chicago, IL: Moody Press, 1988. 410–11.

Walvoord, John F., and Roy B. Zuck, eds. *The Bible Knowledge Commentary: New Testament*. Wheaton, IL: Victor Books, SP Publications, Inc., 1983. 327–29.

*Zondervan Study Bible*. New International Version. Grand Rapids, MI: Zondervan Publishers, 2002. 1661–62.

## Say It Correctly

Expedient. eks-**PEE**-dee-ent.
Reprove. ri-**PROOV**.
Zebedee. **ZEH**-buh-dee.

## Daily Bible Readings

**MONDAY**
Where There is No Prophecy
(Proverbs 29:12–18)

**TUESDAY**
The Lord Has Closed Your Eyes
(Isaiah 29:8–14)

**WEDNESDAY**
Speak, for Your Servant is Listening
(1 Samuel 3:1–10)

**THURSDAY**
A Trustworthy Prophet of the Lord
(1 Samuel 3:11–21)

**FRIDAY**
I Commit My Spirit
(Psalm 31:1–8)

**SATURDAY**
Worship in Spirit and Truth
(John 4:21–26)

**SUNDAY**
The Spirit of Truth Will Guide You
(John 16:4b–15)

# Notes

# Teaching Tips

## Words You Should Know

**A. Remit** (John 20:23) *aphiemi* (Gk.)—To dismiss, forsake, leave, to forgive debts or sins.

**B. Retain** (v. 23) *krateo* (Gk.)—To hold onto, not remit, or seize control of.

## Teacher Preparation

**Unifying Principle—Peace, Power, Presence**. A charismatic speaker can often lift and inspire an attentive audience. What is done and said to bring about such an effect? Jesus speaks peace to and empowers the disciples with the gift of the Holy Spirit.

**A.** Pray for clarity and application, for you and your students.

**B.** Preview and prepare a clip from the film *The Great Debaters*. Specifically, use the scene in which James Farmer Jr. speaks about lynching and the rule of law in the Jim Crow South.

## O—Open the Lesson

**A.** Introduce and show the clip from *The Great Debaters*. Point out how James Farmer Jr.'s speech affects the people listening and how he uses his power and influence to touch minds and hearts in the audience.

**B.** Introduce today's lesson title and Aim for Change.

**C.** Have students read the Keep in Mind verse and the In Focus story.

## P—Present the Scriptures

**A.** Give students a few minutes to silently read The People, Places, and Times; and Background.

**B.** Have students read Focal Verses (aloud or silently).

**C.** Use the In Depth content and Search the Scriptures to facilitate discussion on the Focal Verses.

## E—Explore the Meaning

**A.** As a class, explore Discuss the Meaning, Lesson in Our Society, and Make it Happen.

## N—Next Steps for Application

**A.** Pray that God will reveal the barriers preventing students from fulfilling their purposes.

**B.** Have students share with a neighbor what they believe are their barriers.

**C.** As a class, discuss some of the common barriers and what role the Holy Spirit plays in overcoming these.

## Worship Guide

For the Superintendent or Teacher
Theme: Receive the Holy Spirit
Song: "Sweet, Sweet Spirit"
Devotional Reading: Romans 14:13–19

# Receive the Holy Spirit

**Bible Background • JOHN 20:19–23; ACTS 1:4–8, 2:1–4**
**Printed Text • JOHN 20:19–23**
**Devotional Reading • ROMANS 14:13–19**

## Aim for Change

By the end of the lesson, we will: EXPLORE the importance of Jesus' appearance to the disciples; DESCRIBE our feelings from times when the words of others calmed our fears; and PERFORM the mission God has for our lives as empowered by the Holy Spirit.

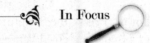 In Focus

It started out as just volunteering at the local crisis pregnancy center. Joy wanted young ladies to know that there was hope for them as they faced unplanned pregnancies. One woman, Ama, who came to America on a school visa, entered into a relationship and found herself pregnant, alone, and ashamed. But, Joy gave her hope. Ama went on to raise her son, telling him stories of his heritage and his homeland. When he was old enough, he decided he wanted to return to their home country to attend university. Ama decided to go with him. Once there, she developed relationships with young women who were in similar situations that she had been in. She grieved, knowing there was more to be done, but unsure of what and how to do it. So she prayed for wisdom, and Joy came to mind. They reconnected, and from one conversation a vision was born. Today, Ama's organization provides shelter, job training, Bible studies, and parenting support for young ladies in four different countries.

*Today's lesson shows how the Holy Spirit can empower us to make a difference, for God's glory.*

## Keep in Mind

"And when he had said this, he breathed on them, and saith unto them, Receive ye the Holy Ghost" (John 20:22).

"And when he had said this, he breathed on them, and saith unto them, Receive ye the Holy Ghost" (John 20:22).

## Focal Verses

**KJV** **John 20:19** Then the same day at evening, being the first day of the week, when the doors were shut where the disciples were assembled for fear of the Jews, came Jesus and stood in the midst, and saith unto them, Peace be unto you.

**20** And when he had so said, he shewed unto them his hands and his side. Then were the disciples glad, when they saw the LORD.

**21** Then said Jesus to them again, Peace be unto you: as my Father hath sent me, even so send I you.

**22** And when he had said this, he breathed on them, and saith unto them, Receive ye the Holy Ghost:

**23** Whose soever sins ye remit, they are remitted unto them; and whose soever sins ye retain, they are retained.

**NLT** **John 20:19** That Sunday evening the disciples were meeting behind locked doors because they were afraid of the Jewish leaders. Suddenly, Jesus was standing there among them! "Peace be with you," he said.

**20** As he spoke, he showed them the wounds in his hands and his side. They were filled with joy when they saw the Lord!

**21** Again he said, "Peace be with you. As the Father has sent me, so I am sending you."

**22** Then he breathed on them and said, "Receive the Holy Spirit.

**23** If you forgive anyone's sins, they are forgiven. If you do not forgive them, they are not forgiven."

### The People, Places, and Times

**The Resurrection.** The Resurrection occurred on the third day after Christ's crucifixion, and was an awesome demonstration of God's power and Christ's deity. While it had been prophesied, it was not necessarily expected, even by the disciples. In fact, John writes, "For until [they saw the empty tomb] they still hadn't understood the Scriptures that said Jesus must rise from the dead" (20:9, NLT). There has been age-old debate regarding whether the Resurrection was bodily or spiritual. However, several facts point to bodily. First, the grave was empty. Next, there were witnesses. He appeared to Mary, the disciples and more than five hundred other people over forty days (see Acts 1:3; 1 Corinthians 15:3–7). Finally, when He appeared, His body still had the actual wounds, He was able to be touched, and He ate (John 21:9–15).

**The Jews.** "The Jews" (20:19, KJV) were the Jewish leaders—Pharisees, chief priests, scribes, etc.—who were the religious and moral authorities during Jesus' time. The Gospel writers tend to highlight their arrogance, legalism, hypocrisy, and unbelief, though John does also show at least one, a Pharisee named Nicodemus, hearing Jesus out (3:1–21). The majority of these leaders, however, were responsible for provoking the people to call for Jesus' death. As Christ warned the disciples though, the hatred that was directed toward Him during His life was redirected toward His followers afterward. Soon after the Resurrection, the disciples witnessed or experienced hostility, false imprisonment, false accusations, beatings, murder, bribery, and deception—all committed by these key religious and moral leaders of their society.

## Background

After spending several years with the man claiming to be the Messiah and Son of God and seeing Him perform untold numbers of miracles (so many that "if they should be written every one ... the world itself could not contain the books that should be written," from John 21:25), it was disheartening for the disciples to witness His death. The disciples knew Christ's miraculous power. They had seen Him escape from His enemies several times. They, like many Jews, were expecting Him to be a triumphant King who would free them from their oppressors, the Romans, and usher in a new worldly kingdom (Luke 24:21; John 6:15). But He was dead. Not only that, but because of the hostility of the Jewish leaders, they feared for their lives, locking themselves behind closed doors. Christ's promises that they would go on to "greater works" (John 14:12) looked grim.

Amid grief, mourning, doubt, chaos, fear, and unbearable shame, the disciples would need a great deal of hope, encouragement, and strength to go forward on the mission for which He had prepared them.

## Say It Correctly

1. Christ Appears to the Disciples (John 20:19–20)
2. Christ Commissions the Disciples (vv. 21–23)

## In Depth

### 1. Christ Appears to the Disciples (John 20:19–20)

After appearing to Mary Magdalene at the tomb very early Sunday morning, Christ pays a visit to the majority of His disciples, although Thomas is not there (v. 24). This would be one of many visits that Christ would give to His disciples before ascending to heaven. What makes this visit special are the words that Christ speaks to them that foretell their upcoming mission. As they gather in fear, Jesus arrives—despite locked doors—and brings a greeting of peace. While "Peace be unto you" was a common Jewish greeting in those days, Christ's words carry several meanings.

First, He who was dead is now alive. The disciples can be at peace and relieved from grief and mourning. Next, they can rest knowing that the man with them is still God, and in spite of having a physical body capable of dying, He still transcends time and space, unhindered by locked doors. Finally, it was common to believe in ghosts and spirits. His greeting of "peace," followed by revealing His wounds, assures them that He is not a ghost, so they have no need to be afraid. They are overjoyed!

### 2. Christ Commissions the Disciples (vv. 21–23)

In the Bible, phrases that are repeated are often important. In this short passage, Christ exhorts His disciples to be at peace twice. He has proven that He has risen. He now encourages them: "Peace be unto you!" They no longer need to fear their persecutors because God is with them. And, despite abandoning Him, they are not disqualified from service. He assures them that just as God sent Him to earth to fulfill a mission, He is sending them into the world to do the same. But He not only sends them, He equips them.

The word used for Spirit here is *pneuma* (Gk., **puh-NEW-ma**), as opposed to *parakletos* (Gk., **pa-RAH-klay-tose,** helper) in last week's lesson. *Pneuma* is also translated as breath and wind. In a play on words reminiscent of God breathing life into Adam, Christ breathes on the disciples and equips them with the Holy Spirit, who He previously told them would lead, guide, instruct, and comfort them. Now is the time for them to go forth to fulfill their mission—sharing the Gospel. Those who choose to believe their message would be forgiven and granted eternal life. Those who reject Christ, would not.

## Search the Scriptures

1. What phrase does Christ use twice (John 20:19, 21)?

2. What is the disciples' mission (vv. 22–23)?

## Discuss the Meaning

There are many obstacles that can prevent us from fulfilling our mission. Fear is a major one. While we may attempt to overcome fear in a variety of ways, Christ demonstrates that only one Person is needed. How did He equip the disciples? Do we tend to view the Holy Spirit as powerful? Why do we sometimes act with limited views of the Holy Spirit's work and powerful existence?

## Lesson in Our Society

We have the tendency to underestimate the power of one and the power of the tongue. Genocide has occurred because one person determined that certain people were not worthy of living and convinced others to go along with his views. In other instances, one man or woman with a vision has sparked movements, inspired change, and positively altered the course of history. Just one.

## Make It Happen

There is work to be done for God's glory. What passion has God given you? What problems do you see that you sense God has wired you to be part of solving? What stops you? Write this out, and place it somewhere you will see it often. Pray that God would equip you with His Spirit to fulfill the mission He has given you.

## Follow the Spirit

What God wants me to do:

_____

_____

_____

_____

## Remember Your Thoughts

Special insights I have learned:

_____

_____

_____

_____

## More Light on the Text

John 20:19–23

**19 Then the same day at evening, being the first day of the week, when the doors were shut where the disciples were assembled for fear of the Jews, came Jesus and stood in the midst, and saith unto them, Peace be unto you.**

In these verses, the resurrected Jesus appears to a group of disciples for the first time. First, Jesus appeared to Mary alone as she visited the tomb. Then Peter and the other disciple (assumed to be John) arrived at the empty tomb. Although they did not see Jesus, the empty tomb and His grave clothes neatly wrapped and laid to the side had been enough to cause them to believe. This occurred on Sunday, suggesting the practice of Christians gathering on that day, the first day of the week, corresponding with verse 1. Ten of the eleven disciples are gathered together after the crisis of seeing their rabbi

Jesus arrested and executed by the Jewish rulers and Roman government. As a result, the disciples are fearful of the Jewish leaders and have hidden themselves from public sight. They do not want to risk being seen in public since their previous association with Jesus is widely known.

The doors are shut. Having the doors locked was a measure of precaution, but here it is mentioned with a reference to the appearance of Jesus. Locked doors prove to not be a barrier to His resurrected body. This suggests that the normal limitations of our bodies will be removed in the Resurrection. It also suggests that nothing can keep Jesus from engaging our human condition. Our fears and anxieties cannot keep Jesus from coming to stand with us in whatever situation we find ourselves in. "Peace be unto you" was a common Jewish greeting (*Shalom*), meaning "May all be well with you." As a Jew speaking to Jews, this word had additional connotations of prosperity, health, and blessing. Although this word was common in Jewish culture, when spoken by the Messiah, it means infinitely more. When Jesus says "peace," He actively gives what the word means. Peace is here presented as a gift from the risen Christ.

**20 And when he had so said, he shewed unto them his hands and his side. Then were the disciples glad, when they saw the LORD.**

The risen Christ now reveals the genuineness of this gift before the eyes of the disciples. Jesus shows them the price with which He bought their peace: His pierced hands, His spear-pierced side, evidence of His death by crucifixion. These holy wounds proclaim that Jesus is at peace with the believers. The word *deiknuo* (Gk., **dayk-NOO-oh**), to show, is a word that also means to give evidence or proof of a thing. Showing His hands and His

side would be unmistakable evidence that the same Jesus who walked with them and who was crucified is now appearing among them. The disciples are glad because they see the Lord. They heard secondhand of Jesus' resurrection from Mary, Peter, and John, but this time they see it for themselves. In the risen Jesus, their heavenly, divine Lord, they experience peace. Doubt did not disappear all at once. Jesus appear again and again, intensifying faith and joy, until nothing could ever disturb the solid certainty of their belief.

**21 Then said Jesus to them again, Peace be unto you: as my Father hath sent me, even so send I you.**

"Peace be unto you" is a repetition of the first greeting. Jesus repeats this phrase for a number of possible reasons. One possibility is that the first time was intended to take away fear, while the second time is to call attention to the seriousness of His commission. Another possibility is that Jesus wants to encourage them in the mission that He is sending them to do. He wants them to know that although they would experience trials and difficulties, His peace would be with them. Jesus then commissions the disciples using relational analogies: "As my Father hath sent me, even so send I you." By this commission, the believers now bear the same divine authorization as Christ. Jesus has been sent into the world for a specific task and purpose, mainly His death and resurrection. The disciples are now authorized for the specific purpose of witnessing to His death and resurrection. They are authorized and commissioned to the task of dispensing this gift of peace in a troubled world. Jesus' Gospel is the Gospel of peace. Jesus Himself is our peace. He gives it to the disciples because those who bring peace must have peace.

Here the word *apostello* (Gk. **ah-poe-STEL-loh**) is used for the Father sending

Jesus. Jesus uses another word for His sending of the disciples into the world: *pempo* (Gk. **PEHM-poe**). This word means to send or thrust, but does not carry authoritative connotation. The emphasis is on the specific action of sending or thrusting out. Jesus is saying just as the Father authorized and commissioned Him for a specific task, He would send or thrust His disciples out into the world. In the use of *apostello*, the emphasis is on the relationship between the sender and the sent one, while in the use of *pempo*, the emphasis is on the specific action of the verb. Jesus Christ, risen from the dead and glorified, tells the disciples that God's mission becomes their mission as well.

**22 And when he had said this, he breathed on them, and saith unto them, Receive ye the Holy Ghost.**

He who sends enables those whom He sends, by the empowerment of the Holy Spirit. "Breathed on them" (Gk. *emphusao*, **em-foo-SAH-oh**) recalls the ancient association of spirit with breath and invokes Genesis 2:7. Jesus breathes on them in the same way that God breathed on Adam after shaping and forming him from the dust. This signifies that the church would be a new humanity created in the image of Christ. By breathing on them, Jesus foreshadows what would happen some weeks later on the day of Pentecost as the Spirit filled the house where they were praying like a mighty rushing wind. They would be empowered by the Holy Spirit for the commission that He has just given them. Jesus was filled with the Spirit at the start of His ministry; it would be no less so for the disciples.

The word for receive (Gk. *lambano*, **lam-BAH-no**) is in the imperative mood, which indicates a command. Jesus is not inviting them to receive the Holy Spirit. It is not an option. He is commanding them to receive the Holy Spirit. By using this form of the verb, Jesus implies that the Holy Spirit is indispensable, necessary for the task that He has given them.

**23 Whose soever sins ye remit, they are remitted unto them; and whose soever sins ye retain, they are retained.**

With this act comes responsibility to execute the divine will among believers and all humanity in the form of forgiveness. By this act, the risen Christ transforms fear into a great joy. The gift of the Spirit is to empower the disciples to proclaim the terms of forgiveness. Jesus wants the remission of sins announced to sinners excluding only those who refuse remission.

Two words are significant: "remit" and "retain." To remit (Gk. *aphiemi*, **ah-FEE-ey-mee**) means to send away. Here the sins are removed from the sinner, as far as the east is from the west (see Psalm 103:12), blotting out the transgressions so that the Lord Himself will not remember them (see Isaiah 43:25). Forgiveness is infinite. To retain (Gk. *krateo*, **krah-TEH-oh**) is to hold fast with strength. The sins committed are not able to be let go. The moment a sin is committed, that sin with all its guilt adheres to the sinner and no human effort can possibly blot it out. Only one person is able to remove that sin, to remove it as though it had never existed: Jesus Christ our Lord. It is still Jesus who dismisses or holds sins, yet by this act that empowers the disciples, He makes them His agents of reconciliation.

Sources:
*Hebrew-Greek Key Word Study Bible.* King James Version. Chattanooga, TN: AMG Publishers, Inc., 1991.
Keener, Craig S. *The IVP Bible Background Commentary: New Testament.* Downers Grove, IL: InterVarsity Press, 1993. 315–17.
Radmacher, Earl D., ed. *Nelson Study Bible.* New King James Version. Nashville, TN: Thomas Nelson Publishers, 1997. 1807–1808.

Ryrie, Charles C. *Ryrie Study Bible.* New International Version. Chicago, IL: Moody Press. 1986. 1487–89.

Unger, Merrill F. *The New Unger's Bible Dictionary.* Chicago, IL: Moody Press, 1988. 1074–75.

Walvoord, John F., and Roy B. Zuck, eds. *The Bible Knowledge Commentary: New Testament.* Wheaton, IL: Victor Books, SP Publications, Inc., 1983. 341–43.

*Zondervan Study Bible.* New International Version. Grand Rapids, MI: Zondervan Publishers, 2002. 1669–70.

# Say It Correctly

Pentecost. **PEN**-teh-cost.
Shalom. sha-**LOME**.

# Daily Bible Readings

**MONDAY**
The Holy Spirit Speaks
(Mark 13:5–11)

**TUESDAY**
Gentiles Receive the Holy Spirit
(Acts 10:39–48)

**WEDNESDAY**
Full of the Spirit and Faith
(Acts 11:19–26)

**THURSDAY**
Joy in the Holy Spirit
(Romans 14:13–19)

**FRIDAY**
Power from the Holy Spirit
(Acts 1:4–8)

**SATURDAY**
Be Filled with the Spirit
(Ephesians 5:15–21)

**SUNDAY**
Receive the Holy Spirit
(John 20:19–23)

# Teaching Tips

## Words You Should Know

**A. Hosanna** (Mark 11:9–10) *hosanna* (Gk.)—From the Hebrew words *yasha'* (**ya-SHAW**, to save) and *na'* (**NAH**, now).

**B. Blessed** (vv. 9–10) *eulogeo* (Gk.)—To praise, celebrate with praises.

## Teacher Preparation

**Unifying Principle—Hail to the Chief**. People want to be in the presence of and pay homage to important people. Why are celebrity events important to us? The people celebrated Jesus' arrival in Jerusalem as the coming of God's kingdom.

**A.** Pray for you and your students to understand the lesson.

**B.** Study Mark 11 using at least three Bible versions.

**C.** Study the lesson in the *Precepts for Living Personal Study Guide®*.

## O—Open the Lesson

**A.** Open with prayer and the Aim for Change.

**B.** Have a volunteer read the In Focus story aloud.

**C.** Ask the class to discuss the ways in which they are like the characters in the story.

## P—Present the Scriptures

**A.** Read the Focal Verses aloud.

**B.** Have volunteers read The People, Places, and Things and Background sections aloud.

**C.** Use the In Depth and More Light on the Text sections to do an exposition of each text verse.

**D.** Have the students answer the questions in the Search the Scriptures section and discuss.

## E—Explore the Meaning

**A.** Discuss the Discuss the Meaning and Lesson in Our Society and then share with the rest of the class.

**B.** Have the students silently read the Keep in Mind verse and the Devotional Reading.

## N—Next Steps for Application

**A.** Have the students write on sticky notes concrete ways they can start to honor God. Ask them to take these notes home and stick them where they'll see them.

**B.** Each time the students do one of these tasks, they can take the note down.

## Worship Guide

For the Superintendent or Teacher
Theme: The One Who Comes
Song: "Victory Chant (Hail Jesus)"
Devotional Reading: Isaiah 45:20–25

# The One Who Comes

**Bible Background • MARK 11:1–11**
**Printed Text • MARK 11:1–11**
**Devotional Reading • ISAIAH 45:20–25**

## Aim for Change

By the end of the lesson, we will: SURVEY the story of Jesus' Triumphal Entry into Jerusalem; DISCUSS our feelings about the kingdom of God; and FIND creative ways to pay homage to Jesus.

## In Focus

Donna was an avid basketball fan. She bought season tickets every year and did not mind paying a small fortune for them. One player in particular was her favorite. She would spend another fortune on any sports gear with her player's number on it. She called in sick so she could go to the parade after he and his team won the championship. She just had to be in the crowd, waving his jersey and shouting his name. One day Donna's mother asked her, "If Jesus were to come to town, would you be as fanatical about Him as you are about your favorite player?" After much thought, Donna honestly said she probably would not. This disturbed her a great deal, and she decided to devote more time to finding ways to honor Jesus for His love and salvation. Donna still watches basketball and still admires her favorite player, but now gives greater effort to celebrating the Lord of her life.

*We should all live to honor Christ as the One who came to save us. In today's lesson, we will examine how and why the people honored Him.*

## Keep in Mind

"And they that went before, and they that followed, cried, saying, Hosanna; Blessed is he that cometh in the name of the Lord" (Mark 11:9).

"And they that went before, and they that followed, cried, saying, Hosanna; Blessed is he that cometh in the name of the Lord" (Mark 11:9).

# Focal Verses

**KJV** **Mark 11:1** And when they came nigh to Jerusalem, unto Bethphage and Bethany, at the mount of Olives, he sendeth forth two of his disciples,

**2** And saith unto them, Go your way into the village over against you: and as soon as ye be entered into it, ye shall find a colt tied, whereon never man sat; loose him, and bring him.

**3** And if any man say unto you, Why do ye this? say ye that the Lord hath need of him; and straightway he will send him hither.

**4** And they went their way, and found the colt tied by the door without in a place where two ways met; and they loose him.

**5** And certain of them that stood there said unto them, What do ye, loosing the colt?

**6** And they said unto them even as Jesus had commanded: and they let them go.

**7** And they brought the colt to Jesus, and cast their garments on him; and he sat upon him.

**8** And many spread their garments in the way: and others cut down branches off the trees, and strawed them in the way.

**9** And they that went before, and they that followed, cried, saying, Hosanna; Blessed is he that cometh in the name of the Lord:

**10** Blessed be the kingdom of our father David, that cometh in the name of the Lord: Hosanna in the highest.

**11** And Jesus entered into Jerusalem, and into the temple: and when he had looked round about upon all things, and now the eventide was come, he went out unto Bethany with the twelve.

**NLT** **Mark 11:1** As Jesus and his disciples approached Jerusalem, they came to the towns of Bethphage and Bethany on the Mount of Olives. Jesus sent two of them on ahead.

**2** "Go into that village over there," he told them. "As soon as you enter it, you will see a young donkey tied there that no one has ever ridden. Untie it and bring it here.

**3** If anyone asks, 'What are you doing?' just say, 'The Lord needs it and will return it soon.'"

**4** The two disciples left and found the colt standing in the street, tied outside the front door.

**5** As they were untying it, some bystanders demanded, "What are you doing, untying that colt?"

**6** They said what Jesus had told them to say, and they were permitted to take it.

**7** Then they brought the colt to Jesus and threw their garments over it, and he sat on it.

**8** Many in the crowd spread their garments on the road ahead of him, and others spread leafy branches they had cut in the fields.

**9** Jesus was in the center of the procession, and the people all around him were shouting, "Praise God! Blessings on the one who comes in the name of the LORD!

**10** Blessings on the coming Kingdom of our ancestor David! Praise God in highest heaven!"

**11** So Jesus came to Jerusalem and went into the Temple. After looking around carefully at everything, he left because it was late in the afternoon. Then he returned to Bethany with the twelve disciples.

## The People, Places, and Times

**Victory Processions.** In ancient times, after wars were won, the generals, soldiers, and in some instances kings would participate in victory processions. Generals would don laurel crowns and stand in horse-drawn chariots while soldiers, flaunting their weaponry, walked before crowds of cheering citizens. Prisoners of war were forced to also walk shackled before the people. When Saul and David returned home after the latter had killed Goliath, the women danced, sang, and played tambourines (1 Samuel 18:7). When Jehu was anointed king of Israel, soldiers "spread out their cloaks on the bare steps and blew the ram's horn, shouting, 'Jehu is king!'" (from 2 Kings 9:13, NLT).

**Palm Tree.** The palm tree was a symbol of victory. The Romans carried palm leaves during their victory processions. Each day of the Feast of Tabernacles, a Jewish holiday that commemorates the harvest and God's protection in the wilderness after the Jews escaped bondage in Egypt, participants wave palms and shout "Hosanna." Our Palm Sunday is so called because the people laid palm branches on the road before Jesus as He entered Jerusalem, signifying that He is the Messiah. In Revelation 7:9, "Apostle John beheld in vision those who had overcome by the blood of the lamb standing 'before the Lamb, clothed with white robes, and palms in their hands'" (Watson 927).

**Gospel of Mark.** Mark, mentioned in Acts 12:12, 25, 15:37–39; Colossians 4:10; Philemon 24; 2 Timothy 4:11; and 1 Peter 5:13, penned his Gospel in Rome between A.D. 66 and 70, during the Jewish war with Rome that ended with the destruction of the temple. During that time, many Jewish people were claiming that the Messiah would come to defeat the Romans and restore their national independence. Mark's Gospel reaffirmed for Christians that Jesus was and is the Messiah, whose purpose was to suffer, die, and rise again to ensure eternal salvation for believers. Most of the material for this gospel is believed to have been gathered from the apostle Peter.

## Background

Jesus and His disciples journeyed to Jerusalem for the upcoming Passover. At this point in Jesus' earthly ministry, whenever He went, crowds gathered, curious about the miracles He has performed. During one such stop, a few Pharisees in the crowd questioned Jesus about divorce to trap Him, but instead He clarified the issue for them. He later gave private teaching on divorce to the disciples. As Jesus and the disciples continued to journey on, parents brought their children to Him for a blessing, and a rich man approached, inquiring what he should do to gain eternal life. When Jesus told him he must give away all his riches and follow Him, the man sadly departed. Jesus taught His disciples that "it is easier for a camel to go through the eye of a needle than for a rich person to enter the Kingdom of God" (from Mark 10:25, NLT). However, Jesus added, although it is impossible with man, all things are possible with God (v. 27). Once they reached the direct road to Jerusalem, Jesus pulled the twelve aside and predicted His death a third time. James and John requested to be leaders in Jesus' kingdom, but He taught them all that in His kingdom, the leader must serve all. Finally, Jesus healed blind Bartimaeus who sat on the road just outside of Jericho. Once healed, he joined the crowd that had been following Jesus to Jerusalem.

## At-A-Glance

1. Supernatural Knowledge Confirmed
   (Mark 11:1–6)
2. The Promised One Comes (vv. 7–11)

## In Depth

### 1. Supernatural Knowledge Confirmed (Mark 11:1–6)

Jesus and His disciples are finally within reach of Jerusalem as they approach Bethphage and Bethany at the Mount of Olives. Instead of continuing, He stops and sends two disciples ahead to find a colt, or young donkey. Those with Jesus may have wondered why He stopped instead of pushing through the last mile to His destination The initial readers of this text, first-century Christians, may have wondered why Mark stopped the story of Jesus' journey here, especially since he seemed to push time steadily along until this point. At this moment in the story, Jesus is poised to reveal a crucial fact about Himself. Perhaps He is very detailed with His instructions because those currently with Him and those who would read of Him later would need to understand that these details revealed His identity. Saying the colt would be tied speaks to Jesus' identity because it mirrors one of the earliest Messianic prophecies: "The scepter will not depart from Judah, nor the ruler's staff from his descendants, until the coming of the one to whom it belongs, the one whom all nations will honor. He ties his foal to a grapevine, the colt of his donkey to a choice vine" (from Genesis 49:10–11, NLT).

Mark primarily depicts Jesus as the Suffering Servant (cf. Isaiah 53). However, in this passage, we witness His authority in His detailed instructions and supernatural knowledge. The two find everything to be as Jesus said it would be. Who but the Messiah, the everlasting King, could speak with such authority and know that everything would be aligned to the smallest detail? For the first-century Christian, this would have been reassurance that the One they served is the true Messiah.

### 2. The Promised One Comes (vv. 7–11)

Jesus sitting on the colt is fulfillment of Messianic prophecy as well (see Zechariah 9:9). Often, Jesus would not reveal His identity (Mark 1:34, 7:36, 8:26, 11:33), but now His actions declare that He is the Messiah. The people treat Him as a king by throwing their garments on the road (cf. 2 Kings 9:13). They also show that they recognize that He is not just any king, but rather the One promised to save, by laying down palm branches on the road and shouting the praise word "Hosanna" (Save now! or Please save us!). This is reminiscent of the Feast of Tabernacles, during which this praise is said with the waving of palms.

In the context of this holiday, "Hosanna" means salvation is coming, and in the context of Jesus' entry, the Messiah is here. Victory is imminent. To further emphasize that the crowd believes Jesus is the Messiah, the people shout, "Blessed is he that cometh in the name of the Lord: Blessed be the kingdom of our father David, that cometh in the name of the Lord: Hosanna in the highest" (from Mark 11:9–10). This is part of the Hallel praise taken from Psalm 118:25–26, which is spoken during Passover and Pentecost holidays as well as the Feast of Tabernacles. The fact that the scene had all the fanfare of a victory procession conveys the crowd's misunderstanding that the Messiah would be a political leader bringing salvation through militaristic means. They seem to want to crown Jesus king immediately. However, He merely enters the temple, looks around, and returns to Bethany for the night. This emphasizes that Jesus will not be the Messiah they were expecting. He came on a donkey, not a horse, which meant He had come with a peaceful agenda to procure eternal salvation. Although many of those present would later develop disdain for Jesus' brand of salvation, the first-century Christians in Mark's initial audience would find comfort in it while living in a society that was hostile to their beliefs.

## Search the Scriptures

1. What were Jesus' instructions for finding the colt (Mark 11:2–3)?

2. What were the people doing and shouting as Jesus entered Jerusalem (vv. 8–10)?

## Discuss the Meaning

Sometimes our view of God is limited to our present wants. We forget that Jesus came so we could have eternal life. What are some ways we try to shape God to meet our wants? How can we learn to express our gratitude for eternal salvation?

## Lesson in Our Society

We live in a society that engages in celebrity worship. We spend hundreds of dollars buying tickets to see our star athletes. We camp out for hours to hear our favorite singers. We stand in long lines to get our pictures taken with movie stars. We want to dress and act like celebrities. We love and honor them. However, Jesus is the only One who truly loves us. He loved us so much He suffered, died, and rose again for our salvation. We should strive to live lives that honor Him.

## Make It Happen

We often pray for a house, a promotion, or a mate. There is nothing wrong with looking to God to take care of our every need. However, we should not only limit Him to what we perceive is important. Jesus came so that we could have eternal life, and for this, we should honor Him. For your daily devotion, ask God to show you ways you can honor Him and whatever He reveals, do it.

## Follow the Spirit

What God wants me to do:

_____

_____

_____

_____

## Remember Your Thoughts

Special insights I have learned:

_____

_____

_____

_____

## More Light on the Text

Mark 11:1–11

**1 And when they came nigh to Jerusalem, unto Bethphage and Bethany, at the mount of Olives, he sendeth forth two of his disciples.**

Jesus and the disciples arrive at Bethphage and Bethany. These two villages were a Sabbath day's journey (approximately one thousand yards) from Jerusalem. It was a fitting staging point for Jesus' next act of ministry. The Mount of Olives held a special significance in the history of Israel. It was the place that David fled to when Absalom took over Jerusalem. This same place would be the launching pad for Jesus' entry to Jerusalem as its rightful King and Lord. He would not conquer with an army, but with His death on the Cross and subsequent resurrection. Now it was time for Jesus to enter Jerusalem and fulfill what was spoken about Him in the Old Testament.

The Greek word *apostello* (**ah-poe-STEL-loh**), "sendeth," denotes the sending of a messenger with a special task or commission, and full authority. The disciples were sent as ambassadors with a precise message, speaking in the name of their Master. They were not going in their own authority, but that of Jesus. Their mandate is described in the next verse. Jesus sent the two in order to accomplish a prophecy from Zechariah 9:9, thus giving this event messianic significance.

**2 And saith unto them, Go your way into the village over against you: and as soon as ye be entered into it, ye shall find a colt tied, whereon never man sat; loose him, and bring him.**

The Greek word *polos* (**POH-lohs**) means a young colt. The description of the young animal as one "whereon never man sat" is significant in the light of many Old Testament passages. Animals that were unyoked and unused were sometimes consecrated to a unique and holy use (see Numbers 19:2; Deuteronomy 21:3; 1 Samuel 6:7). This animal was fitting to be the one the Messiah would ride on as He entered Jerusalem. In Western countries, the donkey is considered to be stubborn and dumb. However, in the Middle East, the donkey is considered to possess the qualities of patience, intelligence, and submission. It was also ridden by royalty and nobility. The donkey was usually mounted during peacetime, as opposed to a horse mounted and used during times of war. We read of the prophet Balaam riding on a donkey (Numbers 22:21) and of the seventy sons of the judge Abdon riding on seventy donkeys (Judges 12:13–14). It was the animal used for nobility in peacetime and also for those who stood in the office of judge. Jesus chooses an animal that fit into the bigger picture of His role as Messiah. He is coming as a King but with a different kind of kingdom. His kingdom is a kingdom of peace, not war. He rides into Jerusalem not as a conquering lion, but the Prince of Peace.

What is also fascinating is Jesus' knowledge of the age and location of the colt. This event is not only messianic but supernatural. By describing the colt and predicting that it would be given to Him, Jesus exercises the wisdom and knowledge from the Holy Spirit. This foreknowledge of the location and age of the colt would be seen as further proof that Jesus truly is the Messiah. The disciples would definitely be amazed at finding the young donkey in the right location and condition, unused. In their minds this would have solidified Jesus' claim to being Messiah. Here, Jesus is acting as the now reigning King of the Jews, and His prophetic insight into how to fulfill this symbolic act supports that claim, and confirms to the disciples that God confirms this claim as well.

**3 And if any man say unto you, Why do ye this? say ye that the Lord hath need of him; and straightway he will send him hither.**

The Greek word *kurios* (**KOO-ree-ose**), meaning "Lord," refers to Jesus Himself, showing His supreme authority over all things. In any case, Jesus arms His two emissaries against possible difficulties by furnishing them with what to say. He predicts that they will send the animal promptly after the disciples give this answer. The colt is already under the authority and ownership of the Lord, who now needs him.

**4 And they went their way, and found the colt tied by the door without in a place where two ways met; and they loose him. 5 And certain of them that stood there said unto them, What do ye, loosing the colt? 6 And they said unto them even as Jesus had commanded: and they let them go.**

Jesus' ambassadors find the young animal exactly as He had said. It is outside the house and fastened by the door. Precisely what Jesus said would happen happens. The two disciples waste no time and loose the colt. They are obedient to their Master and are probably encouraged by seeing the colt exactly as described. They do encounter some difficulty as some nearby people—the owners or villagers—question them regarding the colt. The people are satisfied with the disciples' answer, probably because Jesus is well-known for His miraculous deeds and for teaching with authority (see John 7:46; Mark 11:18). They know that this Master can be trusted. They might even be proud that He wants to use the young colt.

**7 And they brought the colt to Jesus, and cast their garments on him; and he sat upon him. 8 And many spread their garments in the way: and others cut down branches off the trees, and strawed them in the way.**

The disciples place their outer garments on the colt in place of a saddle. Jesus sits and begins His ride to the gates of Jerusalem. He is met by a spontaneous expression of homage. The crowd provides a "red carpet" for Him, their King. They throw their garments "in the way." The Greek word here, *eis* (**ACE**), meaning "into," denotes that the crowd threw their garments into the way and spread them there for Jesus to ride over. The picture of Christ riding into Jerusalem on a donkey provokes immediate action, as the people are inspired by this show of humility.

The carpeted way is not made of garments only. The crowd also cut down branches from the trees and strew them on the road. The Greek word *stibas* (**stee-BAHS**) speaks of a mass of straw, rushes, or leaves beaten together or strewn loosely so as to form a carpet. John's Gospel account speaks specifically of palm branches being spread out and waved (12:12–13). This may have come from the memory of Judas Maccabeus, or Judah the Hammer, who lived almost two hundred years before Christ. When Judas defeated the Seleucid Empire and gained control of the temple, the crowds celebrated by waving palm branches.

**9 And they that went before, and they that followed, cried, saying, Hosanna; Blessed is he that cometh in the name of the Lord.**

The Greek word *Hosanna* comes from the Aramaic phrase *Hoshiah na* (**hoh-SHEE-ah NAH**). Its original meaning is a cry for help: "O save" or "Help, I pray," (cf. Psalm 118:25). Coupled with the blessing that follows, as in Mark, it denotes an expression of praise, rejoicing, or greeting. This psalm is one of the Hallel psalms of praise. It is also known as the "Egyptian Hallel" because it praises God's saving act of delivering Israel from Egypt. The Greek word *eulogeo* (**ew-loh-GEH-oh**) or "blessed" means to speak well of or to praise. The blessing is from God, the source of all blessings. He who comes is blessed by the Lord God to whom He belongs. Jesus is "eulogized" by the crowd, which subjects itself to Him and recognizes Him as the Messiah (cf. Psalm 118:26). Some evidence suggests the phrase "he that cometh" refers to the Messiah, especially as one who rides a young donkey's colt (Genesis 49:10). The crowd recognizes Jesus' riding on a donkey as the fulfillment of the prophecy in Zechariah 9:9 and Genesis 49:11.

This event shows that Jesus is indeed coming as a King and Messiah. Many of the Jewish people are eager for freedom from Roman rule. The garments and branches in the road and the cries of "Hosanna" in the air are the responses of a people who need and seek a Savior. Jesus' riding into Jerusalem on a donkey is more than just a fulfillment of Messianic prophecy; it is also a symbolic action in the manner of the Old Testament prophets. By riding into Jerusalem on a donkey, He publicly shows that He is the King the Jews have been waiting for. This act defies the Romans, who had political authority over Palestine at the time. It also defies the local Jewish ruler Herod and the high priests who ruled alongside Rome.

Many refer to this as the Triumphal Entry, but it is very different from the triumphal entry of a Roman general. The Romans honored generals who had won a complete and decisive victory over a foreign enemy with a "triumph." This consisted of riding into Rome in a parade followed by captured treasure, enemy prisoners, and all of his military units. At the end of the parade, some of the enemy prisoners were ritualistically executed or thrown to wild animals for the crowd's entertainment.

**10 Blessed be the kingdom of our father David, that cometh in the name of the Lord: Hosanna in the highest.**

The crowds understand this entry to be a sign that God is now in charge. The expectation is that the Messiah would rule as a representative of God and that He would come from the line of David. Their cries focus on the kingdom because they understand that this new King would not continue with business as usual. The Jewish expectation of a Messiah is that God would now be King and turn the whole world upside down.

Hosanna means "O save" or "Help, I pray," but this time it is in the superlative: "Hosanna in the highest." The Greek word *hupsistos* (**HOOP-sees-tose**) means to the highest regions or highest degree possible. It is a word that is often used for God as "the Most High." The crowds gives Jesus praise to the highest degree possible. It is praise that is reserved for God. This is a measure of how much the Jewish people are expecting a Messianic Deliverer and how much they believe that right now, Jesus is that Deliverer.

**11 And Jesus entered into Jerusalem, and into the temple: and when he had looked round about upon all things, and now the eventide was come, he went out unto Bethany with the twelve.**

Jesus goes into the temple and looks around. The reign of the Messiah is intricately bound with the temple, since the temple was a symbol of God's presence on earth. It is fitting for Jesus to go into the temple although He does not cleanse it at the moment. He and the disciples had journeyed for a day uphill and the text says that it was "already late." With this and after so much excitement had been created with His entry into Jerusalem, Jesus decides to conclude His day. So after looking into the temple and inspecting the premises, He and the twelve spend the night in Bethany. Business in the temple would have to wait.

Sources:
Black, Clifton. "Gospel According to Mark: Introduction and Mark 11:1–11 notes." *The Harper Collins Study Bible.* NRSV. San Francisco, CA: Harper Collins Publishers, 2006. 1722–24, 1745–46.
Henry, Matthew. "Mark 11." *Matthew Henry's Commentary on the Whole Bible.* Vol. 5: Matthew to John. Peabody, MA: Hendrickson Publishers, 1991.
Hurtado, Larry W. "Jesus Enters Jerusalem and the Temple." *Understanding the Bible Commentary Series: Mark.* Grand Rapids, MI: Baker Books, 2011.
Jensen, Richard A. *Preaching Mark's Gospel: A Narrative Approach.* Lima, OH: CSS Publishing Co., Inc. 1996. 168–70.

Shanks, Hershel, ed. *Ancient Israel from Abraham to the Roman Destruction of the Temple.* Washington, DC: Prentice Hall, 1999. 286.

Unger, Merrill F. "Festivals: Feast of Booths (or Tabernacles)." *The New Unger's Bible Dictionary.* R.K. Harrison, ed. Chicago, IL: Moody Press, 1988. 417–21.

——. "Mark, Gospel of." *The New Unger's Bible Dictionary.* R.K. Harrison, ed. Chicago, IL: Moody Press, 1988. 816.

——. "Palm Tree." *The New Unger's Bible Dictionary.* R.K. Harrison, ed. Chicago, IL: Moody Press, 1988. 957–58.

Watson, Richard, and Nathan Bangs. *A Biblical and Theological Dictionary: Explanatory of the History, Manners, and Customs of the Jews, and Neighbouring Nations.* New York: B. Waugh and T. Mason, 1832. 927.

# Daily Bible Readings

**MONDAY**
God Judges the Peoples with Equity
(Psalm 67)

**TUESDAY**
A Righteous God and a Savior
(Isaiah 45:20–25)

**WEDNESDAY**
God Highly Exalted Him
(Philippians 2:9–16)

**THURSDAY**
Beware, Keep Alert
(Mark 13:30–37)

**FRIDAY**
The Coming Son of Man
(Mark 14:55–62)

**SATURDAY**
The World Has Gone After Him
(John 12:14–19)

**SUNDAY**
Blessed is the Coming Kingdom
(Mark 11:1–11)

# Say It Correctly

Bethphage. **BAYTH**-fah-gay.
Bethany. **BE**-tha-nee.
Hosanna. ho-**ZA**-na.

# Notes

# Teaching Tips

## Words You Should Know

**A. Firstfruits** (1 Corinthians 15:20) *aparche* (Gk.)—The best produce, picked first at harvest and usually offered to God; term is also used for people consecrated to God for all time.

**B. Resurrection** (v. 21) *anastasis* (Gk.)—A rise in status; rising from the dead, specifically that of Christ or all men at the end of this present age.

## Teacher Preparation

**Unifying Principle—Fully Alive.** People need to be reminded of important events that shape their identities and actions. What kind of event can make such an influence on their lives? Jesus' resurrection provided tangible evidence of the possibility of the same for those whose identity is formed by Christ Jesus.

**A.** Pray for yourself and your students to understand the lesson.

**B.** Study 1 Corinthians 15 using at least three Bible versions.

**C.** Examine a commentary and study Bible notes on 1 Corinthians 15.

**D.** Study the lesson in the *Precepts for Living Personal Study Guide®*.

## O—Open the Lesson

**A.** Open with prayer and the Aim for Change.

**B.** Have volunteers read the In Focus story aloud.

**C.** Ask the students to talk about the last huge gathering they had to celebrate a life-changing event.

**D.** Tell the class in today's lesson they will learn about another life-changing event, the Resurrection of Christ.

## P—Present the Scriptures

**A.** Have volunteers read the Focal Verses; The People, Places, and Things; and Background sections aloud.

**B.** Use the In Depth and More Light on the Text sections to do an exposition of each verse.

**C.** Have the students answer the questions in the Search the Scriptures section and discuss.

## E—Explore the Meaning

**A.** Have the students discuss their answers to the Discuss the Meaning section.

## N—Next Steps for Application

**A.** Go over Lesson in Our Society and Make It Happen section.

**B.** Close in prayer.

## Worship Guide

For the Superintendent or Teacher
Theme: Resurrection Guaranteed
Song: "Blessed Assurance"
Devotional Reading: John 11:20–27

# Resurrection Guaranteed

**Bible Background • 1 CORINTHIANS 15:1–22**
**Printed Text • 1 CORINTHIANS 15:1–11, 20–22**
**Devotional Reading • JOHN 11:20–27**

## ———————— Aim for Change ————————

By the end of the lesson, we will: EXPLORE the meaning of Christ's resurrection; VALUE and appreciate our identity in Jesus Christ; and WITNESS personally and corporately to the resurrection of Jesus Christ.

## ———————— In Focus ————————

"Family" for Melissa had been just her and her father when she was growing up. Her mother had passed away when she was very young. Life with her father had been good, but she always wondered what it would have been like to grow up with a huge family around her. One day Melissa received an invitation to the Parker Family Reunion. She was really excited about attending because it would be the first time she would be meeting her mother's family. Over the next few months, Melissa booked her hotel room, paid all the reunion fees, and bought the coveted family reunion T-shirt. Finally, the reunion weekend arrived, and as Melissa and her father walked into the park, she was filled with emotion when she saw the sea of people wearing the very same T-shirt. She met all her mother's uncles, aunts, and cousins, who all said she had her mother's smile. As the reunion ended, everyone exchanged hugs, numbers, and promises to keep in touch. Melissa felt a sense of peace because she now had the huge family she had always wanted and her identity was now complete.

*In today's lesson, we learn that the resurrection of Christ defines our identity as Christians and guarantees our resurrection as well.*

## ———————— Keep in Mind ————————

"For as in Adam all die, even so in Christ shall all be made alive"
(1 Corinthians 15:22).

"For as in Adam all die, even so in Christ shall all be made alive"
(1 Corinthians 15:22).

## Focal Verses

**KJV** **1 Corinthians 15:1** Moreover, brethren, I declare unto you the gospel which I preached unto you, which also ye have received, and wherein ye stand;

**2** By which also ye are saved, if ye keep in memory what I preached unto you, unless ye have believed in vain.

**3** For I delivered unto you first of all that which I also received, how that Christ died for our sins according to the scriptures;

**4** And that he was buried, and that he rose again the third day according to the scriptures:

**5** And that he was seen of Cephas, then of the twelve:

**6** After that, he was seen of above five hundred brethren at once; of whom the greater part remain unto this present, but some are fallen asleep.

**7** After that, he was seen of James; then of all the apostles.

**8** And last of all he was seen of me also, as of one born out of due time.

**9** For I am the least of the apostles, that am not meet to be called an apostle, because I persecuted the church of God.

**10** But by the grace of God I am what I am: and his grace which was bestowed upon me was not in vain; but I laboured more abundantly than they all: yet not I, but the grace of God which was with me.

**11** Therefore whether it were I or they, so we preach, and so ye believed.

**20** But now is Christ risen from the dead, and become the firstfruits of them that slept.

**21** For since by man came death, by man came also the resurrection of the dead.

**22** For as in Adam all die, even so in Christ shall all be made alive.

**NLT** **1 Corinthians 15:1** Let me now remind you, dear brothers and sisters, of the Good News I preached to you before. You welcomed it then, and you still stand firm in it.

**2** It is this Good News that saves you if you continue to believe the message I told you—unless, of course, you believed something that was never true in the first place.

**3** I passed on to you what was most important and what had also been passed on to me. Christ died for our sins, just as the Scriptures said.

**4** He was buried, and he was raised from the dead on the third day, just as the Scriptures said.

**5** He was seen by Peter and then by the Twelve.

**6** After that, he was seen by more than 500 of his followers at one time, most of whom are still alive, though some have died.

**7** Then he was seen by James and later by all the apostles.

**8** Last of all, as though I had been born at the wrong time, I also saw him.

**9** For I am the least of all the apostles. In fact, I'm not even worthy to be called an apostle after the way I persecuted God's church.

**10** But whatever I am now, it is all because God poured out his special favor on me—and not without results. For I have worked harder than any of the other apostles; yet it was not I but God who was working through me by his grace.

**11** So it makes no difference whether I preach or they preach, for we all preach the same message you have already believed.

**20** But in fact, Christ has been raised from the dead. He is the first of a great harvest of all who have died.

**21** So you see, just as death came into the world through a man, now the resurrection from the dead has begun through another man.

**22** Just as everyone dies because we all belong to Adam, everyone who belongs to Christ will be given new life.

---

## The People, Places, and Times

**Gospel.** The Gospel is literally "good news." The equivalent Greek word, *euangelion* (**ehoo-an-GHEL-ee-on**), was used in relation to the announcement that Augustus Caesar was now ruler over the Roman empire and would bring peace and joy. The biblical writers used this word to announce God's grace and the coming of His kingdom in the life, death, and resurrection of Christ. This is the substance of the message the apostles preached. In the Gospel's bare essentials, it is the telling of Jesus' life, death, and resurrection and how we can be forgiven and welcomed into His kingdom.

**Paul.** Paul is often called the great apostle because of his extensive mission to bring the Gospel to the Gentiles, but prior to his conversion, he was a member of the Pharisees. With as much zeal as he would later exhibit in spreading the Gospel, Paul persecuted Christians. He not only sought imprisonment but favored death for men and women who defected from Judaism to Christianity. He condoned the stoning of Stephen (Acts 8:1, 22:20). Paul not only wanted to end Christianity in Jerusalem, but wanted to end it throughout the whole known world. He was on the road to Damascus because he heard there were Christians there (9:1–2), and he had asked for special permission to bring them to Jerusalem for punishment. But on that road he encountered Christ and the trajectory of his life was forever changed.

## Background

Throughout 1 Corinthians, Paul dealt with issue after issue. He addressed the divisions in the church (1:10–4:21), sexual immorality including incest (5:1–13) and fornication (6:12–20), marriage and divorce (7:1–40), idolatry (8:1–11:1), and different aspects of public worship (11:2–13:13). In 1 Corinthians 14, Paul addressed the spiritual gifts of speaking in tongues and prophecy. The apostle instructed that the Corinthians should pursue love and the gift of prophecy because it builds up the whole church. Tongues only build up the individual. The only way tongues can edify the church is if the one speaking has the gift to interpret. Paul wrote that proper worship will result in even unbelievers admitting, "God is truly here among you" (from 1 Corinthians 14:25, NLT). The chapter ends with Paul describing the proper order of worship. With all of these other issues dealt with, Paul finally launched into explaining the significance of Christ's resurrection.

## At-A-Glance

1. Resurrection Clarified (1 Corinthians 15:1–4)
2. Resurrection Witnessed (vv. 5–11)
3. Resurrection Guaranteed (vv. 20–22)

# In Depth

## 1. Resurrection Clarified (1 Corinthians 15:1–4)

There were some in the Corinthian church who did not believe in the resurrection of the dead. Paul reminds them that he had already preached the Good News to them and they had, or so it seemed, fully accepted it. He writes, "It is this Good News that saves you if you continue to believe the message I told you—unless, of course, you believed something that was never true in the first place" (1 Corinthians 15:2, NLT). Before explaining the foundation of the Gospel message, Paul asserts that the message he had given them and he had received himself was valid. He then explains the foundation of the Christian faith: (1) Christ died for our sins. If this had not occurred, eternal damnation would await us all, "for everyone has sinned; we all fall short of God's glorious standard. ... God presented Jesus as the sacrifice for sin. People are made right with God when they believe that Jesus sacrificed his life, shedding his blood" (from Romans 3:23, 25, NLT). (2) Christ was buried. To ensure Jesus was dead, a rock was sealed across the tomb and guards placed outside (Matthew 27:62–66). (3) Christ rose on the third day. Death needed to be conquered so that salvation could be secured (2 Timothy 1:10). Paul notes that the Scriptures support what he says, and though Paul does not indicate specific verses, they could have included Psalm 69:9; Isaiah 53:4–12; Hosea 6:2–3; Jonah 1:17; and others.

## 2. Resurrection Witnessed (vv. 5–11)

Paul offers even more validity to the Resurrection by listing the witnesses. Peter and the Twelve saw the resurrected Jesus (John 20:19–29). They had been chosen to be witnesses (Acts 10:40–43). More than five hundred of His followers saw Jesus, including Jesus' half-brother James and other apostles (v. 6; Luke 24:33, 36–53). Perhaps a criterion for being an apostle, from Paul's perspective, was that one had to have been divinely chosen to see the resurrected Christ. They were sent out to preach the Gospel because they could personally testify to its truth. Paul was the last witness. Although, he had not lived and journeyed with Jesus, he too had been chosen when Jesus appeared to him on the road to Damascus. Of himself, Paul writes, "Last of all he was seen of me also, as of one born out of due time" (1 Corinthians 15:8). The phrase "born out of due time" refers to a miscarried or stillborn baby. In essence, Paul was someone who was spiritually dead and therefore unfit to be an apostle because he had persecuted believers. However, God, in His grace, still chose Paul to be a witness. This fact was in response to those in Corinth who were questioning his authority (1 Corinthians 9). Whether the other apostles or Paul preached the Gospel, it was the same message that the Corinthians had already believed.

## 3. Resurrection Guaranteed (vv. 20–22)

In verses 12–19, Paul refutes the people's belief that there is no resurrection of the dead. Paul's line of reasoning in essence concludes that if there is no resurrection, Christ did not rise and their faith would be useless. They would all still be in their sin, condemned forever. However, Paul reassures his audience that Jesus had indeed risen from the dead. He continues to explain the benefit of this fact. Jesus did not conquer death only for Himself. He is the first of all who have died. His resurrection ensures that all who believe in Him shall have eternal life. To illustrate this truth, Paul compares Jesus to Adam. Just as Adam brought death for all, Jesus has brought eternal life for those who believe in Him. This was Christ's purpose all along; the Father sent Him so "that whosoever believeth in him should not perish, but have everlasting life" (from John 3:16).

## Search the Scriptures

1. What is the Gospel message (1 Corinthians 15:3–4)?

2. How does Paul describe himself (vv. 8–9)?

3. How do Jesus and Adam differ (vv. 21–22)?

## Discuss the Meaning

Many engage in frivolous activities searching for who they are. However as believers, the resurrection has already determined our identity. How has the resurrection of Christ impacted your life? How can you begin to value your identity in Christ?

## Lesson in Our Society

Certain events define our identities. On the wedding day, we become a spouse. Giving birth to a child, we become a parent. We cherish these life-changing events and commemorate them every year with anniversaries and birthday celebrations. As believers, another event that deserves our devotion is the Resurrection of Christ. The Resurrection is the foundation of our faith. It is the fuel that motivates us to want to live right and treat others with love and kindness. Without it, we would be eternally lost. Let's remember to celebrate the Resurrection not just once a year, but every day of our lives.

## Make It Happen

We love to celebrate life-changing events with others. We book banquet halls a year in advance and hire the best caterers so people can spend a few hours with us on our special day. The greatest event to ever happen to us is the Resurrection, and we should find ways

to share it. Pray about at least three people with whom you can share the Good News and create a special occasion for the sharing. For example, meet for breakfast, schedule time at the gym, or invite them to a church function.

## Follow the Spirit

What God wants me to do:

_____

_____

_____

_____

## Remember Your Thoughts

Special insights I have learned:

_____

_____

_____

_____

## More Light on the Text

**1 Corinthians 15:1–11, 20–22**

**1 Moreover, brethren, I declare unto you the gospel which I preached unto you, which also ye have received, and wherein ye stand; 2 By which also ye are saved, if ye keep in memory what I preached unto you, unless you have believed in vain.**

The opening of this chapter introduces Paul's concerns and lays the foundation for the argument he develops in the verses that follow. Some in the Corinthian church exalted the spiritual so much that they devalued the physical. Consequently, this path led to denial of bodily resurrection.

Paul begins with what they have in common. Paul uses the Greek word *euaggelion* (**ew-an-GHEL-ee-on**), which means good news message or Gospel, to describe what he preached and they in turn received as a means for salvation. They owe their existence as a community of faith to the Gospel he brought them. He warns if they cannot hold on to the same Gospel that saved them, their faith is in jeopardy of being ineffective and producing no fruit.

tradition, Scripture, and apostolic authority. First, he appeals to tradition by referencing an early church creed. Then, he asserts that these things have happened according to Scripture. Last, he states that Cephas, or Peter, and the Twelve can attest to the validity of his claims. The twelve apostles had an especially close relationship with Jesus and a special role in the founding of the church. Perhaps Peter is singled out because he has followers in the church of Corinth.

**3 For I delivered unto you first of all that which I also received, how that Christ died for our sins according to the scriptures; 4 And that he was buried, and that he rose again the third day according to the scriptures: 5 And that he was seen of Cephas, then of the twelve.**

Paul presents the basics of the Gospel by highlighting three points of emphasis: Jesus died, was buried, and rose again on the third day, all in accordance with the Scriptures. This essence of the Gospel was passed down to Paul. It is generally accepted that these verses reflect an early creed. Being of primary importance, the creed was in turn passed along by Paul to the church in Corinth.

Although Paul covers a wide range of subjects, not everything he discusses is central to the Gospel. Nor does every instruction carry equal weight. In this passage, Paul highlights the elements of the Gospel message that are critical to the church and its health and vitality.

The death, burial, and resurrection of Jesus are presented as an objective reality. There is a grave, and there were witnesses. It is not merely a spiritual phenomenon.

In addition to misconceptions about the Resurrection, it is likely that the church in Corinth had some misgivings about Paul's authority. Paul grounds his argument in

**6 After that, he was seen of above five hundred brethren at once; of whom the greater part remain unto this present, but some are fallen asleep. 7 After that, he was seen of James; then of all the apostles. 8 And last of all he was seen of me also, as of one born out of due time.**

Paul continues to build the credibility of his position by adding an additional source of authority—eyewitness testimony of believers, apostles, and him. Paul affirms that Jesus was seen by a number of people in a variety of settings after his resurrection, more than five hundred believers, according to Paul. Many of the witnesses were still alive at the time of the writing and their accounts could be verified firsthand, although some had already "fallen asleep," a common euphemism at the time for death.

Next Paul says that the resurrected Jesus was seen by James, Jesus' half-brother. He was also a major leader in the Jerusalem church. This would have given Paul even more credibility, as James had major influence with the church at large due to his natural relation to Jesus. Paul also speaks of the resurrected Jesus being seen by the apostles. This is obviously not the Twelve because they were just mentioned in verse 5. Paul must have been referring to others outside of the Twelve who had been commissioned to represent Christ, perhaps those mentioned in Luke 10:1–20.

Paul establishes a connection between the apostolic tradition and himself, even though there is no evidence he was regarded as one of the Twelve. He is likely referring to his encounter with the risen Lord on the road to Damascus. Paul uses the Greek word *ektroma* (**EHK-troh-ma**), which is often translated abnormally born, to describe his apostolic calling. The Twelve had years of mentoring and close relationship with Jesus during His time on earth. Paul, however, did not become an apostle this way. He may have been expressing feelings of being born out of season since his apostolic calling was out of the ordinary.

**9 For I am the least of the apostles, that am not meet to be called an apostle, because I persecuted the church of God. 10 But by the grace of God I am what I am: and his grace which was bestowed upon me was not in vain; but I labored more abundantly than they all: yet not I, but the grace of God which was with me. 11 Therefore whether it were I or they, so we preach, and so ye believed.**

Paul explains that he is "least" of the apostles because he formerly persecuted the church. He is unworthy of the calling, and did nothing to earn it. His standing before God as the "least" of the apostles and the "chief" of sinners (see 1 Timothy 1:15) provides the foundation for his deep experience of the grace of God in Jesus Christ.

The grace Paul discusses is best understood as twofold: saving and empowering. By the saving grace of God, Paul was transformed from an enemy of God and the church to a friend. His faith flourished and he was empowered to bear fruit. Paul mentions he "labored more abundantly" than all the Twelve. Grace should not be confused with meritorious effort, as indicated by his

assertion that the agent of these works is "yet not I, but the grace of God which was with me." Hard work is not the means of achieving results in his ministry, but a manifestation of God's empowering grace.

The language he uses in verse 11, "I or they," hints that there was debate in the Corinthian church about the authority of various itinerant apostles. He ties together what he preached and all the other apostles' teaching, suggesting it is commonly accepted by all believers. His point is that they all preached the same thing! It allows him to show that the Corinthians were departing from the Gospel message and traditional sources of authority for the church, not just him.

**20 But now is Christ risen from the dead, and become the firstfruits of them that slept. 21 For since by man came death, by man came also the resurrection of the dead. 22 For as in Adam all die, even so in Christ shall all be made alive.**

Paul emphasizes the benefits of the resurrection for believers. Christ's resurrection made the resurrection of the dead necessary and inevitable. God raised Christ from the dead based on His own authority and sovereignty. It is required for the final victory over death so God can be "all in all" (v. 28).

Paul uses the Greek word *aparkhe* (**ah-par-KHAY**), meaning a sacrifice of the harvest's firstfruits to sanctify the whole harvest, to describe the work of Christ. He is the first fruit of a larger harvest (2 Thessalonians 2:13, NIV; 1 Corinthians 16:15, KJV). This agricultural metaphor has eschatological significance. Christ's resurrection is not bound to one annual harvest, but it sanctifies the resurrection of all believers for eternity. For this to happen, Christ had to be human because death is a part of humankind, not divine. Christ reversed what Adam set in motion, ushering in a new order. New life and resurrection for believers is inevitable because we share in the new nature of the Resurrected Christ through the grace of God.

Sources:

Fee, Gordon D. *The First Epistle to the Corinthians.* New International Commentary on the New Testament. Grand Rapids, MI: Eerdmans, 1987.

Furnish, Paul Victor. "First Letter of Paul to the Corinthians: Introduction and 1 Corinthians 15:1–11; 20–22 notes." *The Harper Collins Study Bible.* NRSV. San Francisco, CA: Harper Collins Publishers, 2006. 1932–34, 1952–53.

Keener, Craig S. *The IVP Bible Background Commentary: New Testament.* Downers Grove, IL: InterVarsity Press, 1993. 647–50, 670–71.

Horsley, Richard A. *1 Corinthians.* Abingdon New Testament Commentaries. Nashville, TN: Abingdon Press, 1998.

Lane, William L. *Hebrews 9–13.* Word Biblical Commentary, Vol. 47B. Dallas, TX: Word Inc., 1991.

*Life Application Study Bible.* King James Version. Wheaton, IL: Tyndale House Publishers, Inc., 1997. 2154–55, 2170–72.

Radmacher, Earl D., ed. *Nelson's New Illustrated Bible Commentary: Spreading the Light of God's Word into Your Life.* Nashville, TN: Thomas Nelson Publishers, 1999. 1648–53.

Soards, Marion L. "Back to the Basics: 1 Corinthians 15:1–11." *Understanding the Bible Commentary Series.* Grand Rapids, MI: Baker Books. 2011.

Unger, Merrill F. *The New Unger's Bible Dictionary.* R.K. Harrison, ed. Chicago, IL: Moody Press, 1988. 255–56, 968–69.

## Say It Correctly

Apostolic. ah-po-**STOL**-ik.
Eschatological. es-ka-to-**LAH**-gi-cal.

## Daily Bible Readings

**MONDAY**
Jesus Has Died
(Matthew 27:45–50)

**TUESDAY**
Christ Has Risen
(Matthew 28:1–8)

**WEDNESDAY**
Christ Will Come Again
(1 Thessalonians 4:13–18)

**THURSDAY**
The Resurrection and the Life
(John 11:20–27)

**FRIDAY**
The Hope of Eternal Life
(Titus 3:1–7)

**SATURDAY**
If Christ Has Not Been Raised
(1 Corinthians 15:12–19)

**SUNDAY**
In Fact, Christ Has Been Raised
(1 Corinthians 15:1–11, 20–22)

# Notes

_____

_____

_____

# Teaching Tips

## Words You Should Know

**A. Laid down** (1 John 3:16) *tithemi* (Gk.)—To place, to put, to set or appoint.

**B. Beloved** (v. 21) *agapetos* (Gk.)—Dearly loved one.

## Teacher Preparation

**Unifying Principle—All We Need is Love.** People wonder whether life is a random sequence of events or has an ordered purpose. How do believers measure meaning in life? John's letter indicates that the measure of people's lives is calculated by their faith in Christ and their love for one another.

**A.** Study the More Light on the Text, Background, and In Depth sections to gain insight and become more familiar with the text.

**B.** Prepare the At-A-Glance outline for display. This will help focus the class as you proceed through the activities for the day.

**C.** Have one or two people work as a team to prepare a skit based on the In Focus story.

**D.** Have one student prepare to read the Focal Verses as a dramatic monologue.

## O—Open the Lesson

**A.** Read the In Focus story and have the students perform the prepared skit.

**B.** Read the Aim for Change and Keep in Mind verse.

## P—Present the Scriptures

**A.** Read the Focal Verses aloud as a class.

**B.** Ask the class to be mindful of the commandments emphasized in the lesson's text and open class discussion.

**C.** Brainstorm various ways we tend to treat one another in the church, home, community, and work.

## E—Explore the Meaning

**A.** Review the Discuss the Meaning and Search the Scriptures questions.

**B.** Ask the class what strategies this lesson has inspired that will help them focus on the commandment to love.

## N—Next Steps for Application

**A.** Review the Make It Happen section. Ask the class members for suggestions regarding how to implement ideas. Encourage members to make a personal commitment in the area in the coming weeks.

**B.** Close in prayer.

## Worship Guide

For the Superintendent or Teacher
Theme: Love One Another
Song: "Oh, How I Love Jesus"
Devotional Reading: John 13:31–35

# Love One Another

**Bible Background • 1 JOHN 3:11–24**
**Printed Text • 1 JOHN 3:11–24**
**Devotional Reading • JOHN 13:31–35**

## Aim for Change

By the end of the lesson, we will: UNDERSTAND John's message about loving one another; AFFIRM the fundamental discipleship principle of love for God and others; and EXPRESS unconditional love to others.

## In Focus

Marcy held a part-time job at the local grocery store. Her goal was to save enough money to purchase a new bicycle. Every morning on her way to school, she would gaze through the bicycle shop's window, admiring the new bikes. When Marcy finally saved enough money to purchase the bicycle, she could hardly contain her excitement. Yet something deep inside told her to postpone purchasing the bike, so she waited. The students chose Washington, D.C., as their annual class trip, and every student signed up to go. One particular student named Candice could not attend the trip because her family could not afford to send her. Candice was heartbroken. When Marcy heard about Candice's predicament, she was moved with compassion and immediately knew what to do with the extra money. With joy and without hesitation, she gave the money she had saved for her new bicycle to her classmate. With tears in her eyes, Candice gladly accepted Marcy's unexpected gift and traveled with the class to Washington, D.C.

*Christians should give sacrificially to those in need. In this lesson, we will learn that love is more than mere words; it involves taking action.*

## Keep in Mind

"For this is the message that ye heard from the beginning, that we should love one another" (1 John 3:11).

"For this is the message that ye heard from the beginning, that we should love one another" (1 John 3:11).

## Focal Verses

**KJV** 1 John 3:11 For this is the message that ye heard from the beginning, that we should love one another.

12 Not as Cain, who was of that wicked one, and slew his brother. And wherefore slew he him? Because his own works were evil, and his brother's righteous.

13 Marvel not, my brethren, if the world hate you.

14 We know that we have passed from death unto life, because we love the brethren. He that loveth not his brother abideth in death.

15 Whosoever hateth his brother is a murderer: and ye know that no murderer hath eternal life abiding in him.

16 Hereby perceive we the love of God, because he laid down his life for us: and we ought to lay down our lives for the brethren.

17 But whoso hath this world's good, and seeth his brother have need, and shutteth up his bowels of compassion from him, how dwelleth the love of God in him?

18 My little children, let us not love in word, neither in tongue; but in deed and in truth.

19 And hereby we know that we are of the truth, and shall assure our hearts before him.

20 For if our heart condemn us, God is greater than our heart, and knoweth all things.

21 Beloved, if our heart condemn us not, then have we confidence toward God.

22 And whatsoever we ask, we receive of him, because we keep his commandments, and do those things that are pleasing in his sight.

23 And this is his commandment, That we should believe on the name of his Son Jesus

**NLT** 1 John 3:11 This is the message you have heard from the beginning: We should love one another.

12 We must not be like Cain, who belonged to the evil one and killed his brother. And why did he kill him? Because Cain had been doing what was evil, and his brother had been doing what was righteous.

13 So don't be surprised, dear brothers and sisters, if the world hates you.

14 If we love our Christian brothers and sisters, it proves that we have passed from death to life. But a person who has no love is still dead.

15 Anyone who hates another brother or sister is really a murderer at heart. And you know that murderers don't have eternal life within them.

16 We know what real love is because Jesus gave up his life for us. So we also ought to give up our lives for our brothers and sisters.

17 If someone has enough money to live well and sees a brother or sister in need but shows no compassion—how can God's love be in that person?

18 Dear children, let's not merely say that we love each other; let us show the truth by our actions.

19 Our actions will show that we belong to the truth, so we will be confident when we stand before God.

20 Even if we feel guilty, God is greater than our feelings, and he knows everything.

21 Dear friends, if we don't feel guilty, we can come to God with bold confidence.

22 And we will receive from him whatever we ask because we obey him and do the things that please him.

23 And this is his commandment: We must believe in the name of his Son, Jesus

Christ, and love one another, as he gave us commandment.

**24** And he that keepeth his commandments dwelleth in him, and he in him. And hereby we know that he abideth in us, by the Spirit which he hath given us.

Christ, and love one another, just as he commanded us.

**24** Those who obey God's commandments remain in fellowship with him, and he with them. And we know he lives in us because the Spirit he gave us lives in us.

## The People, Places, and Times

**Cain**. The eldest son of Adam and Eve, Cain was responsible for murdering his brother Abel. Cain became the tiller of the soil while his brother was a keeper of sheep. Both had brought a sacrifice to the Lord (Genesis 4:3–4). Abel acted in faith by bringing a sacrifice more suitable than that of Cain (Hebrews 11:4). The latter's rage burned out of control against God's rejection. In retaliation, he slaughtered his brother, whose gift had been accepted (Genesis 4:5–8). The Lord confronted Cain with his guilt, judged him, and marked him, sending him out of the land of Nod, east of Eden. When he protested that his chastisement exceeded his ability to stand under it and feared someone would kill him, the Lord promised to take sevenfold vengeance on anyone who dared to kill him (vv. 9–16).

**Commandment.** In previous books of the Bible, specifically the Gospels, our Lord had already charged His disciples to love their enemies (Matthew 5:43–45) and love their neighbors as themselves (Luke 10:25–37). The "new commandment" required that Christians love each other (John 15:12, 17). This did not overrule the other two love commandments. Jesus' command to love those within the church was initiated to create persuasive evidence for those outside the church. It would provide them discernible proof (1) that His followers were Christ-like in their love toward one another, (2) that the foundation for vigorous human community could be found in Christ, and (3) that, by extension, Jesus' declaration about Himself in concert with the miracles He accomplished were really true (John 13:35, 17:20–23, 21:24–25).

## Background

This letter was written to members of the churches in Asia Minor. The epistle served as a reminder to the children of God to love one another. The devil is the originator of sin and has sinned from the beginning of time. Those who belong to Satan reveal their essential nature by living lawless lives. This lawlessness is clearly seen in the blatant disregard for human life. John restated that Jesus laid the foundation on how we should treat one another. When Jesus died on the Cross, He demonstrated the greatest, truest, and most unselfish kind of love. His death validated that love is more than mere words; it must be followed by actions. When we say we love someone, our actions should prove our declaration. Displaying love for one another is evidence that we belong to God. Children of God should live to please the Lord in accordance with His commandments. To show indifference to the needs of others is in complete contradiction to the teachings of Christ.

In Jesus' day, many assumed that by obeying the commandments, they could show themselves worthy of God's blessings (Galatians 3:2). However, Jesus made it very clear that love was a natural result of God's blessing, not a pre-condition for it. The commandment to love is an expression of how Christ's disciples should act. The disciples were commanded to love in the same sense that branches were "commanded" to bear fruit (cf. John 15:4).

## At-A-Glance

1. Operating in Love (1 John 3:11–20)
2. Motivated by Love (vv. 21–24)

## In Depth

### 1. Operating in Love (1 John 3:11–20)

Caring for others in accordance to God's will usually means doing the opposite of what is favorable in the eyes of the world. Some may retaliate against our good works, especially if our deeds glorify and illuminate the righteousness of Christ. Showing love toward another person should be prompted by genuine sincerity. In these Scriptures, Cain's reaction to God's rejection is murderous intent. It is difficult to fathom how one act of rejection could spur such violence against another. One might assume that these feelings of hatred and jealousy were dormant in Cain's heart, and God's rejection was the final straw. An unchecked attitude of anger, jealousy, and hatred can harden the heart, making it implacable. Our harsh words may not result in a person's death; however, words and actions can assassinate someone's character and destroy self-esteem.

The Holy Spirit is a filtering system that checks the contents of our hearts and purifies us through the Word of God. Real love is an attribute of God, seen magnificently in the life of Christ. When we lay down our lives for someone else, it means we serve expecting God to reward us. Love is action, not just words. Those of us who can give generously to support the needs of others ought to do so with an honest heart, not grudgingly or expecting favors in return. Our actions indicate our connection and affiliation to Christ.

Demonstrating a life of generosity in our church, communities, homes, and workplaces lets others know we belong to Him. There are times when we will fall short of God's expectations. Fear and uncertainty can hinder our ability to lovingly serve others; we may feel guilty and unworthy. This kind of condemnation is not from God. The Lord understands our apprehension. When we earnestly ask God to check our motives, we will discern the difference between godly and ungodly intentions.

### 2. Motivated by Love (vv. 21–24)

When our actions are motivated by love, we can approach God in boldness and confidence. Pure intentions glorify and please God, and a clean heart gives room for His love to flourish. When genuine love occupies our hearts, Christians express prayers that encompass both personal and community needs. These kinds of prayers include fellow Christians, our nation, the church, and the less fortunate. God answers prayers from hearts willing to see the fulfillment of His Word in both private and public arenas.

The love commandment requires that we believe in the name of Jesus and acknowledge that He is the Son of God, our Savior and Lord. This commandment also requires that we love each other, especially those in the body of Christ. This command also states that we remain in fellowship with God, which means staying connected to Him through personal devotion, meditating on the Word, and in prayer. This also includes staying connected with other Christians. Sometimes we are tempted to "do church" via the Internet; however, fellowship cannot be accomplished via satellite. We need to affirm one another through physical human sight and touch! Sometimes a person's smile and embrace can make a world of difference in someone's life.

When the Spirit of God radiates through our lives, we feel something exploding inside us. The living and breathing Spirit ignites us with joy and energizes the desire to love. Love is contagious! When we obey God's commandments and live in intimate fellowship with Jesus, others will witness a change and ask what fuels our joy. There is no greater witness to the saved and unsaved than expressing the love of God!

## Search the Scriptures

1. What proves that we have passed from death to life (1 John 3:14)?

2. What shows that we love one another (vv. 18–20)?

## Discuss the Meaning

Living in a narcissistic society confounds our ability to love others, especially when individuality and self-centeredness are valued and rewarded. What can we do to combat these obstacles?

## Lesson in Our Society

Tragedy dominates media attention. The more horrific the crime, the more news coverage it receives. With this kind of media frenzy, wickedness appears to have taken an exalted position in our society, leaving many to question the true value of love. It is no wonder so many of us feel love is trivial and irrelevant. Yet, this lesson tells us no matter what goes on in the world, we are commanded to love one another.

## Make It Happen

Love is a basic human desire and the evidence that we belong to the body of Christ.

Love is more than a word, it is a repeated commandment from the Creator: Love one another. How can you express love? Make a list of things you can do in your church and community. Volunteer and serve today.

## Follow the Spirit

What God wants me to do:

_____

_____

_____

_____

## Remember Your Thoughts

Special insights I have learned:

_____

_____

_____

_____

## More Light on the Text

1 John 3:11–24

**11 For this is the message that ye heard from the beginning, that we should love one another.**

John's message is clear: Love for one another is an integral part of the Gospel message. It is a command that Jesus gave to the disciples during the Upper Room discourse. It is also the command that He declared was the second greatest commandment outside of loving God Himself. From the outset, love was a vital part of Jesus' teachings. If love for one another was absent in a community, then they were not following the way of Jesus.

In this verse, John states that love should not be an afterthought. Obedience to Jesus' command to love one another as He loves us is expected of anyone who accepts the Gospel message. Love shows us that the Gospel includes both the benefits of salvation and the responsibility of Christians to love one another. It goes hand in hand and is not separate or tangential to the Christian faith. The message of the Christian faith is love, obedience to the command, and imitation of the life of Jesus Christ.

**12 Not as Cain, who was of that wicked one, and slew his brother. And wherefore slew he him? Because his works were evil, and his brother's righteous.**

Cain is cited here as an example of one who did not show love for his brother. Cain is characterized as "that wicked one." The word "wicked" (Gk. *poneros*, **poh-nay-ROHS**) is also translated as "hurtful" or "evil" and refers to someone who is bad or would cause harm. John is explicitly saying that Cain belonged to Satan. Saying Cain belonged to Satan is John's way of pointing out that the way we treat each other is part of the larger cosmic battle between good and evil. If we are characterized by love, it will affect our behavior. Likewise, if we are characterized by hatred, it will certainly show in our behavior. Hence the saying that we sin because we are, by nature, sinners. We are not sinners because we sin.

Cain slew his brother Abel because his "works were evil." Notice that same Greek word, *poneros* (**poh-nay-ROHS**), translated earlier in the verse as "wicked one," is now also used to describe the quality of Cain's works. Cain's murderous act was most assuredly not motivated by love, like his brother Abel, but by hatred.

From the example of Cain, we see that hatred facilitates envy, violence, and murder. While we may not literally murder people, we may assassinate their character and reputation because of hatred (cf. Matthew 5:21–22). We must avoid hating others, especially Christians, because of the murderous and devilish nature of hatred.

**13 Marvel not, my brethren, if the world hate you. 14 We know that we have passed from death unto life, because we love the brethren. He that loveth not his brother abideth in death.**

"The world" here is representative of all those opposed to God. John is saying that we as Christians should not be surprised because the world hates us. It is the expectation for Christians to love one another in obedience to Christ's command. Such acts of love, then, translate into acts of righteousness.

Obeying Christ's command to love one another gives Christians an inner knowledge and assurance of their passage from spiritual death to spiritual life. Love for fellow Christians is a dynamic experience that testifies to the reality of the spiritual journey from death to life in Christ. Metaphorically, John compares brotherly love as a rite of passage representative of a significant change or progress in one's spiritual life. It is crucial to note that John does not say that one can pass simply by loving others—that would be salvation by works. Rather, his point is that having love for others is evidence of one's maturity and passage from death of sin to a life based on faith in Christ. So love is the evidence of, and not the means of, salvation.

A nominal Christian who does not demonstrate love has not embarked on this spiritual journey; that person is still in a static state of death. The absence of love for others shows that one has yet to come alive spiritually;

they have not allowed the Holy Spirit, who enables us to produce the fruit of love, to come into their hearts.

**15 Whosoever hated his brother is a murderer: and ye know that no murderer hath eternal life abiding in him.**

This is an echo of Cain's experience from verse 12. John presents to his readers the serious consequence of hatred and establishes the parallel between hate and murder: anyone who, like Cain, hates his brother is also a murderer. One could assume that this verse means that a true Christian cannot hate his fellow Christian. But it is a fallacy to believe that the people of God are incapable of hatred and murder. The Bible records several instances of murder by those who were His people. Moses, who killed an Egyptian (Exodus 2:12), and David, who had Uriah killed to conceal his adultery with Bathsheba (2 Samuel 12:9), are two major examples. Having established this link with Cain, John now concludes that hatred of others is the spiritual equivalent of murder and that no murderer is entitled to eternal life.

The word for "abiding" is from the Greek word *meno* (**MEH-noh**), which means to remain, last, or endure. Its use here by John is very important. John says that although believers possess eternal life, those who hate or murder do not have Christ's Spirit residing within them. Thus, hatred is the equivalent of moral murder.

**16 Hereby perceive we the love of God, because he laid down his life for us: and we ought to lay down our lives for the brethren.**

The love of God for others is made known not just in words but in concrete acts of love. The Greek word *ginosko* (**ghee-NOOS-koh**), translated here as "perceive," refers to obtaining knowledge. John is saying that we will obtain knowledge of the love of God by looking at the life of Jesus. Very practically, God demonstrated His love to us by sending His Son to lay down His life on our behalf. This demonstration of divine love is the heart of the Gospel. Christ gave His own sinless life to pay the penalty incurred by our sins. He now offers the pardon resulting from this sacrificial act of love to all who will accept it by faith in Him. Divine love is a giving love. God gave His Son for love. The Son gave His life for love. The Greek word *agape* (**ah-GAH-pay**), translated here as "love," finds its ultimate definition in Jesus' unconditional act of giving.

If Christians follow this model of divine love, then they too ought to give something of themselves to express their love for one another. Jesus says, there is no greater love than this self-sacrificing love (John 15:13). That is why Christians are called to a self-sacrificing love rather than a self-preserving love. As beneficiaries of this kind of love, it is incumbent on us to love others in the same way.

**17 But whoso hath this world's good, and seeth his brother have need, and shutteth up his bowels of compassion from him, how dwelleth the love of God in him?**

John says when anyone has the material means to help the needy but refuses to give compassionately, the existence of a Christlike love in such a Christian is open to question. Using a rhetorical question, John shows that God's love does not exist in anyone who can refuse to help those in need. At issue is not whether God loves the person, but whether such a person possesses God's kind of love toward others.

Our material possessions are not given to us only for self-indulgence. God's command to love others requires that we use our possessions to obey that command. Some regard worldly possessions as an end in themselves.

But John says they are a means for expressing God's love in us, opening the door of compassion in us, enabling us to reach out to others in need.

The Greek word *splagchnon* (**SPLANG-KH-non**) literally means "bowels" or "intestines," but figuratively means "tender mercy or inward affection" and here indicates that compassion is a quality of one's inner emotions. Now, we use similar metaphors when we talk about feeling something deep down, in our "gut," or with our heart. As such, love must unlock it from inside before it can show outwardly. Anybody can perceive a need, but not everybody has the compassion to help others.

**18 My little children, let us not love in word, neither in tongue; but in deed and in truth.**

Addressing his readers as children not only suggests that John is advanced in years, but also shows the family atmosphere he is trying to create among his readers. There is no better institution that reflects the kind of sacrificial love John is writing about than the family. Including himself in the admonition, he says, "Let us not love in word, neither in tongue." The construction suggests like a father giving advice, John was asking them to stop merely talking about love, but show it in deed and truth.

Christian love is more than a feeling: It involves the essential ingredient of giving. Many times when people say they love another, their only real action is from their mouth (i.e., "in tongue"). An expression of love that is backed up by only the tongue is not true love like Christ's self-sacrificing love. True love engages in actions centered on others. The world is tired of passive love; only active love will attract outsiders and make them want to join God's family.

**19 And hereby we know that we are of the truth, and shall assure our hearts before him.**

The word "hereby" (Gk. *en touto*, **ehn TOO-toe**, here meaning "by this") refers to verse 18 and points to an active expression of love that corresponds to Christ's self-sacrifice. When Christians demonstrate this kind of active love, they know they belong to the "truth" (Gk. *aletheia*, **ah-LAY-thay-ah**, what is true in things pertaining to God and the duties of man, morality, and religious truth). In the parable of the sheep and the goats, the sheep on Christ's right were commended for their acts of love toward others and were rewarded accordingly by Christ (Matthew 25:31–46). In the future, when Christ returns, we will all stand before Him to be judged and rewarded according to our deeds.

**20 For if our heart condemn us, God is greater than our heart, and knoweth all things.**

The Greek word *kardia* (**kar-DEE-ah**) refers to the heart organ, but here it figuratively denotes the center of all physical and spiritual life. Therefore, if the testimony of our hearts is negative, then we have not been sacrificially reaching out to love others like Christ. Fortunately, God is greater than our hearts and knows better our motives for service. The Greek word for "condemn" is *kataginosko* (**kah-tah-ghee-NOHS-koh**), which means to find fault, blame, accuse, or condemn. Our motives may be unknown to others, but deep inside we know our reasons. Just as we cannot deceive ourselves, we cannot deceive God, who knows all things.

**21 Beloved, if our heart condemn us not, then have we confidence toward God. 22 And whatsoever we ask, we receive of him,**

because we keep his commandments, and do those things that are pleasing in his sight.

As Christians, we must learn to listen to our inner voice so we can have confidence before God. The Greek word for "confidence" is *parresia* (**par-ray-SEE-ah**), which means openness, or speaking or acting without concealment. It may be easy to deceive others, but God knows our hearts. Therefore, John says, if our hearts are open and honest, we can go confidently before the throne of grace and petition God.

Verse 22 discusses the benefits of a positive testimony of the heart. If we have a confident heart because we keep God's commandments and do the things that please Him, then we also have assurance that we shall receive whatever we pray for that is in line with His will. John's point is that disobeying Christ's command to love can hinder our prayers, so we should obey Him.

**23 And this is his commandment, That we should believe on the name of his Son Jesus Christ, and love one another, as he gave us commandment.**

In this verse, John provides the crux of his epistle. When Christians act in obedient, self-sacrificing love, we gain confidence toward God. Faith in Christ and love for one another bring us into a new relationship with God where we become His children. Believing on the name of Jesus Christ includes accepting the fact that He is the Son of God who gave His life to pay the penalty for our sins, reconciling us back to God.

The second part of the commandment is to love one another. The sequence is important. The command is that we both have faith in Christ and also love one another. Faith in Jesus Christ is the basis of our new relationship with God, and love for one another is the expression of that saving faith in us.

**24 And he that keepeth his commandments dwelleth in him, and he in him. And hereby we know that he abideth in us, by the Spirit which he hath given us.**

To keep God's commands, which includes loving one another, is to abide in Him and to have Him abide in us. As referenced previously in verse 15, the word "abideth" (Gk. *meno*, **MEH-noh**) means to continually be present. This mutual indwelling characterizes the relationship between God and His Son Jesus and points to their unity (John 17:21). The believers' mutual indwelling with God is also a reference to the familial union between God and His believing children.

God is present in believers through His Holy Spirit, who dwells in them (cf. Romans 8:9, 11). Through the presence of the Holy Spirit within believers, they have a sense of belonging in God's family. Paul says, "For ye have not received the spirit of bondage again to fear; but ye have received the Spirit of adoption, whereby we cry, Abba, Father" (v. 15). This context shows that by the Spirit we know we are children of God (v. 16). Since God is love, His children should also be characterized by love. Just as we love members of our earthly family and enjoy getting together with them, so believers will enjoy helping others if they have the love of Christ in them.

Sources:

Comfort, Philip W., and Walter A. Elwell, eds. *Tyndale Bible Dictionary.* Wheaton, IL: Tyndale House Publishers, 2001. 719–728.

*Key Word Study Bible.* New International Version. Grand Rapids, MI: Zondervan Bible Publishers, 1996. 1437.

*Life Application Study Bible.* New International Version. Wheaton, IL: Tyndale House Publishers, 1991. 1909, 2279–80.

*The New Oxford Annotated Bible.* New Revised Standard Version. New York: Oxford University Press, 2001. 386.

*Rainbow Study Bible.* New International Version. Grand Rapids, MI: Zondervan Bible Publishers, 1992. 1375.

Unger, Merrill F. *The New Unger's Bible Handbook.* Chicago, IL: Moody Press, 1998. 634.

## Say It Correctly

Sacrificial. sa-kri-**FI**-shul.
Bowels. **BOW**-uls.

## Daily Bible Readings

**MONDAY**
God So Loved the World
(John 3:16–21)

**TUESDAY**
Love Given Us by God
(1 John 3:1–5)

**WEDNESDAY**
Loved to the End
(John 13:1–15)

**THURSDAY**
Great Love Shown
(Luke 7:44–48)

**FRIDAY**
Those Who Do Not Love
(1 John 3:6–10)

**SATURDAY**
A New Commandment
(John 13:31–35)

**SUNDAY**
Love Made Possible by the Spirit
(1 John 3:11–24)

# Notes

# Teaching Tips

## Words You Should Know

**A. Made perfect** (1 John 4:17) *teleioo* (Gk.)—To complete, finish, reach a goal; be fulfilled.

**B. Grievous** (5:3) *barus* (Gk.)—Heavy, important, savage, and fierce.

## Teacher Preparation

**Unifying Principle—Beloved Child.** Community is built on unity and mutuality. What holds the members of a community together? The writer of 1 John says believers are made complete when as a community they abide in God's love and the Spirit of God's love abides in them.

**A.** Pray over today's lesson.

**B.** Read the Daily Bible Readings as part of your daily devotions. Meditate on these verses, allowing God to reveal eternal truths to your heart concerning this week's lesson.

**C.** Read the companion lesson in the *Precepts for Living Personal Study Guide®.*

**D.** Read applicable commentaries on this week's passage.

## O—Open the Lesson

**A.** Open with prayer and reemphasize the unifying principle.

**B.** Have students read aloud the Aim for Change and Keep in Mind verse.

**C.** Have a student read the In Focus story out loud; discuss and allow students to share their responses.

## P—Present the Scriptures

**A.** Assign The People, Places, and Times to one group of students and Background to another.

**B.** After each group meets, discuss their findings with the class.

**C.** Using the At-A-Glance outline, In Depth, and More Light on the Text, clarify the focal verses.

## E—Explore the Meaning

**A.** Have the students respond to the questions in the Search the Scriptures section.

**B.** Have a volunteer lead a discussion of the Discuss the Meaning Section.

## N—Next Steps for Application

**A.** Use the Keep in Mind verse to sum up the lesson.

**B.** Summarize the Lesson in Our Society and Make It Happen sections.

**C.** Close in prayer.

## Worship Guide

For the Superintendent or Teacher
Theme: Believe God's Love
Song: "Jesus, the Light of the World"
Devotional Reading: Romans 8:31–39

# Believe God's Love

**Bible Background • 1 JOHN 4–5**
**Printed Text • 1 JOHN 4:13–5:5**
**Devotional Reading • ROMANS 8:31–39**

## —————— Aim for Change ——————

By the end of the lesson, we will: COMPREHEND what is required to live in community; TALK about experiences of love within the community that exemplify love and faith in God; and CELEBRATE the community's contribution to our formation as disciples of Jesus.

## In Focus

Whenever Deidra got to church on Sunday morning, Ricky was right in her face. He was overbearing and hardly gave her space to talk to anyone else. Deidra tolerated Ricky because he was a member of her Sunday School and a fellow brother in Christ. Though Deidra appeared to be kind, inside she was fuming with anger at Ricky's inability to take what she was sure were obvious clues—verbal and otherwise—that she was not comfortable with his attentiveness. Deidra began to feel guilty about being nice to Ricky and then mocking him behind his back. Deidra understood her behavior did not reflect the teachings of Christ, which meant loving our fellow brothers and sisters in the family of God. This meant she had to be honest and forthright with Ricky and stop her cruel remarks about him to others. The following Sunday, Deidra talked to Ricky and related her own discomfort. She felt the resentment leave, replaced by a greater appreciation for Ricky, who graciously received her message.

*If we cannot love our fellow Christian who is visible, we cannot love God who is invisible. In this week's lesson we will learn how God's love is made real in our relationships with others.*

## —————— Keep in Mind ——————

"Whosoever believeth that Jesus is the Christ is born of God: and every one that loveth him that begat loveth him also that is begotten of him" (1 John 5:1).

"Whosoever believeth that Jesus is the Christ is born of God: and every one that loveth him that begat loveth him also that is begotten of him" (1 John 5:1).

## Focal Verses

**KJV** **1 John 4:13** Hereby know we that we dwell in him, and he in us, because he hath given us of his Spirit.

**14** And we have seen and do testify that the Father sent the Son to be the Saviour of the world.

**15** Whosoever shall confess that Jesus is the Son of God, God dwelleth in him, and he in God.

**16** And we have known and believed the love that God hath to us. God is love; and he that dwelleth in love dwelleth in God, and God in him.

**17** Herein is our love made perfect, that we may have boldness in the day of judgment: because as he is, so are we in this world.

**18** There is no fear in love; but perfect love casteth out fear: because fear hath torment. He that feareth is not made perfect in love.

**19** We love him, because he first loved us.

**20** If a man say, I love God, and hateth his brother, he is a liar: for he that loveth not his brother whom he hath seen, how can he love God whom he hath not seen?

**21** And this commandment have we from him, That he who loveth God love his brother also.

**5:1** Whosoever believeth that Jesus is the Christ is born of God: and every one that loveth him that begat loveth him also that is begotten of him.

**2** By this we know that we love the children of God, when we love God, and keep his commandments.

**3** For this is the love of God, that we keep his commandments: and his commandments are not grievous.

**4** For whatsoever is born of God overcometh the world: and this is the victory that overcometh the world, even our faith.

**NLT** **1 John 4:13** And God has given us his Spirit as proof that we live in him and he in us.

**14** Furthermore, we have seen with our own eyes and now testify that the Father sent his Son to be the Savior of the world.

**15** All who confess that Jesus is the Son of God have God living in them, and they live in God.

**16** We know how much God loves us, and we have put our trust in his love. God is love, and all who live in love live in God, and God lives in them.

**17** And as we live in God, our love grows more perfect. So we will not be afraid on the day of judgment, but we can face him with confidence because we live like Jesus here in this world.

**18** Such love has no fear, because perfect love expels all fear. If we are afraid, it is for fear of punishment, and this shows that we have not fully experienced his perfect love.

**19** We love each other because he loved us first.

**20** If someone says, "I love God," but hates a Christian brother or sister, that person is a liar; for if we don't love people we can see, how can we love God, whom we cannot see?

**21** And he has given us this command: Those who love God must also love their Christian brothers and sisters.

**5:1** Everyone who believes that Jesus is the Christ has become a child of God. And everyone who loves the Father loves his children, too.

**2** We know we love God's children if we love God and obey his commandments.

**3** Loving God means keeping his commandments, and his commandments are not burdensome.

5 Who is he that overcometh the world, but he that believeth that Jesus is the Son of God?

4 For every child of God defeats this evil world, and we achieve this victory through our faith.

5 And who can win this battle against the world? Only those who believe that Jesus is the Son of God.

## The People, Places, and Times

**John.** The writer of the book of 1 John is thought to be John the apostle. John, along with his brother James, was a fisherman until he was called by Jesus to join the other eleven disciples. For three years, he followed and learned from Christ. John, along with Peter and James, was a part of Jesus' inner circle. In his self-titled Gospel, he refers to himself as the "disciple whom Jesus loved" (John 21:20). After Pentecost, John was said to have led the church in Ephesus and eventually was exiled during the reign of Domitian to the island of Patmos. He is known as the one apostle who died a natural death, although it is also reported that he was thrown into a pot of boiling oil.

**Day of Judgment.** This judgment refers to the final and ultimate judgment of God. It involves the final appearance of Christ when He judges the actions of all humankind. This phrase finds its roots in the Old Testament concept of the Day of the Lord. The Hebrews believed this would be the day when God would judge the nations and vindicate His people. In the New Testament, it loses its nationalistic tone and refers to God's solemn condemnation of all evil. On that day, Christians will inherit eternal life and unbelievers the ill-fated choice of eternal damnation (hell).

## Background

The letters of John are three brief epistles. The succinctness is misleading, for they deal with insightful and significant questions about the fundamental nature of Christian spiritual experience. The Johannine letters also provide fascinating insight to the condition of the church at the end of the first century. Heresy played a critical and deceptive role in the church. Autonomy and church organization are reflected. The genuine nature of a committed and obedient relationship to God through Christ is strongly and affectionately depicted and commanded.

In his first epistle, John described how love is evidence of our relationship to God (1 John 4:14–21). The present assurance is so obvious that even the fear of Judgment Day is eliminated (vv. 17–18). In the final chapter, John turned to the interrelationship of love and righteousness. Those who are born of God do not find His commandments to be troublesome (5:3). The faith of the children of God gives them power to discover victory over the world that would obstruct the execution of commands (v. 4). That faith rests in Jesus as the Son of God (v. 5). Again, accurate belief enters the picture: Jesus was fully human (v. 6) and the Spirit bears witness to the reality of Jesus (vv. 7–8). The result is a great inner confidence that God "has given us eternal life, and this life is in his Son" (from v. 11, NLT). Again, the line of demarcation between the one who has life and the one who does not is made crystal clear (v. 12).

## At-A-Glance

1. Living Proof (1 John 4:13–17)
2. Loving Proof (vv. 18–19)
3. Lasting Proof (4:20–5:5)

## In Depth

### 1. Living Proof (1 John 4:13–17)

All Christians receive the Holy Spirit as living proof of God's presence in our lives. The Holy Spirit gives us power to love and confess Jesus Christ as Lord, and provides assurance that we are connected to our Heavenly Father. Perfect love does not mean we love perfectly; it is a description of our Savior's love for us. Jesus loves flawlessly because He accepts us with all our imperfections and mistakes, and regardless of our gender; sex; race; marital, educational, or economic status; physical, mental, or emotional qualities; age; or cultural background. He loves us! Knowing we are loved by God diminishes our apprehension of Judgment Day, increases our need to see others saved, and supplies us freedom to love indiscriminately and do the work God called us to do. The confidence we receive in acknowledging God's love is not arrogant. Arrogance is when we depend and boast in our own abilities. The confidence that the Bible describes is a declaration of our relationship with Jesus and evidence of the abiding Holy Spirit within us.

### 2. Loving Proof (vv. 18–19)

The love of God eradicates all fear. If we operate from fear, it is a sign that we have not fully grasped the concept of God's unconditional love. Many Christians function in fear and live as prisoners of anxiety, even though the Lord cannot use us when we walk in apprehension. If we fear Judgment Day, are we certain of our salvation? There needs to be a level of confidence in knowing we are saved and eternally secure with Christ.

We cannot explain why God loves us; He just does! It is human nature to want justification for our feelings and actions; however, the Bible tells us Jesus loved us before we became Christians (Romans 5:8). So if a sovereign God can love imperfect people, then who are we to refuse to love another imperfect being? Christians have experienced the fullness of Christ's love and have testimonies of His kindness. The greatest tragedy is to hoard the love of God and miss opportunities to pour this precious gift into the lives of others.

### 3. Lasting Proof (4:20–5:5)

John's emphasis on loving others is nowhere more clearly reflected than in this passage of Scripture. We are lying if we say we love God but actually hate our brothers and sisters in Christ. Many Bible teachers skate over these verses because they are too direct. Yet, these verses force us to examine our actions. How can we claim to love the invisible Lord and still be seen to hate the visible inhabitants of His kingdom? We cannot love God apart from loving one another. How we treat each other is in direct correlation with how much we love God. This principle should alter the way we view the body of Christ. Our love for God confirms our love for others; if we love the Father, we must love the siblings. This sounds simple; however, it is not always an easy task. Still, loving others is not an option; it is a commandment. The commandments of God are not burdensome when we rely on the Holy Spirit to love through us. The world is full of evil, yet we have total victory when we believe in the name of Jesus and trust God to fight our battles for us.

## Search the Scriptures

1. How do we know God lives in us (1 John 4:13)?

2. What gives proof that we love God (vv. 16–17)?

## Discuss the Meaning

1. Why is it important that we love one another?

2. Why do we fear judgment or punishment from God?

3. How is God's love made perfect?

## Lesson in Our Society

Society teaches us to love conditionally. Some people live in fear of rejection from those who claim to love them. This is not real love. One of the most remarkable attributes of God is His ability to love unconditionally and completely. No matter what we face in life, God's love is everlasting and nothing can separate us from His love! Not only do we have God's promise of love but also the promise of eternal life. With this kind of reassurance, what keeps us from loving others?

## Make It Happen

The Lord has high regards for the community of believers, and we should too. All we can do is learn to love and obey God's command. Pray and ask God to reveal where you can extend love to someone in the family of God. After God shows you, act! Write in a journal about how the incident impacted your life and share your experience with the class.

## Follow the Spirit

What God wants me to do:

_____

_____

_____

_____

## Remember Your Thoughts

Special insights I have learned:

_____

_____

_____

_____

## More Light On the Text

1 John 4:13–5:5

**13 Hereby know we that we dwell in him, and he in us, because he hath given us of his Spirit.**

Two themes dominate John's exhortation in verses 13–21: faith and love. In verse 13, John affirms that the assurance of the presence of God in the life of a Christian (cf. vv. 12, 15) is proved by the residence of the Holy Spirit in him or her. Since love is the first of the fruit produced by the Spirit, John's connection of love with the Holy Spirit is obvious, in addition to the other work of the Spirit in the life of a believer.

**14 And we have seen and do testify that the Father sent the Son to be the Saviour of the world.**

Although no one has seen God, He has revealed Himself visibly in His Son Jesus Christ. As one of the apostolic eyewitnesses,

John bears testimony to this fact (cf. 1:1–3). The Greek word *soter* (**soh-TARE**), which means savior or deliverer, defines both the purpose and the result of Christ's mission (cf. Matthew 1:21; John 1:29).

**15 Whosoever shall confess that Jesus is the Son of God, God dwelleth in him, and he in God.**

Emphasis is placed on the test of (doctrinal) faith in Christ as evidence of God's indwelling. The Greek word *homologeo* (**ho-mo-lo-GEH-oh**, confess) indicates that confession involves the intellectual acknowledgment of the human-divine nature of Christ and a personal acceptance of Him.

**16 And we have known and believed the love that God hath to us. God is love; and he that dwelleth in love dwelleth in God, and God in him.**

John effectively connects faith with works (action). Belief must find expression in behavior. Here, believing and loving are intimately joined. They are proof of God's Spirit in the believer.

**17 Herein is our love made perfect, that we may have boldness in the day of judgment: because as he is, so are we in this world. 18 There is no fear in love; but perfect love casteth out fear: because fear hath torment. He that feareth is not made perfect in love.**

By dwelling in love and consequently in God, and by God dwelling in us, love will be made perfect (Gk. *teleioo*, **teh-lay-OH-oh**, to complete or accomplish). This word refers to completion of a goal or maturity. Love will be made complete, mature, and perfect once for all in us. This perfection refers to a complete, fully accomplished state. John is stating that the ongoing action of God's dwelling in us and our dwelling in God perfects our love. The phrase "because as he is, so are we in this world" refers to God's abiding in us (v. 16). If we dwell in God and God in us, despite being in this imperfect world, we are like God, who is love. This should give us confidence on the Day of Judgment, which comes from loving as Jesus loved us. It does not mean that we will love perfectly, but that we will have evidence that we are believers, and we will have confidence that our hearts are right before God.

John then goes on further to clarify that love is absent of fear. Mature and complete love casts out all fear. The word for "casteth out" literally means to lay or throw aside something. Christians should not experience fear of punishment in their life. The punishment that John refers to is the judgment, which is clear because it is mentioned in the context of the Day of Judgment. Because fear has punishment (the two are inevitably intertwined), the person who fears punishment does not have the love in verses 16–17. The same Greek verb appears again here as "perfect" (*teleioo*), confirming the connection. John seals his point by stating that whoever fears has not matured in love. Those who fear that they will receive the final judgment have not experienced the complete work of God's love in their life.

**19 We love him, because he first loved us. 20 If a man say, I love God, and hateth his brother, he is a liar: for he that loveth not his brother whom he hath seen, how can he love God whom he hath not seen?**

Next we see the motivation behind the Christian's love. It is because we have experienced the love of God in Jesus Christ. This verse points to the detailed description and explanation of the preceding verses. It summarizes what John has said concerning the love of Christ and its effect in the life of a believer. We love God because He has shown His love to us in Christ. We love one another because we have experienced God's love in our hearts.

John says that if believers say they love God and hate their brother, they are more than walking contradictions: they are liars. This may not mean they are intentionally deceiving others. At the most basic level, they are deceiving themselves. They are not walking consistent with the truth. Those who do not love someone who is physically visible to them cannot love God, who is invisible to their natural senses. For John, the real test of true love is loving those who are right in front of you. Loving people whom you can see is the litmus test of loving the God whom you cannot see.

**21 And this commandment have we from him, That he who loveth God love his brother also.**

Not only is loving your brother a litmus test for loving God, but not loving your brother is disobedience to the Lord's command. John appeals to the direct command of Jesus (John 13:34). If we do not love our brother, we are not obeying the command of Jesus. Jesus has given us this command, and Christians must fulfill it or risk disobeying the Lord who loves them.

**1 John 5:1–5**

This Scripture passage is a part of John's final elaboration of the three principle tests of authentic Christianity: belief (faith), righteousness (obedience), and love. He has devoted sections of his letter to treating the subjects in turn. Here, all three are closely related, integrated, and woven together into one theological fabric, within the overriding idea of Christian confidence and assurance through the new birth. The text shows the

Christian's confidence in victory, witnesses, eternal life, and prayer.

**1 Whosoever believeth that Jesus is the Christ is born of God: and every one that loveth him that begat loveth him also that is begotten of him.**

John connects belief and love mutually and spiritually. The Greek word *pisteuo* (**pees-TEW-oh**) means to trust or to believe. It is more than a mere profession of a creed; it means personal faith in and personal union with Christ. Our proof of the new birth is shown as a continual belief in the humanity and deity of Christ and His redemptive mission. The logical consequence of the new birth is an expression of love for God, who is the source of the spiritual birth, as well as for all others He has given spiritual birth

**2 By this we know that we love the children of God, when we love God, and keep his commandments.**

In the preceding verse, John connects belief and love. In this verse and the next, the connection is made between love and obedience (righteousness), indicating how intertwined the themes are. John reverses the relationship by stating that our love for one another is made manifest when we love God and keep His commandments. Previously John declared that we cannot love God if we hate one another. Now John is saying that loving God reveals our love for one another. The two are intimately related, so that both should flow from each other.

**3 For this is the love of God, that we keep his commandments: and his commandments are not grievous.**

John takes a step further to link love and obedience. This verse is obviously an echo of the precept of Christ Himself: "If ye love me, keep my commandments. ... He that hath my commandments, and keepeth them, he it is that loveth me" (from John 14:15, 21). Love for God is both a basis and motivation for obedience. The Greek word *barus* (**ba-ROOS**), translated as "grievous," also carries the idea of something difficult or burdensome. For example, some of the regulations of the scribes and the Pharisees were heavy burdens hard to bear. Jesus' yoke, on the contrary, is easy and His burden light (Matthew 11:30). Furthermore, divine resources are made available to equip Christians to do the will of God. John directly references the impartation of divine nature and the indwelling presence of the Holy Spirit in all who have been born of God (see 1 John 3:24).

**4 For whatsoever is born of God overcometh the world: and this is the victory that overcometh the world, even our faith. 5 Who is he that overcometh the world, but he that believeth that Jesus is the Son of God?**

John's confidence in the believer's victory is contagious. Within two verses he uses the words "overcome" and "victory" four times (vv. 4–5). The Greek verb *nikao* (**nee-KAH-oh**) means to conquer, to overcome, or to prevail, while its related noun *nike* (**NEE-kay**) means victory or conquest. Anything that has been born of God conquers the world, but here John focuses on our faith as the victory that has already conquered the world. John uses a present tense verb to begin with because there are always obstacles to face in this world, but in talking of faith, he uses a verb that expresses certainty that our faith is complete in its victory. The way might not be full of roses, yet the Christian life is one of victory from start to finish, not a life of defeat, discouragement, or dread.

Two aspects of the believers' conquest are implied in these verses. First, Christ's victory becomes the believers' own upon their belief in the person and work of Christ, acceptance of Christ as Lord and Savior by faith, and consequent union with Christ (cf. John 1:12, 16:33). Second, the abiding presence of the Holy Spirit enables the believer to live in daily victory over the flesh, the world, and the devil. In everyday experience, the Christian can constantly express thanks to God "which giveth us the victory through our Lord Jesus Christ" (from 1 Corinthians 15:57; cf. 1 John 4:4; Romans 8:37). The person who is born of God is born to win; he or she does not live like a coward or become dominated and defeated by circumstances. The born-again believer lives confidently by faith and has complete trust in God from victory to victory. God's promises are never realized by the fearful but given to those who are overcomers, conquerors through Jesus Christ (Revelation 2:7, 11, 17, 26; 3:5, 12, 21; 12:11, KJV).

Sources:
Comfort, Philip W., and Walter A Elwell. *Tyndale Bible Dictionary.* Wheaton, IL: Tyndale House Publishers, Inc., 2001. 719–28.
*International Bible Lesson Commentary.* King James Version. Colorado Springs, CO: David C. Cook Publishers, 2008.
*Key Word Study Bible.* New International Version. Grand Rapids, MI: Zondervan Bible Publishers, 1996. 1440–41.
*Life Application Study Bible.* New International Version. Wheaton, IL: Tyndale House Publishers, Inc., 1991. 1909, 2282–83.
*The New Oxford Annotated Bible.* New Revised Standard Version. New York: Oxford University Press, Inc., 2001. 386–87.
*Rainbow Study Bible.* New International Version. Grand Rapids, MI: Zondervan Bible Publishers, 1992. 1378–79.
Unger, Merrill F. *The New Unger's Bible Handbook.* Chicago, IL: Moody Press, 1998. 635–36.

## Say It Correctly

Johannine. joe-**HA**-nine.
Grievous. **GREE**-vus.

## Daily Bible Readings

**MONDAY**
Prophetic Discernment by Christ's Spirit
(1 Peter 1:8–12)

**TUESDAY**
Seeking Unity of Spirit
(1 Peter 3:8–12)

**WEDNESDAY**
Be Steadfast in the Spirit
(Romans 12:9–18)

**THURSDAY**
Nothing Can Separate Us
(Romans 8:31–39)

**FRIDAY**
Test the Spirits
(1 John 4:1–6)

**SATURDAY**
Since God Loved Us So Much
(1 John 4:7–12)

**SUNDAY**
Love God, Love Others
(1 John 4:13–5:5)

# Notes

# Teaching Tips

## Words You Should Know

**A. Deceiver** (2 John 7) *planos* (Gk.)—An imposter or misleader; seducer.

**B. Antichrist** (v. 7) *antichristos* (Gk.)—An opponent of the Messiah.

## Teacher Preparation

**Unifying Principle—Fraud Alert.** People who spread lies and heresies are a threat to the faith community's integrity. How does the community deal with this threat? The Apostle John suggests that those who remain faithful in their belief in Christ will have eternal life; in 2 John he warns them to beware of deceivers, lest they corrupt the community of believers.

**A.** Pray and seek the Holy Spirit's help in presenting this lesson.

**B.** Study each section.

**C.** Be prepared to talk about some current events of people being hurt by the fraudulent actions of others.

## O—Open the Lesson

**A.** Open up with prayer, keeping the Aim for Change in mind.

**B.** After prayer, begin the class with your current events presentation.

**C.** Ask the question, "Have you ever misrepresented yourself to get something you wanted?"

**D.** Summarize the In Focus Story, and discuss how remaining faithful to the truth of God's Word and walking in love offer great rewards to the community of faith.

## P—Present the Scriptures

**A.** Have volunteers read the Focal Verses.

**B.** Use The People, Places, and Times; Background; At-A-Glance; In Depth; Search the Scriptures questions; and More Light on the Text to further help clarify meaning.

## E—Explore the Meaning

**A.** Use the Discuss the Meaning and Lesson in Our Society sections to explore the meaning of the text for life today, stressing the power of walking in love and truth.

**B.** Allow the class members to give their own input.

## N—Next Steps for Application

**A.** Examine the relevant points in the Make It Happen section.

**B.** Finally, summarize what is required to observe Christ's teachings.

**C.** Close in prayer.

## Worship Guide

For the Superintendent or Teacher
Theme: Watch Out for Deceivers!
Song: "God So Loved the World"
Devotional Reading: Galatians 6:6–10

# Watch Out for Deceivers!

**Bible Background • 1 JOHN 5:6–12, 18–20; 2 JOHN**
**Printed Text • 2 JOHN**
**Devotional Reading • GALATIANS 6:6–10**

—————————— Aim for Change ——————————

By the end of the lesson, we will: RESEARCH John's caution to beware of those who do not abide in Christ's teachings; REFLECT on the emotional response to teachings that are contrary to what we have been previously taught; and TESTIFY that walking in Jesus' commandment to love protects the faith community from deceivers and corruption. ———————— In Focus ————————

Trina was secretly excited to see a new face in church Sunday. He was tall and handsome and wore a very nice Italian suit. She hoped that somehow they would get a chance to meet, and they did. Ron was an educated and well-spoken businessman. During their conversation, she realized they had a lot in common, including growing up in the same hometown. He suggested they get together for dinner later in the week. Trina couldn't resist a man who seemed to have it all together and shared her love for the Lord. Maybe she had finally found the one, but she didn't want to get ahead of herself. Once they sat down for coffee, he began to tell Trina how he believed in Jesus as a concept and how absurd it was to believe that Jesus actually existed. He went on further to say that the Bible was an outdated book with a few timeless truths, and we needed to be aware of its limits. Trina couldn't believe what she was hearing. It seemed that the one thing Ron didn't have together was his beliefs. She tried to speak the truth in love to him, but he just responded with arrogance. She definitely didn't want a second date.

*In this lesson, we will learn the value of walking in truth and in love.*

—————————— Keep in Mind ——————————

"Look to yourselves, that we lose not those things which we have wrought, but that we receive a full reward" (2 John 8).

"Look to yourselves, that we lose not those things which we have wrought, but that we receive a full reward" (2 John 8).

# Focal Verses

**KJV** **2 John 1** The elder unto the elect lady and her children, whom I love in the truth; and not I only, but also all they that have known the truth;

**2** For the truth's sake, which dwelleth in us, and shall be with us for ever.

**3** Grace be with you, mercy, and peace, from God the Father, and from the Lord Jesus Christ, the Son of the Father, in truth and love.

**4** I rejoiced greatly that I found of thy children walking in truth, as we have received a commandment from the Father.

**5** And now I beseech thee, lady, not as though I wrote a new commandment unto thee, but that which we had from the beginning, that we love one another.

**6** And this is love, that we walk after his commandments. This is the commandment, That, as ye have heard from the beginning, ye should walk in it.

**7** For many deceivers are entered into the world, who confess not that Jesus Christ is come in the flesh. This is a deceiver and an antichrist.

**8** Look to yourselves, that we lose not those things which we have wrought, but that we receive a full reward.

**9** Whosoever transgresseth, and abideth not in the doctrine of Christ, hath not God. He that abideth in the doctrine of Christ, he hath both the Father and the Son.

**10** If there come any unto you, and bring not this doctrine, receive him not into your house, neither bid him God speed:

**11** For he that biddeth him God speed is partaker of his evil deeds.

**12** Having many things to write unto you, I would not write with paper and ink: but I trust to come unto you, and speak face to face, that our joy may be full.

**NLT** **2 John 1** This letter is from John, the elder. I am writing to the chosen lady and to her children, whom I love in the truth—as does everyone else who knows the truth—

**2** because the truth lives in us and will be with us forever.

**3** Grace, mercy, and peace, which come from God the Father and from Jesus Christ—the Son of the Father—will continue to be with us who live in truth and love.

**4** How happy I was to meet some of your children and find them living according to the truth, just as the Father commanded.

**5** I am writing to remind you, dear friends, that we should love one another. This is not a new commandment, but one we have had from the beginning.

**6** Love means doing what God has commanded us, and he has commanded us to love one another, just as you heard from the beginning.

**7** I say this because many deceivers have gone out into the world. They deny that Jesus Christ came in a real body. Such a person is a deceiver and an antichrist.

**8** Watch out that you do not lose what we have worked so hard to achieve. Be diligent so that you receive your full reward.

**9** Anyone who wanders away from this teaching has no relationship with God. But anyone who remains in the teaching of Christ has a relationship with both the Father and the Son.

**10** If anyone comes to your meeting and does not teach the truth about Christ, don't invite that person into your home or give any kind of encouragement.

**11** Anyone who encourages such people becomes a partner in their evil work.

**13** The children of thy elect sister greet thee. Amen.

**12** I have much more to say to you, but I don't want to do it with paper and ink. For I hope to visit you soon and talk with you face to face. Then our joy will be complete.

**13** Greetings from the children of your sister, chosen by God.

---

## The People, Places, and Times

**Elect Lady.** Many scholars believe the term "elect lady" refers to a Christian matron named Lady Electa (a Greek name meaning "chosen"). This matron lived somewhere in Asia Minor where the Johannine churches were located. It is also possible that this is the title John used to address the church itself, with the children being the church members. One reason for writing this missive was to warn this cherished lady (vv. 1–2) against deceitful teachers. She apparently hosted traveling preachers or maybe even church meetings in her home (v. 10), similar to Nympha in Laodicea (Colossians 4:15). John encouraged her and cautioned against erroneous doctrine. He proposed that she not support anyone who teaches less than the full deity and humanity of Christ.

**Elder.** The New Testament church's development of the office of elders originated in Jewish and Old Testament tradition. The term "elder" is an expression that could indicate that John held the office of presbyter in a house church. The term was also used as a reminder of the respect due to elders in the community. In the ancient world, an elder exercised leadership and judicial functions in both religious and secular spheres. The title of elder was given to someone by virtue of position in the family, clan, and tribe or by reason of personality, prowess, influence, or through a process of appointment and ordination.

## Background

In 2 John, the aging apostle bolstered, warned, and encouraged. He talked about deceptive influences, who had traveled through the area at the expense of both the church's material and spiritual welfare. In the days of the early church, not everybody believed Jesus was fully human and fully divine. Some only proclaimed His divinity, while others only His humanity. In 2 John, the issue lay with those who did not profess Jesus to be fully human (such as the docetists who thought Jesus' physical form was a phantasm of God). John's second epistle battled this ungodly perspective and the wicked behavior that stemmed from its teaching. The apostle encouraged true believers to keep the faith. He warned followers to exclude dissidents from fellowship so as not to be accused of sharing in their diabolical work. John's christology and ethics represent a challenging, affirming, and crucial commandment for believers. The message emphasizes that those who have the wrong teaching do not belong to God. He reiterated God's commandment of love and the necessity of walking in love and truth. He gingerly reminded the congregation of his desires to visit them soon. His message was not written in a stern, threatening, supervisory voice, yet was concise and powerful. This epistle was relevant not only to the John's audience, but also to modern-day Christians. To obscure the truth, practice erroneous doctrine, and partner with deceitful instructors violates the fundamental principles of the Gospel. This principle does not originate with the Apostle John; it is traceable to an idea Jesus established (John 3:20–21).

## In Depth

### 1. Walk in Truth (2 John 1–3)

The truth John refers to contains several components. First, the truth acknowledges that Jesus Christ is the Son of God, fully human and fully divine. Second, John's truth also implies that Jesus, who is the one true God, came in the flesh so that we can know God. Finally, acknowledging these truths means believers can through Him attain eternal life (cf. 1 John 5:20). Understanding that Christ is both God and human is of great importance to the author. Believers need to know this truth and remain in it. Holding on to this understanding of who Christ is allows us to abide in the Son of God and not be taken away from Him by heretical teachings. False prophets are easily identified because one of their major christological mistakes is the renunciation of Christ's humanity and the insinuation that He is not the Messiah.

### 2. Walk in Love (vv. 4–6)

The love described in this epistle is not the love portrayed in cinema. It is unconditional love that nullifies selfishness and epitomizes genuine concern for others. We cannot mimic God's love without the sustaining power of the Holy Spirit. John understands that love is a powerful motivation. Our capacity to love

is often fashioned by our experiences. John pens declarations about God's loving character because he experienced His love firsthand. He called himself "the disciple whom Jesus loved" (John 21:20). Jesus' love is clearly communicated by all the Gospel writers, yet it is more prominent in John's literature. John was sensitive to those words and actions of Jesus that illustrated how the One who is love loved others.

Christians have an obligation to love. When we focus on the enormous sacrifice Jesus made on the Cross, how can we not love one another?

### 3. Walk in Obedience (vv. 7–13)

False teachers do not walk in obedience to God's truth. Moral irresponsibility, acceptance of sin, and disregard for the spiritual, mental, and emotional welfare of others are common outcomes of fallacious doctrine. John's letter reminds Christians to live ethically, compassionately, and discerningly. To deny the humanity and deity of Jesus Christ is heresy. The apostle warns faithful believers to forfeit all association with false teachers. His message is relevant in our communities today. We should not lend ourselves to opposing philosophies. Keeping company with false teachers allows them to propagate their doctrine and can signify our approval of what they do. We should not be disrespectful or condemn cordiality toward unbelievers. However, fellowship with apostates is a serious matter to God. This letter serves as a warning to cherish sound doctrinal truth. To identify an imposter is to know the truth. Meditating on God's Word opens our spiritual eyes to learning the truth.

## Search the Scriptures

1. What is the meaning of love (2 John 6)?
2. What are the consequences of wandering from the truth (vv. 9–11)?

## Discuss the Meaning

Chronic exposure to deception alters our understanding and leads to sinful actions. Is it safe to conclude that knowing the truth about Jesus helps us live obedient and victorious lives?

## Lesson in Our Society

Financial scandals, fueled by deception and greed, have crushed the American people's perception of our nation's financial stability. Financial crises caused many to lose their livelihood, sense of security, self-esteem, and dignity. Lives were ruined and many never recovered economically or emotionally. Believing a lie is dangerous and costly. Christ's teaching is in direct opposition to the deception and selfishness that are rampant in our society. Jesus commands that we live in love and honesty. Anyone who claims devotion to Christ must live by these directives.

## Make It Happen

To remain faithful to Jesus' teaching requires tenacity and a commitment to study God's Word. It also means obeying His commandments. We can also help others who do not know the truth through our testimonies and sharing the Good News of the Gospel. Make a decision to share your testimony about how God transformed your life!

## Follow the Spirit

What God wants me to do:

_____

_____

_____

_____

## Remember Your Thoughts

Special insights I have learned:

_____

_____

_____

_____

## More Light on the Text

### 2 John

The important themes of belief, obedience, and love treated in the first letter of John are also central to his second and third letters. John's second letter contains this main message. John manifests concern for the inner life of the church and for the doctrinal danger that threatens it externally. He urges his readers to be watchful and walk in the truth.

**1 The elder unto the elect lady and her children, whom I love in the truth; and not I only, but also all they that have known the truth; 2 For the truth's sake, which dwelleth in us, and shall be with us for ever. 3 Grace be with you, mercy, and peace, from God the Father, and from the Lord Jesus Christ, the Son of the Father, in truth and love.**

John begins this letter with the common introductory greeting of an epistle. He addresses himself as the elder. The recipient is the elect lady. This woman could have been the host or leader of a particular Christian church. John declares his love for her and "her children." This love is qualified by being in the truth. It is not clear whether these are her biological children or children in the Lord. He then states that this love is not particular to him but universal to all who know the truth. This love is motivated by the truth that dwells in all who know it. John here gives personal qualities to "the truth," perhaps as a way to refer to Jesus Christ, who described Himself as "the way, the truth, and the life" (John 14:6). John says this "truth" will be with us forever. It is an eternal truth that lives with them. It is more than just objective facts; it is living, breathing truth. John concludes his introductory greeting with the standard well wishes of grace, mercy, and peace. What distinguishes him from other New Testament writers is that he includes himself in the well wishes. He says this "grace, mercy, and peace ... will continue to be with us"—the ones who know the truth (2 John 3, NLT). This grace, mercy, and peace are not just from John and do not rest in his mere human words; they come from God the Father and the Lord Jesus Christ.

**4 I rejoiced greatly that I found of thy children walking in truth, as we have received a commandment from the Father.**

Characteristically as a shepherd, John's heart is highly elated at the consistent Christian life of members of the congregation to whom he writes. "Walking" here is from the Greek word *peripateo* (**peh-ree-pah-TEH-oh**), which literally means to walk around, and is figuratively used to signify the habits of the individual life. The use of the word "truth" (*aletheia*, **ah-LAY-thay-ah**) implies its doctrinal and ethical denotations. To walk in the truth involves belief and behavior. Walking in the truth conveys the imagery of a path that one walks on and keeps on course without deviating. The tense of the word indicates a perpetual pattern of healthy spiritual life. The truth that John talks about did not originate with humankind, not even with the apostles themselves, who originally received it. The truth originated in divine revelation, and so is the command (Gk. *entole*, **en-tow-LAY**) to obey it. Indeed, in John's epistle,

both the truth and the commandments are synonymous (cf. vv. 5–6).

**5 And now I beseech thee, lady, not as though I wrote a new commandment unto thee, but that which we heard from the beginning, that we love one another.**

John proceeds from commendation to exhortation, based on personal request (Gk. *erotao*, **eh-roh-TAH-oh**, to ask, beg, appeal, or entreat). The commandment he affirms and urges on his readers is not new; it is as old as the Gospel (cf. John 13:34–35) or the time of their hearing and receiving of the same. Here, the command to believe is added to the command to love. To believe in the full humanity and divinity of Christ and His redemptive mission and to demonstrate brotherly love are proof of the new birth (1 John 4:7, 5:1).

**6 And this is love, that we walk after his commandments. This is the commandment, That, as ye have heard from the beginning, ye should walk in it.**

John pursues the line of argument of his first letter—that Christian love is more than emotion; it is action (demonstration). Love for God and Christ is expressed in practical obedience (John 14:15, 21, 15:10; 1 John 5:2–3; cf. Romans 8:8). Jesus summarized the whole Law in the greatest commandment: love (Matthew 22:37–40). Here, John urges a continual walk in love: "that you follow love" (RSV).

In the second part of this message (vv. 7–11), John draws the attention of the church to the threat from without: false teaching. He shifts focus from the true believers to the false teachers—from the wheat to the tares (Matthew 13:24–30, 36–43). John describes the heretics, identifies their error, and warns to neither be deceived by them nor give any encouragement to them. In this Scripture passage, John commands watchfulness. He urges the believers to remain loyal not only in love, but also to the teaching of Christ.

**7 For many deceivers are entered into the world, who confess not that Jesus Christ is come in the flesh. This is a deceiver and an antichrist.**

John affirms the appearance of false teachers in the world. He describes the false teachers as "deceivers" and "an antichrist." The Greek word *planos* (**PLAH-nohs**), translated as "deceiver," implies an impostor or corrupter, signifying wandering or leading astray. This is a repeat of his earlier warning against "deceivers" and "many antichrists" (1 John 2:18, 26, 4:1–6). An antichrist is literally someone who is against the Messiah (Gk. *anti*, **ahn-TEE**, against, instead of; *Christos*, **khrees-TOSE**, Messiah, Anointed One). This is not a separate category of people from the decievers, but instead those who deceive concerning Christ's nature are opposed to Christ and are described with both of these terms. The errors of the heretic are both moral and doctrinal; the latter is in focus here. The Greek word *homologeo* (**ho-mo-lo-GEH-oh**), translated as "confess," also means to acknowledge, admit, or affirm. A heretic denies the incarnation of Christ as fully man and fully deity.

**8 Look to yourselves, that we lose not those things which we have wrought, but that we receive a full reward.**

This is the first command of the letter: a warning to be on guard. The present imperative of the Greek word, *blepo* (**BLEH-poh**), implies continual watchfulness to prevent disaster. John commands readers to reject the enticement of error for two reasons: to prevent the ruin of what both they and John had

worked for, and to ensure that they would be paid their reward in full.

**9 Whosoever transgresseth, and abideth not in the doctrine of Christ, hath not God. He that abideth in the doctrine of Christ, he hath both the Father and the Son.**

Two contradictory consequences of heterodoxy (or false doctrine) and orthodoxy are stated. The negative is first mentioned. The Greek word *parabaino* (**pah-rah-BYE-no**), rendered "transgresseth," literally means to lead before. The false teachers were trying to change the core doctrine the Christians had received—he who fails to abide (Gk. *meno*, **MEHN-oh**, to stay or remain) by the doctrine cannot have the Christ and His salvation. The opposite is also true. To remain continually in the doctrine (Gk. *didache*, **dee-dah-KAY**) or teaching of Christ, showing belief in and obedience of the same, is the proof of the believer's personal relationship to both the Father and the Son.

**10 If there come any unto you, and bring not this doctrine, receive him not into your house, neither bid him God speed: 11 For he that biddeth him God speed is partaker of his evil deeds.**

John adds a practical note after warning about deceivers. He says that the church is not to receive (Gk. *lambano*, **lam-BAH-noh**) these deceivers into their houses. He then goes even further to say that they should not even bid them "God speed" (Gk. *chairo*, **KHEYE-roh**). This is the word for "rejoice" or "be glad." It became a common greeting or salutation that essentially meant to be well.

The reason behind this action toward false teachers is that by receiving them into your home or wishing them well, you partake (Gk. *koinoneo*, **koy-noh-NEH-oh**) in the false teachers' evil deeds.

389

**12 Having many things to write unto you, I would not write with paper and ink: but I trust to come unto you, and speak face to face, that our joy may be full. 13 The children of thy elect sister greet thee. Amen.**

John concludes the letter by letting the church know that he has so much he wants to say that he would rather tell them in person. He does not want any confusion or misunderstanding concerning what he says so that "our joy may be full." He includes himself in the experience of having this joy full (Gk. *pleroo*, **play-ROH-o**). This word means to be complete or filled to the brim. John and the church's joy will be completed once they talk face to face. John finally ends with a salutation from the children of the elect sister. These might have been the biological children of a woman related to the elect lady or fellow converts of the church.

Sources:

Comfort, Philip W., and Walter A. Elwell, eds. *Tyndale Bible Dictionary*. Wheaton, IL: Tyndale House Publishers, Inc., 2001. 719–28.

*Key Word Study Bible*. New International Version. Grand Rapids, MI: Zondervan Bible Publishers, 1996. 1442.

*Life Application Study Bible*. New International Version. Wheaton, IL: Tyndale House Publishers, Inc., 1991. 1909, 2285–87.

*The New Oxford Annotated Bible*. New Revised Standard Version. New York: Oxford University Press, Inc., 2001. 395–400.

*Rainbow Study Bible*. New International Version, Grand Rapids, MI: Zondervan Bible Publishers, 1992. 1381.

Unger, Merrill F. *The New Unger's Bible Handbook*. Chicago, IL: Moody Press, 1998. 640.

## Say It Correctly

Transgresseth. trans-**GRESS**-ith.
Beseech. bih-**SEECH**.

## Daily Bible Readings

**MONDAY**
They Refuse to Know the Lord
(Jeremiah 9:1–7)

**TUESDAY**
Don't Listen to Impostors
(Acts 15:22–35)

**WEDNESDAY**
False Prophets Will Lead Many Astray
(Matthew 24:3–14)

**THURSDAY**
Avoid Those Who Cause Dissensions
(Romans 16:16–20)

**FRIDAY**
The Boldness We Have in Christ
(1 John 5:6–15)

**SATURDAY**
God Protects Those Born of God
(1 John 5:16–21)

**SUNDAY**
Be on Your Guard
(2 John)

# Notes

# Teaching Tips

## Words You Should Know

**A. Fellowhelpers** (3 John 8) *sunergos* (Gk.)—Companions in work, fellow workers.

**B. Truth** (v. 8) *aletheia* (Gk.)— Dependability, fidelity; moral and religious truth; what is true in things relating to God and the duties of man.

## Teacher Preparation

**Unifying Principle—Let's Work Together.** John encourages the church to set an example of selfless cooperation and hospitality that ultimately benefits both the giver and receiver.

**A.** Pray for the class to receive the lesson's intent and inspiration.

**B.** Complete the companion lesson in the *Precepts For Living Personal Study Guide®*.

**C.** Prepare to discuss your individual church's current practices of hospitality and areas that may be improved following the study of this lesson.

## O—Open the Lesson

**A.** Open with prayer, including the Aim for Change.

**B.** Ask the class to read the Aim for Change, In Focus story, and Keep in Mind verse together.

**C.** Instruct the class to begin thinking why hospitality may have been important to the early church, and why it is important today.

## P—Present the Scriptures

**A.** Ask volunteers to read the Focal Verses.

**B.** Use The People, Places, and Times; Background; Search the Scriptures; At-A-Glance outline; In Depth; and More Light on the Text to clarify the verses.

**C.** If time permits, ask students if any of the Scriptures presented are among their favorites. If so, allow them a moment to expound.

## E—Explore the Meaning

**A.** Ask the class to discuss ways in which the church can seem unwelcoming.

**B.** A recurring theme in all the Scripture readings is truth. Discuss how God's truth applies to the commandment to be hospitable.

## N—Next Steps for Application

**A.** Summarize the lesson.

**B.** Close with prayer.

## Worship Guide

For the Superintendent or Teacher
Theme: Coworkers with the Truth
Song: "What a Fellowship"
Devotional Reading: 2 Timothy 2:14–19

# Coworkers with the Truth

**Bible Background • 3 JOHN**
**Printed Text • 3 JOHN**
**Devotional Reading • 2 TIMOTHY 2:14–19**

## —————— Aim for Change ——————

By the end of the lesson, we will: LEARN the importance of hospitality as written in 3 John; TELL of experiences of hospitality and the reactions to it; and PRACTICE acts of hospitality.

————— In Focus —————

Two young and dynamic ministers were invited to preach a revival series on alternating nights at a small church. At the conclusion of the revival, the host pastor invited the young preachers to his study with the promise that the church had something very special for them. Before long, one of the ladies came into the study gushing thanks and presented them each with a package. She said, "This is a small gift and it's not what you're used to, but we wanted to give you something special before you go home." The ministers opened their packages. They expected them to be filled with at least a modest amount of cash. However, when they pulled out the contents, they found their envelopes contained the whopping sum of exactly... two cookies. One sugar and one chocolate chip, and nothing more. No $100 bill, no $20, not even a $5 or a $1. Two cookies! They each took a deep breath, then burst into uncontrollable laughter. They had preached as though they would be paid royally, yet they had been paid as children who had simply performed their regularly assigned chores.

*As believers in Christ, we are called to show hospitality to God's servants in whatever way we can.*

## —————— Keep in Mind ——————

"We therefore ought to receive such, that we might be fellowhelpers to the truth"
(3 John 8).

"We therefore ought to receive such, that we might be fellowhelpers to the truth" (3 John 8).

## Focal Verses

**KJV** **3 John 1** The elder unto the wellbeloved Gaius, whom I love in the truth.

**2** Beloved, I wish above all things that thou mayest prosper and be in health, even as thy soul prospereth.

**3** For I rejoiced greatly, when the brethren came and testified of the truth that is in thee, even as thou walkest in the truth.

**4** I have no greater joy than to hear that my children walk in truth.

**5** Beloved, thou doest faithfully whatsoever thou doest to the brethren, and to strangers;

**6** Which have borne witness of thy charity before the church: whom if thou bring forward on their journey after a godly sort, thou shalt do well:

**7** Because that for his name's sake they went forth, taking nothing of the Gentiles.

**8** We therefore ought to receive such, that we might be fellowhelpers to the truth.

**9** I wrote unto the church: but Diotrephes, who loveth to have the preeminence among them, receiveth us not.

**10** Wherefore, if I come, I will remember his deeds which he doeth, prating against us with malicious words: and not content therewith, neither doth he himself receive the brethren, and forbiddeth them that would, and casteth them out of the church.

**11** Beloved, follow not that which is evil, but that which is good. He that doeth good is of God: but he that doeth evil hath not seen God.

**12** Demetrius hath good report of all men, and of the truth itself: yea, and we also bear record; and ye know that our record is true.

**13** I had many things to write, but I will not with ink and pen write unto thee:

**NLT** **3 John 1** This letter is from John, the elder. I am writing to Gaius, my dear friend, whom I love in the truth.

**2** Dear friend, I hope all is well with you and that you are as healthy in body as you are strong in spirit.

**3** Some of the traveling teachers recently returned and made me very happy by telling me about your faithfulness and that you are living according to the truth.

**4** I could have no greater joy than to hear that my children are following the truth.

**5** Dear friend, you are being faithful to God when you care for the traveling teachers who pass through, even though they are strangers to you.

**6** They have told the church here of your loving friendship. Please continue providing for such teachers in a manner that pleases God.

**7** For they are traveling for the Lord, and they accept nothing from people who are not believers.

**8** So we ourselves should support them so that we can be their partners as they teach the truth.

**9** I wrote to the church about this, but Diotrephes, who loves to be the leader, refuses to have anything to do with us.

**10** When I come, I will report some of the things he is doing and the evil accusations he is making against us. Not only does he refuse to welcome the traveling teachers, he also tells others not to help them. And when they do help, he puts them out of the church.

**11** Dear friend, don't let this bad example influence you. Follow only what is good. Remember that those who do good prove that they are God's children, and those who do evil prove that they do not know God.

14 But I trust I shall shortly see thee, and we shall speak face to face. Peace be to thee. Our friends salute thee. Greet the friends by name.

12 Everyone speaks highly of Demetrius, as does the truth itself. We ourselves can say the same for him, and you know we speak the truth.

13 I have much more to say to you, but I don't want to write it with pen and ink.

14 For I hope to see you soon, and then we will talk face to face.

15 Peace be with you. Your friends here send you their greetings. Please give my personal greetings to each of our friends there.

## The People, Places, and Times

**Gaius.** Gaius' name could mean "lord" or "man of the earth." He was a Christian in Asia Minor who was highly commended by John. John wrote of him as "wellbeloved." He also appreciated that Gaius was walking in the truth and doing a faithful work. He was known for his hospitality toward "the brethren, and to strangers" (3 John 5). Gaius has been identified by some scholars as the Gaius mentioned in the Apostolic Constitution and may have been ordained as the bishop of Pergamum.

**Diotrephes.** His name means "nourished by Jupiter." Diotrephes is mentioned by John as resisting John's authority. He also used his authority in the church to refuse hospitality to Christian workers. John wrote that he was one who "loveth to have the preeminence among them." From this we can assume that Diotrephes was a leader in the church. Diotrephes was also known for speaking malicious words against John and other leaders in the church.

## Background

John named himself "the elder" in his outreach to Gaius. Although not explicit in his epistle, tradition suggests that he wrote from Ephesus. What is clear, however, in this letter is the importance of strong relationships within the early church. Far different from modern Western culture's obsession with individualism and isolation, the world of John, Gaius, and even Diotrephes depended heavily on a network of closely intertwined community connections. While we are able to choose how deeply we will become involved with people different from ourselves, the early church was a blend of people from various walks of life. As John wrote this third epistle, his words conveyed a key element of hospitality, which is genuine appreciation. He was both a spiritual elder in the church, and a physical elder of advanced age. This has earned him a wealth of experience with people at their best and worst.

John's prior epistles warned against challenges the church faced from outside forces (1 John 2:22; 2 John 7) and spiritual forces (1 John 4:4). As the church is open to anyone who may confess Christ, the church is rendered vulnerable to those who may either make a false confession (2 John 10–11), or those who like Diotrephes (3 John 9) may present a threat to the church's survival from within. John knew that the church could only survive by supporting its own network of traveling ministers from already established communities. Those who were preachers and evangelists, committed to honoring Jesus' Great Commission, needed a system of support as they ventured out carrying the Gospel as their precious cargo. John relied on his personal experience with Christ to guide his instruction to those who would carry on the Lord's name and work long after the elder himself would be gone. The theme of hospitality is important because it reminds those within the church to care for each other. It also helps the church to see and seek opportunities to share Christian compassion as a way to bind us together in the truth of God's Word.

## At-A-Glance

1. The Heart of Hospitality (3 John 1–4)
2. Working Together Requires Work (vv. 5–8)
3. Challenges to the Truth (vv. 9–14)

## In Depth

### 1. The Heart of Hospitality (3 John 1–4)

John the elder begins his letter to Gaius, and by extension the church, by expressing love, prosperity, health, and selfless congratulations. The common bond in all these positive acclamations is the truth. In John's Gospel and letters, "truth" (Gk. *aletheia*, **ah-LAY-thay-ah**) includes freedom from affectation, pretense, simulation, falsehood, and deceit. Truth in the Christian faith adds a profound respect for God and His Word, and for the principles of our faith. Since John greets his friend in the truth, loves him in truth, walks with him in truth, and encourages the church to be cooperative in the truth, we know that truth is at the heart of Christian hospitality (vv. 1–4). This recognition of truth may tempt us to say that we should only associate with others who walk

likewise in the truth. While it is important that we as believers connect ourselves with others who hold the truth of Christ at heart, we should also be mindful that our Christian obligation is not just to hold the truth secret. Our job as ministers of Christ is to take and share His truth (vv. 3–4). The heart of hospitality is to have something good and be willing to share it without concern for loss. To share the truth of Christ costs us nothing. Yes, there are expenses for traveling and preparing materials and facilities for the spread and study of the Gospel. Yet, to give to Christ is to increase the family of faith, rather than to lose resources. John desires prosperity and health for his friends and spiritual children. It is important to note that this is John's desire and not necessarily a mandate or promise from God to all believers. This prosperity is not for their own selfish desires but so that they may have strength and ability to continue sharing the most important truth of all (vv. 1–2).

### 2. Working Together Requires Work (vv. 5–8)

John continues his epistle by providing specific recognition of the hard work Gaius and his congregation have performed. Often in church life we find ourselves giving until it hurts. Sometimes this is financial. Other times, our contributions are in large amounts of time spent or in providing supplies and resources for the work at hand. While most of what we do is on a voluntary basis, we continue to work hard knowing that ultimately we are in service to God and our ultimate goal is to support the spread of the Gospel. Still, we are human and it is quite normal for us to feel that our great sacrifices are not recognized. John acknowledges that Gaius' flock is diligent and faithful to the ministers and missionaries they have served. He has received good reports from them and he has firsthand knowledge of their good reputation for superior care (vv. 5–6). Knowing that there may be challenges to their ability to provide accommodations, John praises the church for what they have done, confirming their reputation is sure. He reminds them, however, that whatever the cost of their hospitality, it is still no greater than the price Jesus paid for our sins.

Verse 7 reminds us of the early church's limitations, as "they went forth, taking nothing of the Gentiles." This statement rings sharply to contemporary ears. Our transportation is mechanical. Our funds are easy to access via ATMs or credit cards. In John's day, the average person could literally go only as far as a day's walk. They would eat generally what they could carry, then rely on the kindness of strangers for sustenance each night of their journey. He mentions that many new believers would be traveling without sponsorship, meaning there could be many closed doors. The church could have asked for support from "the Gentiles" (v. 7), but the implication is that believers should not have to seek financial support from non-believers. John emphasizes this in verse 8, saying that we should be "fellowhelpers to the truth." Notice that John focuses attention on the mission, not the missionary. He gives preference to the cargo, not the caravan. The Bible certainly allows for the care and feeding of ministers, but the reason for that is the overall mission to spread the truth. John acknowledges that it will not be easy, and may not be cheap, but the value of this task is beyond price and worth all necessary effort.

### 3. Challenges to the Truth (vv. 9–14)

John boldly calls out Diotrephes (v. 9), who is in church leadership, yet defies the commandment of hospitality. This is a most distressing error that unfortunately can happen even today. The church must have leaders who exercise the administration of affairs and provide structure to the Christian organization. Yet, when we exercise iron rule, or when we lead without compassion, that is a fundamental assault against Christ's example. By contrast, Diotrephes represents an even worse threat to the church than the false teachers John warned against in his earlier epistles. As a result, although Diotrephes has taken a position and no doubt made himself lord within the church, we should be cautious not to allow our earthly authority to supersede the truth of Christ, which encompasses Jesus' examples and explicit teaching. To call oneself Christian yet refuse hospitality to believers is to commit a disastrous sin. Not only is that person shunning a brother or sister in the Gospel, he or she is also setting a poor representation of the entire church. The church needs to reflect God, who welcomes us all to the table. Diotrephes needed to be a better example like Gaius and Demetrius (v. 12), remembering that despite rank, there is no division in Christ; we are all one (Galatians 3:28).

John closes his message with the same sense of fellowship with which he began. He specifically mentions that he has many things to write, but he prefers to meet in person—something we sometimes lack in our modern world of text messages, e-mails, and other impersonal methods of communication. He closes by expressing peace, friendship, and a desire to share communion. The mission of hospitality cannot be maintained by manifestos and mandates. Giving cannot be out of necessity or by obligation. All that we do for each other must come from the heart and a genuine desire to care for the sister and brother as well as the "other" (cf. Hebrews 13:2). As we encounter frustrations and inconveniences on our journey, we will also encounter hospitable folks who go out of their way to help us. Therefore, we should pay it forward and believe that God may also bless us in our time of need.

## Search the Scriptures

1. What does it mean to walk in the truth (3 John 3)?

2. What was significant about acting faithfully toward the brethren and to strangers (v. 5)?

## Discuss the Meaning

1. What does it mean for us to prosper even as our soul prospers (v. 2)? Is this a promise from God?

2. How can we offer correction to someone who is found behaving inhospitably, like Diotrephes?

## Lesson in Our Society

John the elder desires that his friends prosper. He writes a message of love and encouragement and expects that they treat others with the same kindness and compassion. Despite our good intentions or the results of our good works, the task of caring for others can still present risks. Whether we care for traveling evangelists, orphaned children, relatives, or even non-believers who ask for our help, there will always be challenges to our Christian compassion. Thankfully, as God presents us with opportunities to minister, He will open doors for us to include others who desire to help. We are not alone in our time of need or of sharing with others.

## Make It Happen

We have all missed opportunities to show hospitality. Whether we overlooked someone's need or deliberately ignored a situation we could have easily assisted, we have all dropped the ball at some point. With John's message in mind, take time this week to show hospitality to strangers. Invite someone who is not like you to your home for a meal. At the end of the meal, offer to pray for them.

## Follow the Spirit

What God wants me to do:

_____

_____

_____

_____

## Remember Your Thoughts

Special insights I have learned:

_____

_____

_____

_____

## More Light On The Text

3 John

1 The elder unto the wellbeloved Gaius, whom I love in the truth. 2 Beloved, I wish above all things that thou mayest prosper and be in health, even as thy soul prospereth.

John addresses this letter to Gaius, who appears to be a leader in the church. He states his love for Gaius in the same way that he states his love for the elect lady and her children in 2 John. His love is "in the truth." This is the truth of Jesus Christ. He adds to his well wishes toward Gaius by saying that he wishes "above all things that thou mayest prosper (*euodoo* **ew-oh-DOH-oh**) and be in health, even as thy soul prospereth." The word prosper means to grant a successful journey or to be lead by a direct and easy way. Many have used this to justify the prosperity teaching that God wants all people to be rich, when in fact this verse does not communicate material prosperity for all. These are actually general well wishes and not a promise from God. John puts these general well wishes in a Christian context by also desiring the prosperity or health of Gaius' soul.

**3 For I rejoiced greatly, when the brethren came and testified of the truth that is in thee, even as thou walkest in the truth. 4 I have no greater joy than to hear that my children walk in truth.**

John was overwhelmed with joy (twice in two verses) over the report of the balanced spiritual life of Gaius. The first characteristic of the latter's faith is underscored in these verses: he possesses and lives the truth, the fact of which is attested by the external testimony of fellow Christians.

**5 Beloved, thou doest faithfully whatsoever thou doest to the brethren, and to strangers; 6 Which have borne witness of thy charity before the church: whom if thou bring forward on their journey after a godly sort, thou shalt do well.**

The second characteristic of the balanced spiritual life of Gaius is his love, demonstrated practically among Christians, especially in warm and rich hospitality toward Christian missionaries. Such care for missionaries was a great service, particularly at a time when inns and guest houses were scarce and uncomfortable (cf. Hebrews 13:2).

Beneficiaries of Gaius' hospitality gave testimonies, confirming the quality of his faith and love publicly in the church (Gk. *ekklesia*, **ehk-klay-SEE-ah**, the assembly).

He is further encouraged to remain committed to this labor of love. The Greek word *propempo* (**pro-PEHM-poh**), translated "bring forward," indicates that the missionaries are to be provided with necessities and escorts for the next stage of their journey.

The phrase translated "after a godly sort" or "in a manner that honors God" (NIV) describes the manner in which the traveling missionaries are to be sent on their journey They are messengers of God, and as such, they are to be treated with the same type of honor that God is worthy of. This is an extraordinary standard of hospitality!

**7 Because that for his name's sake they went forth, taking nothing of the Gentiles.**

John here offers as examples reasons for encouraging such support. First, the traveling Christians were missionaries: they went out on a Gospel mission. Christ, not money, was their motive. The phrase "for his name's sake" is a common Semitic (or Hebrew) reference to God. Because God's actual name was so holy, Jews would say "the name" rather than "Yahweh" when talking about God. Thus, the verse could be translated "Because that for Yahweh's sake..." Second, they were not "funded" by the Gentiles. They had no means of support other than the Christians.

**8 We therefore ought to receive such, that we might be fellowhelpers to the truth.**

The pronoun "we" (referring to Christians) is emphatic. The Greek word *opheilo* (**oh-FAY-loh**, "ought") carries a sense of obligation. Christians have the moral duty to actively support the work of God. A third reason is that such support is actually a partnership in the truth.

**9 I wrote unto the church: but Diotrephes, who loveth to have the preeminence among them, receiveth us not.**

Now John shuns a contrasting example: Diotrephes is the self-seeking church leader who exhibited a bad example. He refused hospitality to delegates from John. He was motivated not by truth and love like Gaius, but by personal ambition. The word "preeminence" is translated from the Greek word *philoproteuo* (**feel-oh-pro-TEW-oh**) which means the desire to be first. Diotrephes actions stemmed from the desire to put himself first instead of Christ.

**10 Wherefore, if I come, I will remember his deeds which he doeth, prating against us with malicious words: and not content therewith, neither doth he himself receive the brethren, and forbiddeth them that would, and casteth them out of the church.**

Other antitheses of truth and love demonstrated by Diotrephes are listed here. First, he spread slanderous gossip against John. Second, he went from words to action: he refused hospitality to delegates who came from John. Third, he prevented others in the church from entertaining the traveling missionaries. And finally, he expelled those who resisted his authority.

**11 Beloved, follow not that which is evil, but that which is good. He that doeth good is of God: but he that doeth evil hath not seen God.**

The first command of this letter is contained in this verse. John's exhortation to Gaius in view of the bad example of Diotrephes is expressed negatively and positively. The Greek word *mimeomai* (**mee-MEH-oh-my**) means to use as a model, imitate, emulate, or follow. Negatively, Gaius is to forsake the bad example just cited. The Greek word *kakos* (**kah-KOHS**) describes what is bad, evil, or harmful. Positively, he is to follow the good model (i.e., Demetrius in the next verse).

The Greek word *agathos* (**ah-gah-THOHS**) defines what is morally and spiritually good. John also states the reason for his command: A tree is known by its fruit (cf. Matthew 7:20). A Christian's behavior is evidence of his or her spiritual condition.

**12 Demetrius hath good report of all men, and of the truth itself: yea, and we also bear record; and ye know that our record is true.**

There is much speculation on the identity of Demetrius. Some believe that he was the one who carried this letter to the congregation. As such, John wanted the local church to give him a good reception. The phrase "hath good report" is a single verb in Greek (*martureo*, **mar-too-REH-oh**, to confirm or testify to). A better translation would be "well spoken of." This verb is in the perfect tense and implies that this good report of Demetrius had been given over a period of time and continued to be up to date. John also adds that not only do people in the church speak well of Demetrius, but his life and teaching is also aligned with the truth of the Gospel itself. To complete the list of Gaius' recommendation, John lets Gaius know that Demetrius is well spoken of by John and the local church. This personal recommendation along with all the others would carry weight in the eyes of Gaius and the recipients of the letter.

**13 I had many things to write, but I will not with ink and pen write unto thee: 14 But I trust I shall shortly see thee, and we shall speak face to face. Peace be to thee. Our friends salute thee. Greet the friends by name.**

John concludes the letter by stating there is more to be said. He writes that he will tell them in person rather than by letter. This may be due to the credibility attached to speaking in person rather than in writing. John uses the word "friends" twice. The Epicurean philosophers of the time also called each other "friends." John could be utilizing this terminology to emphasize the unity and harmony that he and the local churches shared in regards to the truth.

Sources:
Akin, Daniel, ed. *The New American Commentary*. Nashville, TN: Broadman and Holman, 2001.
Anders, Max, and David Walls, eds. *Holman New Testament Commentary*. Nashville, TN: Broadman and Holman, 2000.
Keener, Craig S., ed. *IVP Bible Background Commentary*. Downers Grove, IL: InterVarsity Press, 1991.

## Say It Correctly

Malicious. ma-**LIH**-shus.
Preeminence. pre-**EM**-in-ins.
Demetrius. deh-**MEE**-tree-us.
Diotrephes. **DEE**-ah-tray-phays.

## Daily Bible Readings

**MONDAY**
All God's Works are Truth
(Daniel 4:34–37)

**TUESDAY**
Walk Before God in Faithfulness
(1 Kings 2:1–4)

**WEDNESDAY**
Truth is in Jesus
(Ephesians 4:17–25)

**THURSDAY**
Knowledge of the Truth
(Hebrews 10:23–27)

**FRIDAY**
Rightly Explain the Word of Truth
(2 Timothy 2:14–19)

**SATURDAY**
A Teacher in Faith and Truth
(1 Timothy 2:1–7)

**SUNDAY**
Coworkers with the Truth
(3 John)

## Notes

_____

_____

_____

_____

# Teaching Tips

## Words You Should Know

**A. Administration** (1 Corinthians 12:5) *diakonia* (Gk.)—service or office, ministering, especially those who execute the commands of others.

**B. Operations** (v. 6) *energema* (Gk.)—activity, experience.

## Teacher Preparation

**Unifying Principle—Unity in Diversity.** Most humans seek opportunities to become loyal, contributing members of their societies. What motivates and empowers them to work together? Paul says that because one person does not possess all of the spiritual gifts, believers must work together for the church's common good.

**A.** Read the Bible Background and Devotional Readings.

**B.** Complete Lesson 1 in the *Precepts For Living Personal Study Guide®*.

**C.** Reread the Focal Verses in a modern translation.

## O—Open the Lesson

**A.** Open with prayer.

**B.** Ask for a volunteer to read the In Focus story.

**C.** Discuss the meaning and purpose of spiritual gifts.

## P—Present the Scriptures

**A.** Ask for volunteers to read the Focal Verses and The People, Places, and Times. Discuss.

**B.** Read and discuss the Background section.

**C.** Encourage students to give thanks for the opportunity today to serve God through their spiritual gifts.

## E—Explore the Meaning

**A.** Review and discuss the Search the Scriptures and Discuss the Meaning questions and the Lesson in Our Society section.

**B.** Ask students to share the most significant point they learned and how to use that point this week.

## N—Next Steps for Application

**A.** Complete the Follow the Spirit and Remember Your Thoughts sections.

**B.** Remind students to read the Daily Bible Readings in preparation for next week's lesson.

**C.** Close in prayer, thanking God for His gifts in our life.

## Worship Guide

For the Superintendent or Teacher
Theme: Gifts of the Spirit
Song: "Spirit"
Devotional Reading: Romans 12:1–8

# Gifts of the Spirit

**Bible Background • 1 CORINTHIANS 12:1–11**
**Printed Text • 1 CORINTHIANS 12:1–11**
**Devotional Reading • ROMANS 12:1–8**

## Aim for Change

By the end of the lesson, we will: OUTLINE the purpose of spiritual gifts according to 1 Corinthians 12:1–11; APPRECIATE individual spiritual gifts and the ways they are used; and UNCOVER the spiritual gifts of the faith community and the ways they can be used for its benefit.

 In Focus

Joe turned on the TV to the Christian television station. He hadn't been to church in a while and preferred to get his weekly dose of spirituality from the televangelists he saw on the screen. Oftentimes Joe dreamed of becoming one of the preachers that he saw on TV. He thought that if only God had given him a way with words and the charisma that some of them had, then he would definitely do something amazing for God. Just then he heard the doorbell ring. He got up and looked through the peephole. It was Deacon Ron. Joe opened the door. "Joe," Deacon Ron said as he smiled. "We've been missing you at the church. How have you been?" "I've been alright," Joe responded as he folded his arms. "Well, we miss you and I just wanted to let you know that we are recruiting for folks to serve in our volunteer ministries. It's one thing to receive from the church, but you are a real member when you contribute your spiritual gifts to the body too." Joe stood there convicted. Those words hit close to home. Maybe it was time to get off the couch.

*As members of the body of Christ, we are called to contribute to the church through the spiritual gifts that God has given each of us.*

## Keep in Mind

"But the manifestation of the Spirit is given to every man to profit withal"
(1 Corinthians 12:7).

"But the manifestation of the Spirit is given to every man to profit withal"
(1 Corinthians 12:7).

## Focal Verses

**KJV** **1 Corinthians 12:1** Now concerning spiritual gifts, brethren, I would not have you ignorant.

**2** Ye know that ye were Gentiles, carried away unto these dumb idols, even as ye were led.

**3** Wherefore I give you to understand, that no man speaking by the Spirit of God calleth Jesus accursed: and that no man can say that Jesus is the Lord, but by the Holy Ghost.

**4** Now there are diversities of gifts, but the same Spirit.

**5** And there are differences of administrations, but the same Lord.

**6** And there are diversities of operations, but it is the same God which worketh all in all.

**7** But the manifestation of the Spirit is given to every man to profit withal.

**8** For to one is given by the Spirit the word of wisdom; to another the word of knowledge by the same Spirit;

**9** To another faith by the same Spirit; to another the gifts of healing by the same Spirit;

**10** To another the working of miracles; to another prophecy; to another discerning of spirits; to another divers kinds of tongues; to another the interpretation of tongues:

**11** But all these worketh that one and the selfsame Spirit, dividing to every man severally as he will.

**NLT** **1 Corinthians 12:1** Now, dear brothers and sisters, regarding your question about the special abilities the Spirit gives us. I don't want you to misunderstand this.

**2** You know that when you were still pagans, you were led astray and swept along in worshiping speechless idols.

**3** So I want you to know that no one speaking by the Spirit of God will curse Jesus, and no one can say Jesus is Lord, except by the Holy Spirit.

**4** There are different kinds of spiritual gifts, but the same Spirit is the source of them all.

**5** There are different kinds of service, but we serve the same Lord.

**6** God works in different ways, but it is the same God who does the work in all of us.

**7** A spiritual gift is given to each of us so we can help each other.

**8** To one person the Spirit gives the ability to give wise advice; to another the same Spirit gives a message of special knowledge.

**9** The same Spirit gives great faith to another, and to someone else the one Spirit gives the gift of healing.

**10** He gives one person the power to perform miracles, and another the ability to prophesy. He gives someone else the ability to discern whether a message is from the Spirit of God or from another spirit. Still another person is given the ability to speak in unknown languages, while another is given the ability to interpret what is being said.

**11** It is the one and only Spirit who distributes all these gifts. He alone decides which gift each person should have.

## The People, Places, and Times

**Idols.** An idol is anything that is worshiped other than God. In ancient times and in some cultures now, many worship at the feet of statues. These statues represent the deity that they worship and serve. The city of Corinth was full of idolatry—the worship of idols and the false gods they represent. There was a well-trafficked temple to the goddess Aphrodite. There was also a large following of worshipers of Poseidon, the Greek sea god. These idols often led the worshipers into immoral acts in order to imitate the behavior and character of the deities they represented.

**Gentiles.** Gentiles are non-Jewish people. Initially, God dealt more with the Jews in His plan of salvation. After the death and resurrection of Christ, the Gentiles were welcomed into the family of God without having to become Jews themselves. The task of preaching this Good News was given to the Apostle Paul. Paul's journeys led him to Corinth, where he preached to a mostly Gentile audience. Consequently, although some Jews received Paul's message at Corinth, the majority of the converts were Gentiles.

## Background

The Corinthian church had been wrapped up in all kinds of immorality and unethical practices. Although it was a very gifted church in one of the most cosmopolitan cities in the Roman empire, they were lacking in some basic Christian theology and behavior. In order to help them, Paul wrote the letter that we know as 1 Corinthians. In 1 Corinthians, we see Paul address a list of issues in the life of the church. This list of issues included celebrity worship of Christian ministers, sexual immorality, eating foods offered to idols, head covering for women, and the proper way to host communion. Next he addressed the spiritual gifts and specifically the gift of tongues. In order to introduce the topic, Paul taught the Corinthians the proper perspective on spiritual gifts.

## At-A-Glance

1. The Test of the Spirit (1 Corinthians 12:1–3)
2. The Unity of the Spirit (vv. 4–7)
3. The Gifts of the Spirit (vv. 8–11)

## In Depth

**1. The Test of the Spirit (1 Corinthians 12:1–3)**

Paul starts off this chapter by stating that he does not want the Corinthians to be ignorant about spiritual gifts. His desire is that they would be mature in their knowledge about what spiritual gifts are and how they operate in the church. He then reminds them of their life as Gentiles. As Gentiles, they worshiped idols. Many of them probably participated in the worship of Aphrodite and Poseidon, two popular gods. Paul says they were led and guided to worship these mute idols. From a Jewish perspective, these idols were blind and could not speak in the same dynamic way as the God of Israel (Habakkuk 2:18–20; Psalm 135:16).

Next he lets the Corinthians know the litmus test of whether someone is speaking by the Spirit of God so they can discern the activity of the Holy Spirit in their gatherings. Paul says that no one can speak by the Spirit of God and at the same time call Jesus cursed. To do so would mean that they were not really speaking by the Spirit of God. In contrast, he says that no one can say that Jesus is Lord except through the Holy Spirit. The purpose of the Holy Spirit is to glorify

Jesus (John 15:26, 16:14), and therefore proclaiming His lordship is the approved sign of the Spirit's activity.

## 2. The Unity of the Spirit (vv. 4–7)

The argument is furthered with a discussion centered on the unity of the Spirit. God grants many different spiritual gifts, which operate and serve the body of Christ in different ways. Paul underscores the fact that they all have the same source and they are all working toward the same purpose under the same leadership. There are many different kinds of gifts, but they all are from the same Spirit. There are many different kinds of ways to serve God, but they are all under the same Lord. There are many different ways that the gifts of the Spirit operate, but it is the same God who works through them.

Here Paul is highlighting the unity of the spiritual gifts. They are given out to every believer and work in different ways, but they are all for the same purpose of glorifying Jesus as Lord and building up the body of Christ. Different people can exercise the same gifts multiple different ways, but it is all for one purpose and from one source. God through the Holy Spirit uses the gifts to proclaim Jesus as Lord and build up His church.

## 3. The Gifts of the Spirit (vv. 8–11)

Paul then lists the gifts of the Spirit. These gifts come from the Holy Spirit as opposed to natural talents and endowments. He begins with the word of wisdom. This is a message of wisdom that comes directly from God, as opposed to human wisdom. Next is the word of knowledge. This is knowledge or facts that can only be known through supernatural means. After this, Paul mentions the gift of faith. Everyone has faith, but the gift of faith listed here is the ability to believe God for impossible things on a consistent basis. Next, Paul lists supernatural healing. Then

he goes on to mention the working of miracles. Miracles are acts that defy the laws of nature. Prophecy is listed after this and can be described as telling a message from God. Often these messages are predictive, but they do not have to be and can pertain to the present. Then Paul mentions discerning of spirits. This is the gift to recognize whether a message or messenger is from God or from Satan. Last, he mentions the gifts of tongues and interpretation of tongues. This is the ability to speak in an unknown language and the ability to interpret that language.

Paul concludes this list with a reminder that it is the Spirit of God that gives out these gifts. They cannot be possessed at our whim but are given by the will of the Holy Spirit. They are given to each person as the Holy Spirit sees fit. He also highlights the fact that they all are given by the same Spirit. They are not given to divide the church but to unite it in glorifying Christ. This is a reminder to us as believers not to be divisive when it comes to spiritual gifts, but to celebrate and receive the gifts of others as they endeavor to build up the body of Christ and testify to His lordship.

## Search the Scriptures

1. What is the reason Paul says, "no man can say that Jesus is the Lord, but by the Holy Ghost" (1 Corinthians 12:3)?

2. How can spiritual gifts be used to defend the doctrine of the Trinity (vv. 4–6)?

## Discuss the Meaning

1. How can believers discover and grow in their spiritual gifts?

2. What gifts do you believe cause the most division in the church and why?

## Lesson in Our Society

Those who are gifted often use their talents for their own profit and success. We can see this in the lives of famous entertainers and politicians. The gifts that God has given them are used to glorify themselves and afford extravagant, luxurious lifestyles. This way of thinking has infiltrated the church, and many have sought to use their spiritual gifts to amass wealth and fame. Paul lets us know this is not what the gifts are for. They are for building up the church and serving others. The spiritual gifts are not ours. We are called to steward what the Holy Spirit has given us for the good of others.

## Make It Happen

Our spiritual gifts are learned in community and experience. If you are not involved in a ministry of your church, then volunteer for a limited time to serve in a ministry you have been interested in. It could be the children's ministry, hospitality, or outreach to the community. After serving for a while, ask for feedback from the leader of the ministry and others whom you have served with about what spiritual gift they may see in you. Be sure to let others know what spiritual gifts you see in them and encourage them as well.

## Follow the Spirit

What God wants me to do:

_____

_____

_____

_____

## Remember Your Thoughts

Special insights I have learned:

_____

_____

_____

_____

## More Light on the Text

1 Corinthians 12:1–11

**1 Now concerning spiritual gifts, brethren, I would not have you ignorant.**

To be "ignorant" (Gk. *agnoeo*, **ag-no-EH-o**) means not only a lack of knowledge, but also a lack of understanding that leads to error or even sin through mistake. In this instance, to be ignorant is to be wrong. Often we sin because we do not know or understand correctly. Concerning spiritual matters, this can have grave consequences for the body of Christ. Most disunity, bigotry, and other errors in the body of Christ are committed by well-meaning, devoted Christians who are either ignorant of the truth or wrong, concerning spiritual or other things of God. This is especially true concerning "spiritual gifts" (Gk. *pneumatikos*, **puh-new-mah-tee-KOSE**) which are special abilities God gives His people to serve the church.

**2 Ye know that ye were Gentiles, carried away unto these dumb idols, even as ye were led.**

Paul is not impressed by their enthusiastic worship and religious frenzy. Idol worshipers (which many of them were) could boast of the same religious excitement. Spirited worship services are not necessarily evidence of the Holy Spirit. There are many kinds of spirits related to pagan idols. The Holy Spirit is the Spirit of Christ. Only one's attitude toward Christ and consideration for those in the body can distinguish which spirit you worship. Some who worship are gifted in music, others with enticing speech, many with elegant liturgical dance, and still others lively praise while paying little attention to the doctrines being taught—whether they are of Christ or not.

**3 Wherefore I give you to understand, that no man speaking by the Spirit of God calleth Jesus accursed: and that no man can say that Jesus is the Lord, but by the Holy Ghost.**

Under persecution, distress, or religious frenzy, believers were often forced or led to curse the name of Jesus. "Accursed be Jesus" could not come from the lips of one under the influence of the Holy Spirit (the Spirit of Christ). On the other hand, "Jesus is the Lord" (Gk. *kurios*, **KOO-ree-ose**) was the battle cry of Christians. *Kurios* was the same title that the Romans demanded everybody who came under their power ascribe to Caesar, saying, "Caesar is lord!" But *kurios* was also the title given to Yahweh by Jews, God-fearers, and Christians alike. To say "Jesus is the Lord" was to commit to ultimate loyalty to Jesus. Thus, those who would not be ignorant or wrong about the Holy Spirit must examine their confession of faith.

**4 Now there are diversities of gifts, but the same Spirit.**

There are "diversities" (Gk. *diairesis*, **dee-EYE-reh-sis**) or allocations of gifts, but they are derived from the same Holy Spirit. Paul wants to make it plain that there can be unity in diversity. It is the Spirit's function to connect, not divide. These gifts are given not for individual glory, but to glorify or edify the body of Christ as a whole. If one does not want to be ignorant or go wrong, one must

understand the underlying unity of the operations of the Holy Spirit, remembering that these people once worshiped many gods according to their function (i.e., war gods, fertility gods, gods of the harvest). This was not so with the Spirit of Christ. With the Holy Spirit, there is unity in diversity.

**5 And there are differences of administrations, but the same Lord.**

There are a variety or "differences" (the same Greek word as "diversities" in v. 4) of "adminstrations" (Gk. *diakonia*, **dee-ah-koh-NEE-ah**) rendered at the command of the same Lord. As each has a different gift given by the same Spirit, each performs a different service command by the same Lord and Master. Once again, Paul emphasizes unity in diversity because the church is in danger of being fractured by the very instruments of God that should have brought them together. Monotheism (belief in one God) was relatively new outside of the Jewish faith in this region of the world. Thus, among the Corinthian church, who were largely not former Jews but instead former Greeks who worshiped many gods, it is necessary to emphasize oneness of the Lord and operations of the Holy Spirit.

**6 And there are diversities of operations, but it is the same God which worketh all in all.**

There is again the same *diairesis* of "operations" (Gk. *energema*, **en-ER-gay-mah**, energy, efficacy, actions, or activities), but it is the same God who is active in all that happens. The Corinthians are divided by those who brought them to Christ and baptized them (3:5–9). Paul faults their immaturity in the faith. Using the metaphor of building a house, he shows how God is the general contractor, and he, Apollos, Cephas (Peter), and others who brought them the Gospel and nurtured them were mere subcontractors in building the temple of God (3:10–23).

The same principle is at work in Paul's rhetorical argument that all gifts are mere tools put into their hands by God to build up the body of Christ. Each member is a part of God's construction crew.

**7 But the manifestation of the Spirit is given to every man to profit withal.**

The spiritual gifts are given by the Spirit to be used in service of the Lord. With power and efficacy made possible by God, they are the manifestation of the Spirit in the Christian community for the good of all. It is not a benefit to the individual, but the whole community. It is a benefit to the individual only insofar as it enhances one's value to the community. However, the manifestation of the Spirit is given to each expressly for the benefit of the whole community. The body of Christ is Paul's metaphor for the functioning Christian community.

**8 For to one is given by the Spirit the word of wisdom; to another the word of knowledge by the same Spirit.**

Paul begins to list the toolbox of gifts given by the Spirit to build the temple of God, the body of Christ. He painstakingly emphasizes to these newcomers in Christ (3:2), who see their gifts as a source of personal pride, that spiritual unity is the foundation for these diverse spiritual tools that have been given as gifts.

The first gifts are the tools for the teaching ministry of the church. The word or utterance of "knowledge" (Gk. *gnosis*, **GNO-sees**) is the knowledge of general items in relation to spiritual things, and "wisdom" (Gk. *sophia*, **soh-FEE-ah**) is the knowledge of the best things to do according to God's

will. They both come from the same Spirit and are used to build up the church with knowledge of what Jesus Christ would do in any given situation (John 14:26), and wisdom to understand the will of God for their mission in the world (2 Peter 3:9). This is the wisdom and knowledge that did not come from academic achievement alone, but from communion with God and the study of His Word.

**9 To another faith by the same Spirit; to another the gifts of healing by the same Spirit.**

Paul names faith as a gift and tool. Everyone has a measure of faith, especially those who claim personal salvation, which comes by faith. Paul has in mind here an all-encompassing trust in God that can move mountains (Matthew 17:20–21), cause blind people to see (9:29), and lame people to walk (Mark 2:5–12). It was the faith of former slaves in America who built institutions of higher learning and great churches while bearing the burden of racism and slavery. This kind of faith is a gift and a mighty tool.

The gifts of faith and healing are closely associated throughout the Gospels. The gifts of healing, along with faith and prayer, are important tools in building Christian fellowship because they demonstrate the unity of the mind, body, and spirit. Even more than that, the laying on of hands, anointing with oil, and mutual prayer build intimacy as they bring healing both individually and communally.

**10 To another the working of miracles; to another prophecy; to another discerning of spirits; to another divers kinds of tongues; to another the interpretation of tongues.**

The Greek word for "miracles" is *dunamis*, (**DOO-nah-meese**), or power. Miracles were a demonstration of power as evidenced by the Messianic age. When John sent his disciples to inquire whether Jesus was the Messiah or not, Jesus responded with a recitation of His demonstrations of power as evidence (Matthew 11:2–5).

The gift of prophecy is the ability to reveal the will of God for our lives and communities. The prophet through the Spirit knows the mind of God and speaks it into the lives of His people. The Spirit works either to rebuke those people or institutions who are not in the will of God by foretelling the dire consequences of their actions, or by advising people or institutions who seek God's guidance to live according to His will.

The discerning of spirits is the ability to distinguish whether a miracle or prophecy is from the Holy Spirit or some other spirit. It is necessary to understand the source of a demonstration or message to know its intent.

Diverse kinds of "tongues" (Gk. *glossa*, **GLOHS-sah**) were not exactly the same as the Pentecost experience (Acts 2:4), where the Spirit enabled them to speak known foreign languages. In Corinth, they spoke unlearned languages that no one understood, except perhaps the one speaking or someone who had the gift of interpreting unknown tongues.

**11 But all these worketh that one and the selfsame Spirit, dividing to every man severally as he will.**

Again Paul reminds us that all the diversity of gifts has one source: the Spirit of God, who chooses who gets what gift. Therefore, no one has reason to boast. More importantly, one does not choose a gift; the Spirit chooses the person for the gift. The same Spirit that gives the gift, gives according to the will of God.

Sources:
Hays, Richard B. *First Corinthians: Interpretation, A Bible Commentary for Teaching and Preaching.* Louisville, KY: John Knox, 1997.
Henry, Matthew. *Matthew Henry's Commentary on the Whole Bible: Complete and Unabridged in One Volume.* Peabody, MA: Hendrickson, 1994.
Utley, Robert James. *Paul's Letters to a Troubled Church: I and II Corinthians.* Study Guide Commentary Series, vol. 6. Marshall, TX: Bible Lessons International, 2002.

## Say It Correctly

Discerning. dih-**SER**-ning.
Diversities. di-**VER**-si-tees.

## Daily Bible Readings

**MONDAY**
Not Exalted Over Other Members
(Deuteronomy 17:14–20)

**TUESDAY**
God's Gifts and Calling are Irrevocable
(Romans 11:25–32)

**WEDNESDAY**
God Distributed Gifts of the Spirit
(Hebrews 2:1–9)

**THURSDAY**
Grace Gifts Given to Us
(Romans 12:1–8)

**FRIDAY**
Understanding the Gifts God Bestows
(1 Corinthians 2:11–16)

**SATURDAY**
Gifts that Build Up the Church
(1 Corinthians 14:1–5)

**SUNDAY**
One Spirit, a Variety of Gifts
(1 Corinthians 12:1–11)

# Teaching Tips

May 17
Bible Study Guide 12

## Words You Should Know

**A. Tempered** (1 Corinthians 12:24) *sugker-annumi* (Gk.)—Mixed together, commingled, united one thing to another.

**B. Schism** (v. 25) *schisma* (Gk.)—A rent, division, or dissension.

## Teacher Preparation

**Unifying Principle—The Sum is Greater than Its Parts.** Organizations are composed of several interrelated, interdependent functional parts. Why is it important to value all the parts? In his letter, Paul tells the Corinthian church that all spiritual gifts are necessary for its efficient operation.

**A.** Read the companion lesson in *Precepts for Living Personal Study Guide®*.

**B.** Pray for the class to be unified in their reception of the lesson.

## O—Open the Lesson

**A.** Ask the class to recite the Lord's Prayer together.

**B.** Introduce the Lesson Title and Aim for Change.

**C.** Ask the class their various definitions of unity.

**D.** Review Galatians 3:23–29 and draw comparisons with the primary text.

## P—Present the Scriptures

**A.** Ask volunteers to read the Focal Verses.

**B.** Use The People, Places, and Times; Background; and In Depth to clarify the verses.

## E—Explore the Meaning

**A.** Discuss what it means that extra honor and care are given to those parts that have less dignity.

**B.** The reading in Galatians 3:23–29 speaks of the change from our various designations to becoming children of God by faith, by putting on Christ. Ask the class to share some things they had to "take off" in order to "put on" Christ.

## N—Next Steps for Application

**A.** Review the lesson.

**B.** Pray that the class and the church be committed members of the body of Christ.

## Worship Guide

For the Superintendent or Teacher
Theme: The Spirit Creates One Body
Song: "We Have Come Into This House"
Devotional Reading: Galatians 3:23–29

# The Spirit Creates One Body

**Bible Background • 1 CORINTHIANS 12:12–31**
**Printed Text • 1 CORINTHIANS 12:14–31**
**Devotional Reading • GALATIANS 3:23–29**

## ————————— Aim for Change —————————

By the end of the lesson, we will: LEARN how each member of the body supports the other members; VALUE the different gifts operating within the church; and USE spiritual gifts in cooperation with others for building up the body of Christ.

## ———————— In Focus ————————

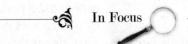

For many years Mrs. Parker had been a member of the church. Like clockwork she attended every Sunday service and was always on time. She attended special programs and was faithful in her tithes and offerings. Yet, Mrs. Parker came to church, sat quietly, smiled, shook hands, and went on her way without becoming notable. While discussing church affairs one day, several members began to discuss members and their various activities. When Mrs. Parker's name came up, everyone mentioned how faithful her attendance was but how unproductive her membership seemed to be. Shortly thereafter, one evening she appeared at choir rehearsal. The music director attempted to stifle her shock, but the members could not contain their excitement. As she settled into her section and the music began, it was immediately clear that Mrs. Parker was not just able to carry a tune, she was actually gifted to sing! After the rehearsal was over, several members surrounded her, asking why she had kept her gifts secret for so long. She replied, "Well, nobody ever asked me to join, so I decided to give it a try. I hope you let me stay."

*If we are to be unified in our faith, we cannot overlook the value of our Christian family. We must never forget that we all have a part to play in the body of Christ.*

## ———————— Keep in Mind ————————

"But now are they many members, yet but one body" (1 Corinthians 12:20).

"But now are they many members, yet but one body" (1 Corinthians 12:20).

## Focal Verses

**KJV** **1 Corinthians 12:14** For the body is not one member, but many.

**15** If the foot shall say, Because I am not the hand, I am not of the body; is it therefore not of the body?

**16** And if the ear shall say, Because I am not the eye, I am not of the body; is it therefore not of the body?

**17** If the whole body were an eye, where were the hearing? If the whole were hearing, where were the smelling?

**18** But now hath God set the members every one of them in the body, as it hath pleased him.

**19** And if they were all one member, where were the body?

**20** But now are they many members, yet but one body.

**21** And the eye cannot say unto the hand, I have no need of thee: nor again the head to the feet, I have no need of you.

**22** Nay, much more those members of the body, which seem to be more feeble, are necessary:

**23** And those members of the body, which we think to be less honourable, upon these we bestow more abundant honour; and our uncomely parts have more abundant comeliness.

**24** For our comely parts have no need: but God hath tempered the body together, having given more abundant honour to that part which lacked.

**25** That there should be no schism in the body; but that the members should have the same care one for another.

**26** And whether one member suffer, all the members suffer with it; or one member be honoured, all the members rejoice with it.

**27** Now ye are the body of Christ, and members in particular.

**NLT** **1 Corinthians 12:14** Yes, the body has many different parts, not just one part.

**15** If the foot says, "I am not a part of the body because I am not a hand," that does not make it any less a part of the body.

**16** And if the ear says, "I am not part of the body because I am not an eye," would that make it any less a part of the body?

**17** If the whole body were an eye, how would you hear? Or if your whole body were an ear, how would you smell anything?

**18** But our bodies have many parts, and God has put each part just where he wants it.

**19** How strange a body would be if it had only one part!

**20** Yes, there are many parts, but only one body.

**21** The eye can never say to the hand, "I don't need you." The head can't say to the feet, "I don't need you."

**22** In fact, some parts of the body that seem weakest and least important are actually the most necessary.

**23** And the parts we regard as less honorable are those we clothe with the greatest care. So we carefully protect those parts that should not be seen,

**24** while the more honorable parts do not require this special care. So God has put the body together such that extra honor and care are given to those parts that have less dignity.

**25** This makes for harmony among the members, so that all the members care for each other.

**26** If one part suffers, all the parts suffer with it, and if one part is honored, all the parts are glad.

**27** All of you together are Christ's body, and each of you is a part of it.

**28** And God hath set some in the church, first apostles, secondarily prophets, thirdly teachers, after that miracles, then gifts of healings, helps, governments, diversities of tongues.

**29** Are all apostles? are all prophets? are all teachers? are all workers of miracles?

**30** Have all the gifts of healing? do all speak with tongues? do all interpret?

**31** But covet earnestly the best gifts: and yet shew I unto you a more excellent way.

**28** Here are some of the parts God has appointed for the church: first are apostles, second are prophets, third are teachers, then those who do miracles, those who have the gift of healing, those who can help others, those who have the gift of leadership, those who speak in unknown languages.

**29** Are we all apostles? Are we all prophets? Are we all teachers? Do we all have the power to do miracles?

**30** Do we all have the gift of healing? Do we all have the ability to speak in unknown languages? Do we all have the ability to interpret unknown languages? Of course not!

**31** So you should earnestly desire the most helpful gifts. But now let me show you a way of life that is best of all.

## The People, Places, and Times

**Helps.** This is the special ability to aid, assist, and support others. It is closely related to the gift of mercy, which is caring for those who are distressed and disadvantaged. In 1 Thessalonians 5:14 the phrase "support the weak" could refer to this ministry in particular. The men who were selected to feed the poor widows in Jerusalem could have possessed this gift (Acts 6:1–7). This gift could also be used in an unofficial capacity as those who gave alms and fed the poor without an official role or title.

**Governments.** This word is related to the word for a captain or pilot of a ship. It is the special ability to organize and make decisions that lead to the church operating efficiently and effectively. It is the ability to administrate people and details in order to accomplish goals. Those with this gift usually have an eye for detail and an ability to problem solve.

## Background

Paul likened the church to a human body. He emphasized that every member has an important function just like the parts of the body. Each and every member contributes to the health and functioning of the whole body. This makes every believer a necessary part of the body of Christ. Paul began 1 Corinthians 12 with an explanation of spiritual gifts. He reminded the church that they were not to take their relatively new Christian faith and make it equal to the other religions, cults, and practices in the Corinthian community. He reminded them that God is the provider of all gifts, and that the Holy Spirit is the source (1 Corinthians 12:2–5). Moreover, he helped the church understand that due to the indivisibility of God, He is able to provide a unified motivation for multiple manifestations (v. 11). The apostle had already advised the church that their individual bodies were the temple of the Holy

Spirit (6:19). As a balance, he illustrated the similarity of the human body to the body of Christ (12:13). By breaking down the importance of each member, he made it clear that the church's body cannot afford to be divided for any reason, whether from outside influence or internal disagreement. Even as the various parts serve differing functions, they have a common source and a common goal and cannot operate separate from one another.

## At-A-Glance

1. The Purpose of the Parts
(1 Corinthians 12:14–20)
2. The Danger of Division (vv. 21–26)
3. The Mission of Membership
(vv. 27–31)

## In Depth

### 1. The Purpose of the Parts (1 Corinthians 12:14–20)

Paul begins his analogy of the body of Christ by using very common language regarding the human body. He blends humor and a hint of irony to describe the rather silly way that people can treat each other. Paul uses rhetorical questions to state the fact that the church is one body. The eye cannot be considered separate from the hand because it is not the hand; they are both a part of the body. Likewise, the ear cannot be considered a separate member from the body. Next Paul asks, what if the whole body was one body part? He further explains that if this were the case, then we would miss out on many important body functions. In the same way, if the church is made up of only one member or one spiritual gift, then it would miss out on some important things that it needs. In

contrast, God has placed all of the members of the church into one body; thus the diversity of gifts can profit the whole church. Paul says that these many members are a part of one body. These many members are necessary for the whole body to function; without them, the body would be incapacitated. All the members with all of their gifts are a part of the one body. This shows the diversity as well as the unity of the church.

### 2. The Danger of Division (vv. 21–26)

Paul continues his conversation about the body parts by shedding light on very common attitudes. He supposes the eye and hand suffer a disagreement in which they attempt to cast each other off (v. 21). While it is quite possible for a body to survive an amputation of an eye or hand (or foot or arm, etc.), the point is that a seeing eye still has nothing with which to grasp. Likewise, a hand without an eye to guide it will do more bumbling and destruction rather than productive handiwork. Far too often, arguments arise in the church wherein members work harder to find fault in each other than they do to find alternate solutions to a common problem. More serious is the idea of "schism" (Gk. *schisma*, **SKHEES-mah**). This word describes a division or dissension. More seriously, it represents a tear or a rip, as in a garment. Whenever we look upon our brothers and sisters as being less valuable—either to God or mankind—we are forgetting our own personal need for salvation. After the argument between the eye and the hand, the head and feet erupt into an outright dismissal of one another. As ludicrous as it would be for one body part to dismiss another, we are quick to seek separation from other Christians, regardless of our common call to life in Christ. Paul acknowledges that there are those among us who may have less favorable

417

attributes (vv. 23–24), yet we have no right to dismiss them or devalue their presence within the body. Schism represents a painful rip among humans, and also rips us from God's will.

### 3. The Mission of Membership (vv. 27–31)

As Paul concludes this portion of his letter, he calls the discorporated body parts into a unified vision of hope. He addresses them directly, saying, "Now ye are the body of Christ, and members in particular" (v. 27). As such he outlines that rather than lowly feet or eye or hand, the members of the church are actually far more vital. Naming gifts like prophecy, teaching, healing, preaching, and administration, he makes it clear that there is no person or gift that is without value in God's eyes (vv. 27–31). More than a simple call to mend fences, Paul is actually empowering individuals to know their place in the body of Christ so that their individual gifts may be put to their best use for God, rather than personal or individual gain. To be a member of the body of Christ is a serious responsibility, but that responsibility is made bearable by support and care from the other members connected to us.

## Search the Scriptures

1. What is the reason that God set the members in one body (1 Corinthians 12:18)?

2. What is the reason Paul gives for honoring less honorable members in the body of Christ (vv. 24–25)?

## Discuss the Meaning

1. How can we show honor to those church members who serve behind the scenes?

2. What makes believers worship Christian celebrities? Is this the proper way to view other brothers and sisters and their spiritual gifts?

## Lesson in Our Society

Often people separate from a church after a negative experience. Sometimes people can be put off by a well-intentioned but poorly placed comment. The news is unfortunately replete with accounts of people suffering tragic abuse at the hands of church leaders. Our natural reaction may be to say how much better we are than a particular denomination. We may go so far as to speak negatively about that particular group's theology based on human failures. Our task in striving for unity is not to condone or cover misdeeds done in or around the church. Instead, we should hold each other up via upholding standards and accountability. While it is hard to subject ourselves to each other, it is best that we determine that we will submit together to the will of God.

## Make It Happen

In some church cultures, the idea of spiritual gifts is only understood to be evident by certain worship activities. In the African American culture, it is no secret that exuberant singing, shouting, dancing, or displays of emotion may indeed reflect the power of the Holy Spirit upon someone's life and physical body. Still, Paul's letter makes certain that our gifts are not simply to be seen or heard within the assembly. Seek out those people in your church body who contribute behind the scenes. Make a point to show them appreciation through words of encouragement, a card, or a gift.

418

## Follow the Spirit

What God wants me to do:

_____

_____

_____

_____

## Remember Your Thoughts

Special insights I have learned:

_____

_____

_____

_____

## More Light on The Text

### 1 Corinthians 12:14–31

**14 For the body is not one member, but many.**

The body metaphor was widely used in the ancient world. Many politicians used it to create peace and harmony between the different social classes. The argument was usually that the lower parts needed to be subordinated under the more superior or noble parts. In other words, the poor and working classes must submit to the rich and noble classes. This was not the case with Paul. The metaphor of the body is used in a more egalitarian way for Paul to show what true Christian community looks like. It can be safe to infer that for Paul, the idea of the church as the body of Christ was more than a metaphor but an actual reality.

Here Paul uses the body metaphor to highlight the necessity of diversity. Everyone cannot have the same gift if the body of Christ is to operate effectively. The body must consist of many members with diverse gifts. The oneness of the body does not take away from the diversity of its members.

**15 If the foot shall say, Because I am not the hand, I am not of the body; is it therefore not of the body? 16 And if the ear shall say, Because I am not the eye, I am not of the body; is it therefore not of the body?**

In many cultures, the foot is regarded as being very lowly. To touch another person with the foot would be considered disrespectful, if not insulting. But the touching of hands is considered a gesture of friendship. Thus, if the foot did not wish to belong to the body because it did not have the status of a hand, that would not change that it is still a vital part of the body in reality.

The ear and the eye both occupy a position upon the head, so there is not as great a difference in status as the foot and the hand. However, the difference lies in function. These two organs have distinct purposes, neither of which the body would gladly do without.

**17 If the whole body were an eye, where were the hearing? If the whole were hearing, where were the smelling?**

The argument for diversity continues. The body of Christ cannot function properly with prophecy only, but also healing, hospitality, teaching, etc. Paul's point is that if the whole consisted of only one thing, the body would lose many functions, if not its very existence. The body is not meant to just pursue one function. Paul argues that a diversity of gifts is needed for the church to do all the work it is meant to do.

**18 But now hath God set the members every one of them in the body, as it hath pleased him. 19 And if they were all one**

member, where were the body? 20 But now are they many members, yet but one body.

Paul credits God with having arranged each member of the body by plan. The body is organized for God's purpose. There would not be a body if He had not planned it, if all the members were the same. Diversity is necessary. According to God's purpose, many diverse members work together for the good of the whole body.

**21 And the eye cannot say unto the hand, I have no need of thee: nor again the head to the feet, I have no need of you.**

One member or body part does not equal a body. Paul ties the existence of the body to the diversity of its members such that the Corinthian church could not protest his argument for diversity and interdependence. The many members make up the one body. Since the existence of the body is wrapped up in its diversity, then interdependence becomes necessary. None of the parts can exist alone; they all need each other to function as one body.

**22 Nay, much more those members of the body, which seem to be more feeble, are necessary: 23 And those members of the body, which we think to be less honourable, upon these we bestow more abundant honour; and our uncomely parts have more abundant comeliness.**

Here Paul overturns the Corinthians' attitude of pride and boasting. The parts of the body that seem feeble (Gk. *asthenes*, **AS-they-nays**) or weak and least powerful are the most necessary. The parts with less honor and dignity are also the ones given the most care. They are the parts that have more abundant comeliness (Gk. *euschemosune*, **ew-skay-mo-SOO-nay**) which means "elegance of figure", gracefulness, and attractiveness. Those that are weakest are those we clothe

with the greatest care. The parts that are stronger do not receive the same kind of care and attention.

For the Corinthian church, this means that those members they deem less dignified and lacking in knowledge are the ones to be treated with honor. The ones they despise for being weaker and an embarrassment were actually placed there by God to receive greater honor and care. This profound statement is rooted in the design of the body and therefore a part of God's plan.

**24 For our comely parts have no need: but God hath tempered the body together, having given more abundant honour to that part which lacked. 25 That there should be no schism in the body; but that the members should have the same care one for another.**

Continuing with the theme of interdependence and unity, Paul says that God has tempered (Gk. *sygkerranymi*, **sun-kair-RA-noo-me**) or mixed the body together and given more honor to the parts that naturally lack it so that there would not be a schism in the body. The opposite of division is that the different members would provide the same care for one another. There would be no member who is isolated and does not receive the same care as the others. That would be detrimental for the health of the body and contrary to their existence as the body of Christ.

**26 And whether one member suffer, all the members suffer with it; or one member be honoured, all the members rejoice with it.**

With our physical bodies, an injury to any part is felt throughout the body. So it is with the body of Christ. The word to suffer (*pascho*, **pahs-SKO**) is to experience something in a positive or negative sense. Whatever one person in the body experiences everyone else experiences it as well. Similarly, if one member exercises his or her gifts for the glory of the Lord, the whole of the church is edified. We see this edification in how the presence of a single member in a church can make an enormous difference in the quality of worship, in the feeling of hospitality visitors receive, even in the effectiveness of the church's administrative functions.

**27 Now ye are the body of Christ, and members in particular.**

Paul underlines what he has been teaching throughout this passage. The members of the Corinthian church are the body of Christ. As individuals, they are members or parts of that body. Their existence as the body of Christ is based on their unity and interdependence. It is not an either/or proposition, but a both/and proposition. As individual body parts, Paul highlights their diversity of function. As the corporate body of Christ, their interdependence and unity is highlighted. Paul says that this is what it means to be the church; it is a diversity in unity that exists through the interdependence of all the members functioning in their gifts.

**28 And God hath set some in the church, first apostles, secondarily prophets, thirdly teachers, after that miracles, then gifts of healings, helps, governments, diversities of tongues. 29 Are all apostles? are all prophets? are all teachers? are all workers of miracles? 30 Have all the gifts of healing? do all speak with tongues? do all interpret?**

Now Paul goes back to the beginning of his argument in verse 12. There are many members but one body. He states that God has set some in the church with different gifts. Four gifts are mentioned here that are not mentioned in the beginning of the chapter: apostles, prophets, teachers, and governments. All four are stated as roles or leader-

ship positions with the final one potentially encompassing a number of types of leadership including administration. Paul includes them all here as spiritual gifts.

To be an apostle (Gk. *apostolos*, **ah-PO-stole-ose**) is literally to be "one who is sent." This applies to the twelve apostles who traveled with Jesus during His earthly ministry, as well as others, including Paul, who came after Jesus who have been specially commissioned by Him to be His witnesses and lay the foundation for the church. The other three gifts Paul mentions here have similarly important roles in spreading the Gospel. The prophet is one who hears from and speaks for God. Teachers regularly educate the members of the emerging church. "Governments" can be defined as the gift of administration or organizing.

He next asks some rhetorical questions. All of them can be answered with an emphatic "No!" The main point he is making is that not everyone can be every gift. He is continuing his argument for the diversity of gifts within the church. Everyone should not have the same gifts, or the church would cease to be a functioning body. This is the practical application of Paul's earlier statements about the whole body being an ear or an eye; there would be a loss of function. Paul is now making it plain that we do not all have, and should not all seek to have, the same gifts.

**31 But covet earnestly the best gifts: and yet shew I unto you a more excellent way.**

The word for covet earnestly (Gk. *zeloo*, **zeh-LO-oh**) means to burn with zeal. Here Paul says to seek after the best gifts with intense passion. We can see that Paul wants to encourage spiritual gifts actively functioning in the church. He says to covet earnestly the best gifts. From this text, we cannot see what the best gifts are. It could be a way to appeal to the Corinthians' fascination with the more ecstatic supernatural gifts, or linked to his preference of prophecy as the best gift (cf. 14:1).

Paul adds a qualifier to his encouragement to seek out the best gifts. He says that he will show them a more excellent (Gk. *huperbole*, **hoo-pair-bow-LAY**) way. Literally, this Greek word means "throwing beyond." Metaphorically it is an adjective describing something beyond measure. Paul is now about to show them a way that is beyond all measure of goodness. This is a transition into Paul's famous passage about love. It is clear from this transition that Paul's chapter on the qualities and the importance of love are set in the context of the spiritual gifts and his teaching on the diversity and unity of the body of Christ.

Sources:

Hays, Richard B. *First Corinthians: Interpretation, A Bible Commentary for Teaching and Preaching.* Louisville, KY: John Knox, 1997.

Henry, Matthew. *Matthew Henry's Commentary on the Whole Bible: Complete and Unabridged in One Volume.* Peabody, MA: Hendrickson, 1994.

Prime, Derek. *Opening Up 1 Corinthians.* Opening Up Commentary. Leominster, UK: Day One Publications, 2005.

Utley, Robert James. *Paul's Letters to a Troubled Church: I and II Corinthians.* Study Guide Commentary Series, vol. 6. Marshall, TX: Bible Lessons International, 2002.

## Daily Bible Readings

**MONDAY**
Speaking with One Voice
(Exodus 19:1–8)

**TUESDAY**
We Will Be Obedient
(Exodus 24:1–7)

**WEDNESDAY**
Sincere and Pure Devotion
(2 Corinthians 11:1–5)

**THURSDAY**
Living in Harmony
(Romans 15:1–7)

**FRIDAY**
One Spirit, One Mind
(Philippians 1:21–30)

**SATURDAY**
One in Christ Jesus
(Galatians 3:23–29)

**SUNDAY**
Many Members, One Body
(1 Corinthians 12:14–31)

## Say It Correctly

Schism. **SKIH**-zim.
Feeble. **FEE**-bul.

## Notes

# Teaching Tips

## Words You Should Know

**A. Utterance** (Acts 2:4) *apophthengomai* (Gk.)—To speak out, speak forth, pronounce.

**B. Unlearned** (1 Corinthians 14:16) *idiotes* (Gk.)—One who is unskilled in a particular art, knowledge, profession or craft; a layman and not a religious official.

## Teacher Preparation

**Unifying Principle—From Nonsense to Sense.** Communication is important as groups implement programs that will affect the lives of others. What is needed to achieve the best communication possible? The need for finding a common understanding is necessary whether people are speaking in different native languages, as in Acts 2, or unknown spiritual languages, as in 1 Corinthians 14.

**A.** Reread the Focal Verses in a modern translation.

**B.** Complete the companion lesson in the *Precepts For Living Personal Study Guide®*.

## O—Open the Lesson

**A.** Open with prayer.

**B.** Have students read Aim for Change in unison.

**C.** Ask for a volunteer to read the In Focus story.

**D.** Discuss the need for common understanding in worship gatherings.

## P—Present the Scriptures

**A.** Ask for volunteers to read the Focal Verses and The People, Places, and Times. Discuss.

**B.** Read and discuss the Background section.

**C.** Encourage students to give thanks for God's empowerment to communicate clearly.

## E—Explore the Meaning

**A.** Review and discuss the Search the Scriptures and Discuss the Meaning questions and the Lesson in Our Society section.

**B.** Ask students to share the most significant point they learned and how to use that point this week.

## N—Next Steps for Application

**A.** Complete the Follow the Spirit and Remember Your Thoughts sections.

**B.** Remind students to read the Daily Bible Readings in preparation for next week's lesson.

## Worship Guide

For the Superintendent or Teacher
Theme: Gift of Languages
Song: "O for a Thousand Tongues to Sing"
Devotional Reading: Deuteronomy 4:32–40

# Gift of Languages

**Bible Background • ACTS 2:1–21; 1 CORINTHIANS 14:1–25**
**Printed Text • ACTS 2:1–7, 12; 1 CORINTHIANS 14:13–19**
**Devotional Reading • DEUTERONOMY 4:32–40**

## Aim for Change

By the end of the lesson, we will: DISCOVER how the Holy Spirit helped people communicate in both different native and spiritual languages; EMPATHIZE with people in situations in which language inhibits communication; and FIND ways to communicate with diverse people to foster common understanding.

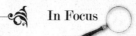 In Focus

Karen walked through the doors of the church. She looked all around and noticed the different people scurrying to their places before the service started. Her friend Mark had invited her to his church this Sunday when he had heard her say she was spiritual but not religious. Mark was a member of a Pentecostal church where they believed in the supernatural gifts of the Holy Spirit, including speaking in tongues. She had wondered what an actual service would be like.

She saw Mark and quickly sat next to him. Pretty soon the service started. At first it seemed quite uneventful. The praise and worship was lively, and the leaders invited people to worship God. Toward the end of one of the songs, the worship leader began to speak in tongues. Soon many in the congregation began to speak in tongues. After the service, she questioned Mark about her experience at his church. They had an interesting dialogue.

*Within the body of Christ, churches differ in their views of speaking in tongues. While some interpret the scriptural statements about the experience as referring only to spoken languages that aid in communicating God's Word, others believe speaking in tongues is a worship experience for those who possess the gift. What does your church teach?*

## Keep in Mind

"What is it then? I will pray with the spirit, and I will pray with the understanding also: I will sing with the spirit, and I will sing with the understanding also" (1 Corinthians 14:15).

"What is it then? I will pray with the spirit, and I will pray with the understanding also: I will sing with the spirit, and I will sing with the understanding also" (1 Corinthians 14:15).

## Focal Verses

**KJV** **Acts 2:1** And when the day of Pentecost was fully come, they were all with one accord in one place.

**2** And suddenly there came a sound from heaven as of a rushing mighty wind, and it filled all the house where they were sitting.

**3** And there appeared unto them cloven tongues like as of fire, and it sat upon each of them.

**4** And they were all filled with the Holy Ghost, and began to speak with other tongues, as the Spirit gave them utterance.

**5** And there were dwelling at Jerusalem Jews, devout men, out of every nation under heaven.

**6** Now when this was noised abroad, the multitude came together, and were confounded, because that every man heard them speak in his own language.

**7** And they were all amazed and marvelled, saying one to another, Behold, are not all these which speak Galilaeans?

**12** And they were all amazed, and were in doubt, saying one to another, What meaneth this?

**1 Corinthians 14:13** Wherefore let him that speaketh in an unknown tongue pray that he may interpret.

**14** For if I pray in an unknown tongue, my spirit prayeth, but my understanding is unfruitful.

**15** What is it then? I will pray with the spirit, and I will pray with the understanding also: I will sing with the spirit, and I will sing with the understanding also.

**16** Else when thou shalt bless with the spirit, how shall he that occupieth the room of the unlearned say Amen at thy giving of thanks, seeing he understandeth not what thou sayest?

**NLT** **Acts 2:1** On the day of Pentecost all the believers were meeting together in one place.

**2** Suddenly, there was a sound from heaven like the roaring of a mighty windstorm, and it filled the house where they were sitting.

**3** Then, what looked like flames or tongues of fire appeared and settled on each of them.

**4** And everyone present was filled with the Holy Spirit and began speaking in other languages, as the Holy Spirit gave them this ability.

**5** At that time there were devout Jews from every nation living in Jerusalem.

**6** When they heard the loud noise, everyone came running, and they were bewildered to hear their own languages being spoken by the believers.

**7** They were completely amazed. "How can this be?" they exclaimed. "These people are all from Galilee."

**12** They stood there amazed and perplexed. "What can this mean?" they asked each other.

**1 Corinthians 14:13** So anyone who speaks in tongues should pray also for the ability to interpret what has been said.

**14** For if I pray in tongues, my spirit is praying, but I don't understand what I am saying.

**15** Well then, what shall I do? I will pray in the spirit, and I will also pray in words I understand. I will sing in the spirit, and I will also sing in words I understand.

**16** For if you praise God only in the spirit, how can those who don't understand you praise God along with you? How can they join you in giving thanks when they don't understand what you are saying?

**17** You will be giving thanks very well, but it won't strengthen the people who hear you.

**17** For thou verily givest thanks well, but the other is not edified.

**18** I thank my God, I speak with tongues more than ye all:

**19** Yet in the church I had rather speak five words with my understanding, that by my voice I might teach others also, than ten thousand words in an unknown tongue.

**18** I thank God that I speak in tongues more than any of you.

**19** But in a church meeting I would rather speak five understandable words to help others than ten thousand words in an unknown language.

## The People, Places, and Times

**Tongues.** The phenomenon of speaking in tongues is prominent in the book of Acts and refers to the ability to speak in a known or unknown language. This was first seen at Pentecost, where the twelve apostles experienced the empowerment of the Holy Spirit and praised God in different languages that were understood by the pilgrims residing in Jerusalem at the time. The ability to speak in tongues is also referenced throughout Acts and the book of 1 Corinthians. In these instances, it refers to the ability to speak to God in a language unknown to man. Some in the congregation were not only gifted by the Spirit to speak in unknown tongues, but also gifted to give the interpretation of what was said.

**Pentecost.** The Feast of Pentecost was celebrated in the Jewish calendar fifty days after Passover. Pentecost was an agricultural celebration and consisted of thanking God for the firstfruits of the harvest. It was also a time when the Israelites remembered the giving of the Law at Mount Sinai. For Christians, Pentecost has special significance as the day that the Holy Spirit was poured out on the disciples and the church was born.

## Background

Paul has given a thorough treatment of the place of spiritual gifts in the body of Christ. He listed all the gifts and let the Corinthians know that one gift was not above the other. They all had their place in the church. By using the metaphor of the body of Christ, Paul let them know that they were united as one. Next, he went on to show them that no matter what gift God had given to them, love was their highest priority. Christianity is not about the gifts and talents they had, but exhibiting love. After the chapter on love, Paul turned to the place of tongues in the church gathering. Some had prided themselves on speaking in tongues. This led them to cause chaos in their gatherings. Those who were new to the church could not understand what was going on. Paul attempted to guide the Corinthian church in how to use the gift of tongues and what gifts they ought to be seeking. His main goal in the whole matter was that any contribution a member made in the church would be strengthened and encouraged.

## At-A-Glance

1. A Case of Clear Communication
(Acts 2:1–7, 12)
2. The Call to Clear Communication
(1 Corinthians 14:13–15)
3. The Conviction for Clear
Communication (vv. 16–19)

## In Depth

### 1. A Case of Clear Communication (Acts 2:1–7, 12)

At the beginning of Acts, we see God's heart communicate clearly His salvation to all the nations. The apostles had been told to wait in Jerusalem until they are empowered by the Holy Spirit. The sign of this is tongues of fire resting over their heads. We do not know whether these tongues actually consisted of real fire or were just a metaphor. Regardless, these tongues of fire are a symbol of the fact that the apostles are empowered to speak for the Lord. Immediately they begin to praise God as "the Spirit gave them utterance," and the crowd of Jewish pilgrims who had come from all over for the Feast of Pentecost hear them speak in their own languages (vv. 4–6).

The Jewish pilgrims have two questions regarding this encounter. First they question that the apostles, who are not educated, could speak in their language. "Behold, are not all these which speak Galilaeans?" they ask with amazement. The apostles are from Galilee and the Galilean accent was famous among the Jews as being distinctive (cf. Matthew 26:73; Mark 14:70). Hearing Galileans speak their language clearly and fluently excite them and must have aroused their curiosity. The next question they ask is "What meaneth this?" (Act 2:12). To hear untrained Galileans speak in Persian, Arabic, Egyptian, Libyan, and a multitude of other languages had to mean something. This is a case of God using the apostles to cross language barriers to communicate to humanity. Through this scene at Pentecost, we see a demonstration of clear communication and also the need to take it a step further as the Jewish pilgrims need to have this event interpreted for them.

### 2. The Call to Clear Communication (1 Corinthians 14:13–15)

Years later, in the Corinthian church, Paul discusses the need for clear communication. The church had been blessed with miraculous gifts, including the ability to speak in unknown tongues. From the text here and in 1 Corinthians 12, we can see that this ability to speak in unknown tongues was different from what the apostles experienced at Pentecost. These are tongues that are not known and need miraculous or supernatural interpretation (12:10, 14:5, 27). The Corinthians were placing a higher priority on speaking in tongues than other gifts that brought more clarity and built up the whole church. They are more interested in gifts that build up and elevate self.

Paul instructs the Corinthians that whoever speak in tongues needs to pray for interpretation. He further explains that when people speak in an unknown tongue, their spirit prays, but their mind has no idea what is being communicated. Their spirit is being built up and empowered, but their mind is at a loss for the meaning of the communication. He then declares that he will pray in an unknown tongue, but with understanding. He adds that he will sing with an unknown tongue, but with understanding. Here we see Paul is not forbidding speaking in tongues, but regulating it so that the church would benefit from clarity in communication.

### 3. The Conviction for Clear Communication (vv. 16–19)

Paul then makes it more personal and brings it to the Corinthians' neighborhood. He asks how someone who belongs to a different church or is new to the Christian faith will be able to say "Amen" at what they are saying when they speak in unknown tongues. New Christians can't because they don't understand. Paul further adds that they are giving thanks well, but the result is that the other person, and in a wider sense the whole church, is not edified or strengthened. His point is that the gift of tongues in a public meeting has little value is not worth unless it brings about clarity through the use of an interpreter. They can speak in unknown tongues in a public meeting, and it wouldn't help anyone but themselves.

Paul then takes it a step further and makes it more personal by stating his own experience of speaking in tongues. He says he thanks God that he speaks in tongues more than them all. Here we see Paul again not advocating for abolishing this practice. He says that this is part of his own experience of the Holy Spirit. The point is not to stop speaking in tongues, but to encourage clear communication when the people of God are gathered together. In order to drive this point home further, Paul says that he would rather speak five understandable words than ten thousand words in an unknown tongue. It is obvious that the priority for Paul is clear communication. This needs to be our priority as well.

## Search the Scriptures

1. What did Paul tell the Corinthians to pray for when they spoke in unknown tongues (1 Corinthians 14:13)?

2. What is the goal of our communication in a church setting (v. 17)?

## Discuss the Meaning

1. What makes people want to speak in an unknown tongue in a public setting?

2. How can we as believers make sure we are understood by those who are new to the church?

## Lesson in Our Society

There are approximately 6,500 languages in the world, not counting unspoken languages or codes. There is also the particular dialect and slang of numerous subcultures. With all of these different languages, it is not hard to believe that we live in a world where people do not understand one another. As followers of Christ, we are called to bridge the language gap. Whether it is a spoken language or what some may call "Christianese," we are called to interpret and make clear what God wants to say to the world. If people cannot understand at first, it is our responsibility to relay God's message so that they can receive it.

## Make It Happen

We as Christians have our own theological and church language. This week, make a list of those words or phrases that would sound strange to those who have no understanding of the Christian faith. Write out ways that you can communicate these concepts to others who are not in the church without losing the meaning.

## Follow the Spirit

What God wants me to do:

_____

_____

_____

_____

## Remember Your Thoughts

Special insights I have learned:

_____

_____

_____

_____

## More Light On The Text

Acts 2:1–7, 12

**1 And when the day of Pentecost was fully come, they were all with one accord in one place.**

The narrative opens with a reference to the time and place of the coming of the Holy Spirit. The time is precise: "when the day of Pentecost was fully come." The word "Pentecost" (Gk. *pentekoste*, **pen-tay-kohs-TAY**) literally means "fiftieth," because it was celebrated fifty days after Passover. It was the second of the three great Jewish annual feasts (Deuteronomy 16:16), falling between Passover and the Feast of Tabernacles, or Feast of Booths. Pentecost was also called the Feast of Weeks because it was held seven weeks after Passover (Exodus 34:22). It had a double meaning. Pentecost celebrated the end of the grain harvest and was also known as the Feast of Harvest (23:16). In later Judaism (toward the first century A.D.), it was observed as the anniversary of the giving of the Law to Moses at Sinai. It is possible to draw out from the two meanings of Pentecost a double symbolism for Christians. The coming of the Holy Spirit occurred fifty days after the crucifixion and resurrection of Christ, marking the beginning of the new covenant and the harvesting of the firstfruits of the Christian missionary enterprise.

The Day of Pentecost "was fully come" (Gk. *sumpleroo*, **soom-play-ROH-oh**), which means that it is in the process of fulfillment or coming to an end.

The expression "in one place" probably refers to their usual meeting place somewhere within the temple area, such as one of the many rooms or halls of the temple (cf. Acts 2:46, 3:11, 5:12).

**2 And suddenly there came a sound from heaven as of a rushing mighty wind, and it filled all the house where they were sitting.**

The place where the disciples are gathered is suddenly filled with what sounds like "a rushing mighty wind" from heaven. The word "wind" (Gk. *pnoe*, **pno-AY**) is frequently used in the Bible as a symbol of the Spirit (1 Kings 19:11; Ezekiel 37:9-14; John 3:8). The Spirit comes on them with great power. This is the power promised by Jesus for witnessing (Luke 24:49; Acts 1:8).

**3 And there appeared unto them cloven tongues like as of fire, and it sat upon each of them.**

The disciples not only hear the sound of a rushing mighty wind, but they see "tongues like as of fire." The word "fire" (Gk. *pur*, **poor**) also denotes the divine presence (Exodus 3:2) and the Spirit who purifies and sanctifies (cf. Matthew 3:11; Luke 3:16).

The expression "cloven tongues" (Gk. *diamerizo glossa*, **dee-ah-meh-REED-zo GLOHS-sah**) refers to tongues dividing, distributing, or parting themselves. Then the tongues "sat" (Gk. *kathizo*, **kah-THEED-zo**) on the disciples. The verb is singular, giving the understanding that a tongue of fire is sitting on each person.

**4 And they were all filled with the Holy Ghost, and began to speak with other tongues, as the Spirit gave them utterance.**

The disciples are all filled with the Holy Spirit (cf. Acts 4:8, 13:9; Ephesians 5:18), and they "began to speak with other tongues." Speaking in tongues is also called glossolalia, from two Greek words: *glossa* (**GLOHS-sah**), tongue, and *laleo* (**lah-LEH-oh**), to speak. It is not an unparalleled manifestation (cf. Acts 10:46, 19:6). It is also a spiritual gift that is highly valued by some (1 Corinthians 12–14). Without denying that it is a manifestation of the Holy Spirit, Paul censures the undue importance that some people of the Corinthian church attach to it. Some believe the glossolalia in Corinth is uttered in speech that cannot be understood until someone present receives the corresponding spiritual gift of interpretation. Such speaking in tongues is similar to the prophetic utterances of people possessed by the Spirit of God in the Old Testament (Numbers 11:25–29; 1 Samuel 10:5–6).

Most believe that in Acts 2, the disciples speak in tongues that are completely different from their native languages, as prompted by the Holy Spirit. The words they speak are immediately recognized by immigrants and visitors from many parts of the world. The following verse (v. 5) shows that the purpose of the Spirit-inspired glossolalia was to symbolize the universality of the Gospel (1:8). It shows that people from all nations will be brought into a unity of understanding through the preaching of the Gospel in the power of the Holy Spirit.

**5 And there were dwelling at Jerusalem Jews, devout men, out of every nation under heaven.**

The verb translated as "were dwelling" (Gk. *katoikeo*, **kat-oy-KEH-oh**) means to dwell or settle. These were not tourists for temporary dwellers who had come for Pentecost from "every nation under heaven"

to stay in Jerusalem near the temple within the city walls as permanent residents. This was due to the long journey it would take for pilgrims to celebrate Jewish festivals. In the absence of plane flights, trains, and motor travel the pilgrims would more than likely stay in Jerusalem for all the festivals. The expression "every nation under heaven" also stresses the international nature of the crowd. The crowd is composed of permanent residents of Jerusalem and visitors who have come to celebrate the feast.

**6 Now when this was noised abroad, the multitude came together, and were confounded, because that every man heard them speak in his own language.**

They are "confounded" (Gk. *sugcheo*, **soon-KHEH-oh**) which means to disturb the mind. Their minds cannot fathom the loud praises to God uttered by the disciples in the indigenous languages and dialects of their native lands. The word "language" (Gk. *dialektos*, **dee-AH-lek-tohs**) means the language of a particular nation or region. It can refer to a whole language or even dialects within a language. The diversity of language is stressed here and in the following verses (vv. 7–12). The desire of God is that every tribe and nation will be reached with the Gospel (cf. 1 Timothy 2:4–7; Revelation 5:9).

**7 And they were all amazed and marvelled, saying one to another, Behold, are not all these which speak Galilaeans?**

They are "amazed" (Gk. *existemi*, **ex-EES-tay-mee**), which literally means to be beside oneself or out of place, denoting an overwhelming surprise. They "marvelled" (Gk. *thaumazo*, **thow-MAHD-zo**), denoting a continuing wonder and speculation as they hear loud praises to God uttered in languages and dialects other than the speakers' native

Galilaean. The Galilaeans used a peculiar dialect that distinguished them from other Judeans (cf. Matthew 26:73; Mark 14:70).

**12 And they were all amazed, and were in doubt, saying one to another, What meaneth this?**

Again we see that the visitors present on the Day of Pentecost are amazed. This verse also adds that they are in doubt (Gk. *diaporeo*, **dee-ah-poh-REH-oh**). This word means to be totally at a loss. They are at a loss for an explanation of the events they are experiencing. As a result, they ask themselves, "What meaneth this?" The Greek verb *thelo* (**THEH-lo**) can specifically mean to intend or to purpose. In essence, the travelers are asking, "What is the purpose of our being able to hear and see this phenomenon?"

**1 Corinthians 14:13–19**
**13 Wherefore let him that speaketh in an unknown tongue pray that he may interpret.**

The "wherefore" (Gk. *dioper*, **dee-OH-pare**) connects this sentence with Paul's preceding thoughts. Since those who earnestly desire spiritual gifts must seek to edify the church, then the one speaking in an unknown tongue must pray for God to give him or her the interpretation of what he or she is saying. The word for tongue here is *glossa*, the generic word for tongue or language. This is translated as "unknown" tongue because the one speaking it does not need to study a known foreign language to understand what is being said. Instead, the one speaking in a tongue is encouraged to pray or ask for divine help to interpret what he or she is saying.

**14 For if I pray in an unknown tongue, my spirit prayeth, but my understanding is unfruitful. 15 What is it then? I will pray with the spirit, and I will pray with the un-** derstanding also: I will sing with the spirit, and I will sing with the understanding also.**

Next Paul describes the dynamics of unknown tongues. When worshipers speak in unknown tongues, their spirit or inner self is praying. At the same time, they have not understood anything that they have said. The word "unfruitful" is *akarpos* (Gk. **AH-kar-pohs**) and means to be barren or not yielding what it ought to yield. Paul is saying that speaking in tongues is unproductive as far as the mind's understanding is concerned.

Paul then states his own approach to unknown tongues. He will pray "with the spirit," another way of saying praying in unknown tongues. This will be accompanied by praying with understanding as well. He also states that he will sing in unknown tongues, but with understanding.

**16 Else when thou shalt bless with the spirit, how shall he that occupieth the room of the unlearned say Amen at thy giving of thanks, seeing he understandeth not what thou sayest? 17 For thou verily givest thanks well, but the other is not edified.**

One of the results of speaking in unknown tongues is obvious. The one who is a novice or unlearned in the Christian faith (*idiotes*) will not be able to understand what is being said. Paul uses the word *eulogeo* (Gk. **ew-loh-GEH-oh**), which means to speak well of someone or something. It is commonly translated as bless. Here he is saying that the person speaking in tongues is doing a good thing by speaking well of God, but at the same time, it is not good for the assembly or worship gathering when no one understands.

**18 I thank my God, I speak with tongues more than ye all: 19 Yet in the church I had rather speak five words with my understanding, that by my voice I might

**teach others also, than ten thousand words in an unknown tongue.**

Here we see that Paul participates in speaking in unknown tongues. In order to drive the point home to the Corinthian church, he boasts that he speaks in tongues more than all of them. Although this is the case, he would rather speak a small amount with understanding so that he can teach others, than ten thousand words in an unknown tongue which neither he nor his hearers could understand. The word for ten thousand (Gk. *murios*, **MOO-ree-ohs**) was the largest number the Greek language of the time had. Paul uses this hyperbole to show just how much he desires communication in the church to be intelligible.

Sources:
Hays, Richard B. *First Corinthians: Interpretation, A Bible Commentary for Teaching and Preaching.* Louisville, KY: John Knox, 1997.
Henry, Matthew. *Matthew Henry's Commentary on the Whole Bible: Complete and Unabridged in One Volume.* Peabody, MA: Hendrickson, 1994.
Prime, Derek. *Opening Up 1 Corinthians.* Opening Up Commentary. Leominster, UK: Day One Publications, 2005.
Utley, Robert James. *Paul's Letters to a Troubled Church: I and II Corinthians.* Study Guide Commentary Series, vol. 6. Marshall, TX: Bible Lessons International, 2002.

## Say It Correctly

Galileans. ga-lih-**LEE**-ins.
Occupieth. ok-yu-**PIE**-ith.

## Daily Bible Readings

**MONDAY**
Made You Hear God's Voice
(Deuteronomy 4:32–40)

**TUESDAY**
A Small Member, Great Boasting
(James 3:1–5)

**WEDNESDAY**
All Languages, One Loud Voice
(Revelation 7:9–12)

**THURSDAY**
We Hear in Our Own Languages
(Acts 2:8–13)

**FRIDAY**
They Shall Prophesy
(Acts 2:14–21)

**SATURDAY**
Excel in Your Gifts
(1 Corinthians 14:6–12)

**SUNDAY**
Building Up Others
(Acts 2:1–7, 12; 1 Corinthians 14:13–19)

# Teaching Tips

May 31
Bible Study Guide 14

## Words You Should Know

**A. Charity** (1 Corinthians 13:1–4) *agape* (Gk.)—Love, fellowship, affection, benevolence, or specifically divine kindness.

**B. Hope** (v. 13) *elpis* (Gk.)—Expectation, confidence, or what is longed for.

## Teacher Preparation

**Unifying Principle—Love Never Ends**. Love is the primary requirement for societies attempting to have a positive influence on the world around them. What is it about love that is so indispensable? In 1 Corinthians 13, Paul says that love is needed to fully achieve the benefit of all spiritual gifts.

**A.** Read the Bible Background and Devotional Readings.

**B.** Complete Lesson 14 in the *Precepts For Living Personal Study Guide®*.

**C.** Reread the Focal Verses in a modern translation.

## O—Open the Lesson

**A.** Open with prayer.

**B.** Ask for a volunteer to read the Aim for Change section.

**C.** Ask for another volunteer to read the In Focus story.

**D.** Ask students to share a time when someone ministered to them in a loving manner.

## P—Present the Scriptures

**A.** Ask for volunteers to read the Focal Verses and The People, Places, and Times. Discuss.

**B.** Read and discuss the Background section.

**C.** Encourage students to thank God for His love and the opportunity to show love using spiritual gifts.

## E—Explore the Meaning

**A.** Review and discuss the Search the Scriptures and Discuss the Meaning questions and the Lesson in Our Society section.

**B.** Ask students to share the most significant point they learned and how to use that point this week.

## N—Next Steps for Application

**A.** Complete the Follow the Spirit and Remember Your Thoughts sections.

**B.** Remind students to read the Daily Bible Readings in preparation for next week's lesson.

**C.** Close in prayer, thanking God for His love toward us.

## Worship Guide

For the Superintendent or Teacher
Theme: The Greatest Gift is Love
Song: "They Will Know We Are Christians By Our Love"
Devotional Reading: Ephesians 3:14–21

434

# The Greatest Gift is Love

**Bible Background • 1 CORINTHIANS 13**
**Printed Text • 1 CORINTHIANS 13**
**Devotional Reading • EPHESIANS 3:14–21**

## Aim for Change

By the end of this lesson, we will EXPLORE the meaning of love as seen in 1 Corinthians 13; FEEL appreciation for one another in love; and SEEK a variety of ways to express love.

## In Focus

Christie had lived next door to an old woman for three months. Every time Christie said "Hello," or tried to start a conversation with her, the woman just scowled and looked away. After three months, Christie didn't even know this woman's name. One Saturday, Alison was visiting her friend Christie. As usual, the woman was sitting on her balcony. "Why do you even bother?" Alison asked. "She never even speaks to you." Christie smiled. "I keep hoping she will." That afternoon, Christie and Alison made peanut butter cookies. "Let's take a couple of cookies next door." Christie suggested. They packed the cookies in a small plastic container and walked over to the woman's door. They rang the bell and waited. After a while, the woman cracked the door and peeked out. "What is it?" she asked. "My name is Christie. I live next door," she said. "My friend and I made cookies, and we wanted to offer you some." The old woman opened the door a little farther and took the cookies. "Enjoy!" Christie said as she and Alison walked away. "Wait," the old woman called after them. "You can come inside."

*Love is patient and love is kind. Love brings out the best in others and always seeks to do good.*

## Keep in Mind

"And now abideth faith, hope, charity, these three; but the greatest of these is charity" (1 Corinthians 13:13).

"And now abideth faith, hope, charity, these three; but the greatest of these is charity" (1 Corinthians 13:13).

# Focal Verses

**KJV** **1 Corinthians 13:1** Though I speak with the tongues of men and of angels, and have not charity, I am become as sounding brass, or a tinkling cymbal.

**2** And though I have the gift of prophecy, and understand all mysteries, and all knowledge; and though I have all faith, so that I could remove mountains, and have not charity, I am nothing.

**3** And though I bestow all my goods to feed the poor, and though I give my body to be burned, and have not charity, it profiteth me nothing.

**4** Charity suffereth long, and is kind; charity envieth not; charity vaunteth not itself, is not puffed up,

**5** Doth not behave itself unseemly, seeketh not her own, is not easily provoked, thinketh no evil;

**6** Rejoiceth not in iniquity, but rejoiceth in the truth;

**7** Beareth all things, believeth all things, hopeth all things, endureth all things.

**8** Charity never faileth: but whether there be prophecies, they shall fail; whether there be tongues, they shall cease; whether there be knowledge, it shall vanish away.

**9** For we know in part, and we prophesy in part.

**10** But when that which is perfect is come, then that which is in part shall be done away.

**11** When I was a child, I spake as a child, I understood as a child, I thought as a child: but when I became a man, I put away childish things.

**12** For now we see through a glass, darkly; but then face to face: now I know in part; but then shall I know even as also I am known.

**13** And now abideth faith, hope, charity, these three; but the greatest of these is charity.

**NLT** **1 Corinthians 13:1** If I could speak all the languages of earth and of angels, but didn't love others, I would only be a noisy gong or a clanging cymbal.

**2** If I had the gift of prophecy, and if I understood all of God's secret plans and possessed all knowledge, and if I had such faith that I could move mountains, but didn't love others, I would be nothing.

**3** If I gave everything I have to the poor and even sacrificed my body, I could boast about it; but if I didn't love others, I would have gained nothing.

**4** Love is patient and kind. Love is not jealous or boastful or proud

**5** or rude. It does not demand its own way. It is not irritable, and it keeps no record of being wronged.

**6** It does not rejoice about injustice but rejoices whenever the truth wins out.

**7** Love never gives up, never loses faith, is always hopeful, and endures through every circumstance.

**8** Prophecy and speaking in unknown languages and special knowledge will become useless. But love will last forever!

**9** Now our knowledge is partial and incomplete, and even the gift of prophecy reveals only part of the whole picture!

**10** But when the time of perfection comes, these partial things will become useless.

**11** When I was a child, I spoke and thought and reasoned as a child. But when I grew up, I put away childish things.

**12** Now we see things imperfectly, like puzzling reflections in a mirror, but then we will see everything with perfect clarity. All that I know now is partial and incomplete, but then I will know everything completely, just as God now knows me completely.

**13** Three things will last forever—faith, hope, and love—and the greatest of these is love.

---

## The People, Places, and Times

**Corinth.** The city of Corinth was a major trade city located on an isthmus that connects mainland Greece with the Peloponnesian peninsula. Its location made Corinth a bustling trade and cultural center. As a result, there was a mixture of religious beliefs in Corinth. During the time in which Paul wrote, Corinth was a Roman colony. The ancient city of Corinth, known for its artistry, wealth, and rampant sexual immorality, was destroyed in 146 B.C. It was reestablished by Rome in 44 B.C. Under Roman rule, Corinth continued to be known for its wanton sexuality.

## Background

Paul wrote 1 Corinthians while he was living and ministering in the city of Ephesus. The letter was written between A.D. 53 and 55. During his time in Ephesus, Paul wrote a letter to the church in Corinth that is not present in the Bible (cf. 1 Corinthians 5:9). In that letter Paul addressed sexual immorality, which continued to be a problem.

In 1 Corinthians, the first letter to the Corinthians that is included in the Christian canon, Paul wrote to further address sexual immorality and divisions in the church. He had also received a letter from the church at Corinth (7:1) expressing confusion about marriage, divorce, corporate worship, bodily resurrection, and living in a pagan society. Paul wrote to encourage the Corinthians and to emphasize the importance of holiness. He also wrote to correct their misunderstanding and abuse of spiritual gifts, which he discussed in chapter 12.

This chapter is often misinterpreted, which leads to improper application as a mere ode to the virtues of love. Paul was using 1 Corinthians 13 to address specific issues in the Corinthian church: selfishness, division, abuse of gifts, and envying of others' gifts.

The Greek term for love used in this chapter is *agape* (**ah-GAH-pay**). This word is closely associated with the Hebrew word *khesed* (**KHESS-ed**) which refers to God's covenant love for His people. Because of this association, *agape* became a key word for describing God's character and took on the meaning of a divine love that is deeply loyal. Believers should emulate this love, and Paul highlighted its importance in this letter to the Corinthians.

## At-A-Glance

1. Love is Superior to Other Spiritual Gifts (1 Corinthians 13:1–3)
2. Characteristics of Love (vv. 4–7)
3. Love Endures (vv. 7–13)

## In Depth

**1. Love is Superior to Other Spiritual Gifts (1 Corinthians 13:1–3)**

Paul begins by demonstrating the superiority of love. The Corinthians held eloquence in especially high esteem and were somewhat preoccupied with the gift of tongues. However, even the most sophisticated gift of tongues, speaking the languages of men and angels, is just noise if not exercised in love.

The use and exercise of the other spiritual gifts is pointless without love. Prophecy, though a desirable gift (14:1), is useless without love. Knowledge of the deepest mysteries of God has no value apart from love. Faith, even when great enough to move mountains, is nothing apart from love. Likewise, boundless generosity is not profitable without love. Willingness to suffer, even to the point of martyrdom, is worthless in the absence of love.

Love is essential. Spiritual gifts are nothing without love; they can even be destructive when not practiced in love. Love is what enriches the gifts and gives them value. Therefore, spiritual gifts must be founded and exercised only in genuine love for God and His people.

## 2. Characteristics of Love (vv. 4–7)

In the King James Version, *agape* is translated "charity." When we think of charity, we usually think of giving to others, an active expression of Christian love. This was not the limit of the meaning of "charity" in King James' time, however. Back then, "charity" was understood as it related to the similar word "cherish." To show charity to someone was to show that you cherished them. This includes, but also goes far beyond, giving alms, as Paul further explains.

Love is patient and kind. It is patient with people and treats others gently, even when mistreated. Further, love waits to see the effect of that kindness when wronged. It is courteous and seeks for opportunities to do good or be of service. Love is steadfast and protective. It does not seek retaliation when wronged. Rather than seeking and broadcasting others' faults, love sees the best in people.

Further, love is not jealous or proud. It is not angered by the good fortune of others.

Love does not desire to gain possessions or control others. It is not boastful, proud, or rude. Instead, love honors and cherishes others. It is not irritable, selfish, resentful, or malicious. Love is incompatible with ill will. It does not seek its own honor, profit, or pleasure. Instead, love focuses on the well-being of others. It is not quarrelsome or vindictive. Instead, love "thinketh no evil," meaning that it keeps no account of wrongs.

In verse 7, Paul writes that love bears, believes, hopes, and endures all things. His use of language implies that love does these things at all times. Love "beareth all things." It covers and protects. Love "believeth all things." It has faith in others and is always willing to give the benefit of the doubt. Love "hopeth all things." It does not despair, but is always hopeful for the growth and development of other believers. Love "endureth all things." This communicates a strong sense of enduring temptation or testing. Love does not retaliate or reject, but is patient.

Paul highlights the character of love as it should be expressed by Christians. His descriptions of love are active, indicating that love is something one does, not merely an emotion. As Christians who have received the love of God, we are to love others. The indwelling Holy Spirit empowers us to demonstrate this kind of love.

## 3. Love Endures (vv. 7–13)

Love surpasses all the other spiritual gifts because they will pass away, but it endures forever. Prophecy, tongues, and knowledge are limited (v. 9). Further, a time will come when those gifts will not be necessary. They are given by the Spirit for the building and maturation of the church. We will not need such things in heaven, but will experience love there.

Corinth was well known for its bronze artistry and bronze mirrors. Paul's illustration in verse 12 would have been particularly meaningful for the Corinthians. We exercise our gifts imperfectly. Our knowledge is imperfect, like seeing indirectly, as if through a bronze mirror. However, imperfection will give way to perfection, enabling us to see perfectly.

In the perfection of heaven, we will experience love eternally. Because love is eternal and is superior to the other spiritual gifts, it is childish to focus on spiritual gifts in the absence of love.

Not only is faith superior to the spiritual gifts, but also faith and hope. Just as in heaven we will no longer need prophecy or tongues, we will also no longer need faith (because we will see God) or hope (because all hopes will be fulfilled; cf. Romans 8:24). Since love outlasts all of these good things, it is the greatest.

## Search the Scriptures

1. What are some of the characteristics of love (1 Corinthians 13:4–7)?

2. Why is love superior to the other spiritual gifts (v. 8)?

## Discuss the Meaning

1. As we continually experience the love of God, how can we show His love to others? How can we demonstrate more love in our relationships? How can we express love in difficult situations?

2. Paul writes to the Corinthians in response to their abuse and misunderstanding of spiritual gifts. What are some of the practical ways we can work to ensure that all members of the body of Christ, regardless of their spiritual gifts, are loved and valued?

## Lesson in Our Society

The Holy Spirit is the source of all the spiritual gifts and He decides which gifts each person will have (1 Corinthians 12:11). The spiritual gifts are given to strengthen other believers (v. 7), not to gain personal status and position.

The gifts themselves should not be our primary focus. Love is an essential element in the exercise of spiritual gifts. It is good to desire spiritual gifts (14:1). However, love is superior to every gift. Prophecy, knowledge, and the demonstration of great faith must all reflect a genuine love and affection for people.

Websites and bookstores abound with assessments to help people discover their spiritual gifts. While the understanding and use of spiritual gifts is important, we must always exercise them in love.

## Make It Happen

Spiritual gifts cannot be effective if not used in love. Grow in your relationship with Christ. Show His love to those around you. Demonstrate the love of God as you use your spiritual gifts to help others grow and mature.

## Follow the Spirit

What God wants me to do:

_____

_____

_____

_____

## Remember Your Thoughts

Special insights I have learned:

_____

_____

_____

_____

## More Light on the Text

### 1 Corinthians 13

"Charity" (Gk. *agape*, **ah-GAH-pay**) is the lifeblood of the body of Christ. It builds up the body of Christ by providing each member the life forces that animate the individual spiritual gifts as instruments of God rather than the inanimate tools of people. Having spiritual gifts without love is like a fish out of water, a bee without honey, or an automobile without wheels.

**1 Though I speak with the tongues of men and of angels, and have not charity, I am become as sounding brass, or a tinkling cymbal.**

The word "charity" here means love, heavenly love, affection, goodwill, or benevolence. Agape love means the decentering of the ego. The person is no longer the center of his or her universe or ultimate concern; "the other" is now in the center. Love is a radical reordering of priorities and ultimate values. Without love, everything we do is for our own self-glorification and benefit. With love, what we do is for God and others. Love is not a feeling; it is what we do for others without regard for self. It is partaking in the very nature of God, because He is love (1 John 4:8).

Spirit-inspired speech spoken in ecstasy, different languages, brilliant human rhetoric, or superhuman entreaties mean nothing if they are not of God. Any intention whose source is not the God of love is in vain. If the Spirit of God animates the body, love holds it together. Tongues without love are only noise.

**2 And though I have the gift of prophecy, and understand all mysteries, and all knowledge; and though I have all faith, so that I could remove mountains, and have not charity, I am nothing.**

The gift of prophecy or preaching is mere entertainment or scolding and has no effect if the speaker is not motivated by love. The gift of intellectual accomplishment without love leads to contempt and snobbery. The gift of great faith that achieves or sacrifices much can lead to false pride. Without love, none of these gifts edifies the body of Christ or pleases God.

**3 And though I bestow all my goods to feed the poor, and though I give my body to be burned, and have not charity, it profiteth me nothing.**

Benevolence and even self-sacrifice can be great for those on the receiving end or in the eyes of the world. In terms of our own spiritual maturity it means nothing. To give out of obligation, self-promotion, or even contempt can profit those who are poor and needy but it does not profit the giver. Likewise, to seek persecution or make sacrifice for selfish intentions may very well hurt one's cause more than it helps.

Paul has made it clear that agape love is more important than spiritual gifts. In this passage, he explains exactly what agape is. Love is that which connects us to God and one another. Like the blood that circulates through the body's veins carrying oxygen and nutrients from cell to cell, so love also brings us into a life-giving relationship to God and one another.

**4 Charity suffereth long, and is kind; charity envieth not; charity vaunteth not itself, is not puffed up,**

Love "suffereth long" (Gk. *makrothumeo*, **mah-kro-thoo-MEH-oh**), or endures patiently, the errors, weaknesses, and even meanness of people. Love makes us slow to anger or repay hurt for hurt. It will suffer many things for the sake of the relationship. Love is kind (Gk. *chresteuomai*, **khray-STEH-oo-oh-meye**); it shows kindness whenever possible. Love "envieth not" (Gk. *zeloo*, **zay-LOH-oh**); it does not earnestly covet another's good fortune. Love does not get angry at another's success. Love does "vaunteth not" (Gk. *perpereuomai*, **pair-pair-EW-oh-my**), or brag, about itself. It is not boastful or stuck up. Love does not have a swollen head and is not "puffed up" (Gk. *phusioo*, **foo-see-OH-oh**), snobbish, or arrogant. Loving people esteem others higher than themselves.

**5 Doth not behave itself unseemly, seeketh not her own, is not easily provoked, thinketh no evil;**

Love is never rude; it is full of grace and charm. It does not go around hurting others' feelings. It always uses tact and politeness whenever possible. Love never demands its rights, but seeks its responsibilities toward others. It is not self-centered or self-assertive. Love does not fly off the handle. It does not lose its temper. It is not easily exasperated at people. Love does not keep the books on the wrong done to it. Love does not keep score in order to repay wrong for wrong. It forgives the evil that people do to it. It does not carry a grudge.

**6 Rejoiceth not in iniquity, but rejoiceth in the truth;**

Love does not like to hear about the moral failures of others. It does not get pleasure out of the misfortune of others. There is a sick joy from witnessing or hearing gossip about the misdeeds of others. We often judge our own righteousness and well-being as measured by the failings of others. However, love is happy to hear the truth (or what is right), no matter how painful. Love rejoices when what is true, correct, and righteous wins the day regardless of how that may impact it directly.

**7 Beareth all things, believeth all things, hopeth all things, endureth all things.**

If God is love and He created all things good, then love also is the progenitor of all things good. Love is our participation in God's nature. Thus, love is the only foundation for Christian community and relationships. Love, like God, is eternal. It "beareth" (Gk. *stego*, **STEH-goh**) the errors and faults of others. Love does not expose one's weakness because it does not rejoice in the misfortune of others. Yet it does not excuse sin or wrongdoing, because it equally rejoices in truth. Instead, as Christ bore our sin on the Cross, we take on the weakness and faults of others as though they were our own.

Love believes the best, trusts in the object of its love, has confidence in him or her, and gives credit to the object of love that may not be self-evident except through the eyes of love. Love can bear all things because it believes all things with the special insight that only a loving relationship can bring. Love "hopeth" (Gk. *elpizo*, **el-PEED-zo**) with joy, full of confidence in eager expectation the salvation of the Lord to come. It bears all things because it believes with only the insight of God the Maker, thus it can wait for the true nature of people to reveal itself. Love trusts in the eventual reconciliation with God. It "endureth" (Gk. *hupomeno*, **hoo-po-MEN-oh**) and continues to be present; it does not perish or depart in spite of errors, faults, or wrongs done.

**8 Charity never faileth: but whether there be prophecies, they shall fail; whether there be tongues, they shall cease; whether there be knowledge, it shall vanish away.**

Love is eternal; it never comes to an end. It is absolutely permanent. Whereas all the gifts in which the Corinthians pride themselves are transitory at best, love is transcendent. Love is—exists only in and for—relationship, yet is more than the sum of its parts; like life itself, it is always renewed, even in the age to come.

The gifts, on the other hand, have no such guarantee. They were given by the Spirit as instruments to be used in this age. Paul anticipates that these gifts will no longer be needed when the next age occurs, marked by the return of Christ and fulfillment of the reign of God. They will pass away with the old age. Love, on the other hand, is essential, not instrumental; it will never pass away. In contrast, when all prophecy has been fulfilled, tongues will no longer be necessary as a language; signs, missions, and knowledge will vanish because there will be no more mysteries.

**9 For we know in part, and we prophesy in part.**

Love, like God, is complete. On the other hand, we are imperfect creatures who can only comprehend reality—both material and spiritual—in an incomplete manner. Therefore, we can only preach or prophesy in an imperfect and partial way. For Paul, the kingdom of God is near, but not yet. It is not fully revealed in this age, so our knowledge and prophecy of it can only be partial.

**10 But when that which is perfect is come, then that which is in part shall be done away.**

The "perfect" (Gk. *teleios*, **TEH-lay-ose**) maturity or completeness will come with the end of this present, imperfect age and the beginning of the new, perfect age—namely the "eschaton" (Gk. *eschatos*, **ES-khah-tose**, last, uttermost). Paul describes the times the Corinthians lived in as transitory at best. Thus they should not make gods or idols out of the gifts they esteem so highly, because their gifts are both imperfect and temporary.

**11 When I was a child, I spake as a child, I understood as a child, I thought as a child: but when I became a man, I put away childish things.**

Paul uses the metaphor of the maturing spiritual human being who grows from childhood to adulthood. The spiritual gifts become mere toys or childish things in people who do not love. Paul, who had called the Corinthians "babes in Christ," chides them once again to grow up and put away their toys, in this case, using their gifts for the wrong reasons (3:1).

**12 For now we see through a glass, darkly; but then face to face: now I know in part; but then shall I know even as also I am known.**

The word translated as glass (Gk. *esoptron*, **eh-SOHP-trone**) is another word for mirror. Mirrors were a primary industry in the city of Corinth. Mirrors made in Corinth were finely polished silver and bronze. The image was often concave and distorted, much like the amusement park house of mirrors. Thus we see only dimly through the distorted reflections of our own limited apprehensions. However, when Jesus returns and God makes His dwelling place among His people, we will see face to face (cf. Revelation 21:22–23).

When we look through a mirror, we see only a reflection of ourselves and have only a knowledge that is filtered through our senses. However, when we come face-to-face with another, we see clearly, but are also seen. We not only come to know, but also are known by another.

**13 And now abideth faith, hope, charity, these three; but the greatest of these is charity.**

After everything that has been said, we come to the conclusion of the matter. Spirit gifts are transient, given to a particular community, for a particular purpose, and for the particular time. It is childish to esteem them too highly. However, by faith we are saved according to the grace of God. In hope, we wait upon the return of Jesus and the coming of the reign of God. All this is due to God's love for us. These are what remain when one matures in Christ.

However, when Jesus returns, the reign of God is fulfilled. We have no need of hope. When we stand face-to-face with God and clearly see all that there is to see, then we will have no need of faith. Yet we will continue to love and be loved by God. Love never ends; it is eternal.

Love has revealed itself completely in the revelation of Jesus Christ in His life, death, and resurrection. Thus we can love the Holy One. Jesus says, "This is my commandment, That ye love one another, as I have loved you. Greater love hath no man than this, that a man lay down his life for his friends" (John 15:12–13). Love is the greatest.

Sources:
*English Standard Version Study Bible.* Wheaton, IL: Crossway, 2007.
Henry, Matthew. *Matthew Henry's Commentary on the Whole Bible: Complete and Unabridged in One Volume.* Peabody, MA: Hendrickson, 1994.
Prime, Derek. *Opening Up 1 Corinthians.* Opening Up Commentary. Leominster, UK: Day One Publications, 2005.
Utley, Robert James. *Paul's Letters to a Troubled Church: I and II Corinthians.* Study Guide Commentary Series, vol. 6. Marshall, TX: Bible Lessons International, 2002.
Walvoord, John F., and Roy B. Zuck. *The Bible Knowledge Commentary: An Exposition of the Scriptures.* Dallas Theological Seminary. Wheaton, IL: Victor Books, 1985.
Wiersbe, Warren W. *The Bible Exposition Commentary.* Wheaton, IL: Victor Books, 1996.

## Say It Correctly

Vaunteth. **VON**-teth.
Bestow. bi-**STOW**.

## Daily Bible Readings

**MONDAY**
Love and the Knowledge of God
(Hosea 6:1–6)

**TUESDAY**
Abounding in Steadfast Love
(Jonah 3:10–4:11)

**WEDNESDAY**
Guided by the Spirit
(Galatians 5:19–26)

**THURSDAY**
Increasing Love for One Another
(2 Thessalonians 1:1–5)

**FRIDAY**
Love and Steadfastness
(2 Thessalonians 3:1–5)

**SATURDAY**
Filled with the Fullness of God
(Ephesians 3:14–21)

**SUNDAY**
Love Never Ends
(1 Corinthians 13)

# God's Prophets Demand Justice

This quarter has three units discussing justice and injustice. Lessons covering seven different prophets investigate the perpetrators of injustice, the nature of injustice, and the victims of injustice. It steadily moves toward repentance, redemption, and restoration.

## UNIT I • AMOS RAILS AGAINST INJUSTICE

**Lesson 1: June 7, 2015**
**Judgment on Israel and Judah**
**Amos 2:4–8**
Even though they know right from wrong, some people treat others unjustly. What can unjust people expect will be the result of their misdeeds? God will not overlook injustice but will punish the unjust.

**Lesson 2: June 14, 2015**
**God is Not Fooled**
**Amos 5:14–15, 18–27**
Some people cover their evil ways with outward acts of goodness. Who will uncover their deceit and demand justice? The people learned through Amos that God will not be fooled by insincere offerings and will severely punish all sinners.

**Lesson 3: June 21, 2015**
**Rebuked for Selfishness**
**Amos 6:4–8, 11–14**
Some people care only about accumulating lavish possessions for themselves and care nothing for those who possess little. What happens to greedy and selfish people? God will dispossess the greedy and selfish and thus demonstrate His justice.

**Lesson 4: June 28, 2015**
**God Will Never Forget**
**Amos 8:1–6, 9–10**
Some people are so deep into deceit and cheating others that they ignore warnings and must live with the consequences of their wicked ways. What happens to those who do not heed a warning? Amos says that God will no longer overlook their misdeeds and will destroy them for all time.

## UNIT II • MICAH CALLS FOR JUSTICE AMONG UNJUST PEOPLE

**Lesson 5: July 5, 2015**
**No Rest for the Wicked**
**Micah 2:4–11**
People do not want to be confronted with their social and moral abuse of others. What is the result of their failure to acknowledge their evil ways? Micah prophesied that God would give no rest to those who practice evil against His faithful ones.

**Lesson 6: July 12, 2015**
**No Tolerance for Corrupt Leaders and Prophets**
**Micah 3:5–12**

Some leaders are corrupt, lie to the people they are charged to protect, and then find associates who will support their evil ways. What can be done to end this dishonesty? God will judge and punish corrupt leaders and prophets.

**Lesson 7: July 19, 2015**
**Justice, Love, and Humility**
**Micah 6:3–8**

People sometimes forget what a benefactor has done for them or they make insincere efforts to show gratitude. How will benefactors react to such forgetfulness or ingratitude? God instructs the unjust to be just, love kindness, and walk humbly with Him.

**Lesson 8: July 26, 2015**
**God Shows Clemency**
**Micah 7:14–20**

Sometimes evil and injustice are not met with corrective justice but trumped by mercy. Who will meet evil and injustice with mercy rather than with punishment? God will show compassion and faithfulness to His people, even to the unjust.

**UNIT III • ADVOCATES OF JUSTICE FOR ALL**

**Lesson 9: August 2, 2015**
**Our Redeemer Comes**
**Isaiah 59:15b–21**

Sometimes everything around us seems violent, cruel, and immoral. Who will bring justice and righteousness to a troubled world? Isaiah promises a time when God will come as a Redeemer with a foundation of righteousness and justice and place His spirit on those who repent of their sins.

**Lesson 10: August 9, 2015**
**A Choice to Be Just**
**Jeremiah 7:1–15**

Many people show partiality, oppress the weak, and break the law as though they are unaware of the error of their ways. What are the consequences for people who will not change their ways? Through Jeremiah, God sent messages of hope to those who will amend their ways and messages of doom to those who will not.

**Lesson 11: August 16, 2015**
**A Call for Repentance**
**Ezekiel 18:1–13, 31–32**

People are aware of behavior that is harmful to the life of a community. What can be done to build and maintain the health of a community? Ezekiel advises confession and exhorts the people to do the right thing, and thereby build a just community.

**Lesson 12: August 23, 2015**
**God Demands Justice**
**Zechariah 7:8–14**

Some people show no kindness, mercy, or justice to others. Who will protect the weak from their oppressors? Zechariah says that God requires kindness and mercy for the widows, orphans, aliens, and the poor—a message He has long been sharing with His people.

**Lesson 13: August 30, 2015**
**Return to a Just God**
**Malachi 3:1–10**

Fairness and philanthropy are most apparent during times of great tragedy and loss. How do the faithful demonstrate the same benevolent and just spirit all the time? Malachi informs the faithful that God requires justice and faithfulness and will bestow bountiful blessings in proportion to what they are willing to give.

# Fighting for Justice in an Unjust World

*Unjust* is a very fitting adjective to describe the world that we live in. Natural disasters take lives and damage property indiscriminately. Many suffer from abuse and oppression through no fault of their own. Wars are fought and innocent people die because of the greed and callousness of misguided leaders. From the day we are born, we recognize that the world doesn't just yield to our way and does not seem fair. Moreover, we recognize that the world is a dangerous place, hostile to our well-being. It seems as though evil has the last say and the scales are tipped in its favor.

So we search for justice. Many take up this quest and fight against those who would oppress and take advantage of others. Others seek to relieve the suffering caused by disease and natural disasters. Deep down within us, we know that the world is not right and the most noble of us seek to help heal it. This can be done through confronting those in authority who abuse their power or establishing places of refuge for those whose lives have been ravaged. Something inside pulls us to not wallow in the mess but build a better world and be better people.

This oftentimes becomes a futile effort. We say to ourselves, "What can one person do to solve this problem?" Whether concerned about clean water or neighborhood gangs, we feel overwhelmed by the task at hand. This drives us to either give up and let the situation go on as it is, or become more determined and double our efforts. The first option leaves us in the same oppressive and unjust conditions. It not only keeps the condition the same, but makes it worse because now we are a part of the problem, not the solution. Why do neighborhood gangs continue to dominate a neighborhood? Because good people don't speak up. This silence continues to multiply and increases the gang's power in the community. The second option soon makes us tired and self-righteous. We wonder why others are not joining the cause and helping us out. We become exhausted or just as oppressive and unjust as the injustice we are fighting against. There has got to be a better way.

A better way can be found in the pages of the Bible. God has the market cornered on justice. He is just and righteous inside and out. He saw the needs of this world way before you and I were ever thought of in our parents' minds. God knew that this world would need justice. His solution to this dilemma was not a homeless shelter or a rally in the streets. It wasn't a boycott or a voter's drive. God's solution to the injustice of this world is Jesus Christ. Jesus Christ came to bring justice to a world that was unjust. Throughout His ministry, Jesus healed the sick and raised the dead. He fed the poor and taught people how to live righteously and not oppress others. Jesus spoke out against the unjust systems in first-century Palestine. It was His stance against injustice that finally caused Him to be executed by the Romans on a cross outside Jerusalem. The Bible speaks of Jesus' pursuit of justice this way:

He shall not strive, nor cry; neither shall any man hear his voice in the streets. A bruised reed shall he not break, and smoking flax shall he not quench, till he send forth judgment unto victory. And in his name shall the Gentiles trust. (Matthew 12:19–21)

These verses say that Jesus will make justice victorious. Justice will be realized through His pursuit of it. How is that possible when Jesus died as an outcast criminal and an enemy of Rome? The answer can be found in some verses written by Paul in Romans. Here Paul addresses our unrighteousness and sin and how God made atonement for our sins through Jesus, saying:

For God presented Jesus as the sacrifice for sin. People are made right with God when they believe that Jesus sacrificed his life, shedding his blood. This sacrifice shows that God was being fair when he held back and did not punish those who sinned in times past, for he was looking ahead and including them in what he would do in this present time. God did this to demonstrate his righteousness, for he himself is fair and just, and he declares sinners to be right in his sight when they believe in Jesus. (Romans 3:25–26, NLT)

Paul says that it was through Jesus that God demonstrated His righteousness and justice toward the world. Through Christ's death on the Cross, all of us who are sinners are made right in His sight. That's true justice. Jesus could rest in not solving all the world's problems and dying on the Cross because His death is what brought genuine justice to the world. Poverty, crime, sickness and government corruption are all symptoms of a deeper problem. The sacrifice of Jesus on the Cross attacked the root of injustice: sin.

When sin was released into the world, everything was thrown off balance. We see a small glimpse of this as the Lord curses the ground, which is symbolic of the whole created order (Genesis 3:17–19). We also see that creation is groaning, waiting for our redemption in order to be freed from decay and corruption (Romans 8:20–22). The man and woman's bond is also cursed as strife and conflict become their normal way of relating. This then becomes the normal relationship for coming generations. This is why we have natural disasters, sickness, and disease. This is why there is corruption and oppression and an abuse of power. Sin is the root of all these problems. Jesus' death released us from sin so we can fight against injustice. We do not have to give up and throw in the towel, because we have His Spirit empowering us. We do not have to become exhausted and burned out, because we can rest in His promise of a new heaven and earth. We can fight for injustice, because Jesus has already destroyed the root of injustice on the Cross. He has given us His Spirit so we can fight injustice with His energy and wisdom. He has given us the promise of victory so we can rest in His work and not our own.

There are many problems to tackle out there. Injustice is pervasive throughout society and many are affected by it, whether they are the oppressors or the oppressed. As followers of Jesus, we must take hold of His promise and receive His Spirit for daily empowerment to fight for a just and fair world. Only then can we model and imitate our Savior, who caused justice to triumph on the Cross.

# Christian Education in Action

# Fostering Justice
# in Christian Education

by Melvin Banks Sr., Litt. D.

After teaching a Bible lesson that focused on God's desire that His people show justice to the poor, the Sunday School teacher led a brainstorming session on what the class members might do to show their concern for the poor and less fortunate. Someone remembered injustice that a racist group of people had inflicted on a community two hundred miles away. A class member suggested that their group might consider doing something for the families in that community.

With encouragement from their teacher, the class formed a committee, drove to the community, and interviewed families to determine their needs. They brought back to their Sunday School class a list of needs that included food, clothing, and shoes for children. The class raised funds and purchased clothes and supplies. Then the group drove the two hundred miles back to the community to deliver the items they had purchased.

This was just a tangible way one Sunday School class put into practice a lesson on justice they gleaned from the study of God's Word.

Not only did the class learn that a study of God's Word could have tangible outcomes, they also discovered that they could experience a great sense of fulfillment in doing it. It is why UMI lesson aims include a component that we not only KNOW a truth and FEEL deeply about it, but also DO something to put that truth into practice. The DOING leaves a long-lasting impact on the memory and the character development. It helps fulfill the biblical injunction, "Anyone who *does* what pleases God will live forever" (from 1 John 2:17, NLT, emphasis added).

The Gospel of Matthew records that after Jesus spent considerable time teaching and demonstrating ministry principles to His disciples, He sent them out to preach, heal, and cast out demons from people (Matthew 10). We can profitably follow Jesus' example.

Addressing injustice and fostering justice may take multiple forms. The goal of justice is to right wrongs and foster fairness. Sometimes in Scripture, the focus is on how we ourselves treat others fairly. At other times, it may mean we come to the rescue of those whom others have mistreated. It may involve writing letters or voting for people who will work for justice.

Someone has developed this list of guidelines that both young and older people may use as a sort of checklist for practicing fairness in one-on-one relationships:

- Treat people the way you want them to treat you
- Take turns
- Tell the truth
- Think about how your actions will affect others
- Listen to others with an open mind
- Do not blame others for your mistakes
- Do not take advantage of other people
- Do not play favorites

Let us take a closer look at justice...

### Justice—What is It?

Justice is an objective standard of righteousness and right behavior that has its origin in God. Our Lord both personified and exemplified His passion for justice as He "went about doing good" (from Acts 10:38). In His life, teachings, ministry, and atoning sacrifice, Christ reversed the wrongs that Satan and his demons and followers had inflicted upon people.

### Why is Justice Important for Us to Address?

God calls us to practice righteousness and fairness because He is righteous and fair. Jesus said, "But you are to be perfect, even as your Father in heaven is perfect" (Matthew 5:48, NLT). God Himself is our model. Jesus tells us to "do to others as you would like them to do to you" (Luke 6:31, NLT).

### How Can We Convey the Idea of Justice to Others?

As teachers, we transmit to others best what we firmly believe and practice ourselves. Of course, we know some people in the role of "teacher" may attempt to burden others with what they do not firmly believe or model, but Jesus calls them hypocrites (Matthew 23:1–4).

We best communicate justice and righteousness when it becomes a burning desire in us. Then that fire for justice in us will likely ignite a desire in those we touch.

Having said that, we can proceed to fashion a teaching plan that seeks to communicate justice to our students. Bear in mind that one can extend the outline below to be not only a plan for a class but also for a church-wide initiative.

*We begin by creating an instructional or teaching aim.*

For example: By the end of our teaching session, we will know that Christ expects His followers to practice fairness and justice; be deeply convinced that showing fairness is both a personal and corporate duty; and identify and implement a project where we can foster justice.

*We plan an attention-getting way to focus the class on the issue of justice.*

Pair up students and have them share an example of injustice. After three minutes, get their responses to build a list of situations they have identified.

*We make a promise to the class.*

With a list of unjust situations, the teacher can now make a promise to the class. For example: Today, we will explore what God has to say about justice and what we might possibly do to right some wrong or encourage righteous behavior.

*We present biblical facts about justice.*

We derive our objective standard of justice from God and His revelation of truth recorded in the Scriptures. Here are a few biblical texts that highlight God's concern for justice:

"Will not the Judge of all the earth do right?" (from Genesis 18:25, NIV).

"He rules the world in righteousness and judges the peoples with equity" (Psalm 9:8, NIV).

"All he does is just and good, and all his commandments are trustworthy. They are forever true, to be obeyed faithfully and with integrity" (Psalm 111:7–8, NLT).

"Look at my servant, whom I strengthen. He is my chosen one, who pleases me. I have put my Spirit upon him. He will bring justice to the nations. He will not shout or raise his voice in public. He will not crush the weakest reed or put out a flickering candle. He will bring justice to all who have been wronged. He will not falter or lose heart until justice prevails throughout the earth. Even distant lands beyond the sea will wait for his instruction" (Isaiah 42:1–4, NLT).

"He has shown you, O mortal, what is good. And what does the LORD require of you? To act justly and to love mercy and to walk humbly with your God" (Micah 6:8, NIV).

About each of these texts, the teacher or facilitator might ask these questions:
- What does this text say?
- What does this text mean by what it says?
- What does this text mean for us today?
- What might we do differently if we were to take this text seriously?

*We can apply the truth.*

Go back to your list of unjust situations and ask students to pick one situation that disturbs them most and that they would like to address individually or as a class. Discuss what they might possibly do. Then ask who would like to serve on a project committee to address the issue. Appoint someone to serve as temporary chairperson until the group convenes its first meeting and selects a chairperson.

*Urge the calls to complete a "justice project."*

Monitor the progress of the group and ask them to report their results to the class. Depending on the project, the committee may complete it by the following week, or may require several weeks to complete.

NOTE: This project would not replace the church's Commission for Social Justice, unless there is no such provision at present. This project is just a teaching device to show how we can translate learning into doing, to make it a part of our experience. It may or may not become an ongoing commission for the church.

So go ahead, make it happen!

# Justice: Just Live It

### by Kimberly Gillespie

No Justice. No Peace
We want justice!!!
Justice for _____!!!

Justice.

We chant, protest, and fight for it. But, what is "justice"? Why do we insist on it? Justice is the principle or action of treating people in a way that is good, fair, moral, and unbiased.

Good. Fair. Moral. Unbiased.

Individually, we all want this, and fight for aspects of it, daily. While driving, someone cuts you off, causing you to miss the light. You get frustrated because what she did was not good. You have been overcharged on a bill, and you call to reconcile it, because the charges were not fair. A co-worker takes credit for a task you completed, so you confront him because it was not morally right. You enter into a restaurant at the same time as another customer of a different ethnicity, but they are served, while you are left waiting. You complain, because you believe the server was biased. We all want our form of justice. But true justice, specifically godly justice, is much loftier than our individual ambitions.

We live in a world of injustices. I have lived on the East and West coasts, in the South and the Midwest, and have traveled several times to Africa. Let me assure you, injustice is everywhere. Wherever I am, I notice that the common thread that connects the oppressed—whether children, various ethnic groups, the homeless, etc.—is poverty. When people lack financial resources, they are left without a voice. As a result, they are susceptible to being overlooked, exploited, judged, and treated unfairly. Briefly consider some of the topics that are prevalent these days—education, childhood obesity, immigration, human trafficking, universal health care, taxes, unemployment. Woven throughout the debates about these are the injustices often experienced because people lack sufficient resources.

Over the years, I have had the opportunity to teach in schools and organizations that serve the underprivileged. While there was a certain level of compassion that developed as I served, a greater understanding came as a result of recent experiences. A year ago, my family relocated from a suburb of Nashville, Tennessee, to Richmond, California, to serve at an urban neighborhood church being revitalized. Prior to relocating, we prayed, we researched, we saved, and we planned. However, our best-laid plans fell by the wayside. Six weeks after arriving in California, we found ourselves homeless and jobless with a 22-month-old son, and twins on the way.

Over the course of seven months, we stayed in five different homes. We applied for and received various resources allocated for "the poor." While we were grateful for the provision, those experiences were overwhelming, humbling, and quite educational. Unfortunately, we became well acquainted with certain injustices.

For one thing, all things are not created equal. Many of the resources allocated for the poor are substandard—from spoiled food to overcrowded and undersupplied classrooms to segregated medical facilities with inadequate, dirty, and outdated medical equipment.

Next, there is a certain bias against the poor that has developed as a result of the vicious cycle of poverty. Ignorance begets ignorance, but not knowing is not necessarily a reflection of lack of capacity, but lack of exposure and often fear. However, those who lack resources are often treated as if they are unintelligent, lazy, and incapable of or uninterested in learning. Therefore, there can be a mentality of governing, but not educating. While resources are available, accessing them can be a daunting task, requiring knowledge, access, time, and support, among other things. For example, there are employers that require a physical address, impossible if a person is homeless. Some resources require completing lengthy applications, and providing "proof" of various things—a challenge for those who cannot read, refugees and immigrants who speak other languages, or transients who travel with their entire lives in a cart, suitcase, or vehicle.

Poverty subjects people to situations they would normally not consider. For example, in recent years, more attention has been given to human trafficking. Previously, it was considered a foreign vice, as stories were told of families giving children over to "employers"

in hopes of better lives and money. However, over time, it has been revealed that the United States is a destination for traffickers.

Injustice is everywhere. And God is not silent.

## God's View of Justice

"For the LORD loves justice, and he will never abandon the godly. He will keep them safe forever, but the children of the wicked will die" (Psalm 37:28, NLT).

"He gives justice to the oppressed and food to the hungry. The LORD frees the prisoners" (Psalm 146:7, NLT).

"The LORD gives righteousness and justice to all who are treated unfairly" (Psalm 103:6, NLT).

"He ensures that orphans and widows receive justice. He shows love to the foreigners living among you and gives them food and clothing" (Deuteronomy 10:18, NLT).

"Even common people oppress the poor, rob the needy, and deprive foreigners of justice" (Ezekiel 22:29, NLT).

So, He makes provisions. God sees what we refuse to see, and commands in principle and in practice what is good, fair, moral, and unbiased.

*Good*

"When you are harvesting your crops and forget to bring in a bundle of grain from your field, don't go back to get it. Leave it for the foreigners, orphans, and widows. Then the LORD your God will bless you in all you do" (Deuteronomy 24:19, NLT).

*Fair*

"Do not twist justice in legal matters by favoring the poor or being partial to the rich and powerful. Always judge people fairly" (Leviticus 19:15, NLT).

"True justice must be given to foreigners living among you and to orphans, and you must never accept a widow's garment as security for her debt. Always remember that you were slaves in Egypt and that the LORD your God redeemed you from your slavery. That is why I have given you this command" (Deuteronomy 24:17–18, NLT).

*Moral*

"Never take advantage of poor and destitute laborers, whether they are fellow Israelites or foreigners living in your towns. You must pay them their wages each day before sunset because they are poor and are counting on it. If you don't, they might cry out to the LORD against you, and it would be counted against you as sin" (Deuteronomy 24:14–15, NLT).

*Unbiased*

"My dear brothers and sisters, how can you claim to have faith in our glorious Lord Jesus Christ if you favor some people over others? For example, suppose someone comes into your meeting dressed in fancy clothes and expensive jewelry, and another comes in who is poor and dressed in dirty clothes. If you give special attention and a good seat to the rich person, but you say to the poor one, 'You can stand over there, or else sit on the floor'—well, doesn't this discrimination show that your judgments are guided by evil motives?" (James 2:1–4, NLT).

But how does this apply to us?

The unfortunate reality is that we have ample opportunities to fight for true justice.

Perhaps your heart is pricked when you hear of orphans' struggles, both here and abroad: "Learn to do good. Seek justice. Help the oppressed. Defend the cause of orphans" (from Isaiah 1:17, NLT).

Maybe you are burdened by the ill-treatment of senior citizens because of a bad experience with a parent or grandparent: "Fight for the rights of widows" (from Isaiah 1:17, NLT).

You weep when you hear of those involved in trafficking: "Speak up for those who cannot speak for themselves; ensure justice for those being crushed" (Proverbs 31:8, NLT).

You wonder what can be done about the homeless family you pass daily: "Give justice to the poor and the orphan; uphold the rights of the oppressed and the destitute" (Psalm 82:3, NLT).

You are angered when you see or hear of any injustice. "Yes, speak up for the poor and helpless, and see that they get justice" (Proverbs 31:9, NLT).

At any rate, as followers of Christ, James reminds us that we do not have the option of doing nothing: "What good is it, dear brothers and sisters, if you say you have faith but don't show it by your actions? Can that kind of faith save anyone? Suppose you see a brother or sister who has no food or clothing, and you say, 'Good-bye and have a good day; stay warm and eat well'—but then you don't give that person any food or clothing. What good does that do? So you see, faith by itself isn't enough. Unless it produces good deeds, it is dead and useless. Now someone may argue, 'Some people have faith; others have good deeds.' But I say, 'How can you show me your faith if you don't have good deeds? I will show you my faith by my good deeds'" (James 2:14–18, NLT).

I part with these words from Micah 6:8: "No, O people, the LORD has told you what is good, and this is what he requires of you: to do what is right, to love mercy, and to walk humbly with your God" (NLT).

Justice—Just live it.

# GORDON PARKS

## (November 30, 1912–March 7, 2006)

### Photographer and filmmaker

Some would call Gordon Parks a renaissance man. As a talented photographer, filmmaker, writer, composer, novelist, and poet, he achieved greatness by refusing to limit himself. Gordon was born on November 30, 1912, in Fort Scott, Kansas. Life was hard for the son of Jackson Parks, a vegetable farmer. He was the youngest of fifteen children,

and the family lived in poverty. On top of that, Gordon faced severe discrimination in the segregated schools he attended. He also was not allowed to participate in high school activities because of his race. One high school teacher actually discouraged the class from going to college because of their being Black. Around this time, Gordon's mother died, and he subsequently left home at the age of fourteen. He managed to sustain himself financially by picking up odd jobs wherever he could find them, including waiting tables, playing piano in a brothel, and mopping floors. Gordon managed to keep himself afloat however he could.

One day while working as a Pullman porter, Gordon picked up a magazine on the train. A story inside highlighted the plight of migrant workers. The pictures moved Gordon to buy his own camera and begin taking pictures himself. His first camera was a Voigtlander Brilliant, which he bought in a Seattle pawn shop for $12.50. Little did he know that purchase would change his life. Gordon stated, "I bought what was to become my weapon against poverty and racism." His first roll of film was admired so much by the photography clerks who developed it that they encouraged Gordon to apply for a job at a women's clothing store in Minneapolis, Minnesota. While working at the clothing store, Marva Louis, the wife of heavyweight boxing champ Joe Louis, saw his work. She suggested that Gordon go to Chicago in 1940. There he started a portrait business and photographed many rich society women.

While in Chicago, Gordon began freelance work, including pictures of the city's South Side. These pictures, which chronicled life in the ghetto, won him a fellowship with the Farm Security Administration to photograph Dust Bowl farmers and sharecroppers. Gordon began to work under Roy Stryker and created his best known photograph, "American Gothic, Washington D.C." The picture is of a Black domestic worker with a mop in one hand and a broom in the other against the backdrop of the American flag. The picture was inspired by Gordon's experience of racism in the city. After the FSA disbanded, Gordon worked for the Office of War Information and had a brief stint with the Standard Oil Photography Project. During this time, Gordon longed to do fashion photography and began freelancing for *Vogue*, becoming their first Black photographer. In 1948 Gordon created a photographic essay of a young Harlem gang leader, earning him a staff job at *Life* magazine, making him the first African American to work at the company. During this time, Gordon worked on three hundred assignments, producing portraits of Stokely Carmichael, Malcolm X, Muhammad Ali, Langston Hughes, and Duke Ellington along with many other celebrities. Gordon was also the first Black photographer at *Glamour* magazine as well.

Gordon is also known for his career in writing and film. His first film, *The Learning Tree*, was based on his autobiographical novel of the same name. The film was based on his childhood in Kansas and earned him the reputation of being the first African American to direct a major Hollywood film. His next film was *Shaft*, which succeeded at the box office in 1971. Although followed by a string of films in the blaxplotiation genre, Gordon wanted *Shaft* to be a depiction of a positive Black role model. In 2005, he made a cameo in the John Singleton remake of the same name. Gordon went on to follow *Shaft* with two sequels and the film *LeadBelly* in 1976. In addition, Gordon has written over fourteen books, including works of fiction, poetry, photography instruction, and a three-volume memoir.

Gordon died of cancer on March 7, 2006, in his Manhattan apartment. By the time of his death, he had received forty-five honorary doctorate degrees. He also was awarded numerous film and photography awards. Using art and film, he battled racism and oppression. Gordon's work continues to influence artists today. By achieving many firsts in his life and trailblazing with new mediums, he continued to learn and grow in multiple crafts. He was truly a renaissance man.

# Teaching Tips

## Words You Should Know

**A. Transgressions** (Amos 2:4, 6) *pesha'* (Heb.)—Willful deviation from, and therefore rebellion against, the path of moral or godly living.

**B. Despised** (v. 4) *ma'as* (Heb.)—To reject, refuse, despise.

## Teacher Preparation

**Unifying Principle—Injustice is Intolerable!** Even though they know right from wrong, some people treat others unjustly. What can unjust people expect to result from their misdeeds? God will not overlook injustice but will punish the unjust.

**A.** Read Amos 1–2 in multiple translations.

**B.** Read the Bible Background and Devotional Reading.

**C.** Pray for your students and for lesson clarity.

## O—Open the Lesson

**A.** Open with prayer and introduce today's lesson title.

**B.** Have your students read the Aim for Change and Keep in Mind verse together. Discuss.

**C.** Instruct your students to read the In Focus story silently. Discuss.

**D.** Discuss how the poor and powerless are treated in our society.

## P—Present the Scriptures

**A.** Use The People, Places, and Times and Background to provide context.

**B.** Ask volunteers to read the Focal Verses. Ask the students to share how the Background and The People, Places, and Times inform their understanding of the text.

**C.** Use In Depth to clarify the verses.

## E—Explore the Meaning

**A.** Review and discuss the Search the Scriptures and Discuss the Meaning questions.

**B.** Read the Lesson in Our Society section. Ask the students if they've shared a similar experience, or observed the same thing in our society.

## N—Next Steps for Application

**A.** Summarize the lesson and use the Make It Happen section to provide practical steps that students can take for change.

**B.** Close with prayer.

## Worship Guide

For the Superintendent or Teacher
Theme: Judgment on Israel and Judah
Song: "The Lord Will Make a Way Somehow"
Devotional Reading: Psalm 75

# Judgment on Israel and Judah

**Bible Background • AMOS 2:4–8**
**Printed Text • AMOS 2:4–8**
**Devotional Reading • PSALM 75**

## —————— Aim for Change ——————

By the end of the lesson, we will: REVIEW God's judgment of Judah and Israel; ENCOURAGE sensitivity toward social injustice; and ADDRESS issues of injustice in our local and global communities.

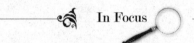

In Focus

Tony had lived in his neighborhood for ten years. He tried to take an active role in helping the neighborhood be a safe and welcoming place. One afternoon while resting on his front porch, Tony's neighbor Kodjo stopped by to chat. Kodjo was planning to rent a local storefront to sell furniture and antiques. However, Kodjo was a little uncomfortable with the contract that he had been asked to sign as a part of the lease agreement. English wasn't Kodjo's first language, so some of the contract wording was difficult to understand. Tony agreed to take a look at the lease paperwork. After reviewing Kodjo's paperwork, Tony discovered that several of the rules in the lease were unusual and seemed to favor the landlord. He suspected that the landlord was trying to take advantage of Kodjo. Tony worked with Kodjo to renegotiate the lease so that the terms were reasonable. The following week, Kodjo happily reported that the landlord had agreed to the new terms. He thanked Tony with a big hug. "Thanks for looking out! You're a true friend!"

*In today's lesson, we'll learn about God's view of injustice and discuss ways that we can fight social injustice in our own community.*

## —————— Keep in Mind ——————

"Thus saith the LORD; For three transgressions of Judah, and for four, I will not turn away the punishment thereof; because they have despised the law of the LORD, and have not kept his commandments, and their lies caused them to err, after the which their fathers have walked" (Amos 2:4).

"Thus saith the LORD; For three transgressions of Judah, and for four, I will not turn away the punishment thereof; because they have despised the law of the LORD, and have not kept his commandments, and their lies caused them to err, after the which their fathers have walked" (Amos 2:4).

# Focal Verses

**KJV** **Amos 2:4** Thus saith the LORD; For three transgressions of Judah, and for four, I will not turn away the punishment thereof; because they have despised the law of the LORD, and have not kept his commandments, and their lies caused them to err, after the which their fathers have walked:

**5** But I will send a fire upon Judah, and it shall devour the palaces of Jerusalem.

**6** Thus saith the LORD; For three transgressions of Israel, and for four, I will not turn away the punishment thereof; because they sold the righteous for silver, and the poor for a pair of shoes;

**7** That pant after the dust of the earth on the head of the poor, and turn aside the way of the meek: and a man and his father will go in unto the same maid, to profane my holy name:

**8** And they lay themselves down upon clothes laid to pledge by every altar, and they drink the wine of the condemned in the house of their god.

**NLT** **Amos 2:4** This is what the LORD says: "The people of Judah have sinned again and again, and I will not let them go unpunished! They have rejected the instruction of the LORD, refusing to obey his decrees. They have been led astray by the same lies that deceived their ancestors.

**5** So I will send down fire on Judah, and all the fortresses of Jerusalem will be destroyed."

**6** This is what the LORD says: "The people of Israel have sinned again and again, and I will not let them go unpunished! They sell honorable people for silver and poor people for a pair of sandals.

**7** They trample helpless people in the dust and shove the oppressed out of the way. Both father and son sleep with the same woman, corrupting my holy name.

**8** At their religious festivals, they lounge in clothing their debtors put up as security. In the house of their gods, they drink wine bought with unjust fines."

## The People, Places, and Times

**Tekoa.** Tekoa was a small village located west of the Dead Sea, ten miles from Jerusalem. Situated on a 2,700-foot hill, the city was at one point used as a lookout and defensive fortification. From Tekoa, one could look down across the Judean wilderness. However, it was most commonly known as a city of farmers and shepherds. The village still remains today, as Tekua, six miles south of Bethlehem. The city still contains large pastures upon which sheep and goats graze.

**Slavery in the Ancient Near East.** The concept of slavery depicted in the Old Testament is not the equivalent of the North Atlantic slave trade, although there are certain parallels between the two. Slavery was a customary practice throughout the ancient Near East. Individuals could be sold into slavery to repay a personal debt or a debt to society. In war, citizens of conquered countries were often made slaves. Mosaic Law governed how Israel was to treat slaves, given the practice was already a custom in Near Eastern culture. These laws detailed how masters were to treat slaves humanely, and how slaves could be freed. For example, in Exodus 21:2–4, it is indicated that a Hebrew who sold himself to another Hebrew should be released after six years of service.

## Background

The prophet Amos was born in the city of Tekoa. He prophesied in Israel around 750 B.C. He was not the descendant of prophets; rather he was from "among the herdman of Tekoa" (from Amos 1:1). He was a shepherd and also tended and gathered sycamore figs. He received his call to ministry while he was out in the pastures, with his sheep (Amos 7:14–15). His career as a shepherd and a common working man informed his view of the world and the way he communicated his prophetic message. He used images from nature and agriculture in his prophecies. Amos lived during an era of relative peace and prosperity. This prosperity led to an atmosphere of indulgent luxury, corrupt power, and moral depravity in Israel. Many had turned to the worship of idols and other gods. Some religious practices were still maintained; however, these had deteriorated into empty rituals. Israel's religion didn't have the intended impact on how they lived their lives.

The book of Amos begins with the prophet's message of judgment to the nations surrounding Israel. Syria, Philistia, Tyre, Edom, Ammon, and Moab were each to be punished for their various sins. The Syrians were judged for being particularly barbaric in their dealings with conquered nations. Philistia treated its people as if they were a commodity, selling men, women, and children for nothing more than profit. Tyre was admonished for violating covenant agreements, and Edom for maintaining an angry rage against neighboring countries. In its unchecked desire to gain more land, Ammon had waged war on Gilead. And the Moabites desecrated a corpse, warranting God's judgment on their nation. It was not unusual for a prophet of God to declare His judgment on the idolatrous nations surrounding Israel and Judah. However, Amos' message to Israel also concerned the sins of God's people as well. Judah and Israel were also to be held accountable for their sin.

## At-A-Glance

1. Judah's Sin and God's Judgment
(Amos 2:4–5)
2. Israel's Sin (vv. 6–8)

## In Depth

### 1. Judah's Sin and God's Judgment (Amos 2:4–5)

Amos delivers his message from the Lord, explaining the sins that Judah has committed. Judah's sin is repetitive, a continual pattern of disobedience. Their sins are numerous and God's patience with Judah has run out. In this regard, Judah is no different than the other nations that God has judged. The same pattern, "for three transgressions ... and for four" used to judge pagan nations, is used here as well. However, Judah's sin is different in that they had received God's laws and chosen not to follow them. Rather than keeping His laws, they have "despised the law of the LORD." The word translated "despised" in the KJV is the Hebrew word *ma'as* (**mah-AHS**), also meaning to reject or refuse. Judah knows what to do, but refuses to do it.

Judah has chosen to follow in the lies and falsehoods of their ancestors. They have continued a historical pattern of preferring false teaching over the divine instruction provided to them. For their sin, Judah will be judged in the same manner as the surrounding pagan nations: They will be destroyed in warfare, consumed by fire.

### 2. Israel's Sin (vv. 6–8)

Amos completes his message with a stern rebuke of Israel. Israel's spiritual climate has fallen to the point that they resemble the foreign nations around them. Their sin and rejection of God's Law places them squarely in the company of nations that haven't even received it. Again, the prophecy indicates an identical pattern of judgement: "For three transgressions … and for four."

The innocent and the poor are being abused in Israel. Though slavery is a customary practice, Amos speaks to the rigged and unjust practice of driving debtors to slavery for the sole purpose of benefiting the powerful and wealthy. Rather than being merciful and allowing them more time to repay, people are driven into slavery. For as little as the cost of a pair of sandals, the poor and innocent are dealt with harshly. Additionally the people are participating in ritual prostitution. Amos records that "a man and his father will go in unto the same maid" which is the result of religious prostitution and idol worship. Their lack of total allegiance to the one true God is connected to their blatant disregard for the weak and vulnerable.

Israel's sin is not merely negligent abuse. The innocent are actively being denied justice in the courts and are taken advantage of in the name of power and greed (v. 7). The poor, rather than being helped and protected, are pushed down even further. These practices have become commonplace in Israel.

Verse 8 further describes the indulgent and immoral behavior of the Israelites. It was common to give a coat as a pledge to repay a debt. However, garments given as a pledge were to be given back to debtors in the evening, to keep them warm at night (Exodus 22:26–27). Rather than returning these garments, the rich were seen wearing them in the temple. Similarly, wines used to pay debts to the state were stolen and used as drink or offerings in the temple.

Israel's rejection of God's Law has resulted in horrible abuses against its people. The majority of these involve the powerful using the system to benefit themselves and push down the needy and less powerful. They have perverted legitimate political and legal systems to enrich themselves.

## Search the Scriptures

1. What conditions do you think contributed to Judah's rejection of God's Law and reliance on the false teaching of their ancestors (Amos 2:4)? *Refusing to obey his word*

2. The poor are sold into slavery for what amounted to the cost of a pair of sandals. Do you think greed motivated the actions of the wealthy? What other evil rationale may have driven their actions (v. 6)?

## Discuss the Meaning

1. Judah and Israel looked just like the other nations, despite having received God's Law and being His chosen people. Can you cite modern-day examples of God's people resembling non-believers?

2. God's judgment of Israel centered on its treatment of the innocent, poor, and oppressed. How do you feel today's Christian church is doing in comparison?

## Lesson in Our Society

The powerful and wealthy in Israel used legitimate political and legal systems to enrich themselves and hold down the less fortunate. A parallel to this type of behavior is the modern-day practice of predatory lending in America. Predatory lending occurs when wealthy banking institutions provide loans under terms that are misleading or abusive. Often the loan terms make it impossible for a borrower to repay the loan or make the required payments. This results in the debtor losing land, money, or property to the bank. The poor and less educated are often the primary targets of such lending practices. Rather than taking advantage of the less fortunate, God calls us to minister to those who need help (Matthew 25:34–36).

## Make It Happen

As a nation and as the church, when it comes to social injustice, we often point the finger at others. Prayerfully make a list of the ways our nation and the church contribute to social injustice. Commit to practicing justice in these areas of life as an individual.

## Follow the Spirit

What God wants me to do:

_____

_____

_____

_____

## Remember Your Thoughts

Special insights I have learned:

_____

_____

_____

_____

## More Light on The Text

Amos 2:4–8

**4 Thus saith the LORD; For three transgressions of Judah and for four, I will not turn away the punishment thereof; because they have despised the law of the LORD, and have not kept his commandments, and their lies caused them to err, after the which their fathers have walked.**

By moving from neighboring nations on to Judah, Amos begins to zero in on the goal of prophesying against Israel. His hearers would have heard the repeated phrase "for three transgressions and for four" with anticipation of who Amos would condemn next. Judah is condemned for rejecting the Law of God and for idolatry. Although the actual word "idolatry" is not mentioned, we can infer this from the reference to lies (Heb. *kazav*, **kah-ZAHV**) making them err. The word "lies" is often used in reference to idols or anything that gives them false hope (Psalm 4:2; Ezekiel 13:6). The idols of the nations only lead people into deception. The sin of idolatry is also alluded to with the phrase "after the which their fathers have walked." "Walking after" is often used in reference to idol worship or following the commands and statutes of Yahweh (Deuteronomy 8:19; Jeremiah 8:2). It is obvious Amos is referring to the former since he has already stated that Judah has "despised" (Heb. *ma'as*, **mah-AHS**) God's Law.

This oracle against Judah stands out from the prophetic oracles against the other nations because Judah is closest to Israel and Judah's sins are of a covenantal nature, not just crimes against humanity. They are indicted for their breach of covenant with God by going after idols. This is something that God does not take lightly with His covenant people.

**5 But I will send a fire upon Judah, and it shall devour the palaces of Jerusalem.**

Amos announces that Judah's sins will not go unpunished. The Lord will send a fire on Judah and the palaces (Heb. *'armon*, **ar-MONE**) of Jerusalem. Most likely, Amos is referring to the citadels and strongholds that made up the king's palace and temple complex, since this word for "palace" can also mean citadel or fortress. The word comes from a root meaning high and lofty. These high and lofty places would be brought down by fire. This happened in 586 B.C. when Nebuchadnezzar and the Babylonian army defeated Jerusalem through siege.

**6 Thus saith the LORD; For three transgressions of Israel, and for four, I will not turn away the punishment thereof; because they sold the righteous for silver, and the poor for a pair of shoes.**

Now Amos turns his prophetic gaze toward Israel. As Amos prophesied against the other nations like Tyre, Edom, Moab, and Judah, Israel must have savored and enjoyed hearing their neighbors' condemnation. Now it was their turn. The Lord would not be partial but would judge fairly. If the other nations received prophetic pronouncements of judgment, then Israel would receive judgment as well.

Amos repeats the same prophetic formula "for three transgressions of Israel, and for four." This is an acknowledgment of God's patience toward their sin. Adding "for four" show that God is at His limit and cannot restrain His punishment for their wrongdoing. This wrongdoing manifested itself in selling "the righteous for silver, and the poor for a pair of shoes." The word "righteous" (Heb. *tsaddiq*, **tsahd-DEEK**) here may be used in a legal sense, referencing those who are religiously upright. It could also be referring to those sold into slavery for a debt. Mosaic law reveals that God calls for civil and religious uprightness. Both meanings could be in view here. A pair of sandals could be referring to land transfer (see Ruth 4) or a very small, insignificant debt. In addition, Amos is using a Hebrew literary form called parallelism which aligns two closely related ideas in order to challenge the audience to consider the relationship. In this case, both the righteous and the poor are objects of the same verb (sell). Amos is not saying that one must be poor to be righteous, but he is acknowledging that fact that it is the wealthy who are using their excess of power corruptly in order to further oppress those who are already vulnerable. Even if some of the righteous are not poor financially, by selling them for silver, those in power are subjecting them to the same destitution as the poor. Amos is pointing out how the Israelites are devaluing human life.

**7 That pant after the dust of the earth on the head of the poor, and turn aside the way of the meek: and a man and his father will go in unto the same maid, to profane my holy name.**

Israel is accused of having little or no regard for the poor. The word "pant" (Heb. *sha'af*, **shah-AHF**) is often rendered "swallow up" or "trample." The actual verb in the Hebrew text means to pant or gasp, but translations often read with the Greek (Septuagint) which understood a different verb (a homonym that is spelled differently; Heb. *shof*, **SHOHF**, to bruise, snatch someone's heel). To trample or force to the ground makes more sense with the phrases "the head of the poor" and "on the dust of the earth." However, both the Hebrew and the Greek indicate a lot of force pressing the poor into submission. They trample the head of the poor into the earth, meaning they provide no means for the poor to better themselves. Instead, Israel is accused of wanting the poor to remain poor for their own benefit and personal gain. They also push the meek or afflicted out of the way and do not give alms or financial, social, or physical assistance.

In addition, many are participating in ritual or religious prostitution. This is what is meant by "father and son go in unto the same maid" The scope of corruption includes whole households. Such acts profane, defile, or stain the Lord's holy name. The Hebrew word *khalal* (**khah-LAHL**) expresses the hideous act of desecrating that which belongs to God. It is making unholy that which is deemed holy. The Israelites are particularly accused of defiling the Lord's name through religious and social sins.

**8 And they lay themselves down upon clothes laid to pledge by every altar, and they drink the wine of the condemned in the house of their god.**

Amos continues to show how Israel has sinned. They are accused of laying "themselves down upon clothes laid to pledge by every altar." Their sexual immorality and injustice (v. 7) is connected to their religious sin and unfaithfulness to their covenant with God. Part of their idolatrous practices is to worship through sexual acts. Their crime is even more serious, as they commit these acts on clothes that have been taken as collateral for a loan. The law stated that these garments (usually the outer garments or cloaks) were to be returned for the night (Exodus 22:26). Instead they were kept to be used for shameful acts. The perpetrators also drank wine, which was paid for by "unjust fines" (NLT). It is not clear whether these fines are unjust taxes or part of the tithe to the "house of their god." During this time, ancient Israel had set up shrines and temples to replace the temple of Yahweh at Jerusalem. At these shrines, Yahweh was represented as a bull, which was also the representation of Baal. It is not surprising that because of this syncretistic mix of ideas, their worship was also patterned after the worship of Baal to include orgiastic rituals.

Sources:

Alexander, David, and Pat Alexander. *Zondervan Handbook to the Bible.* Grand Rapids, MI: Zondervan, 1999. 490.

Burge, Gary M., and Andrew E. Hill, eds. *Baker Illustrated Bible Commentary.* Grand Rapids, MI: Baker Books, 2012. 834.

Butler, Trent C., ed. *Holman Bible Dictionary.* Electronic Edition, QuickVerse. Nashville, TN: Holman Bible Publishers, 1991. S.vv. "Amos," "Slavery in the Old Testament," and "Tekoa."

Carson, D. A., R. T. France, J. A. Motyer, and G. J. Wenham, eds. *New Bible Commentary.* Downers Grove, IL: InterVarsity Press, 1994. 796–797.

Easton, M. G. *Easton's Bible Dictionary.* 1st ed. Oklahoma City: Ellis Enterprises, 1993. S.vv. "Amos," "Slave," and "Tekoa."

Motyer, J. A. *The Message of Amos.* Downers Grove, IL: InterVarsity Press, 1974. 49–60.

Orr, James, ed. "Tekoa." *International Standard Bible Encyclopedia.* Electronic Edition. Omaha, NE: QuickVerse, 1998.

Strong, James. *The New Strong's Exhaustive Concordance of the Bible Expanded Edition.* Nashville, TN: Thomas Nelson, 2001. S.vv. "Ma'ac" and "Pasha."

Stuart, Douglas. *Word Biblical Commentary: Hosea–Jonah.* Nashville, TN: Thomas Nelson, 1987. 304–305, 315–318.

Walton, John H., Victor H. Matthews, and Mark W. Chavalas. *The IVP Bible Background Commentary: Old Testament.* Downers Grove, IL: InterVarsity Press, 2000. 764.

## Say It Correctly

Devour. di-**VOW**-er.
Profane. pro-**FAYN**.

## Daily Bible Readings

**MONDAY**
I Will Judge with Equity
(Psalm 75)

**TUESDAY**
I Will Press You Down
(Amos 2:9–16)

**WEDNESDAY**
I Will Punish Your Iniquities
(Amos 3:1–8)

**THURSDAY**
I Will Punish Your Transgressions
(Amos 3:9–15)

**FRIDAY**
Judgment is Surely Coming
(Amos 4:1–6)

**SATURDAY**
You Did Not Return to Me
(Amos 4:7–13)

**SUNDAY**
I Will Not Revoke Punishment
(Amos 2:4–8)

# Teaching Tips

## Words You Should Know

**A. Gracious** (Amos 5:15) *khanan* (Heb.)—To bend or stoop in kindness to an inferior; to be considerate; to show favor.

**B. Righteousness** (v. 24) *tsedaqah* (Heb.)—Being in the right, justified, just.

## Teacher Preparation

**Unifying Principle— Justice is Not "Just Us."** Some people cover their evil ways with outward acts of goodness. Who will uncover their deceit and demand justice? The people learned through Amos that God will not be fooled by insincere offerings and will severely punish all sinners.

**A.** Read Amos 5, and research Amos 5:14–15, 18–27 in a good commentary.

**B.** Read the Bible Background and Devotional Readings.

**C.** Pray for your students and for lesson clarity.

## O—Open the Lesson

**A.** Open with prayer and introduce today's lesson title.

**B.** Have your students read the Aim for Change and Keep in Mind verse together. Discuss.

**C.** Instruct your students to read the In Focus story silently. Discuss.

**D.** Discuss the connection between outward displays of worship and one's inner spiritual life.

## P—Present the Scriptures

**A.** Use The People, Places, and Times and Background to provide context.

**B.** Ask volunteers to read the Focal Verses.

**C.** Use the In Depth section to clarify the verses.

## E—Explore the Meaning

**A.** Review and discuss the Search the Scriptures and Discuss the Meaning questions.

**B.** Read the Lesson in Our Society section. Ask the students if they can think of other examples of how these concepts are relevant to modern living.

## N—Next Steps for Application

**A.** Summarize the lesson and use the Make It Happen section to provide practical steps that students can take for change.

**B.** Close with prayer.

## Worship Guide

For the Superintendent or Teacher
Theme: God is Not Fooled
Song: "Create in Me a Clean Heart"
Devotional Reading: Psalm 14

# God is Not Fooled

**Bible Background • AMOS 5**
**Printed Text • AMOS 5:14–15, 18–27**
**Devotional Reading • PSALM 14**

## —————————— Aim for Change ——————————

By the end of the lesson, we will: KNOW how God establishes justice for the righteous and punishes deceivers; RECOGNIZE and REFLECT on actions of injustice within the community of faith; and IDENTIFY unjust practices, commit to stop our participation in them, and help others do the same.

 In Focus

Jenna's check engine light had been blinking at her for a week, so she finally took her car in for service. While waiting, Jenna noticed a young woman and her three children get off at a nearby bus stop and make their way toward the auto shop. The young woman made a payment toward the repair of her vehicle that was stored behind the shop. The shop owner told the woman, "I've held your car here as long as I can. I'm within my legal rights to sell that vehicle. If you don't pay your balance by tomorrow, I'm selling it." As the woman left the shop, Jenna heard the shop owner mutter to himself, "It'll be hard to pay up without a bus to get you here." Jenna realized tomorrow was a Sunday and the buses wouldn't be servicing this particular route. The woman would have no way to get her payment to the shop. On her way home, Jenna saw the woman and her children walking to the supermarket a few blocks away. Jenna pulled alongside them and offered to give the woman a ride back to the shop the next day.

*God desires that we would pursue justice and oppose evil. In today's lesson, we will discuss how we can do this in our own lives.*

## —————————— Keep in Mind ——————————

"But let judgment run down as waters, and righteousness as a mighty stream" (Amos 5:24).

"But let judgment run down as waters, and righteousness as a mighty stream"
(Amos 5:24).

# Focal Verses

**KJV** **Amos 5:14** Seek good, and not evil, that ye may live: and so the LORD, the God of hosts, shall be with you, as ye have spoken.

**15** Hate the evil, and love the good, and establish judgment in the gate: it may be that the LORD God of hosts will be gracious unto the remnant of Joseph.

**18** Woe unto you that desire the day of the LORD! to what end is it for you? the day of the LORD is darkness, and not light.

**19** As if a man did flee from a lion, and a bear met him; or went into the house, and leaned his hand on the wall, and a serpent bit him.

**20** Shall not the day of the LORD be darkness, and not light? even very dark, and no brightness in it?

**21** I hate, I despise your feast days, and I will not smell in your solemn assemblies.

**22** Though ye offer me burnt offerings and your meat offerings, I will not accept them: neither will I regard the peace offerings of your fat beasts.

**23** Take thou away from me the noise of thy songs; for I will not hear the melody of thy viols.

**24** But let judgment run down as waters, and righteousness as a mighty stream.

**25** Have ye offered unto me sacrifices and offerings in the wilderness forty years, O house of Israel?

**26** But ye have borne the tabernacle of your Moloch and Chiun your images, the star of your god, which ye made to yourselves.

**27** Therefore will I cause you to go into captivity beyond Damascus, saith the LORD, whose name is The God of hosts.

**NLT** **Amos 5:14** Do what is good and run from evil so that you may live! Then the LORD God of Heaven's Armies will be your helper, just as you have claimed.

**15** Hate evil and love what is good; turn your courts into true halls of justice. Perhaps even yet the LORD God of Heaven's Armies will have mercy on the remnant of his people.

**18** What sorrow awaits you who say, "If only the day of the LORD were here!" You have no idea what you are wishing for. That day will bring darkness, not light.

**19** In that day you will be like a man who runs from a lion—only to meet a bear. Escaping from the bear, he leans his hand against a wall in his house—and he's bitten by a snake.

**20** Yes, the day of the LORD will be dark and hopeless, without a ray of joy or hope.

**21** "I hate all your show and pretense—the hypocrisy of your religious festivals and solemn assemblies.

**22** I will not accept your burnt offerings and grain offerings. I won't even notice all your choice peace offerings.

**23** Away with your noisy hymns of praise! I will not listen to the music of your harps.

**24** Instead, I want to see a mighty flood of justice, an endless river of righteous living.

**25** Was it to me you were bringing sacrifices and offerings during the forty years in the wilderness, Israel?

**26** No, you served your pagan gods—Sakkuth your king god and Kaiwan your star god—the images you made for yourselves.

**27** So I will send you into exile, to a land east of Damascus," says the LORD, whose name is the God of Heaven's Armies.

470

## The People, Places, and Times

**Feast Days.** There were three major feast days in the nation of Israel: the Feast of Unleavened Bread (Passover), the Feast of Harvest (Pentecost), and the Feast of Ingathering (Tabernacles). These were pilgrimage festivals that required participation from the entire Israelite community. All work was to cease and travelers made their way from all over Israel to celebrate these festivals in Jerusalem.

**Sikkuth (Moloch).** Sikkuth is another name for the Mesopotamian astral deity Sakkut (Ninib). This god was also associated with the planet Saturn. It was commonly believed that this god was not introduced until after the Assyrian conquest, but recent scholarship has revealed that Aramean merchants and other foreign travelers helped to spread the worship of Sikkuth in Israel.

**Kaiwan (Chiun).** Kaiwan was the Babylonian Saturn god. The name actually means "the steadiest one" and is taken from the planet Saturn's slow-moving orbit. The differences in spelling are likely because when foreign gods were referenced, the original vowels were often replaced with the vowels from the Hebrew word for "abomination." The Phoenicians were thought to offer human sacrifices to this god.

## Background

Amos begins chapter 5 as a eulogy for the "dead" nation of Israel. Israel was not yet dead, but the lament was meant to impress on the nation the severe danger it was in. The death of Israel is described as the death of a virgin (v. 2). The death of a virgin would have been considered particularly tragic because she had no children to carry on her memory. This type of death is distinctly permanent. Furthermore, the dead virgin is described as having been left lying in a field,

unburied. To leave a body unburied would have been a shocking and appalling image to consider, yet this is how the demise of Israel is described. Its depraved moral climate and refusal to turn back to God had indeed set it on the path of destruction.

Israel could not trust in the power of its armies to defend them against the coming destruction. Amos declared that their armies will be systematically cut down in battle (v. 3). Their trust in false gods was misplaced. The Israelites were known to visit idol temples in Bethel, Gilgal, and Beersheba. But Amos announced that each of these is set for destruction as well. Their only hope was to return to God. Amos repeatedly declared the way of escape for some. If they will seek after God, they will live (vv. 4, 6). Despite Amos' lament, he presented God's offer to save a remnant who will turn to Him.

## At-A-Glance

1. Love Good, Hate Evil (Amos 5:14–15)
2. A Day of Darkness (vv. 18–20)
3. God Desires Justice, Not Empty Rituals (vv. 21–24)
4. Israel's Idolatry Results in Exile (vv. 25–27)

## In Depth

**1. Love Good, Hate Evil (Amos 5:14–15)**

Israel has become complacent in their presumption of God's favor (v. 14). Israel has mistakenly believed that, despite their sinful ways and their worship of other gods, they can still count on God's protection. However, Amos has declared to them that their actions have displeased God and will result in the destruction of their nation. In order for some to be spared, they must both seek good and avoid evil. The two-fold action of seeking and avoiding is emphasized in verse 15. They are to "hate" the evil and "love" the good. The terms "hate" and "love" indicate decisions that one must make. Seeking good is connected with choosing to love good. Avoiding evil is connected to choosing to hate evil.

## 2. A Day of Darkness (vv. 18–20)

Again, the prophet's message seizes on Israel's presumption of God's favor. It was common in times of trouble for the Israelites to long for "the day of the LORD," when God would rescue them from their enemies. But "the day of the LORD" will now be a day of reckoning. For those who have turned to idols and denied justice to the poor, there will be no rescue, but rather darkness and judgment waiting for them. This will be a jarring turn of events for Israel. It is described metaphorically like escaping a lion, only to find that you must escape a bear; then resting at home, only to find that a snake is waiting to bite you.

## 3. God Desires Justice, Not Empty Rituals (vv. 21–24)

The worship of other gods had seeped into Israel's religious practices, but the people still maintained their Israelite rituals and festivals too. However, God is not fooled by their empty worship. True worship flows out of the hearts of those who earnestly seek to follow God's will. A true worshiper's relationships and personal life will be consistent with his or her public worship. Israel's worship is hypocritical. They publicly give offerings to God and worship Him with their music, but they continue to reject justice and righteousness in their everyday lives. Their religious practices have become distasteful to God, and He refuses their show of piety. Rather than continued injustice and hypocrisy, the Lord desires a continual, daily flow of justice and righteousness.

## 4. Israel's Idolatry Results in Exile (vv. 25–27)

Israel's unfaithfulness is called out here. In addition to making offerings to Yahweh, they have begun worshiping foreign deities. Idol worship often included parades in which the people would carry handmade representations of their gods. Amos describes an image that depicts Israel, the chosen people of Yahweh the one true God, carrying around idols made to worship other gods (v. 26). It is a sad betrayal of the God who had redeemed them. Idolatry leads to injustice. It is at the root of their oppression of others and their choosing to love evil and not good. As a result, the Lord will send them into exile—what happens to all those who choose other gods.

## Search the Scriptures

1. What do you think it would have looked like for an Israelite to love good and hate evil during this time in Israel's history (Amos 5:14–15)?

2. What were the attitudes and motives of the Israelite worshipers (vv. 21–23)? Why did God refuse their worship?

## Discuss the Meaning

1. Amos declared that God desires justice and righteousness, not religious practices that have no impact on how we live. How does your public worship inform your desire for social justice in our society?

2. Amos instructed Israel to love good and hate evil. How might you love good and hate evil in your daily life? How would others know that you love good and hate evil?

## Lesson in Our Society

Most Christians have no problem determining the difference between good and evil. In fact, even non-believers often choose to do the right thing. But merely choosing not to do evil is different than actively opposing evil. Opposing evil requires a level of conviction that goes beyond a simple understanding of right and wrong. This concept has been examined in social experiments and hidden camera television shows. During these experiments, an unsuspecting participant is presented with a scenario that requires that he or she make a moral determination of what is right or wrong. Generally, participants will choose to do the right thing. The scenario is then changed slightly. Now the participant is presented with a scenario in which someone is doing wrong to another person. The participant must decide to either intervene or ignore the injustice that they are witnessing. It is often the case that only certain individuals will go out of their way to oppose an injustice. Most people are content to sit by while others are treated unfairly. It is God's desire that Christians would not only seek to do good, but also oppose evil and injustice. We are charged with standing for justice in our communities and in our world.

## Make It Happen

It is often difficult in the moment to choose to love good and hate evil. One way to be prepared for those times and situations where we have decisions to make is to determine what is good or evil. Get a piece of paper and on one side write "Love Good" and on the other side write "Hate Evil." On the "Love Good" side, write all the ways that you can seek good in your daily life. On the "Hate Evil" side, write all the ways that you can hate evil in your daily life. Think-

ing about these things beforehand can help us to not only avoid falling into sin, but also move us forward in serving others in our community.

## Follow the Spirit

What God wants me to do:

_____

_____

_____

_____

## Remember Your Thoughts

Special insights I have learned:

_____

_____

_____

_____

## More Light On The Text

**Amos 5:14–15, 18–27**

**14 Seek good, and not evil, that ye may live: and so the LORD, the God of hosts, shall be with you, as ye have spoken.**

Amos continues with the refrain of seeking. The word seek (Heb. *darash*, **dah-RASH**) is used in verse 4 and 6 to refer to the people seeking the idol sanctuaries and then to refer to seeking God. Now Amos uses it in reference to good as opposed to evil. The good that the people are to seek is justice for the poor. Amos holds out the promise of the Lord's presence if they seek good. This highlights the fact that the Lord is not with them to begin with because of their injustice and oppression.

**15 Hate the evil, and love the good, and establish judgment in the gate: it may be that the LORD God of hosts will be gracious unto the remnant of Joseph.**

This seeking of good is more than just an outward action. It must radiate from an attitude of the heart. Amos uses strong words here. Seeking good is spelled out as hating (Heb. *sane'*, **sah-NAY**) evil. In other passages of the Old Testament, this word is used to refer to an enemy. The Israelites had been friends with evil and stood on the side of injustice. By using this word, Amos confronts them and challenges them to choose sides. Being on the side of good means establishing "judgment in the gate." The gates of the town were often used for courts of justice and centers of trade, and there the Israelites did most of their oppression of the poor. So this is where they could show that they love good and hate evil instead.

If the people would seek Him and seek good instead of seeking the sanctuaries at Bethel and Gilgal, then maybe he would be gracious (Heb. *khanan*, **khah-NAHN**) to them. Amos is communicating that there is still the possibility of God showing favor and mercy to them. A remnant of Joseph is offered grace. After breaking away from the Southern Kingdom of Judah, the ten tribes were often referred to as Joseph. To refer to the remnant of Joseph is to appeal to those who will choose to seek good.

**18 Woe unto you that desire the day of the LORD! to what end is it for you? the day of the LORD is darkness, and not light. 19 As if a man did flee from a lion, and a bear met him; or went into the house, and leaned his hand on the wall, and a serpent bit him. 20 Shall not the day of the LORD be darkness, and not light? even very dark, and no brightness in it?**

"The day of the LORD" is a term that refers to the Lord appearing and waging a holy war with His enemies. This is the first reference to the Day of the Lord in the Old Testament. Amos implies that those Israelites who are involved in oppressing the poor longed for this Day of Judgment. He lets them know that it will not be a good time for them; it will be darkness and not light. The images of running from a lion only to meet a bear or running into a house only to be bitten by a serpent describe the Day of the Lord as a time where they will not be able to escape God's judgment.

**21 I hate, I despise your feast days, and I will not smell in your solemn assemblies. 22 Though ye offer me burnt offerings and your meat offerings, I will not accept them: neither will I regard the peace offerings of your fat beasts.**

Outwardly impressive religious acts of good will that are selfishly done do not move the heart of God. The phrase "your feast days" (Heb. *khag*, **KHAG**) refers to the three main festivals that God established in Israel: Passover, Pentecost, and the Feast of Tabernacles (Exodus 23:14–19; Deuteronomy 16:16–17). Israel was abusing all of these festivals at this time. God rejected what Israel did in these feasts, which had a form of godliness but lacked the power thereof. The implication is that God Himself may establish events, activities, or procedures, but His people can pervert, abuse, and misuse them to achieve their own selfish ends. The Lord says He will not smell in their assemblies (Heb. *'atsarah*, **ah-tsah-RAH**). Amos is possibly referring to the solemn assembly on the seventh day of Feast of Unleavened Bread and the eighth day of the Feast of Tabernacles (Leviticus 23:8, 36). The Lord would not be pleased with any of the worship practiced on those days because of the absence of justice and right living.

None of the offerings prescribed in the law would please God. The Lord would not accept their burnt offerings (Heb. *'olah*, **oh-LAH**), in which the whole animal was consumed with fire. This was a symbol of the total commitment of the worshiper's life to God. He would not accept their meat offerings (Heb. *minkhah*, **min-KHAH**). These were sacrifices devoid of blood and intended as gifts to the Lord. Lastly, He would not accept their peace offerings (Heb. *shelem*, **SHEH-lehm**), as these gifts were a sign of reconciliation or friendship, and this was not the state of their relationship with God. All of the worship rituals here were to be symbols of the people's real-life walk with the Lord, and offering them without the true reality behind them was hypocritical. This made their offerings unacceptable to the Lord.

**23 Take thou away from me the noise of thy songs; for I will not hear the melody of thy viols.**

Celebrations and rejoicing in God's presence played an important part in Israel's temple worship, which God had established. The Israelites used many kinds of musical instruments to praise God for His goodness and faithfulness (2 Chronicles 7; Psalm 149). In this instance the Lord actually calls their songs noise (Heb. *hamon*, **hah-MONE**). It is not the joyful noise of Psalm 100:1, but the noise and confusion of a host of people—noise that the Lord does not want to hear.

**24 But let judgment run down as waters, and righteousness as a mighty stream.**

God illustrates the nature of judgment (justice) and righteousness by using the phrases "run down as waters" and "as a mighty stream," which speak of the ongoing and unobstructed movement of an ever-flowing body of water. The word for stream, *nakhal* (Heb. **NAH-khall**), is the word for the desert wadi. These small narrow valleys laid dry and barren for much of the year until a torrent of rain flooded them and made them into flowing streams. The Lord has already laid out the stipulations of justice in His covenant, and He is waiting for His people to fill the dry and barren land with justice and righteousness as the rains fill up a desert wadi.

**25 Have ye offered unto me sacrifices and offerings in the wilderness forty years, O house of Israel? 26 But ye have borne the tabernacle of your Moloch and Chiun your images, the star of your god, which ye made to yourselves. 27 Therefore will I cause you to go into captivity beyond Damascus, saith the LORD, whose name is The God of hosts.**

The Lord ends His pronouncement of judgment upon Israel's hypocritical worship with a rhetorical question. He asks if the Israelites have offered sacrifices to Him in the wilderness. While there were sacrifices made to the Lord in the wilderness, they were not a regular feature in Israel's religious life until after the conquest. The Lord is affirming that His relationship with them was not dependent on sacrifices and offerings. He had been with them in the wilderness without regular sacrifices.

Next, He confronts them on their worship of idols. They have paraded images of foreign gods through their streets to their shrines. Sacrifices, sacred dancing, and other perverse forms of worship followed this parade. Many translations say the "tabernacle of your Moloch and Chiun your images." Other translations say "Sikkuth your king and Kaiwan your star god." Sikkuth is more probable as Sikkuth and Kaiwan were worshiped as astral deities in Mesopotamia, while Moloch was associated more with Syria-Palestine, and the worship practices here seem to be associated with Mesopotamia and the influences of the Assyrians. Since this is the only time Sikkuth is mentioned in the Bible but Moloch is mentioned numerous times, the Greek and Latin translators probably provided the more familiar name for the astral deity so that their audiences would understand. The meaning of the text does not change as either epithet refers to a deity associated with Saturn in the ancient world. In ancient times, Saturn was observed as being a star and influencing agriculture. This explains the reference to "the star of your god" (v. 26). In the next verse, Amos predicts that instead of them carrying their gods to the shrine to worship, they will be carried away captive. The phrase "beyond Damascus" points toward the coming Assyrian invasion that would take place, and the resulting demise of the Northern Kingdom.

Sources:

Alexander, David, and Pat Alexander. *Zondervan Handbook to the Bible.* Grand Rapids, MI: Zondervan, 1999. 490.

Burge, Gary M., and Andrew E. Hill, eds. *Baker Illustrated Bible Commentary.* Grand Rapids, MI: Baker Books, 2012. 834–835, 837–838.

Butler, Trent C., ed. *Holman Bible Dictionary.* Electronic Edition, QuickVerse. Nashville, TN: Holman Bible Publishers, 1991. S.vv. "Kaiwan" and "Prophet."

Easton, M. G. "Chiun." *Easton's Bible Dictionary.* 1st ed. Oklahoma City: Ellis Enterprises, 1993.

Kaiser, Walter C., and Duane Garrett, eds. "Prophets in the Bible and Pagan Nations." *Archaeological Study Bible.* Grand Rapids, MI: Zondervan, 2005.

Keck, Leander, ed. *The Twelve Prophets.* The New Interpreter's Bible. Vol. 7. Nashville, TN: Abingdon Press, 1996. 384–397.

Orr, James, ed. "Chiun." *International Standard Bible Encyclopedia.* Electronic Edition. Omaha, NE: QuickVerse, 1998.

Strong, James. *The New Strong's Exhaustive Concordance of the Bible Expanded Edition.* Nashville, TN: Thomas Nelson, 2001. S.vv. "Chanan" and "Tsadaqah."

Stuart, Douglas. *Word Biblical Commentary: Hosea–Jonah.* Nashville, TN: Thomas Nelson, 1987. 340–356.

Walton, John H., Victor H. Matthews, and Mark W. Chavalas. *The IVP Bible Background Commentary: Old Testament.* Downers Grove, IL: InterVarsity Press, 2000. 769–771.

## Say It Correctly

Tabernacle. **TA**-ber-na-hul.
Damascus. da-**MAS**-kus.
Moloch. **MOE**-lokh.
Sikkuth. see-**KOOTH**.

## Daily Bible Readings

**MONDAY**
Fools Say, "There is No God"
(Psalm 14)

**TUESDAY**
Can You Deceive God?
(Job 13:7–12)

**WEDNESDAY**
Full of Hypocrisy and Lawlessness
(Matthew 23:23–28)

**THURSDAY**
To Obey is Better than Sacrifice
(1 Samuel 15:17–23)

**FRIDAY**
I Know Your Transgressions and Sins
(Amos 5:7–13)

**SATURDAY**
Seek the Lord and Live
(Amos 5:1–6)

**SUNDAY**
Love Good and Establish Justice
(Amos 5:14–15, 18–27)

# Teaching Tips

## Words You Should Know

**A. Chant** (Amos 6:5) *parat* (Heb.)—To improvise carelessly; to stammer.

**B. Afflict** (v. 14) *lakhats* (Heb.)—To squeeze or oppress.

## Teacher Preparation

**Unifying Principle—A Deadly Trio: Selfishness, Greed, and Pride.** Some people care only about accumulating lavish possessions for themselves and care nothing for those who possess little. What happens to greedy and selfish people? God will dispossess them to demonstrate His justice.

**A.** Pray for students and the upcoming lesson.

**B.** Read Amos 6 in multiple translations

**C.** Find media (videos or articles) that show excessive spending, luxurious living, and poverty.

## O—Open the Lesson

**A.** Open with prayer and introduce today's lesson title.

**B.** Have your students read the Aim for Change and Keep in Mind verse together.

**C.** Share the articles or video clips featuring lavish living (e.g., celebrity reality shows).

**D.** Ask, "Is it wrong or sinful to be wealthy?"

**E.** Allow students to share their responses.

**F.** Tell the class to read the In Focus story silently, and then discuss it.

## P—Present the Scriptures

**A.** Have volunteers take turns reading Focal Verses.

**B.** Use The People, Places, and Times; Background; Search the Scriptures; At-A-Glance; In Depth; and More Light on the Text to clarify the verses.

## E—Explore the Meaning

**A.** Divide the class into small groups to go over the Discuss the Meaning, Lesson in Our Society, and Make It Happen sections.

**B.** Have groups share what they discussed.

## N—Next Steps for Application

**A.** Summarize the lesson.

**B.** Ask students to consider how they could use their resources to help others in need.

**C.** Close with prayer.

## Worship Guide

For the Superintendent or Teacher
Theme: Rebuked for Selfishness
Song: "Lead Me, Guide Me"
Devotional Reading: Psalm 119:31–38

# Rebuked for Selfishness

**Bible Background • AMOS 6**
**Printed Text • AMOS 6:4–8, 11–14**
**Devotional Reading • PSALM 119:31–38**

—————————— Aim for Change ——————————

By the end of the lesson, we will: EXPLORE God's response to injustice as recorded by Amos; REFLECT on ways people practice greed and selfishness; and UNCOVER and DISCOVER ways God does justice amid injustice and ways humans can join God in the fight against injustice.

———————  In Focus ———————

Michael was a successful businessman who worked for a large corporation. He lived in a huge mansion with a four-car garage in a gated community. He had attended several prestigious universities, attaining the necessary degrees to promote him to a high position at his company. He had risen to an upper-level management position quickly and had a huge office. Michael made over seven figures each year in salary, not including an annual bonus. He was living the good life. Every day, Michael's driver would pick him up from his mansion and drive him to work. When the driver would get off the exit, the car would pass a poorer neighborhood. Michael would often see people on the streets who looked as if they were homeless and suffering from different addictions. One day as the car was approaching the office, Michael saw a younger mother trying to walk her children to school. He saw that she was struggling to manage pushing a stroller and tend to two smaller children. Yet, he chose to ignore her and instructed the driver to proceed.

*God invites us to participate in ending the injustices that oppress other humans. In today's lesson, we will learn how God desires for us to have radical compassion for others.*

——————————— Keep in Mind ———————————

"Shall horses run upon the rock? will one plow there with oxen? for ye have turned judgment into gall, and the fruit of righteousness into hemlock" (Amos 6:12).

"Shall horses run upon the rock? will one plow there with oxen? for ye have turned judgment into gall, and the fruit of righteousness into hemlock" (Amos 6:12).

# Focal Verses

**KJV** **Amos 6:4** That lie upon beds of ivory, and stretch themselves upon their couches, and eat the lambs out of the flock, and the calves out of the midst of the stall;

**5** That chant to the sound of the viol, and invent to themselves instruments of musick, like David;

**6** That drink wine in bowls, and anoint themselves with the chief ointments: but they are not grieved for the affliction of Joseph.

**7** Therefore now shall they go captive with the first that go captive, and the banquet of them that stretched themselves shall be removed.

**8** The Lord GOD hath sworn by himself, saith the LORD the God of hosts, I abhor the excellency of Jacob, and hate his palaces: therefore will I deliver up the city with all that is therein.

**11** For, behold, the LORD commandeth, and he will smite the great house with breaches, and the little house with clefts.

**12** Shall horses run upon the rock? will one plow there with oxen? for ye have turned judgment into gall, and the fruit of righteousness into hemlock:

**13** Ye which rejoice in a thing of nought, which say, Have we not taken to us horns by our own strength?

**14** But, behold, I will raise up against you a nation, O house of Israel, saith the LORD the God of hosts; and they shall afflict you from the entering in of Hemath unto the river of the wilderness.

**NLT** **Amos 6:4** How terrible for you who sprawl on ivory beds and lounge on your couches, eating the meat of tender lambs from the flock and of choice calves fattened in the stall.

**5** You sing trivial songs to the sound of the harp and fancy yourselves to be great musicians like David.

**6** You drink wine by the bowlful and perfume yourselves with fragrant lotions. You care nothing about the ruin of your nation.

**7** Therefore, you will be the first to be led away as captives. Suddenly, all your parties will end.

**8** The Sovereign LORD has sworn by his own name, and this is what he, the LORD God of Heaven's Armies, says: "I despise the arrogance of Israel, and I hate their fortresses. I will give this city and everything in it to their enemies."

**11** When the LORD gives the command, homes both great and small will be smashed to pieces.

**12** Can horses gallop over boulders? Can oxen be used to plow them? But that's how foolish you are when you turn justice into poison and the sweet fruit of righteousness into bitterness.

**13** And you brag about your conquest of Lo-debar. You boast, "Didn't we take Karnaim by our own strength?"

**14** "O people of Israel, I am about to bring an enemy nation against you," says the LORD God of Heaven's Armies. "They will oppress you throughout your land—from Lebo-hamath in the north to the Arabah Valley in the south."

## The People, Places, and Times

**Viol.** These were instruments similar to a harp or lyre. They were often used in temple worship and had ten strings (Psalm 33:2). The Hebrew word is also used for bottles or pitchers, probably because they had the same conical or triangular shape. They were plucked by hand instead of a pick and were mainly used during times of feasting and celebration.

**Ointments.** In biblical times, people used ointments for medicinal, cosmetic, and even religious purposes. These ointments served the purpose of not only healing the skin but also masking odors. They were similar to our modern lotion and made the skin glisten. Rubbing ointment on the body was often done in preparation for a festival and was a mark of sanctification. Oils or ointments were also used to prepare bodies for burial, and they marked various types of leaders as ordained by God (priests, prophets, kings). They could signify both luxury and holiness.

**Hemath to the River of the Wilderness.** Hemath was situated on the Orontes River and was the northern boundary of ancient Israel. Hemath represented the farthest north you could go before you ventured outside of Israel (Numbers 13:21). The river of wilderness was a desert wadi or brook that ran through the Arabah valley, which was a barren depression on the southern side of the Dead Sea. This brook flowed on the border of Moab and Edom. The river of the wilderness represented the farthest southern border of undivided Israel that could be inhabited. Thus the phrase "Hemath unto the river of the wilderness" encompassed the entirety of the undivided kingdom of Israel.

## Background

The upper crust of Israel had become very complacent and comfortable with their wealthy lives. They were secure in the strength of their army and able to maintain a certain lifestyle that made them oblivious to the world around them. Those in leadership believed that Israel's cities were superior to others because of their extravagant and materialistic luxuries. They had become so focused on their wealth that they had forgotten those who were suffering and less fortunate. Israel had forgotten that God had blessed them tremendously over the years. God had delivered them from oppressors and had shown them favor. Unfortunately, they sinned against God by rejecting His call for love and obedience. They had also sinned against God by oppressing others and therefore violating His Law. Israel's blatant disregard for others and overindulgence in their wealth angered God, provoking His wrath.

Amos proclaimed prophecies from God that convict leaders for a lack of social justice and warning them of the "day of the LORD" when judgment would come to Israel. He had opposed the nation's sins and had encouraged them to repent for their evil and unjust ways. However, Israel had refused to turn away from their wickedness and remember the God they worshiped when they were in bondage. They were at risk for God's divine punishment.

## At-A-Glance

1. A Selfish Lifestyle (Amos 6:4–8)
2. Punishment for the Self-Indulgent (vv. 11–14)

## In Depth

### 1. A Selfish Lifestyle (Amos 6:4–8)

The rich leaders of Samaria completely turn all of their attention to their material wealth. They are consumed with a lifestyle that is rich, elegant, exquisite, lavish, and excessive. They are only concerned with a higher standard of living that requires the finest and best. From dining selections, fine clothing, wild parties, extravagant celebrations, grand mansions, and expensive skin creams, the influential people of Israel are accustomed to a lifestyle that only served an elite class. Their lifestyle causes them to lose focus on real-life issues around them. They are blind to the fact that as the elite become richer, the poor become poorer. Often when we experience an increase of wealth, we forget about God and the plight of others. The elite of Israel had only used their wealth for selfish and luxurious needs, forsaking those who were suffering among them. Amos declares an oath from the Sovereign Lord that God is angry at their conceited and arrogant way of living. God holds the wealthy accountable for the use of their resources and whether they use it for the blessing of others instead of selfishness.

### 2. Punishment for the Self-Indulgent (vv. 11–14)

The Lord has promised to enact severe punishment on Israel because of their refusal to repent. God will not only punish individuals, but plans to completely destroy their houses and buildings. The prophet explains that God will punish them because they twisted justice into a poison doing more harm than good. God mocks Israel for their prideful celebration over smaller cities that they had successfully conquered. Finally, their ultimate judgment is given as God announces that another force will be raised up against them to return the oppression that they have afflicted on others. Selfishness always ends with judgment; the selfish can expect to reap the fruits of what they have sown.

## Search the Scriptures

1. What are the the signs of the people of Israel's selfishness (Amos 6:4–6)?

2. What does the Lord despise and hate about Israel (v. 8)?

## Discuss the Meaning

There is a huge debate on whether it is possible to be a follower of God and also have great wealth. Should Christians have nice things (cars, houses, clothing, etc.)? Does serving God mean that we can't spend our money on the things we can enjoy?

## Lesson in Our Society

In many places around the world, people are living in underserved and impoverished areas. They are suffering from lack of clean water, fresh produce, safe living conditions, and other resources that affect their everyday lives. There is not an equal distribution of wealth in our world. The powerful will continue to get rich, while the poor and working class will continue to suffer. The issue with wealth that is mentioned in this text is not the possession of wealth, but the dangers of being selfish, prideful, and sinful in the ways we use it. If we choose to ignore the injustices of the poor and needy, then we are at risk of God's punishment.

## Make It Happen

We are tempted to ignore injustice when we are wealthy and comfortable. To combat this tendency, we can show solidarity with those who are disadvantaged. As a class, make a commitment to eat only one meal a day as an act of solidarity with those who live in hunger. While you are doing that, research ways in which you as a class can help fight global hunger. You can find many resources for this at the Bread for the World website (http://www.bread.org/help).

## Follow the Spirit

What God wants me to do:

_____

_____

_____

_____

## Remember Your Thoughts

Special insights I have learned:

_____

_____

_____

_____

## More Light on the Text

### Amos 6:4–8, 11–14

To understand what Amos is saying in his sixth chapter, it is necessary to explore the wider social context of Israel and Judah in his day. His prophetic ministry took place during the reign of Jeroboam II in Israel (793–753 B.C.) and of Uzziah, also called Azariah, in Judah (792–740 B.C.), both of whom were strong monarchs with outstanding military prowess (Dunn 694). The main part of Amos' ministry probably occurred between 760 and 755 B.C., when both kingdoms enjoyed great prosperity and reached new political and military heights (2 Kings 14:23–25; 2 Chronicles 26:1–15). For instance, during his reign, Jeroboam managed to extend the borders of Israel as far north as Hamath (2 Kings 14:25; Amos 6:14).

This political and military success shaped the social conditions of Israel and Judah. Commerce was good and an upper class of prosperous merchants emerged. The rich became more materialistic, indulging deeply in luxury while the poor continued to be grossly taken advantage of. This was a time of rampant idolatry, immorality, corruption of judicial procedures, and oppression of the needy. In his commentary on Amos, David Hubbard observes that "at particular fault were the powerful, the landed, the wealthy, and the influential ... the leadership who had not only seduced the underprivileged from obedient worship of Yahweh but had conscripted their lands, confiscated their goods, violated their women and cheated them in business" (87).

It was also a time of complacency. The kingdom of Israel—the primary audience of Amos' prophecy—was politically secure and spiritually smug. About forty years earlier, at the end of his ministry, Elisha had prophesied the resurgence of Israel's power (2 Kings 13:17–19), and more recently, Jonah had prophesied her restoration to a glory not known since the days of Solomon (2 Kings 14:25). Israel seemed and felt undefeatable (Amos 6:13, 9:10). Her leaders wrongly believed that the political and economic success was evidence that she was in God's good graces. This sense of security, in turn, increased Israel's religious and moral corruption. They lived like there was no judgment—like there was no tomorrow to face God. His past punishments for unfaithfulness were forgotten, and His patience was at an end—which Amos was sent to announce. In judgment, God would soon—in less than forty years—bring about the Assyrian captivity of the Northern Kingdom (722–721 B.C.).

In Amos 6, the prophet continues to denounce the sinful condition of the nation of Israel and the spiritual and moral decay of its leaders. Until now, they have been able to disregard and postpone the day of the Lord's judgment. Amos describes them in a rather grim and disturbing prophetic image of the complacent powerful reclining upon expensive couches, enjoying their entertainments, anointing themselves and their guests with the finest perfumes, indulging lavishly in expensive wines, with vocal and instrumental music, all while neglecting the true worship of Jehovah. So, the prophet indicts (6:1), warns (v. 2), rebukes (vv. 3–6), pronounces impending judgment (vv. 7–11), and declares that the judgment is inevitable (vv. 12–14). His prophecy continues the doom that was pronounced upon Israel at the conclusion of Amos 2 (vv. 6–16). This chapter begins with an exclamation of "Woe," the second in this series of such indictments, the first one being at 5:18.

✓ **4 That lie upon beds of ivory, and stretch themselves upon their couches, and eat the lambs out of the flock, and the calves out of the midst of the stall; 5 That chant to the sound of the viol, and invent to themselves instruments of musick, like David; 6 That drink wine in bowls, and anoint themselves with the chief ointments: but they are not grieved for the affliction of Joseph.**

Verse 4 continues the woe that was declared in verse 1. In essence, he is saying, "Woe to you who put far off the day of doom . . . who sing idly to the sound of stringed instruments . . . who drink wine from bowls . . . but are not grieved." The leaders of Israel lie on ivory divans, sprawl on couches, feast on tender lamb and veal, amuse themselves by improvising babbling sounds of the harp. Each one of these items would have earlier been only possible for royalty, being so distant to actual village life. Amos had earlier prophesied against the houses of ivory, and now, it was the beds overlaid with ivory that invoked judgment (3:15). The eating of meat

(lambs) with any regularity was the privilege of the wealthy. "The general population lived on wheat and barley and whatever fruits and vegetables were at hand, and if they had meat at all, reserved it for times of high celebration. ... In contrast, Samaria's elite not only ate animals at random but also put their calves in special stalls to fatten them, undoubtedly on grain wrested from the poor" (Hubbard 193). Of course, Amos had earlier said that this luxury is obtained through robbery and violence against the poor (3:10).

The reclining (or lying down) and sprawling in verses 4 and 7 depict not just comfort but drunken torpor—possibly of the religious kind like those mentioned in Isaiah 65:11 and Jeremiah 44:17. The traditional custom in Israel at the time was to eat while sitting on rugs or seats. The practice of reclining at meals that Amos describes here is foreign. The Hebrew *sarakh* (**sah-RAHKH**), translated "sprawl" (NLT), means to "go free, unrestrained," and is used in Arabic for camels left loose to pasture where they choose and of hair hanging loose (Snaith 112). Hubbard adds that it may also mean "free fall" from weakness or fatigue (Hubbarb 193). The word *parat* (Heb., **pah-RAHT**), generally translated "to chant," "to improvise," or "to sing extemporaneously," suggests a flow of trivial words in which the rhythm of words and music was everything but the sense and meaning nothing (Hubbard 193). Amos attacks the wealthy for overindulgence in food, drink, luxurious ointments and leisure to the point that they neglect those in need. They think that because they live a luxurious lifestyle and practice music, they are like David, God's beloved, but they deceive themselves in their thoughts and practices. *Mizraq* (Heb., **meez-RAHK**) suggests that they used special bowls or basins for their wine-drinking, not ordinary cups. However we under-

484

stand Amos' imagery, their parties feature extreme extravagance and careless ease.

The whole chapter pictures an upper class too self-centered and intent on its own pleasure as to find Amos' prediction of catastrophe credible. We see their apathy expressed in the clause, "they are not grieved for the affliction of Joseph," i.e., their own Northern Kingdom. Hubbard interprets this to say they have been sick for the wrong reasons: their drunkenness and their mourning of the dead (6:9–10). As they enjoyed all their luxuries, they had not even the slightest concern for the broken-down state of the nation of Israel. Much like today, selfishness and greed cause people to only look for their own comfort, often at the expense of the needy. The sufferings of the oppressed and wronged do not touch them at all. If anything, the presence of the underprivileged is advantageous to the greedy leaders, who made their wealth by oppressing them.

**7 Therefore now shall they go captive with the first that go captive, and the banquet of them that stretched themselves shall be removed. 8 The Lord GOD hath sworn by himself, saith the LORD the God of hosts, I abhor the excellency of Jacob, and hate his palaces: therefore will I deliver up the city with all that is therein.**

The prophet's "therefore" begins to conclude the rebuke. Everything—all their drunken gluttonous orgies—will come to an end. Their God, the Great I AM, who revealed Himself to Israel in Egypt as One who heard their cry and knew their sufferings there (Exodus 3:7), cannot bear this revelry. God will intervene and judge the oppressors. Just as He rejects the sound of their worship (Amos 5:21–24), God also finds the noise of their amusement nauseous. These careless leaders of today will tomorrow lead the

pitiful column of captives who go into exile. Thus, with tragic irony, Amos declares that they will be first to the bitter end. These notables of the "chief of the nations" (v. 1) who used "chief ointments" (v. 6) are now to be "first that go captive." Where revelry fills the air, there shall remain only ominous silence (Mays 117). This prophecy emphasizes the unusually strong announcement of judgment that Amos also gives in 4:2, "The Lord GOD hath sworn by his holiness." Mays observes, "That Yahweh takes oath on his own person (as in Jeremiah 22:5, 49:13, 51:14) makes the decree more final, because the total force of Yahweh's integrity is invested in this solemn oath—the ancient Near East's most binding form of commitment" (118).

The language used here is "the strongest possible language God used to express wrath … the language of abhorrence, hatred and chiasm" (Hubbard 195). The Lord abhors the "excellency of Jacob." This pride of Jacob—which might actually be the city of Samaria (Dunn 694)—speaks of Israel's national self-confidence, which meant their displacement of Yahweh as the foundation of their national existence. In the season of great prosperity and success, Israel's leaders have lifted their hearts high in overconfidence, putting their pride in their fortified cities. However, God is about to judge their pride by sending an army that will bring them low. In addition, God hates the palaces of Jacob—the strongholds that give Israel a sense of self-sufficiency and security but are filled with the spoils of robbery and violence. They are like a monument before God as constant reminders of the pride of the rich and the plight of the poor. Mays adds, "The city and its strongholds … enshrines the worst of Israel's guilt. The powerful rich may think themselves invulnerable against any foe, but when Yahweh is against them, their strength is useless and their defenses already breached" (119). Thus, when all has been said and done, God will deliver the city and everything inside to a foreign army. This chapter concludes with the promise that God will raise up a nation against Israel to afflict them (v. 14). Assyria defeated Israel in 721/722 B.C., during the reign of King Hoshea of Israel.

**11 For, behold, the LORD commandeth, and he will smite the great house with breaches, and the little house with clefts.**

In judgment, God will smite the great house with breaches and the small house with clefts. Some scholars have said that the great house stands for Israel and the small house is Judah. For instance, Jerome interprets the former being reduced to branches or ruins, literally, "small drops"; the latter, though injured with "clefts" or rents, which threaten its fall, is still permitted to stand (Mays 120). Other scholars believe that "great house" and "small house" have nothing to do with Israel and Judah. This is because Amos primarily prophesied to the former and not the latter, and there is no other evidence of these terms being used for Israel and Judah. A better interpretation of the verse is that the judgment would come to both wealthy and poor. Both great and small suffered equally. No distinction will be made; the rich and the poor will fall together. When the great houses are all carried away by their captors, the small houses will not escape. Why? Not only are the poor abused and neglected by the wealthy during times of national prosperity, but they will be implicated in the punishment as well, either because they are led astray in worship or because they are politically associated with those in power. Destruction and death do not spare anyone.

**12 Shall horses run upon the rock? will one plow there with oxen? for ye have turned judgment into gall, and the fruit of righteousness into hemlock: 13 Ye which rejoice in a thing of nought, which say, Have we not taken to us horns by our own strength?**

Horses do not run on cliffs like mountain goats, nor can one plough through boulders with an ox. These are both absurd scenarios. In turning "judgement into gall, and the fruit of righteousness into hemlock" (a bitter and noxious plant), the Israelites are acting perversely. Thus, as horses and oxen are useless on a rock, so the Israelites are making justice poisonous. The absurd is happening in Israel. Arnold Schultz interprets this verse as saying, "There is a spiritual and moral order in the universe that is just as impossible to ignore as the natural order. It is as senseless to pervert justice as it is to expect horses to run on the rocks, or for oxen to plow on rock" (835). It is, thus, easier to change the course of nature than the course of God's providence or the laws of His just retribution.

The national leaders feel proud and confident because under Jeroboam, Israel had recaptured some territory that it had formerly lost to Aram (2 Kings 14:25). These recaptured lands included the town of Lodebar in Transjordan (2 Samuel 9:4, 17:27). Amos, however, cleverly make light of this feat by deliberately misspelling the city's name as "Lo-debar" (v. 13, NLT), which means "not a thing" (Mays 122). They have taken nothing of much value. The people are also claiming that they took the town of Karnaim (whose name means "a pair of horns," symbols of strength) by their own strength. It is not they but Yahweh, however, who had strengthened them to achieve this victory over a symbolically strong town. Therefore, Israel's leaders celebrate the capture of nothing and think they have captured it by their own strength (Mays 122).

**14 But, behold, I will raise up against you a nation, O house of Israel, saith the LORD the God of hosts; and they shall afflict you from the entering in of Hemath unto the river of the wilderness.**

Archaeological reports suggest that the capture was exactly and terribly fulfilled just as God had promised. Less than forty years after Amos wrote this prophecy, the Northern Kingdom was destroyed by Sargon of Assyria. "Behold" indicates God's resolute emphasis, as Yahweh had sworn by Himself (v. 8). God, through His power and sovereignty, raises up Sargon and the Assyrian empire to defeat and oppress the nation of Israel. "With power, he identifies himself as the Lord of all armies and with specificity, he directs his announcement to the whole house of Israel" (Hubbard 200). Selfishness, greed, and pride do not only affect the leaders of the nation; they affect everyone. The influence of Israel's leaders has corrupted the nation. Thus, the whole house of Israel is doomed to disaster by the complacency and corruption of their leaders.

Sources:
Anderson, Francis I., and David Noel Freedman. *The Anchor Bible*. 1st Edition. New York: Doubleday, 1989.
Bitrus, Daniel. *Africa Bible Commentary*. Ed. Tokunboh Adeyemo. Grand Rapids, MI: Zondervan, 2006.
Boling, Robert G. *The Anchor Bible: Judges*. Vol. 6A. Garden City, NY: Doubleday & Company, Inc., 1975.
Dunn, James D. G., and J. W. Rogerson. *Eerdmans Commentary on the Bible*. Grand Rapids, MI: W.B. Eerdmans, 2003.
Gowan, Donald E. *The New Interpreter's Bible: A Commentary in Twelve Volumes*. Nashville, TN: Abdingdon Press, 1996.
Hubbard, David Allan. *Joel and Amos: An Introduction and Commentary*. Downers Grove, IL: InterVarsity Press, 1989.
Mays, James Luther. *Amos: A Commentary*. Philadelphia: Westminster, 1969.
Schultz, Arnold. *Wycliffe Bible Commentary*. Chicago: Moody Press, 1962.
Snaith, Norman Henry. *The Book of Amos*. London: Epworth Press, 1945.

# Say It Correctly

Lo-Debar. lo-de-**BAR**.
Karnaim. kar-**NAH**-yim.

# Daily Bible Readings

**MONDAY**
Israel's Guilt and Punishment
(Amos 3:1–11)

**TUESDAY**
Jeroboam II's Reign
(2 Kings 14:23–28)

**WEDNESDAY**
Israel Carried Captive to Assyria
(2 Kings 17:5–23

**THURSDAY**
Judah Carried Captive to Babylon
(2 Kings 25:1–21)

**FRIDAY**
Warning to Rich Oppressors
(James 5:1–6)

**SATURDAY**
The Deserted City
(Lamentations 1)

**SUNDAY**
God Has Got a Plan for This
(Jeremiah 29:10–14)

# Teaching Tips

## Words You Should Know

**A. Lamentation** (Amos 8:10) *kinah* (Heb.)—Dirge, elegy.

**B. Sackcloth** (v. 10) *sak* (Heb.)—Rough woven cloth worn in humiliation and mourning.

## Teacher Preparation

**Unifying Principle—So Done With You!** Some people are so deep into deceit and cheating others that they ignore warnings and must live with the consequences of their wicked ways. What happens to those who do not heed a warning? Amos says that God will no longer overlook their misdeeds and will destroy them for all time.

**A.** Read the Bible Background and Devotional Readings.

**B.** Complete Lesson 4 in the *Precepts For Living Personal Study Guide®*.

**C.** Reread the Focal Verses in a few other translations.

## O—Open the Lesson

**A.** Open with prayer.

**B.** Have a student read Aim for Change.

**C.** Ask for a volunteer to read the In Focus story.

**D.** Discuss how Christians can be faithful in our dealings.

## P—Present the Scriptures

**A.** Ask for volunteers to read the Focal Verses and The People, Places, and Times. Discuss.

**B.** Read and discuss the Background section.

**C.** Encourage students to give thanks for the opportunity today to study God's Word freely in our present society.

## E—Explore the Meaning

**A.** Review and discuss the Search the Scriptures and Discuss the Meaning questions.

**B.** Ask students to share the most significant point they learned and how to use that point this week.

## N—Next Steps for Application

**A.** Discuss the Lesson in Our Society and Make It Happen sections.

**B.** Have the students complete the Follow the Spirit and Remember Your Thoughts sections individually.

**C.** Remind students to read the Daily Bible Readings in preparation for the coming week.

**D.** Close in prayer.

## Worship Guide

For the Superintendent or Teacher
Theme: God Will Never Forget
Song: "Soon and Very Soon"
Devotional Reading: Hosea 11:1–7

# God Will Never Forget

**Bible Background • AMOS 8**
**Printed Text • AMOS 8:1–6, 9–10**
**Devotional Reading • HOSEA 11:1–7**

## Aim for Change

By the end of the lesson, we will: EXPLORE unjust practices and their consequences during Amos' time; REFLECT on how the church practices injustices and seems to be oblivious; ENCOURAGE the church to address injustices practiced within our community of faith.

 In Focus

As Monique pushed her cart down the aisles, she kept scanning the shelves for more bargains. She couldn't believe how much she was saving. "All of these microwave meals for $1.99. I have to stock up on these." Her daughter Keira and son Malik kept bothering her about buying junk food, toys, and video games. Monique kept walking down the aisle and piling food into her cart. "We gon' be eating good this week, y'all. I should've been shopping here all along." When she arrived at the checkout, Monique noticed Lakisha, one of the new church members, working there. As they caught up on old times, Lakisha let her know that it was hard with her schedule to get to all the public assistance appointments she had to go to. "Why do you need public assistance if you are working so much?" "They don't pay me enough," Lakisha said. As Monique finished putting her bags back in her cart, she couldn't help but think about why Lakisha was not getting paid enough and why she could find so many great deals at that store. Something wasn't adding up.

*In this week's lesson, we learn that those who practice injustice will face the consequence of God's judgment.*

## Keep in Mind

"And he said, Amos, what seest thou? And I said, A basket of summer fruit. Then said the LORD unto me, The end is come upon my people of Israel; I will not again pass by them any more" (Amos 8:2).

"And he said, Amos, what seest thou? And I said, A basket of summer fruit. Then said the LORD unto me, The end is come upon my people of Israel; I will not again pass by them any more" (Amos 8:2).

## Focal Verses

**KJV** **Amos 8:1** Thus hath the Lord GOD shewed unto me: and behold a basket of summer fruit.

**2** And he said, Amos, what seest thou? And I said, A basket of summer fruit. Then said the LORD unto me, The end is come upon my people of Israel; I will not again pass by them any more.

**3** And the songs of the temple shall be howlings in that day, saith the Lord GOD: there shall be many dead bodies in every place; they shall cast them forth with silence.

**4** Hear this, O ye that swallow up the needy, even to make the poor of the land to fail,

**5** Saying, When will the new moon be gone, that we may sell corn? and the sabbath, that we may set forth wheat, making the ephah small, and the shekel great, and falsifying the balances by deceit?

**6** That we may buy the poor for silver, and the needy for a pair of shoes; yea, and sell the refuse of the wheat?

**9** And it shall come to pass in that day, saith the Lord GOD, that I will cause the sun to go down at noon, and I will darken the earth in the clear day:

**10** And I will turn your feasts into mourning, and all your songs into lamentation; and I will bring up sackcloth upon all loins, and baldness upon every head; and I will make it as the mourning of an only son, and the end thereof as a bitter day.

**NLT** **Amos 8:1** Then the Sovereign LORD showed me another vision. In it I saw a basket filled with ripe fruit.

**2** "What do you see, Amos?" he asked. I replied, "A basket full of ripe fruit." Then the LORD said, "Like this fruit, Israel is ripe for punishment! I will not delay their punishment again.

**3** In that day the singing in the Temple will turn to wailing. Dead bodies will be scattered everywhere. They will be carried out of the city in silence. I, the Sovereign LORD, have spoken!"

**4** Listen to this, you who rob the poor and trample down the needy!

**5** You can't wait for the Sabbath day to be over and the religious festivals to end so you can get back to cheating the helpless. You measure out grain with dishonest measures and cheat the buyer with dishonest scales.

**6** And you mix the grain you sell with chaff swept from the floor. Then you enslave poor people for one piece of silver or a pair of sandals.

**9** "In that day," says the Sovereign LORD, "I will make the sun go down at noon and darken the earth while it is still day.

**10** I will turn your celebrations into times of mourning and your singing into weeping. You will wear funeral clothes and shave your heads to show your sorrow—as if your only son had died. How very bitter that day will be!"

### The People, Places, and Times

**Amos.** His personal name means "one who is carried," and he was a prophet from Judah who ministered in Israel around 750 B.C. Some might describe the prophet Amos as a "burden bearer." He carried a heavy burden for his people, or his people were a burden he carried.

As a prophet, Amos was a primary figure among the series of courageous men known as the minor prophets. They are called "minor" only because their books are far shorter than the major prophets such as Isaiah, Jeremiah, and Ezekiel. In Judaism, the minor prophets' writings are commonly known as the "Book of the Twelve."

**New Moon.** The New Moon was a festival held at the beginning of every lunar month. The priests would offer a burnt offering. This consisted of two male calves, one ram, and seven spotless lambs combined with a drink offering of wine. These offerings were accompanied by the blowing of the trumpet or shofar. All trade and commerce were stopped as on the Sabbath. The spiritual significance of the New Moon festival can be found in the setting apart of a natural division of time.

## Background

Amos documented the reasons for God's judgment against Israel being legal injustice, economic exploitation, religious hypocrisy, luxurious indulgence, and boastful complacency. The violations resulted in the nation being doomed, but sparing individuals who repented.

The Lord gave Amos a series of visions that described Israel's complete destruction. The first vision that Amos received was a swarm of locusts. These locusts would come at the most inopportune time, right after the king's portion had been harvested and the next crop was beginning to grow. If locusts came, then there would be a famine for the people. After Amos pleaded to spare the people, the Lord relented and showed him a devouring fire that consumed the land. Amos pleaded again and the Lord relented. Next Amos was shown a plumb line. This was a weight that builders used to make sure that walls were constructed properly. Israel would be shown to not be in line with God's standards and torn down. Before Amos could plead for God's mercy, the Lord confirmed that the nation of Israel would be judged.

Then Amos was confronted by Amaziah, the priest of Bethel. This confrontation resulted in Amos being charged with conspiracy against the king. Amos had denounced the legitimacy of the shrine at Bethel and the people's worship. As a result, Amaziah told Amos to go back to Judah and earn a living as a prophet there. Amos responded to this by stating that he was a farmer and a shepherd and that his prophetic calling was not for monetary gain, but a divine mandate from the Lord. He prophesied that Amaziah's family would die and that foreigners would claim his property. Amos added that Amaziah himself would die in a foreign land. After this the Lord showed Amos a vision of a basket of ripe fruit and predicted the end of Israel.

## At-A-Glance

1. Human Grief (Amos 8:1–3)
2. Cosmic Grief (vv. 4–6, 9–10)

## In Depth

### 1. Human Grief (Amos 8:1–3)

Amos' vision begins with a basket of summer fruit. This fruit is a symbol of Israel's impending judgment. The summer fruit was the fruit gathered in the harvest season. God is communicating a message to Israel through Amos: the time is ripe. The end has come for Israel and they are ripe for God's wrath. The Lord will spare them no longer. He can no longer offer them grace and show patience in the face of their persistent injustice and disobedience.

The Lord goes on to say that Israel's temple songs would turn into the sounds of grief and misery. The temple in Bethel was the foundation of the nation. It was the spiritual foundation to the political kingdom. The destruction of this temple would definitely mean the destruction of the Northern Kingdom. The "dead bodies" everywhere would only elicit the response of silence. It suggests that because of the horror of this scene, anyone who is left will be at a loss for words.

### 2. Cosmic Grief (vv. 4–6, 9–10)

After the Lord shows them the grief they will experience, He shows them the reason for the coming judgment. They will be grieved because He has been grieved. He has put up with their trampling of the poor and needy. They anticipate the end of the New Moons and Sabbaths so they can go on cheating the people by selling inferior products and creating dishonest scales so they can make a profit. Instead of seeking justice for the poor, they seek ways to enslave them for negligible amounts of money: the price of sandals. They clearly have a low perspective on human life.

The Lord announces what will happen to them on the day of punishment. It will be cosmic in scope. The sun will go down at noon. The earth will be darkened in broad daylight. In 763 B.C. there was a solar eclipse, and in 759 there was an earthquake. The two events were historically distinct, but Amos speaks of them both happening on the Day of the Lord. Rather than these two events fulfilling Amos' prophecy, he is appealing to their recent occurrence in order to shock the people into realizing that God will bring both natural "disasters" at once rather than separately next time. The darkness announced here will remind Israel of the judgment on Egypt. Where before the Lord's judgment fell on Pharaoh and his kingdom, now the Lord's judgment falls on the Northern Kingdom for their own stubbornness and disobedience. It will be a day of mourning. Feasting and celebration will cease; all the songs they sing will be gloomy funeral dirges. The Lord's judgment will cause them to wear sackcloth and shave their heads, a sign of repentance toward God. By then it will be too late. They will mourn just like the Egyptians mourned for their firstborn children. God will remember their sins of injustice and oppression and judge accordingly.

## Search the Scriptures

1. What did God show Amos (Amos 8:1)?

2. When will God cause the sun to go down and what will happen to the earth (v. 9)?

3. What was God going to turn their feasts into (v. 10)?

## Discuss the Meaning

1. How are we currently experiencing injustice due to the hunger for more profits?

2. What is our motivation for fighting injustice since the Scriptures say that God will ultimately judge those who oppress others?

## Lesson in Our Society

The profit motive drives most of what we do in a capitalist economy. While this has created many blessings for those with no opportunity, it has also created a culture in which we worship at the god of "profit." Whatever will sell, we will sell it regardless of whether it affects our fellow citizens negatively. As long as we can find a way to boost our finances, we buy and sell with no regard for the consequences. The Lord calls us to seek justice even in our commerce. These things brought judgment on the nation of Israel and may bring judgment on us as well.

## Make It Happen

The greed and injustice of many corporate and business leaders is all around us if we open our eyes to see it. In the coming week, find an example online or in a newspaper of injustice. Study it to discover ways greed has led to oppression of the weak and vulnerable.

## Follow the Spirit

What God wants me to do:

_____

_____

_____

_____

## Remember Your Thoughts

Special insights I have learned:

_____

_____

_____

_____

## More Light on the Text

Amos 8:1–6, 9–10

1 Thus hath the Lord GOD shewed unto me: and behold a basket of summer fruit. 2 And he said, Amos, what seest thou? And I said, A basket of summer fruit. Then said the LORD unto me, The end is come upon my people of Israel; I will not again pass by them any more. 3 And the songs of the temple shall be howlings in that day, saith the Lord GOD: there shall be many dead bodies in every place; they shall cast them forth with silence.

In the closing verses of chapter 7, Amos had confronted the priest Amaziah and pronounced an oracle of judgment against him for his failure to believe the Word of God (vv. 6–17). Now he resumes where he left off and continues the account of his visions. He begins by authenticating his fourth vision the same way as the previous ones, by declaring that the Lord showed him a vision (7:1, 4, 7). In the last vision in 7:7–9, Amos declared that the end was certain but here he declares its imminence. The present vision is to reiterate and make final the previous one. He sees a basket of summer fruit (Heb. *kayits*, **KAH-yeets**) and heard a response from the Lord that the "end" (Heb. *kets*, **KEHTS**) has come. Usually, summer fruit was not preserved but eaten as soon as it was gathered. So the Lord hints by this symbol and the pun on the word "end" that the kingdom of Israel is now ripe for destruction, and punishment must descend on it without delay. The Lord "will not again pass by them any more," that is, He will spare them no longer. However, the Hebrew word "end" here does not merely refer to its ripeness for judgment in a temporal sense, but also its destruction and devastation.

There will be two responses. First, all the joy shall be turned into mourning. The songs of joy would be turned into yells, that is, into sounds of lamentation because of the multitude of the dead on the ground on every side. The word "howlings" describes an inarticulate, shattering scream common during funerals, particularly in times of sudden devastation. Second, there will be silence, an appropriate response to God's severe judgment, accompanied by a destruction of untold proportions—"there shall be many dead bodies in every place."

4 Hear this, O ye that swallow up the needy, even to make the poor of the land to fail, 5 Saying, When will the new moon be gone, that we may sell corn? and the sabbath, that we may set forth wheat, making the ephah small, and the shekel great, and

494

falsifying the balances by deceit? **6 That we may buy the poor for silver, and the needy for a pair of shoes; yea, and sell the refuse of the wheat?**

Amos gives the reasons for the judgment and punishment. Israel fails to take care of its needy and poor, but instead exploit them and swallow them up. The poor, vulnerable, and unprotected members of the society are treated harshly and unjustly. The rich grow richer on the back of the poor, and the poor become poorer. Yet these oppressive merchants keep going on with their religious activities, observing the Sabbath and other festivals. Worship, fraud, exploitation, and oppression go on simultaneously. However, they keep the Sabbath and the festivals as mere formal rituals; their minds are not engaged. Their worship is superficial, formal, and hypocritical. They detest the rest of the Sabbath, wanting to keep it as short as possible if they can, so as not to rest from their frauds. They consider the time spent for the festivals as business time lost. Amos quotes the merchants to show their attitude toward worship, "When will the new moon be gone, that we may sell corn? and the sabbath, that we may set forth wheat…?" For them, the day of rest is a day wasted, when the poor could be exploited and profit added. There is an anxious longing for the religious observances to end so that they can resume their unethical commerce. Their greed causes them to use deception to increase their profits. On the one hand, they reduce the weight, "making the ephah small," and on the other hand, they make "the shekel great," that is, increased the prices both ways by paring down the quantity which they sold and by obtaining more silver by fictitious weights, and weighing in uneven balances. Customers have no choice but to pay more than what the items they purchase are worth.

Merchants buy the poor and confiscate their property as payment for debts. It sounds like modern-day "payday lending." Israel's sins are descriptive of our contemporary society.

For those living in the Western world, materialism is a value system that often leads to injustice. Possessiveness is a great challenge. It is a world of opulence, one drowned in affluence. It raises several questions: At whose expense are we being enriched? Are workers being underpaid? What of those who rig the market, speculate with currency, or specialize in the financial subterfuge that falls only just short of outright theft? We must also remember that human greed for profit at the expense of the innocent destroys a society. In fact, one could say that of all the evils that plague human society, greediness is perhaps one of the most common and the most dangerous. It is an insatiable desire for money and power, a predatory impulse that makes the lives of others mere prey in the path of one's own advancement, and an acceptance of extortion as normal business. Its goal is entirely the satisfaction of self, its victims being all those weak enough to be used for personal ends. It is indeed akin to a kind of religion, evoking profound love of self and happy acceptance of the ruin of others, neglecting God's command to love God and neighbors first (Matthew 22:36–40). But insatiable greed is so fundamentally foreign to the whole truth of God that it must not be tolerated but seriously condemned. But as Amos sees it, the foundations of avarice are so firm that only something earth-shattering could weaken its proud structures.

**9 And it shall come to pass in that day, saith the Lord GOD, that I will cause the sun to go down at noon, and I will darken the earth in the clear day.**

The first phrase "and it shall come to pass" here translates the Hebrew word *vehaya* (**veh-hah-YAH**), usually denoting that what follows as occurring in the future. "In that day" points to a time of the Lord's visitation to bring additional judgment and disasters on Israel. Israel needs to know that what is going to happen to them is the Day of the Lord. Amos refers to a devastation, namely a total eclipse of the sun. The Lord will create a day of darkness that will turn their merriment into misery, and transform their happy days into lamentation and mourning. The day of light will become a day of darkness, the eclipsed sun symbolizing that the light of God's face will be hidden from Israel. There are similar images of the Lord bringing darkness in times of judgment in several passages (see Isaiah 59:10; Jeremiah 13:16, 15:9). The imagery here of darkness on a clear day is shocking and symbolically expresses the sudden and unexpected end of Israel's prosperity and the darkening of her glory days, just when the nation seems at its pinnacle of power. Nations today must be warned because God has not changed.

With the media making news available every hour of every day, we hear about so many natural disasters around the world on a daily basis. On the one hand, we need to be careful not to be desensitized by the overabundance of images. We must respond with awe and lamentation at each disaster, just as the Israelites would have. On the other hand, we must also take care not to understand every natural disaster as a punishment and everyone affected by a disaster as deserving. Amos is making a point: Injustice will ultimately be eradicated by God because God has both the power and compassion to do so, even to darken the day at noon if He chooses because the poor are being oppressed.

**10 And I will turn your feasts into mourning, and all your songs into lamentation; and I will bring up sackcloth upon all loins, and baldness upon every head; and I will make it as the mourning of an only son, and the end thereof as a bitter day.**

The consequences of Israel's failure to follow the Lord continue to reverberate in verse 10. Because of God's judgments, happy days will become harrowing days, festivals will be turned into mourning and joy to sadness. Because Israel has turned God's justice and righteousness into bitterness and poison (cf. 5:7, 6:12), He will turn their joy into grief. One cannot celebrate light and live in darkness. Baldness on every head suggests that every person in Israel will be touched by the grief-causing calamity. The Lord vows to make the coming grief "as the mourning of an only son." The loss of an only son produces an unspeakable grief. Such great sorrow attends the loss of an only son because not only is all hope for continuing one's family gone, but also the provision for one's old age (cf. Jeremiah 6:26; Zechariah 12:10). Mourning an only son is always a bitter experience—it is a picture of hopelessness. The day that starts out with mourning an only son is sure to end as bitter as it began. If we really desire the light of God to shine on us, then we must walk in the light.

Sources:

Achtemmeier, Elizabeth. *Minor Prophets 1.* Understanding the Bible Commentary Series. Grand Rapids, MI: Baker Books, 1996.

Craigie, Peter C. *Twelve Prophets.* The Daily Study Bible Series. Vol. 1. Louisville, KY: Westminster John Knox Press, 1984.

Nogalski, James D. *The Book of the Twelve: Hosea–Jonah.* Macon, GA: Smyth and Helwys Publishing, Inc., 2011.

Smith, Billy K., and Franklin S. Page. *Amos, Obadiah, Jonah. The New American Commentary.* Vol. 19B. Nashville, TN: Broadman & Holman Publishers, 1995.

Stuart, Douglas. *Hosea–Jonah.* Word Biblical Commentary. Vol. 31. Dallas: Word Publishers, 2002.

Waard, Jan de, and William Allen Smalley. *A Translator's Handbook on the Book of Amos.* UBS Handbook Series. Stuttgart, Germany: United Bible Societies, 1979.

## Say It Correctly

Amaziah. am-uh-**ZEE**-uh.
Ephah. ee-**FAH**.

## Daily Bible Readings

**MONDAY**
A Famine of Hearing God's Word
(Amos 8:11–14)

**TUESDAY**
Reaping the Whirlwind
(Hosea 8:7–14)

**WEDNESDAY**
Days of Punishment Have Come
(Hosea 9:5–9)

**THURSDAY**
Israel's Sin Shall Be Destroyed
(Hosea 10:1–8)

**FRIDAY**
Israel Refused to Return to Me
(Hosea 11:1–7)

**SATURDAY**
God Will Remember Their Iniquity
(Jeremiah 14:1–10)

**SUNDAY**
A Day of Mourning and Lamentation
(Amos 8:1–6, 9–10)

# Notes

_____

_____

_____

_____

# Teaching Tips

## Words You Should Know

**A. Parable** (Micah 2:4) *mashal* (Heb.)—A proverb or byword.

**B. Prophesy** (v. 11) *nataf* (Heb.)—To cause to drip or make words flow.

## Teacher Preparation

**Unifying Principle—You've Got to Change Your Evil Ways**. People do not want to be confronted with their social and moral abuse of others. What is the result of their failure to acknowledge their evil ways? Micah prophesied that God would give no rest to those who practice evil against His faithful ones.

**A.** Read the Bible Background and Devotional Readings.

**B.** Complete Lesson 5 in the *Precepts For Living Personal Study Guide®*.

**C.** Reread the Focal Verses in a modern translation.

## O—Open the Lesson

**A.** Open with prayer.

**B.** Ask for a volunteer to read the Aim for Change section.

**C.** Ask for another volunteer to read the In Focus story.

## P—Present the Scriptures

**A.** Ask for volunteers to read the Focal Verses and The People, Places, and Times. Discuss.

**B.** Read and discuss the Background section.

**C.** Encourage students to earnestly seek and follow the Lord's instruction.

## E—Explore the Meaning

**A.** Review and discuss the Search the Scriptures and Discuss the Meaning questions and the Lesson in Our Society section.

**B.** Ask students to share the most significant point they learned and how to use that point this week.

## N—Next Steps for Application

**A.** Complete the Follow the Spirit and Remember Your Thoughts sections.

**B.** Remind students to read the Daily Bible Readings in preparation for next week's lesson.

**C.** Close in prayer, thanking God for His love and instruction.

## Worship Guide

For the Superintendent or Teacher
Theme: No Rest for the Wicked
Song: "I Have Decided to Follow Jesus"
Devotional Reading: Proverbs 11:1–10

# No Rest for the Wicked

**Bible Background • MICAH 2**
**Printed Text • MICAH 2:4–11**
**Devotional Reading • PROVERBS 11:1–10**

## Aim for Change

By the end of the lesson, we will: EXPLORE Micah's depiction of people who deny their wrongdoing in the community; EXPRESS feelings about people who attempt to justify the evil and harm they commit; and RESPOND with appropriate opposition to those engaged in wrongdoing in the community.

### In Focus

Bill ran to his office in a panic. He didn't think this could ever happen to him. His plan had been working for the last three years, and he had no idea it would all come crashing down on him today. He immediately started emptying file cabinets. His secretary Doris came in with her notepad. "You won't need that notepad, Doris. There's only one thing I need you to do for me right now," he said. "What's that, Bill?" she asked. "See all this stuff?" He motioned toward all the papers on the floor. "Get rid of it." Bill wasted no time and did not even check to see if she comprehended what he said. He did not have time. They were coming, and if they found any shred of evidence, he would be indicted. Bill thought about what this would mean for his career, his family, his reputation. After all, he had to do what he'd done to further his political career. Right? His stomach began to churn and he became nauseated. They had to get these records out of here. "Hurry up, Doris," Bill said. "Now is not the time to hesitate." Just then, they heard a knock on the door. Could it be that Bill was going to reap what he had sown?

*In today's lesson, we learn that we cannot justify evil and wrongdoing in our communities and those who do will face the judgment of God.*

## Keep in Mind

"O thou that art named the house of Jacob, is the spirit of the LORD straitened? are these his doings? do not my words do good to him that walketh uprightly?" (Micah 2:7).

"O thou that art named the house of Jacob, is the spirit of the LORD straitened? are these his doings? do not my words do good to him that walketh uprightly?" (Micah 2:7).

## Focal Verses

**KJV** **Micah 2:4** In that day shall one take up a parable against you, and lament with a doleful lamentation, and say, We be utterly spoiled: he hath changed the portion of my people: how hath he removed it from me! turning away he hath divided our fields.

**5** Therefore thou shalt have none that shall cast a cord by lot in the congregation of the LORD.

**6** Prophesy ye not, say they to them that prophesy: they shall not prophesy to them, that they shall not take shame.

**7** O thou that art named the house of Jacob, is the spirit of the LORD straitened? are these his doings? do not my words do good to him that walketh uprightly?

**8** Even of late my people is risen up as an enemy: ye pull off the robe with the garment from them that pass by securely as men averse from war.

**9** The women of my people have ye cast out from their pleasant houses; from their children have ye taken away my glory for ever.

**10** Arise ye, and depart; for this is not your rest: because it is polluted, it shall destroy you, even with a sore destruction.

**11** If a man walking in the spirit and falsehood do lie, saying, I will prophesy unto thee of wine and of strong drink; he shall even be the prophet of this people.

**NLT** **Micah 2:4** In that day your enemies will make fun of you by singing this song of despair about you: "We are finished, completely ruined! God has confiscated our land, taking it from us. He has given our fields to those who betrayed us."

**5** Others will set your boundaries then, and the LORD's people will have no say in how the land is divided.

**6** "Don't say such things," the people respond. "Don't prophesy like that. Such disasters will never come our way!"

**7** Should you talk that way, O family of Israel? Will the LORD's Spirit have patience with such behavior? If you would do what is right, you would find my words comforting.

**8** Yet to this very hour my people rise against me like an enemy! You steal the shirts right off the backs of those who trusted you, making them as ragged as men returning from battle.

**9** You have evicted women from their pleasant homes and forever stripped their children of all that God would give them.

**10** Up! Begone! This is no longer your land and home, for you have filled it with sin and ruined it completely.

**11** Suppose a prophet full of lies would say to you, "I'll preach to you the joys of wine and alcohol!" That's just the kind of prophet you would like!

### The People, Places, and Times

**Micah.** His name is actually a sentence that befittingly proclaims "Who is like Yah(weh)?" Very little is known about the prophet. He was from the town of Moresheth-Gath, which is approximately twenty miles southwest of Jerusalem and centrally located halfway between Jerusalem and Gaza. The prophet ministered from 740–690 B.C. during the reigns of Jotham, Ahaz, and Hezekiah. The prophet informs us that the word of "I Am" (Yahweh/The Lord) came to him through a vision. As such, Micah boldly proclaims, "I am full of power by the spirit of the Lord, and of judgment, and of might" (from 3:8), all of which are reflected in his oracles (messages from God). These oracles concerned the destruction of Jerusalem and Samaria due to injustice, corrupt government, idolatry, and dishonest economic principles. One of Micah's most amazing feats was that even within his prophecy of doom, he was able to remain hopeful regarding Jerusalem's future. He foretold of the Messiah and even the city of His birth. Micah is known as one of the twelve minor prophets, a category based solely on the length of the author's work, not their importance or status.

**House of Jacob.** Jacob was a a patriarch of the nation of Israel. The name Jacob means "heel grabber." God renamed Jacob as a result of spiritual transformation (Genesis 35:10). He is no longer Jacob the heel grabber but Israel, or "he who strives with God."

**Lamentation.** A lamentation is an elegy or dirge. The first biblical example of a lamentation is the lament of David over Saul and Jonathan (2 Samuel 1:17–27). The lamentation was a frequent accompaniment of mourning (Amos 8:10). Prophecy sometimes took the form of a lament when it predicted calamity (Ezekiel 27:32; Isaiah 47:1).

## Background

Micah ministered during a time in which Assyria enjoyed great power and influence. The Northern Kingdom of Israel had already fallen. King Ahaz of Judah made an arrangement with Assyria to prevent the fall of Judah. The Southern Kingdom would pay large tribute and honor Assyria's gods. As a result, idol worship spread throughout Judah.

In the opening chapter of Micah, the Lord invited the nations to be witnesses as He judged His people. Micah 1 describes the Lord being roused from His throne to execute judgment in response to the transgressions of His people. He brought judg-

ment on Samaria, the capital of Israel and the center of idol worship. Likewise, He brought judgment on Jerusalem, which was rife with idolatry.

Micah uttered oracles of judgment against Samaria and then against Jerusalem. While most of the oracles were directed at Judah, Israel was also mentioned in the pronouncement of judgment in order to serve as an example and warning of what will happen to Judah.

Samaria would be destroyed. The walls would be broken down, the foundations would be laid bare, and vineyards would be planted where their streets once were (Micah 1:6). Her destruction came in 722 B.C., after a three-year siege by the Assyrian army.

The Lord also named specific cities in Judah where His judgment would be visited. The Lord gave His reasons for His judgment against Judah: the greed and covetousness of the rich and the oppression of the lower class.

Micah 2 begins with the description of the deeds of the wealthy land barons and their wanton greed. The rich seized the houses and land of the poor and stole their possessions. The Lord promised to reward their evil with evil and that the oppressors would themselves be oppressed.

## At-A-Glance

1. The Land Divided (Micah 2:4–5)
2. The Lord Incited (vv. 6–9)
3. The Lies Invited (vv. 10–11)

# In Depth

## 1. The Land Divided (Micah 2:4–5)

The rich are getting richer at the expense of the poor. Greedy land barons confiscate the lands, homes, and goods of the poor. The Lord promises judgment for this injustice and tells them that they will suffer the same injustice (vv. 4–5). Assyria will confiscate the lands, homes, and goods that the rich have taken. Further, they will taunt Judah with their own lamentations.

The people of Judah will lament that they are "utterly spoiled" and that the Lord has taken away their inheritance. Their lands will be taken from them and given to their enemies. The "fields" that have been unjustly acquired will be divided among their conquerors.

Though their lament is in response to divine judgment, the elements of the lament include charges against the Lord. They accuse the Lord of unjustly giving their rightful possession, or portion, to others. They also lament that He has turned away from them, giving their enemies the fields that once belonged to the house of Jacob.

## 2. The Lord Incited (vv. 6–9)

The people of Judah have no interest in Micah's message of judgment. "Don't prophesy like that," they say (v. 6, NLT). They do not believe that any calamity will befall them. During this time, there are false prophets in Judah that only prophesy peace and blessing. The wealthy people of Judah prefer to hear the false messages. They do not want to hear any prophecies that expose their faults or demand change.

So, the Lord challenges them: "Is the spirit of the LORD straitened? are these his doings?" (from v. 7). In other words, "Has the patience of the Lord run short? Are these His deeds?" The false prophets have been preaching messages of the Lord's patience and long-suffering without preaching about His willingness to judge and discipline His people. When God established His covenant with Israel on Mount Sinai, He stated that He is "slow to anger" (Exodus 34:6, NLT). The belief that God is patient and forgiving was central to Israel's theology. Many believe that love will prevent the Lord from punishing them, and false teachers of Micah's time encourage this belief (v. 11). The people do not want to be confronted with their sin and prefer to continue in their wicked ways.

The Lord continues, "Do not my words do good to him that walketh uprightly?" The righteous have no fear of judgment; those who walk uprightly can expect to be rewarded. This also implies that judgment can be averted with a behavioral change. Judah, however, has not been walking uprightly; they have engaged in wicked behavior characterized by greed and covetousness. They evicte widows from their property and strip children of their inheritance. They take personal possessions from the unsuspecting and leave them with nothing. Instead of becoming instruments of the Lord's justice, Judah has engaged in social violence toward the weak and vulnerable.

## 3. The Lies Invited (vv. 10–11)

The Lord gives His sentence against Judah: "Up! Begone! This is no longer your land and home, for you have filled it with sin and ruined it completely" (v. 10, NLT). The powerful land barons will be evicted from the very property they stole. In the same way that they stripped the poor, widows, and orphans of their lands and possessions, the Lord will strip them.

The people of Judah have no regard for the Lord's message (v. 11). They prefer the false teachings of the prophets. Wine and strong drink represent prosperity. The people are looking for someone who will give only messages of peace and prosperity, rather than change and judgment. Instead of the truth, they would rather hear lies. This is a definite sign that they are truly not interested in doing God's will and seeking justice; they only seek their own selfish ends.

## Search the Scriptures

1. How does the Lord punish Judah for their evil practices (Micah 2:4–5)?

2. What evil does the Lord judge them for (vv. 8–9)?

3. What is the message the people would like to hear (v. 11)?

## Discuss the Meaning

1. Judah could not reconcile the Lord's patience and His promise of judgment. How can we develop an accurate and balanced understanding of God as Righteous Judge and Loving Father?

2. The people of Judah only wanted to hear words of prosperity. How can we make sure that we listen to all God's words and not just what we want to hear?

## Lesson in Our Society

The effects of greed can be felt throughout our society. Corporations have crushed the lives of countless people in their quest to make a profit. As a society, we have sought luxuries at the expense of workers and their wages. We put our material comforts ahead of justice for others. God is not pleased with this. Instead of wanting to hear the truth, we would rather hear preachers tell us about how much more money we are going to get or what expensive house or car God is going to give us. The Lord wants us to repent of our evil ways so we can hear the truth and seek justice for the oppressed.

## Make It Happen

Greed was the driving force behind Judah's unjust ways. So often, the world prompts us to get all we can, even at the expense of others. Instead God calls us to seek out the welfare of the poor and weak. One way that we can do that is fight against modern slavery. Take some time to learn more about the conditions and what you can do at the "Not For Sale" website (http://www.notforsalecampaign.org/about/slavery/slavery-faq).

## Follow the Spirit

What God wants me to do:

_____

_____

_____

_____

## Remember Your Thoughts

Special insights I have learned:

_____

_____

_____

_____

## More Light on the Text

### Micah 2:4–11

**4 In that day shall one take up a parable against you, and lament with a doleful lamentation, and say, We be utterly spoiled: he hath changed the portion of my people: how hath he removed it from me! turning away he hath divided our fields. 5 Therefore thou**

**shalt have none that shall cast a cord by lot in the congregation of the LORD.**

Beginning with verse 2, the prophet Micah presents a portrait of God's reversal of Judah's situation. In verses 1–2, the oppressing classes ruined others; they had used violence to deprive others of their possessions and take the fields of the poor. Now in verse 4, the tables are turned: the oppressors will become the oppressed, and their enemies will divide up their land. The Lord will take the fields away from the scheming land-grabbers in Israel and give them to the treacherous Assyrians. The rich had seized the fields of their helpless victims (v. 2); now the Lord will take those fields and turn them over to enemies. So the rich are dispossessed of their ill-gotten property. Micah quotes the rich as saying, "We be utterly spoiled: he hath changed the portion of my people: how hath he removed it from me!" When the disaster comes, the rich landowners will be mocked. "People will ridicule you" (NIV) is literally "he will lift up against you a parable." The Hebrew word *mashal* (**mah-SHAHL**), translated as "parable," is used here with the negative sense of a byword.

The prophet speaks on behalf of God (v. 5). He uses the word "therefore" to link this verse with the preceding verses, showing both the result and extent of the judgment. In the Old Testament, there were two ways in which land was returned to its original owner: first in the year of Jubilee (Leviticus 25), second by lot at the time of Joshua (Joshua 14:2), a practice that continued and was alluded to in Psalm 16:6 (KJV). The latter is what Micah refers to here. The families of the oppressors will have no representation. The punishment fits the crime. What a solemn warning against greed, materialism and oppression. Because the guilty parties have dealt with their neighbors' fields unjustly, none of their

descendants will be left in the Lord's covenant community who can use a cord (measuring line) to divide up the land by lot. So they will be cut off from the promises of the Lord's people. They will have no one to claim their inheritance, either because their family will be completely wiped out or they will all be in exile. People who have a desperate greed for land and material wealth put their own desires far above the more basic needs of others, but such people will also learn the emptiness of riches, lands, and materials at their loss.

**6 Prophesy ye not, say they to them that prophesy: they shall not prophesy to them, that they shall not take shame. 7 O thou that art named the house of Jacob, is the spirit of the LORD straitened? are these his doings? do not my words do good to him that walketh uprightly?**

How true is the axiom that truth hurts! It is hardly surprising that Micah's stern message to the rich did not bring him popularity. Instead, it aroused opposition and earned for him mockery and rebuke, just as it did for Isaiah (Isaiah 28:9–10, 30:9–11) and Amos (Amos 7:12–13). Micah's audience, particularly the wealthy and land-grabbers, cannot accept his message. The message sounds offensive to them, so they command him to stop saying such things as he had said in 2:1–5. The verb used for prophesy is *nataf* (Heb., **nah-TAHF**), which means "to drip." Used in this context, it has a connotation of driveling or foaming at the mouth. The false prophets are really telling the Lord's prophets, "Stop foaming at the mouth," which refers to ecstatic prophecy. Ironically, the false prophets are described as doing the same thing. In their rejection of the prophets' message and the ensuing shame, the false prophets in fact mock themselves. The same is true today:

charlatans reject all judgment, prophecy, and proclamation. They cannot believe that disaster and disgrace will overtake them because they think God will not do such things. It is, to them, a figment of Micah's imagination, but they are wrong. The greedy oppressors are confident that no evil will trouble them. They believed that Micah is wrong when he says that God is devising evil against them and that the day will come when these swindlers will have no representative in the Lord's assembly.

Micah's opponents use rhetorical questions to say, "Do not even mention judgment. God is not annoyed." The word *katsar* (Heb., **kah-TSAR**), translated "straitened," literally means "short." Here Micah turns the words of the evildoers against them by asking of the Lord is "short of spirit," an idiom for "impatient" or "quick-tempered." The false prophets are teaching erroneously that the Lord's patience has no limits (cf. Exodus 34:6–7a). They cannot believe that the Lord would really lose His patience, especially with them. Surely, He must be able to put up easily with them despite their sins. So, they ask, "Is the Lord short-tempered," "Does the Lord get angry quickly?" Without waiting for an answer, they ask another question, "Are these things that you say will happen the deeds of God?" The final question admits that God is righteous, but if this question comes from the mouths of the oppressors, it shows that they assume that they also are among those who walk uprightly, and can thus expect that God will speak kindly to them. This assumption underlines their moral blindness. The point is that God's words or promises cause good to happen to the one who walks uprightly.

**8 Even of late my people is risen up as an enemy: ye pull off the robe with the garment from them that pass by securely as men averse from war. 9 The women of my people have ye cast out from their pleasant houses; from their children have ye taken away my glory for ever.**

Micah continues to describe the offenses of his hearers. He lists the specific sins of the people. God calls them "my people." However, their behavior does not reflect that of those who belong to God. It is a sad case of God's people living ungodly lives. He says, "Even of late," that is, only recently you have pulled off the robe of those who walked securely and men who were averse to war, a reference to the innocent and peaceful travellers. The women and children were not spared the humiliation and atrocities. The former were driven away from their houses, suggesting that these women might have been widows. The wealthy not only dispossessed women but also disinherited their children. Thus, the children are left without property, money, or security. Doubtless, a society cannot be in a lower state of morality than when it oppresses and exploits the vulnerable in it. Micah's denouncements retain a pressing relevance in a world where such conditions continue. Covetousness and greed still have the same devastating results for defenseless women and children and the unprotected poor. For those who are called Christians, it is important that our character mirrors that of Christ.

**10 Arise ye, and depart; for this is not your rest: because it is polluted, it shall destroy you, even with a sore destruction.**

This verse takes up again the theme of verse 4 and announces the fate of the rich oppressors. The rich must get up and go into exile. The oppressors among God's people rise up like an enemy to increase their wealth and power at the expense of others among their own people; now the Lord tells them to prepare to leave their ill-gotten land and possessions behind. They who had evicted others from their land are about to be evicted themselves; they will go away into exile. Their wrongfully acquired land will no longer be their possession. The reason is that they polluted (Heb. *tame'*, **tah-MEH**) the land which means to become unclean sexually, religiously, or ceremonially. As the Promised Land it was meant to be their resting place (Heb. *menukhah*, **meh-noo-KHAH**) but they had defiled it with their sins and ruined it beyond all remedy. Others will take over their property acquired by fraud and oppression.

**11 If a man walking in the spirit and falsehood do lie, saying, I will prophesy unto thee of wine and of strong drink; he shall even be the prophet of this people.**

The section ends in verse 11 as the prophet returns to practice of false prophecy. Micah says that his hearers are so deluded that if a preacher or prophet are to come along preaching the gospel of wine and strong drink, or prosperity gospel as it is known today, they will hire him immediately. Here, such a prophet is called a liar and deceiver, obviously because he does not tell the truth and so leads others astray. His message is one of peace and prosperity, "plenty of wine and beer" (NIV). The sinful, covenant-breaking people deserve that kind of prophet. Anyone who promises greater affluence will gain a hearing. False prophets are happy to oblige with "feel-good messages" so long as their hearers feed them and give them money (3:5, 11). The tests of true prophets are given in Deuteronomy 13:1–3, 18:17–22: A prophet's message must not contradict or disagree with the previous revelation of truth through true prophets (cf. Isaiah 8:19–20), and his predic-

tions must come true. These prophets fail on both counts.

Today there are still false prophets and teachers both inside and outside the church. In recent years, some preachers throughout the world have not only made predictions about the coming of the Lord but also about those who might be elected to certain political offices. Unfortunately they have been proven wrong. There are still swindlers and hucksters who "peddle the word of God for profit" (from 2 Corinthians 2:17, NIV). Jesus issued a warning about them (Matthew 24:4–5, 10–11, 23–24); so did Paul and John (1 Timothy 4:1–2; 1 John 2:18–19, 4:1–3). Such so-called ministers may masquerade as "apostles of Christ," but in reality they are "false apostles" and servants of Satan (2 Corinthians 11:13–15). They will exist as long as there are people who "will gather around them a great number of teachers to say what their itching ears want to hear" (from 2 Timothy 4:3, NIV).

Sources:
Allen, Leslie C. *The Books of Joel, Obadiah, Jonah and Micah*. New International Commentary of the Old Testament. Grand Rapids, MI: Wm. B. Eerdmans, 1976.
Barker, Kenneth L. *Micah, Nahum, Habakkuk, Zephaniah*. The New American Commentary. Vol. 20. Nashville, TN: Broadman & Holman Publishers, 1999.
Boice, J. M. *The Minor Prophets*. 2 vols. Complete in one edition. Grand Rapids, MI: Kregel, 1996.
Clark, David J., and Norm Mundhenk. *A Translator's Handbook on the Book of Micah*, UBS Handbook Series. London: United Bible Societies, 1982.
Craigie, P. C. *Twelve Prophets*. 2 vols. Philadelphia: Westminster, 1985. S.v. 2:19.
Dockery, David S., ed. *Holman Concise Bible Commentary*. Nashville, TN: Broadman & Holman Publishers, 1998.
Easton, M. G. *Easton's Bible Dictionary*. New York: Harper & Brothers, 1893.
Feinberg, Charles L. *The Minor Prophets*. Chicago: Moody Press, 1976.
Henry, Matthew. *Matthew Henry's Commentary on the Whole Bible: Complete and Unabridged in One Volume*. Peabody, MA: Hendrickson, 1994.
Jamieson, Robert, A. R. Fausset, and David Brown. *Commentary Critical and Explanatory on the Whole Bible*. Oak Harbor, WA: Logos Research Systems, Inc., 1997.
Myers, Allen C. *The Eerdmans Bible Dictionary*. Grand Rapids, MI: Eerdmans, 1987.
Smith, James E. *The Minor Prophets*. Old Testament Survey Series. Joplin, MO: College Press, 1994.

Smith, Ralph L. *Micah–Malachi.* Word Biblical Commentary. Vol. 32. Dallas: Word, Inc., 1998.

Walvoord, John F., and Roy B. Zuck. *The Bible Knowledge Commentary: An Exposition of the Scriptures.* Wheaton, IL: Victor Books, 1985.

## Say It Correctly

Doleful. **DOL**-ful.
Averse. a-**VERS**.

## Daily Bible Readings

**MONDAY**
Good Deeds for the Oppressed
(Job 29:7–17)

**TUESDAY**
Attention to the Needs of Others
(Job 31:13–22)

**WEDNESDAY**
Judge Me, O Lord
(Psalm 7:1–8)

**THURSDAY**
Test My Mind and Heart
(Psalm 7:9–17)

**FRIDAY**
The Lord Executes Judgment
(Psalm 9:15–20)

**SATURDAY**
The Righteous and the Wicked
(Proverbs 11:1–10)

**SUNDAY**
A Day of Bitter Lamentation
(Micah 2:4–11)

# Notes

# Teaching Tips

## Words You Should Know
**A. Confounded** (Micah 3:7) *khafer* (Heb.)—To be ashamed, to be embarrassed.

**B. Equity** (v. 9) *yashar* (Heb.)—Upright, straight, level.

## Teacher Preparation
**Unifying Principle—Public Trust Betrayed.** Some leaders are corrupt, lie to the people they are charged to protect, and then find associates who will support their evil ways. What can be done to end this dishonesty? God will judge and punish corrupt leaders and prophets.

**A.** Think about the various effects a corrupt leader can have on a community.

**B.** Pray and ask God to lead you as you facilitate this lesson.

**C.** Read through the entire lesson.

## O—Open the Lesson
**A.** Introduce the title of the lesson and read the Aim for Change.

**B.** Have the class take three minutes to think about the devastating effects of a corrupt leader in each of the following categories: government both in the U.S. and abroad, schools (compulsory and collegiate), churches, work. Pause between each category, allowing them time to think before introducing the next.

## P—Present the Scriptures
**A.** Instruct the class to read the Focal Verses silently.

**B.** Use The People, Places, and Times; Background; Search the Scriptures; At-A-Glance Outline; and In Depth to clarify the verses if necessary.

**C.** Solicit a volunteer to read In Focus and Keep in Mind.

## E—Explore the Meaning
**A.** Complete the Discuss the Meaning. Allow the class to refer to the In Focus story when necessary. Remember the participation aspect of the lesson; seek as many different opinions as time permits.

## N—Next Steps for Application
**A.** Depending on the size of the class and time left, divide participants into groups and instruct them to complete the Lesson in Our Society and Make It Happen sections. Each group should select a representative to report their conclusions.

**B.** Summarize the lesson.

**C.** Close with prayer.

## Worship Guide

For the Superintendent or Teacher
Theme: No Tolerance for Corrupt
Leaders and Prophets
Song: "Leaning on the Everlasting
Arms"
Devotional Reading: Matthew 7:15–20

509

# No Tolerance for Corrupt Leaders and Prophets

**Bible Background • MICAH 3**
**Printed Text • MICAH 3:5–12**
**Devotional Reading • MATTHEW 7:15–20**

## Aim for Change

By the end of the lesson, we will: EXPLORE how Micah confronted corrupt leaders; REFLECT on reactions to leaders who mislead and deceive people; and ADDRESS corruptions in leadership within the church and the broader community.

 In Focus

Kim didn't know what to think about Pastor Hindley's newly bought house and car. He owned several businesses, but he had never bought extravagant things before. Plus she knew Pastor Hindley had done so much work for the community. Outside of being a pastor, he was also a congressional representative for the district. That's what moved her to join the church and also volunteer for his latest political campaign. He always talked about justice and the well-being of the people in the community. He couldn't possibly be misappropriating money. She kept her thoughts to herself and prayed that the Lord would reveal the true source of Pastor Hindley's recent purchases. One day, while Kim was going through the records, she noticed some discrepancies in the books. She approached Pastor Hindley about them, but he just ignored her and muttered something about, "We can't be saddled down with details." Was he trying to evade her question? Could he be skimming money from his campaign funds to buy luxuries for himself?

*In today's lesson, we will discuss the effects of leaders who abandon the interests of the people they are positioned to support.*

## Keep in Mind

"But truly I am full of power by the spirit of the LORD, and of judgment, and of might, to declare unto Jacob his transgression, and to Israel his sin" (Micah 3:8).

"But truly I am full of power by the spirit of the LORD, and of judgment, and of might, to declare unto Jacob his transgression, and to Israel his sin" (Micah 3:8).

# Focal Verses

**KJV** **Micah 3:5** Thus saith the LORD concerning the prophets that make my people err, that bite with their teeth, and cry, Peace; and he that putteth not into their mouths, they even prepare war against him.

**6** Therefore night shall be unto you, that ye shall not have a vision; and it shall be dark unto you, that ye shall not divine; and the sun shall go down over the prophets, and the day shall be dark over them.

**7** Then shall the seers be ashamed, and the diviners confounded: yea, they shall all cover their lips; for there is no answer of God.

**8** But truly I am full of power by the spirit of the LORD, and of judgment, and of might, to declare unto Jacob his transgression, and to Israel his sin.

**9** Hear this, I pray you, ye heads of the house of Jacob, and princes of the house of Israel, that abhor judgment, and pervert all equity.

**10** They build up Zion with blood, and Jerusalem with iniquity.

**11** The heads thereof judge for reward, and the priests thereof teach for hire, and the prophets thereof divine for money: yet will they lean upon the LORD, and say, Is not the LORD among us? none evil can come upon us.

**12** Therefore shall Zion for your sake be plowed as a field, and Jerusalem shall become heaps, and the mountain of the house as the high places of the forest.

**NLT** **Micah 3:5** This is what the LORD says: "You false prophets are leading my people astray! You promise peace for those who give you food, but you declare war on those who refuse to feed you.

**6** Now the night will close around you, cutting off all your visions. Darkness will cover you, putting an end to your predictions. The sun will set for you prophets, and your day will come to an end.

**7** Then you seers will be put to shame, and you fortune-tellers will be disgraced. And you will cover your faces because there is no answer from God."

**8** But as for me, I am filled with power—with the Spirit of the LORD. I am filled with justice and strength to boldly declare Israel's sin and rebellion.

**9** Listen to me, you leaders of Israel! You hate justice and twist all that is right.

**10** You are building Jerusalem on a foundation of murder and corruption.

**11** You rulers make decisions based on bribes; you priests teach God's laws only for a price; you prophets won't prophesy unless you are paid. Yet all of you claim to depend on the LORD. "No harm can come to us," you say, "for the LORD is here among us."

**12** Because of you, Mount Zion will be plowed like an open field; Jerusalem will be reduced to ruins! A thicket will grow on the heights where the Temple now stands.

## The People, Places, and Times

**Heads.** The heads of Israel were the heads of families. The elders of the tribes became the judges. This system was based on the cultural custom of the time. During the Exodus, Moses established a system that organized the heads in groups of tens, fifties, hundreds, and thousands in order to better manage and give leadership to the people (Exodus 18:13–24). By the time of David, these heads or judges began to be organized as a circuit court with delegated royal authority (1 Chronicles 23:4, 26:29, 28:1). This made it easy for them to become corrupt and dishonest. By the time of the prophets, the heads were known for taking bribes and being partial to the rich.

**False Prophets.** While there were many true prophets in Israel, there were also false prophets. These false prophets often offered messages of hope and peace. These messages comforted the people without pointing out their sin or challenging them to repent from their evil ways. The false prophets became rich from the fees they charged for their services. Often they would use pagan methods of divination or fortune-telling, which were strictly forbidden in the Law of the Old Testament. The Lord had given the people of Israel ways to evaluate a false prophet: one was if the message they had spoken came to pass (Deuteronomy 18:21–22), the other if they enticed the people to worship idols (v. 20).

### Background

The Neo-Assyrian Empire was a very dominant and real threat to Jerusalem at Micah's time. One of many ways Jerusalem prepared for conflict was to strengthen the economy so they would have the necessary resources to fight off both foreign and domestic threats. As today's text suggests, the ways they pursued economic stability were immoral and did not align with the precepts of the Lord. Their stimulus plan was based on greed, exploitation, and senseless taxes, and as a result, moral corruption slowly crept in.

The rulers and leaders convinced themselves that their methods of governing were necessary because of the impending dangers. If you do something long enough, it becomes a part of who are; thus, treachery soon became merely business as usual. The

culture spread, and soon landowners began taking advantage of farmers. The poor were subjugated, and they had no social or economic power to resist.

One of the ironies of this era is that individually and collectively the people claimed to depend on God, whom they knew and believed to be the ultimate lover of justice; however, the leaders were cynical and perverted righteousness.

## At-A-Glance

1. Corrupt Prophets (Micah 3:5–7)
2. The Man of God (vv. 8–10)
3. Corrupt Leaders (vv. 11–12)

### In Depth

**1. Corrupt Prophets (Micah 3:5–7)**

Micah is speaking on behalf of God and unveiling the sinister practices of the prophets in Jerusalem and Samaria. Micah not only classifies them as deceivers, but specifically identifies their transgressions (wrongdoings). War is imminent and the prophets are capitalizing on Jerusalem's concerns by structuring their messages to benefit their paying audience, while those who cannot pay receive detrimental messages.

Micah explain that the punishment for misusing their gifts will be to stop hearing from God altogether. Those who continue to communicate these messages will be shown to have no knowledge of God and false. Those who claim to speak for the Lord and only talk of peace in order to gain a profit are not speaking for the Lord but only for themselves.

**2. The Man of God (vv. 8–10)**

Amid all of this, Micah stands up for justice. He proclaims his strength and courage so all will know he knows the depth of their corruption. He also informs them he understands the magnitude of the danger that he is in by speaking out. The eighth century B.C. was not very different from today's society as far as the extent of corruption; someone seeking to change the economic and social structure would face social, political, and religious opposition much as Jesus, Medgar Evers, and Martin Luther King Jr. did.

Like many prophets before him and those who would follow, Micah is very clear that the power he speaks with is not his own. When God commissions an individual to carry out a task, it does not matter how monumental the task, what type of challenges are ahead, or how strong the opposition. God will fill His messengers with power, strength, and the Holy Spirit so they can complete the given assignment.

### 3. Corrupt Leaders (vv. 11–12)

Micah says the leaders are attempting to build up the city, but at the expense of the poor. There is no respect for justice or righteousness. The false prophets are not the only corrupt citizens in Samaria and Jerusalem; leaders in almost every area of their society has gone astray (vv. 9–12). As a nation and individually for many leaders, the focus quickly became prosperity by any means necessary.

Despite the fact that the nation has adopted a culture of cheating, lying, stealing, and marginalizing the poor, they profess that their "growth and success" is due to their dependence on and protection by God. Micah ends by telling people that the city they are working so hard to build will ultimately be destroyed.

### Search the Scriptures

1. What were the prophets doing to the people (Micah 3:5)?
2. Based on Micah's prophecy, what was the primary source of motivation during this period in Jerusalem (v. 11)?

### Discuss the Meaning

1. How can we tell whether a preacher is leading us astray?
2. What makes a leader corrupt? Be sure to consider thoughts, words, and actions.

### Lesson in Our Society

It can be very difficult to speak against leadership at any level. Some people naturally believe that if someone has been given a title or responsibility, they have integrity and will maintain the best interest of the people they represent. However, the Bible and life have provided us with many examples of leaders who have ill intentions, succumb to temptation, and take advantage of their positions. As children of God, our instructions are simple: do justice, love kindness, and walk humbly with our God (Micah 6:8). Every group that we are members of—our country, civic organization, religious institution, or sorority/fraternity—should follow the same statutes.

### Make It Happen

After reading the Lesson in Our Society, discuss what we should do as Christians if we suspect a political leader is corrupt. Make a list of appropriate and inappropriate response methods. One way to respond is to confront the leader and withhold votes or cooperation with unjust policies and practices. With this in mind, consider your own community and whether this response is needed.

## Follow the Spirit

What God wants me to do:

_____

_____

_____

_____

## Remember Your Thoughts

Special insights I have learned:

_____

_____

_____

_____

## More Light on the Text

### Micah 3:5–12

The prophet Micah, a contemporary of Isaiah, speaks to the Southern Kingdom of Judah. At this time, the Northern Kingdom of Israel has been under threat of destruction and will eventually fall into the hands of the Assyrians in 722 B.C. Micah's warning to Judah is that the same could happen to them if they continue in their evil ways.

**5 Thus saith the LORD concerning the prophets that make my people err, that bite with their teeth, and cry, Peace; and he that putteth not into their mouths, they even prepare war against him.**

After an analogy comparing the leaders of Judah to cannibalistic shepherds, Micah then focuses on Judah's prophets, who are causing the people to err (Heb. *ta'ah*, **tah-AH**) or wander. The prophets cause the people to go astray and wander from God

and His truth—the opposite of their true role as spokesmen for God. Instead of speaking for God, they speak on their own and draw people away from God. Micah says that they "bite with their teeth." The word "bite" can also be used figuratively as "to vex" and "to oppress." The image is of a snake or other sharp-fanged creature causing harm through biting. The prophets vex and oppress the people by offering prophecies for money. Ironically, after committing such a poisonous and potentially lethal practice, they cry "Peace!" The Hebrew word for peace is shalom (**shah-LOME**), which refers to peace, prosperity, and general welfare. Such a cry is a double-entendre because although there is no peace for the people, the leaders prosper from their swindling. In addition, shalom is sandwiched between two acts of violence (biting and war), making it an even more deceptive promise for the people. The prophets' message of peace is their selling point; they tell the people that everything will be well and receive the people's money and applause. However, this is a false peace; those who will not give to them will be the objects of their hostility.

**6 Therefore night shall be unto you, that ye shall not have a vision; and it shall be dark unto you, that ye shall not divine; and the sun shall go down over the prophets, and the day shall be dark over them.**

As a result of their false prophecies and oppression, God will judge the prophets, manifesting itself in their lack of prophetic sight. Micah says that the prophets will experience darkness, and they will not be able to divine (Heb. *kasam*, **kah-SAHM**). Divination was a common way to understand the will of the gods. This was done through various methods; some would read and interpret the liver of animals or the position of fired arrows, while others studied dreams and vi-

515

sions. The latter is probably the method used by these false prophets of Judah. The sun going down and the day turning dark are metaphors for the loss of the prophets' gifts.

**7 Then shall the seers be ashamed, and the diviners confounded: yea, they shall all cover their lips; for there is no answer of God.**

Micah announces the fate of the seers (Heb. *khozeh*, **kho-ZEH**) and diviners (Heb. *kasam*, **kah-SAHM**): they will be ashamed and confounded, and experience the humiliation of lepers by having to cover their lips (Leviticus 13:45). The prophets will be considered unclean like lepers because they have "no answer of God." Their lack of honesty and true relationship with God will be evident. Because their falsehood is on display, they will cover their lips and feel the same shame as those considered outcasts to the covenant community.

**8 But truly I am full of power by the spirit of the LORD, and of judgment, and of might, to declare unto Jacob his transgression, and to Israel his sin.**

Micah declares his distinction from the false prophets. He says that he is full of power (Heb. *koach*, **KOH-akh**) by the spirit of the Lord. He is also full of judgment (Heb. *mishpat*, **mish-PAWT**) and might (Heb. *gevurah*, **geh-voo-RAH**). Micah's "judgment" here is the establishment of right through fair and legal procedures in accordance with the will and laws of God. Micah has aligned himself with the cause of justice, and by using the words "power" and "might," he states that this cause is God's cause and he is equipped to be victorious.

**9 Hear this, I pray you, ye heads of the house of Jacob, and princes of the house of Israel, that abhor judgment, and pervert all equity.**

Micah particularly addresses the political and religious groups of Judah. He calls out the heads and princes responsible for establishing the religious and political moral standards for the people. The Lord, through Micah, accuses them of hating or abhorring what is just. The word "abhor," or *ta'av* (Heb., **tah-AHV**, to loathe, detest, or make abominable) is a strong indication of how far those who rule over the Hebrews have fallen from God. They are not instructing people with fairness, but seeking their own gain and pursuing personal agendas.

Not only do these rulers and chiefs abhor justice, they also pervert equity (Heb. *yashar*, **yah-SHAR**, that which is straight, right, or just). This word also denotes fairness and being honest and aboveboard. Those who rule over Judah do not practice such honesty.

**10 They build up Zion with blood, and Jerusalem with iniquity.**

The prophet continues to personalize the accusation against Judah. In the name of religion and sacrifice to God, the people have erected buildings using perverse and deceitful means. Instead of using tithes and offerings to establish places of worship, the religious leaders have taken from the poor and, in some instances, killed to expand Jerusalem. Archaeology testifies to the building activities underway in Jerusalem during Micah's prophecy. Such capital activities were performed at the expense of the oppressed and less fortunate. Jeremiah makes reference to similar activities, mentioning those who build their homes by unrighteousness (22:13). The prophet Habakkuk also records official building with bloodshed (2:12).

The name "Zion" refers to the hill between the Kidron and Tyropean valleys that David captured from the Jebusites (2 Samuel

5:7). After the building of the temple to the north of the hill, Zion became the center of the Lord's activity, since the temple was where Yahweh dwelt. The term "Zion" may refer specifically to the temple vicinity or Jerusalem in general. Thus, Micah's reference to the people building Zion up with blood shows how this holy habitation had been defamed and desecrated.

**11 The heads thereof judge for reward, and the priests thereof teach for hire, and the prophets thereof divine for money: yet will they lean upon the LORD, and say, Is not the LORD among us? none evil can come upon us.**

Micah again compels Judah to reexamine its political and social ethics. The rulers who govern civic and state affairs are corrupt. The priests who dictate religious standards practice evil. The prophets who speak the Word of the Lord only do it for money. Micah contends that Judah's leadership has turned away from the Lord. Those in power only want to be compensated by humankind for what God has gifted and instructed them to do. Rulers give judgment for a bribe, priests teach for a price, and prophets give oracles for money. Micah stresses the greed and insatiable materialism pervading Judah.

These leaders, however, believe that what they do is good and pleasing in the eyes of the Lord. They are convinced that since Zion is the dwelling place of God and that since the Hebrews are God's chosen people, all is well and their transgressions can be overlooked. Speaking rhetorically, Micah states that those in authority did not lean on the Lord. The word "lean" (Heb. *sha'an*, **shah-AWN**), means to lie, rely on, or rest on, often with reference to God (2 Chronicles 14:11). Isaiah uses another verb for leaning in stating how Judah must depend on God (48:2).

Such leaning implies a need to find favor and obtain support. Judah wishes to engage in wrongdoing while depending on the Lord for safety. The leaders, despite their unscrupulous conduct, believe that God will protect them because of His faithfulness and promises. The people do not see the error of their ways; they are so obstinate and spiritually blind that they are convinced that because the Lord dwells in Zion, no harm can come to them even when they sin against God.

**12 Therefore shall Zion for your sake be plowed as a field, and Jerusalem shall become heaps, and the mountain of the house as the high places in the forest.**

Because Judah has become prideful and sinful, the Lord, through Micah, predicts its ensuing destruction. The crassness of the leaders will result in the leveling of Jerusalem and its temple. Micah made a similar pronouncement earlier stating that Samaria would be a heap and a place for planting vineyards, i.e., a desolate, open land (1:6). This prophecy is remembered a century later when the people of Israel observe its fulfillment (Jeremiah 26:18–19). Both prophets were foretelling the captivity of Judah by the Babylonians and the exile afterward. Judah, during Micah's time, was already a vassal state of the Assyrians; further enslavement was the next step.

Again the prophet specifically names Zion and Jerusalem, the center of Israelite worship, as places to be destroyed. No place was beyond God's wrath when evil has been committed. Micah personalizes the message and the plans of God to show Judah's leaders their ill behavior.

Sources:

Achtemeier, Paul J., ed. *The HarperCollins Bible Dictionary.* New York: HarperCollins Publishing, 1996. 680, 888.

Smith, Ralph L. *Micah–Malachi.* Word Biblical Commentary. Waco, TX: World Books Publishers, 1984. 32–34.

Waltke, Bruce K. *A Commentary on Micah.* Grand Rapids, MI: Eerdmans 2007. 181–183.

## Say It Correctly

Diviners. di-**VIE**-ners.
Equity. **EH**-kwi-tee.

## Daily Bible Readings

**MONDAY**
Do Not Pervert Justice
(Exodus 23:1–8)

**TUESDAY**
False Prophecies of Peace
(Ezekiel 13:15–20)

**WEDNESDAY**
Act in the Fear of the Lord
(2 Chronicles 19:4–10)

**THURSDAY**
Walk Blamelessly, Do Right,
Speak Truth
(Psalm 15)

**FRIDAY**
Known by Their Fruits
(Matthew 7:15–20)

**SATURDAY**
Woe to Those Striving with God
(Isaiah 45:5–13)

**SUNDAY**
Sold Out Religion
(Micah 3:5–12)

# Notes

_____

_____

_____

_____

# Teaching Tips

## Words You Should Know

**A. Redeemed** (Micah 6:4) *padah* (Heb.)— To ransom, rescue, or deliver.

**B. Mercy** (v. 8) *khesed* (Heb.)—Goodness or kindness (especially as extended to the lowly, needy, miserable, or in a lower position of power).

## Teacher Preparation

**Unifying Principle—What God Wants.** People sometimes forget what a benefactor has done for them or they make insincere efforts to show gratitude. How will benefactors react to such forgetfulness or ingratitude? God instructs the unjust to be just, love kindness, and walk humbly with Him.

**A.** Read Micah 1–7.

**B.** Read the Bible Background and Devotional Readings.

**C.** Pray for your students and for lesson clarity.

## O—Open the Lesson

**A.** Open with prayer and introduce today's lesson title.

**B.** Have your students read the Aim for Change and Keep in Mind verse together. Discuss.

**C.** Instruct your students to read the In Focus story silently. Discuss.

## P—Present the Scriptures

**A.** Use The People, Places, and Times and Background to provide context.

**B.** Ask volunteers to read the Focal Verses. Ask the students to share how the Background and The People, Places, and Times inform their understanding of the text.

**C.** Use the At-A-Glance outline and In Depth section to clarify the verses. Be sure to acknowledge any themes that the students have noticed.

## E—Explore the Meaning

**A.** Review and discuss the Search the Scriptures and Discuss the Meaning questions.

**B.** Review and discuss the Lesson in Our Society section.

## N—Next Steps for Application

**A.** Complete the Follow the Spirit and Remember Your Thoughts sections.

**B.** Summarize the lesson and use the Make It Happen section to provide practical ideas for change.

**C.** Close with prayer.

## Worship Guide

For the Superintendent or Teacher
Theme: Justice, Love, and Humility
Song: "Walk with Me Lord"
Devotional Reading: Deuteronomy
10:12–22

# Justice, Love, and Humility

**Bible Background • MICAH 6**
**Printed Text • MICAH 6:3–8**
**Devotional Reading • DEUTERONOMY 10:12–22**

## Aim for Change

By the end of the lesson, we will: KNOW how to honor God gratefully by exhibiting the character traits that God requires; EXPRESS feelings about living up to God's expectations for us to be just, loving, and humble; and LEAD the community into making God's requirements a reality.

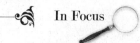 In Focus

Edward has owned and operated his restaurant for eighteen years. What started as a small diner in a strip mall has grown to three successful locations in their city. But over the past few years, the stress of running his restaurants has begun to wear on him. He has also been more short and less forgiving with his staff. Just last week, he yelled at a waitress because she was five minutes late for her shift. Employees began to fear his angry outbursts. One night, an old friend of Edward's walked into the restaurant. Quincy Tipp had been Edward's partner at his first location. Edward's face brightened and he smiled broadly, "Hey, Tipp! It's great to see you, man!" He gave Quincy a big hug and ushered him over to their best table. Over dinner and for several hours after, the two friends laughed and reminisced. They had sacrificed and worked long hours in the hopes that someday the restaurant would be a grand success. Most of all, they had wanted to honor God with their business. Edward realized that he had been led astray from their initial purpose in opening the restaurant.

*As Christians, when we remember all that God has done for us, we can extend His love and mercy to others. In today's lesson, we'll discuss how God desires that we would respond to His blessings in our lives.*

## Keep in Mind

"He hath shewed thee, O man, what is good; and what doth the LORD require of thee, but to do justly, and to love mercy, and to walk humbly with thy God?" (Micah 6:8).

"He hath shewed thee, O man, what is good; and what doth the LORD require of thee, but to do justly, and to love mercy, and to walk humbly with thy God?" (Micah 6:8).

## Focal Verses

**KJV** **Micah 6:3** O my people, what have I done unto thee? and wherein have I wearied thee? testify against me.

**4** For I brought thee up out of the land of Egypt, and redeemed thee out of the house of servants; and I sent before thee Moses, Aaron, and Miriam.

**5** O my people, remember now what Balak king of Moab consulted, and what Balaam the son of Beor answered him from Shittim unto Gilgal; that ye may know the righteousness of the LORD.

**6** Wherewith shall I come before the LORD, and bow myself before the high God? shall I come before him with burnt offerings, with calves of a year old?

**7** Will the LORD be pleased with thousands of rams, or with ten thousands of rivers of oil? shall I give my firstborn for my transgression, the fruit of my body for the sin of my soul?

**8** He hath shewed thee, O man, what is good; and what doth the LORD require of thee, but to do justly, and to love mercy, and to walk humbly with thy God?

**NLT** **Micah 6:3** "O my people, what have I done to you? What have I done to make you tired of me? Answer me!

**4** For I brought you out of Egypt and redeemed you from slavery. I sent Moses, Aaron, and Miriam to help you.

**5** Don't you remember, my people, how King Balak of Moab tried to have you cursed and how Balaam son of Beor blessed you instead? And remember your journey from Acacia Grove to Gilgal, when I, the LORD, did everything I could to teach you about my faithfulness."

**6** What can we bring to the LORD? What kind of offerings should we give him? Should we bow before God with offerings of yearling calves?

**7** Should we offer him thousands of rams and ten thousand rivers of olive oil? Should we sacrifice our firstborn children to pay for our sins?

**8** No, O people, the LORD has told you what is good, and this is what he requires of you: to do what is right, to love mercy, and to walk humbly with your God.

---

### The People, Places, and Times

**Balaam.** Balaam was an example of one of the ancient Near Eastern prophets who did not serve the Israelite God. Rather, he worshiped the many other false gods in the region. Balaam was highly regarded among the Midianites, and possessed a great deal of power and influence. King Balak of Moab tried to get Balaam to curse Israel as the Israelites traveled through the Moabite countryside. While traveling to meet Balak, God spoke to Balaam through his donkey, commanding him to only deliver God's message to King Balak (Numbers 22:21–30). Instead of a curse, God used Balaam to speak a blessing on Israel.

**Human Sacrifice.** There is some evidence of child sacrifice in ancient Syria-Palestine and Carthage. The nations surrounding Israel also worshiped fertility gods who demanded a portion of what they helped produce: crops, animals, and children. The child sacrifice was usually the firstborn son, because he would be the most precious thing to a family as the heir of all the wealth and possessions of the family. This practice was a temptation for the Israelites and forbidden by the Lord (2 Kings 3:27, 23:10). Although the firstborn of every man and animal belonged to the Lord, Israel was given specific commands for redeeming the firstborn (Numbers 18:15–17). This was Israel's way of distinguishing themselves from the different nations around them.

## Background

Micah's prophecy began with a general announcement to Samaria and Jerusalem that God had a case to present against the nations of Israel and Judah. He then laid out the first of two series of judgments against Israel and Judah. Micah described the sins that they had committed against God as well as their fellow man.

Israel had allowed the worship of idols and other gods to take root in their religious practices. Pagan practices had become a part of Israel's worship to Yahweh. For example, they engaged in the pagan ritual of temple prostitution. They presented the money earned by prostitutes to God as an offering (Micah 1:7; cf. Deuteronomy 23:17–18).

The wealthy had oppressed the poor to gain more wealth and power. They lay awake at night, devising how they would collect more land by defrauding others (Micah 2:1–2). In their greed, they stole from the poor, women, and children. As a punishment for their sin, their possessions would be taken from them and they would be humiliated.

Israel's leaders had neglected their duties and led the people astray. Rather than protecting and instructing their citizens, they exploited and misled them. Micah used the image of cannibalism to describe how the leaders fed off those they were called to protect. Jerusalem's leaders were accused of increasing their power by using violence and oppression. Similarly, the prophets chose to seek after money, rather than speak God's truth to the people. They prophesied according to how much money their words might bring them. Israel's leaders were not directed by God; their actions were driven by greed and ambition (3:11).

Micah's first series of judgments was followed by a hopeful look to a distant future, when Israel would be restored. God would eventually redeem His exiled people once again. He would lift Israel up above all other nations.

It was against this backdrop that Micah's second series of judgments began in chapter 6. This second series of judgments also concerned the issue of social justice in Israel.

## At-A-Glance

1. God Reminds Israel of His Benevolence (Micah 6:3–5)
2. God Requires Justice, Love, and Humility (vv. 6–8)

## In Depth

### 1. God Reminds Israel of His Benevolence (Micah 6:3–5)

Through the prophet Micah, God questions why Israel has turned against Him. Why have they turned to false gods? What did God do to deserve their indifference? He recounts how He delivered Israel from the slavery of Egypt. It would seem that Israel has forgotten the significance of their freedom from Egypt and His hand in delivering them. God has done nothing to provoke their negative attitude toward Him. He graciously rescued them from a life of cruel slavery and provided leaders to guide them.

God has also acted on their behalf with those who sought to harm them. He recounts how He disrupted King Balak's plot to have Balaam curse Israel. God's intervention resulted instead in a blessing over Israel. He has rescued Israel and acted to assure their continued freedom. He has maintained His commitment to the Israelites. These accounts are a reminder of what God has done for them in the past, as well as a reminder of His continued presence among them.

### 2. God Requires Justice, Love, and Humility (vv. 6–8)

What can Israel do to correct their broken relationship with God? Their immediate response is to offer sacrifices to God. They first suggest reasonable sacrifices of calves and burnt offerings. However, they exponentially increase their offer of sacrifice to ridiculous levels. They ultimately offer the human sacrifice of a firstborn child, which was customary of pagan sacrifice but prohibited by the covenant law (Leviticus 18:21; 20:2–5). The ridiculous nature of their offers seems to imply that there might be no pleasing Yahweh. However, Micah's prophecy, in keeping with other Israelite prophecies, clearly indicates that the inward condition of one's heart is of more concern to God than outward religiosity. God doesn't require outrageous sacrifice; He has already told them what He requires. As communicated earlier in Micah's prophecy, God requires that His people would once again be a just society that loves mercy. He desires protection for the oppressed and poor. He desires that His people would act mercifully toward one another. He requires that they would continue to walk in covenant fellowship with Himself.

### Search the Scriptures

1. Why do you think Israel had forgotten the significance of their miraculous deliverance from Egyptian slavery (Micah 6:4)?

2. Why do you think their first response was outward sacrifice, rather than inward change (vv. 6–7)?

### Discuss the Meaning

1. Micah's message to the people indicated that God is more concerned with the inward state of one's heart than outward shows of piety. What causes us to try to look spiritual outwardly, while secretly knowing that we're out of step with God's will?

2. What does it mean for today's Christian to do justly, love mercy, and walk humbly with God? Do you find these requirements easy or difficult to live out in your own life?

### Lesson in Our Society

We live in a world where we are bombarded with advertisements daily. It has been said that the average person today sees more ads in a day than people in the 1950s saw in their lifetime. These ads have a subtle way of making us ungrateful and dissatisfied, so we crave new products and luxuries and pursue them no matter what the cost—even injustice. God wants us to be satisfied with the blessings He has given us. By remembering what God has already done for us and who He is, we will be motivated to seek justice for others, not wealth and comfort for ourselves.

### Make It Happen

Consider the ways that God has blessed you. Do you sometimes forget all that He has done in your life? In order to get out of yourself this week and focus on God, create a list of things that God has done for you. As you create this list, think about one thing that you can do for others who are treated unjustly.

## Follow the Spirit

What God wants me to do:

_____

_____

_____

_____

## Remember Your Thoughts

Special insights I have learned:

_____

_____

_____

_____

## More Light On The Text

### Micah 6:3–8

**3 O my people, what have I done unto thee? and wherein have I wearied thee? testify against me.**

Here the Lord pleads His case. He asks the people of Judah the reason they have become so unfaithful as His covenant people. Specifically, He asks what He has done to them and how He has wearied (Heb. *la'ah*, **lah-AH**) them. This word means to be tired or to give up. The Lord asks, "How have I offended you? How could you become dissatisfied with Me?" He gives them an opportunity to testify (Heb. *'anah*, **ah-NAH**, to answer or, in a legal suit, to provide opposing testimony) against Him.

**4 For I brought thee up out of the land of Egypt, and redeemed thee out of the house of servants; and I sent before thee Moses, Aaron, and Miriam.**

Next the Lord rehearses His blessings and how gracious He has been toward His people. He brought them out of Egypt. He redeemed them from slavery. He sent Moses, Aaron, and Miriam. They were not left without leaders, but were guided to the Promised Land.

**5 O my people, remember now what Balak king of Moab consulted, and what Balaam the son of Beor answered him from Shittim unto Gilgal; that ye may know the righteousness of the LORD.**

Next the Lord brings up the incident with Balak the king of Moab and Balaam the prophet. Balak feared the Israelites coming out of Egypt, so he hired Balaam to pronounce a curse on them (Numbers 22:1–6). Quite the opposite happened, as the Lord caused a donkey to speak to Balaam and refuse to go any farther (vv. 22–30). This opened Balaam's eyes to an angel of the Lord in the middle of the road, who told him not to follow through with the king's orders (vv. 31–35). After this, Balaam could do nothing but bless them. Each time he opened his mouth, he blessed God's people. The Lord here shows them that even when their enemies tried to curse them, God fulfilled His promise and they were blessed instead.

Shittim and Gilgal are references to the Israelites' conquest of the land. Shittim was the place where Joshua camped east of the Jordan River, and Gilgal is where they crossed to take over the land. It was quite common in military annals of the ancient Near East to summarize the itinerary of the conquering king as a way to summarize the whole conquest. The reference to these places was God's way of reminding them of all that He had done to give them the land they now enjoyed.

**6 Wherewith shall I come before the LORD, and bow myself before the high God? shall I come before him with burnt offerings, with calves of a year old?**

Micah establishes a courtroom setting in which the Lord is the accuser (plaintiff) who charges Israel, the accused (defendant), with social and religious injustice. Judah attempts to respond to God's indictment by asking how they can approach God, who is so high and mighty, under the shadow of their own sin and transgressions.

The act of bowing (Heb. *kafaf*, **kah-FAHF**) shows homage or respect to royalty. It is similar to the Greek word *proskuneo* (**pro-skoo-NEH-oh**), which means to lie prostrate as a form of worship. The people of Judah acknowledge the royal and lofty nature of God and realize that the King of kings is worthy to receive their obeisance. Because of the greed of the religious and political leadership, they have not paid God the respect and honor He deserves.

Not only does God deserve their honor as the King of kings, He must be offered sacrifices, particularly burnt offerings. The burnt offering (Heb. *'olah*, **oh-LAH**) is a gift that ascends to the heavens. A portion is given to the priest to offer to God and the remainder is consumed or burned. The offering is dedicated completely to God. Young calves, or any animal less than a year old, were often sacrificed to render this type of offering. By their question, Judah knows they should have been engaging in these sacrifices. Yet their questions also indicate how far they have strayed from the Lord's covenant promise.

**7 Will the LORD be pleased with thousands of rams, or with ten thousands of rivers of oil? shall I give my firstborn for my transgression, the fruit of my body for the sin of my soul?**

Judah continues an arrogant defense of their crimes by sarcastically asking what the Lord requires. The people know that sacrifices of rams are pleasing to the Lord. Yet they exaggerate how many sacrifices they should give to God by asking if thousands of rams will do. The Hebrews are aware that oil is used in anointing royalty and in presenting gifts to God. Yet they are overzealous in their need to repent and ask if many rivers, not vials, of oil will suffice. Micah again uses this rhetorical line of reasoning to show how far the people are removed from God. They are not aware repentance needs to occur.

The line of questioning and sarcasm continues with Judah even offering "the fruit of my body" or their firstborn as restitution for sin. Micah alludes to the importance of the Lord receiving the firstfruits of the harvest for sacrifice. This passage also alludes to God delivering the firstborn of the Hebrew children from the angel of death during Israel's enslavement in Egypt (Exodus 12). This giving of the firstborn also refers to human sacrifices practiced at times by the Israelites' neighbors (Leviticus 18:21; 20:2–5).

**8 He hath shewed thee, O man, what is good; and what doth the LORD require of thee, but to do justly, and to love mercy, and to walk humbly with thy God?**

Micah now offers a response to the questions of verses 6 and 7. None of what Judah has offered is what the Lord desires. God does not seek sacrifices, offerings, or rituals. The Lord wants the people to treat each other fairly and to walk according to His way. Obedience is better than sacrifice (1 Samuel 15:22).

To do justly or carry out justice comes from the Hebrew word *mishpat* (**mish-PAHT**). It means judgment or a right sentence. It is the establishment of right through fair and legal procedures in accordance with the will of God. Mercy is translated from the Hebrew word *khesed* (**KHEH-sed**, pity, lovingkindness, or doing good for those in a lower position) and is similar to the Greek word for grace. Some scholars distinguish grace as favor God bestows "just because," whereas mercy is favor "in spite of" sinful behavior. God's mercy withholds the punishment despite our guilt. The idea of walking humbly with God is juxtaposed with Judah's arrogance and refusal to lean on the Lord (Micah 3:11). Because the people have allowed their lust for money to interfere with their relationship with God and have chosen their own selfish gain, Micah warns that He wants them to submit, to return to the commandments and the way of the Lord.

Sources:

Brown, Francis, S. R. Driver, and Charles Briggs. *The Brown-Driver-Briggs Hebrew and English Lexicon*. Peabody, MA: Hendrickson Publishers, 2007. S.vv. "Chesed" and "Padah."

Burge, Gary M., and Andrew E. Hill, eds. *Baker Illustrated Bible Commentary*. Grand Rapids, MI: Baker Books, 2012. 860–870.

Butler, Trent C., ed. "Balaam." *Holman Bible Dictionary*. Electronic Edition, QuickVerse. Nashville, TN: Holman Bible Publishers, 1991.

Carson, D. A., R. T. France, J. A. Motyer, G. J. Wenham, eds. *New Bible Commentary*. Downers Grove, IL: InterVarsity Press, 1994. 830.

Easton, M. G. "Balaam." *Easton's Bible Dictionary*. 1st ed. Oklahoma City, OK: Ellis Enterprises, 1993.

Hill, Andrew E., and John H. Walton. *A Survey of the Old Testament*. Grand Rapids, MI: Zondervan. 2009. 642–647.

Keck, Leander, ed. *The Twelve Prophets*. The New Interpreter's Bible. Vol. 7. Nashville, TN: Abingdon Press, 1996. 533–534, 577–580.

Orr, James, ed. "Balaam." *International Standard Bible Encyclopedia*. Electronic Edition. Omaha, NE: QuickVerse, 1998.

## Say It Correctly

Shittim. shee-**TEEM**.
Beor. be-**OR**.

## Daily Bible Readings

**MONDAY**
What Does the Lord Require?
(Deuteronomy 10:12–22)

**TUESDAY**
Who Gives Speech to Mortals?
(Exodus 4:10–17)

**WEDNESDAY**
The Word the Lord Speaks
(Numbers 22:1–14)

**THURSDAY**
Do Only What I Tell You
(Numbers 22:15–21)

**FRIDAY**
Speak Only What I Tell You
(Numbers 22:31–38)

**SATURDAY**
You Have Blessed My Enemies
(Numbers 23:1–12)

**SUNDAY**
Justice, Kindness, and Humility
(Micah 6:3–8)

# Teaching Tips

## Words You Should Know
**A. Iniquity** (Micah 7:18) *'avon* (Heb.)—Perversity or guilt.

**B. Remnant** (v. 18) *she'erit* (Heb.)—The rest, what is left, remaining descendants.

## Teacher Preparation
**Unifying Principle—Mercy Me!** Sometimes evil and injustice are not met with corrective justice but are trumped by mercy. Who will meet evil and injustice with mercy rather than with punishment? God will show compassion and faithfulness to His people, even to the unjust.

**A.** Pray for guidance as you prepare.

**B.** As you read through the lesson, think of ways to smoothly transition through each section with the class.

## O—Open the Lesson
**A.** Ask for a volunteer to pray.

**B.** Read the Aim for Change.

**C.** Instruct the class to read the Keep in Mind verse silently.

## P—Present the Scriptures
**A.** Instruct participants to read the Focal Verses silently to themselves.

**B.** Request a volunteer to read the In Focus story.

**C.** Use The People, Places, and Times; Background; Search the Scriptures; At-A-Glance; and In Depth to clarify the verses.

## E—Explore the Meaning
**A.** Complete the Lesson in Our Society, Search the Scriptures, and Discuss the Meaning activities as a group.

**B.** Ensure there is ample time for participants to complete the Make It Happen activity individually. Ask for volunteers to share, but instruct them not to mention the names associated with their scenarios.

## N—Next Steps for Application
**A.** Summarize the lesson and be sure to highlight any significant revelations the group discovered.

**B.** Ask the group to read the Daily Bible Reading in preparation for the next lesson.

**C.** Close in prayer.

## Worship Guide

For the Superintendent or Teacher
Theme: God Shows Clemency
Song: "Great is Your Mercy"
Devotional Reading: Psalm 13

# God Shows Clemency

**Bible Background • MICAH 7:11–20**
**Printed Text • MICAH 7:14–20**
**Devotional Reading • PSALM 13**

## —————————— Aim for Change ——————————

By the end of the lesson, we will: LEARN of God's mercy even when punishment seems in order; REFLECT on experiences when God's mercy and compassion were more than expected; and CARRY out acts of mercy and compassion.

## ————————— In Focus —————————

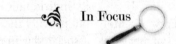

Lane and Lin were twin sisters. Since their childhood, they had dreamed of buying a house together after graduating college. After graduation, they both saved enough for the down payment and found a builder. The twins had to have doors that reminded them of their grandfather's farmhouse. The builder was not sure if he could have the doors manufactured according to the ladies' request, but he needed the money, so he assured them there would not be any problems. A week before their move-in was scheduled, the twins went to take a peek at their home. They immediately noticed the doors were not customized to their request. Without hesitation, Lane called the builder and explained the actions she would pursue based on what was outlined in the contract. Lin stopped Lane, took the phone, and allowed the builder to explain. Once he was finished, she informed him that if he could build a shed behind the house that looked like their grandfather's farmhouse, all would be forgiven.

*While consequences are essential to maintaining order, they are not always necessary to maintain relationship. In today's lesson, we learn of God's unexpected mercy and compassion.*

## ——————————— Keep in Mind ———————————

"Who is a God like unto thee, that pardoneth iniquity, and passeth by the transgression of the remnant of his heritage? he retaineth not his anger for ever, because he delighteth in mercy" (Micah 7:18).

"Who is a God like unto thee, that pardoneth iniquity, and passeth by the transgression of the remnant of his heritage? he retaineth not his anger for ever, because he delighteth in mercy" (Micah 7:18).

# Focal Verses

**KJV** **Micah 7:14** Feed thy people with thy rod, the flock of thine heritage, which dwell solitarily in the wood, in the midst of Carmel: let them feed in Bashan and Gilead, as in the days of old.

**15** According to the days of thy coming out of the land of Egypt will I shew unto him marvellous things.

**16** The nations shall see and be confounded at all their might: they shall lay their hand upon their mouth, their ears shall be deaf.

**17** They shall lick the dust like a serpent, they shall move out of their holes like worms of the earth: they shall be afraid of the LORD our God, and shall fear because of thee.

**18** Who is a God like unto thee, that pardoneth iniquity, and passeth by the transgression of the remnant of his heritage? he retaineth not his anger for ever, because he delighteth in mercy.

**19** He will turn again, he will have compassion upon us; he will subdue our iniquities; and thou wilt cast all their sins into the depths of the sea.

**20** Thou wilt perform the truth to Jacob, and the mercy to Abraham, which thou hast sworn unto our fathers from the days of old.

**NLT** **Micah 7:14** O LORD, protect your people with your shepherd's staff; lead your flock, your special possession. Though they live alone in a thicket on the heights of Mount Carmel, let them graze in the fertile pastures of Bashan and Gilead as they did long ago.

**15** "Yes," says the LORD, "I will do mighty miracles for you, like those I did when I rescued you from slavery in Egypt."

**16** All the nations of the world will stand amazed at what the LORD will do for you. They will be embarrassed at their feeble power. They will cover their mouths in silent awe, deaf to everything around them.

**17** Like snakes crawling from their holes, they will come out to meet the LORD our God. They will fear him greatly, trembling in terror at his presence.

**18** Where is another God like you, who pardons the guilt of the remnant, overlooking the sins of his special people? You will not stay angry with your people forever, because you delight in showing unfailing love.

**19** Once again you will have compassion on us. You will trample our sins under your feet and throw them into the depths of the ocean!

**20** You will show us your faithfulness and unfailing love as you promised to our ancestors Abraham and Jacob long ago.

## The People, Places, and Times

**Bashan.** The area east of the Jordan River was divided into three parts: the plain, Gilead, and Bashan. This place is most known from a passage in Deuteronomy 3. In the text, Moses was facing war with King Og of Bashan and God's instructions were, "Do not be afraid of him, for I have delivered him into your hands, along with his whole army and his land" (from v. 2, NIV). And that is exactly what transpired.

**Gilead.** This is the land that borders Bashan. It was also among the land seized during the battle with King Og, but it is famous for other reasons. The Bible talks about the healing balm that was able to soothe and remedy sickness and this is what the area was known for (Jeremiah 8:22). Gilead became synonymous for God's healing power. Both David and Jesus knew it as a place of retreat.

**Staff.** The shepherd's staff has a vast amount of significance in the Bible. Not only does it represent guidance and stability, it also represents an extension of power. The staff was also used for support, much like a walking stick. Because shepherds have the daunting task of controlling something that is much larger than them (an entire flock of sheep), it was necessary to have an extension of their hand that would give them the ability to prod and pull the flock when they went astray or needed direction. Another reason the staff came to symbolize an extension of powers was its use in defending the flock from predatory animals.

## Background

Micah began chapter 7 lamenting the evil and injustice done in Judah. He saw so much that he declared, "Woe is me!" (Micah 7:1). The crimes of the people were so appalling that he likens this season to the time after the summer harvest when no more fruit was left. He wanted to "taste" and experience good things, but none remained; there was violence and extortion, oppression and injustice everywhere he looked.

From this point, Micah spoke a psalm of trust and salvation for Israel. He let them know that the Lord would not let their enemies gloat over them. This was probably a prophecy of the fall of Jerusalem in 586 B.C. Additionally, he informed them that one day their walls would be rebuilt and foreigners from Assyria to Egypt would come to be part of Israel. At the same time, the rest of the nations would be uninhabited as punishment for what they did to God's people. This led Micah to speak of God's mercy and faithfulness to His people.

## At-A-Glance

1. The Lord is My Shepherd (Micah 7:14–15)
2. Embarrassment (vv. 16–17)
3. Who is Like God? (vv. 18–20)

## In Depth

### 1. The Lord is My Shepherd (Micah 7:14–15)

Micah is asking God to care for His people in the same tender and affectionate manner that a shepherd oversees his flock. More specifically, he requests divine provision because they are God's children. He uses the imagery of lush pastures in Gilead and Bashan to further urge God to restore not only the people, but the land. Although it may appear to be a monologue, God responds. He interjects a quick, comforting word to assure Micah that He will forgive and restore. Similar to Micah drawing from their history, God cites a past experience to confirm that He will continue to intervene on the side of Israel.

### 2. Embarrassment (vv. 16–17)

After Micah requests favor for Israel, he then asks God to punish their enemies by shaming them and having them acknowledge the limitations of their power compared to the Lord. Micah is very specific when he relays to God the wrath he wants them to receive. Micah's petition is for all of their enemies to experience God in such a way that His dominance and authority cannot be doubted or disputed. When Micah suggests "they will come out to meet the LORD" (from v. 17, NLT), this could signify repentance because the nations would have to change their ways. However, Micah wants them to approach God as humbly as snakes, which symbolize the lowest position possible.

### 3. Who is Like God? (vv. 18–20)

How fitting is it that Micah would begin to praise God? He recognizes that there is no being on Earth or in heaven as merciful as God, and begins praising Him. After considering the nation's immorality in comparison to God's grace, Micah boasts of the love and compassion God repeatedly extends through His never-ending forgiveness. Micah rejoices in the covenant between his ancestors and God. He knows that God will honor His promises to Abraham and Jacob, and as such Israel will always know the covenantal love of God.

## Search the Scriptures

1. What is the writer comparing God's people to (Micah 7:14)?

2. What does God take delight in doing (v. 18)?

## Discuss the Meaning

1. In what ways are God's love and compassion more than we expect?

2. What type of limits do we place on the compassion we extend to others when they have done wrong?

## Lesson in Our Society

Just like chivalry, some may say that compassion is a thing of the past. While this may appear true at first glance, innumerable examples of empathy, forgiveness, and reconciliation suggest otherwise. Every day we face situations where we can turn the other cheek and extend compassion, or subject someone to the consequences of their actions. In the same way, although God demands justice, He also has mercy for those who repent. This is fully demonstrated by Jesus' work on the Cross.

## Make It Happen

Think of a specific person you know who has done something wrong. Should that person receive mercy or punishment? Make a point to offer forgiveness to this person, and if possible, alleviate the consequences of the original wrong.

## Follow the Spirit

What God wants me to do:

_____

_____

_____

_____

## Remember Your Thoughts

Special insights I have learned:

_____

_____

_____

_____

## More Light on the Text

Micah 7:14–20

**14 Feed thy people with thy rod, the flock of thine heritage, which dwell solitarily in the wood, in the midst of Carmel: let them feed in Bashan and Gilead, as in the days of old.**

Starting with the relational image of a shepherd, Micah prays for the fulfillment of the promised salvation and restoration of verses 11–13 (v. 14). The prayer is reminiscent of Psalm 23:4, where David portrays the Lord as a Shepherd, who with loving care, leads His sheep with the rod and the staff. The people of God are called the flock of His inheritance or possession. They belong to Him (cf. Micah 7:14; Psalms 94:14, 100:3). But Israel is dwelling solitarily in the field. Dwelling "solitarily in the woods" is probably used to stress that they were not living in a good situation. Not only is their ground poor, but they are also cut off from other peoples and cannot get goods or help from them. So, Micah prays that their Shepherd will once again let them feed in Bashan and Gilead, cities that had proverbially fruitful pasturelands. This may also have been a prayer for the return of that rich and fertile land to the people of Zion (Zechariah 10:10). "As in the days of old" could refer to the time of Moses and Joshua, when those regions were first occupied by the Israelites (Deuteronomy 3:1–4), or to the kingdoms of David and Solomon, when those areas were securely in their possession (cf. 1 Kings 4:7–13).

**15 According to the days of thy coming out of the land of Egypt will I shew unto him marvellous things.**

God gives an answer to the prophet's prayer. He will protect, save, defend, and work miracles for them in their restoration, such as He did for their fathers in their return from Egypt to the Promised Land. God showed them His wonders then, and He will do it again. His future acts for them will include similar displays of His redemptive grace and power on their behalf. With the restoration of Israel, Micah anticipates manifestations of God's power and leadership like those at the Red Sea, Sinai, and other cities along the Exodus out of Egypt.

**16 The nations shall see and be confounded at all their might: they shall lay their hand upon their mouth, their ears shall be deaf.**

When the Lord begins to work miracles for His people again, His activity will have a dramatic effect on the nations around them, just as it did on the Egyptians at the time of the Exodus. They will see this and be confounded in spite of all their might, because when they see the mighty acts of God, they will realize how weak they really are. The nations, who thought they were so strong, will realize that their strength is nothing compared to God's power, and they will be ashamed of their strength instead of proud. They will be so dismayed that they can neither speak nor hear. They will lay their hands on their mouths in awe and amazement. Their ears will become deaf, perhaps meaning that they will turn a deaf ear to all this; they do not want to hear anything more about the Lord's powerful redemptive acts for His people.

**17 They shall lick the dust like a serpent, they shall move out of their holes like worms of the earth: they shall be afraid of the LORD our God, and shall fear because of thee.**

Micah continues with his description of the heathen nations' reaction to the Lord's miracles, and again uses symbolic actions. "They shall lick the dust like a serpent, they shall move out of their holes like worms of the earth" are two parallel lines expressing a single idea. It is a graphic way to show the humiliation of the nations, and lying with their faces in the dust (like snakes) shows how weak and lowly they are. The expression "lick the dust like a snake" may have Genesis 3:14 as its background and may also be compared to the modern idiom "to bite the dust," symbolizing death in defeat (cf. Psalm 72:9). Finally the nations will come trembling out of their hiding places, and they will turn in fear to the Lord and will be afraid of him.

**18 Who is a God like unto thee, that pardoneth iniquity, and passeth by the transgression of the remnant of his heritage? he retaineth not his anger for ever, because he delighteth in mercy.**

Verse 18 opens with a rhetorical question, "Who is a God like unto thee…?" The answer expected is clearly that there is no one like God. The question here is a way of affirming God's incomparability, particularly in His forgiving love and grace. The characteristic that sets Him apart is His ability and willingness to forgive sin. God's forgiveness "pardoneth iniquity" (Heb. *nasa'*, **NAH-sah**) which means to lift, carry, raise or take away. The enormous weight of our sins is lifted up and taken away by a merciful God. It is not like the imperfect forgiveness that people offer, but instead full, free, bottomless, boundless, and absolute. The magnitude of God's forgiveness is underscored by the use of three different, common words in this verse and the next for sin ("iniquity" and "transgression" in verse 18, and "iniquities" and "sins" in verse 19), their purpose and effect are to emphasize the completeness of God's ability to forgive all kinds of sin.

God does not retain His anger forever. He may be angry with His people when they sin, but once they have repented or been punished, He instead delighteth (Heb. *khafets*, **KHAH-fets**) or takes pleasure in showing mercy. He is more ready to save than to destroy. Nothing can please Him better than having the opportunity to show mercy to the sinner.

**19 He will turn again, he will have compassion upon us; he will subdue our iniquities; and thou wilt cast all their sins into the depths of the sea. 20 Thou wilt perform the truth to Jacob, and the mercy to Abraham,**

**which thou hast sworn unto our fathers from the days of old.**

Because He is such a God as described in verse 18, "he will turn again." His face has been long turned from His people because of their sins. But He will have compassion on them, pitying our state and feeling for our sorrows. He will defeat the iniquities of His people and demonstrate His complete victory over their sin. Though they have been mighty, He will bring them down. The theme recalls the treatment of their enemies in verse 10. To further accentuate the extent of His forgiveness, He will cast all their sins into the depths of the sea—He will fully pardon them. The word "compassion" suggests a tender, maternal love. In the Hebrew it is a verb (*rakham*, **rah-KHAHM**; to show mercy or compassion), and it comes from the same root as the word "womb" (Heb. *rekhem*, **REH-khem**; womb, compassion, mercy). This root is frequently used to describe God's feminine characteristics of care and nurture in the Old Testament (Exodus 33:19; Isaiah 14:1; Zechariah 10:6). The word "subdue" paints the picture of sin as an enemy that God conquers and liberates His people from (cf. Romans 6:14). God overcomes sin and sets His people free.

The book of Micah, despite its threats of punishment and judgment in the earlier chapters, ends on a note of joy and confidence that the nation will eventually enjoy a restored relationship with the Lord. In concluding his prophecy, Micah sees God's future work as a continuation of His covenants and promises to the Israelites' ancestors. He knows that the same love, compassion, and mercy He showed to their parents was available to them, if they received it in faith. Regardless of the moral and spiritual decline of His people, God can be relied on to be faithful to His covenant promises.

Sources:

Achtemeier, Paul J., ed. *The HarperCollins Bible Dictionary.* New York: HarperCollins Publishing, 1996. 919, 923, 1026.

Allen, Leslie C. *The Books of Joel, Obadiah, Jonah and Micah.* New International Commentary of the Old Testament. Grand Rapids, MI: Wm. B. Eerdmans, 1976.

Barker, Kenneth L. *Micah, Nahum, Habakkuk, Zephaniah.* The New American Commentary. Vol. 20. Nashville, TN: Broadman & Holman Publishers, 1999.

Boice, J. M. *The Minor Prophets.* Complete in one edition, 2 volumes. Grand Rapids, MI: Kregel, 1996. S.v. 2:24.

Clark, David J., and Norm Mundhenk. *A Translator's Handbook on the Book of Micah, UBS Handbook Series.* London: United Bible Societies, 1982.

Craigie, P. C. *Twelve Prophets.* 2 vols. Philadelphia: Westminster, 1985. 2:19.

Smith, Ralph L. *Micah–Malachi.* Word Biblical Commentary. Vol. 32. Dallas: Word Books Publishers, Inc., 1984. 58–59.

Waltke, Bruce K. *A Commentary on Micah.* Grand Rapids, MI: Eerdmans 2007. 181-183.

Wolfendale, James. "Minor Prophets." *The Preacher's Homiletical Commentary.* New York: Funk and Wagnalls, 1892.

## Say It Correctly

Solitarily. so-li-**TA**-ri-lee.
Pardoneth. **PAR**-dun-ith.
Retaineth. ree-**TAYN**-ith.

## Daily Bible Readings

**MONDAY**
I Trusted in Your Steadfast Love
(Psalm 13)

**TUESDAY**
My Sheep Were Scattered
(Ezekiel 34:1–6)

**WEDNESDAY**
The Lord Will Shepherd His Sheep
(Ezekiel 34:7–16)

**THURSDAY**
You are My Sheep
(Ezekiel 34:23–31)

**FRIDAY**
Troubling Times of Woe
(Micah 7:1–6)

**SATURDAY**
I Will Look to the Lord
(Micah 7:7–11)

**SUNDAY**
God Delights in Showing Clemency
(Micah 7:14–20)

# Notes

# Teaching Tips

August 2
Bible Study Guide 9

## Words You Should Know

**A. Intercessor** (Isaiah 59:16) *paga'* (Heb.)—One who intervenes or interposes oneself.

**B. Recompence** (v. 18) *gemul* (Heb.)—Punishment or reward to someone for an action; benefit.

## Teacher Preparation

**Unifying Principle—The Rescuer Comes.** Sometimes everything around us seems violent, cruel, and immoral. Who will bring justice and righteousness to a troubled world? Isaiah promises a time when God will come as a Redeemer with a foundation of righteousness and justice and place His spirit on those who repent of their sins.

**A.** Pray for clarity as you prepare.

**B.** Read the Background section for further insight.

**C.** Complete the companion lesson in the *Precepts For Living Personal Study Guide®*.

## O—Open the Lesson

**A.** Begin by asking the class to define two separate terms. First define "justice," then discuss and define "the oppressed."

**B.** Introduce the Aim for Change.

## P—Present the Scriptures

**A.** Instruct participants to silently read the Focal Verses.

**B.** Have a volunteer read the In Focus story.

**C.** Use The People, Places, and Times; Background; Search the Scriptures; and In Depth to clarify the verses.

## E—Explore the Meaning

**A.** Divide the class into groups to complete the Discuss the Meaning and Search the Scripture activities. Instruct each group to select a representative to report their findings to the group.

**B.** Read and discuss Lesson in Our Society.

## N—Next Steps for Application

**A.** Summarize the lesson.

**B.** Read and discuss the Make It Happen section with a plan to practice suggested exercise.

**C.** Close with prayer.

## Worship Guide

For the Superintendent or Teacher
Theme: Our Redeemer Comes
Song: "My Redeemer Lives"
Devotional Reading: Exodus 6:2–8

# Our Redeemer Comes

**Bible Background • ISAIAH 59:15–21; PSALM 89:11–18**
**Printed Text • ISAIAH 59:15b–21**
**Devotional Reading • EXODUS 6:2–8**

## —————— Aim for Change ——————

By the end of the lesson, we will: EXPLORE how God promises a renewed covenant relationship; REVEAL our feelings about the cruelty and violence of society; and EXPRESS gratitude and joy for God's salvation from worldly dangers and work toward a renewed community.

## In Focus

Mya could not believe her ears when she heard two co-workers tell Juan, another employee, that he should work somewhere that had people "like him"—as though because he was of another ethnicity, they did not want to work with him. Juan did not respond; he simply hung his head and continued to work. Mya regretted her co-workers' being maliciously cruel and decided to comfort Juan. When she apologized to Juan for the behavior she witnessed, she also mentioned that it went against their company's policy. Juan looked at Mya and told her not to put too much faith in the company's policies because the human resources manager had done something similar to him. He also told her that he was used to maltreatment; he had experienced it even as a child. Mya was furious. She went back to her office and wrote the vice president of employee relations a letter demanding that something be done to assist Juan.

*Sometimes all it takes is one person to be concerned and stand for what is right. In this lesson, we will learn how to partner with God to work for a renewed society.*

## —————— Keep in Mind ——————

"And the Redeemer shall come to Zion, and unto them that turn from transgression in Jacob, saith the LORD" (Isaiah 59:20).

"And the Redeemer shall come to Zion, and unto them that turn from transgression in Jacob, saith the LORD" (Isaiah 59:20).

# Focal Verses

**KJV** **Isaiah 59:15b** The LORD saw it, and it displeased him that there was no judgment.

**16** And he saw that there was no man, and wondered that there was no intercessor: therefore his arm brought salvation unto him; and his righteousness, it sustained him.

**17** For he put on righteousness as a breastplate, and an helmet of salvation upon his head; and he put on the garments of vengeance for clothing, and was clad with zeal as a cloak.

**18** According to their deeds, accordingly he will repay, fury to his adversaries, recompence to his enemies; to the islands he will repay recompence.

**19** So shall they fear the name of the LORD from the west, and his glory from the rising of the sun. When the enemy shall come in like a flood, the Spirit of the LORD shall lift up a standard against him.

**20** And the Redeemer shall come to Zion, and unto them that turn from transgression in Jacob, saith the LORD.

**21** As for me, this is my covenant with them, saith the LORD; My spirit that is upon thee, and my words which I have put in thy mouth, shall not depart out of thy mouth, nor out of the mouth of thy seed, nor out of the mouth of thy seed's seed, saith the LORD, from henceforth and for ever.

**NLT** **Isaiah 59:15b** The LORD looked and was displeased to find there was no justice.

**16** He was amazed to see that no one intervened to help the oppressed. So he himself stepped in to save them with his strong arm, and his justice sustained him.

**17** He put on righteousness as his body armor and placed the helmet of salvation on his head. He clothed himself with a robe of vengeance and wrapped himself in a cloak of divine passion.

**18** He will repay his enemies for their evil deeds. His fury will fall on his foes. He will pay them back even to the ends of the earth.

**19** In the west, people will respect the name of the LORD; in the east, they will glorify him. For he will come like a raging flood tide driven by the breath of the LORD.

**20** "The Redeemer will come to Jerusalem to buy back those in Israel who have turned from their sins," says the LORD.

**21** "And this is my covenant with them," says the LORD. "My Spirit will not leave them, and neither will these words I have given you. They will be on your lips and on the lips of your children and your children's children forever. I, the LORD, have spoken!

## The People, Places, and Times

**Islands.** The "islands" were not just simply dry lands in the middle of the sea. This term was used to denote the Mediterranean coastlands or a maritime region. For the Israelites, these coastlands, such as Greece and Italy, represented the far ends of the earth. Gentiles inhabited these lands, so they were also known as the isles of the Gentiles (Genesis 10:5).

**Redeemer.** In the Old Testament, the word "redeemer" can have one of three meanings. The first meaning refers to a person who recovers ownership by purchasing something that has been sold, usually property or a family member who has fallen into slavery or destitution by being a widow or orphan. The second meaning is of the avenger of blood who takes revenge for the murder of a deceased relative. The third use applies solely to God acting in relation with His people and reestablishing relationship after acts of rebellion, disobedience, or transgression.

## Background

The events that were transpiring around him inspired Isaiah to give his prophecies during a crucial time in the history of Judah. In approximately 791 B.C., Uzziah became king of Judah. Forty years into his reign, he was stricken with leprosy, so his son Jotham became co-regent, helping him rule. Around 745 B.C., Assyria, a dominant and opposing empire, began to shift its focus in an attempt to conquer the Mediterranean area, including Judah and many other nations. In the year that King Uzziah died, Jotham began to rule alone and Isaiah had one of his greatest visions. The prophet saw the Lord lifted up in the temple (Isaiah 6:1). In 736 B.C., Jotham died and Ahaz became king. Soon after Ahaz assumed power, Israel and Syria pressured him to join the anti-Assyrian coalition. In 722, the Northern Kingdom was abolished at the hands of Assyria. By 715, Hezekiah had become the newest king of Judah, and subsequently disavowed the relationship that had been forged to prevent Assyria from attacking Judah. Moreover, Hezekiah led a rebellion against the empire, and by the conclusion of Isaiah's ministry in 701 B.C., forty-three of Judah's cities were destroyed, though Judah as a whole was not captured.

## At-A-Glance

1. Intercession (Isaiah 59:15b–16)
2. God's Wrath (vv. 17–21)

## In Depth

### 1. Intercession (Isaiah 59:15b–16)

The writer discloses that there is a paradigm shift in the land. His report reveals that the people have abandoned truth and embraced wickedness because harsh retaliation is the consequence for siding with righteousness. The historical truth is that people are physically persecuted and even killed for following the Lord. However, this is not a foreign or antiquated premise because even today, people suffer and die for righteousness in countries like China and Syria. According to Isaiah, God will survey the situation and realize that human intervention is not possible because the people lack the strength and tenacity to oppose injustice. God will act on behalf of the oppressed with extraordinary power and ensure their recovery.

### 2. God's Wrath (vv. 17–21)

God's intervention will not be diplomatic; Judah's adversaries will know God's wrath and fury. Here we get our first glimpse of the armor of God. Paul tells his readers that they should guard themselves by donning this holy battle gear (Ephesians 6:10–18), but in this text it is used as a metaphor to describe the intensity with which God will admonish the enemy. It is no surprise that Isaiah uses warrior metaphors to describe God; He was often known as a battle-ax, conqueror, and divine warrior to the people of Israel, and they are confident that He will intervene on their behalf.

Isaiah makes it clear that those who oppose justice and truth will be held accountable. The Lord's vengeance will be swift and strong. The prophet paints a vivid picture of the Lord's retribution. Isaiah, like so many other prophets, makes the claim that as a result of God's judgment, they will fear and acknowledge the Lord.

## Search the Scriptures

1. What is the purpose of the Lord putting on armor and robes of vengeance (Isaiah 59:17)?

2. What did God promise would not depart out of their mouth, and why is this important (v. 21)?

## Discuss the Meaning

1. What type of injustices are present in our society that would be displeasing to God?

2. What would God's redemption look like in the present day?

## Lesson in Our Society

Morals and socioeconomic perspectives are two of the primary contributors to ideas of justice. Apart from individual premises of justice, nations have a prevailing interpretation of justice that shapes policy, governance, and culture. Justice does not solely address law; it addresses moral questions of right and wrong in humanity. Words such as accountability, equity, access, representation, and opportunity are key when analyzing justice in a society.

## Make It Happen

Israel was to be very diligent in sharing their experiences with God with their children. Isaiah says, "[The words I have given you] will be on your lips and on the lips of your children and your children's children forever" (from 59:21, NLT). For this to happen, there must be an exchange of information from one generation to the next. Share your spiritual encounters and experiences in seeking justice with your children or others in the neighborhood. Not only will they know God through their personal experience, but they will know God through yours as well.

## Follow the Spirit

What God wants me to do:

_____

_____

_____

_____

## Remember Your Thoughts

Special insights I have learned:

_____

_____

_____

_____

## More Light on the Text

**Isaiah 59:15b–21**

**15 The LORD saw it, and it displeased him that there was no judgment. 16 And he saw that there was no man, and wondered that there was no intercessor: therefore his arm brought salvation unto him; and his righteousness, it sustained him.**

These verses portray the social degradation of the people of God. They directly follow verses 14–15a, where we see the consequence of what happens when people live in lies and assume that it is alright to oppress those who are weaker, neglect God, and turn away from His commandments and the path of righteousness. First, truth has been left behind or abandoned. People do not care for the truth but tell lies with impunity. Although not limited to politicians, people say the lies over and over until they are somehow convinced that the lies are truth. Second, whoever turns away from sin is victimized by those in power. One would expect that everyone departing from evil would feel not hatred and censure, but commendation and appreciation. Unfortunately, this is not the case; on the contrary, the person who takes this step "maketh himself a prey" (v. 15a). In a society that is increasingly morally bankrupt, turning aside from evil could easily make one seem the most apparent loser. Third, there is injustice—that is, no social justice, no sense of the "right" manifestly ruling in the common relations of life. Not only are people mistreating one another, but nobody intervenes to protect the abused and stop the injustice.

The only comforting hope of the world is that God sees. He is neither oblivious nor insensitive. He not only sees, but also hears the clamor of the wicked societies of this world and decrees that their sin will be put to an end. He did it in Sodom (Genesis 18:21, 19:24–25). He saw the oppression of His people in Egypt and put an end to it (Exodus 2:24–25). Here God sees the helplessness of His people and cares about it. The word "intercessor," from the Hebrew root word *paga'* (**pah-GAH**), which also occurred in 53:12 means to cover the breach with one's body. In the same manner as in Isaiah 53, God has to intervene on behalf of His people. God looks down and sees the degenerate and hopeless condition of His people. He knows how far the evil spread, until the whole people are corrupted. To make matters worse, God saw no one stood for truth and righteousness—none such as Abraham, Moses, or Phinehas (Genesis 15:6; Exodus 33:11–14; Numbers 25:7–8). That God wonders does not suggest a surprise or ignorance of the situation, but rather astonishment. As no human intercessor can be found among the exiles, God Himself brings salvation. Isaiah uses the word arm (Heb. *zeroah*, **zeh-ro-AH**), which theologically describes God's work in creation, freeing His people from Egyptian

bondage, fighting against His enemies, and judging His own people. The arm is the primary instrument in working and fighting. As such it is a dynamic metaphor for the saving action of God. He is patient and waits for a disobedient Israel to turn to Him. He waits and longs for a man to lead them back to Him, but none defend His cause or proclaim His truth, so the Lord does it Himself. If an intercessor had stepped forth, it would have saved Israel a lot of calamity, but the lack of an intercessor did not derail God's plan. His work will still go forth if none arose (cf. Esther 4:14). It is His own righteousness that sustains (Heb. *samak*, **sah-MAHK**) or supports Him. This word is used over twenty times for the act of the high priest laying his hands on offerings and sacrifices. This especially applies the sin offering on the Day of Atonement, which alludes to the work of Christ as an atoning sacrifice satisfying the justice of God.

**17 For he put on righteousness as a breastplate, and an helmet of salvation upon his head; and he put on the garments of vengeance for clothing, and was clad with zeal as a cloak.**

Using metaphorical language, Isaiah continues showing how the Lord will help His people. God appears as a man of war and puts on His arms—righteousness as breastplate, helmet and garments of salvation, and zeal as a cloak. The imagery is a prototype of Ephesians 6:13–17, where Paul exhorts his hearers to prepare for spiritual battle. The absence of offensive weapons such as bows or spears is striking; perhaps all God needs to execute vengeance on His enemies is His mighty arm. He will proceed in righting the wrongs and avenging the injuries of His people. Both in saving them and destroying their enemies, He will secure the honor of His faithfulness and justice, and by preserving His people, He maintains the honor and glory of His name. Since the heart and inward parts are protected by the breastplate, He calls righteousness His breastplate, to show the justness of His cause and His faithfulness in making good on His promises. In putting on the garments of vengeance, He is determined to punish His and His people's enemies. Zeal (Heb. *kin'ah*, **kin-AH**) or the passionate ardent love of God toward his people (Isaiah 26:11, Isaiah 9:7) is to be His cloak (Heb. *me'il*, **meh-EEL**). This was the outer garment worn by men of rank and by the high priest. In this verse, God comes to the defense of His people.

**18 According to their deeds, accordingly he will repay, fury to his adversaries, recompence to his enemies; to the islands he will repay recompence.**

The Lord will deal with the enemies of His people according to the laws of retribution and retaliation. God will judge and repay His foes; He will execute vengeance on all those who have opposed Him. Fury (Heb. *khemah*, **KHEH-mah**) is a word referring to heat or the venom of the snake. Sin's havoc on creation will be fully and richly repaid. Nothing will be left unrequited.

**19 So shall they fear the name of the LORD from the west, and his glory from the rising of the sun. When the enemy shall come in like a flood, the Spirit of the LORD shall lift up a standard against him.**

The negative picture gives way to positive results. The verse begins with a general statement that people from all over the world will fear the Lord. Here "fear" is understood as godly, reverent, childlike fear from the acknowledgement of His name. The last part of the verse gives further reasons for the reverential awe displayed toward the Lord—his overwhelming justice for his people. This overwhelming justice is described as a pent up flood washing out a desert wadi or small narrow valley. The last part of the verse gives further reasons for the reverential awe displayed toward the Lord—His overwhelming justice for His people. This overwhelming justice is described as a pent-up flood washing out a desert wadi or small narrow valley. The last sentence is poorly translated in the King James Version. The word "enemy" (Heb. *tsar*, **TSAHR**) can also be translated as the adjective "oppressive" or "raging." This would describe the "flood" or rushing stream. The word translated "lift up a standard" also causes confusion. It could either be from *nus* (Heb., **NOOS**), meaning "to drive at or to put to flight," or from the rare verb *nasas* (Heb., **nah-SAHS**) meaning "to raise up (as a standard)." Thus, more modern translations will render the sentence: "For he will come like a raging flood tide driven by the breath of the LORD" (NLT). This seems to fit better with the image in the first half of the verse. In summary, the flood or rushing stream flowing through the wadi will increase in force because of the wind or breath of God driving it. This is a picture of God's pent-up justice finally being executed on His enemies. For this reason, people from across the world will fear the name of the Lord.

**20 And he the Redeemer shall come to Zion, and unto them that turn from transgression in Jacob, saith the LORD. 21 As for me, this is my covenant with them, saith the LORD; My spirit that is upon thee, and my words which I have put in thy mouth, shall not depart out of thy mouth, nor out of the mouth of thy seed, nor out of the mouth of thy seed's seed, saith the LORD, from henceforth and for ever.**

Verses 15–19 provide a description of how the Lord deals with the enemies of His people. He will be stern and just. There is a marked shift in tone in verse 20. Now He describes how differently He will deal with His own people and the generations that follow. First, God, acting as the Redeemer, shall come to Zion, but only to those who turn and repent from their sins. As such, turning from sin is the entry point into the covenant. God's judgment on His people was a foreshadowing of that final Day of the Lord, when all the nations will be judged. When it is ended, then "the Redeemer shall come to Zion" and the glorious kingdom will be established. Israel will be God's chosen and purified people, and the glory of the Lord will radiate from Mount Zion. God's dealings are based on the covenant, which embodies the mercies that He has repeatedly promised to them. The substance of the covenant is encapsulated in two words—spirit and words. The words here may be the Torah. Israel will become a people that truly meditate on the Torah day and night. Both the words and the spirit belong together and constitute testimony that characterizes God's people not only in its momentary fulfillment but "from henceforth and for ever." The people of God must continue to embrace the Word by constantly hearing, saying, and learning it. They also have the responsibility to teach the Word to their "seed" and their "seed's seed," that is, to their children and grandchildren, as in the case of Timothy (cf. 2 Timothy 1:5).

Sources:
Achtemeier, Paul J., ed. *The HarperCollins Bible Dictionary.* New York: HarperCollins Publishing, 1996. 918.
Brueggemann, Walter. *Isaiah 40–66.* Louisville, KY: Westminster John Knox Press, 1998.
Goldingay, John. *Isaiah.* New International Bible Commentary. Peabody, MA: Hendrickson Publishers, 2001.
Hanson, Paul D. *Isaiah 40–66.* Interpretation. Louisville, KY: Westminster John Knox Press, 1995.
Leupold, H. C. *Exposition of Isaiah.* Grand Rapids, MI: Baker Books House, 1976.
Oswald, John N. *The Book of Isaiah, Chapters 44–66.* The New International Commentary on the Old Testament. Grand Rapids, MI: Wm. B. Eerdmans, 1998.
Simeon, Charles. *Isaiah, XXVII–LXVI.* Horae Homileticae. Vol. 8. London: Holdsworth and Ball, 1832.
Spence-Jones, H. D. M., ed. *Isaiah, Vol. II.* The Pulpit Commentary. London: Funk & Wagnalls Company, 1910.
Warren W. Wiersbe. *Be Comforted.* "Be" Commentary Series. Wheaton, IL: Victor Books, 1996.
Watts, John D. *Isaiah 34–66.* Word Biblical Commentary. Waco, TX: World Books Publishers., 1987. 286–87.
Young, Edward J. *The Book of Isaiah, Vol. 3.* Grand Rapids, MI: Wm. B. Eerdmans, 1972.

## Say It Correctly

Recompence. **REH**-kum-pence.
Maritime. me-ri-**TIME**.

## Daily Bible Readings

**MONDAY**
Our Sins Testify Against Us
(Isaiah 59:1–14)

**TUESDAY**
Taught for Our Own Good
(Isaiah 48:12–19)

**WEDNESDAY**
God's Everlasting Love
(Isaiah 54:1–8)

**THURSDAY**
Our Redeemer is Strong
(Jeremiah 50:28–34)

**FRIDAY**
Walking in the Light
(Psalm 89:11–18)

**SATURDAY**
Redeemed with an Outstretched Arm
(Exodus 6:2–8)

**SUNDAY**
The Lord Will Come as Redeemer
(Isaiah 59:15–21)

# Teaching Tips

## Words You Should Know

**A. Amend** (Jeremiah 7:3, 5) *yatav* (Heb.)— To reform; to make well or right.

**B. Abominations** (v. 10) *to'evah* (Heb.)— Idolatrous practices; various kinds of wickedness.

## Teacher Preparation

**Unifying Principle—Doing Justice**. Many people show partiality, oppress the weak, and break the law as though they are unaware of the error of their ways. What are the consequences for people who will not change their ways? Through Jeremiah, God sent messages of hope to those who will amend their ways and messages of doom to those who will not.

**A.** Pray for your students and for lesson clarity.

**B.** Read 1 Samuel 1–4 for historical context about the sanctuary at Shiloh.

**C.** Gather newspaper articles that deal with issues of doing justice or harm for the community.

## O—Open the Lesson

**A.** Open with prayer, including asking God to reveal ways that we may need to amend our lives.

**B.** Introduce today's lesson title and subject text.

**C.** Have your students read the Aim for Change and Keep in Mind verse together.

**D.** Share your newspaper articles with the class. Discuss the advantages of doing justice and the consequences of doing harm.

## P—Present the Scriptures

**A.** Have a volunteer read the Focal Verses.

**B.** Discuss differences between KJV and NLT translations of the passages.

**C.** Use The People, Places, and Times; Background; Search the Scriptures; and In Depth to clarify the verses.

## E—Explore the Meaning

**A.** Have the class answer the Discuss the Meaning questions.

**B.** Have the class review the Lesson in Our Society.

## N—Next Steps for Application

**A.** Have students write down at least one thing they resolve to change in their own lives.

**B.** Close in prayer.

## Worship Guide

For the Superintendent or Teacher
Theme: A Choice to Be Just
Song: "Get Right Church"
Devotional Reading: Jeremiah 26:8–15

# A Choice to Be Just

**Bible Background: JEREMIAH 7:1–15; EZRA 7:6, 21–28**
**Printed Text: JEREMIAH 7:1–15**
**Devotional Reading: JEREMIAH 26:8–15**

## Aim for Change

By the end of the lesson, we will: REVIEW the messages of doom and hope found in Jeremiah; REGRET the error of our ways and resolve to change; and ADDRESS our personal unfaithfulness and our community's corruption.

## In Focus

Upon moving into his new house, Jeff quickly made friends with two of his neighbors. Jeff invited his friends to attend church with him, but they always politely declined. When the new sanctuary at his church was completed, Jeff tried once more to invite Jorge and Alonzo to church. They again told Jeff no because of things they knew about him and some of the other members. It bothered them that Jeff had contributed a lot of money toward the new building, yet his mother lived in inadequate housing and subsisted on government assistance. Another member had recently evicted a young mother from one of his rental homes following the disability of her husband. Still others had adulterous affairs and abused spouses or children. Jeff went home and considered all they had said. They were right. His deeds had not matched his professed faith. He repented of his sins and resolved to change his attitude and his ways. He also resolved to talk with his fellow church members about their actions and lifestyles. He asked God to change his heart and give him the courage to lead others to change as well.

*In today's lesson, Jeremiah warns the people of Judah that their actions are evil, and they need to amend their ways or face judgment.*

## Keep in Mind

"Thus saith the LORD of hosts, the God of Israel, Amend your ways and your doings, and I will cause you to dwell in this place" (Jeremiah 7:3).

"Thus saith the LORD of hosts, the God of Israel, Amend your ways and your doings, and I will cause you to dwell in this place" (Jeremiah 7:3).

## Focal Verses

**KJV** **Jeremiah 7:1** The word that came to Jeremiah from the LORD, saying,

**2** Stand in the gate of the LORD's house, and proclaim there this word, and say, Hear the word of the LORD, all ye of Judah, that enter in at these gates to worship the LORD.

**3** Thus saith the LORD of hosts, the God of Israel, Amend your ways and your doings, and I will cause you to dwell in this place.

**4** Trust ye not in lying words, saying, The temple of the LORD, The temple of the LORD, the temple of the LORD, are these.

**5** For if ye throughly amend your ways and your doings; if ye throughly execute judgment between a man and his neighbour;

**6** If ye oppress not the stranger, the fatherless, and the widow, and shed not innocent blood in this place, neither walk after other gods to your hurt:

**7** Then will I cause you to dwell in this place, in the land that I gave to your fathers, for ever and ever.

**8** Behold, ye trust in lying words, that cannot profit.

**9** Will ye steal, murder, and commit adultery, and swear falsely, and burn incense unto Baal, and walk after other gods whom ye know not;

**10** And come and stand before me in this house, which is called by my name, and say, We are delivered to do all these abominations?

**11** Is this house, which is called by my name, become a den of robbers in your eyes? Behold, even I have seen it, saith the LORD.

**12** But go ye now unto my place which was in Shiloh, where I set my name at the first, and see what I did to it for the wickedness of my people Israel.

**NLT** **Jeremiah 7:1** The LORD gave another message to Jeremiah. He said,

**2** "Go to the entrance of the LORD's Temple, and give this message to the people: 'O Judah, listen to this message from the LORD! Listen to it, all of you who worship here!

**3** This is what the LORD of Heaven's Armies, the God of Israel, says: Even now, if you quit your evil ways, I will let you stay in your own land.

**4** But don't be fooled by those who promise you safety simply because the LORD's Temple is here. They chant, "The LORD's Temple is here! The LORD's Temple is here!"

**5** But I will be merciful only if you stop your evil thoughts and deeds and start treating each other with justice;

**6** only if you stop exploiting foreigners, orphans, and widows; only if you stop your murdering; and only if you stop harming yourselves by worshiping idols.

**7** Then I will let you stay in this land that I gave to your ancestors to keep forever.

**8** Don't be fooled into thinking that you will never suffer because the Temple is here. It's a lie!

**9** Do you really think you can steal, murder, commit adultery, lie, and burn incense to Baal and all those other new gods of yours,

**10** and then come here and stand before me in my Temple and chant, "We are safe!"— only to go right back to all those evils again?

**11** Don't you yourselves admit that this Temple, which bears my name, has become a den of thieves? Surely I see all the evil going on there. I, the LORD, have spoken!

**12** Go now to the place at Shiloh where I once put the Tabernacle that bore my name.

**13** And now, because ye have done all these works, saith the LORD, and I spake unto you, rising up early and speaking, but ye heard not; and I called you, but ye answered not;

**14** Therefore will I do unto this house, which is called by my name, wherein ye trust, and unto the place which I gave to you and to your fathers, as I have done to Shiloh.

**15** And I will cast you out of my sight, as I have cast out all your brethren, even the whole seed of Ephraim.

See what I did there because of all the wickedness of my people, the Israelites.

**13** While you were doing these wicked things, says the LORD, I spoke to you about it repeatedly, but you would not listen. I called out to you, but you refused to answer.

**14** So just as I destroyed Shiloh, I will now destroy this Temple that bears my name, this Temple that you trust in for help, this place that I gave to you and your ancestors.

**15** And I will send you out of my sight into exile, just as I did your relatives, the people of Israel.'"

## The People, Places, and Times

**Shiloh.** Shiloh was a place in Northern Israel where the tabernacle resided from the time of the judges until the Philistines captured it. It was located in the area allotted to the tribe of Ephraim, ten miles north of Bethel. The name Shiloh means "place of rest." The evidence of Shiloh's destruction and desolation can be seen to this day, as the land where this city once was is secluded and uninhabited.

**The temple in Jerusalem**. The eastern gate of the temple in Jerusalem was most likely the place where Jeremiah delivered the sermon found in Jeremiah 7. This was the magnificent temple Solomon had built some 350 years earlier, where the people worshiped and where the Ark of the Covenant, the symbolic presence of God, resided. Jerusalem had withstood many attacks over the years, and the people of Jerusalem believed that because God resided in the temple, He would never allow His temple or His people to fall.

## Background

The occasion for Jeremiah's sermon was most likely the beginning of one of the Israelite pilgrimage festivals, when great crowds of people would be pouring into the temple courts for worship. Most scholars date the chapter 7 sermon to around 609 B.C., during the first year of the reign of King Jehoiakim (Jeremiah 26:1). This is significant because it was some 110 years after the Northern Kingdom of Israel had fallen to the Assyrians. Jeremiah frequently pointed to the fall of Israel as an example of God's judgment upon a sinful and unrepentant nation, and he repeatedly warned that Judah and Jerusalem were destined for the same fate if they did not repent. The people of Judah were well aware of Israel's fate, but they had come to believe that because they had the temple, God would never judge them in the same way. Just a few years earlier, Josiah, a godly king of Judah, had renewed the covenant with God. Hoping to restore God's blessing and avoid His judgment for the people's idolatrous acts, Josiah cleansed the temple, ordered the destruction of all idols and altars to other gods, and attempted to restore proper worship at the temple. The people had pledged themselves to the covenant and all its laws and festivals (2 Kings 23:1–4). But after Josiah's death, as Jeremiah's sermon indicates, the people's reforms and pledges proved to be superficial. They did not change their immoral behaviors. Jeremiah's preaching fell on deaf ears and hardened hearts, and Jerusalem and Judah fell to the Babylonians fewer than twenty-five years after Jeremiah issued his sermon of warning and hope.

## At-A-Glance

1. The Lord of the Temple
(Jeremiah 7:1–4)
2. The Longing for Change (vv. 5–7)
3. The Litany of Sins (vv. 8–11)
4. The Last Warning (vv. 12–15)

## In Depth

### 1. The Lord of the Temple (Jeremiah 7:1–4)

During the pilgrimage festivals, it would not have been unusual for pilgrims entering the temple area to be greeted by a representative of the temple asking them to examine their lives before going in for worship. On this particular day, that representative is Jeremiah. But his pleas on that day has a sense of urgency about them. Beyond the usual call for repentance, Jeremiah conveys that their words of repentance must be accompanied by actions of abandoning their evil ways. So great is God's anger against them that their privilege of staying in the land is contingent on radical and immediate amending of their immoral ways. Additionally, in verse 4, he challenges them to examine the superficial nature of their worship and their false sense of security associated with the temple. They are convinced that God will never allow anything bad to happen to His temple or to the people who worship there. They put their faith in the temple of the Lord instead of the Lord of the temple.

### 2. The Longing for Change (vv. 5–7)

Through His servant Jeremiah, God makes it very clear that continued blessings are conditional on the people's making drastic changes in their attitudes and actions. If the people stop their evil deeds, He will allow them to continue to live in the land and have access to the temple. It is clearly the people's choice: they must choose to do justice and treat those around and among them with respect and honor. So important is this issue of justice, and its conditional tie to living in the Promised Land, that it is included in the Ten Commandments: "Honor your father and your mother, so that you may live long in the land the LORD your God is giving you" (Exodus 20:12, NIV). God's requirements of justice comprise a large part of His elaboration on the Law in Exodus 20–23. The Israelites in Jeremiah's day are openly violating God's laws of justice, yet He still offers mercy (v. 7) if they will turn from their evil ways.

### 3. The Litany of Sins (vv. 8–11)

Here God shows that He not only knows His people's evil deeds, but He also knows their corrupt view of the temple and their worship there. The people are guilty of violating at least five of the Ten Commandments, yet they confidently flock to the temple, where they believe their mere attendance and participation in rituals will atone for their sins. God is obviously angry both at their sins and at their attitude that temple worship give them indulgence to keep on sinning. He says they have turned His temple into a "den of robbers" (Jeremiah 7:11). The prophet's audience would have certainly known about the many limestone caves in the mountains surrounding Jerusalem where gangs of thieves sought temporary safety between their robberies. For the people to treat the temple as a place of sanctuary, where they think they are safe from the consequences of their sins, is such an abomination in God's eyes that He will rain judgment down on them.

### 4. The Last Warning (vv. 12–15)

Shiloh, located about thirty miles north of Jerusalem in the Northern Kingdom of Israel, was an important place of worship during the time of the judges (c. 1300–1030 B.C.), as the tabernacle was set up there for a time. The hearers of Jeremiah's temple gate sermon are well aware that the tabernacle, an earlier forerunner to the Jerusalem temple, had been destroyed in Shiloh many hundreds of years previous. Psalm 78:59–60 records the fate of that once sacred place of worship: "God ... was wroth ... so that he forsook the tabernacle of Shiloh." God would not be bound to any physical building, location, or place of worship. In 722 B.C., God gave all of Israel over to destruction and exile at the hands of the Assyrians. Jeremiah makes it very clear that unless the people of Judah amend their ways and turn from their abominations, that their fate will be like that of Shiloh and Israel. Clearly, the choice is theirs. The sad reality of their response is recorded later in Jeremiah's ministry (26:8–15).

### Search the Scriptures

1. What did it mean for the people of Judah to amend their ways (Jeremiah 7:3)?

2. What did the people's chant say about their attitude toward God and their sin (vv. 4, 10)?

### Discuss the Meaning

1. How do our attitudes toward church reflect those of the worshipers at the temple?

2. What does it mean when we continue to commit abominations against God and claim to be "safe"?

### Lesson in Our Society

Like the Israelites of Jeremiah's day, each of us daily faces temptations to perpetuate injustices and commit sinful acts. We must make choices and face their consequences. This text should also inform our attitudes and practices concerning worship and redemption. Sometimes we treat our church the way the Israelites treated their temple. We are sometimes focused on appearances and rituals rather than the God who is supposed to be the object of our worship.

### Make It Happen

Often our attempts at repentance and reform fall short because we simply forget what God requires of us and only talk about change in a general way. In order to combat this tendency, write down a list of resolutions and practices that will specifically help you to to "throughly amend your ways" (Jeremiah 7:5).

### Follow the Spirit

What God wants me to do:

_____

_____

_____

_____

## Remember Your Thoughts

Special insights I have learned:

_____

_____

_____

_____

## More Light on the Text

Jeremiah 7:1–15

**1 The word that came to Jeremiah from the LORD, saying, 2 Stand in the gate of the LORD's house, and proclaim there this word, and say, Hear the word of the LORD, all ye of Judah, that enter in at these gates to worship the LORD. 3 Thus saith the LORD of hosts, the God of Israel, Amend your ways and your doings, and I will cause you to dwell in this place.**

When Josiah became king of Israel, a priest found a copy of the Word of God in the temple, and Josiah led the nation in a religious revival that sought to restore the people's worship of God to its rightful place. However, King Josiah was slain in a battle with an Egyptian pharaoh, and when Jehoiakim replaced Josiah as king, he immediately began to reverse the religious reforms that had been instituted. Judah was caught in the middle of a battle between Egypt and Babylon over who would control Palestine, raising questions of national security and prosperity. Under Jehoiakim, worship within the temple had become ritualistic with more emphasis on the external matters of the temple than proper worship of God. The people had a form of godliness, but it was only external. They attended the temple as required, paid their tithes, and submitted their sacrificial offerings, but it was only for show. When they were not in the temple, the people commit-

ted the same evils as the heathens around them. It was under these circumstances that God instructs Jeremiah to stand in the gate of the Lord's house to proclaim a word to the entering people of Judah. The gate where Jeremiah stands is the gate that leads into the court of the women and the outer court of the temple, or the court of the Gentiles. The prophet's message, then, is directed toward all those religious people within the nation who are still attempting to worship God. For preaching this message, called the Temple Sermon, Jeremiah's life is threatened (see 26:7–9).

**4 Trust ye not in lying words, saying, The temple of the LORD, The temple of the LORD, The temple of the LORD, are these. 5 For if ye throughly amend your ways and your doings; if ye throughly execute judgment between a man and his neighbor; 6 If ye oppress not the stranger, the fatherless, and the widow, and shed not innocent blood in this place, neither walk after other gods to your hurt: 7 Then will I cause you to dwell in this place, in the land that I gave to your fathers, for ever and ever.**

Many in Judah have collectively embraced a misunderstanding of God's relationship with them. Because they are His chosen people and He has located His temple among them, they believe that no harm can befall them. Almost like a charm, the people reply "the temple of the LORD" whenever they feel threatened. By doing so, they are asserting that they can do as they please and "trust" (Heb. *batakh*, **bah-TAHKH**, to feel safe or confident in) God will protect them because His home is with them. Further, the nation of Israel is under the impression that they cannot be displaced from "the land" (Heb. *'erets*, **EH-rets**, land, country or territory) because God promised it to their "fathers"

(Heb. *'av*, **AHV**) and they believe it is their inheritance forever. Jeremiah seeks to make them understand that God did not bestow the nation with a covenant without obligation. Only as the nation faithfully observes the requirements of their covenant with the Lord, will He honor His portion of the covenant with them. They will have to "throughly amend [their] ways" and "throughly execute judgment." These two phrases are examples of the Hebrew infinitive absolute. This form of verb is meant to convey intensity. In other words, the Lord wants the people to "really amend their ways" and "truly execute judgment." Jeremiah, here, begins a representative listing of the sins Judah has committed.

**8 Behold, ye trust in lying words, that cannot profit. 9 Will ye steal, murder, and commit adultery, and swear falsely, and burn incense unto Baal, and walk after other gods whom ye know not; 10 And come and stand before me in this house, which is called by my name, and say, We are delivered to do all these abominations? 11 Is this house, which is called by my name, become a den of robbers in your eyes? Behold, even I have seen it, saith the LORD.**

It is easy to imagine that as Jeremiah stands in the gate of the temple and continues his sermon to the nation of Israel, the people and their leadership becoming angrier with him. They have been coming to the temple to bring their offerings as they believed the Law demanded; what then was God's problem? Jeremiah tries to show them that they have an outward show of religiosity but are inwardly corrupt. The nation of Judah assumes that their presence in the temple is all that is needed. "We are delivered" (Heb. *natsal*, **nah-TSALL**, to take away or snatch away, e.g., from violence) is the phrase used as license for them to live as they please

when not in the temple. God will deliver them out of harm's way because His house is among them. The list of sins Jeremiah recounts for the people accuses them of violating nearly all the Ten Commandments God handed down (Exodus 20; Deuteronomy 5), and though they retreat to God's house as though it were a "den" (Heb. *me'arah*, **meh-ah-RAH**, hideout) to which robbers would escape once they committed their evil deeds, it is not enough to protect them from God's wrath. God has been watching and has "seen" (Heb. *ra'ah*, **rah-AH**, to inspect, perceive, or consider) their wrongdoings.

**12 But go ye now unto my place which was in Shiloh, where I set my name at the first, and see what I did to it for the wickedness of my people Israel. 13 And now, because ye have done all these works, saith the LORD, and I spake unto you, rising up early and speaking, but ye heard not; and I called you, but ye answered not; 14 Therefore will I do unto this house, which is called by my name, wherein ye trust, and unto the place which I gave to you and to your fathers, as I have done to Shiloh. 15 And I will cast you out of my sight, as I have cast out all your brethren, even the whole seed of Ephraim.**

Jeremiah now seeks to reinforce for the nation of Judah the truth: trusting in a location will not preserve them from God's wrath. God challenges the people to visit Shiloh (Heb. *Shiloh*, **shee-LOH**), a city in Ephraim and temporary home of the Ark of the Covenant and the tabernacle, and view how He permitted it to be destroyed because of the wickedness of the leaders of Israel. The Israelite leaders at that time even brought out the Ark of the Covenant before their enemy, the Philistines, in an effort to secure their victory over them. However, the Israelites were defeated and the Ark had been carried off into the land of the Philistines (1 Samuel 4:10–11). Jeremiah is seeking to teach the people of Judah that God's favor is not tied to a location, but rather the covenant made with His people. Violation of the covenant, regardless of the location, will result in punishment.

At Shiloh, God demonstrated that He would remove His tabernacle to Jerusalem, where it now resided, and He could just as easily remove His temple from Jerusalem. God declares then that He tried to reason with the nation of Judah, "rising up early" (implying an earnestness) and speaking to them, only to have His plea for a return to righteousness fall on deaf ears. Therefore, God promises to do two things to them because of their rebellious state: 1) He will permit the enemies of Judah to conquer them, and 2) He will permit His chosen people to be carried off into captivity the same way that He permitted the seed of Ephraim (i.e, the Northern Kingdom) to be carried off.

Sources:
Brown, Francis. *The Brown-Driver-Briggs Hebrew and English Lexicon.* Peabody, MA: Hendrickson, 2010.
Burton, James. *Coffman Commentaries on the Old Testament and New Testament.* Abilene, TX: Abilene Christian University Press, n.d.
Craigie, Peter, Page Kelley, and Joel Drinkard Jr. *Jeremiah 1–25.* Word Biblical Commentary. Vol. 6. Nashville, TN: Thomas Nelson, 1991.
Dunn, James D. G., and John W. Rogerson. *Commentary on the Bible.* Grand Rapids, MI: Wm. B. Eerdmans, 2003.
English, E. Schuyler, and Marian Bishop Bower, eds., *The Holy Bible: Pilgrim Edition.* New York: Oxford University Press, Inc., 1952.
Espinosa, Eddie. *Songs of Faith and Praise.* Alton H. Howard, ed. West Monroe, LA: Howard Publishing, 1994.
Feinberg, Charles. Jeremiah. *The Expositor's Bible Commentary.* Vol. 6. Frank Gaebelein, ed. Grand Rapids: Zondervan, 1986.
Howley, G. C. D., F. F. Bruce, and H. L. Ellison. *The New Layman's Bible Commentary.* Grand Rapids, MI: Zondervan Publishing, 1979.
*Life Application Study Bible.* New Living Translation. Carol Stream, IL: Tyndale House Publishers, 2007.
Strong, James. *Strong's Exhaustive Concordance of the Bible.* Nashville, TN: Thomas Nelson, 1990.
Wolf, Herbert. *Judges.* The Expositor's Bible Commentary. Vol. 3. Frank Gaebelein, ed. Grand Rapids, MI: Zondervan, 1992.

## Say It Correctly

Throughly. thru-**LEE.**
Shiloh. **SHY-**lo.

## Daily Bible Readings

**MONDAY**
Justice for the Poor
(Psalm 140:6–13)

**TUESDAY**
My People Have Forgotten Me
(Jeremiah 18:11–17)

**WEDNESDAY**
Judgment for the Disobedient
(Ezra 7:21–28)

**THURSDAY**
If You Will Not Listen
(Jeremiah 26:1–7)

**FRIDAY**
Amend Your Ways and Your Doings
(Jeremiah 26:8–15)

**SATURDAY**
God Abandoned Shiloh
(Psalm 78:56–62)

**SUNDAY**
Let Me Dwell with You
(Jeremiah 7:1–15)

# Teaching Tips

## Words You Should Know

**A. Soul** (Ezekiel 18:4) *nefesh* (Heb.)—Life, creature, the inner being of a person.

**B. Cast away** (v. 31) *shalak* (Heb.)—To throw away, cast off, shed, cast down.

## Teacher Preparation

**Unifying Principle—The Error of Our Ways**. People are aware of behavior that is harmful to the life of a community. What can be done to build and maintain the health of a community? Ezekiel advises confession and exhorts the people to do the right thing and thereby build a just community.

**A.** Pray for your students and for lesson clarity.

**B.** Read Ezekiel 1:1–3, and the introductory material to the book of Ezekiel in a good commentary.

## O—Open the Lesson

**A.** Open with prayer.

**B.** Read the In Focus story.

**C.** Introduce the lesson title, Aim for Change, and Keep in Mind verses.

## P—Present the Scriptures.

**A.** Have a volunteer read the Focal Verses.

**B.** Discuss the differences between the KJV and NLT.

**C.** Use The People, Places, and Times; Background; Search the Scriptures; In Depth; and More Light on the Text to clarify the verses.

## E—Explore the Meaning

**A.** Divide the class into groups to discuss the Discuss the Meaning, Lesson in Our Society, and Make It Happen sections. Have the students select a representative to report their responses.

**B.** Have another representative from each group discuss how these lessons can be put into action in their individual lives.

## N—Next Steps for Application

**A.** Have each student consider whether there is any area in their lives where they are blaming their situation on the actions of others.

**B.** Lead the students in a prayer in which they ask God to help them take responsibility for their own actions, forgive others, and make changes in their lives in order to promote justice in the community.

**C.** Close in prayer.

## Worship Guide

For the Superintendent or Teacher
Theme: A Call for Repentance
Song: "I'm So Glad Jesus Lifted Me!"
Devotional Reading: Hosea 14

# A Call for Repentance

**Bible Background: EZEKIEL 18; PROVERBS 21:2–15**
**Printed Text: EZEKIEL 18:1–13, 31–32**
**Devotional Reading: HOSEA 14**

## Aim for Change

By the end of the lesson, we will: REVIEW the message of Ezekiel that God holds each person responsible for his or her own actions; FEEL accountability for personal acts of omission that damage the community; and PRAY for discernment in how to amend our ways and build communities of justice.

## In Focus

Philip couldn't help but feel depressed. That's all he had known since he could remember. The neighborhood he and his family lived in brought him down just by looking at it. Graffiti covered the walls and trash covered the streets. Liquor stores seemed to be on every corner along with check cashing places and winos begging for change. He could not help but get angry with his parents for not making enough money to move out. He felt like this was the reason he did so poorly in school and why he was fired from his last job. He was thirty years old and still living at home with his mother. He could not stand it any longer. He decided that he would begin to deal drugs. After all, that's what it seemed he was born to do. That's what many of his friends did. Most of them had either been killed or locked up in prison. Philip thought about a few of his friends who had gone to college and had determined to not let their past determine their future. Maybe he could do the same thing. Was there a better way for him?

*In today's lesson, Ezekiel warns the people of Judah of approaching danger and pleads with them to take responsibility for their actions, repent, and live.*

## Keep in Mind

"Cast away from you all your transgressions, whereby ye have transgressed; and make you a new heart and a new spirit" (Ezekiel 18:31).

"Cast away from you all your transgressions, whereby ye have transgressed; and make you a new heart and a new spirit" (Ezekiel 18:31).

## Focal Verses

**KJV** **Ezekiel 18:1** The word of the LORD came unto me again, saying,

**2** What mean ye, that ye use this proverb concerning the land of Israel, saying, The fathers have eaten sour grapes, and the children's teeth are set on edge?

**3** As I live, saith the Lord GOD, ye shall not have occasion any more to use this proverb in Israel.

**4** Behold, all souls are mine; as the soul of the father, so also the soul of the son is mine: the soul that sinneth, it shall die.

**5** But if a man be just, and do that which is lawful and right,

**6** And hath not eaten upon the mountains, neither hath lifted up his eyes to the idols of the house of Israel, neither hath defiled his neighbour's wife, neither hath come near to a menstruous woman,

**7** And hath not oppressed any, but hath restored to the debtor his pledge, hath spoiled none by violence, hath given his bread to the hungry, and hath covered the naked with a garment;

**8** He that hath not given forth upon usury, neither hath taken any increase, that hath withdrawn his hand from iniquity, hath executed true judgment between man and man,

**9** Hath walked in my statutes, and hath kept my judgments, to deal truly; he is just, he shall surely live, saith the Lord GOD.

**10** If he beget a son that is a robber, a shedder of blood, and that doeth the like to any one of these things,

**11** And that doeth not any of those duties, but even hath eaten upon the mountains, and defiled his neighbour's wife,

**12** Hath oppressed the poor and needy, hath spoiled by violence, hath not restored

**NLT** **Ezekiel 18:1** Then another message came to me from the LORD:

**2** "Why do you quote this proverb concerning the land of Israel: 'The parents have eaten sour grapes, but their children's mouths pucker at the taste'?

**3** As surely as I live, says the Sovereign LORD, you will not quote this proverb anymore in Israel.

**4** For all people are mine to judge—both parents and children alike. And this is my rule: The person who sins is the one who will die.

**5** Suppose a certain man is righteous and does what is just and right.

**6** He does not feast in the mountains before Israel's idols or worship them. He does not commit adultery or have intercourse with a woman during her menstrual period.

**7** He is a merciful creditor, not keeping the items given as security by poor debtors. He does not rob the poor but instead gives food to the hungry and provides clothes for the needy.

**8** He grants loans without interest, stays away from injustice, is honest and fair when judging others,

**9** and faithfully obeys my decrees and regulations. Anyone who does these things is just and will surely live, says the Sovereign LORD.

**10** But suppose that man has a son who grows up to be a robber or murderer and refuses to do what is right.

**11** And that son does all the evil things his father would never do—he worships idols on the mountains, commits adultery,

**12** oppresses the poor and helpless, steals from debtors by refusing to let them redeem the pledge, and hath lifted up his eyes to the idols, hath committed abomination,

**13** Hath given forth upon usury, and hath taken increase: shall he then live? he shall not live: he hath done all these abominations; he shall surely die; his blood shall be upon him.

**31** Cast away from you all your transgressions, whereby ye have transgressed; and make you a new heart and a new spirit: for why will ye die, O house of Israel?

**32** For I have no pleasure in the death of him that dieth, saith the Lord GOD: wherefore turn yourselves, and live ye.

their security, worships idols, commits detestable sins,

**13** and lends money at excessive interest. Should such a sinful person live? No! He must die and must take full blame.

**31** Put all your rebellion behind you, and find yourselves a new heart and a new spirit. For why should you die, O people of Israel?

**32** I don't want you to die, says the Sovereign LORD. Turn back and live!"

---

## The People, Places, and Times

**Proverbs.** Proverbs are a way of summarizing wisdom and real-life truth. Those compiled and written by King Solomon are preserved as the Bible book Proverbs. These phrases are usually structured according to parallelism. One line is compared or contrasted with the following line, to reinforce the point being made. Although Solomon had the most famous collection of proverbs in Israel, many others were quoted and cited in the everyday life of the common people.

**Usury.** This is the act of giving a loan with exorbitant interest. The Israelites were forbidden to charge interest to one another, but they could charge interest to strangers. The practice of charging interest was evidently practiced by the religious and civic leaders that returned from Babylon. This prompted Nehemiah to command those who had charged interest to give back 1 percent monthly of the interest they took from their fellow Israelites (Nehemiah 5:9–12).

## Background

Ezekiel's sermon in this lesson was preached to an audience of Israelites living in exile in Babylonia. They were foreigners living in a strange land, having a very hard time making sense of all the bad things that had happened to them.

They had placed their hope in the temple and the God of their forefathers. They felt both helpless and hopeless. They blamed their current fate on the failures and sins of the generations before them. They no doubt just felt like giving up on their past, including their faith and their God, and were just trying to make the best of a bad situation.

God had called Ezekiel to minister to these people of little hope. God had told him that this would not be an easy assignment. He had said these people were rebellious, obstinate, and stubborn and not likely to listen (Ezekiel 2:3–5). Ezekiel would need to employ some creative ways of communicating to the Israelites, including using dramatic object lessons and speaking in parables, as he does here. Through it all, Ezekiel was fearlessly faithful as God's prophet. We can only hope that some of his original audience heeded his warnings, and that we heed them ourselves today.

## In Depth

### 1. The Proverb from the Past (Ezekiel 18:1–4)

The people of Judah, exiles in a foreign land, rationalize that they are being punished for the sinful deeds of their ancestors. There was a popular proverb in those days that reflected this sentiment: "The fathers have eaten sour grapes, and the children's teeth are set on edge." Apparently God was tired of hearing this proverb tossed about as a fatalistic and irresponsible view of the consequences of sin (vv. 2–3). He says He has heard it enough and He doesn't want to hear it any more, so He bans its use.

### 2. The Parable: Promise of Life for a Righteous Man (vv. 5–9)

Ezekiel uses a parable to illustrate his point about individual responsibility and punishment for sins. He describes a man who is righteous in conduct and character (vv. 5–9). In three broad areas of godly morality (piety, chastity, and charity), he displays the attributes of one who is just and right. For piety, he does not involve himself in any idolatrous acts or even look upon idols. He is faithful to God's Law and obeys it to the best of his ability. As for chastity, he is faithful to his wife and treats her with respect. As for charity, he is fair in his business dealing,

merciful to those who are poor, and gracious to those in need. He practices justice and is fair and honest in all his dealings and judgments. As a result, this man, when judged by God, will surely live, and receive blessings from Him.

### 3. The Parable Continued: Punishment for an Unrighteous Son (vv. 10–13)

Ezekiel continues his parable by presenting the imaginary son who is the antithesis of all his father's good characteristics. He is not faithful to God, and he treats his neighbors with contempt. He is a thief and a liar, oppresses the poor, and withholds justice. Ezekiel says God will judge this man for his sins, and he deserves death. His father's righteousness could not save him from bearing responsibility and punishment for his own actions. This parable illustrates the fact that the earlier proverb had no application to the Judean people's present circumstance, nor was it a proper understanding of the justice of God. Ezekiel clearly makes the point that although the present exiled generation is indeed suffering because of the sins of the previous generations, they are not guiltless, and they are fully responsible for their own actions. The people of the exiled generation are not innocent bystanders, but actually guilty participants in many sins.

### 4. The Pleading for Repentance (vv. 31–32)

The destruction of Israel, Jerusalem, and the temple was God's judgment and punishment for the spiritual apostasy and moral decay of the previous generations. But He speaks through Ezekiel to tell the exiled Israelites that their situation is as much a judgment of their sins as a national punishment for their fathers' sins. God justly judges each person individually. One person's sins may affect other lives, even the entire community.

But God does not punish anyone for another's sins. Each person is responsible for his or her own actions.

Ezekiel does not leave the people without hope. They can continue to blame their situation on previous generations and use that as an excuse to continue in their own sin. Or they can repent of their own sins and change course, and the result will be life, not death. It is not too late! When any individual sincerely repents of his sins, God will not only forgive him, but He will give him a new heart and a new spirit. This new heart will move him to be righteous and promote justice.

## Search the Scriptures

1. What does God say about the souls of the father and the son (Ezekiel 18:4)?

2. What does Ezekiel show as the appropriate response when we are tempted to blame others for our situation (v. 31)?

## Discuss the Meaning

Each individual's actions affect the whole community, for good or for bad. What types of actions hurt community? What can individuals do to build and maintain a sense of fairness and justice in our communities?

## Lesson in Our Society

Perhaps you or someone you know feels like they are suffering because of the actions of others. Perhaps your parents were substance abusers or were absent during your formative years. Perhaps you were abused physically or emotionally. Perhaps you just don't feel loved and appreciated and have given up hope for a better future.

When people are without hope, it is easy to blame someone else and turn to gangs, drugs, or alcohol as an escape. Your situation may indeed be miserable. But God's Word assures us that we are not bound to our present condition. There is hope, life, and joy to be found in the loving community of faith that is the family of God.

## Make It Happen

Sometimes taking responsibility for our own actions, acknowledging our sin, and turning from it is very difficult to do. If you are struggling with this, seek the guidance of a spiritually mature trusted friend. Jesus has already won the victory over our sin and the penalty of death. What joy there is in allowing Him to transform your thinking from that of victim to victor! He will give you a new heart and a new spirit, one in which you will find joy in helping others and in building and maintaining healthy relationships in a healthy community.

## Follow the Spirit

What God wants me to do:

_____

_____

_____

_____

## Remember Your Thoughts

Special insights I have learned:

_____

_____

_____

_____

## More Light on the Text
Ezekiel 18:1–13, 31–32

**1 The word of the LORD came unto me again, saying, 2 What mean ye, that ye use this proverb concerning the land of Israel, saying, The fathers have eaten sour grapes, and the children's teeth are set on edge?**

When things do not go as well as one might want, the natural tendency is to complain and try to put the blame on another. This had occurred so often within the land of Israel that it had developed into a "proverb" (Heb. *mashal*, **mah-SHALL**, a proverbial saying or aphorism) (see Jeremiah 31:29–30). Because of the sins of the "fathers" (Heb. *'av*, **AHV**, the father, head, or founder of a household, group, or clan), the children were being made to pay the penalty. Plenty of support for the belief that the children were being made to pay the penalty for the sins of their fathers can be found in Exodus 20:5, 34:7 (cf. Joshua 7:19–25; 2 Kings 24:1–4). The nation of Israel was conquered and driven into exile because of the apostasy of Manasseh. Only by this means could the sin be removed. However, within the nation of Israel, the teaching had been carried to excess and was being used to remove personal responsibility for sins.

**3 As I live, saith the Lord GOD, ye shall not have occasion any more to use this proverb in Israel. 4 Behold, all souls are mine; as the soul of the father, so also the soul of the son is mine: the soul that sinneth, it shall die.**

God as the Creator and Father of all affirms that all "souls" are His (Heb. *nefesh*, **NEH-fesh**, a living being with life in the blood) and that He has the right to impose penalty for wrongdoing. God knew that there was a natural tendency in people for the son to follow the sins of the father and thereby share the father's guilt. For that reason, there

was no room for the children to complain that they were being punished unfairly. The prophet Jeremiah offered that the sins of the father would be visited on the children (see 32:18). If the father lived in rebellion to God and His precepts, then there was every possibility that the son would follow in the same rebellion. There is a certain amount of truth to such theology because often what we do impacts not only us but those around us, and promising to punish multiple generations for the same sin was a way of reminding the people that they were not the only ones who would suffer for their sins. However, such retribution is a problem when turned around to place blame on others for our suffering. Beginning with this verse, Ezekiel begins to offer a corrective to the misunderstanding of God's intent, which had grown into a common proverb by stating that "the soul that sinneth" would be the soul that "shall die" (Heb. *mut*, **MOOT**, to perish). In other words, the individual person was responsible for his or her own sin and its consequences.

**5 But if a man be just, and do that which is lawful and right.**

The laws determining what was "lawful" (Heb. *mishpat*, **mish-PAHT**, justice or fairness) and "right" (Heb. *tsedakah*, **tseh-dah-KAH**, honesty, loyalty, or justness) were spelled out in Mosaic Torah, including Exodus, Deuteronomy, and the Holiness Code in Leviticus 17–26. Many of these laws were more detailed expressions of the Ten Commandments (Exodus 20:1–17) and the greatest commandments of loving God and loving neighbor (Deuteronomy 6:5; Leviticus 19:18). In this way, a man was to be righteous in the eyes of God but also deal justly with those around him.

**6 And hath not eaten upon the mountains, neither hath lifted up his eyes to the**

idols of the house of Israel, neither hath defiled his neighbor's wife, neither hath come near to a menstruous woman, 7 And hath not oppressed any, but hath restored to the debtor his pledge, hath spoiled none by violence, hath given his bread to the hungry, and hath covered the naked with a garment; 8 He that hath not given forth upon usury, neither hath taken any increase, that hath withdrawn his hand from iniquity, hath executed true judgment between man and man, 9 Hath walked in my statutes, and hath kept my judgments, to deal truly; he is just, he shall surely live, saith the Lord GOD.

The righteous man is one who does not participate in ritual meals on mountaintop sanctuaries, which is the common practice of the pagans (cf. 6:2–4, 20:28–29), nor indulges in the worship of idols (cf. Leviticus 19:4), does not commit adultery (cf. Exodus 20:14), does not approach a menstruating woman (cf. Leviticus 18:19), does not violate the laws governing business practices (cf. Exodus 22:25), feeds the hungry, clothes the naked, and judges fairly (cf. Leviticus 19:15). God declares that this individual shall live.

10 If he beget a son that is a robber, a shedder of blood, and that doeth the like to any one of these things, 11 And that doeth not any of those duties, but even hath eaten upon the mountains, and defiled his neighbour's wife, 12 Hath oppressed the poor and needy, hath spoiled by violence, hath not restored the pledge, and hath lifted up his eyes to the idols, hath committed abomination, 13 Hath given forth upon usury, and hath taken increase: shall he then live? he shall not live: he hath done all these abominations; he shall surely die; his blood shall be upon him.

However, if the same individual has a son who is guilty of being a thief, a killer, of any of those things expressly forbidden in the Torah, then this son "shall surely die," reinforcing the principle that the consequence of his actions will only be upon him.

31 Cast away from you all your transgressions, whereby ye have transgressed; and make you a new heart and a new spirit: for why will ye die, O house of Israel?

Ezekiel pleads on God's behalf for the nation of Israel to turn away from all its "transgressions." They are to do their part to "make you a new heart" (Heb. *lev*, **LEV**, heart, mind, or inclination) and also to make a "new spirit" (Heb. *ruakh*, **ROO-akh**, spirit, breath, mental and spiritual essence of the human or divine). The prophet wants the people to understand that the cause of their sin resides within themselves and that the only sure way to escape sin's consequences is to be reconciled to God (see Romans 7:21–8:2). Ezekiel implores the people to acquire a new heart, a task that is impossible for us to do, but trying to do so teaches us what God desires of us and brings with it the realization that God alone can make our hearts new. So too with the spirit: we do not have the ability to make a new spirit for ourselves, but the effort drives us to see our own helplessness and seek God's Holy Spirit to accomplish the task. Ezekiel is telling the people that they need not die, because God will honor their sincere repentance with an abundance of His grace.

32 For I have no pleasure in the death of him that dieth, saith the Lord GOD: wherefore turn yourselves, and live ye.

Ezekiel concludes this entreaty by reminding the nation of Israel that God takes no "pleasure" (Heb. *chafets*, **khah-FEHTS**, to delight or take joy in) in the death of the wicked. All that is required is to sincerely turn from wickedness, repent, and experience God's grace. God is merciful and desires that all find life in Him and "live" (Heb. *khayah*, **khah-YAH**, to restore to life or quicken) (see 2 Peter 3:9).

Sources:

Brown, Francis. *The Brown-Driver-Briggs Hebrew and English Lexicon.* Peabody MA: Hendrickson, 2010.

Burton, James. *Coffman Commentaries on the Old Testament and New Testament.* Abilene, TX: Abilene Christian University Press, n.d.

Duguid, Iain M. *Ezekiel.* The NIV Application Commentary. Grand Rapids, MI: Zondervan, 1999.

Dunn, James D. G., and John W. Rogerson. *Commentary on the Bible.* Grand Rapids, MI: Wm. B. Eerdmans, 2003.

English, E. Schuyler, and Marian Bishop Bower, eds. *The Holy Bible: Pilgrim Edition.* New York: Oxford University Press, 1952.

Howley, G.C.D., F.F. Bruce, and H.L. Ellison. *The New Layman's Bible Commentary.* Grand Rapids, MI: Zondervan, 1979.

*Life Application Study Bible.* New Living Translation. Carol Stream, IL: Tyndale House Publishers, 2007.

Rainer, Thom S. *Baptist Hymnal.* Nashville, TN: LifeWay, 2008.

Strong, James. *Strong's Exhaustive Concordance of the Bible.* Nashville, TN: Thomas Nelson, 1990.

# Say It Correctly

Usury. **USE**-uh-ree.
Executed. **EK**-se-kyu-tid.

# Daily Bible Readings

**MONDAY**
Justice, Righteousness, and Repentance
(Isaiah 1:24–28)

**TUESDAY**
Justice: A Joy to the Righteous
(Proverbs 21:10–15)

**WEDNESDAY**
Avoiding a Parent's Negative Example
(Ezekiel 18:14–19)

**THURSDAY**
The Consequences of Changing
Behaviors
(Ezekiel 18:21–28)

**FRIDAY**
The Lord Weighs the Heart
(Proverbs 21:2–8)

**SATURDAY**
Walking in the Lord's Ways
(Hosea 14)

**SUNDAY**
The Person Who Sins Shall Die
(Ezekiel 18:1–13, 31–32)

# Notes

# Teaching Tips

## Words You Should Know

**A. Wrath** (Zechariah 7:12) *ketsef* (Heb.)— Great anger or fierce rage.

**B. Desolate** (v. 14) *shamem* (Heb.)—Laid waste, uninhabited, or deserted.

## Teacher Preparation

Unifying Principle—Making a Difference. Some people show no kindness, mercy, or justice to others. Who will protect the weak from their oppressors? Zechariah says that God requires kindness and mercy for the widows, orphans, aliens, and the poor.

**A.** Pray for your students' understanding and application of the lesson.

**B.** Research Zechariah 7 in a good commentary.

**C.** Read several Bible translations of this passage.

## O—Open the Lesson

**A.** Open with prayer.

**B.** Give the lesson title and the Scriptures.

**C.** Have students read the Aim for Change and Keep in Mind verses and discuss.

**D.** Have the class read the In Focus story.

## P—Present the Scriptures

**A.** Have volunteers read the Focal Verses.

**B.** Use The People, Places, and Times; Background; and Search the Scriptures.

**C.** Look at the At-A-Glance outline, and In Depth.

## E—Explore the Meaning

**A.** Divide the class into groups to review the Discuss the Meaning and Lesson in Our Society sections. Have the students give highlights from their group discussion to the class.

**B.** Have students review again the Aim for Change and the Keep in Mind verses.

## N—Next Steps for Application

**A.** Plan to apply the Make It Happen section.

**B.** Summarize the lesson.

**C.** Close with prayer.

## Worship Guide

For the Superintendent or Teacher
Theme: God Demands Justice
Song: "Since Jesus Came Into My Heart"
Devotional Reading: Psalm 147:1–11

# God Demands Justice

**Bible Background • ZECHARIAH 7:8–14, ISAIAH 30:18–26**
**Printed Text • ZECHARIAH 7:8–14**
**Devotional Reading • Psalm 147:1–11**

## ———————— Aim for Change ————————

By the end of the lesson, we will: STUDY the punishment meted out by God for those who reject His demands; MAKE confessions concerning how we abandon the weak; and SHOW kindness to the oppressed and the weak.

————— In Focus —————

John and Kevin walked through the aisles of the new grocery co-op in their neighborhood. It had been there for about a year and neither one of them had been inside. "This stuff is expensive," said Kevin. "You know you could get this stuff cheaper at E-Z Mart." "I know I could," said John, "but I'd rather pay for food that I can trust." Kevin looked puzzled. "What do you mean 'food you can trust'?" John explained to Kevin how when he shops at the co-op, he can trust where his food comes from and the quality of it. He also explained how his money helps to pay the workers a livable wage. "I know I can do more, but this is my first step in the journey toward living a lifestyle of justice." John paused. He knew that just a few years ago, he would have been asking the same questions as Kevin. The Lord had led him toward significant change in this area little by little, and now he was hoping his friend would begin this journey of change as well.

*We may not be able to change the world overnight, but we must start with hearing God's voice when He speaks to us. In this week's lesson, we learn what it means to change in the areas of justice and compassion.*

## ———————— Keep in Mind ————————

"Thus speaketh the LORD of hosts, saying, Execute true judgment, and shew mercy and compassions every man to his brother: and oppress not the widow, nor the fatherless, the stranger, nor the poor; and let none of you imagine evil against his brother in your heart" (Zechariah 7:9–10).

"Thus speaketh the LORD of hosts, saying, Execute true judgment, and shew mercy and compassions every man to his brother: and oppress not the widow, nor the fatherless, the stranger, nor the poor; and let none of you imagine evil against his brother in your heart" (Zechariah 7:9–10).

# Focal Verses

**KJV** **Zechariah 7:8** And the word of the LORD came unto Zechariah, saying,

**9** Thus speaketh the LORD of hosts, saying, Execute true judgment, and shew mercy and compassions every man to his brother:

**10** And oppress not the widow, nor the fatherless, the stranger, nor the poor; and let none of you imagine evil against his brother in your heart.

**11** But they refused to hearken, and pulled away the shoulder, and stopped their ears, that they should not hear.

**12** Yea, they made their hearts as an adamant stone, lest they should hear the law, and the words which the LORD of hosts hath sent in his spirit by the former prophets: therefore came a great wrath from the LORD of hosts.

**13** Therefore it is come to pass, that as he cried, and they would not hear; so they cried, and I would not hear, saith the LORD of hosts:

**14** But I scattered them with a whirlwind among all the nations whom they knew not. Thus the land was desolate after them, that no man passed through nor returned: for they laid the pleasant land desolate.

**NLT** **Zechariah 7:8** Then this message came to Zechariah from the LORD:

**9** "This is what the LORD of Heaven's Armies says: Judge fairly, and show mercy and kindness to one another.

**10** Do not oppress widows, orphans, foreigners, and the poor. And do not scheme against each other.

**11** Your ancestors refused to listen to this message. They stubbornly turned away and put their fingers in their ears to keep from hearing.

**12** They made their hearts as hard as stone, so they could not hear the instructions or the messages that the LORD of Heaven's Armies had sent them by his Spirit through the earlier prophets. That is why the LORD of Heaven's Armies was so angry with them.

**13** Since they refused to listen when I called to them, I would not listen when they called to me, says the LORD of Heaven's Armies.

**14** As with a whirlwind, I scattered them among the distant nations, where they lived as strangers. Their land became so desolate that no one even traveled through it. They turned their pleasant land into a desert."

## The People, Places, and Times

**Zechariah.** Zechariah was likely a young boy when he first began to prophesy. It appears that the second part of his book belongs to his old age. Zechariah was the son of Berechiah, the son of Iddo the prophet (1:1). He was an enthusiast for the rebuilding of the temple in 520 B.C.

**Post-exilic period.** Malachi, Zechariah, and Haggai all prophesied during the post-exilic period. This was a time in Israel's history after the returning of the exiles to Jerusalem in 538 B.C. up until the time of Christ. During the post-exilic period, the Palestinian Jewish leaders main concern was the building up of Jerusalem and the second temple. At various times there were enemies who tried to stop the restoration and rebuilding of the temple. There was also complacency at times concerning the worship of the Lord, and there was often doubt about the future of the nation that had been wiped out by the Assyrians and Babylonians and only reinstated as a Persian and Greco-Roman province after the exile. Because of this, the Lord raised up prophets to stir the people to action and to give them a vision and hope for the future.

**Whirlwind.** Whirlwinds were common in the ancient Near East. They are the result of two currents from opposite directions combining to create a circular motion of wind. Oftentimes in Scripture, a whirlwind is used as a figurative expression for destruction (Psalm 58:9, KJV; Habukkuk 3:14), quickness (Isaiah 5:28, 66:15; Jeremiah 4:13), or anger (Jeremiah 23:19). Storms often came from the southwest, although Ezekiel had a vision of a whirlwind from the north (Ezekiel 1:4). On the sea, they were known to capsize small ships. In the desert, traveling caravans feared them, as they were a threat to health and property.

## Background

Zechariah prophesied during a time of great upheaval in the Persian empire. Cambyses, the son of Cyrus the Great, succeeded his father, who died in 530 B.C. Then Darius took the throne after Cambyses' sudden death in 522 B.C., inheriting the job of extinguishing several rebellions that sprang up throughout the empire. At the same time, the Jews who had returned to their homeland were rebuilding the temple in Jerusalem. Zechariah was a contemporary of Haggai and they both preached to encourage the people to continue the work of rebuilding this second temple.

It is in this context that a delegation was sent to Zechariah from Bethel, the former site of idolatrous worship in the Northern Kingdom. The delegation was sent to ask whether they should continue fasting now since their seventy-year exile would soon be completed (7:3). Zechariah began a series of prophetic oracles concerning the time of the Messiah and the renewed righteousness of the people of God. Ultimately he concluded this series of prophetic oracles with the pronouncement that their fasting will be turned into feasting (8:19). It was in this context that Zechariah spoke his oracle concerning God's demands for justice from His people and repentance from past acts of injustice. This is concluded with the observation that it was the people's unrighteousness and injustice that caused the land to become desolate.

## At-A-Glance

1. The Calling (Zechariah 7:8–10)
2. The Rejection (vv. 11–12)
3. The Scattering (vv. 13–14)

## In Depth

### 1. The Calling (Zechariah 7:8–10)

This passage begins with God's calling for the Israelites. It is a formula that is often used in reference to their basic duties as God's covenant people. They are to "execute true judgment, and shew mercy and compassions every man to his brother." These two admonitions are prominent in Scripture, especially in the prophetic writings (Micah 6:6–8; Hosea 12:6–7). Zechariah's prophecy gets at the heart of true covenant loyalty to God, which is not found in blindly following religious rituals such as fasting at a certain time of year, but in dealing justly with others and showing them the kindness and compassion of God.

This justice and compassion are spelled out in detail in verse 10. The poor and marginalized are to be the objects of this justice and compassion. They are commanded to "oppress not the widow, nor the fatherless, the stranger, nor the poor." These groups were landless and without inherited rights in Israelite society and could not plead their case in the courts of law, making them vulnerable to oppression. As a result, the Law of Moses had several stipulations to protect them from those who would take advantage of them (Exodus 22:22, 23:6–9; Deuteronomy 10:18–19, 24:14). Zechariah also zeroes in on the internal state of the heart with the words "Let none of you imagine evil against his brother in your heart." It is not just about external righteousness, but the attitude we have toward our brother and sister. These words echo similar admonitions in the Torah (Leviticus 19:15–18) and Jesus' focus on the internal attitudes that produce outward sinful actions (Matthew 5:28, 15:19).

### 2. The Rejection (vv. 11–12)

Zechariah recalls the people's past disobedience. First he goes over their initial actions in response to the words of God concerning their covenant duties of justice and compassion. Zechariah says they "refused to hearken, and pulled away the shoulder"— the image of someone who turns his or her back and will not turn around to hear what the other person is saying. The people were stubborn and would not listen to the Word of God concerning their behavior. Zechariah says that they "stopped their ears." They made it so that they did not even have the ability to hear what God was saying.

Zechariah continues his description with the condition of their hearts in light of God's Word to them. He describes their hearts as adamant stone or flint. Flint was a form of quartz that was abundant in the land of Palestine. It is a very sharp, hard stone that can be used for starting fires. This was a pic-

ture of Judah's collective heart. They were firm and resolute in turning away from God and rejecting His Law and the words of the prophets. This resulted in the wrath of God on the whole nation.

### 3. The Scattering (vv. 13–14)

Zechariah concludes this oracle with a description of God's wrath on the nation of Judah as they refused to hear His Word. Judah's deafness to God's Word receives a reciprocal response from God to their prayers. Since they will not listen to His Word, He will not listen to their prayers. This is similar to the words of Proverbs 28:9: "He that turneth away his ear from hearing the law, even his prayer shall be abomination" (KJV). This is a clear example of what happens when we refuse to obey God's Word: He will refuse our prayers.

The Lord eventually cannot tolerate the wickedness of His people and decides to scatter them like a whirlwind "among all nations whom they knew not." This happened in the Babylonian captivity. Judah was invaded by Nebuchadnezzar, and Jerusalem was sacked in 586 B.C. Most of the people were exiled to Babylonia or fled to other surrounding nations. Because of this scattering, the "pleasant land" would be laid "desolate." This pleasant land promised to God's people was flowing with milk and honey (Exodus 3:8, 17) but it would remain barren and empty due to their disobedience. The land was a symbol of a people's livelihood. Their disobedience resulted in their livelihood being made unfruitful and unproductive. Instead of being filled with farms and vineyards and people moving about to work and play, this land would remain empty, a symbol of what happens when we do not show justice and compassion to our neighbors.

## Search the Scriptures

1. Whom did God command them to show mercy, kindness, and tender compassion toward (Zechariah 7:9)?

2. What did the people do with the word that they heard through the prophet (v. 11)?

3. What did God say He would do when the people cried (v. 13)?

## Discuss the Meaning

1. We often want to hear from God, but are we always happy about what He says when we ask Him about our situations?

2. What are the good things that we can lose as Christians because of our own stubbornness and hard hearts?

## Lesson in Our Society

There are numerous problems in our society. Gangs and drugs plague our urban areas. Our national economy is unstable. Wars with other nations are a constant threat. We pray and cry out to God and observe all the outward rituals of religion, but we do not have a high priority on justice and compassion for our neighbor. If these two things had priority in our lives, then we would be able to eradicate these problems. Instead we cry out to God without listening to His Word. As a result, He does not listen to our words. Continuing down the path of coldhearted selfishness to those around us may cause us to miss out on the good things that God has for us. It is important for us not only to cry out to God, but also do what He says. Sometimes the solution to our problems lies within our own hearts as we turn back to Him.

## Make It Happen

Often justice issues are separate from our prayer life. It is possible that we have cried out to God, but He does not hear because we have not obeyed His call to show justice and compassion to those less fortunate. As an experiment, before your private times of prayer, list out ways that you can personally show justice and compassion to those around you. Once you make this list, pray for the people you will serve. Make note in the days to come whether God answers your other requests as well. Sometimes He isn't hearing us because we aren't hearing Him.

## Follow the Spirit

What God wants me to do:

_____

_____

_____

_____

## Remember Your Thoughts

Special insights I have learned:

_____

_____

_____

_____

## More Light on the Text

Zechariah 7:8–14

**8 And the word of the LORD came unto Zechariah, saying.**

The people of Bethel (an important and symbolic town; its name means "house of God") had sought out the priest and prophets to see if they should fast during a certain month, as was their custom. Jehovah takes this opportunity to recall to the people's minds the former prophets and their messages. Zechariah realizes that

Bethel's religious practice is similar to that of Israel and Judah before the exile: They were practicing religious rituals but did not have any true heart involvement or genuine repentance behind it. Zechariah likely knows of the people of Bethel and suspects that their religious practice reflects this same kind of empty formalism. In light of this suspicion, he reminds the people that the prophets had, for years, warned them about practicing ritual without true worship.

**9 Thus speaketh the LORD of hosts, saying, Execute true judgment, and shew mercy and compassions every man to his brother.**

At this point in the book of Zechariah, the building of the temple is well underway, so that in one sense, God's people are showing responsiveness and obedience to His command. However, it is clear from God's word through Zechariah that true covenant faithfulness is absent, as evidenced by the failure of the people to demonstrate justice and kindness in community. God's voice thunders with a verb-noun combination: *shaphat* (Heb. **shah-FAHT**) and *mishpat* (Heb. **meesh-PAHT**). These words are from the same Hebrew tri-consonantal root, *sh-p-t*, and are linked together in a phrase that might be literally translated as "judge a judgment." This word combination has a variety of meanings that, taken together, speak not only of "judgment" but of "judgment according to truth." Although the people have apparently shown some discernment and wisdom, the forceful repetition of this word group indicates that they have not extended true justice and mercy to their neighbor, even though the Lord has shown remarkable mercy to them. As a result, Jehovah demands conduct that simply reflects the way He has treated His people. "Mercy" and "compassions" do not refer to

some heroic act or unreasonable demand, but the natural and proper outgrowth of the mercy the people had received from the Lord's hand.

**10 And oppress not the widow, nor the fatherless, the stranger, nor the poor; and let none of you imagine evil against his brother in your heart.**

Zechariah's call for justice rather than oppression repeats the calls of the prophets before the exile, as well as God's command to show mercy to the helpless (Deuteronomy 14:29, 16:11, 24:19–21). Although the verb *'ashak* (Heb. **ah-SHAHK**) can often mean "defraud," "oppress" is a better translation here because, in this context, the word emphasizes the position of power in which the Israelites find themselves relative to the helpless among them. Once again, these commands are full of sad irony: Although the Jews found themselves utterly helpless in Babylon and Persia, God showed them mercy and made a way for them to return to Jerusalem and build the temple. Yet, shockingly, the Jews have turned and looked on the powerless in their community with contempt, perhaps even taking advantage of their lowly position.

The New Testament contains similar themes. The parable of the unmerciful servant (Matthew 18:21–35) graphically portrays the crimes the Israelite leaders are guilty of here, and James 1:27 again speaks of widows and orphans in describing what "pure religion" looks like. The covenant context provides the background in both cases: God's covenant people are supposed to mirror the covenant faithfulness He has shown them. In light of the Gospel revealed through Christ, the perfect Covenant Keeper, we understand that our failings are covered in the blood of the new covenant, shed by the Lamb. Because of Christ's sacrifice, we should strive to demonstrate His faithfulness to us in our dealings with each other!

**11 But they refused to hearken, and pulled away the shoulder, and stopped their ears, that they should not hear.**

The word "hearken" in the King James Version, although not commonly used today, brings out the sense of the Hebrew word *kashav* (**kah-SHAHV**), which means more than just listening. It does not merely indicate that the Israelites had failed to hear the prophets' warnings; it means that they had heard these warnings all too well, but had stubbornly refused to repent and obey. Nevertheless, the focus on hearing is obvious; the phrase "pulled away the shoulder" might be expressed in more modern terms as "turned their backs" (implying a breaking of relationship and disobedience, but also making it harder to hear). The phrase translated "stopped their ears" literally means "made their ears heavy," suggesting that the act of listening was burdensome to them. The final clause shows the purpose of these actions on their part: They did not want to hear the warnings of the prophets, and although they no doubt heard the warnings, they made every effort to pretend that they hadn't. Zechariah's warning gains added force in that his hearers could hardly claim not to have heard him! The actions of their ancestors and the resulting destruction and despair would have made God's warning utterly impossible to ignore.

**12 Yea, they made their hearts as an adamant stone, lest they should hear the law, and the words which the LORD of hosts hath sent in his spirit by the former prophets: therefore came a great wrath from the LORD of hosts.**

The description of the covenant people's faithlessness continues, with a natural transition from the ears to the heart (which in the Bible always represents the center of both understanding and affections). There is no doubt who the guilty party is in this covenant violation. God did not harden their hearts, as He did with pharaoh (Exodus 9:12, 10:1, 20); they hardened their own hearts. On the contrary, the prophets before the exile portray a God longing for His people to return to Him, pining for His adulterous bride. The intentional hardening described here was heartbreaking, coming from a people who had seen the disastrous consequences of disobedience. The word used for "adamant stone" *shamir* (**shah-MEER**) is the word used for the hard point of a stylus, usually made of a kind of quartz. The people had made their hearts as hard as flint.

Zechariah mentions the Spirit as the agent of the former prophets' inspiration. This reference brings out the seriousness of not heeding their commands and warnings—to do so was to deny the very Spirit of God. The New Testament shows us that denying the Spirit is blasphemy (Mark 3:22–30). Ananias and Sapphira paid with their lives for their "lie to the Holy Ghost" (see Acts 5:1–10). It is no wonder that the military phrase "LORD of hosts" reappears, with God pictured as going to war against His own people! Their treason has brought about the King's inevitable response, despite centuries of patience.

**13 Therefore it is come to pass, that as he cried, and they would not hear; so they cried, and I would not hear, saith the LORD of hosts.**

The verbs in this passage suggest repeated, customary actions; the Lord's call to His people was, of course, repeated many times over, as was their unbelieving response. God in His mercy patiently offered restoration far beyond what His people deserved. Eventually, however, He executed His justice in a perfectly proportional way. Because He had called to them and they had not listened, he would not hear their cries. Yet, God provided safety and security (albeit in Babylonia) for those who truly repented. Many of these same people have returned to Jerusalem and are being addressed by Zechariah. For them, the importance of hearing the Lord's call is abundantly clear.

**14 But I scattered them with a whirlwind among all the nations whom they knew not. Thus the land was desolate after them, that no man passed through nor returned: for they laid the pleasant land desolate.**

The term translated "scattered . . . with a whirlwind" occurs seven times in the Old Testament (cf. Isaiah 54:11; Habakkuk 3:14), and in all but two cases, it refers to a violent storm. This is not a literal storm, however, but the worst kind of curse imaginable: exile from the Promised Land, where the people had rest, and forcible removal into the terrible strangeness of foreign lands, with strange customs and foreign gods. It is no accident that the curses of Deuteronomy 28 focus primarily on assault and capture by a foreign people; this was the worst kind of judgment imaginable for a people whose very lifeblood, blessedness, and shalom depended on the land that had been promised to their great forefather Abraham hundreds of years earlier. And so the worst kind of upheaval took place: Whereas back in the glory days of Israel—the reigns of David and Solomon—the whole world traveled through the blessed land, now it had become desolate, without the hum of merchants traveling through it. Given that this land at the eastern end of the Mediterranean was a key crossroads, its

desolation would have been a terribly striking reminder of God's rejection of His people.

As Zechariah now stands among the people to whom God has shown great mercy and restored their land, his warnings and promises focus on making sure that the people retain the blessedness promised to them. Such warnings and promises are wonderfully relevant to people who are richly blessed in Christ. Believers must both hear and obey God's commands.

Sources:
Burton, James. *Coffman Commentaries on the Old Testament and New Testament.* Abilene, TX: Abilene Christian University Press, n.d.
Dunn, James D. G., and John W. Rogerson. *Commentary on the Bible.* Grand Rapids, MI: Wm. B. Eerdmans, 2003.
Howley, G.C.D., F.F. Bruce, and H.L. Ellison. *The New Layman's Bible Commentary.* Grand Rapids, MI: Zondervan, 1979.

## Say It Correctly

Hearken. **HAR**-ken.
Adamant. **AH**-duh-ment.

## Daily Bible Readings

**MONDAY**
You Behaved Worse than Your Ancestors
(Jeremiah 16:9–13)

**TUESDAY**
I Call Upon the Lord
(2 Samuel 22:1–7)

**WEDNESDAY**
Hope in God's Steadfast Love
(Psalm 147:1–11)

**THURSDAY**
Walking in the Way
(Judges 2:16–23)

**FRIDAY**
Pursue Justice and Only Justice
(Deuteronomy 16:16–20)

**SATURDAY**
The Lord Waits to Be Gracious
(Isaiah 30:18–26)

**SUNDAY**
The Results of Not Listening
(Zechariah 7:8–14)

# Notes

_____

_____

_____

_____

# Teaching Tips

## Words You Should Know

**A. Purge** (Malachi 3:3) *zakak* (Heb.)—Purify, distill, strain, refine.

**B. Ordinance** (v. 7) *khok* (Heb.)—Civil enactment prescribed by God, a prescribed limit.

## Teacher Preparation

**Unifying Principle—The Change Agent.** Fairness and philanthropy are most apparent during times of great tragedy and loss. How do the faithful demonstrate the same benevolent and just spirit all the time? Malachi informs the faithful that God requires justice and faithfulness and will bestow bountiful blessings in proportion to what they are willing to give.

**A.** Pray for your students' understanding and application of the lesson.

**B.** Research Malachi 3:1–10 in a few good commentaries.

**C.** Read the Focal Verses in several different Bible translations.

## O—Open the Lesson

**A.** Open with a song and prayer, including the Aim for Change.

**B.** Give the lesson title and the Scriptures.

**C.** Have students read the Aim for Change and Keep in Mind verse and discuss.

**D.** Ask, "What groups of people need justice today?" Discuss.

**E.** Have the class read the In Focus story.

## P—Present the Scriptures

**A.** Have volunteers read the Focal Verses.

**B.** Use The People, Places, and Times; Background; and Search the Scriptures to clarify the verses.

**C.** Look at the At-A-Glance outline, In Depth, and More Light on the Text to answer any lingering questions about the lesson.

## E—Explore the Meaning

**A.** Divide the class into groups to review the Discuss the Meaning and Lesson in Our Society sections. Have the students give highlights from their group discussion to the class.

**B.** Have students review again the Aim for Change and the Keep in Mind verse.

## N—Next Steps for Application

**A.** Plan to apply the Make It Happen section.

**B.** Summarize the lesson.

**C.** Close with prayer.

## Worship Guide

For the Superintendent or Teacher
Theme: Return to a Just God
Song: "You Can't Beat God Giving"
Devotional Reading: Psalm 24:4–11

# Return to a Just God

**Bible Background • MALACHI 3:1–10; MATTHEW 7:12**
**Printed Text • MALACHI 3:1–10**
**Devotional Reading • PSALM 24:4–11**

## —————— Aim for Change ——————

By the end of this lesson, we will: REVIEW Malachi's prophecy about possessions, wealth, and hospitality in light of our faithfulness and justice; CONFESS personal unfaithfulness to God and pray for forgiveness; and INSTITUTE a personal plan for charitable living.

## In Focus

Stanley couldn't believe what he was hearing from the pulpit. The pastor was talking about how the church was raising money to buy backpacks of school supplies for the poor kids in the community. All he heard was another call for money. It seemed like that's all they wanted. He had joined this church because his former church had turned giving into a competition and a get-rich-quick scheme. *Now I'm giving my tithe faithfully… well, sort of. So, I'm giving 7 percent instead of 10 percent. I mean, I can't quite give 10 percent because I have so much that I need to take care of. Why should I give to these poor kids whose parents probably didn't care about their education anyway? Next thing you know, they will ask us to pay for people's rent and groceries. There are government programs to help kids like this. Besides that's where all of my taxes go. Why does God have to tax me because of other people's irresponsibility?* It seemed to Stanley as if God just wanted to rob him of his finances. He worked hard for his money. Did he have to give all of it to the church?

*Our commitment to justice is shown in how we give to the Lord and His work. In this week's lesson, we will learn how faithfulness to a just God can be shown in our giving.*

## —————— Keep in Mind ——————

"Even from the days of your fathers ye are gone away from mine ordinances, and have not kept them. Return unto me, and I will return unto you, saith the LORD of hosts. But ye said, Wherein shall we return?" (Malachi 3:7).

"Even from the days of your fathers ye are gone away from mine ordinances, and have not kept them. Return unto me, and I will return unto you, saith the LORD of hosts. But ye said, Wherein shall we return?" (Malachi 3:7).

# Focal Verses

**KJV** Malachi 3:1 Behold, I will send my messenger, and he shall prepare the way before me: and the LORD, whom ye seek, shall suddenly come to his temple, even the messenger of the covenant, whom ye delight in: behold, he shall come, saith the LORD of hosts.

**2** But who may abide the day of his coming? and who shall stand when he appeareth? for he is like a refiner's fire, and like fullers' soap:

**3** And he shall sit as a refiner and purifier of silver: and he shall purify the sons of Levi, and purge them as gold and silver, that they may offer unto the LORD an offering in righteousness.

**4** Then shall the offering of Judah and Jerusalem be pleasant unto the LORD, as in the days of old, and as in former years.

**5** And I will come near to you to judgment; and I will be a swift witness against the sorcerers, and against the adulterers, and against false swearers, and against those that oppress the hireling in his wages, the widow, and the fatherless, and that turn aside the stranger from his right, and fear not me, saith the LORD of hosts.

**6** For I am the LORD, I change not; therefore ye sons of Jacob are not consumed.

**7** Even from the days of your fathers ye are gone away from mine ordinances, and have not kept them. Return unto me, and I will return unto you, saith the LORD of hosts. But ye said, Wherein shall we return?

**8** Will a man rob God? Yet ye have robbed me. But ye say, Wherein have we robbed thee? In tithes and offerings.

**9** Ye are cursed with a curse: for ye have robbed me, even this whole nation.

**10** Bring ye all the tithes into the storehouse, that there may be meat in mine house,

**NLT** Malachi 3:1 "Look! I am sending my messenger, and he will prepare the way before me. Then the Lord you are seeking will suddenly come to his Temple. The messenger of the covenant, whom you look for so eagerly, is surely coming," says the LORD of Heaven's Armies.

**2** "But who will be able to endure it when he comes? Who will be able to stand and face him when he appears? For he will be like a blazing fire that refines metal, or like a strong soap that bleaches clothes.

**3** He will sit like a refiner of silver, burning away the dross. He will purify the Levites, refining them like gold and silver, so that they may once again offer acceptable sacrifices to the LORD.

**4** Then once more the LORD will accept the offerings brought to him by the people of Judah and Jerusalem, as he did in the past.

**5** At that time I will put you on trial. I am eager to witness against all sorcerers and adulterers and liars. I will speak against those who cheat employees of their wages, who oppress widows and orphans, or who deprive the foreigners living among you of justice, for these people do not fear me," says the LORD of Heaven's Armies.

**6** "I am the LORD, and I do not change. That is why you descendants of Jacob are not already destroyed.

**7** Ever since the days of your ancestors, you have scorned my decrees and failed to obey them. Now return to me, and I will return to you," says the LORD of Heaven's Armies. "But you ask, 'How can we return when we have never gone away?'

**8** Should people cheat God? Yet you have cheated me! But you ask, 'What do you mean? When did we ever cheat you?' You

and prove me now herewith, saith the LORD of hosts, if I will not open you the windows of heaven, and pour you out a blessing, that there shall not be room enough to receive it.

have cheated me of the tithes and offerings due to me.

**9** You are under a curse, for your whole nation has been cheating me.

**10** Bring all the tithes into the storehouse so there will be enough food in my Temple. If you do," says the LORD of Heaven's Armies, "I will open the windows of heaven for you. I will pour out a blessing so great you won't have enough room to take it in! Try it! Put me to the test!"

## The People, Places, and Times

**Refiner.** In order to separate the dross or impurities from the pure metal, a refiner would heat it until the dross burned off and the metal was purified or refined. Most mentions of refining in the Bible are for silver (Proverbs 25:4; Zechariah 13:9; Isaiah 48:10). Smelting lead sulfide ore and then blowing hot air over the surface of the melted metal usually did this. The refiner's tools were a crucible or furnace and some bellows or a blow pipe. He would usually sit and carefully watch for the right time to let the melted metal run off (Malachi 3:3).

**Fuller.** A fuller was someone who cleaned clothes. It literally means "to trample." This referred to how fullers laundered clothes by beating or stepping on them. There were many cleaning agents in biblical times, including white clay, urine, and alkali powder from indigenous plants. Malachi 3:2 refers to alkali powder. The fuller would take soda powder from the iceplant, found in Mesopotamia, and wash clothes. Afterward he would stomp on them or beat them with sticks. This process would not only clean the clothes but also make them dazzling white (Mark 9:3).

**Hireling.** A hireling was a hired servant. This servant was different than a slave in that he was paid wages. A hireling was similar to a day laborer in that he would be hired out

for different jobs at an hourly rate. Often the hired servant was a stranger or foreigner living in Israel or someone who was poor and in debt. Because a hireling had no land rights of their own, they were vulnerable to exploitation, so the Lord provided protection in the Law of Moses for them (Leviticus 19:13; Deuteronomy 24:14).

**Tithes and Offerings.** A tithe was a tenth of someone's possessions that was offered to God. Tithing was practiced in patriarchal times and existed before the Law was given on Mount Sinai. Once the Law was established in Israel, tithes were required annually and every third year. These offerings would help provide for the Levites, poor, fatherless, widows, and foreigners in the land. Offerings were the obligatory sacrifices to God that were taken from the flock or herd. The people of Israel were often complacent concerning both of these institutions during the time of Malachi.

## Background

Malachi was written during the post-exilic period. This was the time after the Jews returned from exile in Babylonia to rebuild their nation and the temple of God. Malachi was a contemporary of Zechariah and Haggai. All three prophets were concerned with the people's neglect and complacency concerning the worship of God and the people's repetition of the sins and injustice that caused them to be scattered in the first place. Malachi spoke out against a corrupt priesthood. He also indicted the people of Judah for their lack of faith, which was shown in the neglect of worship, particularly in withholding tithes and sacrificial offerings. This meant that the priests who officiated worship were not adequately provided for. It also meant that worship was not continuous and therefore not a priority among the majority of the people. Malachi condemned this attitude and announced that God's messenger would come to refine His people so that they worship Him in righteousness.

## At-A-Glance

1. The Messenger of God
(Malachi 3:1–4)
2. The Message of God (vv. 5–7)
3. The Maintenance of God's House
(vv. 8–10)

## In Depth

### 1. The Messenger of God (Malachi 3:1–4)

Malachi begins this oracle with an announcement concerning God's messenger, who will prepare the way before Him. It is a prophecy concerning the time of the Messiah. The people needed to change their ways in order to receive the Messiah, so a messenger would be sent to prepare them for His coming. Although they long for a Messiah who will bring justice, they are not in a moral state to be ready for Him. Malachi's announcement lets them know that a Messiah is coming, and they need to be ready for Him when He comes.

This Messiah or "messenger of the covenant" will come to the temple and will refine

and purify His people. Malachi shows them that their cries for justice are hypocritical (Malachi 2:17) because they themselves will not be able to stand the refining fire of this coming Messiah. He will purify the sons of Levi so that their offerings to God will be pleasant to Him. The Lord wants to purify them like silver and gold, or the whitening soap of a launderer. He desires pure worship from a righteous people.

### 2. The Message of God (vv. 5–7)

Malachi then takes the people into the heavenly law courts. The Lord is the chief witness testifying against them. He will not be hesitant but swift in His judgment of their unrighteousness. He has seen their adultery, oppression, sorcery, lying, and idolatry. They have no excuse for their behavior, and the Lord will see to it that they are judged accordingly. He then states, "I am the LORD, I change not" (v. 6). He is not a wishy-washy God. His character is steadfast and faithful, therefore they "are not consumed" (v. 6).

Next, the Lord points out the irony of the situation. He has not changed, but they have changed by not being faithful to His ordinances. The laws and limits He has given them were part of the covenant He made with the nation. The Lord has not strayed from His covenant, but His people have. Their cries for justice are a moot point since they have been disloyal to God. He says if they return to Him, then He will return to them. The people of Judah want justice, but God wants them to repent. Now the question on the people's lips is "Wherein shall we return?" (v. 7).

### 3. The Maintenance of God's House (vv. 8–10)

Malachi points out that they are the ones in the wrong. He pronounces them as cursed by the Lord. Although they demanded justice, they have robbed God by not giving the tithes of their crops and herds and by not giving the proper worship sacrifices or offerings (Malachi 1:6–14). They give blind, diseased, and sometimes even stolen animals to the temple. This is shameful and disrespectful in God's eyes. They also have not given the tithe, which is designed to support the priests and others who have no land rights (Deuteronomy 14:28–29, 26:12).

Lastly, the Lord then issues them a challenge: He calls them to put Him to the test by giving their full tithe. By giving pure whole animals from their flocks and herds and tithing the best of their crops, they would be placing their trust in the Lord. Their tithe would be placed in the storehouse for the priests, and God's house would be properly maintained. The Lord says if they do this, then He would bless them beyond what they would ever need. Instead of being cursed, they would be blessed so much they would not have room for the abundance that He would give them. This is the reward for their returning to Him.

## Search the Scriptures

1. What is the purpose and role of the "messenger of the covenant" (Malachi 3:1)?

2. How could the people properly return to the Lord (vv. 8–10)?

## Discuss the Meaning

1. In what ways does the Lord refine and purify His people?

2. Since we do not live in an agricultural society, we do not have crops and flocks and herds of animals. How does God bless us in the twenty-first century when we give to Him?

## Lesson in Our Society

Many people today cry out hypocritically for justice. The same people who demand jus-

tice are quick to dish out injustice. We fight with others and look down on those who are disadvantaged. We cheat and steal from others in order to claw our way to success. Then we complain to God when someone cheats and steals from us. We are quick to point the finger and pray to God to make things right. We only pray when we need something and neglect God in our everyday life. The lesson for us today is that making things right has to start with us. We cannot think that God will take care of our house when we do not take care of His house.

## Make It Happen

Oftentimes we want God to be there for us in our time of need, yet we don't ask how we can serve Him. This week in your prayer times, instead of asking the Lord for things that benefit you, ask Him how you can serve Him and be a blessing to those around you. If you are not being faithful in your financial giving to your local church, make a commitment to give. If you have been faithful, consider what charities or non-profits could be blessed by your financial giving. Ask your pastor or church leader whether there is a missionary you can help support through your financial contribution.

## Follow the Spirit

What God wants me to do:

_____

_____

_____

_____

## Remember Your Thoughts
Special insights I have learned:

_____

_____

_____

_____

## More Light on the Text
### Malachi 3:1–10

**1 Behold, I will send my messenger, and he shall prepare the way before me: and the LORD, whom ye seek, shall suddenly come to his temple, even the messenger of the covenant, whom ye delight in: behold, he shall come, saith the LORD of hosts.**

The name "Malachi" (Heb. *mal'aki*, **mal-ah-KEE**) means "my messenger." However, scholars generally agree that the prophet who goes by that name is not being referred to here. Rather, Jewish scholars believe that the person being identified is Elijah the prophet (see Malachi 4:5), while Christian New Testament scholars believe that the person identified is John the Baptist (see Matthew 11:10), who heralded the coming of the Lord Jesus in the spirit and power of Elijah (see Matthew 11:14, 17:11–12; Luke 1:17). This messenger "shall prepare" (Heb. *panah*, **pah-NAH**, to remove, to clear a path) "the way" (Heb. *derek*, **DEH-rehk**, a road, distance, journey or manner) for Him. Many scholars debate whether the individual identified as "my messenger" differs from the individual referred to as the messenger "of the covenant" (Heb. *berit*, **beh-REET**, promise or agreements). Some believe that the person being spoken of as "the messenger of the covenant" is the Messiah. The message that Malachi the prophet was to deliver to the people seems to be in response

to their question in Malachi 2:17 when they inquire, "Where is the God of judgment?" Malachi responds that the Lord they "seek" (Heb. *bakash*, **bah-KASH**, to seek, demand, or find) and in whom they find "delight" (Heb. *khafets*, **khah-FEHTS**, having pleasure in) will come "suddenly" (Heb. *pit'om*, **pit-OME**, any moment now or unexpectedly) to His temple. The question of those who are seeking to live and do right is rhetorical. The priests of the temple are corrupt and many of the people have stopped taking issues of right or wrong seriously. Malachi warns that the Sovereign Ruler will come unannounced and bring judgment with Him.

**2 But who may abide the day of his coming? and who shall stand when he appeareth? for he is like a refiner's fire, and like fullers' soap.**

Because the Lord will bring judgment with Him, Malachi asks the people, who will be able to "abide" (Heb. *kul*, **KOOL**, to survive or endure) the day "of his coming" (Heb. *bo'*, **BOE**, to fall or light upon). Further, he inquires who will be able to "stand" (Heb. *'amad*, **ah-MAHD**, to stand up) when He "appeareth" (Heb. *ra'ah*, **rah-AH**, to present oneself or to be visible). The suggestion is that no one will be able to continue as before, because the Lord will come like a "refiner's" (Heb. *tsaraf*, **tsah-RAHF**, to purge away or to smelt) fire or even like the "fullers'" (Heb. *kavas*, **kah-VAHS**, to launder or wash by treading) "soap" (Heb. *borit*, **bo-REET**, lye or potash). It is noteworthy that Christ did not come initially to bring judgment but God's grace. Like many of the Old Testament prophets, Malachi did not distinguish between Christ's first coming in grace and His second advent for judgment. These two occurrences of Christ were merged by the prophets into a single appearance, with the need to satisfy the demands of justice having prominence.

**3 And he shall sit as a refiner and purifier of silver: and he shall purify the sons of Levi, and purge them as gold and silver, that they may offer unto the LORD an offering in righteousness. 4 Then shall the offering of Judah and Jerusalem be pleasant unto the LORD, as in the days of old, and as in former years.**

Such a "purge" (Heb. *zakak*, **zah-KAHK**, to distill or strain) will be harsh on all who are found to be lacking moral or ethical standards. The Lord's purpose, once He appears, will be to "purify" (Heb. *taher*, **tah-HAIR**, to pronounce clean) His temple, and its leadership, the Levites. Malachi tells the people that the Lord will begin His work of purification with the priests. He will "sit" (Heb. *yashav*, **yah-SHAHV**, to dwell or remain) as one who refines silver, because it is more difficult than refining gold. The refining of silver requires hotter fires and takes more time and patience. Once the temple and its leadership have been cleansed, the expectation is that the priests will once again return to the offering of sacrifices as spelled out in the laws of the Old Testament, and the people will follow their leadership. The end result of all of these actions will be a restoration of the relationship between God and His chosen people (see Philippians 1:8–11).

**5 And I will come near to you to judgment; and I will be a swift witness against the sorcerers, and against the adulterers, and against false swearers, and against those that oppress the hireling in his wages, the widow, and the fatherless, and that turn aside the stranger from his right, and fear not me, saith the LORD of hosts. 6 For I am the LORD, I change not; therefore ye sons of Jacob are not consumed.**

Malachi continues to respond to the people's question (2:17). He informs them that God will appear, and in addition to being a refining fire on some, will be the God of "judgment" (Heb. *mishpat*, **meesh-PAHT**, justice, legal decision before a judge) they asked for. The continual presence of so many within the community of returned exiles practicing acts condemned by the Law serves as an indication that they do not fear God, and His punishment will be their reward. When God does appear to judge, there will be no need for others to be witnesses against the wrongdoers; God has declared that He Himself will be the witness. However, because God is unchanging and always remains true to His word, His people will not be "consumed" (Heb. *kalah*, **kah-LAH**, to come to an end) even in their faithlessness and rebellion.

**7 Even from the days of your fathers ye are gone away from mine ordinances, and have not kept them. Return unto me, and I will return unto you, saith the LORD of hosts. But ye said, Wherein shall we return?**

The rebellion in the Jewish nation had been going on for a very long time. Like their "fathers" (Heb. *'av*, **AHV**, the head or founder of a household, group, family or clan) before them, the people have turned away from the ordinances of God and embraced evil (see Matthew 15:3), which is resulting in the ruin of the nation. Malachi, speaking for God, implores them to return to the "ordinances" (Heb. *khok*, **KHOKE**, rules or commands) of the Law so that the Lord of hosts would reward them by returning to them. The people have shown themselves deserving of God's wrath, and as the righteous judge, He has every right to consume them, but God demonstrates His patience and graciousness to His chosen people by speaking gently to them and offering for them to return. The people only need to repent. This was the message of John the Baptist, too (see Matthew 3:2, 4:17). However, rather than repentance, the Lord's plea is met with continued denial and rebellion. The self-righteous Pharisees do not feel the need for repentance because they believe that they have kept the whole Law and are blameless before God. In asking "wherein shall we return" (Heb. *shuv*, **SHOOV**, to turn back) to God, they are justifying themselves and their behavior in their own eyes. The parallels between Malachi's confrontation of the priests and other leaders and John's confrontation of the Pharisees reminds us that in all times and places, people have a tendency to become complacent about worshiping God and doing justice.

**8 Will a man rob God? Yet ye have robbed me. But ye say, Wherein have we robbed thee? In tithes and offerings. 9 Ye are cursed with a curse: for ye have robbed me, even this whole nation.**

Through the prophet, God answers their inquiry. The people are guilty of robbing (Heb. *kaba'*, **kah-VAH**, to defraud) God because they have stopped bringing their tithes and offerings for sacrifice to the temple. The nation is to take care of the needs of the priests and the Levites; however, by not giving their tithes and not offering sacrifices, or by doing either grudgingly, they are guilty of robbing God. The people's lack of giving with a cheerful spirit is viewed by God as a lack of gratitude for how He favored them or lack of acknowledgement of Him as Lord. The "curse" (Heb. *'arar*, **ah-RAR**, to condemn or call judgment down on) God inflicts on them is the withholding of rain so their crops will not grow (see 3:11).

**10 Bring ye all the tithes into the storehouse, that there may be meat in mine house, and prove me now herewith, saith the LORD of hosts, if I will not open you the windows of heaven, and pour you out a blessing, that there shall not be room enough to receive it.**

Finally, God challenges the people to put Him to the test. They are to once again bring their tithes to the "storehouse" (Heb. *'otsar*, **oh-TSAR**, treasure-house or armory), a repository which was attached to the temple and over which the priest exercised control, and "prove" (Heb. *bakhan*, **bah-KHAN**, to examine or try) if God would in fact open the windows of heaven so that an overabundance of "blessing" (Heb. *berakah*, **beh-rah-KAH**, gift, prosperity) might flow down. Malachi suggests that the people who did bring tithes to the storehouse were guilty of withholding a portion of those tithes, thereby robbing God further. He implores the populace to bring all their tithes so that they might receive God's favor.

Sources:

Burton, James. *Coffman Commentaries on the Old Testament and New Testament.* Abilene, TX: Abilene Christian University Press, n.d.

Dunn, James D. G., and John W. Rogerson. *Commentary on the Bible.* Grand Rapids, MI: Wm. B. Eerdmans Publishing House, 2003.

Howley, G.C.D., F.F. Bruce, and H.L. Ellison. *The New Layman's Bible Commentary.* Grand Rapids, MI: Zondervan, 1979.

## Say It Correctly

Sorcerer. **SOR**-seh-rer.
Ordinance. **OR**-di-nens.

## Daily Bible Readings

**MONDAY**
Teach Me Your Paths, O Lord
(Psalm 25)

**TUESDAY**
How Shall We Treat Others?
(Matthew 7:7–14)

**WEDNESDAY**
How Have We Spoken Against You?
(Malachi 3:11–18)

**THURSDAY**
How Shall We Be Judged?
(Joel 3:9–16)

**FRIDAY**
How Shall We Repent?
(Jeremiah 6:26–30)

**SATURDAY**
The Contrite and Humble in Spirit
(Isaiah 57:10–21)

**SUNDAY**
Return to a Just God
(Malachi 3:1–10)

## Notes

_____

_____

_____

_____

## A

**Abomination:** A foul and detestable thing

**Affliction:** Anguish, burden, persecution, tribulation, or trouble

**Angels:** God's messengers; they are not eternal or all-knowing, and are sometimes referred to as winged creatures known as "cherubim" and "seraphim"

**Atonement:** To "propitiate" (to satisfy the demands of an offended holy God) or "atone" (being reconciled to a holy God) because of sin

**Avenger:** One who takes revenge, one who punishes

## B

**Be Baptized:** To dip repeatedly, to immerse, to submerge

**Blameless:** Irreproachable, faultless, flawless

**Blessedness:** Happiness, joy, prosperity. It is not based on circumstance but is rooted in the deep abiding hope shared by all who have received salvation through Jesus Christ.

**Bless the Lord:** To simply speak well of Him

**Blood of the Lamb:** The blood that Jesus shed on the Cross of Calvary when He suffered and died for humanity's sin

**Bowels:** The place of emotions, distress, or love

## C

**Called:** Appointed or commissioned by God to fulfill a task

**Charge:** Admonish, order, command

**Chosen:** To be elected or selected

**Christ:** The Anointed One

**Commandments:** God's mandates; the entire body of Laws issued by God to Moses for Israel

**Conduct:** Manner of living

**Confess:** To acknowledge or to fully agree

**Consider:** To determine, make out

**Covenant:** An agreement with God based on God's character, strength, and grace; an agreement and promise between God and humankind

**Crucifixion:** Jesus suffered and died on the Cross

## D

**Decalogue:** The Ten Commandments; the words translated "Ten Commandments" literally mean "ten words"

**Desolation:** Making something deserted or uninhabited

**Disciples:** Learners, students, followers

**Dominion:** Rule or reign

**Dwelling place:** A location that is a person's refuge, home

## E

**El:** The Hebrew word for "god" or "mighty one"

**Even from everlasting to everlasting:** "Indefinite or unending future, eternity" (Strong)

**Evil:** To do "bad, unpleasant, displeasing" things

**Evil doer:** A malefactor, wrongdoer, criminal, troublemaker

**Evil spirits:** Messengers and ministers of the devil

**Exalt:** To raise up; to raise to the highest degree possible

**Exhortation:** Giving someone motivation to change his or her behavior; it can imply either rebuke or encouragement.

## F

**Faithfulness:** Steadfastness, steadiness

**Fear of the Lord:** Reverence or awe of who God is

## G

**Gittith:** A musical instrument resembling a Spanish guitar that, in ancient times, provided a musical tune or tempo during a ceremony or festival

**Glory:** Splendor, unparalleled honor, dignity, or distinction; to honor, praise, and worship

**God called:** To commission, appoint, endow

**God's Bride:** The Church

**God's own hand:** God's strength, power

**God's protection:** Conveys the idea of staying in God's abode, staying constantly in His presence, getting completely acquainted or connected with Him, and resting permanently in Him

**Gospel:** "The glad tidings of the kingdom of God soon to be set up, and later also of Jesus the Messiah, the founder of this kingdom" (Strong).

**Graven image:** An idol or likeness cut from stone, wood, or metal and then worshiped as a god

**Great Tribulation:** A time of great suffering (Daniel 12:1, Revelation 6–18)

## H

**Hallowed:** Consecrated, dedicated, or set apart

**Hear:** Listen to, yield to, to be obedient

**Hearken:** Pay attention to, give attention to

**Heart:** The place, figuratively, where our emotions and passions exist

**Heathen:** Literally means "nations" and is used in the Old Testament to refer to the Gentiles, all those who are not a part of the people of God

**Holy:** Anything consecrated and set aside for sacred use; the place made sacred because of God's presence; set apart from sin

**Honor:** To revere, value

**Hosts:** Those which go forth; armies

## I

**Idolatry:** The worship of anything other than God, our Creator

**Infidel:** One who is unfaithful, unbelieving, not to be trusted

**Iniquities:** Perversity, depravity, guilt

**In vain:** A waste, a worthless thing, or simply emptiness

## J

**Jesus' ascension:** Forty days after Jesus' death, burial, and Resurrection, He ascended or went back to heaven to sit at the right hand of the Father (Acts 1:9–11).

**Jesus' transfiguration:** While on the Mount of Olives with His closest disciples—Peter, James, and John—Jesus changed into another form. His face shone with the brightness like the sun and His raiment was white as snow (Matthew 17:2; Mark 9:2; Luke 9:29).

**Just:** A word often rendered as "righteous"; that which is right and fair

**Justice:** Righteousness in government

## K

**Kingdom of Christ:** It is the same as the "Kingdom of Heaven (Matthew 18:1–4); it is where Jesus reigns in "glory" (i.e., in "dignity or honor").

**Know:** To ascertain by seeing, have understanding, to acknowledge

**Knowledge:** Discernment, understanding, wisdom

## L

**Labor:** To toil to the point of exhaustion or weariness

**Logos (LOG-os):** The entire Word of God

## M

**"Make a joyful noise":** A command that literally means "shout"

**Manna:** Food from heaven

**Messiah:** The Promised One; the Anointed One

**Minister:** "A servant, an attendant, one who executes the commands of another" (Strong)

## O

**Omnipotent:** All powerful

**Omnipresent:** All present, present everywhere

**Omniscient:** All knowing

**Ordained:** Established and founded by God; founded, fixed, appointed, or established

## P

**Parousia (par-oo-SEE-ah):** Christ's Second Coming

**Path:** Connotes an ongoing process of taking dynamic steps toward an expected end

**Peace:** Denotes "wholeness, quietness, contentment, health, prosperity" (Strong); it is far more than an absence of conflict or problems, but that every part of life would be blessed.

**Pentateuch:** The Mosaic Law or Divine Law; The first five books of the Old Testament, as well as the Old Testament as a whole, reveal the entire set of legal and religious instructions which God gave, through Moses, for God's people. Terms that are synonymous for "Law" include commandments, ordinances, statutes, legal regulations, authoritative instructions, and teachings.

**People(s):** Most English versions translate "people" as "peoples." The New Living Translation goes even further: "Let the whole world bless our God."

**Power:** Boldness, might, strength, especially God's

**Prophets:** They were filled with the Spirit of God and under the authority and command of God, pleaded God's cause and urged humanity to be saved

**Profit:** To gain, benefit, avail

**Prosperous:** To make progress, to succeed, especially in spiritual things. It often did not refer to personal profit. Rather it meant "to move forward or succeed" in one's efforts.

**Proved:** Examined, tested, and tried

**Psalm:** A Hebrew title that means "praise"

**Purity:** "Sinless of life" (Strong)

## R

**Ransom:** To redeem (buy back) from, to pay a price for a person. It is commonly used as a purchase price to free slaves.

**Redeemed:** Ransomed, purchased.

**Refuge:** Place of shelter; stronghold or fortress—a place to which we can run when the enemy threatens and be secure; a shelter from rain, storm, or danger

**Repent:** To change (be transformed) or turn back from sin and turn to God in faith

**Righteous:** To be declared "not guilty"

**Righteousness:** God's justness and rightness, which He works as a gift also in His people; refers to the right way to live as opposed to a lifestyle that treats others unfairly or unjustly

## S

**Sabbath:** In Hebrew, *shabbath* means "ceasing from work." A day set aside to worship God.

**Sanctuary:** A word that means "holy" when used as an adjective. The "holy place" of which David speaks is the tabernacle, the portable temple built under Moses' leadership after the Exodus from Egypt

**Salvation:** Rescue, safety, deliverance

**Satan:** An adversary or devil

**Savior:** A defender, rescuer, deliverer

**Scribes:** They were secretaries, recorders, men skilled in the law

**Secret place:** A refuge, place of safety and a covering from all forms of destructive elements that seek to attack or destroy the children of God and to prevent us from experiencing the fullness of God's blessings, peace, and divine providence

**See:** To behold, consider, discern, perceive

**Selah:** This Hebrew expression (**SEH-lah**) is found almost exclusively in the book of Psalms. Some believe that Selah denotes a pause or a suspension in singing of the psalm or recitation, and the insertion of an instrumental musical interlude. The Greek Septuagint renders the word *dia'psalma*, meaning "a musical interlude." Still others think that the word *Selah* signaled a holding back of singing and allowed for silent meditation.

**Septuagint:** It means "seventy," and it is the ancient Greek translation of the Hebrew Old Testament by 70 Jewish scholars.

**Servant:** A slave, subject, worshiper

**Shalom:** Means "peace"

**Shekinah Glory:** The awesome presence of the Lord; His honor, fame, and reputation

**Shofar (sho-FAR):** Means "ram's horn" and was used in celebration as well as in signaling armies

or large groups of people in civil assembly

**Soul:** Refers to the immaterial part of the human being (what leaves the body when death occurs), or to the whole being—the self, one's life

**Stiffnecked:** Obstinate and difficult

**Strengthen:** To secure, make firm, make strong

**Strive:** To struggle, to exert oneself

**Supplications:** Seeking, asking, entreating, pleading, imploring, and petitioning God

## T

**Tabernacles:** Literally means "dwelling places," the name of the portable temple constructed by Moses and the people of Israel

**Teaching:** Instruction in Christian living

**Tetragrammaton:** Hebrew name for God (YHWH)

**Torah:** The Law, which means "instrument" or "direction"; the first five books of the Old Testament (Genesis, Exodus, Leviticus, Numbers, and Deuteronomy)

**Transfigured:** To change or transform

**Transgressions:** Include sins, rebellion, breaking God's Law

**Tried:** Smelted or refined, purified

**Trumpet:** A ram's horn that was used in celebration as well as in signaling armies or large groups of people in civil assembly

## U

**Understand:** To consider, have wisdom

## W

**Wisdom:** "Prudence, an understanding of ethics" (Strong)

**Woe:** An exclamation of grief

**Worship:** Bow down deeply, show obeisance and reverence

**Wrath:** "Burning anger, rage" (Strong)

## Y

**Yahweh:** Many scholars simply use the Hebrew spelling with consonants only, *YHWH*, which is God's name.

**Source:**

Strong, James. *New Exhaustive Strong's Numbers and Concordance with Expanded Greek-Hebrew Dictionary.* Seattle, WA: Biblesoft, and International Bible Translators, 1994. 2003.

# Notes

# Notes

# Notes

# Notes

# Notes

# Notes

# Notes

# Notes

# Notes

# Notes

# Notes

# Notes

# Notes

# Notes

# Notes

# Notes

# Notes

# Notes

# Notes

# Notes

# Notes